JUVENILE LAW

A COLLECTION OF LEADING
U.S. SUPREME COURT CASES

LARRY J. SIEGEL

University of Massachusetts Lowell

PAUL E. TRACY

University of Texas at Dallas

PEARSON

Prentice
Hall

Upper Saddle River, New Jersey 07458

Library of Congress Cataloging –in-Publication Data

Siegel, Larry J.
  Juvenile law : a collection of leading U.S. Supreme Court cases /
Larry J. Siegel and Paul E. Tracy.
    p. cm.
  ISBN-13: 978-0-13-134778-6
  ISBN-10: 0-13-134778-0
  1. Juvenile courts—United States. 2. United States. Supreme Court.
I. Tracy, Paul E. II. Title.
  KF9794.S54 2008
  345.73'081—dc22

                                    2006101988

Editor-in-Chief: Vernon R. Anthony
Senior Acquisitions Editor: Tim Peyton
Marketing Manager: Adam Kloza
Editorial Assistant: Jillian Allison
Production Editor: Jessica Balch, Pine Tree Composition
Production Liaison: Barbara Marttine Cappuccio
Managing Editor: Mary Carnis
Manufacturing Manager: Ilene Sanford
Manufacturing Buyer: Cathleen Petersen
Senior Design Coordinator: Christopher Weigand
Cover Design: Rob Aleman
Cover Image: Getty Images/Stockbyte
Composition: Laserwords Pvt. Ltd

Pearson Education LTD.
Pearson Education Singapore, Pte. Ltd
Pearson Education, Canada, Ltd
Pearson Education–Japan

Pearson Education Australia PTY, Limited
Pearson Education North Asia Ltd
Pearson Educatión de Mexico, S.A. de C.V.
Pearson Education Malaysia, Pte. Ltd.

ISBN-13 978-0-13-134778-6
ISBN-10 0-13-134778-0

CONTENTS

PREFACE

In 1966 the U.S. Supreme Court rendered its first major decision (*Kent v. United States*) concerning the rights of children in the juvenile justice system. This case marked the beginning of unprecedented revisions to juvenile laws across America, and children were affected in both the juvenile justice and educational systems. There could not have been a more propitious time for the Supreme Court to begin scrutinizing the juvenile court system. One reason for the timeliness of the Court's scrutiny was that juvenile crime would prove to be an enduring problem, as juvenile crime rates began escalating in the 1970s and 1980s. For example, over the thirty years between 1967 and 1996, the violent juvenile crime arrest rate increased by 124 percent for males and 345 percent for females.[1] In 2004, the most recent year for which data are available, there were 1.37 million arrests for persons under the age of eighteen and over one-half million were tried in juvenile courts. Thus, there are hundreds of thousands of juveniles who are being arrested for serious violations of the criminal law and they are entitled to be processed in a juvenile system that is just, fair, and effective.

Juvenile gangs have become a fixture in many metropolitan areas and even in the suburbs and rural areas. Some youth gangs contain thousands of members and have branch chapters around the nation. Adolescent gangs are believed to control the drug trade in inner-city areas and are quite willing to use their automatic weapons to protect and expand their markets.

Concern about adolescent misbehavior is not the only reason that the nature of juvenile law has taken on greater importance. There is concern about the problems of all youth in modern society. Many U.S. teenagers are approaching adulthood unable to adequately meet

---

1. Federal Bureau of Investigation, 1998. *Crime in the United States: Uniform Crime Reports,* p. 288. Washington, DC: U.S. Department of Justice.

the requirements and responsibilities of the workplace, the family, and the neighborhood. They suffer from health problems, are educational underachievers, and are already skeptical about their ability to enter the social mainstream. Too often, these at-risk youths live in neighborhoods where they fear walking to school in the morning and where it is common to begin experimenting with drugs and alcohol at an early age. The number of teenage pregnancies has increased sharply, and many children born to underage mothers are extremely vulnerable to health problems.

U.S. youths also live in families undergoing tremendous strain. About half of all new marriages end in divorce; many family members sacrifice time with each other in order to afford better housing and lifestyles. More than 1 million youths suffer physical, emotional, and sexual abuse at the hands of their parents, guardians, or relatives.

Considering the social problems faced by U.S. youth, the law that controls their activities and defines their legal rights is an important area of study. The need to summarize new juvenile case law and related legal issues has prompted the development of this juvenile law textbook, a version of which was first published thirty years ago. This new edition covers changes in juvenile case law that have evolved since the first edition was published. The book now includes cases that define the legal rights of youth within the juvenile justice process and also the critical cases defining the rights of minors at school. These areas are crucial because the justice system as well as the school system have extensive authority over the lives of minors.

Organization of the Text

This volume contains twelve chapters and covers landmark U.S. Supreme Court cases that had a profound impact on the lives of minors. The text is divided into two sections. Part I covers cases on the justice system, including investigation of crimes, court processing, dispositions, and even the death penalty. Part II focuses on the educational system and includes topics such as school prayer, free speech, discipline, search and seizure in schools, and drug testing of students.

Chapter One, "The Origin of the Juvenile Court," provides a brief discussion of the juvenile justice system and introduces the reader to the particular jurisdiction and philosophy of juvenile and family courts.

Chapter Two, "Due Process for Juvenile Offenders," covers the first two U.S. Supreme Court cases by which juveniles were given "due process" rights.

Chapter Three, "Juvenile Court Processing," addresses cases concerning the standard of proof for the adjudication of juveniles and the right to trial by jury.

Chapter Four, "Double Jeopardy," concerns the issue of whether juveniles can be adjudicated in juvenile court and then transferred to adult court to face further sanctions.

Chapter Five, "Self-Incrimination," focuses on the extent to which juveniles should be entitled to certain *Miranda* warnings when confronted with police interrogations.

Chapter Six, "Detention of Juveniles Prior to Ajudication," covers the constitutionality of detaining a juvenile prior to trial in juvenile court.

Chapter Seven, "Juveniles and Capital Punishment," provides the cases by which the U.S. Supreme Court resolved the issue of whether juveniles can receive the death penalty.

Chapter Eight, "Prayer in School," covers the U.S. Supreme Court rulings on the constitutionality of prayer in school or school-related settings.

Chapter Nine, "Free Speech," covers the extent to which students have constitutional rights to free speech in a school environment.

Chapter Ten, "School Discipline," focuses on the due process considerations that should govern school discipline processes and covers both disciplinary actions and corporal punishment.

Chapter Eleven, "Search and Seizure," addresses the question of whether school students have the same rights to privacy and freedom from unwarranted searches and seizures as adults.

Chapter Twelve, "Drug Testing," covers the constitutionality of exposing school students to random drug testing when they wish to participate in extracurricular programs.

Special Features

While there are hundreds of important court decisions concerning juvenile law from trial courts, state supreme courts, and federal appeals courts, this volume covers U.S. Supreme Court decisions exclusively. Only the U.S. Supreme Court can render rulings that become the "law of the land" all across the country as opposed to other courts, which have limited jurisdiction. Further, this volume is only concerned with the major, landmark U.S. Supreme Court cases pertaining to juveniles as decided by the highest court in the land. The cases that were chosen were the most significant in their subject area; they had a significant impact on juvenile rights; and they are important teaching tools.

Each chapter begins with an introduction to the subject matter. Case comments within each section are used to facilitate the learning process by providing a summary of the key issues within individual cases.

The text for the Supreme Court's majority opinion is always provided, as this opinion reflects the opinion of the Justices that voted in favor of the ruling. Occasionally a concurring opinion is included when such opinions offer something of value beyond the majority opinion. The dissenting opinions are offered when the Supreme Court's ruling goes against the juvenile issue that is the focus of the case. These dissenting opinions serve as a useful comparative basis with which to evaluate the majority opinion that ruled against the particular constitutional issue involving juvenile rights.

Larry J. Siegel
Paul E. Tracy

PART

I

Juveniles and the Justice System

CHAPTER 1

THE ORIGIN OF THE JUVENILE COURT

Introduction

Prior to the creation of the first modern juvenile court in Illinois in 1899, juveniles were tried for violations of the law in criminal courts just like adult offenders. There were no accommodations based on the age of young offenders. The consequences of this procedure were devastating. Having been convicted of a crime, a child was usually treated like any other criminal offender, and many of these youthful criminals were sentenced to adult prisons, as there were no special facilities reserved for juvenile criminals. The *Illinois Juvenile Court Act of 1899* created the first juvenile court in the United States. Soon thereafter, the juvenile court phenomenon spread across the country. By 1912, twenty-two states had copied Illinois's legislation, and by 1925, every state except two had followed suit.[1] The problem of treating criminals the same regardless of age had been resolved, and juveniles would now be accorded their own, separate, and very different court system.

Illinois Juvenile Court Act of 1899

An Act to regulate the treatment and control of dependent, neglected, and delinquent children. 41st General Assembly Laws Regular Session (Illinois 1899).

§ 2. Be it enacted by the People of the State of Illinois, represented in the General Assembly: Definition. This act shall apply only to children under the age of 16 years not now or hereafter inmates of a State institution, or any training school for boys or industrial school for girls or some institution incorporated under the laws of this State. For the purposes of this act the words *dependent child* and *neglected child* shall mean any child who for any reason is destitute or homeless or abandoned; or dependent upon the public for support; or has not proper parental care or guardianship; or who habitually begs or receives alms; or who is found living in any house of ill fame or with any vicious or disreputable person; or whose home, by reason of neglect, cruelty or depravity on the part of its parents, guardian or other person in whose care it may be, is an unfit place for such a child; and any child under the age of 8 years who is found peddling or selling any article or singing or playing any musical instrument upon the streets or giving any public entertainment. The words *delinquent child* shall include any child under the age of 16 years who violates any law of this State or any city or village ordinance.

---

1. Krisberg, B., Austin, J. 1993. *Reinventing Juvenile Justice.* Newbury Park, CA: Sage Publications.

§ 2. Jurisdiction. The circuit and county courts of the several counties in this State shall have original jurisdiction in all cases coming within the terms of this act. In all trials under this act any person interested therein may demand a jury of six, or the judge of his own motion may order a jury of the same number, to try the case.

§ 3. Juvenile Court. In counties having over 500,000 population the judges of the circuit court shall, at such times as they shall determine, designate one or more of their number whose duty it shall be to hear all cases coming under this act. A special court room, to be designated as the juvenile court room, shall be provided for the hearing of such cases, and the findings of the court shall be entered in a book or books to be kept for that purpose and known as the "Juvenile Record," and the court may, for convenience, be called the "Juvenile Court."

§ 4. Petition To The Court. Any reputable person, being resident in the county, having knowledge of a child in his county who appears to be either neglected, dependent or delinquent, may file with the clerk of a court having jurisdiction in the matter a petition in writing, setting forth the facts, verified by affidavit. It shall be sufficient that the affidavit is upon information and belief.

§ 5. Summons. Upon the filing of the petition a summons shall issue requiring the person having custody or control of the child, or with whom the child may be, to appear with the child at a place and time stated in the summons, which time shall be not less than 24 hours after service. The parents of the child or its legal guardian shall be notified of the proceedings, and in any case the judge may appoint some suitable person to act on behalf of the child. If the person summoned as herein provided shall fail, without reasonable cause, to appear or to bring the child, he may be proceeded against as in case of contempt of court. In case the summons cannot be served or the party fails to obey the same, and in any where when it shall be made to appear to the court that such summons will be ineffectual, a warrant may issue on order of the court, either against the parent or guardian or against the child itself. On the return of the summons or other process, or as soon thereafter as may be, the court shall proceed to hear and dispose of the case in a summary manner. Pending the final disposition of any case the child may be retained in the possession of the person having the charge of same, or may be kept in some suitable place provided by the city or county authorities.

§ 6. Probation Officers. The court shall have authority to appoint or designate one or more discreet persons of good character to serve as probation officers during the pleasure of the court; said probation officers to receive no compensation from the public treasury. In case a probation officer shall be appointed by any court, it shall be the duty of the clerk of the court to notify the said probation officer in advance when any child is to be brought before the said court; it shall be the duty of the said probation officer to make such investigation as may be required by the court; to be present in court in order to represent the interests of the child when the case is heard; to furnish to the court such information and assistance as the judge may require; and to take such charge of any child before and after trial as may be directed by the court.

§ 9. Disposition of Delinquent Children. In the case of a delinquent child the court may continue the hearing from time to time, and may commit the child to the care and guardianship of a probation officer duly appointed by the court, and may allow said child to remain in its own home, subject to the visitation of the probation officer: such child to report to the probation officer as often as may be required and subject to be returned to the court for further proceedings, whenever such action may appear to be necessary; or the court may commit the child to the care and guardianship of the probation officer, to be placed in a suitable family home, subject to the friendly supervision of such probation officer; or it may authorize the said probation officer to board out the said child in some suitable family home, in case provision is made by voluntary contribution or otherwise for the payment of the board of such child, until a suitable provision may be made for the child in a home without such payment: or the court may commit the child, if a boy, to a training school for boys, or if a girl, to an industrial school for girls. Or, if the child is found guilty of any criminal offense, and the judge is of the opinion that the best interest require it, the court may commit the child to any institution within said county incorporated under the laws of this State for the care of delinquent children, or provided by a city for the care of such offenders, or may commit the child, if a boy over the age of ten years, to the State reformatory, or if a girl over the age of ten years, to the State Home for Juvenile Female Offenders. In no case shall a child be committed beyond his or her minority. A child committed to such an institution shall be subject to the control of the board of managers thereof, and the said board shall have power to parole such child on such conditions as it may prescribe, and the court shall, on the recommendation of the board, have power to discharge such child from custody whenever in the judgment of the court his or her reformation shall be complete; or the court may commit the child to the care and custody of some association that will receive it embracing in its objects the care of neglected and dependent children and that has been duly accredited as hereinafter provided.

§ 10. Transfer From Justices and Police Magistrates. When a child under the age of 16 years is arrested with or without warrant, such child may, instead of being taken before a justice of the peace or police magistrate, be taken directly before such court; or if the child is taken before a justice of the peace or police magistrate, it shall be the duty of such justice of the peace or police magistrate to transfer the case to such court, and the officer having the child in charge to take such child before that court, and in any such case the court may proceed to hear and dispose of the case in the same manner as if the child had been brought before the court upon petition as herein provided.

§ 11. Children Under Twelve Years Not To Be Committed to Jail. No court or magistrate shall commit a child under twelve (12) years of age to a jail or police station, but if such child is unable to give bail it may be committed to the care of the sheriff, police officer or probation officer, who shall keep such children in some suitable placed provided by the city or county outside of the inclosure of any jail or police station. When any child shall be sentenced to confinement in any institution to which adult convicts are sentenced it shall be unlawful to confine such child in the same building with such adult convicts, or to confine such child in the same yard or inclosure with such adult convicts, or to bring such child into any yard or building in which adult convicts may be present.

§ 21. Construction of the Act. This act shall be liberally construed, to the end that its purpose may be carried out, to wit: That the care, custody and discipline of a child shall approximate as nearly as may be that which should be given by its parents, and in all cases where it can properly be done the child be placed in an improved family home and become a member of the family by legal adoption or otherwise.
Approved April 21, 1899.

In 1907, the state of Illinois amended the Juvenile Court Act. The changes primarily involved (1) extending the jurisdiction of the court to age 21; (2) extending the age of delinquency to 17 for males and 18 for females; (3) preventing juvenile court records from being used as evidence in other courts; and (4) allowing a juvenile to be tried in other courts rather than juvenile court exclusively.

Illinois Juvenile Court Act of 1899, As Amended. 45th General Assembly Laws, Regular Session (Illinois 1907). An Act to amend [Illinois Juvenile Court Act of 1899]:

§ 2. [1]. That all persons under the age of twenty-one (21) years, shall, for purposes of this Act only, be considered wards of this State, and their persons shall be subject to the care, guardianship and control of the court as hereinafter provided. The words "delinquent child" shall mean any male child who while under the age of seventeen years or any female child who while under the age of eighteen years, violates any law of this State: or is incorrigible, or knowingly associates with thieves, vicious or immoral persons; or without just cause and without the consent of its parents, guardian or custodian absents itself from its home or place of abode, or is growing up in idleness or crime; or knowingly frequents a house of ill-repute; or knowingly frequents any policy shop or place where any gaming device is operated; or frequents any saloon or dram shop where intoxicating liquors are sold; or patronizes or visits any public pool room or bucket shop; or wanders about the streets in the night time without being on any lawful business or lawful occupation; or habitually wanders about any railroad yards or tracks or jumps or attempt to jump onto any moving train; or enters any car or engine without lawful authority; or uses vile, obscene, vulgar, profane or indecent language in any public place or about any school house; or is guilty of indecent or lascivious conduct; any child committing any of these acts herein mentioned shall be deemed a delinquent child and shall be cared for as such in the manner hereinafter provided.

A disposition of any child under this Act, or any evidence given in such causes, shall not, in any civil, criminal or other cause or proceeding whatever in any court, be lawful or proper evidence against such child for any purposes whatever, except in subsequent cases against the same child under this Act.

§ 9a. The court may in its discretion in any case of a delinquent child permit such child to be proceeded against in accordance with the laws that may be in force in this State governing the commission of crimes or violations of city, village, or town ordinance. In such case the petition filed under this Act shall be dismissed. Approved June 4, 1907.

The Juvenile Court

Jurisdiction

Beginning with the Illinois statute, a significant feature of the criminal justice system in the United States is the existence of a bifurcated or two-track justice system that determines court jurisdiction on the basis of the age of the offender. There is one court system and attendant policies and procedures specifically designed to handle youthful offenders and an entirely different court system for adult criminals. While there is some variation across the states concerning the statutory upper age limit for the jurisdiction of "juvenile" or "family" courts, the majority of states use ages 16 or 17 as the cutoff point for delinquency and juvenile justice jurisdiction.

The modern juvenile court is a specialized court for children. It may be organized as an independent statewide court system, as a special session of a lower court, or even as part of a broader family court. Juvenile courts are normally established by state legislation and exercise jurisdiction over "delinquent" and "incorrigible" children. Delinquent children are those who reach a jurisdictional age, which may vary from state to state, and who commit a violation of the penal code. Incorrigible children include truants and habitually disobedient and ungovernable children. They are characterized in state statutes as children, minors, persons, youths, or juveniles in need of supervision (CHINS, MINS, PINS, YINS, and JINS, respectively), and their actions are often classified as status offenders. Most states distinguish such behavior from delinquent conduct so as to lessen the effect of any stigma on the children as a result of their involvement with the juvenile court. Some juvenile courts may also have jurisdiction over adoption, neglect, and custody proceedings.

Juvenile court jurisdiction is established by state statute and based on age classifications. The states have differed in determining what age brings children under the juvenile court. Many state statutes include all children under 18, others set the upper limit at under 17, and still other states include children under 16. There are also jurisdictions that have a lower age limit, as well as some that provide different age categories for males and females. This latter gender-based distinction has been held to be violative of the equal protection clause of the U.S. Constitution.

Juvenile court jurisdiction is also based on the child's actions. If such action is a crime, this conduct normally falls into the category of delinquency. Definitions of *delinquency* vary from state to state, but most are based on the common element that delinquency is an intentional violation of the criminal law. On the other hand, the juvenile courts also have jurisdiction over status offenders or children without parental supervision. Here, the states differ markedly on defining conduct. Some states provide comprehensive definitions of a status offender, such as are found in the statement "a child who habitually disobeys the order of his parents or guardian, or who is truant, or who may be in danger of boding an idle, dissolute, lurid or immoral life is within the jurisdiction of the court." Other states define a status offender as "one who is beyond the control of his parents."

Having once obtained jurisdiction of a child, however, the court ordinarily retains it until the child reaches a specified age, usually the age of majority (18). Jurisdiction terminates in most states when the child is placed in a public childcare agency.

Philosophy

Despite the lack of a uniform age for the boundaries of juvenile and adult justice, there is considerable consistency surrounding the philosophy, goals, procedures, and thus, the raison d'être of juvenile justice. Since its inception in 1899 in Cook County, Illinois, juvenile or family courts have been easily distinguishable from their adult court counterparts. Fundamentally, juvenile courts are guided by a *parens patriae* doctrine by which the court acts as a surrogate parent for the welfare of the child and the judge is generally guided in his or her actions by the principle of "the best interests of the child." This *parens patriae* doctrine has resulted in a particular form and substance for juvenile justice. By tradition, if not by statute, juvenile courts are (1) informal and nonadversarial; (2) guided by a philosophy of nonintervention; (3) oriented toward the least restrictive sanction, usually community-based treatment rather than custody; and (4) concerned with the rehabilitation of the delinquent and the prevention of subsequent delinquency. On the other hand, adult courts are characteristically more "crime control oriented," and, consequently, adult courts and the criminal justice system are (1) formal and adversarial; (2) intrusive; and (3) focused on punishment, incapacitation, and deterrence.

From its origins in 1899, the basic rationale for such a vastly different court philosophy and procedure was the belief that the phenomenon of delinquency is quite dissimilar from that of adult crime, not only because the acts themselves are different, but also because the offenders are believed to be very different from adult criminals. The typical delinquent is presumed to be young and immature, and his or her misbehavior is generally presumed to be infrequent and nonserious. Most important, the "condition" of delinquency is assumed to be fleeting and temporary and is thus susceptible to remediation through appropriate (and usually *limited*) court interventions. This "typical" delinquent is seen as requiring a very different justice model from his or her adult counterpart.

The creation of the juvenile justice system was an important development in criminal justice. It has often been identified as a byproduct of the Progressive Era of the late eighteenth century. However, a number of commentators have noted that the creation of a special justice system authorized to deal exclusively and differently with problem youth may not have been as benign as supporters would suggest. In one of the definitive accounts of the creation of the juvenile court, Platt has referred to the phenomenon as "The Child Saving Movement," and he raised a number of important issues about the motives of the reformers who spearheaded the movement.[2]

In addition to controversy about its creation, concerns evolved over time about the image of the prototypical delinquent and both the appropriateness and effectiveness of the supposedly "benign hand" of juvenile justice. Consequently, the validity and usefulness of juvenile justice was challenged with special concerns over the absence of due process protections in juvenile court procedures. After about sixty-six years of unfettered discretion, the U.S. Supreme Court stepped in and began to expose the juvenile justice system to judicial scrutiny.

---

2. Platt, A. 1969. *The Child Savers.* Chicago: University of Chicago Press. See also, Myers, D. L. 2005. *Boys Among Men.* Westport, CT: Praeger.

CHAPTER 2

DUE PROCESS FOR JUVENILE OFFENDERS

Introduction

For the first sixty-seven years of the juvenile court, beginning with the original juvenile court in Illinois in 1899, children were denied constitutional protections. The juvenile court operated in what the authorities deemed to be a benevolent, paternalistic, and informal manner. Children were arrested, tried, adjudicated (not convicted), and given a disposition (not a punitive sentence) on the basis of *parens patriae*—the power of the state to act on behalf of the child and to provide care and protection equivalent to that of a parent. Throughout the process, the juvenile court system was guided by a rehabilitation philosophy by which the purpose of the court was therapeutic rather than punitive. The administrative structure of the court, including a juvenile court judge, intake workers, probation staff, government prosecutors, and defense attorneys, worked within a sociolegal framework in which the constitutional protections of due process were deemed not to apply, and further, these protections were viewed as possibly hindering the capacity of the court to function in the best interests of the child.

However, over time, the application of the *parens patriae* doctrine without constitutional safeguards led to arbitrary treatment for many juvenile offenders. Nowhere was the absence of due process more evident and more problematic than in two cases that found their way to the U.S. Supreme Court. The two cases, *Kent v. United States* and *In re Gault,* were characterized by such constitutional flaws that the Supreme Court decided it was finally time to rule on whether juveniles were entitled to due process protections.

The *Kent* case concerned the transfer of a juvenile from the jurisdiction of the juvenile court to the adult criminal justice system. The juvenile justice system recognized that certain forms of criminal conduct require that children be tried as adults in the adult criminal justice rather than the juvenile system. Thus, most jurisdictions had statutes by which certain juveniles would be removed from the juvenile justice system. There were two basic methods: (1) Some states used a "waiver" or "transfer" hearing; and (2) some states excluded certain offenses from the juvenile court's jurisdiction (e.g., capital offenses, such as murder). Thus, whether by a transfer hearing or by excluded offense provisions, almost all states allowed the juvenile court to waive, transfer, or bind over jurisdiction to the criminal court. The transfer of a juvenile to the criminal court was often based on statutory criteria established by the states' juvenile court acts, and waiver provisions were generally quite varied among the jurisdictions. Such criteria included the age of the child and the type of offenses alleged in the petition. For example, some jurisdictions required that the child be over a certain age and be charged with a felony. Others permitted waiver of jurisdiction to the criminal court above a certain age, without regard to the offense. There are also some jurisdictions that permitted waiver not only on the basis of age and type of offense, but also on consideration of the child's prior criminal record and probability of further juvenile conduct.

Because of the nature and effect of the waiver decision on the child in terms of status and disposition, the U.S. Supreme Court used the *Kent* case to consider procedural protections for juveniles in the waiver process. The Supreme Court ruled that the waiver proceeding was a "critically important" stage in the juvenile process and that juveniles must be afforded minimum requirements of due process of law at such proceedings.

The second case concerned the process by which juvenile courts should render a punitive disposition for a juvenile and expose the child to a possibly long period of incarceration for a relatively minor offense. In the *Gault* case, the Supreme Court decided that the concept of "fundamental fairness" must be made applicable to juvenile delinquency proceedings. In other words, the Supreme Court ruled that the due process clause of the Fourteenth Amendment required that certain procedural guarantees were essential to the adjudication of delinquency cases. It then specified the precise nature of due process by indicating that juveniles who have violated a criminal statute and who may be committed to an institution in which their freedom may be curtailed are entitled to: (1) fair notice of charges against them; (2) right to representation by counsel; (3) right to confrontation and cross-examination; and (4) the privilege against self-incrimination.

Gault did not hold that the juvenile offender was entitled to all procedural guarantees applicable in the case of an adult charged with a crime. The Supreme Court did not rule, for instance, on such issues as whether the juvenile had a right to appellate review. Nor was it clear as to what extent the right to counsel should apply to nondelinquent children. *Gault* specifically ruled that a juvenile is entitled to counsel in delinquency actions that may result in institutionalization. In this regard, some states provide juveniles with a right to counsel in all kinds of cases. Other jurisdictions specify that the right to counsel is applicable in delinquency and status offenses. Still other states go beyond *Gault* and provide counsel in neglect and dependency proceedings as well.

The *Gault* decision, and particularly the constitutional right of a juvenile to the assistance of counsel, completely altered the juvenile justice system. Instead of dealing with children in a benign and paternalistic fashion, the court must process juvenile offenders within the framework of appropriate constitutional procedures. And although *Gault* was technically limited to the adjudicatory stage, it has spurred further legal reform throughout the juvenile system. Today, the right to counsel, the privilege against self-incrimination, the right to treatment in detention and correctional facilities, and other elements of the adversary process have come to be applied at all stages of the juvenile process, from investigation through adjudication to parole.

Due Process in Juvenile Waiver

Case Comment

In *Kent v. United States,* the Supreme Court formulated procedural guidelines to be followed in the waiver of a delinquent from juvenile to adult courts. Kent claimed that his waiver from the juvenile court violated his statutory and constitutional right to due process of law. In granting the petition, the Supreme Court formulated procedural guidelines to be followed in the waiver of a delinquent from juvenile to adult courts.

In granting the petition, the Supreme Court argued that the difference between the juvenile and adult courts is so vast that the relief requested by petitioner is necessary to ensure equal protection of law. In its decision, the Court reviewed the purpose of waiver and the procedures to be followed for its just application. The Court's conclusion reflects the belief that although latitude and discretion are important functions of the juvenile court system, its procedures must also satisfy a fundamental fairness doctrine. The Supreme Court ruled that the following conditions must be observed for a valid waiver: (1) A hearing must be held on the motion of waiver; (2) the child is entitled to be represented by counsel; (3) the defense attorney must be given access to all records and reports relied upon to reach a waiver decision; and (4) the court must provide a written statement of the reasons for the waiver decision.

Many jurisdictions have established specific rules of practice for the waiver of a juvenile to the criminal court as a result of the *Kent* case. Most jurisdictions that have waiver proceedings require by statute or court rule a hearing, right to counsel, an investigations by the probation staff into whether the juvenile is amenable to treatment, evidence that reasonable ground exists to believe the child committed the delinquent act, and a statement of reasons for the waiver.

One of the most difficult issues in the waiver process is to decide what standards should be used to support a waiver decision. The appendix in the *Kent* case lists eight objective criteria to be used in determining whether to transfer a child to criminal court. These criteria generally include such factors as: (1) the type of offense; (2) the child's prior record; (3) nature of past treatment efforts; (4) the availability of rehabilitative services; and (5) the reasonable likelihood of the child being rehabilitated in the juvenile court.

KENT V. UNITED STATES

Supreme Court of the United States, 1966.

383 US 541.

Mr. Justice Fortas delivered the opinion of the Court.

This case is here on certiorari to the United States Court of Appeals for the District of Columbia Circuit. The facts and the contentions of counsel raise a number of disturbing questions concerning the administration by the police and the Juvenile Court authorities of the District of Columbia laws relating to juveniles. Apart from raising questions as to the adequacy of custodial and treatment facilities and policies, some of which are not within judicial competence, the case presents important challenges to the procedure of the police and Juvenile Court officials upon apprehension of a juvenile suspected of serious offenses. Because we conclude that the Juvenile Court's order waiving jurisdiction of petitioner was entered without compliance with required procedures, we remand the case to the trial court.

Morris A. Kent, Jr., first came under the authority of the Juvenile Court of the District of Columbia in 1959. He was then aged 14. He was apprehended as a result of several house-breakings and an attempted purse snatching. He was placed on probation, in the custody of his mother, who had been separated from her husband since Kent was two years old. Juvenile Court officials interviewed Kent from time to time during the probation period, and accumulated a "Social Service" file.

On September 2, 1961, an intruder entered the apartment of a woman in the District of Columbia. He took her wallet. He raped her. The police found in the apartment latent fingerprints. They were developed and processed. They matched the fingerprints of Morris Kent, taken when he was 14 years old and under the jurisdiction of the Juvenile Court. At about 3 p.m. on September 5, 1961, Kent was taken into custody by the police. Kent was then 16, and therefore subject to the "exclusive jurisdiction" of the Juvenile Court. D.C.Code § 11-907 (1961), now § 11-1551 (Supp. IV, 1965). He was still on probation to that court as a result of the 1959 proceedings.

Upon being apprehended, Kent was taken to police headquarters, where he was interrogated by police officers. It appears that he admitted his involvement in the offense which led to his apprehension, and volunteered information as to similar offenses involving housebreaking, robbery, and rape. His interrogation proceeded from about 3 p.m. to 10 p.m. the same evening.[1]

Sometime after 10 p.m., petitioner was taken to the Receiving Home for Children. The next morning, he was released to the police for further interrogation at police headquarters, which lasted until 5 p.m.[2]

The record does not show when his mother became aware that the boy was in custody, but, shortly after 2 p.m. on September 6, 1961, the day following petitioner's apprehension, she retained counsel.

Counsel, together with petitioner's mother, promptly conferred with the Social Service Director of the Juvenile Court. In a brief interview, they discussed the possibility that the Juvenile Court might waive jurisdiction under D.C.Code § 11-914 (1961), now § 11-1553 (Supp. IV, 1965), and remit Kent to trial by the District Court. Counsel made known his intention to oppose waiver.

Petitioner was detained at the Receiving Home for almost a week. There was no arraignment during this time, no determination by a judicial officer of probable cause for petitioner's apprehension.[3]

---

1. There is no indication in the file that the police complied with the requirement of the District Code that a child taken into custody, unless released to his parent, guardian or custodian, "shall be placed in the custody of a probation officer or other person designated by the court, or taken immediately to the court or to a place of detention provided by the Board of Public Welfare, and the officer taking him shall immediately notify the court and shall file a petition when directed to do so by the court." D.C.Code § 11-912 (1961), now § 16-2306 (Supp. IV, 1965).

2. The elicited statements were not used in the subsequent trial before the United States District Court. Since the statements were made while petitioner was subject to the jurisdiction of the Juvenile Court, they were inadmissible in a subsequent criminal prosecution under the rule of *Harling v. United States*, 111 U.S.App.D.C. 174, 295 F.2d 161 (1961).

3. In the case of adults, arraignment before a magistrate for determination of probable cause and advice to the arrested person as to his rights, etc., are provided by law, and are regarded as fundamental. Cf. Fed.Rules Crim.Proc. 5(a), (b); *Mallory v. United States*, 354 U.S. 449. In *Harling v. United States*, supra, the Court of Appeals for the Dis-

During this period of detention and interrogation, petitioner's counsel arranged for examination of petitioner by two psychiatrists and a psychologist. He thereafter filed with the Juvenile Court a motion for a hearing on the question of waiver of Juvenile Court jurisdiction, together with an affidavit of a psychiatrist certifying that petitioner "is a victim of severe psychopathology," and recommending hospitalization for psychiatric observation. Petitioner's counsel, in support of his motion to the effect that the Juvenile Court should retain jurisdiction of petitioner, offered to prove that if petitioner were given adequate treatment in a hospital under the aegis of the Juvenile Court, he would be a suitable subject for rehabilitation.

At the same time, petitioner's counsel moved that the Juvenile Court should give him access to the Social Service file relating to petitioner which had been accumulated by the staff of the Juvenile Court during petitioner's probation period, and which would be available to the Juvenile Court judge in considering the question whether it should retain or waive jurisdiction. Petitioner's counsel represented that access to this file was essential to his providing petitioner with effective assistance of counsel.

The Juvenile Court judge did not rule on these motions. He held no hearing. He did not confer with petitioner or petitioner's parents or petitioner's counsel. He entered an order reciting that after "full investigation, I do hereby waive" jurisdiction of petitioner and directing that he be "held for trial for [the alleged] offenses under the regular procedure of the U.S. District Court for the District of Columbia." He made no findings. He did not recite any reason for the waiver.[4] He made no reference to the motions filed by petitioner's counsel. We must assume that he denied, sub silentio, the motions for a hearing, the recommendation for hospitalization for psychiatric observation, the request for access to the Social Service file, and the offer to prove that petitioner was a fit subject for rehabilitation under the Juvenile Court's jurisdiction.[5]

---

trict of Columbia has stated the basis for this distinction between juveniles and adults as follows: "It is, of course, because children are, generally speaking, exempt from criminal penalties that safeguards of the criminal law, such as Rule 5 and the exclusionary *Mallory* rule, have no general application in juvenile proceedings." 111 U.S.App.D.C. at 176, 295 F.2d at 163.

In *Edwards v. United States*, 117 U.S.App.D.C. 383, 384, 330 F.2d 849, 850 (1964) it was said that: ". . . special practices . . . follow the apprehension of a juvenile. He may be held in custody by the juvenile authorities—and is available to investigating officers—for five days before any formal action need be taken. There is no duty to take him before a magistrate, and no responsibility to inform him of his rights. He is not booked. The statutory intent is to establish a nonpunitive, noncriminal atmosphere."

We indicate no view as to the legality of these practices. Cf. *Harling v. United States*, supra, 111 U.S.App.D.C. at 176, 295 F.2d at 163, n. 12.

4. At the time of these events, there was in effect Policy Memorandum No. 7 of November 30, 1959, promulgated by the judge of the Juvenile Court to set forth the criteria to govern disposition of waiver requests. It is set forth in the Appendix. This Memorandum has since been rescinded. See *United States v. Caviness*, 239 F.Supp. 545, 550 (D.C.D.C.1965).

5. It should be noted that, at this time, the statute provided for only one Juvenile Court judge. Congressional hearings and reports attest the impossibility of the burden which he was supposed to carry. See Amending the Juvenile Court Act of the District of Columbia. Hearings before Subcommittee No. 3 of the House Committee on the District of Columbia, 87th Cong., 1st Sess. (1961); Juvenile Delinquency, Hearings before the Subcommittee to Investigate Juvenile Delinquency of the Senate Committee on the Judiciary, 86th Cong., 1st Sess. (1959–1960); Additional Judges for Juvenile Court, Hearing before the House Committee on the District of Columbia, 86th Cong., 1st Sess. (1959); H.R.Rep.No.1041, 87th Cong., 1st Sess. (1961); S.Rep.No.841, 87th Cong., 1st Sess. (1961); S.Rep.No.116, 86th Cong., 1st Sess. (1959). The statute was amended in 1962 to provide for three judges for the court. 76 Stat. 21; D.C. Code § 11-1502 (Supp. IV, 1965).

Presumably, prior to entry of his order, the Juvenile Court judge received and considered recommendations of the Juvenile Court staff, the Social Service file relating to petitioner, and a report dated September 8, 1961 (three days following petitioner's apprehension), submitted to him by the Juvenile Probation Section. The Social Service file and the September 8 report were later sent to the District Court, and it appears that both of them referred to petitioner's mental condition. The September 8 report spoke of "a rapid deterioration of [petitioner's] personality structure and the possibility of mental illness." As stated, neither this report nor the Social Service file was made available to petitioner's counsel.

The provision of the Juvenile Court Act governing waiver expressly provides only for "full investigation." It states the circumstances in which jurisdiction may be waived and the child held for trial under adult procedures, but it does not state standards to govern the Juvenile Court's decision as to waiver. The provision reads as follows:

> If a child sixteen years of age or older is charged with an offense which would amount to a felony in the case of an adult, or any child charged with an offense which if committed by an adult is punishable by death or life imprisonment, the judge may, after full investigation, waive jurisdiction and order such child held for trial under the regular procedure of the court which would have jurisdiction of such offense if committed by an adult; or such other court may exercise the powers conferred upon the juvenile court in this subchapter in conducting and disposing of such cases.[6]

Petitioner appealed from the Juvenile Court's waiver order to the Municipal Court of Appeals, which affirmed, and also applied to the United States District Court for a writ of habeas corpus, which was denied. On appeal from these judgments, the United States Court of Appeals held on January 22, 1963, that neither appeal to the Municipal Court of Appeals nor habeas corpus was available. In the Court of Appeals' view, the exclusive method of reviewing the Juvenile Court's waiver order was a motion to dismiss the indictment in the District Court. *Kent v. Reid*, 114 U.S.App.D.C. 330, 316 F.2d 331 (1963).

Meanwhile, on September 25, 1961, shortly after the Juvenile Court order waiving its jurisdiction, petitioner was indicted by a grand jury of the United States District Court for the District of Columbia. The indictment contained eight counts alleging two instances of housebreaking, robbery, and rape, and one of housebreaking and robbery. On November 16, 1961, petitioner moved the District Court to dismiss the indictment on the grounds that the waiver was invalid. He also moved the District Court to constitute itself a Juvenile Court as authorized by D.C.Code § 11-914 (1961), now § 11-1553 (Supp. IV, 1965). After substantial delay occasioned by petitioner's appeal and habeas corpus proceedings, the District Court addressed itself to the motion to dismiss on February 8, 1963.[7]

The District Court denied the motion to dismiss the indictment. The District Court ruled that it would not "go behind" the Juvenile Court judge's recital that his order was entered "after full investigation." It held that "the only matter before me is as to whether or not the statutory provisions were complied with and the Courts have held . . . with reference to full investigation, that that does not mean a quasi-judicial or judicial hearing. No hearing is required."

---

6. D.C.Code § 11-914 (1961), now § 11-1553 (Supp. IV, 1965).

7. On February 5, 1963, the motion to the District Court to constitute itself a Juvenile Court was denied. The motion was renewed orally and denied on February 8, 1963, after the District Court's decision that the indictment should not be dismissed.

On March 7, 1963, the District Court held a hearing on petitioner's motion to determine his competency to stand trial. The court determined that petitioner was competent.[8]

At trial, petitioner's defense was wholly directed toward proving that he was not criminally responsible because "his unlawful act was the product of mental disease or mental defect." *Durham v. United States,* 94 U.S.App.D.C. 228, 241, 214 F.2d 862, 875, 45 A.L.R.2d 1430 (1954). Extensive evidence, including expert testimony, was presented to support this defense. The jury found as to the counts alleging rape that petitioner was "not guilty by reason of insanity." Under District of Columbia law, this made it mandatory that petitioner be transferred to St. Elizabeth's Hospital, a mental institution, until his sanity is restored.[9] On the six counts of housebreaking and robbery, the jury found that petitioner was guilty.[10]

Kent was sentenced to serve five to 15 years on each count as to which he was found guilty, or a total of 30 to 90 years in prison. The District Court ordered that the time to be spent at St. Elizabeth's on the mandatory commitment after the insanity acquittal be counted as part of the 30- to 90-year sentence. Petitioner appealed to the United States Court of Appeals for the District of Columbia Circuit. That court affirmed. 119 U.S.App.D.C. 378, 343 F.2d 247 (1964).[11]

Before the Court of Appeals and in this Court, petitioner's counsel has urged a number of grounds for reversal. He argues that petitioner's detention and interrogation, described above, were unlawful. He contends that the police failed to follow the procedure prescribed by the Juvenile Court Act in that they failed to notify the parents of the child and the Juvenile Court itself, note 1, supra; that petitioner was deprived of his liberty for about a week without a determination of probable cause which would have been required in the case of an adult, see note 3, supra; that he was interrogated by the police in the absence of counsel or a parent, cf. *Harling v. United States,* 111 U.S.App.D.C. 174, 176, 295 F.2d 161, 163, n. 12

---

8. The District Court had before it extensive information as to petitioner's mental condition, hearing upon both competence to stand trial and the defense of insanity. The court had obtained the "Social Service" file from the Juvenile Court and had made it available to petitioner's counsel. On October 13, 1961, the District Court had granted petitioner's motion of October 6 for commitment to the Psychiatric Division of the General Hospital for 60 days. On December 20, 1961, the hospital reported that "It is the concensus [sic] of the staff that Morris is emotionally ill and severely so . . . ; we feel that he is incompetent to stand trial and to participate in a mature way in his own defense. His illness has interfered with his judgment and reasoning ability. . . ." The prosecutor opposed a finding of incompetence to stand trial, and at the prosecutor's request, the District Court referred petitioner to St. Elizabeth's Hospital for psychiatric observation. According to a letter from the Superintendent of St. Elizabeth's of April 5, 1962, the hospital's staff found that petitioner was "suffering from mental disease at the present time, Schizophrenic Reaction, Chronic Undifferentiated Type," that he had been suffering from this disease at the time of the charged offenses, and that, "if committed by him [those criminal acts] were the product of this disease." They stated, however, that petitioner was "mentally competent to understand the nature of the proceedings against him and to consult properly with counsel in his own defense."

9. D.C.Code § 24-301 (1961).

10. The basis for this distinction—that petitioner was "sane" for purposes of the housebreaking and robbery but "insane" for the purposes of the rape—apparently was the hypothesis, for which there is some support in the record, that the jury might find that the robberies had anteceded the rapes, and, in that event, it might conclude that the housebreakings and robberies were not the products of his mental disease or defect, while the rapes were produced thereby.

11. Petitioner filed a petition for rehearing en banc, but subsequently moved to withdraw the petition in order to prosecute his petition for certiorari to this Court. The Court of Appeals permitted withdrawal. Chief Judge Bazelon filed a dissenting opinion in which Circuit Judge Wright joined. 119 U.S.App.D.C. at 395, 343 F.2d at 264 (1964).

(1961), without warning of his right to remain silent or advice as to his right to counsel, in asserted violation of the Juvenile Court Act and in violation of rights that he would have if he were an adult; and that petitioner was fingerprinted in violation of the asserted intent of the Juvenile Court Act and while unlawfully detained, and that the fingerprints were unlawfully used in the District Court proceeding.[12]

These contentions raise problems of substantial concern as to the construction of and compliance with the Juvenile Court Act. They also suggest basic issues as to the justifiability of affording a juvenile less protection than is accorded to adults suspected of criminal offenses, particularly where, as here, there is an absence of any indication that the denial of rights available to adults was offset, mitigated or explained by action of the Government, as parens patriae, evidencing the special solicitude for juveniles commanded by the Juvenile Court Act. However, because we remand the case on account of the procedural error with respect to waiver of jurisdiction, we do not pass upon these questions.[13]

It is to petitioner's arguments as to the infirmity of the proceedings by which the Juvenile Court waived its otherwise exclusive jurisdiction that we address our attention. Petitioner attacks the waiver of jurisdiction on a number of statutory and constitutional grounds. He contends that the waiver is defective because no hearing was held; because no findings were made by the Juvenile Court; because the Juvenile Court stated no reasons for waiver; and because counsel was denied access to the Social Service file which presumably was considered by the Juvenile Court in determining to waive jurisdiction.

We agree that the order of the Juvenile Court waiving its jurisdiction and transferring petitioner for trial in the United States District Court for the District of Columbia was invalid. There is no question that the order is reviewable on motion to dismiss the indictment in the District Court, as specified by the Court of Appeals in this case. *Kent v. Reid*, supra. The issue is the standards to be applied upon such review.

We agree with the Court of Appeals that the statute contemplates that the Juvenile Court should have considerable latitude within which to determine whether it should retain jurisdiction over a child or—subject to the statutory delimitation[14]—should waive jurisdiction. But this latitude is not complete. At the outset, it assumes procedural regularity sufficient in the particular circumstances to satisfy the basic requirements of due process and fairness, as well as compliance with the statutory requirement of a "full investigation." *Green v. United States*, 113 U.S.App.D.C. 348, 308 F.2d 303 (1962).[15] The statute gives the Juvenile Court a

---

12. *Cf. Harling v. United States*, 111 U.S.App.D.C. 174, 295 F.2d 161 (1961); *Bynum v. United States*, 104 U.S.App.D.C. 368, 262 F.2d 465 (1958). It is not clear from the record whether the fingerprints used were taken during the detention period or were those taken while petitioner was in custody in 1959, nor is it clear that petitioner's counsel objected to the use of the fingerprints.

13. Petitioner also urges that the District Court erred in the following respects:

   (1) It gave the jury a version of the "Allen" charge. See *Allen v. United States*, 164 U.S. 492.
   (2) It failed to give an adequate and fair competency hearing.
   (3) It denied the motion to constitute itself a juvenile court pursuant to D.C.Code § 11-914 (1961), now § 11-1553. (Supp. IV, 1965.)
   (4) It should have granted petitioner's motion for acquittal on all counts, n.o.v., on the grounds of insanity.

   We decide none of these claims.

14. The statute is set out at pp. 547–548, supra.

15. "What is required before a waiver is, as we have said, 'full investigation.' . . . It prevents the waiver of jurisdiction as a matter of routine for the purpose of easing the docket. It prevents routine waiver in certain classes of

substantial degree of discretion as to the factual considerations to be evaluated, the weight to be given them, and the conclusion to be reached. It does not confer upon the Juvenile Court a license for arbitrary procedure. The statute does not permit the Juvenile Court to determine, in isolation and without the participation or any representation of the child, the "critically important" question whether a child will be deprived of the special protections and provisions of the Juvenile Court Act.[16] It does not authorize the Juvenile Court, in total disregard of a motion for hearing filed by counsel, and without any hearing or statement or reasons, to decide—as in this case—that the child will be taken from the Receiving Home for Children and transferred to jail along with adults, and that he will be exposed to the possibility of a death sentence,[17] instead of treatment for a maximum, in Kent's case, of five years, until he is 21.[18]

We do not consider whether, on the merits, Kent should have been transferred; but there is no place in our system of law for reaching a result of such tremendous consequences without ceremony—without hearing, without effective assistance of counsel, without a statement of reasons. It is inconceivable that a court of justice dealing with adults with respect to a similar issue would proceed in this manner. It would be extraordinary if society's special concern for children, as reflected in the District of Columbia's Juvenile Court Act, permitted this procedure. We hold that it does not.

1. The theory of the District's Juvenile Court Act, like that of other jurisdictions,[19] is rooted in social welfare philosophy, rather than in the *corpus juris*. Its proceedings are designated as civil, rather than criminal. The Juvenile Court is theoretically engaged in determining the needs of the child and of society, rather than adjudicating criminal conduct. The objectives are to provide measures of guidance and rehabilitation for the child and protection for society, not to fix criminal responsibility, guilt and punishment. The State is parens patriae, rather than prosecuting attorney and judge.[20] But the admonition to function in a "parental" relationship is not an invitation to procedural arbitrariness.

2. Because the State is supposed to proceed in respect of the child as parens patriae, and not as adversary, courts have relied on the premise that the proceedings are "civil" in nature, and not criminal, and have asserted that the child cannot complain of the deprivation of important rights available in criminal cases. It has been asserted that he can claim only the fundamental due process right to fair treatment.[21] For example, it has been held that he is

---

alleged crimes. It requires a judgment in each case based on an inquiry not only into the facts of the alleged offense but also into the question whether the parens patriae plan of procedure is desirable and proper in the particular case." *Pee v. United States,* 107 U.S.App.D.C. 47, 50, 274 F.2d 556, 559 (1959). *Green v. United States,* supra, at 350, 308 F.2d at 305.

16. See *Watkins v. United States,* 119 U.S.App.D.C. 409, 413, 343 F.2d 278, 282 (1964); *Black v. United States,* 122 U.S.App.D.C. 393, 355 F.2d 104 (1965).

17. D.C.Code § 22-2801 (1961) fixes the punishment for rape at 30 years, or death if the jury so provides in its verdict. The maximum punishment for housebreaking is 15 years, D.C.Code § 22-1801 (1961); for robbery it is also 15 years, D.C.Code § 22-2901 (1961).

18. The jurisdiction of the Juvenile Court over a child ceases when he becomes 21. D.C.Code § 11-907 (1961), now § 11-1551 (Supp. IV, 1965).

19. All States have juvenile court systems. A study of the actual operation of these systems is contained in Note, Juvenile Delinquents: The Police, State Courts, and Individualized Justice, 79 Harv.L.Rev. 775 (1966).

20. See Handler, The Juvenile Court and the Adversary System: Problems of Function and Form, 1965 Wis.L.Rev. 7.

21. *Pee v. United States,* 107 U.S.App.D.C. 47, 274 F.2d 556 (1959).

not entitled to bail; to indictment by grand jury; to a speedy and public trial; to trial by jury; to immunity against self-incrimination; to confrontation of his accusers; and, in some jurisdictions (but not in the District of Columbia, see *Shioutakon v. District of Columbia*, 98 U.S.App.D.C. 371, 236 F.2d 666 (1956), and *Black v. United States*, supra), that he is not entitled to counsel.[22]

While there can be no doubt of the original laudable purpose of juvenile courts, studies and critiques in recent years raise serious questions as to whether actual performance measures well enough against theoretical purpose to make tolerable the immunity of the process from the reach of constitutional guaranties applicable to adults.[23] There is much evidence that some juvenile courts, including that of the District of Columbia, lack the personnel, facilities and techniques to perform adequately as representatives of the State in a parens patriae capacity, at least with respect to children charged with law violation. There is evidence, in fact, that there may be grounds for concern that the child receives the worst of both worlds: that he gets neither the protections accorded to adults nor the solicitous care and regenerative treatment postulated for children.[24]

This concern, however, does not induce us in this case to accept the invitation[25] to rule that constitutional guaranties which would be applicable to adults charged with the serious offenses for which Kent was tried must be applied in juvenile court proceedings concerned with allegations of law violation. The Juvenile Court Act and the decisions of the United States Court of Appeals for the District of Columbia Circuit provide an adequate basis for decision of this case, and we go no further.

3. It is clear beyond dispute that the waiver of jurisdiction is a "critically important" action determining vitally important statutory rights of the juvenile. The Court of Appeals for the District of Columbia Circuit has so held. See *Black v. United States*, supra; *Watkins v. United States*, 119 U.S.App.D.C. 409, 343 F.2d 278 (1964). The statutory scheme makes this plain. The Juvenile Court is vested with "original and exclusive jurisdiction" of the child. This jurisdiction confers special rights and immunities. He is, as specified by the statute, shielded from publicity. He may be confined, but, with rare exceptions, he may not be jailed along with adults. He may be detained, but only until he is 21 years of age. The court is admonished by the statute to give preference to retaining the child in the custody of his parents "unless his welfare and the safety and protection of the public cannot be adequately safeguarded without . . . removal." The child is protected against consequences of adult conviction such as the loss of civil rights, the use of adjudication against him in subsequent proceedings, and disqualification for public employment. D.C.Code §§ 11-907, 11-915, 11-927, 11-929 (1961).[26]

The net, therefore, is that petitioner—then a boy of 16—was, by statute, entitled to certain procedures and benefits as a consequence of his statutory right to the "exclusive" jurisdiction of the Juvenile Court. In these circumstances, considering particularly that decision as to waiver of jurisdiction and transfer of the matter to the District Court was potentially as important to petitioner as the difference between five years' confinement and a death sen-

---

22. *See Pee v. United States*, supra, at 54, 274 F.2d at 563; Paulsen, Fairness to the Juvenile Offender, 41 Minn.L.Rev. 547 (1957).

23. Cf. *Harling v. United States*, 111 U.S.App.D.C. 174, 177, 295 F.2d 161, 164 (1961).

24. See Handler, op. cit. supra, note 20; Note, supra, note 19; materials cited in note 5, supra.

25. See brief of amicus curiae.

26. These are now, without substantial changes, §§ 11-1551, 16-2307, 16-2308, 16-2313, 11-1586 (Supp. IV, 1965).

tence, we conclude that, as a condition to a valid waiver order, petitioner as entitled to a hearing, including access by his counsel to the social records and probation or similar reports which presumably are considered by the court, and to a statement of reasons for the Juvenile Court's decision. We believe that this result is required by the statute, read in the context of constitutional principles relating to due process and the assistance of counsel.[27]

The Court of Appeals in this case relied upon *Wilhite v. United States,* 108 U.S.App.D.C. 279, 281 F.2d 642 (1960). In that case, the Court of Appeals held, for purposes of a determination as to waiver of jurisdiction, that no formal hearing is required and that the "full investigation" required of the Juvenile Court need only be such "as is needed to satisfy that court . . . on the question of waiver."[28] The authority of *Wilhite,* however, is substantially undermined by other, more recent, decisions of the Court of Appeals.

In *Black v. United States,* decided by the Court of Appeals on December 8, 1965, the court held that[29] assistance of counsel in the "critically important" determination of waiver is essential to the proper administration of juvenile proceedings. Because the juvenile was not advised of his right to retained or appointed counsel, the judgment of the District Court, following waiver of jurisdiction by the Juvenile Court, was reversed. The court relied upon its decision in *Shioutakon v. District of Columbia,* 98 U.S.App.D.C. 371, 236 F.2d 666 (1956), in which it had held that effective assistance of counsel in juvenile court proceedings is essential. See also *McDaniel v. Shea,* 108 U.S.App.D.C. 15, 278 F.2d 460 (1960). In *Black,* the court referred to the Criminal Justice Act, enacted four years after *Shioutakon,* in which Congress provided for the assistance of counsel "in proceedings before the juvenile court of the District of Columbia." D.C.Code § 2-2202 (1961). The court held that "The need is even greater in the adjudication of waiver [than in a case like Shioutakon], since it contemplates the imposition of criminal sanctions." 122 U.S.App.D.C. at 395, 355 F.2d at 106.

In *Watkins v. United States,* 119 U.S.App.D.C. 409, 343 F.2d 278 (1964), decided in November, 1964, the Juvenile Court had waived jurisdiction of appellant who was charged with housebreaking and larceny. In the District Court, appellant sought disclosure of the social record in order to attack the validity of the waiver. The Court of Appeals held that in a waiver proceeding a juvenile's attorney is entitled to access to such records. The court observed that

> All of the social records concerning the child are usually relevant to waiver, since the Juvenile Court must be deemed to consider the entire history of the child in determining waiver. The relevance of particular items must be construed generously. Since an attorney has no certain knowledge of what the social records contain, he cannot be expected to demonstrate the relevance of particular items in his request.
>
> The child's attorney must be advised of the information upon which the Juvenile Court relied in order to assist effectively in the determination of the waiver question, by insisting upon

---

27. While we "will not ordinarily review decisions of the United States Court of Appeals [for the District of Columbia Circuit], which are based upon statutes . . . limited [to the District] . . . ," *Del Vecchio v. Bowers,* 296 U.S. 280, 285, the position of that court, as we discuss infra, is self-contradictory. Nor have we deferred to decisions on local law where to do so would require adjudication of difficult constitutional questions. See *District of Columbia v. Little,* 339 U.S. 1.

28. The panel was composed of Circuit Judges Miller, Fahy and Burger. Judge Fahy concurred in the result. It appears that the attack on the regularity of the waiver of jurisdiction was made 17 years after the event, and that no objection to waiver had been made in the District Court.

29. Bazelon, C.J., and Fahy and Leventhal, J.J.

the statutory command that waiver can be ordered only after "full investigation," and by guarding against action of the Juvenile Court beyond its discretionary authority. 119 U.S.App.D.C. at 413, 343 F.2d at 282.

The court remanded the record to the District Court for a determination of the extent to which the records should be disclosed.

The Court of Appeals' decision in the present case was handed down on October 26, 1964, prior to its decisions in *Black* and *Watkins*. The Court of Appeals assumed that, since petitioner had been a probationer of the Juvenile Court for two years, that Court had before it sufficient evidence to make an informed judgment. It therefore concluded that the statutory requirement of a "full investigation" had been met. It noted the absence of "a specification by the Juvenile Court Judge of precisely why he concluded to waive jurisdiction." 119 U.S.App.D.C. at 384, 343 F.2d at 253. While it indicated that, "in some cases, at least," a useful purpose might be served "by a discussion of the reasons motivating the determination," id. at 384, 343 F.2d at 253, n. 6, it did not conclude that the absence thereof invalidated the waiver.

As to the denial of access to the social records, the Court of Appeals stated that "the statute is ambiguous." It said that petitioner's claim, in essence, is "that counsel should have the opportunity to challenge them, presumably in a manner akin to cross-examination." Id. at 389, 343 F.2d at 258. It held, however, that this is "the kind of adversarial tactics which the system is designed to avoid." It characterized counsel's proper function as being merely that of bringing forward affirmative information which might help the court. His function, the Court of Appeals said, "is not to denigrate the staff's submissions and recommendations." Ibid. Accordingly, it held that the Juvenile Court had not abused its discretion in denying access to the social records.

We are of the opinion that the Court of Appeals misconceived the basic issue and the underlying values in this case. It did note, as another panel of the same court did a few months later in *Black* and *Watkins*, that the determination of whether to transfer a child from the statutory structure of the Juvenile Court to the criminal processes of the District Court is "critically important." We hold that it is, indeed, a "critically important" proceeding. The Juvenile Court Act confers upon the child a right to avail himself of that court's "exclusive" jurisdiction. As the Court of Appeals has said, "[I]t is implicit in [the Juvenile Court] scheme that noncriminal treatment is to be the rule—and the adult criminal treatment the exception which must be governed by the particular factors of individual cases." *Harling v. United States*, 111 U.S.App.D.C. 174, 177-178, 295 F.2d 161, 164-165 (1961).

Meaningful review requires that the reviewing court should review. It should not be remitted to assumptions. It must have before it a statement of the reasons motivating the waiver, including, of course, a statement of the relevant facts. It may not "assume" that there are adequate reasons, nor may it merely assume that "full investigation" has been made. Accordingly, we hold that it is incumbent upon the Juvenile Court to accompany its waiver order with a statement of the reasons or considerations therefor. We do not read the statute as requiring that this statement must be formal, or that it should necessarily include conventional findings of fact. But the statement should be sufficient to demonstrate that the statutory requirement of "full investigation" has been met, and that the question has received the careful consideration of the Juvenile Court; and it must set forth the basis for the order with sufficient specificity to permit meaningful review.

Correspondingly, we conclude that an opportunity for a hearing, which may be informal, must be given the child prior to entry of a waiver order. Under *Black,* the child is entitled to counsel in connection with a waiver proceeding, and, under Watkins, counsel is entitled to see the child's social records. These rights are meaningless—an illusion, a mockery—unless counsel is given an opportunity to function.

The right to representation by counsel is not a formality. It is not a grudging gesture to a ritualistic requirement. It is of the essence of justice. Appointment of counsel without affording an opportunity for hearing on a "critically important" decision is tantamount to denial of counsel. There is no justification for the failure of the Juvenile Court to rule on the motion for hearing filed by petitioner's counsel, and it was error to fail to grant a hearing.

We do not mean by this to indicate that the hearing to be held must conform with all of the requirements of a criminal trial, or even of the usual administrative hearing, but we do hold that the hearing must measure up to the essentials of due process and fair treatment. *Pee v. United States,* 107 U.S.App.D.C. 47, 50, 274 F.2d 556, 559 (1959).

With respect to access by the child's counsel to the social records of the child, we deem it obvious that, since these are to be considered by the Juvenile Court in making its decision to waive, they must be made available to the child's counsel. This is what the Court of Appeals itself held in Watkins. There is no doubt as to the statutory basis for this conclusion, as the Court of Appeals pointed out in Watkins. We cannot agree with the Court of Appeals in the present case that the statute is "ambiguous." The statute expressly provides that the record shall be withheld from "indiscriminate" public inspection, "except that such records or parts thereof shall be made available by rule of court or special order of court to such persons . . . as have a legitimate interest in the protection . . . of the child. . . ." D.C.Code § 11-929(b) (1961), now § 11-1586(b) (Supp. IV, 1965).[30] The Court of Appeals has held in *Black,* and we agree, that counsel must be afforded to the child in waiver proceedings. Counsel, therefore, have a "legitimate interest" in the protection of the child, and must be afforded access to these records.[31]

We do not agree with the Court of Appeals' statement, attempting to justify denial of access to these records, that counsel's role is limited to presenting "to the court anything on behalf of the child which might help the court in arriving at a decision; it is not to denigrate the staff's submissions and recommendations." On the contrary, if the staff's submissions include materials which are susceptible to challenge or impeachment, it is precisely the role of counsel to "denigrate" such matter. There is no irrebuttable presumption of accuracy attached to staff reports. If a decision on waiver is "critically important," it is equally of "critical importance" that the material submitted to the judge—which is protected by the statute only against "indiscriminate" inspection—be subjected, within reasonable limits having regard to the theory of the Juvenile Court Act, to examination, criticism and refutation. While the Juvenile Court judge may, of course, receive ex parte analyses and recommendations

---

30. Under the statute, the Juvenile Court has power by rule or order, to subject the examination of the social records to conditions which will prevent misuse of the information. Violation of any such rule or order, or disclosure of the information "except for purposes for which . . . released," is a misdemeanor. D.C.Code § 11-929 (1961), now, without substantial change, § 11-1586 (Supp. IV, 1965).

31. In Watkins, the Court of Appeals seems to have permitted withholding of some portions of the social record from examination by petitioner's counsel. To the extent that Watkins is inconsistent with the standard which we state, it cannot be considered as controlling.

from his staff, he may not, for purposes of a decision on waiver, receive and rely upon secret information, whether emanating from his staff or otherwise. The Juvenile Court is governed in this respect by the established principles which control courts and quasi-judicial agencies of the Government.

For the reasons stated, we conclude that the Court of Appeals and the District Court erred in sustaining the validity of the waiver by the Juvenile Court. The Government urges that any error committed by the Juvenile Court was cured by the proceedings before the District Court. It is true that the District Court considered and denied a motion to dismiss on the grounds of the invalidity of the waiver order of the Juvenile Court, and that it considered and denied a motion that it should itself, as authorized by statute, proceed in this case to "exercise the powers conferred upon the juvenile court." D.C.Code § 11-914 (1961), now § 11-1553 (Supp. IV, 1965). But we agree with the Court of Appeals in *Black* that "the waiver question was primarily and initially one for the Juvenile Court to decide, and its failure to do so in a valid manner cannot be said to be harmless error. It is the Juvenile Court, not the District Court, which has the facilities, personnel and expertise for a proper determination of the waiver issue." 122 U.S.App.D.C. at 396, 355 F.2d at 107.[32]

Ordinarily, we would reverse the Court of Appeals and direct the District Court to remand the case to the Juvenile Court for a new determination of waiver. If, on remand, the decision were against waiver, the indictment in the District Court would be dismissed. See *Black v. United States,* supra. However, petitioner has now passed the age of 21, and the Juvenile Court can no longer exercise jurisdiction over him. In view of the unavailability of a redetermination of the waiver question by the Juvenile Court, it is urged by petitioner that the conviction should be vacated and the indictment dismissed. In the circumstances of this case, and in light of the remedy which the Court of Appeals fashioned in *Black,* supra, we do not consider it appropriate to grant this drastic relief.[33] Accordingly, we vacate the order of the Court of Appeals and the judgment of the District Court and remand the case to the District Court for a hearing de novo on waiver, consistent with this opinion.[34] If that court finds that waiver was inappropriate, petitioner's conviction must be vacated. If, however, it finds that the waiver order was proper when originally made, the District Court may proceed, after consideration of such motions as counsel may make and such further proceedings, if any, as may be warranted, to enter an appropriate judgment. Cf. *Black v. United States,* supra.

Reversed and remanded.

---

32. It also appears that the District Court requested and obtained the Social Service file and the probation staff's report of September 8, 1961, and that these were made available to petitioner's counsel. This did not cure the error of the Juvenile Court. Perhaps the point of it is that it again illustrates the maxim that, while nondisclosure may contribute to the comfort of the staff, disclosure does not cause heaven to fall.

33. Petitioner is in St. Elizabeth's Hospital for psychiatric treatment as a result of the jury verdict on the rape charges.

34. We do not deem it appropriate merely to vacate the judgment and remand to the Court of Appeals for reconsideration of its present decision in light of its subsequent decisions in *Watkins* and *Black,* supra. Those cases were decided by different panels of the Court of Appeals from that which decided the present case, and, in view of our grant of certiorari and of the importance of the issue, we consider it necessary to resolve the question presented instead of leaving it open for further consideration by the Court of Appeals.

Appendix to Opinion of the Court

Policy Memorandum No. 7, November 30, 1959

The authority of the Judge of the Juvenile Court of the District of Columbia to waive or transfer jurisdiction to the U.S. District Court for the District of Columbia is contained in the Juvenile Court Act (§ 11-914 D.C.Code, 1951 Ed.). This section permits the Judge to waive jurisdiction "after full investigation" in the case of any child "sixteen years of age or older [who is] charged with an offense which would amount to a felony in the case of an adult, or any child charged with an offense which if committed by an adult is punishable by death or life imprisonment."

The statute sets forth no specific standards for the exercise of this important discretionary act, but leaves the formulation of such criteria to the Judge. A knowledge of the Judge's criteria is important to the child, his parents, his attorney, to the judges of the U.S. District Court for the District of Columbia, to the United States Attorney and his assistants, and to the Metropolitan Police Department, as well as to the staff of this court, especially the Juvenile Intake Section.

Therefore, the Judge has consulted with the Chief Judge and other judges of the U.S. District Court for the District of Columbia, with the United States Attorney, with representatives of the Bar, and with other groups concerned and has formulated the following criteria and principles concerning waiver of jurisdiction which are consistent with the basic aims and purpose of the Juvenile Court Act.

An offense falling within the statutory limitations (set forth above) will be waived if it has prosecutive merit and if it is heinous or of an aggravated character, or—even though less serious—if it represents a pattern of repeated offenses which indicate that the juvenile may be beyond rehabilitation under Juvenile Court procedures, or if the public needs the protection afforded by such action.

The determinative factors which will be considered by the Judge in deciding whether the Juvenile Court's jurisdiction over such offenses will be waived are the following:

1. The seriousness of the alleged offense to the community and whether the protection of the community requires waiver.

2. Whether the alleged offense was committed in an aggressive, violent, premeditated or willful manner.

3. Whether the alleged offense was against persons or against property, greater weight being given to offenses against persons especially if personal injury resulted.

4. The prosecutive merit of the complaint, i.e., whether there is evidence upon which a Grand Jury may be expected to return an indictment (to be determined by consultation with the United States Attorney).

5. The desirability of trial and disposition of the entire offense in one court when the juvenile's associates in the alleged offense are adults who will be charged with a crime in the U.S. District Court for the District of Columbia.

6. The sophistication and maturity of the juvenile as determined by consideration of his home, environmental situation, emotional attitude and pattern of living.

7. The record and previous history of the juvenile, including previous contacts with the Youth Aid Division, other law enforcement agencies, juvenile courts and other jurisdictions, prior periods of probation to this Court, or prior commitments to juvenile institutions.

8. The prospects for adequate protection of the public and the likelihood of reasonable rehabilitation of the juvenile (if he is found to have committed the alleged offense) by the use of procedures, services and facilities currently available to the Juvenile Court.

It will be the responsibility of any officer of the Court's staff assigned to make the investigation of any complaint in which waiver of jurisdiction is being considered to develop fully all available information which may bear upon the criteria and factors set forth above. Although not all such factors will be involved in an individual case, the Judge will consider the relevant factors in a specific case before reaching a conclusion to waive juvenile jurisdiction and transfer the case to the U.S. District Court for the District of Columbia for trial under the adult procedures of that Court.

Due Process in Adjudication Hearings

Case Comment

The case of *In re Gault* followed the Kent decision by only one year and the Supreme Court's ruling in *Gault* changed the complexion of juvenile justice. It is considered the leading constitutional case in juvenile law. The *Gault* decision established that juvenile offenders must be provided with many basic due process rights, including counsel, notice, confrontation of witnesses, and freedom from self-incrimination, all of which had been accorded only to adult criminals. The *Gault* decision reshaped the constitutional, philosophical, and procedural nature of the juvenile court system. As a result, those working in the system—judges, social workers, attorneys, and so forth—became faced with the problem of reaffirming the rehabilitative ideal of the juvenile court while ensuring that juveniles receive proper procedural due process safeguards.[1] As Justice Hugo Black (387 U.S. 1, 19) stated in the *Gault* case:

> When a person, infant or adult, can be seized by the state, charged and convicted, for violating a criminal law, and then ordered by the state to be confined for six years, I think the Constitution requires that he be tried in accordance with the guarantees of all the provisions of the Bill of rights, made applicable to the states by the Fourteenth Amendment (387 U.S. 1 (1967), 19.

IN RE GAULT

Supreme Court of the United States, 1967.
387 US 1.

Mr. Justice Fortas delivered the opinion of the Court.

This is an appeal under 28 U.S.C. § 1257(2) from a judgment of the Supreme Court of Arizona affirming the dismissal of a petition for a writ of habeas corpus. 99 Ariz. 181, 407 P.2d 760 (1965). The petition sought the release of Gerald Francis Gault, appellants' 15-year-old son, who had been committed as a juvenile delinquent to the State Industrial School by the Juvenile Court of Gila County, Arizona. The Supreme Court of Arizona affirmed dismissal

---

1. See Feld, B. 1989. "The Right to Counsel in Juvenile Court: An Empirical Study of When Lawyers Appeal and the Difference They Make." *Journal of Criminal Law and Criminology* 79:1187–1346.

of the writ against various arguments which included an attack upon the constitutionality of the Arizona Juvenile Code because of its alleged <u>denial of procedural due process rights</u> <u>to juveniles charged with being "delinquents."</u> The court agreed that the constitutional guarantee of due process of law is applicable in such proceedings. It held that Arizona's Juvenile Code is to be read as "impliedly" implementing the "due process concept." It then proceeded to identify and describe "the particular elements which constitute due process in a juvenile hearing." It concluded that the proceedings ending in commitment of Gerald Gault did not offend those requirements. We do not agree, and we reverse. We begin with a statement of the facts.

I

On Monday, June 8, 1964, at about 10 a.m., Gerald Francis Gault and a friend, Ronald Lewis, were taken into custody by the Sheriff of Gila County. Gerald was then still subject to a six months' probation order which had been entered on February 25, 1964, as a result of his having been in the company of another boy who had stolen a wallet from a lady's purse. The police action on June 8 was taken as the result of a verbal complaint by a neighbor of the boys, Mrs. Cook, about a telephone call made to her in which the caller or callers made lewd or indecent remarks. It will suffice for purposes of this opinion to say that the remarks or questions put to her were of the irritatingly offensive, adolescent, sex variety.

At the time Gerald was picked up, his mother and father were both at work. No notice that Gerald was being taken into custody was left at the home. No other steps were taken to advise them that their son had, in effect, been arrested. Gerald was taken to the Children's Detention Home. When his mother arrived home at about 6 o'clock, Gerald was not there. Gerald's older brother was sent to look for him at the trailer home of the Lewis family. He apparently learned then that Gerald was in custody. He so informed his mother. The two of them went to the Detention Home. The deputy probation officer, Flagg, who was also superintendent of the Detention Home, told Mrs. Gault "why Jerry was there," and said that a hearing would be held in Juvenile Court at 3 o'clock the following day, June 9.

Officer Flagg filed a petition with the court on the hearing day, June 9, 1964. It was not served on the Gaults. Indeed, none of them saw this petition until the habeas corpus hearing on August 17, 1964. The petition was entirely formal. It made no reference to any factual basis for the judicial action which it initiated. It recited only that "said minor is under the age of eighteen years, and is in need of the protection of this Honorable Court; [and that] said minor is a delinquent minor." It prayed for a hearing and an order regarding "the care and custody of said minor." Officer Flagg executed a formal affidavit in support of the petition.

On June 9, Gerald, his mother, his older brother, and Probation Officers Flagg and Henderson appeared before the Juvenile Judge in chambers. Gerald's father was not there. He was at work out of the city. Mrs. Cook, the complainant, was not there. No one was sworn at this hearing. No transcript or recording was made. No memorandum or record of the substance of the proceedings was prepared. Our information about the proceedings and the subsequent hearing on June 15, derives entirely from the testimony of the Juvenile Court Judge,[1]

---

1. Under Arizona law, juvenile hearings are conducted by a judge of the Superior Court, designated by his colleagues on the Superior Court to serve as Juvenile Court Judge. Arizona Const., Art. 6, § 15; Arizona Revised Statutes (hereinafter ARS) §§ 8-201, 8-202.

Mr. and Mrs. Gault and Officer Flagg at the habeas corpus proceeding conducted two months later. From this, it appears that, at the June 9 hearing, Gerald was questioned by the judge about the telephone call. There was conflict as to what he said. His mother recalled that Gerald said he only dialed Mrs. Cook's number and handed the telephone to his friend, Ronald. Officer Flagg recalled that Gerald had admitted making the lewd remarks. Judge McGhee testified that Gerald "admitted making one of these [lewd] statements." At the conclusion of the hearing, the judge said he would "think about it." Gerald was taken back to the Detention Home. He was not sent to his own home with his parents. On June 11 or 12, after having been detained since June 8, Gerald was released and driven home.[2] There is no explanation in the record as to why he was kept in the Detention Home or why he was released. At 5 p.m. on the day of Gerald's release, Mrs. Gault received a note signed by Officer Flagg. It was on plain paper, not letterhead. Its entire text was as follows:

"Mrs. Gault:
    Judge McGHEE has set Monday June 15, 1964 at 11:00 A.M. as the date and time for further Hearings on Gerald's delinquency.
    /s/Flagg"

At the appointed time on Monday, June 15, Gerald, his father and mother, Ronald Lewis and his father, and Officers Flagg and Henderson were present before Judge McGhee. Witnesses at the habeas corpus proceeding differed in their recollections of Gerald's testimony at the June 15 hearing. Mr. and Mrs. Gault recalled that Gerald again testified that he had only dialed the number, and that the other boy had made the remarks. Officer Flagg agreed that, at this hearing Gerald did not admit making the lewd remarks.[3] But Judge McGhee recalled that "there was some admission again of some of the lewd statements. He didn't admit any of the more serious lewd statements."[4] Again, the complainant, Mrs. Cook, was not present. Mrs. Gault asked that Mrs. Cook be present "so she could see which boy that done the talking, the dirty talking over the phone." The Juvenile Judge said "she didn't have to be present at that hearing." The judge did not speak to Mrs. Cook or communicate with her at any time. Probation Officer Flagg had talked to her once—over the telephone on June 9.

At this June 15 hearing a "referral report" made by the probation officers was filed with the court, although not disclosed to Gerald or his parents. This listed the charge as "Lewd Phone Calls." At the conclusion of the hearing, the judge committed Gerald as a juvenile delinquent to the State Industrial School "for the period of his minority [that is, until 21], unless sooner discharged by due process of law." An order to that effect was entered. It recites that "after a full hearing and due deliberation the Court finds that said minor is a delinquent child, and that said minor is of the age of 15 years."

---

2. There is a conflict between the recollection of Mrs. Gault and that of Officer Flagg. Mrs. Gault testified that Gerald was released on Friday, June 12, Officer Flagg that it had been on Thursday, June 11. This was from memory; he had no record, and the note hereafter referred to was undated.

3. Officer Flagg also testified that Gerald had not, when questioned at the Detention Home, admitted having made any of the lewd statements, but that each boy had sought to put the blame on the other. There was conflicting testimony as to whether Ronald had accused Gerald of making the lewd statements during the June 15 hearing.

4. Judge McGhee also testified that Gerald had not denied "certain statements" made to him at the hearing by Officer Henderson.

No appeal is permitted by Arizona law in juvenile cases. On August 3, 1964, a petition for a writ of habeas corpus was filed with the Supreme Court of Arizona and referred by it to the Superior Court for hearing.

At the habeas corpus hearing on August 17, Judge McGhee was vigorously cross-examined as to the basis for his actions. He testified that he had taken into account the fact that Gerald was on probation. He was asked "under what section of . . . the code you found the boy delinquent?"

His answer is set forth in the margin.[5] In substance, he concluded that Gerald came within ARS § 201-6(a), which specifies that a "delinquent child" includes one "who has violated a law of the state or an ordinance or regulation of a political subdivision thereof." The law which Gerald was found to have violated is ARS § 13-377. This section of the Arizona Criminal Code provides that a person who "in the presence or hearing of any woman or child . . . uses vulgar, abusive or obscene language, is guilty of a misdemeanor. . . ." The penalty specified in the Criminal Code, which would apply to an adult, is $5 to $50, or imprisonment for not more than two months. The judge also testified that he acted under ARS § 8-201-6(d), which includes in the definition of a "delinquent child" one who, as the judge phrased it, is "habitually involved in immoral matters."[6]

Asked about the basis for his conclusion that Gerald was "habitually involved in immoral matters," the judge testified, somewhat vaguely, that two years earlier, on July 2, 1962, a "referral" was made concerning Gerald, "where the boy had stolen a baseball glove from another boy and lied to the Police Department about it." The judge said there was "no hearing," and "no accusation" relating to this incident, "because of lack of material foundation." But it seems to have remained in his mind as a relevant factor. The judge also testified that Gerald had admitted making other nuisance phone calls in the past, which, as the judge recalled the boy's testimony, were "silly calls, or funny calls, or something like that."

The Superior Court dismissed the writ, and appellants sought review in the Arizona Supreme Court. That court stated that it considered appellants' assignments of error as urging (1) that the Juvenile Code, ARS § 8-201 to § 8-203, is unconstitutional because it does not require that parents and children be apprised of the specific charges, does not require proper notice of a hearing, and does not provide for an appeal, and (2) that the proceedings and order relating to Gerald constituted a denial of due process of law because of the absence

---

5. "Q. All right. Now, Judge, would you tell me under what section of the law or tell me under what section of—of the code you found the boy delinquent?

A. Well, there is a—I think it amounts to disturbing the peace. I can't give you the section, but I can tell you the law, that, when one person uses lewd language in the presence of another person, that it can amount to—and I consider that, when a person makes it over the phone, that it is considered in the presence, I might be wrong, that is one section. The other section upon which I consider the boy delinquent is Section 201, Subsection (d), habitually involved in immoral matters."

6. ARS § 8-201-6, the section of the Arizona Juvenile Code which defines a delinquent child, reads:
"Delinquent child" includes:
  (a) A child who has violated a law of the state or an ordinance or regulation of a political subdivision thereof.
  (b) A child who, by reason of being incorrigible, wayward or habitually disobedient, is uncontrolled by his parent, guardian or custodian.
  (c) A child who is habitually truant from school or home.
  (d) A child who habitually so deports himself as to injure or endanger the morals or health of himself or others.

of adequate notice of the charge and the hearing; failure to notify appellants of certain constitutional rights including the rights to counsel and to confrontation, and the privilege against self-incrimination; the use of unsworn hearsay testimony, and the failure to make a record of the proceedings. Appellants further asserted that it was error for the Juvenile Court to remove Gerald from the custody of his parents without a showing and finding of their unsuitability, and alleged a miscellany of other errors under state law.

The Supreme Court handed down an elaborate and wide-ranging opinion affirming dismissal of the writ and stating the court's conclusions as to the issues raised by appellants and other aspects of the juvenile process. In their jurisdictional statement and brief in this Court, appellants do not urge upon us all of the points passed upon by the Supreme Court of Arizona. They urge that we hold the Juvenile Code of Arizona invalid on its face or as applied in this case because, contrary to the Due Process Clause of the Fourteenth Amendment, the juvenile is taken from the custody of his parents and committed to a state institution pursuant to proceedings in which the Juvenile Court has virtually unlimited discretion, and in which the following basic rights are denied:

1. Notice of the charges;
2. Right to counsel;
3. Right to confrontation and cross-examination;
4. Privilege against self-incrimination;
5. Right to a transcript of the proceedings; and
6. Right to appellate review.

We shall not consider other issues which were passed upon by the Supreme Court of Arizona. We emphasize that we indicate no opinion as to whether the decision of that court with respect to such other issues does or does not conflict with requirements of the Federal Constitution.[7]

---

7. For example, the laws of Arizona allow arrest for a misdemeanor only if a warrant is obtained or if it is committed in the presence of the officer. ARS § 13-1403. The Supreme Court of Arizona held that this is inapplicable in the case of juveniles. See ARS § 8-221, which relates specifically to juveniles. But compare *Two Brothers and a Case of Liquor*, Juv.Ct.D.C. Nos. 66-2652-J, 66-2653-J, December 28, 1966 (opinion of Judge Ketcham); Standards for Juvenile and Family Courts, Children's Bureau Pub. No. 437-1966, p. 47 (hereinafter cited as Standards); New York Family Court Act § 721 (1963) (hereinafter cited as N.Y.Family Court Act).

The court also held that the judge may consider hearsay if it is "of a kind on which reasonable men are accustomed to rely in serious affairs." But compare Note, Juvenile Delinquents: The Police, State Courts, and Individualized Justice, 79 Harv.L.Rev. 775, 794-795 (1966) (hereinafter cited as Harvard Law Review Note):

"The informality of juvenile court hearings frequently leads to the admission of hearsay and unsworn testimony. It is said that 'close adherence to the strict rules of evidence might prevent the court from obtaining important facts as to the child's character and condition which could only be to the child's detriment.' The assumption is that the judge will give normally inadmissible evidence only its proper weight. It is also declared in support of these evidentiary practices that the juvenile court is not a criminal court, that the importance of the hearsay rule has been overestimated, and that allowing an attorney to make 'technical objections' would disrupt the desired informality of the proceedings. But to the extent that the rules of evidence are not merely technical or historical, but, like the hearsay rule, have a sound basis in human experience, they should not be rejected in any judicial inquiry. Juvenile court judges in Los Angeles, Tucson, and Wisconsin Rapids, Wisconsin report that they are satisfied with the operation of their courts despite application of unrelaxed rules of evidence." (Footnotes omitted.)

It ruled that the correct burden of proof is that "the juvenile judge must be persuaded by clear and convincing evidence that the infant has committed the alleged delinquent act." Compare the "preponderance of the evidence"

II

The Supreme Court of Arizona held that due process of law is requisite to the constitutional validity of proceedings in which a court reaches the conclusion that a juvenile has been at fault, has engaged in conduct prohibited by law, or has otherwise misbehaved, with the consequence that he is committed to an institution in which his freedom is curtailed. This conclusion is in accord with the decisions of a number of courts under both federal and state constitutions.[8]

This Court has not heretofore decided the precise question. In *Kent v. United States*, 383 U.S. 541 (1966), we considered the requirements for a valid waiver of the "exclusive" jurisdiction of the Juvenile Court of the District of Columbia so that a juvenile could be tried in the adult criminal court of the District. Although our decision turned upon the language of the statute, we emphasized the necessity that "the basic requirements of due process and fairness" be satisfied in such proceedings.[9] *Haley v. Ohio*, 332 U.S. 596 (1948), involved the admissibility, in a state criminal court of general jurisdiction, of a confession by a 15-year-old boy. The Court held that the Fourteenth Amendment applied to prohibit the use of the coerced confession. MR. JUSTICE DOUGLAS said, "Neither man nor child can be allowed to stand condemned by methods which flout constitutional requirements of due process of law."[10] To the same effect is *Gallegos v. Colorado*, 370 U.S. 49 (1962). Accordingly, while these cases relate only to restricted aspects of the subject, they unmistakably indicate that, whatever may be their precise impact, neither the Fourteenth Amendment nor the Bill of Rights is for adults alone.

We do not in this opinion consider the impact of these constitutional provisions upon the totality of the relationship of the juvenile and the state. We do not even consider the entire process relating to juvenile "delinquents." For example, we are not here concerned with the procedures or constitutional rights applicable to the pre-judicial stages of the juvenile process, nor do we direct our attention to the post-adjudicative or dispositional process. See note 48, infra. We consider only the problems presented to us by this case. These relate to the proceedings by which a determination is made as to whether a juvenile is a "delinquent" as a result of alleged misconduct on his part, with the consequence that he may be committed to a state institution. As to these proceedings, there appears to be little current dissent from the proposition that the Due Process Clause has a role to play.[11] The problem is to ascertain the precise impact of the due process requirement upon such proceedings.

---

test, N.Y.Family Court Act § 744 (where maximum commitment is three years, §§ 753, 758). Cf. Harvard Law Review Note, p. 795.

8. See, e.g., *In the Matters of Gregory W. and Gerald S.*, 19 N.Y.2d 55, 224 N.E.2d 102 (1966); *In the Interests of Carlo and Stasilowicz*, 48 N.J. 224, 225 A.2d 110 (1966); *People v. Dotson*, 46 Cal.2d 891, 299 P.2d 875 (1956); *Pee v. United States*, 107 U.S.App.D.C. 47, 274 F.2d 556 (1959); *Wissenburg v. Bradley*, 209 Iowa 813, 229 N.W. 205 (1930); *Bryant v. Brown*, 151 Miss. 398, 118 So. 184 (1928); *Dendy v. Wilson*, 142 Tex. 460, 179 S.W.2d 269 (1944); Application of Johnson, 178 F.Supp. 155 (D.C.N.J.1957).

9. 383 U.S. at 553.

10. 332 U.S. at 601 (opinion for four Justices).

11. See Report by the President's Commission on Law Enforcement and Administration of Justice, "The Challenge of Crime in a Free Society" (1967) (hereinafter cited as Nat'l Crime Comm'n Report), pp. 81, 85-86; Standards, p. 71; Gardner, The Kent Case and the Juvenile Court: A Challenge to Lawyers, 52 A.B.A.J. 923 (1966); Paulsen, Fairness to the Juvenile Offender, 41 Minn.L.Rev. 547 (1957); Ketcham, The Legal Renaissance in the Juvenile Court, 60 Nw.U.L.Rev. 585 (1965); Allen, The Borderland of Criminal Justice (1964), pp. 19–23; Harvard Law Review Note, p. 791; Note, Rights and Rehabilitation in the Juvenile Courts, 67 Col.L.Rev. 281 (1967); Comment, Criminal Offenders in the Juvenile Court: More Brickbats and Another Proposal, 114 U.Pa.L.Rev. 1171 (1966).

From the inception of the juvenile court system, wide differences have been tolerated—indeed insisted upon—between the procedural rights accorded to adults and those of juveniles. In practically all jurisdictions, there are rights granted to adults which are withheld from juveniles. In addition to the specific problems involved in the present case, for example, it has been held that the juvenile is not entitled to bail, to indictment by grand jury, to a public trial or to trial by jury.[12] It is frequent practice that rules governing the arrest and interrogation of adults by the police are not observed in the case of juveniles.[13]

The history and theory underlying this development are well known, but a recapitulation is necessary for purposes of this opinion. The Juvenile Court movement began in this country at the end of the last century. From the juvenile court statute adopted in Illinois in 1899, the system has spread to every State in the Union, the District of Columbia, and Puerto Rico.[14] The constitutionality of Juvenile Court laws has been sustained in over 40 jurisdictions against a variety of attacks.[15]

The early reformers were appalled by adult procedures and penalties, and by the fact that children could be given long prison sentences and mixed in jails with hardened criminals. They were profoundly convinced that society's duty to the child could not be confined by the concept of justice alone. They believed that society's role was not to ascertain whether the child was "guilty" or "innocent," but "What is he, how has he become what he is, and what had best be done in his interest and in the interest of the state to save him from a downward career."[16] The child—essentially good, as they saw it—was to be made "to feel that he is the object of [the state's] care and solicitude,"[17] not that he was under arrest or on trial. The rules of criminal procedure were therefore altogether inapplicable. The apparent rigidities, technicalities, and harshness which they observed in both substantive and procedural criminal law were therefore to be discarded. The idea of crime and punishment was to be abandoned. The child was to be "treated" and "rehabilitated," and the procedures, from apprehension through institutionalization, were to be "clinical," rather than punitive.

---

12. See *Kent v. United States*, 383 U.S. 541, 555 and n. 22 (1966).

13. See n. 7, supra.

14. See National Council of Juvenile Court Judges, Directory and Manual (1964), p. 1. The number of Juvenile Judges as of 1964 is listed as 2,987, of whom 213 are full-time Juvenile Court Judges. Id. at 305. The Nat'l Crime Comm'n Report indicates that half of these judges have no undergraduate degree, a fifth have no college education at all, a fifth are not members of the bar, and three-quarters devote less than one-quarter of their time to juvenile matters. See also McCune, Profile of the Nation's Juvenile Court Judges (monograph, George Washington University, Center for the Behavioral Sciences, 1965), which is a detailed statistical study of Juvenile Court Judges, and indicates additionally that about a quarter of these judges have no law school training at all. About one-third of all judges have no probation and social work staff available to them; between eighty and ninety percent have no available psychologist or psychiatrist. Ibid. It has been observed that, while "good will, compassion, and similar virtues are . . . admirably prevalent throughout the system . . . expertise, the keystone of the whole venture, is lacking." Harvard Law Review Note, p. 809. In 1965, over 697,000 delinquency cases (excluding traffic) were disposed of in these courts, involving some 601,000 children, or 2% of all children between 10 and 17. Juvenile Court Statistics—1965, Children's Bureau Statistical Series No. 85 (1966), p. 2.

15. See Paulsen, *Kent v. United States:* The Constitutional Context of Juvenile Cases, 1966 Sup.Ct. Review 167, 174.

16. Julian Mack, The Juvenile Court, 23 Harv.L.Rev. 104, 119-120 (1909).

17. Id. at 120.

These results were to be achieved, without coming to conceptual and constitutional grief, by insisting that the proceedings were not adversary, but that the state was proceeding as parens patriae.[18] The Latin phrase proved to be a great help to those who sought to rationalize the exclusion of juveniles from the constitutional scheme; but its meaning is murky, and its historic credentials are of dubious relevance. The phrase was taken from chancery practice, where, however, it was used to describe the power of the state to act in loco parentis for the purpose of protecting the property interests and the person of the child.[19] But there is no trace of the doctrine in the history of criminal jurisprudence. At common law, children under seven were considered incapable of possessing criminal intent. Beyond that age, they were subjected to arrest, trial, and in theory to punishment like adult offenders.[20] In these old days, the state was not deemed to have authority to accord them fewer procedural rights than adults.

The right of the state, as parens patriae, to deny to the child procedural rights available to his elders was elaborated by the assertion that a child, unlike an adult, has a right "not to liberty, but to custody." He can be made to attorn to his parents, to go to school, etc. If his parents default in effectively performing their custodial functions—that is, if the child is "delinquent"—the state may intervene. In doing so, it does not deprive the child of any rights, because he has none. It merely provides the "custody" to which the child is entitled.[21] On this basis, proceedings involving juveniles were described as "civil," not "criminal," and therefore not subject to the requirements which restrict the state when it seeks to deprive a person of his liberty.[22]

Accordingly, the highest motives and most enlightened impulses led to a peculiar system for juveniles, unknown to our law in any comparable context. The constitutional and theoretical basis for this peculiar system is—to say the least—debatable. And in practice, as we

---

18. Id. at 109; *Paulsen*, op. cit. supra, n. 15, at 173-174. There seems to have been little early constitutional objection to the special procedures of juvenile courts. But see Waite, How Far Can Court Procedure Be Socialized Without Impairing Individual Rights, 12 J.Crim.L. & Criminology 339, 340 (1922): "The court which must direct its procedure even apparently to do something to a child because of what he has done, is parted from the court which is avowedly concerned only with doing something for a child because of what he is and needs, by a gulf too wide to be bridged by any humanity which the judge may introduce into his hearings, or by the habitual use of corrective, rather than punitive, methods after conviction."

19. *Paulsen*, op. cit. supra, n. 15, at 173; Hurley, Origin of the Illinois Juvenile Court Law, in The Child, The Clinic, and the Court (1925), pp. 320, 328.

20. Julian Mack, The Chancery Procedure in the Juvenile Court, in The Child, The Clinic, and the Court (1925), p. 310.

21. See, e.g., Shears, Legal Problems Peculiar to Children's Courts, 48 A.B.A.J. 719, 720 (1962) ("The basic right of a juvenile is not to liberty, but to custody. He has the right to have someone take care of him, and if his parents do not afford him this custodial privilege, the law must do so."); *Ex parte Crouse*, 4 Whart. 9, 11 (Sup.Ct.Pa. 1839); *Petition of Ferrier*, 103 Ill. 367, 371-373 (1882).

22. The Appendix to the opinion of Judge Prettyman in *Pee v. United States*, 107 U.S.App.D.C. 47, 274 F.2d 556 (1959), lists authority in 51 jurisdictions to this effect. Even rules required by due process in civil proceedings, however, have not generally been deemed compulsory as to proceedings affecting juveniles. For example, constitutional requirements as to notice of issues, which would commonly apply in civil cases, are commonly disregarded in juvenile proceedings, as this case illustrates.

remarked in the Kent case, supra, the results have not been entirely satisfactory.[23] Juvenile Court history has again demonstrated that unbridled discretion, however benevolently motivated, is frequently a poor substitute for principle and procedure. In 1937, Dean Pound wrote: "The powers of the Star Chamber were a trifle in comparison with those of our juvenile courts. . . ."[24] The absence of substantive standards has not necessarily meant that children receive careful, compassionate, individualized treatment. The absence of procedural rules based upon constitutional principle has not always produced fair, efficient, and effective procedures. Departures from established principles of due process have frequently resulted not in enlightened procedure, but in arbitrariness. The Chairman of the Pennsylvania Council of Juvenile Court Judges has recently observed: "Unfortunately, loose procedures, high-handed methods and crowded court calendars, either singly or in combination, all too often, have resulted in depriving some juveniles of fundamental rights that have resulted in a denial of due process."[25]

---

23. "There is evidence . . . that there may be grounds for concern that the child receives the worst of both worlds: that he gets neither the protections accorded to adults nor the solicitous care and regenerative treatment postulated for children." 383 U.S. at 556, citing Handler, The Juvenile Court and the Adversary System: Problems of Function and Form, 1965 Wis.L.Rev. 7; Harvard Law Review Note, and various congressional materials set forth in 383 U.S. at 546, n. 5.

On the other hand, while this opinion and much recent writing concentrate upon the failures of the Juvenile Court system to live up to the expectations of its founders, the observation of the Nat'l Crime Comm'n Report should be kept in mind:

"Although its shortcomings are many and its results too often disappointing, the juvenile justice system in many cities is operated by people who are better educated and more highly skilled, can call on more and better facilities and services, and has more ancillary agencies to which to refer its clientele than its adult counterpart." Id. at 78.

24. Foreword to Young, Social Treatment in Probation and Delinquency (1937), p. xxvii. The 1965 Report of the United States Commission on Civil Rights, "Law Enforcement—A Report on Equal Protection in the South," pp. 80–83, documents numerous instances in which "local authorities used the broad discretion afforded them by the absence of safeguards [in the juvenile process]" to punish, intimidate, and obstruct youthful participants in civil rights demonstrations. See also Paulsen, Juvenile Courts, Family Courts, and the Poor Man, 54 Calif.L.Rev. 694, 707–709 (1966).

25. Lehman, A Juvenile's Right to Counsel in a Delinquency Hearing, 17 Juvenile Court Judges Journal 53, 54 (1966).

Compare the observation of the late Arthur T. Vanderbilt, Chief Justice of the Supreme Court of New Jersey, in a foreword to Virtue, Basic Structure for Children's Services in Michigan (1953), p. x:

"In their zeal to care for children, neither juvenile judges nor welfare workers can be permitted to violate the Constitution, especially the constitutional provisions as to due process that are involved in moving a child from its home. The indispensable elements of due process are: first, a tribunal with jurisdiction; second, notice of a hearing to the proper parties, and finally, a fair hearing. All three must be present if we are to treat the child as an individual human being and not to revert, in spite of good intentions, to the more primitive days when he was treated as a chattel."

We are warned that the system must not "degenerate into a star chamber proceeding with the judge imposing his own particular brand of culture and morals on indigent people. . . ." Judge Marion G. Woodward, letter reproduced in 18 Social Service Review 366, 368 (1944). Doctor Bovet, the Swiss psychiatrist, in his monograph for the World Health Organization, Psychiatric Aspects of Juvenile Delinquency (1951), p. 79, stated that: "One of the most definite conclusions of this investigation is that few fields exist in which more serious coercive measures are applied, on such flimsy objective evidence, than in that of juvenile delinquency." We are told that "The judge as amateur psychologist, experimenting upon the unfortunate children who must appear before him, is neither an attractive nor a convincing figure." Harvard Law Review Note, at 808.

Failure to observe the fundamental requirements of due process has resulted in instances, which might have been avoided, of unfairness to individuals and inadequate or inaccurate findings of fact and unfortunate prescriptions of remedy. Due process of law is the primary and indispensable foundation of individual freedom. It is the basic and essential term in the social compact which defines the rights of the individual and delimits the powers which the state may exercise.[26] As Mr. Justice Frankfurter has said: "The history of American freedom is, in no small measure, the history of procedure."[27] But, in addition, the procedural rules which have been fashioned from the generality of due process are our best instruments for the distillation and evaluation of essential facts from the conflicting welter of data that life and our adversary methods present. It is these instruments of due process which enhance the possibility that truth will emerge from the confrontation of opposing versions and conflicting data. "Procedure is to law what 'scientific method' is to science."[28]

It is claimed that juveniles obtain benefits from the special procedures applicable to them which more than offset the disadvantages of denial of the substance of normal due process. As we shall discuss, the observance of due process standards, intelligently and not ruthlessly administered, will not compel the States to abandon or displace any of the substantive benefits of the juvenile process.[29] But it is important, we think, that the claimed benefits of the juvenile process should be candidly appraised. Neither sentiment nor folklore should cause us to shut our eyes, for example, to such startling findings as that reported in an exceptionally reliable study of repeaters or recidivism conducted by the Stanford Research Institute for

---

26. The impact of denying fundamental procedural due process to juveniles involved in "delinquency" charges is dramatized by the following considerations: (1) In 1965, persons under 18 accounted for about one-fifth of all arrests for serious crimes (Nat'l Crime Comm'n Report, p. 55) and over half of all arrests for serious property offenses (id. at 56), and, in the same year, some 601,000 children under 18, or 2% of all children between 10 and 17, came before juvenile courts (Juvenile Court Statistics—1965, Children's Bureau Statistical Series No. 85 (1966) p. 2). About one out of nine youths will be referred to juvenile court in connection with a delinquent act (excluding traffic offenses) before he is 18 (Nat'l Crime Comm'n Report, p. 55). Cf. also Wheeler & Cottrell, Juvenile Delinquency—Its Prevention and Control (Russell Sage Foundation, 1965), p. 2; Report of the President's Commission on Crime in the District of Columbia (1966) (hereinafter cited as D.C. Crime Comm'n Report), p. 773. Furthermore, most juvenile crime apparently goes undetected or not formally punished. Wheeler & Cottrell, supra, observe that "[A]lmost all youngsters have committed at least one of the petty forms of theft and vandalism in the course of their adolescence." Id. at 28-29. See also Nat'l Crime Comm'n Report, p. 55, where it is stated that "self-report studies reveal that perhaps 90 percent of all young people have committed at least one act for which they could have been brought to juvenile court." It seems that the rate of juvenile delinquency is also steadily rising. See Nat'l Crime Comm'n Report, p. 56; Juvenile Court Statistics, supra, pp. 2–3. (2) In New York, where most juveniles are represented by counsel (see n. 69, infra) and substantial procedural rights are afforded (see, e.g., nn. 80, 81, 99, infra), out of a fiscal year 1965–1966 total of 10,755 juvenile proceedings involving boys, 2,242 were dismissed for failure of proof at the factfinding hearing; for girls, the figures were 306 out of a total of 1,051. New York Judicial Conference, Twelfth Annual Report, pp. 314, 316 (1967). (3) In about one-half of the States, a juvenile may be transferred to an adult penal institution after a juvenile court has found him "delinquent" (Delinquent Children in Penal Institutions, Children's Bureau Pub. No. 4151964, p. 1). (4) In some jurisdictions, a juvenile may be subjected to criminal prosecution for the same offense for which he has served under a juvenile court commitment. However, the Texas procedure to this effect has recently been held unconstitutional by a federal district court judge, in a habeas corpus action. *Sawyer v. Hauck*, 245 F.Supp. 55 (D.C.W.D.Tex.1965). (5) In most of the States, the juvenile may end in criminal court through waiver (Harvard Law Review Note, p. 793).

27. *Malinski v. New York*, 324 U.S. 401, 414 (1945) (separate opinion).

28. Foster, Social Work, the Law, and Social Action, in Social Casework, July 1964, pp. 383, 386.

29. See Note, Rights and Rehabilitation in the Juvenile Courts, 67 Col.L.Rev. 281, 321, and passim (1967).

the President's Commission on Crime in the District of Columbia. This Commission's Report states:

> In fiscal 1966, approximately 66 percent of the 16- and 17-year-old juveniles referred to the court by the Youth Aid Division had been before the court previously. In 1965, 56 percent of those in the Receiving Home were repeaters. The SRI study revealed that 61 percent of the sample Juvenile Court referrals in 1965 had been previously referred at least once, and that 42 percent had been referred at least twice before. Id. at 773.

Certainly these figures and the high crime rates among juveniles to which we have referred (supra, n. 26), could not lead us to conclude that the absence of constitutional protections reduces crime, or that the juvenile system, functioning free of constitutional inhibitions as it has largely done, is effective to reduce crime or rehabilitate offenders. We do not mean by this to denigrate the juvenile court process or to suggest that there are not aspects of the juvenile system relating to offenders which are valuable. But the features of the juvenile system which its proponents have asserted are of unique benefit will not be impaired by constitutional domestication. For example, the commendable principles relating to the processing and treatment of juveniles separately from adults are in no way involved or affected by the procedural issues under discussion.[30] Further, we are told that one of the important benefits of the special juvenile court procedures is that they avoid classifying the juvenile as a "criminal." The juvenile offender is now classed as a "delinquent." There is, of course, no reason why this should not continue. It is disconcerting, however, that this term has come to involve only slightly less stigma than the term "criminal" applied to adults.[31] It

---

30. Here again, however, there is substantial question as to whether fact and pretension, with respect to the separate handling and treatment of children, coincide. See generally infra.

While we are concerned only with procedure before the juvenile court in this case, it should be noted that, to the extent that the special procedures for juveniles are thought to be justified by the special consideration and treatment afforded them, there is reason to doubt that juveniles always receive the benefits of such a quid pro quo. As to the problem and importance of special care at the adjudicatory stage, cf. nn. 14 and 26, supra.

As to treatment, see Nat'l Crime Comm'n Report, pp. 80, 87; D.C. Crime Comm'n Report, pp. 665–676, 686–687 (at p. 687, the Report refers to the District's "bankruptcy of dispositional resources"), 692–695, 700–718 (at p. 701, the Report observes that "The Department of Public Welfare currently lacks even the rudiments of essential diagnostic and clinical services"); Wheeler & Cottrell, Juvenile Delinquency—Its Prevention and Control (Russell Sage Foundation, 1965), pp. 3235; Harvard Law Review Note, p. 809; Paulsen, Juvenile Courts, Family Courts, and the Poor Man, 54 Calif.L.Rev. 694, 709–712 (1966); Polier, A View From the Bench (1964). Cf. also In the Matter of the Youth House, Inc., Report of the July, 1966, "A" Term of the Bronx County Grand Jury, Supreme Court of New York, County of Bronx, Trial Term, Part XII, March 21, 1967 (cf. New York Times, March 23, 1967, p. 1, col. 8). The high rate of juvenile recidivism casts some doubt upon the adequacy of treatment afforded juveniles. See D.C. Crime Comm'n Report, p. 773; Nat'l Crime Comm'n Report, pp. 55, 78.

In fact, some courts have recently indicated that appropriate treatment is essential to the validity of juvenile custody, and therefore that a juvenile may challenge the validity of his custody on the ground that he is not, in fact, receiving any special treatment. See Creek v. Stone, U.S.App.D.C., 379 F.2d 106 (1967); Kautter v. Reid, 183 F.Supp. 352 (D.C.D.C.1960); White v. Reid, 125 F.Supp. 647 (D.C.D.C.1954). See also Elmore v. Stone, 122 U.S.App.D.C. 416, 355 F.2d 841 (1966) (separate statement of Bazelon, C.J.); Clayton v. Stone, 123 U.S.App.D.C. 181, 358 F.2d 548 (1966) (separate statement of Bazelon, C.J.). Cf. Wheeler & Cottrell, supra, pp. 32, 35; In re Rich, 125 Vt. 373, 216 A.2d 266 (1966). Cf. also Rouse v. Cameron, 125 U.S.App.D.C. 366, 373 F.2d 451 (1966); Millard v. Cameron, 125 U.S.App.D.C. 383, 373 F.2d 468 (1966).

31. "[T]he word "delinquent" has today developed such invidious connotations that the terminology is in the process of being altered; the new descriptive phrase is 'persons in need of supervision,' usually shortened to 'pins.'"

is also emphasized that, in practically all jurisdictions, statutes provide that an adjudication of the child as a delinquent shall not operate as a civil disability or disqualify him for civil service appointment.[32] There is no reason why the application of due process requirements should interfere with such provisions.

Beyond this, it is frequently said that juveniles are protected by the process from disclosure of their deviational behavior. As the Supreme Court of Arizona phrased it in the present case, the summary procedures of Juvenile Courts are sometimes defended by a statement that it is the law's policy "to hide youthful errors from the full gaze of the public and bury them in the graveyard of the forgotten past." This claim of secrecy, however, is more rhetoric than reality. Disclosure of court records is discretionary with the judge in most jurisdictions. Statutory restrictions almost invariably apply only to the court records, and even as to those, the evidence is that many courts routinely furnish information to the FBI and the military, and on request to government agencies and even to private employers.[33] Of more importance are police records. In most States, the police keep a complete file of juvenile "police contacts" and have complete discretion as to disclosure of juvenile records. Police departments receive requests for information from the FBI and other law enforcement agencies, the Armed Forces, and social service agencies, and most of them generally comply.[34] Private employers word their application forms to produce information concerning juvenile arrests and court proceedings, and, in some jurisdictions, information concerning juvenile police contacts is furnished private employers as well as government agencies.[35]

In any event, there is no reason why, consistently with due process, a State cannot continue, if it deems it appropriate, to provide and to improve provision for the confidentiality of records of police contacts and court action relating to juveniles. It is interesting to note, however, that the Arizona Supreme Court used the confidentiality argument as a justification for the type of notice which is here attacked as inadequate for due process purposes. The parents were given merely general notice that their child was charged with "delinquency." No facts were specified. The Arizona court held, however, as we shall discuss, that, in addition to this general "notice," the child and his parents must be advised "of the facts involved in the case" no later than the initial hearing by the judge. Obviously, this does not "bury" the word about the child's transgressions. It merely defers the time of disclosure to a point when it is of limited use to the child or his parents in preparing his defense or explanation.

Further, it is urged that the juvenile benefits from informal proceedings in the court. The early conception of the Juvenile Court proceeding was one in which a fatherly judge touched the heart and conscience of the erring youth by talking over his problems, by paternal advice and admonition, and in which, in extreme situations, benevolent and wise institutions

---

Harvard Law Review Note, p 799, n. 140. The N.Y.Family Court Act § 712 distinguishes between "delinquents" and "persons in need of supervision."

32. See, e.g., the Arizona provision, ARS § 8-228.

33. Harvard Law Review Note, pp. 784–785, 800. Cf. Nat'l Crime Comm'n Report, pp. 87–88; Ketcham, The Unfulfilled Promise of the Juvenile Court, 7 Crime & Delin. 97, 102–103 (1961).

34. Harvard Law Review Note, pp. 785-787.

35. Id. at 785, 800. See also, with respect to the problem of confidentiality of records, Note, Rights and Rehabilitation in the Juvenile Courts, 67 Col.L.Rev. 281, 286–289 (1967). Even the privacy of the juvenile hearing itself is not always adequately protected. Id. at 285–286.

of the State provided guidance and help "to save him from a downward career."[36] Then, as now, goodwill and compassion were admirably prevalent. But recent studies have, with surprising unanimity, entered sharp dissent as to the validity of this gentle conception. They suggest that the appearance as well as the actuality of fairness, impartiality and orderliness—in short, the essentials of due process—may be a more impressive and more therapeutic attitude so far as the juvenile is concerned. For example, in a recent study, the sociologists Wheeler and Cottrell observe that, when the procedural laxness of the "parens patriae" attitude is followed by stern disciplining, the contrast may have an adverse effect upon the child, who feels that he has been deceived or enticed. They conclude as follows: "Unless appropriate due process of law is followed, even the juvenile who has violated the law may not feel that he is being fairly treated, and may therefore resist the rehabilitative efforts of court personnel."[37] Of course it is not suggested that juvenile court judges should fail appropriately to take account, in their demeanor and conduct, of the emotional and psychological attitude of the juveniles with whom they are confronted. While due process requirements will, in some instances, introduce a degree of order and regularity to Juvenile Court proceedings to determine delinquency, and in contested cases will introduce some elements of the adversary system, nothing will require that the conception of the kindly juvenile judge be replaced by its opposite, nor do we here rule upon the question whether ordinary due process requirements must be observed with respect to hearings to determine the disposition of the delinquent child.

Ultimately, however, we confront the reality of that portion of the Juvenile Court process with which we deal in this case. A boy is charged with misconduct. The boy is committed to an institution where he may be restrained of liberty for years. It is of no constitutional consequence—and of limited practical meaning—that the institution to which he is committed is called an Industrial School. The fact of the matter is that, however euphemistic the title, a "receiving home" or an "industrial school" for juveniles is an institution of confinement in which the child is incarcerated for a greater or lesser time. His world becomes "a building with whitewashed walls, regimented routine and institutional hours...."[38] Instead of mother and father and sisters and brothers and friends and classmates, his world is peopled by guards, custodians, state employees, and "delinquents" confined with him for anything from waywardness[39] to rape and homicide.

In view of this, it would be extraordinary if our Constitution did not require the procedural regularity and the exercise of care implied in the phrase "due process." Under our Constitution, the condition of being a boy does not justify a kangaroo court. The traditional ideas of Juvenile Court procedure, indeed, contemplated that time would be available and

36. Mack, The Juvenile Court, 23 Harv.L.Rev. 104, 120 (1909).

37. Juvenile Delinquency—Its Prevention and Control (Russell Sage Foundation, 1966), p. 33. The conclusion of the Nat'l Crime Comm'n Report is similar: "[T]here is increasing evidence that the informal procedures, contrary to the original expectation, may themselves constitute a further obstacle to effective treatment of the delinquent to the extent that they engender in the child a sense of injustice provoked by seemingly all-powerful and challengeless exercise of authority by judges and probation officers." Id. at 85. See also Allen, The Borderland of Criminal Justice (1964), p. 19.

38. Holmes' Appeal, 379 Pa. 599, 616, 109 A.2d 523, 530 (1954) (Musmanno, J., dissenting). See also The *State (Sheerin) v. Governor*, [1966] I.R. 379 (Supreme Court of Ireland); *Trimble v. Stone*, 187 F.Supp. 483, 485-486 (D.C.D.C.1960); Allen, The Borderland of Criminal Justice (1964), pp. 18, 52–56.

39. Cf. the Juvenile Code of Arizona, ARS § 8-201-6.

care would be used to establish precisely what the juvenile did and why he did it—was it a prank of adolescence or a brutal act threatening serious consequences to himself or society unless corrected?[40] Under traditional notions, one would assume that, in a case like that of Gerald Gault, where the juvenile appears to have a home, a working mother and father, and an older brother, the Juvenile Judge would have made a careful inquiry and judgment as to the possibility that the boy could be disciplined and dealt with at home, despite his previous transgressions.[41] Indeed, so far as appears in the record before us, except for some conversation with Gerald about his school work and his "wanting to go to . . . Grand Canyon with his father," the points to which the judge directed his attention were little different from those that would be involved in determining any charge of violation of a penal statute.[42] The essential difference between Gerald's case and a normal criminal case is that safeguards available to adults were discarded in Gerald's case. The summary procedure as well as the long commitment was possible because Gerald was 15 years of age instead of over 18.

If Gerald had been over 18, he would not have been subject to Juvenile Court proceedings.[43] For the particular offense immediately involved, the maximum punishment would have been a fine of $5 to $50, or imprisonment in jail for not more than two months. Instead, he was committed to custody for a maximum of six years. If he had been over 18 and had committed an offense to which such a sentence might apply, he would have been entitled to substantial rights under the Constitution of the United States as well as under Arizona's laws and constitution. The United States Constitution would guarantee him rights and protections with respect to arrest, search and seizure, and pretrial interrogation. It would assure him of specific notice of the charges and adequate time to decide his course of action and to prepare his defense. He would be entitled to clear advice that he could be represented by counsel, and, at least if a felony were involved, the State would be required to provide counsel if his parents were unable to afford it. If the court acted on the basis of his confession, careful procedures would be required to assure its voluntariness. If the case went to trial, confrontation and opportunity for cross-examination would be guaranteed. So wide a gulf between the State's treatment of the adult and of the child requires a bridge sturdier than mere verbiage, and reasons more persuasive than cliche can provide. As Wheeler and Cottrell have put it, "The rhetoric of the juvenile court movement has developed without any necessarily close correspondence to the realities of court and institutional routines."[44]

---

40. Cf., however, the conclusions of the D.C. Crime Comm'n Report, pp. 692–693, concerning the inadequacy of the "social study records" upon which the Juvenile Court Judge must make this determination and decide on appropriate treatment.

41. The Juvenile Judge's testimony at the habeas corpus proceeding is devoid of any meaningful discussion of this. He appears to have centered his attention upon whether Gerald made the phone call and used lewd words. He was impressed by the fact that Gerald was on six months' probation because he was with another boy who allegedly stole a purse—a different sort of offense, sharing the feature that Gerald was "along." And he even referred to a report which he said was not investigated because "there was no accusation" "because of lack of material foundation."

With respect to the possible duty of a trial court to explore alternatives to involuntary commitment in a civil proceeding, cf. *Lake v. Cameron*, 124 U.S.App.D.C. 264, 364 F.2d 657 (1966), which arose under statutes relating to treatment of the mentally ill.

42. While appellee's brief suggests that the probation officer made some investigation of Gerald's home life, etc., there is not even a claim that the judge went beyond the point stated in the text.

43. ARS §§ 201, 202.

44. Juvenile Delinquency—Its Prevention and Control (Russell Sage Foundation, 1966), p. 35. The gap between rhetoric and reality is also emphasized in the Nat'l Crime Comm'n Report, pp. 80–81.

In *Kent v. United States,* supra, we stated that the Juvenile Court Judge's exercise of the power of the state as parens patriae was not unlimited. We said that "the admonition to function in a 'parental' relationship is not an invitation to procedural arbitrariness."[45] With respect to the waiver by the Juvenile Court to the adult court of jurisdiction over an offense committed by a youth, we said that "there is no place in our system of law for reaching a result of such tremendous consequences without ceremony—without hearing, without effective assistance of counsel, without a statement of reasons."[46] We announced with respect to such waiver proceedings that, while "We do not mean . . . to indicate that the hearing to be held must conform with all of the requirements of a criminal trial or even of the usual administrative hearing; but we do hold that the hearing must measure up to the essentials of due process and fair treatment."[47] We reiterate this view, here in connection with a juvenile court adjudication of "delinquency," as a requirement which is part of the Due Process Clause of the Fourteenth Amendment of our Constitution.[48]

We now turn to the specific issues which are presented to us in the present case.

III

Notice of Charges

Appellants allege that the Arizona Juvenile Code is unconstitutional, or, alternatively, that the proceedings before the Juvenile Court were constitutionally defective because of failure to provide adequate notice of the hearings. No notice was given to Gerald's parents when he was taken into custody on Monday, June 8. On that night, when Mrs. Gault went to the Detention Home, she was orally informed that there would be a hearing the next afternoon and was told the reason why Gerald was in custody. The only written notice Gerald's parents received at any time was a note on plain paper from Officer Flagg delivered on Thursday or Friday, June 11 or 12, to the effect that the judge had set Monday, June 15, "for further Hearings on Gerald's delinquency."

A "petition" was filed with the court on June 9 by Officer Flagg, reciting only that he was informed and believed that "said minor is a delinquent minor and that it is necessary that some order be made by the Honorable Court for said minor's welfare." The applicable Arizona statute provides for a petition to be filed in Juvenile Court, alleging in general terms that the child is "neglected, dependent or delinquent." The statute explicitly states that such a

---

45. 383 U.S. at 555.

46. 383 U.S. at 554. THE CHIEF JUSTICE stated in a recent speech to a conference of the National Council of Juvenile Court Judges, that a juvenile court "must function within the framework of law and . . . in the attainment of its objectives it cannot act with unbridled caprice." Equal Justice for Juveniles, 15 Juvenile Court Judges Journal, No. 3, pp. 14, 15 (1964).

47. 383 U.S. at 562.

48. The Nat'l Crime Comm'n Report recommends that "Juvenile courts should make fullest feasible use of preliminary conferences to dispose of cases short of adjudication." Id. at 84. See also D.C. Crime Comm'n Report, pp. 662–665. Since this "consent decree" procedure would involve neither adjudication of delinquency nor institutionalization, nothing we say in this opinion should be construed as expressing any views with respect to such procedure. The problems of pre-adjudication treatment of juveniles, and of post-adjudication disposition, are unique to the juvenile process; hence what we hold in this opinion with regard to the procedural requirements at the adjudicatory stage has no necessary applicability to other steps of the juvenile process.

general allegation is sufficient, "without alleging the facts."[49] There is no requirement that the petition be served, and it was not served upon, given to, or shown to Gerald or his parents.[50]

The Supreme Court of Arizona rejected appellants' claim that due process was denied because of inadequate notice. It stated that "Mrs. Gault knew the exact nature of the charge against Gerald from the day he was taken to the detention home." The court also pointed out that the Gaults appeared at the two hearings "without objection." The court held that, because "the policy of the juvenile law is to hide youthful errors from the full gaze of the public and bury them in the graveyard of the forgotten past," advance notice of the specific charges or basis for taking the juvenile into custody and for the hearing is not necessary. It held that the appropriate rule is that "the infant and his parent or guardian will receive a petition only reciting a conclusion of delinquency."[51] But, no later than the initial hearing by the judge, they must be advised of the facts involved in the case. If the charges are denied, they must be given a reasonable period of time to prepare.

We cannot agree with the court's conclusion that adequate notice was given in this case. Notice, to comply with due process requirements, must be given sufficiently in advance of scheduled court proceedings so that reasonable opportunity to prepare will be afforded, and it must "set forth the alleged misconduct with particularity."[52] It is obvious, as we have discussed above, that no purpose of shielding the child from the public stigma of knowledge of his having been taken into custody and scheduled for hearing is served by the procedure approved by the court below. The "initial hearing" in the present case was a hearing on the merits. Notice at that time is not timely, and even if there were a conceivable purpose served by the deferral proposed by the court below, it would have to yield to the requirements that the child and his parents or guardian be notified, in writing, of the specific charge or factual allegations to be considered at the hearing, and that such written notice be given at the earliest practicable time, and, in any event, sufficiently in advance of the hearing to permit preparation. Due process of law requires notice of the sort we have described—that is, notice which would be deemed constitutionally adequate in a civil or criminal proceeding.[53] It

---

49. ARS § 8-222(b).

50. Arizona's Juvenile Code does not provide for notice of any sort to be given at the commencement of the proceedings to the child or his parents. Its only notice provision is to the effect that, if a person other than the parent or guardian is cited to appear, the parent or guardian shall be notified "by personal service" of the time and place of hearing. ARS § 8-224. The procedure for initiating a proceeding, as specified by the statute, seems to require that, after a preliminary inquiry by the court, a determination may be made "that formal jurisdiction should be acquired." Thereupon, the court may authorize a petition to be filed. ARS § 8-222. It does not appear that this procedure was followed in the present case.

51. No such petition was served or supplied in the present case.

52. Nat'l Crime Comm'n Report, p. 87. The Commission observed that "The unfairness of too much informality is . . . reflected in the inadequacy of notice to parents and juveniles about charges and hearings." Ibid.

53. For application of the due process requirement of adequate notice in a criminal context, see, e.g., *Cole v. Arkansas*, 333 U.S. 196 (1948); *In re Oliver*, 333 U.S. 257, 273-278 (1948). For application in a civil context, see, e.g., *Armstrong v. Manzo*, 380 U.S. 545 (1965); *Mullane v. Central Hanover Tr. Co.*, 339 U.S. 306 (1950). Cf. also *Chaloner v. Sherman*, 242 U.S. 455 (1917). The Court's discussion in these cases of the right to timely and adequate notice forecloses any contention that the notice approved by the Arizona Supreme Court, or the notice actually given the Gaults, was constitutionally adequate. See also Antieau, Constitutional Rights in Juvenile Courts, 46 Cornell L.Q. 387, 395 (1961); Paulsen, Fairness to the Juvenile Offender, 41 Minn.L.Rev. 547, 557 (1957). Cf. Standards, pp. 63–65; Procedures and evidence in the Juvenile Court, A Guidebook for Judges, prepared by the Advisory Council of Judges of the National Council on Crime and Delinquency (1962), pp. 9–23 (and see cases discussed therein).

does not allow a hearing to be held in which a youth's freedom and his parents' right to his custody are at stake without giving them timely notice, in advance of the hearing, of the specific issues that they must meet. Nor, in the circumstances of this case, can it reasonably be said that the requirement of notice was waived.[54]

IV

Right to Counsel

Appellants charge that the Juvenile Court proceedings were fatally defective because the court did not advise Gerald or his parents of their right to counsel, and proceeded with the hearing, the adjudication of delinquency, and the order of commitment in the absence of counsel for the child and his parents or an express waiver of the right thereto. The Supreme Court of Arizona pointed out that "[t]here is disagreement [among the various jurisdictions] as to whether the court must advise the infant that he has a right to counsel."[55] It noted its own decision in *Arizona State Dept. of Public Welfare v. Barlow,* 80 Ariz. 249, 296 P.2d 28 (1956), to the effect "that the parents of an infant in a juvenile proceeding cannot be denied representation by counsel of their choosing." It referred to a provision of the Juvenile Code which it characterized as requiring "that the probation officer shall look after the interests of neglected, delinquent and dependent children," including representing their interests in court.[56] The court argued that "The parent and the probation officer may be relied upon to protect the infant's interests." Accordingly, it rejected the proposition that "due process requires that an infant have a right to counsel." It said that juvenile courts have the discretion, but not the duty, to allow such representation; it referred specifically to the situation in which the Juvenile Court discerns conflict between the child and his parents as an instance in which this discretion might be exercised. We do not agree. Probation officers, in

---

54. Mrs. Gault's "knowledge" of the charge against Gerald, and/or the asserted failure to object, does not excuse the lack of adequate notice. Indeed, one of the purposes of notice is to clarify the issues to be considered, and, as our discussion of the facts, supra, shows, even the Juvenile Court Judge was uncertain as to the precise issues determined at the two "hearings." Since the Gaults had no counsel and were not told of their right to counsel, we cannot consider their failure to object to the lack of constitutionally adequate notice as a waiver of their rights. Because of our conclusion that notice given only at the first hearing is inadequate, we need not reach the question whether the Gaults ever received adequately specific notice even at the June 9 hearing, in light of the fact they were never apprised of the charge of being habitually involved in immoral matters.

55. For recent cases in the District of Columbia holding that there must be advice of the right to counsel, and to have counsel appointed if necessary, see, e.g., *Shioutakon v. District of Columbia,* 98 U.S.App.D.C. 371, 236 F.2d 666 (1956); *Black v. United States,* 122 U.S.App.D.C. 393, 355 F.2d 104 (1965); *In re Poff,* 135 F.Supp. 224 (D.C.D.C.1955). Cf. also *In re Long,* 184 So.2d 861, 862 (1966); *People v. Dotson,* 46 Cal.2d 891, 299 P.2d 875 (1956).

56. The section cited by the court, ARS § 8-204-C, reads as follows:
The probation officer shall have the authority of a peace officer. He shall:
  (1) Look after the interests of neglected, delinquent and dependent children of the county.
  (2) Make investigations and file petitions.
  (3) Be present in court when cases are heard concerning children and represent their interests.
  (4) Furnish the court information and assistance as it may require.
  (5) Assist in the collection of sums ordered paid for the support of children.
  (6) Perform other acts ordered by the court.

the Arizona scheme, are also arresting officers. They initiate proceedings and file petitions which they verify, as here, alleging the delinquency of the child, and they testify, as here, against the child. And here the probation officer was also superintendent of the Detention Home. The probation officer cannot act as counsel for the child. His role in the adjudicatory hearing, by statute and, in fact, is as arresting officer and witness against the child. Nor can the judge represent the child. There is no material difference in this respect between adult and juvenile proceedings of the sort here involved. In adult proceedings, this contention has been foreclosed by decisions of this Court.[57] A proceeding where the issue is whether the child will be found to be "delinquent" and subjected to the loss of his liberty for years is comparable in seriousness to a felony prosecution. The juvenile needs the assistance of counsel to cope with problems of law,[58] to make skilled inquiry into the facts, to insist upon regularity of the proceedings, and to ascertain whether he has a defense and to prepare and submit it. The child "requires the guiding hand of counsel at every step in the proceedings against him."[59] Just as in *Kent v. United States,* supra, at 561-562, we indicated our agreement with the United States Court of Appeals for the District of Columbia Circuit that the assistance of counsel is essential for purposes of waiver proceedings, so we hold now that it is equally essential for the determination of delinquency, carrying with it the awesome prospect of incarceration in a state institution until the juvenile reaches the age of 21.[60]

During the last decade, court decisions,[61] experts,[62] and legislatures[63] have demonstrated increasing recognition of this view. In at least one-third of the States, statutes now provide

---

57. *Powell v. Alabama,* 287 U.S. 45, 61 (1932); *Gideon v. Wainwright,* 372 U.S. 335 (1963).

58. In the present proceeding, for example, although the Juvenile Judge believed that Gerald's telephone conversation was within the condemnation of ARS § 13-377, he suggested some uncertainty because the statute prohibits the use of vulgar language "in the presence or hearing of" a woman or child.

59. *Powell v. Alabama,* 287 U.S. 45, 69 (1932).

60. This means that the commitment, in virtually all cases, is for a minimum of three years since jurisdiction of juvenile courts is usually limited to age 18 and under.

61. See cases cited in n. 55, supra.

62. See, e.g., Schinitasky, 17 The Record 10 (N.Y.City Bar Assn.1962); Paulsen, Fairness to the Juvenile Offender, 41 Minn.L.Rev. 547, 568-573 (1957); Antieau, Constitutional Rights in Juvenile Courts, 46 Cornell L.Q. 387, 404–407 (1961); Paulsen, *Kent v. United States:* The Constitutional Context of Juvenile Cases, 1966 Sup.Ct.Rev. 167, 187–189; Ketcham, The Legal Renaissance in the Juvenile Court, 60 Nw.U.L.Rev. 585 (1965); Elson, Juvenile Courts & Due Process, in Justice for the Child (Rosenheim ed.) 95, 103–105 (1962); Note, Rights and Rehabilitation in the Juvenile Courts, 67 Col.L.Rev. 281, 321–327 (1967). See also Nat'l Probation and Parole Assn., Standard Family Court Act (1959) § 19, and Standard Juvenile Court Act (1959) § 19, in 5 NPPA Journal 99, 137, 323, 367 (1959) (hereinafter cited as Standard Family Court Act and Standard Juvenile Court Act, respectively).

63. Only a few state statutes require advice of the right to counsel and to have counsel appointed. See N.Y.Family Court Act §§ 241, 49, 728, 741; Calif.Welf. & Inst'ns Code §§ 633, 634, 659, 700 (1966) (appointment is mandatory only if conduct would be a felony in the case of an adult); Minn.Stat.Ann. § 260.155(2) (1966 Supp.) (see Comment of Legislative Commission accompanying this section); District of Columbia Legal Aid Act, D.C.Code Ann. § 2-2202 (1961) (Legal Aid Agency "shall make attorneys available to represent indigents . . . in proceedings before the juvenile court. . . ." See *Black v. United States,* 122 U.S.App.D.C. 393, 395-396, 355 F.2d 104, 106-107 (1965), construing this Act as providing a right to appointed counsel and to be informed of that right). Other state statutes allow appointment on request, or in some classes of cases, or in the discretion of the court, etc. The state statutes are collected and classified in Riederer, The Role of Counsel in the Juvenile Court, 2 J.Fam.Law 16, 19–20 (1962), which, however, does not treat the statutes cited above. See also Note, Rights and Rehabilitation in the Juvenile Courts, 67 Col.L.Rev. 281, 321–322 (1967).

for the right of representation by retained counsel in juvenile delinquency proceedings, notice of the right, or assignment of counsel, or a combination of these. In other States, court rules have similar provisions.[64]

The President's Crime Commission has recently recommended that, in order to assure "procedural justice for the child," it is necessary that "Counsel . . . be appointed as a matter of course wherever coercive action is a possibility, without requiring any affirmative choice by child or parent."[65] As stated by the authoritative "Standards for Juvenile and Family Courts," published by the Children's Bureau of the United States Department of Health, Education, and Welfare:

---

64. Skoler & Tenney, Attorney Representation in Juvenile Court, 4 J. Fam.Law 77, 95–96 (1964); Riederer, The Role of Counsel in the Juvenile Court, 2 J. Fam.Law 16 (1962).

Recognition of the right to counsel involves no necessary interference with the special purposes of juvenile court procedures; indeed, it seems that counsel can play an important role in the process of rehabilitation. See Note, Rights and Rehabilitation in the Juvenile Courts, 67 Col.L.Rev. 281, 324–327 (1967).

65. Nat'l Crime Comm'n Report, pp. 86–87. The Commission's statement of its position is very forceful:

"The Commission believes that no single action holds more potential for achieving procedural justice for the child in the juvenile court than provision of counsel. The presence of an independent legal representative of the child, or of his parent, is the keystone of the whole structure of guarantees that a minimum system of procedural justice requires. The rights to confront one's accusers, to cross-examine witnesses, to present evidence and testimony of one's own, to be unaffected by prejudicial and unreliable evidence, to participate meaningfully in the dispositional decision, to take an appeal have substantial meaning for the overwhelming majority of persons brought before the juvenile court only if they are provided with competent lawyers who can invoke those rights effectively. The most informal and well intentioned of judicial proceedings are technical; few adults without legal training can influence or even understand them; certainly children cannot. Papers are drawn and charges expressed in legal language. Events follow one another in a manner that appears arbitrary and confusing to the uninitiated. Decisions, unexplained, appear too official to challenge. But with lawyers come records of proceedings; records make possible appeals which, even if they do not occur, impart by their possibility a healthy atmosphere of accountability.

Fears have been expressed that lawyers would make juvenile court proceedings adversary. No doubt this is partly true, but it is partly desirable. Informality is often abused. The juvenile courts deal with cases in which facts are disputed and in which, therefore, rules of evidence, confrontation of witnesses, and other adversary procedures are called for. They deal with many cases involving conduct that can lead to incarceration or close supervision for long periods, and therefore juveniles often need the same safeguards that are granted to adults. And in all cases children need advocates to speak for them and guard their interests, particularly when disposition decisions are made. It is the disposition stage at which the opportunity arises to offer individualized treatment plans and in which the danger inheres that the court's coercive power will be applied without adequate knowledge of the circumstances.

"Fears also have been expressed that the formality lawyers would bring into juvenile court would defeat the therapeutic aims of the court. But informality has no necessary connection with therapy; it is a device that has been used to approach therapy, and it is not the only possible device. It is quite possible that, in many instances lawyers, for all their commitment to formality, could do more to further therapy for their clients than can the small, overworked social staffs of the courts. . . ."

"The Commission believes it is essential that counsel be appointed by the juvenile court for those who are unable to provide their own. Experience under the prevailing systems in which children are free to seek counsel of their choice reveals how empty of meaning the right is for those typically the subjects of juvenile court proceedings. Moreover, providing counsel only when the child is sophisticated enough to be aware of his need and to ask for one or when he fails to waive his announced right [is] not enough, as experience in numerous jurisdictions reveals."

"The Commission recommends:

"COUNSEL SHOULD BE APPOINTED AS A MATTER OF COURSE WHEREVER COERCIVE ACTION IS A POSSIBILITY, WITHOUT REQUIRING ANY AFFIRMATIVE CHOICE BY CHILD OR PARENT."

As a component part of a fair hearing required by due process guaranteed under the 14th amendment, notice of the right to counsel should be required at all hearings and counsel provided upon request when the family is financially unable to employ counsel. Standards, p. 57.

This statement was "reviewed" by the National Council of Juvenile Court Judges at its 1965 Convention and they "found no fault" with it.[66] The New York Family Court Act contains the following statement:

This act declares that minors have a right to the assistance of counsel of their own choosing or of law guardians[67] in neglect proceedings under article three and in proceedings to determine juvenile delinquency and whether a person is in need of supervision under article seven. This declaration is based on a finding that counsel is often indispensable to a practical realization of due process of law and may be helpful in making reasoned determinations of fact and proper orders of disposition.[68]

The Act provides that "At the commencement of any hearing" under the delinquency article of the statute, the juvenile and his parent shall be advised of the juvenile's "right to be represented by counsel chosen by him or his parent ... or by a law guardian assigned by the court...."[69] The California Act (1961) also requires appointment of counsel.[70]

We conclude that the Due Process Clause of the Fourteenth Amendment requires that, in respect of proceedings to determine delinquency which may result in commitment to an institution in which the juvenile's freedom is curtailed, the child and his parents must be notified of the child's right to be represented by counsel retained by them, or, if they are unable to afford counsel, that counsel will be appointed to represent the child.

At the habeas corpus proceeding, Mrs. Gault testified that she knew that she could have appeared with counsel at the juvenile hearing. This knowledge is not a waiver of the right to

---

66. Lehman, A Juvenile's Right to Counsel in A Delinquency Hearing, 17 Juvenile Court Judge's Journal 53 (1966). In an interesting review of the 1966 edition of the Children's Bureau's "Standards," Rosenheim, Standards for Juvenile and Family Courts: Old Wine in a New Bottle, 1 Fam.L.Q. 25, 29 (1967), the author observes that "The 'standards' of 1966, just like the 'standards' of 1954, are valuable precisely because they represent a diligent and thoughtful search for an accommodation between the aspirations of the founders of the juvenile court and the grim realities of life against which, in part, the due process of criminal and civil law offers us protection."

67. These are lawyers designated, as provided by the statute, to represent minors. N.Y.Family Court Act § 242.

68. N.Y.Family Court Act § 241.

69. N.Y.Family Court Act § 741. For accounts of New York practice under the new procedures, see Isaacs, The Role of the Lawyer in Representing Minors in the New Family Court, 12 Buffalo L.Rev. 501 (1963); Dembitz, Ferment and Experiment in New York: Juvenile Cases in the New Family Court, 48 Cornell L.Q. 499, 508–512 (1963). Since introduction of the law guardian system in September of 1962, it is stated that attorneys are present in the great majority of cases. Harvard Law Review Note, p. 796. See New York Judicial Conference, Twelfth Annual Report, pp. 288–291 (1967), for detailed statistics on representation of juveniles in New York. For the situation before 1962, see Schinitasky, The Role of the Lawyer in Children's Court, 17 The Record 10 (N.Y.City Bar Assn.1962). In the District of Columbia, where statute and court decisions require that a lawyer be appointed if the family is unable to retain counsel, see n. 63, supra, and where the juvenile and his parents are so informed at the initial hearing, about 85% to 90% do not choose to be represented, and sign a written waiver form. D.C.Crime Comm'n Report, p. 646. The Commission recommends adoption in the District of Columbia of a "law guardian" system similar to that of New York, with more effective notification of the right to appointed counsel, in order to eliminate the problems of procedural fairness, accuracy of factfinding, and appropriateness of disposition which the absence of counsel in so many juvenile court proceedings involves. Id. at 681–685.

70. See n. 63, supra.

counsel which she and her juvenile son had, as we have defined it. They had a right expressly to be advised that they might retain counsel and to be confronted with the need for specific consideration of whether they did or did not choose to waive the right. If they were unable to afford to employ counsel, they were entitled, in view of the seriousness of the charge and the potential commitment, to appointed counsel unless they chose waiver. Mrs. Gault's knowledge that she could employ counsel was not an "intentional relinquishment or abandonment" of a fully known right.[71]

V

Confrontation, Self-Incrimination, Cross-Examination

Appellants urge that the writ of habeas corpus should have been granted because of the denial of the rights of confrontation and cross-examination in the Juvenile Court hearings, and because the privilege against self-incrimination was not observed. The Juvenile Court Judge testified at the habeas corpus hearing that he had proceeded on the basis of Gerald's admissions at the two hearings. Appellants attack this on the ground that the admissions were obtained in disregard of the privilege against self-incrimination.[72] If the confession is disregarded, appellants argue that the delinquency conclusion, since it was fundamentally based on a finding that Gerald had made lewd remarks during the phone call to Mrs. Cook, is fatally defective for failure to accord the rights of confrontation and cross-examination which the Due Process Clause of the Fourteenth Amendment of the Federal Constitution guarantees in state proceedings generally.[73]

Our first question, then, is whether Gerald's admission was improperly obtained and relied on as the basis of decision, in conflict with the Federal Constitution. For this purpose, it is necessary briefly to recall the relevant facts.

Mrs. Cook, the complainant, and the recipient of the alleged telephone call, was not called as a witness. Gerald's mother asked the Juvenile Court Judge why Mrs. Cook was not present, and the judge replied that "she didn't have to be present." So far as appears, Mrs. Cook was spoken to only once, by Officer Flagg, and this was by telephone. The judge did not speak with her on any occasion. Gerald had been questioned by the probation officer after having been taken into custody. The exact circumstances of this questioning do not appear, but any admissions Gerald may have made at this time do not appear in the record.[74] Gerald was also questioned by the Juvenile Court Judge at each of the two hearings. The judge testified in the habeas corpus proceeding that Gerald admitted making "some of the lewd statements. . . , [but not] any of the more serious lewd statements." There was conflict and uncertainty among the witnesses at the habeas corpus proceeding—the Juvenile Court Judge, Mr. and Mrs. Gault, and the probation officer—as to what Gerald did or did not admit.

We shall assume that Gerald made admissions of the sort described by the Juvenile Court Judge, as quoted above. Neither Gerald nor his parents were advised that he did not have to

71. *Johnson v. Zerbst*, 304 U.S. 458, 464 (1938); *Carnley v. Cochran*, 369 U.S. 506 (1962); United *States ex rel. Brown v. Fay*, 242 F.Supp. 273 (D.C.S.D.N.Y.1965).

72. The privilege is applicable to state proceedings. *Malloy v. Hogan*, 378 U.S. 1 (1964).

73. *Pointer v. Texas*, 380 U.S. 400 (1965); *Douglas v. Alabama*, 380 U.S. 415 (1965).

74. For this reason, we cannot consider the status of Gerald's alleged admissions to the probation officers. Cf., however, Comment, *Miranda* Guarantees in the California Juvenile Court, 7 Santa Clara Lawyer 114 (1966).

testify or make a statement, or that an incriminating statement might result in his commitment as a "delinquent."

The Arizona Supreme Court rejected appellants' contention that Gerald had a right to be advised that he need not incriminate himself. It said: "We think the necessary flexibility for individualized treatment will be enhanced by a rule which does not require the judge to advise the infant of a privilege against self-incrimination."

In reviewing this conclusion of Arizona's Supreme Court, we emphasize again that we are here concerned only with a proceeding to determine whether a minor is a "delinquent" and which may result in commitment to a state institution. Specifically, the question is whether, in such a proceeding, an admission by the juvenile may be used against him in the absence of clear and unequivocal evidence that the admission was made with knowledge that he was not obliged to speak and would not be penalized for remaining silent. In light of *Miranda v. Arizona*, 384 U.S. 436 (1966), we must also consider whether, if the privilege against self-incrimination is available, it can effectively be waived unless counsel is present or the right to counsel has been waived.

It has long been recognized that the eliciting and use of confessions or admissions require careful scrutiny. Dean Wigmore states:

> The ground of distrust of confessions made in certain situations is, in a rough and indefinite way, judicial experience. There has been no careful collection of statistics of untrue confessions, nor has any great number of instances been even loosely reported . . . , but enough have been verified to fortify the conclusion, based on ordinary observation of human conduct, that, under certain stresses, a person, especially one of defective mentality or peculiar temperament, may falsely acknowledge guilt. This possibility arises wherever the innocent person is placed in such a situation that the untrue acknowledgment of guilt is, at the time, the more promising of two alternatives between which he is obliged to choose; that is, he chooses any risk that may be in falsely acknowledging guilt in preference to some worse alternative associated with silence.
>
> * * * *
>
> The principle, then, upon which a confession may be excluded is that it is, under certain conditions, testimonially untrustworthy. . . . [T]he essential feature is that the principle of exclusion is a testimonial one, analogous to the other principles which exclude narrations as untrustworthy. . . .[75]

This Court has emphasized that admissions and confessions of juveniles require special caution. In *Haley v. Ohio*, 332 U.S. 596, where this Court reversed the conviction of a 15-year-old boy for murder, MR. JUSTICE DOUGLAS said:

> What transpired would make us pause for careful inquiry if a mature man were involved. And when, as here, a mere child—an easy victim of the law—is before us, special care in scrutinizing the record must be used. Age 15 is a tender and difficult age for a boy of any race. He cannot be judged by the more exacting standards of maturity. That which would leave a man cold and unimpressed can overawe and overwhelm a lad in his early teens. This is the period of great instability which the crisis of adolescence produces. A 15-year-old lad, questioned through the dead of night by relays of police, is a ready victim of the inquisition. Mature men possibly might stand the ordeal from midnight to 5 a.m. But we cannot believe that a lad of tender years is a match for the

---

75. 3 Wigmore, Evidence § 822 (3d ed.1940).

police in such a contest. He needs counsel and support if he is not to become the victim first of fear, then of panic. He needs someone on whom to lean lest the overpowering presence of the law, as he knows it, crush him. No friend stood at the side of this 15-year-old boy as the police, working in relays, questioned him hour after hour, from midnight until dawn. No lawyer stood guard to make sure that the police went so far and no farther, to see to it that they stopped short of the point where he became the victim of coercion. No counsel or friend was called during the critical hours of questioning.[76]

In *Haley*, as we have discussed, the boy was convicted in an adult court, and not a juvenile court. In notable decisions, the New York Court of Appeals and the Supreme Court of New Jersey have recently considered decisions of Juvenile Courts in which boys have been adjudged "delinquent" on the basis of confessions obtained in circumstances comparable to those in Haley. In both instances, the State contended before its highest tribunal that constitutional requirements governing inculpatory statements applicable in adult courts do not apply to juvenile proceedings. In each case, the State's contention was rejected, and the juvenile court's determination of delinquency was set aside on the grounds of inadmissibility of the confession. *In the Matters of Gregory W. and Gerald S.*, 19 N.Y.2d 55, 224 N.E.2d 102 (1966) (opinion by Keating, J.), and *In the Interests of Carlo and Stasilowicz,* 48 N.J. 224, 225 A.2d 110 (1966) (opinion by Proctor, J.). The privilege against self-incrimination is, of course, related to the question of the safeguards necessary to assure that admissions or confessions are reasonably trustworthy, that they are not the mere fruits of fear or coercion, but are reliable expressions of the truth. The roots of the privilege are, however, far deeper. They tap the basic stream of religious and political principle, because the privilege reflects the limits of the individual's attornment to the state and—in a philosophical sense—insists upon the equality of the individual and the state.[77] In other words, the privilege has a broader and deeper thrust than the rule which prevents the use of confessions which are the product of coercion because coercion is thought to carry with it the danger of unreliability. One of its purposes is to prevent the state, whether by force or by psychological domination, from overcoming the mind and will of the person under investigation and depriving him of the freedom to decide whether to assist the state in securing his conviction.[78]

It would indeed be surprising if the privilege against self-incrimination were available to hardened criminals, but not to children. The language of the Fifth Amendment, applicable to the States by operation of the Fourteenth Amendment, is unequivocal and without exception. And the scope of the privilege is comprehensive. As MR. JUSTICE WHITE, concurring, stated in *Murphy v. Waterfront Commission,* 378 U.S. 52, 94 (1964):

> The privilege can be claimed in any proceeding, be it criminal or civil, administrative or judicial, investigatory or adjudicatory . . . it protects any disclosures which the witness may reasonably apprehend could be used in a criminal prosecution or which could lead to other evidence that might be so used.[79]

---

76. 332 U.S. at 599-600 (opinion of MR. JUSTICE DOUGLAS, joined by JUSTICES BLACK, Murphy and Rutledge; Justice Frankfurter concurred in a separate opinion).

77. See Fortas, The Fifth Amendment, 25 Cleveland Bar Assn. Journal 91 (1954).

78. See *Rogers v. Richmond,* 365 U.S. 534 (1961); *Culombe v. Connecticut,* 367 U.S. 568 (1961) (opinion of Mr. Justice Frankfurter, joined by MR. JUSTICE STEWART); *Miranda v. Arizona,* 384 U.S. 436 (1966).

79. See also *Malloy v. Hogan,* 378 U.S. 1 (1964); *McCarthy v. Arndstein,* 266 U.S. 34, 40 (1924).

With respect to juveniles, both common observation and expert opinion emphasize that the "distrust of confessions made in certain situations" to which Dean Wigmore referred in the passage quoted supra, at 44-45, is imperative in the case of children from an early age through adolescence. In New York, for example, the recently enacted Family Court Act provides that the juvenile and his parents must be advised at the start of the hearing of his right to remain silent.[80] The New York statute also provides that the police must attempt to communicate with the juvenile's parents before questioning him,[81] and that, absent "special circumstances," a confession may not be obtained from a child prior to notifying his parents or relatives and releasing the child either to them or to the Family Court.[82] In *In the Matters of Gregory W. and Gerald S.*, referred to above, the New York Court of Appeals held that the privilege against self-incrimination applies in juvenile delinquency cases and requires the exclusion of involuntary confessions, and that *People v. Lewis*, 260 N.Y. 171, 183 N.E. 353 (1932), holding the contrary, had been specifically overruled by statute.

The authoritative "Standards for Juvenile and Family Courts" concludes that, "Whether or not transfer to the criminal court is a possibility, certain procedures should always be followed. Before being interviewed [by the police], the child and his parents should be informed of his right to have legal counsel present and to refuse to answer questions or be fingerprinted[83] if he should so decide."[84]

Against the application to juveniles of the right to silence, it is argued that juvenile proceedings are "civil," and not "criminal," and therefore the privilege should not apply. It is true that the statement of the privilege in the Fifth Amendment, which is applicable to the States by reason of the Fourteenth Amendment, is that no person "shall be compelled in any criminal case to be a witness against himself." However, it is also clear that the availability of the privilege does not turn upon the type of proceeding in which its protection is invoked, but upon the nature of the statement or admission and the exposure which it invites. The privilege may, for example, be claimed in a civil or administrative proceeding, if the statement is or may be inculpatory.[85]

It would be entirely unrealistic to carve out of the Fifth Amendment all statements by juveniles on the ground that these cannot lead to "criminal" involvement. In the first place, juvenile proceedings to determine "delinquency," which may lead to commitment to a state institution, must be regarded as "criminal" for purposes of the privilege against self-incrimination. To hold otherwise would be to disregard substance because of the feeble enticement of the "civil" "label of convenience" which has been attached to juvenile proceedings. Indeed, in over half of the States, there is not even assurance that the juvenile will be kept in

---

80. N.Y.Family Court Act § 741.

81. N.Y.Family Court Act § 724(a). In *In the Matter of Williams*, 49 Misc.2d 154, 267 N.Y.S.2d 91 (1966), the New York Family Court held that "The failure of the police to notify this child's parents that he had been taken into custody, if not alone sufficient to render his confession inadmissible, is germane on the issue of its voluntary character. . . ." Id. at 165, 267 N.Y.S.2d at 106. The confession was held involuntary, and therefore inadmissible.

82. N.Y.Family Court Act § 724 (as amended 1963, see Supp. 1966). See *In the Matter of Addison*, 20 App.Div.2d 90, 245 N.Y.S.2d 243 (1963).

83. The issues relating to fingerprinting of juveniles are not presented here, and we express no opinion concerning them.

84. Standards, p. 49.

85. See n. 79, supra, and accompanying text.

separate institutions, apart from adult "criminals." In those States, juveniles may be placed in or transferred to adult penal institutions[86] after having been found "delinquent" by a juvenile court. For this purpose, at least, commitment is a deprivation of liberty. It is incarceration against one's will, whether it is called "criminal" or "civil." And our Constitution guarantees that no person shall be "compelled" to be a witness against himself when he is threatened with deprivation of his liberty—a command which this Court has broadly applied and generously implemented in accordance with the teaching of the history of the privilege and its great office in mankind's battle for freedom.[87]

In addition, apart from the equivalence for this purpose of exposure to commitment as a juvenile delinquent and exposure to imprisonment as an adult offender, the fact of the matter is that there is little or no assurance in Arizona, as in most if not all of the States, that a juvenile apprehended and interrogated by the police or even by the Juvenile Court itself will remain outside of the reach of adult courts as a consequence of the offense for which he has been taken into custody. In Arizona, as in other States, provision is made for Juvenile Courts to relinquish or waive jurisdiction to the ordinary criminal courts.[88] In the present case, when Gerald Gault was interrogated concerning violation of a section of the Arizona Criminal Code, it could not be certain that the Juvenile Court Judge would decide to "suspend" criminal prosecution in court for adults by proceeding to an adjudication in Juvenile Court.[89]

It is also urged, as the Supreme Court of Arizona here asserted, that the juvenile and presumably his parents should not be advised of the juvenile's right to silence because confession is good for the child as the commencement of the assumed therapy of the juvenile court process, and he should be encouraged to assume an attitude of trust and confidence toward the officials of the juvenile process. This proposition has been subjected to widespread challenge on the basis of current reappraisals of the rhetoric and realities of the handling of juvenile offenders.

In fact, evidence is accumulating that confessions by juveniles do not aid in "individualized treatment," as the court below put it, and that compelling the child to answer questions, without warning or advice as to his right to remain silent, does not serve this or any other good purpose. In light of the observations of *Wheeler* and *Cottrell*,[90] and others, it seems probable that, where children are induced to confess by "paternal" urgings on the part of officials and the confession is then followed by disciplinary action, the child's reaction is likely to be hostile and adverse—the child may well feel that he has been led or tricked into confession and that, despite his confession, he is being punished.[91]

---

86. Delinquent Children in Penal Institutions, Children's Bureau Pub. No. 415—1964, p. 1.

87. See, e.g., *Miranda v. Arizona,* 384 U.S. 436 (1966), *Garrity v. New Jersey,* 385 U.S. 493 (1967); *Spevack v. Klein,* 385 U.S. 511 (1967); *Haynes v. Washington,* 373 U.S. 503 (1963); *Culombe v. Connecticut,* 367 U.S. 568 (1961); *Rogers v. Richmond,* 365 U.S. 534 (1961); *Malloy v. Hogan,* 378 U.S. 1 (1964); *Griffin v. California,* 380 U.S. 609 (1965).

88. Arizona Constitution, Art. 6, § 15 (as amended 1960); ARS §§ 223, 8-228(A); Harvard Law Review Note, p. 793. Because of this possibility that criminal jurisdiction may attach, it is urged that "... all of the procedural safeguards in the criminal law should be followed." Standards, p. 49. Cf. *Harlin v. United States,* 111 U.S.App.D.C. 174, 295 F.2d 161 (1961).

89. ARS § 8-228(A).

90. Juvenile Delinquency—Its Prevention and Control (Russell Sage Foundation, 1966).

91. Id. at 33. See also the other materials cited in n. 37, supra.

Further, authoritative opinion has cast formidable doubt upon the reliability and trustworthiness of "confessions" by children. This Court's observations in *Haley v. Ohio* are set forth above. The recent decision of the New York Court of Appeals referred to above, *In the Matters of Gregory W. and Gerald S.*, deals with a dramatic and, it is to be hoped, extreme example. Two 12-year-old Negro boys were taken into custody for the brutal assault and rape of two aged domestics, one of whom died as the result of the attack. One of the boys was schizophrenic, and had been locked in the security ward of a mental institution at the time of the attacks. By a process that may best be described as bizarre, his confession was obtained by the police. A psychiatrist testified that the boy would admit "whatever he thought was expected so that he could get out of the immediate situation." The other 12-year-old also "confessed." Both confessions were in specific detail, albeit they contained various inconsistencies. The Court of Appeals, in an opinion by Keating, J., concluded that the confessions were products of the will of the police, instead of the boys. The confessions were therefore held involuntary, and the order of the Appellate Division affirming the order of the Family Court adjudging the defendants to be juvenile delinquents was reversed.

A similar and equally instructive case has recently been decided by the Supreme Court of New Jersey. *In the Interests of Carlo and Stasilowicz*, supra. The body of a 10-year-old girl was found. She had been strangled. Neighborhood boys who knew the girl were questioned. The two appellants, aged 13 and 15, confessed to the police, with vivid detail and some inconsistencies. At the Juvenile Court hearing, both denied any complicity in the killing. They testified that their confessions were the product of fear and fatigue due to extensive police grilling. The Juvenile Court Judge found that the confessions were voluntary and admissible. On appeal, in an extensive opinion by Proctor, J., the Supreme Court of New Jersey reversed. It rejected the State's argument that the constitutional safeguard of voluntariness governing the use of confessions does not apply in proceedings before the Juvenile Court. It pointed out that, under New Jersey court rules, juveniles under the age of 16 accused of committing a homicide are tried in a proceeding which "has all of the appurtenances of a criminal trial," including participation by the county prosecutor, and requirements that the juvenile be provided with counsel, that a stenographic record be made, etc. It also pointed out that, under New Jersey law, the confinement of the boys after reaching age 21 could be extended until they had served the maximum sentence which could have been imposed on an adult for such a homicide, here found to be second-degree murder carrying up to 30 years' imprisonment.[92] The court concluded that the confessions were involuntary, stressing that the boys, contrary to statute, were placed in the police station and there interrogated;[93] that the parents of both boys were not allowed to see them while they were being interrogated;[94] that inconsistencies appeared among the various statements of the boys and with the objective evidence of the crime, and that there were protracted periods of questioning. The court noted the State's contention that both boys were advised of their constitutional rights

---

92. 92 N.J.Rev.Stat. § 2A:4-37(b)(2) (Supp. 1966); N.J.Rev.Stat. § 2A:113-4.

93. N.J.Rev.Stat. § 2A:4-32-33. The court emphasized that the "frightening atmosphere" of a police station is likely to have "harmful effects on the mind and will of the boy," citing In the Matter of Rutane, 37 Misc.2d 234, 234 N.Y.S.2d 777 (Fam.Ct. Kings County, 1962).

94. The court held that this alone might be enough to show that the confessions were involuntary "even though, as the police testified, the boys did not wish to see their parents" (citing *Gallegos v. Colorado*, 370 U.S. 49 (1962)).

before they made their statements, but it held that this should not be given "significant weight in our determination of voluntariness."[95] Accordingly, the judgment of the Juvenile Court was reversed.

In a recent case before the Juvenile Court of the District of Columbia, Judge Ketcham rejected the proffer of evidence as to oral statements made at police headquarters by four juveniles who had been taken into custody for alleged involvement in an assault and attempted robbery. *In the Matter of Four Youths,* Nos. 28-776-J, 28-778-J, 28-783-J, 28-859-J, Juvenile Court of the District of Columbia, April 7, 1961. The court explicitly stated that it did not rest its decision on a showing that the statements were involuntary, but because they were untrustworthy. Judge Ketcham said:

> Simply stated, the Court's decision in this case rests upon the considered opinion—after nearly four busy years on the Juvenile Court bench during which the testimony of thousands of such juveniles has been heard—that the statements of adolescents under 18 years of age who are arrested and charged with violations of law are frequently untrustworthy, and often distort the truth.

We conclude that the constitutional privilege against self-incrimination is applicable in the case of juveniles as it is with respect to adults. We appreciate that special problems may arise with respect to waiver of the privilege by or on behalf of children, and that there may well be some differences in technique—but not in principle—depending upon the age of the child and the presence and competence of parents. The participation of counsel will, of course, assist the police, Juvenile Courts and appellate tribunals in administering the privilege. If counsel was not present for some permissible reason when an admission was obtained, the greatest care must be taken to assure that the admission was voluntary, in the sense not only that it was not coerced or suggested, but also that it was not the product of ignorance of rights or of adolescent fantasy, fright or despair.[96] The "confession" of Gerald Gault was first obtained by Officer Flagg, out of the presence of Gerald's parents, without counsel and without advising him of his right to silence, as far as appears. The judgment of the Juvenile Court was stated by the judge to be based on Gerald's admissions in court. Neither "admission" was reduced to writing, and, to say the least, the process by which the "admissions" were obtained and received must be characterized as lacking the certainty and order which are required of pro-

---

95. The court quoted the following passage from *Haley v. Ohio,* supra, at 601:
"But we are told that this boy was advised of his constitutional rights before he signed the confession and that, knowing them, he nevertheless confessed. That assumes, however, that a boy of fifteen, without aid of counsel, would have a full appreciation of that advice, and that, on the facts of this record, he had a freedom of choice. We cannot indulge those assumptions. Moreover, we cannot give any weight to recitals which merely formalize constitutional requirements. Formulas of respect for constitutional safeguards cannot prevail over the facts of life which contradict them. They may not become a cloak for inquisitorial practices and make an empty form of the due process of law for which free men fought and died to obtain."

96. The N.Y. Family Court Act § 744(b) provides that "an uncorroborated confession made out of court by a respondent is not sufficient" to constitute the required "preponderance of the evidence." See *United States v. Morales,* 233 F.Supp. 160 (D.C. Mont.1964), holding a confession inadmissible in proceedings under the Federal Juvenile Delinquency Act (18 U.S.C. § 5031 et seq.) because, in the circumstances in which it was made, the District Court could not conclude that it "was freely made while Morales was afforded all of the requisites of due process required in the case of a sixteen year old boy of his experience." Id. at 170.

ceedings of such formidable consequences.[97] Apart from the "admissions," there was nothing upon which a judgment or finding might be based. There was no sworn testimony. Mrs. Cook, the complainant, was not present. The Arizona Supreme Court held that "sworn testimony must be required of all witnesses including police officers, probation officers and others who are part of or officially related to the juvenile court structure." We hold that this is not enough. No reason is suggested or appears for a different rule in respect of sworn testimony in juvenile courts than in adult tribunals. Absent a valid confession adequate to support the determination of the Juvenile Court, confrontation and sworn testimony by witnesses available for cross-examination were essential for a finding of "delinquency" and an order committing Gerald to a state institution for a maximum of six years.

The recommendations in the Children's Bureau's "Standards for Juvenile and Family Courts" are in general accord with our conclusions. They state that testimony should be under oath and that only competent, material and relevant evidence under rules applicable to civil cases should be admitted in evidence.[98] The New York Family Court Act contains a similar provision.[99]

As we said in *Kent v. United States*, 383 U.S. 541, 554 (1966), with respect to waiver proceedings, "there is no place in our system of law for reaching a result of such tremendous consequences without ceremony. . . ." We now hold that, absent a valid confession, a determination of delinquency and an order of commitment to a state institution cannot be sustained in the absence of sworn testimony subjected to the opportunity for cross-examination in accordance with our law and constitutional requirements.

VI

Appellate Review and Transcript of Proceedings

Appellants urge that the Arizona statute is unconstitutional under the Due Process Clause because, as construed by its Supreme Court, "there is no right of appeal from a juvenile court order. . . ." The court held that there is no right to a transcript because there is no right to appeal and because the proceedings are confidential, and any record must be destroyed after a prescribed period of time.[100] Whether a transcript or other recording is made, it held, is a matter for the discretion of the juvenile court.

---

97. Cf. *Jackson v. Denno*, 378 U.S. 368 (1964); *Miranda v. Arizona*, 384 U.S. 436 (1966).

98. Standards, pp. 72–73. The Nat'l Crime Comm'n Report concludes that. "the evidence admissible at the adjudicatory hearing should be so limited that findings are not dependent upon or unduly influenced by hearsay, gossip, rumor, and other unreliable types of information. To minimize the danger that adjudication will be affected by inappropriate considerations, social investigation reports should not be made known to the judge in advance of adjudication." Id. at 87 (bold face eliminated). See also Note, Rights and Rehabilitation in the Juvenile Courts, 67 Col.L.Rev. 281, 336 (1967): "At the adjudication stage, the use of clearly incompetent evidence in order to prove the youth's involvement in the alleged misconduct . . . is not justifiable. Particularly in delinquency cases, where the issue of fact is the commission of a crime, the introduction of hearsay—such as the report of a policeman who did not witness the events—contravenes the purposes underlying the sixth amendment right of confrontation." (Footnote omitted.)

99. N.Y.Family Court Act § 744(a). See also Harvard Law Review Note, p. 795. Cf. *Willner v. Committee on Character*, 373 U.S. 96 (1963).

100. ARS § 238.

This Court has not held that a State is required by the Federal Constitution "to provide appellate courts or a right to appellate review at all."[101] In view of the fact that we must reverse the Supreme Court of Arizona's affirmance of the dismissal of the writ of habeas corpus for other reasons, we need not rule on this question in the present case or upon the failure to provide a transcript or recording of the hearings—or, indeed, the failure of the Juvenile Judge to state the grounds for his conclusion. Cf. *Kent v. United States*, supra, at 561, where we said, in the context of a decision of the juvenile court waiving jurisdiction to the adult court, which by local law, was permissible: "... it is incumbent upon the Juvenile Court to accompany its waiver order with a statement of the reasons or considerations therefor." As the present case illustrates, the consequences of failure to provide an appeal, to record the proceedings, or to make findings or state the grounds for the juvenile court's conclusion may be to throw a burden upon the machinery for habeas corpus, to saddle the reviewing process with the burden of attempting to reconstruct a record, and to impose upon the Juvenile Judge the unseemly duty of testifying under cross-examination as to the events that transpired in the hearings before him.[102]

For the reasons stated, the judgment of the Supreme Court of Arizona is reversed, and the cause remanded for further proceedings not inconsistent with this opinion.

It is so ordered.

---

101. *Griffin v. Illinois*, 351 U.S. 12, 18 (1956).

102. "Standards for Juvenile and Family Courts" recommends "written findings of fact, some form of record of the hearing" "and the right to appeal." Standards, p. 8. It recommends verbatim recording of the hearing by stenotypist or mechanical recording (p. 76) and urges that the judge make clear to the child and family their right to appeal (p. 78). See also Standard Family Court Act §§ 19, 24, 28; Standard Juvenile Court Act §§ 19, 24, 28. The Harvard Law Review Note, p. 799, states that "The result [of the infrequency of appeals due to absence of record, indigency, etc.] is that juvenile court proceedings are largely unsupervised." The Nat'l Crime Comm'n Report observes, p. 86, that "records make possible appeals which, even if they do not occur, impart by their possibility a healthy atmosphere of accountability."

CHAPTER 3

JUVENILE COURT PROCESSING

Introduction

The adjudicatory process, often called the fact-finding hearing in the juvenile court, exists to hear evidence on the allegations in the petition. In its early development, the juvenile court did not emphasize judicial rule-making similar to the criminal trial process. Such basic requirements as standard of proof, rules of evidence, and other adjudicatory formalities were generally kept out of the juvenile court. The reason for this approach was that the traditional juvenile system was designed to diagnose and rehabilitate children appearing before the court. This was consistent with the view that the court should be social-service oriented and that the proceedings be nonadversary, informal, and noncriminal in nature.[1]

Gradually, however, the juvenile court movement became the subject of much criticism and disillusionment. This growing dissatisfaction was based primarily on the inability of the court to rehabilitate the juvenile offender, while at the same time failing to safeguard his or her constitutional rights. Juvenile courts apparently were punishing many children under the pretense of being a social-service agency, while arguing that constitutional protections were not necessary because the juvenile was being "helped" in the name of the state. Because of this *parens patriae* philosophy, in which the state acted in promoting the child's welfare, the adjudicatory proceeding, as well as the subsequent disposition, was conceived to be in the child's best interest. Thus, there generally was no need for legal rules and procedures in the nature of the criminal process nor for the introduction of state prosecutors or defense attorneys, since this was inconsistent with the philosophy of the juvenile court. But these views and practices were severely changed by the U.S. Supreme Court as a result of the landmark case of *In re Gault*. In *Gault*, the Court decided that the concept of fundamental fairness must be made applicable to juvenile delinquency proceedings

After *Gault*, the Supreme Court continued its trend toward "legalizing" and "formalizing" the juvenile adjudication process with its decision in *In re Winship* (1970). In *Winship*, the Court held that the standard in a criminal prosecution of proof beyond a reasonable doubt is also required in the adjudication of a delinquency petition. It is unsettled from the *Winship*

---

1. Krisberg, B. 1988. *The Juvenile Court: Reclaiming the Vision.* San Francisco: National Council on Crime and Delinquency.

decision whether this burden of proof is also applicable to nondelinquent forms of conduct. As a result, some state statutes require proof beyond a reasonable doubt only in delinquency matters. In these jurisdictions, such standards of proof as clear and convincing evidence or a preponderance of the evidence are used for incorrigibility, neglect, or dependency-type cases. Some jurisdictions, however, apply the reasonable-doubt standard to all types of juvenile actions. In spite of various statutory differences, *Winship* does impose the constitutional requirement of proof beyond a reasonable doubt during the adjudicatory stage of a delinquency proceeding.

Although the traditional juvenile court trial has been severely altered by *Gault* and *Winship*, this movement for increased rights for juveniles was somewhat curtailed by the Supreme Court's decision in *McKeiver v. Pennsylvania* (1971). In *McKiever,* the court held that the Fourteenth Amendment's due process clause does not require the states to provide juveniles with a jury trial. This decision, however, does not prevent the various states from giving juveniles a trial by jury as a state constitutional right or by state statute.

Despite the impact of constitutional law in the adjudicatory stage of the juvenile process, many states retain their own standards in such areas as rules of evidence, double jeopardy, and findings of the juvenile court.

Rules of evidence represent the means by which evidentiary matters may be admitted in court to prove or disprove a particular point. Thus, for example, evidence must be relevant, which means it must shed light on the issue, or material, which means it must relate to the importance or proving the issue of the case. One of the most fundamental rules of evidence is the hearsay rule, which generally means that a witness can only testify to matters of his or her own personal knowledge.

Most states do not have a definitive statutory statement of evidentiary rules of juvenile proceedings, as they ordinarily have for the criminal process. Some states do not comply with strict rules of evidence in such major areas as opinion testimony, hearsay evidence, rules of impeachment, and so forth. Other jurisdictions apply those rules of evidence that determine admissibility in a criminal case. Still other states use the rules of evidence of civil law to apply to juvenile proceedings.

There are evidentiary problems, apart from the strict rules of evidence, that spring from constitutional law and procedure. These problem areas include oral testimony or physical evidence obtained from illegal arrests, search and seizure problems, the legality of confessions, lineups, and the rules involving custodial interrogation and right to counsel. As a result of *Gault,* many of these pretrial rights previously available only in criminal proceedings have been extended to juveniles.

In regard to the issue of double jeopardy, at trial children are protected from being tried twice for the same offense by the Fifth Amendment of the U.S. Constitution. More than one adjudicatory hearing in the juvenile court on the same delinquent act would violate the juvenile's constitutional right to be free from double jeopardy. This is unlikely to occur in light of the *Gault* decision and the increased formality in juvenile proceedings. More prevalent is the double jeopardy provision barring the juvenile from subsequent criminal prosecution after adjudication for the same act in the juvenile court.

Standard of Proof

Case Comment

Do the essentials of due process and equal protection require proof beyond a reasonable doubt in determining the culpability of youth in delinquency proceedings? Some states held that merely a "preponderance of the evidence" standard (the standard used in civil cases) was sufficient in determining that a youth could be adjudicated a delinquent. However, in *In re Winship,* the U.S. Supreme Court thought other wise and mandated that the "beyond a reasonable doubt" doctrine must apply to minors as it does to adult criminals. Even if juvenile court had traditionally been considered by some to be a civil procedure, the Supreme Court found it clear that "labels and good intentions" do not obviate the need for procedural safeguards in the trial process.

Although the standard of proof beyond a reasonable doubt is not stated in the Constitution, the U.S. Supreme Court said that *Gault* had established that due process required the essentials of fair treatment, although it did not require that the adjudication process conform to all the requirements of a criminal trial. The Court further indicated that the due process clause recognized proof beyond a reasonable doubt as being among the essentials of fairness required when a child is charged with a delinquent act. The state of New York argued that juvenile delinquency proceedings were civil in nature, not criminal, and that the preponderance of the evidence standard was therefore valid. The Supreme Court indicated that the standard of proof beyond a reasonable doubt plays a vital role in the U.S. criminal justice system and ensures a greater degree of safety for the presumption of innocence of those accused of crimes.

Thus, the *Winship* case required proof beyond a reasonable doubt as the standard for juvenile adjudication proceedings and eliminated the use of lesser standards, such as preponderance of the evidence, clear and convincing proof, and reasonable proof.

IN RE WINSHIP

Supreme Court of the United States, 1970.

397 U.S. 358.

Mr. Justice Brennan delivered the opinion of the Court.

Constitutional questions decided by this Court concerning the juvenile process have centered on the adjudicatory stage at "which a determination is made as to whether a juvenile is a 'delinquent' as a result of alleged misconduct on his part, with the consequence that he may be committed to a state institution." *In re Gault,* 387 U.S. 1, 13, 1436 (1967). *Gault* decided that, although the Fourteenth Amendment does not require that the hearing at this stage conform with all the requirements of a criminal trial or even of the usual administrative proceeding, the Due Process Clause does require application during the adjudicatory hearing of "the essentials of due process and fair treatment." Id., at 30, 87 S.Ct. at 1445. This case presents the single, narrow question whether proof beyond a reasonable doubt is among the "essentials of due process and fair treatment" required during the adjudicatory stage when a juvenile is charged with an act which would constitute a crime if committed by an adult.[1]

Section 712 of the New York Family Court Act defines a juvenile delinquent as "a person over seven and less than sixteen years of age who does any act which, if done by an adult, would constitute a crime." During a 1967 adjudicatory hearing, conducted pursuant to 742 of the Act, a judge in New York Family Court found that appellant, then a 12-year-old boy, had entered a locker and stolen $112 from a woman's pocketbook. The petition which charged appellant with delinquency alleged that his act, "if done by an adult, would constitute the crime or crimes of Larceny." The judge acknowledged that the proof might not establish guilt beyond a reasonable doubt, but rejected appellant's contention that such proof was required by the Fourteenth Amendment. The judge relied instead on 744(b) of the New York Family Court Act which provides that "(a)ny determination at the conclusion of (an adjudicatory) hearing that a (juvenile) did an act or acts must be based on a preponderance of the evidence."[2] During a subsequent dispositional hearing, appellant was ordered placed in a training school for an initial period of 18 months, subject to annual extensions of his commitment until his 18th birthday—six years in appellant's case. The Appellate Division of the New York Supreme Court, First Judicial Department, affirmed without opinion, 30 A.D.2d 781, 291 N.Y.S.2d 1005 (1968). The New York Court of Appeals then affirmed by a four-to-three vote, expressly sustaining the constitutionality of 744(b), 24 N.Y.2d 196, 299 N.Y.S.2d 414, 247 N.W.2d 253 (1969).[3] We noted probable jurisdiction 396 U.S. 885 (1969). We reverse.

---

1. Thus, we do not see how it can be said in dissent that this opinion "rests entirely on the assumption that all juvenile proceedings are 'criminal prosecutions,' hence subject to constitutional limitations." As in *Gault*, "we are not here concerned with . . . the pre-judicial stages of the juvenile process, nor do we direct our attention to the post-adjudicative or dispositional process." 387 U.S., at 13. In New York, the adjudicatory stage of a delinquency proceeding is clearly distinct from both the preliminary phase of the juvenile process and from its dispositional stage. See N.Y. Family Court Act 731-749. Similarly, we intimate no view concerning the constitutionality of the New York procedures governing children "in need of supervision." See id., at 711, 712, 742-745. Nor do we consider whether there are other "essentials of due process and fair treatment" required during the adjudicatory hearing of a delinquency proceeding. Finally, we have no occasion to consider appellant's argument that 744(b) is a violation of the Equal Protection Clause, as well as a denial of due process.

2. The ruling appears in the following portion of the hearing transcript:

Counsel: "Your Honor is making a finding by the preponderance of the evidence."

Court: "Well, it convinces me."

Counsel: "It's not beyond a reasonable doubt, Your Honor."

Court: "That is true . . . Our statute says a preponderance and a preponderance it is."

3. Accord, e.g., In re Dennis M., 70 Cal.2d 444, 75 Cal.Rptr. 1, 450 P.2d 296 (1969); *In re Ellis*, 253 A.2d 789 (D.C.Ct.App. 1969); *State v. Arenas*, 253 Or. 215, 453 P.2d 915 (Or.1969); *State v. Santana*, 444 S.W.2d 614 (Texas 1969). Contra. *United States v. Costanzo*, 395 F.2d 441 (C.A.4th Cir. 1968); In re Urbasek, 38 Ill.2d 535, 232 N.E.2d 716 (1967); *Jones v. Commonwealth,* 185 Va. 335, 38 S.E.2d 444 (1946); N.D.Cent.Code 27-20-29(2) (Supp. 1969); Colo.Rev.Stat.Ann. 22-3-6(1) (1967); Md.Ann.Code, Art. 26, 70-18(a) (Supp. 1969); N.J.Ct.Rule 6:9(1)(f) (1967); Wash.Sup.Ct., Juv.Ct.Rule 4.4(b) (1969); cf. In re Agler, 19 Ohio St.2d 70, 249 N.E.2d 808 (1969).

Legislative adoption of the reasonable doubt standard has been urged by the National Conference of Commissioners on Uniform State Laws and by the Children's Bureau of the Department of Health, Education, and Welfare's Social and Rehabilitation Service. See Uniform Juvenile Court Act 29(b) (1968); Children's Bureau, Social and Rehabilitation Service, U.S. Department of Health, Education and Welfare, Legislative Guide for Drafting Family and Juvenile Court Acts 32(c) (1969). Cf. the proposal of the National Council on Crime and Delinquency that a "clear and convincing" standard be adopted. Model Rules for Juvenile Courts, Rule 26, p. 57 (1969). See generally Cohen, The Standard of Proof in Juvenile Proceedings: Gault Beyond a Reasonable Doubt, 68 Mich.L.Rev. 567 (1970).

I

The requirement that guilt of a criminal charge be established by proof beyond a reasonable doubt dates at least from our early years as a Nation. The "demand for a higher degree of persuasion in criminal cases was recurrently expressed from ancient times, (though) its crystallization into the formula 'beyond a reasonable doubt' seems to have occurred as late as 1798. It is now accepted in common law jurisdictions as the measure of persuasion by which the prosecution must convince the trier of all the essential elements of guilt." C. McCormick, Evidence 321, pp. 681–682 (1954); see also 9 J. Wigmore, Evidence, 2497 (3d ed. 1940). Although virtually unanimous adherence to the reasonable-doubt standard in common-law jurisdictions may not conclusively establish it as a requirement of due process, such adherence does "reflect a profound judgment about the way in which law should be enforced and justice administered." *Duncan v. Louisiana,* 391 U.S. 145, 155, 1451 (1968).

Expressions in many opinions of this Court indicate that it has long been assumed that proof of a criminal charge beyond a reasonable doubt is constitutionally required. See, for example, *Miles v. United States,* 103 U.S. 304, 312 (1881); *Davis v. United States,* 160 U.S. 469, 488, 358 (1895); *Holt v. United States,* 218 U.S. 245, 253, 6 (1910); *Wilson v. United States,* 232 U.S. 563, 569-570, 349, 350 (1914); *Brinegar v. United States,* 338 U.S. 160, 174, 1310 (1949); *Leland v. Oregon,* 343 U.S. 790, 795, 1005, 1006 (1952); *Holland v. United States,* 348 U.S. 121, 138, 136, 137 (1954); *Speiser v. Randall,* 357 U.S. 513, 525-526, 1342 (1958). Cf. *Coffin v. United States,* 156 U.S. 432 (1895). Mr. Justice Frankfurter stated that "(i)t [is] the duty of the Government to establish . . . guilt beyond a reasonable doubt. This notion—basic in our law and rightly one of the boasts of a free society—is a requirement and a safeguard of due process of law in the historic, procedural content of 'due process.'" *Leland v. Oregon,* supra, 343 U.S., at 802-803 (dissenting opinion). In a similar vein, the Court said in *Brinegar v. United States,* supra, 338 U.S., at 174, that "(g)uilt in a criminal case must be proved beyond a reasonable doubt and by evidence confined to that which long experience in the common-law tradition, to some extent embodied in the Constitution, has crystallized into rules of evidence consistent with that standard. These rules are historically grounded rights of our system, developed to safeguard men from dubious and unjust convictions, with resulting forfeitures of life, liberty and property." *Davis v. United States,* supra, 160 U.S., at 488 stated that the requirement is implicit in "constitutions . . . (which) recognize the fundamental principles that are deemed essential for the protection of life and liberty." In *Davis* a murder conviction was reversed because the trial judge instructed the jury that it was their duty to convict when the evidence was equally balanced regarding the sanity of the accused. This Court said: "On the contrary, he is entitled to an acquittal of the specific crime charged, if upon all the evidence, there is reasonable doubt whether he was capable in law of committing crime. . . . No man should be deprived of his life under the forms of law unless the jurors who try him are able, upon their consciences, to say that the evidence before them . . . is sufficient to show beyond a reasonable doubt the existence of every fact necessary to constitute the crime charged." Id., at 484, 493, 360.

The reasonable-doubt standard plays a vital role in the American scheme of criminal procedure. It is a prime instrument for reducing the risk of convictions resting on factual error. The standard provides concrete substance for the presumption of innocence-that bedrock "axiomatic and elementary" principle whose "enforcement lies at the foundation of the administration of our criminal law." *Coffin v. United States,* supra, 156 U.S., at 453.

As the dissenters in the New York Court of Appeals observed, and we agree, "a person accused of a crime . . . would be at a severe disadvantage, a disadvantage amounting to a lack of fundamental fairness, if he could be adjudged guilty and imprisoned for years on the strength of the same evidence as would suffice in a civil case." 24 N.Y.2d, at 205, 299 N.Y.S.2d, at 422, 247 N.E.2d, at 259.

The requirement of proof beyond a reasonable doubt has this vital role in our criminal procedure for cogent reasons. The accused during a criminal prosecution has at stake interest of immense importance, both because of the possibility that he may lose his liberty upon conviction and because of the certainty that he would be stigmatized by the conviction. Accordingly, a society that values the good name and freedom of every individual should not condemn a man for commission of a crime when there is reasonable doubt about his guilt. As we said in *Speiser v. Randall,* supra, 357 U.S., at 525-526: "There is always in litigation a margin of error, representing error in factfinding, which both parties must take into account. Where one party has at stake an interest of transcending value—as a criminal defendant his liberty—this margin of error is reduced as to him by the process of placing on the other party the burden of . . . persuading the factfinder at the conclusion of the trial of his guilt beyond a reasonable doubt. Due process commands that no man shall lose his liberty unless the Government has borne the burden of . . . convincing the factfinder of his guilt." To this end, the reasonable-doubt standard is indispensable, for it "impresses on the trier of fact the necessity of reaching a subjective state of certitude of the facts in issue." Dorsen & Rezneck, *In Re Gault* and the Future of Juvenile Law, 1 Family Law Quarterly, No. 4, pp. 1, 26 (1967).

Moreover, use of the reasonable-doubt standard is indispensable to command the respect and confidence of the community in applications of the criminal law. It is critical that the moral force of the criminal law not be diluted by a standard of proof that leaves people in doubt whether innocent men are being condemned. It is also important in our free society that every individual going about his ordinary affairs have confidence that his government cannot adjudge him guilty of a criminal offense without convincing a proper factfinder of his guilt with utmost certainty.

Lest there remain any doubt about the constitutional stature of the reasonable-doubt standard, we explicitly hold that the Due Process Clause protects the accused against conviction except upon proof beyond a reasonable doubt of every fact necessary to constitute the crime with which he is charged.

II

We turn to the question whether juveniles, like adults, are constitutionally entitled to proof beyond a reasonable doubt when they are charged with violation of a criminal law. The same considerations that demand extreme caution in factfinding to protect the innocent adult apply as well to the innocent child. We do not find convincing the contrary arguments of the New York Court of Appeals, *Gault* rendered untenable much of the reasoning relied upon by that court to sustain the constitutionality of 744(b). The Court of Appeals indicated that a delinquency adjudication "is not a 'conviction' (781); that it affects no right or privilege, including the right to hold public office or to obtain a license (782); and a cloak of protective confidentiality is thrown around all the proceedings (783-784)." 24 N.Y.2d at 200, 299 N.Y.

S.2d, at 417-418, 247 N.E.2d, at 255-256. The court said further: "The delinquency status is not made a crime; and the proceedings are not criminal. There is, hence, no deprivation of due process in the statutory provision (challenged by appellant). . . ." 24 N.Y.2d, at 203, 299 N.Y.S. 2d, at 420, 247 N.E.2d, at 257. In effect the Court of Appeals distinguished the proceedings in question here from a criminal prosecution by use of what *Gault* called the "civil label-of-convenience which has been attached to juvenile proceedings." 387 U.S., at 50. But *Gault* expressly rejected that distinction as a reason for holding the Due Process Clause inapplicable to a juvenile proceeding. 387 U.S., at 50-51, 1456. The Court of Appeals also attempted to justify the preponderance standard on the related ground that juvenile proceedings are designed "not to punish, but to save the child." 24 N.Y.2d, at 197, 299 N.Y.S.2d, at 415, 247 N.E.2d, at 254. Again, however, Gault expressly rejected this justification. 387 U.S., at 27. We made clear in that decision that civil labels and good intentions do not themselves obviate the need for criminal due process safeguards in juvenile courts, for "(a) proceeding where the issue is whether the child will be found to be 'delinquent' and subjected to the loss of his liberty for years is comparable in seriousness to a felony prosecution." Id., at 36.

Nor do we perceive any merit in the argument that to afford juveniles the protection of proof beyond a reasonable doubt would risk destruction of beneficial aspects of the juvenile process.[4] Use of the reasonable-doubt standard during the adjudicatory hearing will not disturb New York's policies that a finding that a child has violated a criminal law does not constitute a criminal conviction, that such a finding does not deprive the child of his civil rights, and that juvenile proceedings are confidential. Nor will there be any effect on the informality, flexibility, or speed of the hearing at which the factfinding takes place. And the opportunity during the post-adjudicatory or dispositional hearing for a wide-ranging review of the child's social history and for his individualized treatment will remain unimpaired. Similarly, there will be no effect on the procedures distinctive to juvenile proceedings that are employed prior to the adjudicatory hearing.

The Court of Appeals ovserved that "a child's best interest is not necessarily, or even probably, promoted if he wins in the particular inquiry which may bring him to the juvenile court." 24 N.Y.2d, at 199, 299 N.Y.S.2d, at 417, 247 N.E.2d, at 255. It is true, of course, that the juvenile may be engaging in a general course of conduct inimical to his welfare that calls for judicial intervention. But that intervention cannot take the form of subjecting the child to the stigma of a finding that he violated a criminal law[5] and to the possibility of institutional confinement on proof insufficient to convict him were he an adult.

---

4. Appellee, New York City, apparently concedes as much in its Brief, page 8, where it states:
"A determination that the New York law unconstitutionally denies due process because it does not provide for use of the reasonable doubt standard probably would not have a serious impact if all that resulted would be a change in the quantum of proof."
And Dorsen & Rezneck, supra, at 27, have observed:
"(T)he reasonable doubt test is superior to all others in protecting against an unjust adjudication of guilt, and that is as much a concern of the juvenile court as of the criminal court. It is difficult to see how the distinctive objectives of the juvenile court give rise to a legitimate institutional interest in finding a juvenile to have committed a violation of the criminal law on less evidence than if he were an adult."
5. The more comprehensive and effective the procedures used to prevent public disclosure of the finding, the less the danger of stigma. As we indicated in *Gault*, however, often the "claim of secrecy . . . is more rhetoric than reality." 387 U.S., at 24.

We conclude, as we concluded regarding the essential due process safeguards applied in *Gault*, that the observance of the standard of proof beyond a reasonable doubt "will not compel the States to abandon or displace any of the substantive benefits of the juvenile process." *Gault*, supra, at 21.

Finally, we reject the Court of Appeals' suggestion that there is, in any event, only a "tenuous difference" between the reasonable-doubt and preponderance standards. The suggestion is singularly unpersuasive. In this very case, the trial judge's ability to distinguish between the two standards enabled him to make a finding of guilt that he conceded he might not have made under the standard of proof beyond a reasonable doubt. Indeed, the trial judge's action evidences the accuracy of the observation of commentators that "the preponderance test is susceptible to the misinterpretation that it calls on the trier of fact merely to perform an abstract weighing of the evidence in order to determine which side has produced the greater quantum, without regard to its effect in convincing his mind of the truth of the proposition asserted." Dorsen & Rezneck, supra, at 26-27. [6]

III

In sum, the constitutional safeguard of proof beyond a reasonable doubt is as much required during the adjudicatory stage of a delinquency proceeding as are those constitutional safeguards applied in *Gault*—notice of charges, right to counsel, the rights of confrontation and examination, and the privilege against self-incrimination. We therefore hold, in agreement with Chief Judge Fuld in dissent in the Court of Appeals, "that, where a 12-year-old child is charged with an act of stealing which renders him liable to confinement for as long as six years, then, as a matter of due process . . . the case against him must be proved beyond a reasonable doubt." 24 N.Y.2d, at 207, 299 N.Y.S.2d, at 423, 247 N.E.2d, at 260.

Reversed.

Mr. Justice Harlan, concurring.

No one, I daresay, would contend that state juvenile court trials are subject to no federal constitutional limitations. Differences have existed, however, among the members of this Court as to what constitutional protections do apply. See *In re Gault*, 387 U.S. 1 d 527 (1967). The present case draws in question the validity of a New York statute that permits a determination of juvenile delinquency, founded on a charge of criminal conduct, to be made on a standard of proof that is less rigorous than that which would obtain had the accused been tried for the same conduct in an ordinary criminal case. While I am in full agreement that this statutory provision offends the requirement of fundamental fairness embodied in the Due Process Clause of the Fourteenth Amendment, I am constrained to add something to what my Brother Brennan has written for the Court, lest the true nature of the constitutional problem presented become obscured or the impact on state juvenile court systems of what the Court holds today be exaggerated.

---

6. Compare this Court's rejection of the preponderance standard in deportation proceedings, where we ruled that the Government must support its allegations with "clear, unequivocal, and convincing evidence." *Woodby v. Immigration and Naturalization Service*, 385 U.S., 276, 285, 488 (1966). Although we ruled in *Woodby* that deportation is not tantamount to a criminal conviction, we found that since it could lead to "drastic deprivations," it is impermissible for a person to be "banished from this country upon no higher degree of proof than applies in a negligence case." Ibid.

I

Professor Wigmore, in discussing the various attempts by courts to define how convinced one must be to be convinced beyond a reasonable doubt, wryly observed: "The truth is that no one has yet invented or discovered a mode of measurement for the intensity of human belief. Hence there can be yet no successful method of communicating intelligibly . . . a sound method of self-analysis for one's belief," 9 J. Wigmore, Evidence 325 (3d ed. 1940).[1]

Notwithstanding Professor Wigmore's skepticism, we have before us a case where the choice of the standard of proof has made a difference: the juvenile court judge below forthrightly acknowledged that he believed by a preponderance of the evidence, but was not convinced beyond a reasonable doubt, that appellant stole $112 from the complainant's pocketbook. Moreover, even though the labels used for alternative standards of proof are vague and not a very sure guide to decisionmaking, the choice of the standard for a particular variety of adjudication does, I think, reflect a very fundamental assessment of the comparative social costs of erroneous factual determinations.[2]

To explain why I think this so, I begin by stating two propositions, neither of which I believe can be fairly disputed. First, in a judicial proceeding in which there is a dispute about the facts of some earlier event, the factfinder cannot acquire unassailably accurate knowledge of what happened. Instead, all the fact-finder can acquire is a belief of what probably happened. The intensity of this belief—the degree to which a factfinder is convinced that a given act actually occurred—can, of course, vary. In this regard, a standard of proof represents an attempt to instruct the fact-finder concerning the degree of confidence our society thinks he should have in the correctness of factual conclusions for a particular type of adjudication. Although the phrases "preponderance of the evidence" and "proof beyond a reasonable doubt" are quantitatively imprecise, they do communicate to the finder of fact different notions concerning the degree of confidence he is expected to have in the correctness of his factual conclusions.

A second proposition, which is really nothing more than a corollary of the first, is that the trier of fact will sometimes, despite his best efforts, be wrong in his factual conclusions. In a lawsuit between two parties, a factual error can make a difference in one of two ways. First, it can result in a judgment in favor of the plaintiff when the true facts warrant a judgment for the defendant. The analogue in a criminal case would be the conviction of an innocent man. On the other hand, an erroneous factual determination can result in a judgment for the defendant when the true facts justify a judgment in plaintiff's favor. The criminal analogue would be the acquittal of a guilty man.

The standard of proof influences the relative frequency of these two types of erroneous outcomes. If, for example, the standard of proof for a criminal trial were a preponderance of the evidence rather than proof beyond a reasonable doubt, there would be a smaller risk of factual errors that result in freeing guilty persons, but a far greater risk of factual errors that result in convicting the innocent. Because the standard of proof affects the comparative frequency of these two types of erroneous outcomes, the choice of the standard to be applied

---

1. See also Paulsen, Juvenile Courts and the Legacy of '67, 43 Ind.L. J. 527, 551–552 (1968).

2. For an interesting analysis of standards of proof see Kaplan, Decision Theory and the Factfinding Process, 20 Stan.L.Rev. 1065, 1071–1077 (1968).

in a particular kind of litigation should, in a rational world, reflect an assessment of the comparative social disutility of each.

When one makes such an assessment, the reason for different standards of proof in civil as opposed to criminal litigation becomes apparent. In a civil suit between two private parties for money damages, for example, we view it as no more serious in general for there to be an erroneous verdict in the defendant's favor than for there to be an erroneous verdict in the plaintiff's favor. A preponderance of the evidence standard therefore seems peculiarly appropriate for, as explained most sensibly,[3] it simply requires the trier of fact "to believe that the existence of a fact is more probable than its nonexistence before (he) may find in favor of the party who has the burden to persuade the (judge) of the fact's existence."[4]

In a criminal case, on the other hand, we do not view the social disutility of convicting an innocent man as equivalent to the disutility of acquitting someone who is guilty. As Mr. Justice Brennan wrote for the Court in *Speiser v. Randall,* 357 U.S. 513, 525-526, 1341-1342 (1958):

> "There is always in litigation a margin of error, representing error in factfinding, which both parties must take into account. Where one party has at stake an interest of transcending value—as a criminal defendant his liberty—this margin of error is reduced as to him by the process of placing on the other party the burden . . . of persuading the fact-finder at the conclusion of the trial of his guilt beyond a reasonable doubt."

In this context, I view the requirement of proof beyond a reasonable doubt in a criminal case as bottomed on a fundamental value determination of our society that it is far worse to convict an innocent man than to let a guilty man go free. It is only because of the nearly complete and long- standing acceptance of the reasonable-doubt standard by the States in criminal trials that the Court has not before today had to hold explicitly that due process, as an expression of fundamental procedural fairness,[5] requires a more stringent standard for criminal trials than for ordinary civil litigation.

---

3. The preponderance test has been criticized, justifiably in my view, when it is read as asking the trier of fact to weigh in some objective sense the quantity of evidence submitted by each side rather than asking him to decide what he believes most probably happened. See J. Maguire, Evidence, Common Sense and Common Law 180 (1947).

4. F. James, Civil Procedure 250-251 (1965); see E. Morgan, Some Problems of Proof Under the Anglo-American System of Litigation 84–85 (1956).

5. In dissent my Brother Black again argues that, apart from the specific prohibitions of the first eight amendments, any procedure spelled out by a legislature—no matter how unfair—passes constitutional muster under the Due Process Clause. He bottoms his conclusion on history that he claims demonstrates (1) that due process means "law of the land"; (2) that any legislative enactment, ipso facto, is part of the law of the land; and (3) that the Fourteenth Amendment incorporates the prohibitions of the Bill of Rights and applies them to the States. I cannot refrain from expressing my continued bafflement at my Brother Black's insistence that due process, whether under the Fourteenth Amendment or the Fifth Amendment, does not embody a concept of fundamental fairness as part of our scheme of constitutionally ordered liberty. His thesis flies in the face of a course of judicial history reflected in an unbroken line of opinions that have interpreted due process to impose restraints on the procedures government may adopt in its dealing with its citizens, see, e.g., the cases cited in my dissenting opinions in *Poe v. Ullman,* 367 U.S. 497, 522, 539-545, 1765, 1774-1778 (1961); *Duncan v. Louisiana,* 391 U.S. 145, 171, 1458, 1459 (1968); as well as the uncontroverted scholarly research (notwithstanding H. Flack, The Adoption of the Fourteenth Amendment (1908)), respecting the intendment of the Due Process Clause of the Fourteenth Amendment, see Fairman, Does the Fourteenth Amendment Incorporate the Bill of Rights? The Original Understanding, 2 Stan.L.Rev. 5 (1949). Indeed, with all respect, the very case cited in Brother Black's dissent as establishing that "due process of law" means "law of the land" rejected the argument that any statute, by the mere process of enactment, met the re-

II

When one assesses the consequences of an erroneous factual determination in a juvenile delinquency proceeding in which a youth is accused of a crime, I think it must be concluded that, while the consequences are not identical to those in a criminal case, the differences will not support a distinction in the standard of proof. First, and of paramount importance, a factual error here, as in a criminal case, exposes the accused to a complete loss of his personal liberty through a state-imposed confinement away from his home, family, and friends. And, second, a delinquency determination, to some extent at least, stigmatizes a youth in that it is by definition bottomed on a finding that the accused committed a crime.[6] Although there are no doubt costs to society (and possibly even to the youth himself) in letting a guilty youth go free, I think here, as in a criminal case, it is far worse to declare an innocent youth a delinquent. I therefore agree that a juvenile court judge should be no less convinced of the factual conclusion that the accused committed the criminal act with which he is charged than would be required in a criminal trial.

III

I wish to emphasize, as I did in my separate opinion in Gault, 387 U.S. 1, 65, 1463, that there is no automatic congruence between the procedural requirements imposed by due process in a criminal case, and those imposed by due process in juvenile cases.[7] It is of great importance, in my view, that procedural strictures not be constitutionally imposed that jeopardize "the essential elements of the State's purpose" in creating juvenile courts, id., at 72, 87

---

quirements of the Due Process Clause. In *Murray's Lessee v. Hoboken Land & Improv. Co.,* 18 How, 272 (1856), an issue was whether a "distress warrant" issued by the Solicitor of the Treasury under an act of Congress to collect money due for taxes offended the Due Process Clause. Justice Curtis wrote: "That the warrant now in question is legal process, is not denied. It was issued in conformity with an Act of Congress. But is it 'due process of law?' The constitution contains no description of those processes which it was intended to allow or forbid. It does not even declare what principles are to be applied to ascertain whether it be due process. It is manifest that it was not left to the legislative power to enact any process which might be devised. The article is a restraint on the legislative as well as on the executive and judicial powers of the government, and cannot be so construed as to leave congress free to make any process 'due process of law,' by its mere will." Id., at 276.

6. The New York statute was amended to distinguish between a "juvenile delinquent," i.e., a youth "who does any act which, if done by an adult, would constitute a crime," N.Y.Family Court Act 712 (1963), and a "(p)erson in need of supervision" (PINS) who is a person "who is an habitual truant or who is incorrigible, ungovernable or habitually disobedient and beyond the lawful control of parent or other lawful authority." The PINS category was established in order to avoid the stigma of finding someone to be a "juvenile delinquent" unless he committed a criminal act. The Legislative Committee report stated: "'Juvenile delinquent' is now a term of disapproval. The judges of the Children's Court and the Domestic Relations Court of course are aware of this and also aware that government officials and private employers often learn of an adjudication of delinquency." N.Y.Jt. Legislative Committee on Court Reorganization, The Family Court Act, pt. 2, p. 7 (1962). Moreover, the powers of the police and courts differ in these two categories of cases. See id., at 7-9. Thus, in a PINS type case, the consequences of an erroneous factual determination are by no means identical to those involved here.

7. In *Gault,* for example, I agreed with the majority that due process required (1) adequate notice of the "nature and terms" of the proceedings; (2) notice of the right to retain counsel, and an obligation on the State to provide counsel for indigents "in cases in which the child may be confined"; and (3) a written record "adequate to permit effective review." 387 U.S., at 72. Unlike the majority, however, I thought it unnecessary at the time of *Gault* to impose the additional requirements of the privilege against self-incrimination, confrontation, and cross-examination.

S.Ct. at 1467. In this regard, I think it worth emphasizing that the requirement of proof be-yond a reasonable doubt that a juvenile committed a criminal act before he is found to be a delinquent does not (1) interfere with the worthy goal of rehabilitating the juvenile, (2) make any significant difference in the extent to which a youth is stigmatized as a "criminal" because he has been found to be a delinquent, or (3) burden the juvenile courts with a procedural requirement that will make juvenile adjudications significantly more time consuming, or rigid. Today's decision simply requires a juvenile court judge to be more confident in his be-lief that the youth did the act with which he has been charged.

With these observations, I join the Court's opinion, subject only to the constitutional reservations expressed in my opinion in *Gault*.

Right to Trial by Jury

Case Comment

McKiever v. Pennsylvania is an important case for two principal reasons: (1) It denied that juveniles have a constitutional right to a jury trial; and (2) it represented a retreat from the practice following *Gault* for the Court to equalize the procedures in the adult court and fam-ily/juvenile courts. In ruling on behalf of the defendants, the Supreme Court recognized that while recent constitutional cases had focused on the issue of fundamental fairness in fact-finding procedures, juries are not actually an essential part of this area of justice, nor are they required for all types of trials. Fearing that the jury would put an end to the informal nature of the juvenile court and introduce open adversary procedures, the Supreme Court decreed that the states themselves must determine whether juries are an acceptable form of procedure in juvenile court.

MCKEIVER V. PENNSYLVANIA

Supreme Court of the United States, 1971.

403 U.S. 528.

Mr. Justice Blackman announced the judgments of the Court and an opinion in which The Chief Justice, Mr. Justice Stewart, and Mr. Justice White join.

These cases present the narrow but precise issue whether the Due Process Clause of the Fourteenth Amendment assures the right to trial by jury in the adjudicative phase of a state juvenile court delinquency proceeding.

I

The issue arises understandably, for the Court in a series of cases already has emphasized due process factors protective of the juvenile:

1. *Haley v. Ohio*, 332 U.S. 596 (1948), concerned the admissibility of a confession taken from a 15-year-old boy on trial for first-degree murder. It was held that, upon the facts there developed, the Due Process Clause barred the use of the confession. Mr. Justice Douglas, in an opinion in which three other Justices joined, said, "Neither man nor child can be allowed to stand condemned by methods which flout constitutional requirements of due process of law." 332 U.S., at 601.

2. *Gallegos v. Colorado*, 370 U.S. 49 (1962), where a 14-year-old was on trial, is to the same effect.

3. *Kent v. United States*, 383 U.S. 541 (1966), concerned a 16-year-old charged with house-breaking, robbery and rape in the District of Columbia. The issue was the propriety of the juvenile court's waiver of jurisdiction "after full investigation," as permitted by the applicable statute. It was emphasized that the latitude the court possessed within which to determine whether it should retain or waive jurisdiction "assumes procedural regularity sufficient in the particular circumstances to satisfy the basic requirements of due process and fairness, as well as compliance with the statutory requirement of a 'full investigation.'" 383 U.S., at 553.

4. *In re Gault*, 387 U.S. 1 (1967), concerned a 15-year-old, already on probation, committed in Arizona as a delinquent after being apprehended upon a complaint of lewd remarks by telephone. Mr. Justice Fortas, in writing for the Court, reviewed the cases just cited and observed,

"Accordingly, while these cases relate only to restricted aspects of the subject, of the subject, they unmistakably indicate that, whatever may be their precise impact, neither the Fourteenth Amendment nor the Bill of Rights is for adults alone." 387 U.S., at 13.

The Court focused on "the proceedings by which a determination is made as to whether a juvenile is a 'delinquent' as a result of alleged misconduct on his part, with the consequence that he may be committed to a state institution" and, as to this, said that "there appears to be little current dissent from the proposition that the Due Process Clause has a role to play." Ibid. *Kent* was adhered to: "We reiterate this view, here in connection with a juvenile court adjudication of 'delinquency,' as a requirement which is part of the Due Process Clause of the Fourteenth Amendment of our Constitution." Id., at 30-31. Due process, in that proceeding, was held to embrace adequate written notice; advice as to the right to counsel, retained or appointed; confrontation; and cross-examination. The privilege against self-incrimination was also held available to the juvenile. The Court refrained from deciding whether a State must provide appellate review in juvenile cases or a transcript or recording of the hearings.

5. *DeBacker v. Brainard*, 396 U.S. 28 (1969), presented, by state habeas corpus, a challenge to a Nebraska statute providing that juvenile court hearings "shall be conducted by the judge without a jury in an informal manner." However, because that appellant's hearing had antedated the decisions in *Duncan v. Louisiana*, 391 U.S. 145 (1968), and *Bloom v. Illinois*, 391 U.S. 194 (1968), and because *Duncan* and *Bloom* had been given only prospective application by *DeStefano v. Woods*, 392 U.S. 631 (1968), DeBacker's case was deemed an inappropriate one for resolution of the jury trial issue. His appeal was therefore dismissed. Mr. Justice Black and Mr. Justice Douglas, in separate dissents, took the position that a juvenile is entitled to a jury trial at the adjudicative stage. Mr. Justice Black described this as "a right which is surely one of the fundamental aspects of criminal justice in the English-speaking world," 396 U.S., at 34, and Mr. Justice Douglas described it as a right required by the Sixth and Fourteenth Amendments "where the delinquency charged is an offense that, if the person were an adult, would be a crime triable by jury." 396 U.S., at 35.

6. *In re Winship*, 397 U.S. 358 (1970), concerned a 12-year-old charged with delinquency for having taken money from a woman's purse. The Court held that "the Due Process Clause protects the accused against conviction except upon proof beyond a reasonable doubt of every fact necessary to constitute the crime with which he is charged," 397 U.S., at 364, and

then went on to hold, at 368, that this standard was applicable, too, "during the adjudicatory stage of a delinquency proceeding."

From these six cases—*Haley, Gallegos, Kent, Gault, DeBacker,* and *Winship*—it is apparent that:

1. Some of the constitutional requirements attendant upon the state criminal trial have equal application to that part of the state juvenile proceeding that is adjudicative in nature. Among these are the rights to appropriate notice, to counsel, to confrontation and to cross-examination, and the privilege against self-incrimination. Included, also, is the standard of proof beyond a reasonable doubt.

2. The Court, however, has not yet said that all rights constitutionally assured to an adult accused of crime also are to be enforced or made available to the juvenile in his delinquency proceeding. Indeed, the Court specifically has refrained from going that far:

> "We do not mean by this to indicate that the hearing to be held must conform with all of the requirements of a criminal trial or even of the usual administrative hearing; but we do hold that the hearing must measure up to the essentials of due process and fair treatment." *Kent,* 383 U.S., at 562; *Gault,* 387 U.S., at 30.

3. The Court, although recognizing the high hopes and aspirations of Judge Julian Mack, the leaders of the Jane Addams School[1] and the other supporters of the juvenile court concept, has also noted the disappointments of the system's performance and experience and the resulting widespread disaffection. *Kent,* 383 U.S., at 555-556; *Gault,* 387 U.S., at 17-19. There have been, at one and the same time, both an appreciation for the juvenile court judge who is devoted, sympathetic, and conscientious, and a disturbed concern about the judge who is untrained and less than fully imbued with an understanding approach to the complex problems of childhood and adolescence. There has been praise for the system and its purposes, and there has been alarm over its defects.

4. The Court has insisted that these successive decisions do not spell the doom of the juvenile court system or even deprive it of its "informality, flexibility, or speed." *Winship,* 397 U.S., at 366. On the other hand, a concern precisely to the opposite effect was expressed by two dissenters in *Winship.* Id., at 375-376.

II

With this substantial background already developed, we turn to the facts of the present cases: No. 322. Joseph McKeiver, then age 16, in May 1968 was charged with robbery, larceny, and receiving stolen goods (felonies under Pennsylvania law, Pa. Stat. Ann., Tit. 18, 4704, 4807, and 4817 (1963)) as acts of juvenile delinquency. At the time of the adjudication hearing he was represented by counsel.[2] His request for a jury trial was denied and his case was heard by Judge Theodore S. Gutowicz of the Court of Common Pleas, Family Division, Juvenile Branch, of Philadelphia County, Pennsylvania. McKeiver was adjudged a delinquent upon findings that he had violated a law of the Commonwealth. Pa. Stat. Ann., Tit. 11, 243 (4) (a)

---

1. See Mr. Justice Fortas' article, Equal Rights—For Whom?, 42 N. Y. U. L. Rev. 401, 406 (1967).

2. At McKeiver's hearing his counsel advised the court that he had never seen McKeiver before and "was just in the middle of interviewing" him. The court allowed him five minutes for the interview. Counsel's office, Community Legal Services, however, had been appointed to represent *McKeiver* five months earlier. App. 2.

(1965). He was placed on probation. On appeal, the Superior Court affirmed without opinion. *In re McKeiver*, 215 Pa. Super. 760, 255 A. 2d 921 (1969).

Edward Terry, then age 15, in January 1969 was charged with assault and battery on a police officer and conspiracy (misdemeanors under Pennsylvania law, Pa. Stat. Ann., Tit. 18, 4708 and 4302 (1963)) as acts of juvenile delinquency. His counsel's request for a jury trial was denied and his case was heard by Judge Joseph C. Bruno of the same Juvenile Branch of the Court of Common Pleas of Philadelphia County. Terry was adjudged a delinquent on the charges. This followed an adjudication and commitment in the preceding week for an assault on a teacher. He was committed, as he had been on the earlier charge, to the Youth Development Center at Cornwells Heights. On appeal, the Superior Court affirmed without opinion. *In re Terry*, 215 Pa. Super. 762, 255 A. 2d 922 (1969).

The Supreme Court of Pennsylvania granted leave to appeal in both cases and consolidated them. The single question considered, as phrased by the court, was "whether there is a constitutional right to a jury trial in juvenile court." The answer, one justice dissenting, was in the negative. *In re Terry*, 438 Pa. 339, 265 A. 2d 350 (1970). We noted probable jurisdiction. 399 U.S. 925 (1970).

The details of the *McKeiver* and *Terry* offenses are set forth in Justice Roberts' opinion for the Pennsylvania court, 438 Pa., at 341-342, nn. 1 and 2, 265 A. 2d, at 351 nn. 1 and 2, and need not be repeated at any length here. It suffices to say that McKeiver's offense was his participating with 20 or 30 youths who pursued three young teenagers and took 25 cents from them; that McKeiver never before had been arrested and had a record of gainful employment; that the testimony of two of the victims was described by the court as somewhat inconsistent and as "weak"; and that Terry's offense consisted of hitting a police officer with his fists and with a stick when the officer broke up a boys' fight Terry and others were watching.

No. 128. Barbara Burrus and approximately 45 other black children, ranging in age from 11 to 15 years,[3] were the subjects of juvenile court summonses issued in Hyde County, North Carolina, in January 1969.

The charges arose out of a series of demonstrations in the county in late 1968 by black adults and children protesting school assignments and a school consolidation plan. Petitions were filed by North Carolina state highway patrolmen. Except for one relating to James Lambert Howard, the petitions charged the respective juveniles with wilfully impeding traffic. The charge against Howard was that he wilfully made riotous noise and was disorderly in the O. A. Peay School in Swan Quarter; interrupted and disturbed the school during its regular sessions; and defaced school furniture. The acts so charged are misdemeanors under North Carolina law. N.C. Gen. Stat. 20-174.1 (1965 and Supp. 1969), 14-132 (a), 14-273 (1969).

The several cases were consolidated into groups for hearing before District Judge Hallett S. Ward, sitting as a juvenile court. The same lawyer appeared for all the juveniles. Over counsel's objection, made in all except two of the cases, the general public was excluded. A request for a jury trial in each case was denied.

The evidence as to the juveniles other than Howard consisted solely of testimony of highway patrolmen. No juvenile took the stand or offered any witness. The testimony was to the effect that on various occasions the juveniles and adults were observed walking along Highway 64 singing, shouting, clapping, and playing basketball. As a result, there was interference

3. In North Carolina juvenile court procedures are provided only for persons under the age of 16. N.C. Gen. Stat. 7A-277 and 7A-278 (1) (1969).

with traffic. The marchers were asked to leave the paved portion of the highway and they were warned that they were committing a statutory offense. They either refused or left the roadway and immediately returned. The juveniles and participating adults were taken into custody. Juvenile petitions were then filed with respect to those under the age of 16.

The evidence as to Howard was that on the morning of December 5, he was in the office of the principal of the O. A. Peay School with 15 other persons while school was in session and was moving furniture around; that the office was in disarray; that as a result the school closed before noon; and that neither he nor any of the others was a student at the school or authorized to enter the principal's office.

In each case the court found that the juvenile had committed "an act for which an adult may be punished by law." A custody order was entered declaring the juvenile a delinquent "in need of more suitable guardianship" and committing him to the custody of the County Department of Public Welfare for placement in a suitable institution "until such time as the Board of Juvenile Correction or the Superintendent of said institution may determine, not inconsistent with the laws of this State." The court, however, suspended these commitments and placed each juvenile on probation for either one or two years conditioned upon his violating none of the State's laws, upon his reporting monthly to the County Department of Welfare, upon his being home by 11 p. m. each evening, and upon his attending a school approved by the Welfare Director. None of the juveniles has been confined on these charges.

On appeal, the cases were consolidated into two groups. The North Carolina Court of Appeals affirmed. *In re Burrus,* 4 N.C. App. 523, 167 S. E. 2d 454 (1969); *In re Shelton,* 5 N.C. App. 487, 168 S. E. 2d 695 (1969). In its turn the Supreme Court of North Carolina deleted that portion of the order in each case relating to commitment, but otherwise affirmed. *In re Burrus,* 275 N.C. 517, 169 S. E. 2d 879 (1969). Two justices dissented without opinion. We granted certiorari. 397 U.S. 1036 (1970).

III

It is instructive to review, as an illustration, the substance of Justice Roberts' opinion for the Pennsylvania court. He observes, 438 Pa., at 343, 265 A. 2d at 352, that "[f]or over sixty-five years the Supreme Court gave no consideration at all to the constitutional problems involved in the juvenile court area"; that *Gault* "is somewhat of a paradox, being both broad and narrow at the same time"; that it "is broad in that it evidences a fundamental and far-reaching disillusionment with the anticipated benefits of the juvenile court system"; that it is narrow because the court enumerated four due process rights which it held applicable in juvenile proceedings, but declined to rule on two other claimed rights, id., at 344-345, 265 A. 2d, at 353; that as a consequence the Pennsylvania court was "confronted with a sweeping rationale and a carefully tailored holding," id., at 345, 265 A. 2d, at 353; that the procedural safeguards "*Gault* specifically made applicable to juvenile courts have already caused a significant 'constitutional domestication' of juvenile court proceedings," id., at 346, 265 A. 2d, at 354; that those safeguards and other rights, including the reasonable-doubt standard established by *Winship,* "insure that the juvenile court will operate in an atmosphere which is orderly enough to impress the juvenile with the gravity of the situation and the impartiality of the tribunal and at the same time informal enough to permit the benefits of the juvenile system to operate" [footnote omitted], id., at 347, 265 A. 2d, at 354; that the "proper inquiry, then, is whether the right to a trial by jury is 'fundamental' within the meaning of *Duncan,* in the context of a juvenile court which operates with all of the above constitutional safeguards," id., at 348, 265 A. 2d, at 354; and that his court's inquiry turned "upon whether there are elements in the juvenile process which render the right to a trial by jury less essential to the protection of an accused's rights in the juvenile system than in the normal criminal process." Ibid.

Justice Roberts then concluded that such factors do inhere in the Pennsylvania juvenile system: (1) Although realizing that "faith in the quality of the juvenile bench is not an entirely satisfactory substitute for due process," id., at 348, 265 A. 2d, at 355, the judges in the juvenile courts "do take a different view of their role than that taken by their counterparts in the criminal courts." Id., at 348, 265 A. 2d, at 354-355. (2) While one regrets its inadequacies, "the juvenile system has available and utilizes much more fully various diagnostic and rehabilitative services" that are "far superior to those available in the regular criminal process." Id., at 348-349, 265 A. 2d, at 355. (3) Although conceding that the post-adjudication process "has in many respects fallen far short of its goals, and its reality is far harsher than its theory," the end result of a declaration of delinquency "is significantly different from and less onerous than a finding of criminal guilt" and "we are not yet convinced that the current practices do not contain the seeds from which a truly appropriate system can be brought forth." (4) Finally, "of all the possible due process rights which could be applied in the juvenile courts, the right to trial by jury is the one which would most likely be disruptive of the unique nature of the juvenile process." It is the jury trial that "would probably require substantial alteration of the traditional practices." The other procedural rights held applicable to the juvenile process "will give the juveniles sufficient protection" and the addition of the trial by jury "might well destroy the traditional character of juvenile proceedings." Id., at 349-350, 265 A. 2d, at 355.

The court concluded, id., at 350, 265 A. 2d, at 356, that it was confident "that a properly structured and fairly administered juvenile court system can serve our present societal needs without infringing on individual freedoms."

IV

The right to an impartial jury "[i]n all criminal prosecutions" under federal law is guaranteed by the Sixth Amendment. Through the Fourteenth Amendment that requirement has now been imposed upon the States "in all criminal cases which—were they to be tried in a federal court—would come within the Sixth Amendment's guarantee." This is because the Court has said it believes "that trial by jury in criminal cases is fundamental to the American scheme of justice." *Duncan v. Louisiana*, 391 U.S. 145, 149 (1968); *Bloom v. Illinois*, 391 U.S. 194, 210-211 (1968).

This, of course, does not automatically provide the answer to the present jury trial issue, if for no other reason than that the juvenile court proceeding has not yet been held to be a "criminal prosecution," within the meaning and reach of the Sixth Amendment, and also has not yet been regarded as devoid of criminal aspects merely because it usually has been given the civil label. *Kent*, 383 U.S., at 554; *Gault*, 387 U.S., at 17, 49-50; *Winship*, 397 U.S., at 365-366.

Little, indeed, is to be gained by any attempt simplistically to call the juvenile court proceeding either "civil" or "criminal." The Court carefully has avoided this wooden approach. Before *Gault* was decided in 1967, the Fifth Amendment's guarantee against self-incrimination had been imposed upon the state criminal trial. *Malloy v. Hogan*, 378 U.S. 1 (1964). So, too, had the Sixth Amendment's rights of confrontation and cross-examination. *Pointer v. Texas,* 380 U.S. 400 (1965), and *Douglas v. Alabama,* 380 U.S. 415 (1965). Yet the Court did not automatically and peremptorily apply those rights to the juvenile proceeding. A reading of *Gault* reveals the opposite. And the same separate approach to the standard-of-proof issue is evident from the carefully separated application of the standard, first to the criminal trial, and then to the juvenile proceeding, displayed in *Winship.* 397 U.S., at 361 and 365.

Thus, accepting "the proposition that the Due Process Clause has a role to play," *Gault,* 387 U.S., at 13, our task here with respect to trial by jury, as it was in *Gault* with respect to other claimed rights, "is to ascertain the precise impact of the due process requirement." Id., at 13-14.

V

The Pennsylvania juveniles' basic argument is that they were tried in proceedings "substantially similar to a criminal trial." They say that a delinquency proceeding in their State is initiated by a petition charging a penal code violation in the conclusory language of an indictment; that a juvenile detained prior to trial is held in a building substantially similar to an adult prison; that in Philadelphia juveniles over 16 are, in fact, held in the cells of a prison; that counsel and the prosecution engage in plea bargaining; that motions to suppress are routinely heard and decided; that the usual rules of evidence are applied; that the customary common-law defenses are available; that the press is generally admitted in the Philadelphia juvenile courtrooms; that members of the public enter the room; that arrest and prior record may be reported by the press (from police sources, however, rather than from the juvenile court records); that, once adjudged delinquent, a juvenile may be confined until his majority in what amounts to a prison (see *In re Bethea,* 215 Pa. Super. 75, 76, 257 A. 2d 368, 369 (1969), describing the state correctional institution at Camp Hill as a "maximum security prison for adjudged delinquents and youthful criminal offenders"); and that the stigma attached upon delinquency adjudication approximates that resulting from conviction in an adult criminal proceeding.

The North Carolina juveniles particularly urge that the requirement of a jury trial would not operate to deny the supposed benefits of the juvenile court system; that the system's primary benefits are its discretionary intake procedure permitting disposition short of adjudication, and its flexible sentencing permitting emphasis on rehabilitation; that realization of these benefits does not depend upon dispensing with the jury; that adjudication of factual issues on the one hand and disposition of the case on the other are very different matters with very different purposes; that the purpose of the former is indistinguishable from that of the criminal trial; that the jury trial provides an independent protective factor; that experience has shown that jury trials in juvenile courts are manageable; that no reason exists why protection traditionally accorded in criminal proceedings should be denied young people subject to involuntary incarceration for lengthy periods; and that the juvenile courts deserve healthy public scrutiny.

VI

All the litigants here agree that the applicable due process standard in juvenile proceedings, as developed by *Gault* and *Winship,* is fundamental fairness. As that standard was applied in those two cases, we have an emphasis on factfinding procedures. The requirements of notice, counsel, confrontation, cross-examination, and standard of proof naturally flowed from this emphasis. But one cannot say that in our legal system the jury is a necessary component of accurate factfinding. There is much to be said for it, to be sure, but we have been content to pursue other ways for determining facts. Juries are not required, and have not been, for example, in equity cases, in workmen's compensation, in probate, or in deportation cases. Neither have they been generally used in military trials. In *Duncan* the Court stated, "We would not assert, however, that every criminal trial—or any particular trial—held before a judge alone is unfair or that a defendant may never be as fairly treated by a judge as he would be by a jury." 391 U.S., at 158. In *DeStefano,* for this reason and others, the Court refrained from retrospective application of *Duncan,* an action it surely would have not taken had it felt that the integrity of the result was seriously at issue. And in *Williams v. Florida,* 399 U.S. 78 (1970), the Court saw no particular magic in a 12-man jury for a criminal case, thus revealing that even jury concepts themselves are not inflexible.

We must recognize, as the Court has recognized before, that the fond and idealistic hopes of the juvenile court proponents and early reformers of three generations ago have not been realized. The devastating commentary upon the system's failures as a whole, contained in the President's Commission on Law Enforcement and Administration of Justice, Task Force Report: Juvenile Delinquency and Youth Crime 7–9 (1967), reveals the depth of disappointment in what has been accomplished. Too often the juvenile court judge falls far short of that stalwart, protective, and communicating figure the system envisaged.[4] The community's unwillingness to provide people and facilities and to be concerned, the insufficiency of time devoted, the scarcity of professional help, the inadequacy of dispositional alternatives, and our general lack of knowledge all contribute to dissatisfaction with the experiment.[5]

The Task Force Report, however, also said, id., at 7, "To say that juvenile courts have failed to achieve their goals is to say no more than what is true of criminal courts in the United States. But failure is most striking when hopes are highest."

Despite all these disappointments, all these failures, and all these shortcomings, we conclude that trial by jury in the juvenile court's adjudicative stage is not a constitutional requirement. We so conclude for a number of reasons:

---

4. "A recent study of juvenile court judges . . . revealed that half had not received undergraduate degrees; a fifth had received no college education at all; a fifth were not members of the bar." Task Force Report 7.

5. "What emerges, then, is this: In theory the juvenile court was to be helpful and rehabilitative rather than punitive. In fact the distinction often disappears, not only because of the absence of facilities and personnel but also because of the limits of knowledge and technique. In theory the court's action was to affix no stigmatizing label. In fact a delinquent is generally viewed by employers, schools, the armed services—by society generally—as a criminal. In theory the court was to treat children guilty of criminal acts in noncriminal ways. In fact it labels truants and runaways as junior criminals.

"In theory the court's operations could justifiably be informal, its findings and decisions made without observing ordinary procedural safeguards, because it would act only in the best interest of the child. In fact it frequently does nothing more nor less than deprive a child of liberty without due process of law—knowing not what else to do and needing, whether admittedly or not, to act in the community's interest even more imperatively than the child's. In theory it was to exercise its protective powers to bring an errant child back into the fold. In fact there is increasing reason to believe that its intervention reinforces the juvenile's unlawful impulses. In theory it was to concentrate on each case the best of current social science learning. In fact it has often become a vested interest in its turn, loathe to cooperate with innovative programs or avail itself of forward-looking methods." Task Force Report 9.

1. The Court has refrained, in the cases heretofore decided, from taking the easy way with a flat holding that all rights constitutionally assured for the adult accused are to be imposed upon the state juvenile proceeding. What was done in *Gault* and in *Winship* is aptly described in *Commonwealth v. Johnson*, 211 Pa. Super. 62, 74, 234 A. 2d 9, 15 (1967):

> "It is clear to us that the Supreme Court has properly attempted to strike a judicious balance by injecting procedural orderliness into the juvenile court system. It is seeking to reverse the trend [pointed out in *Kent*, 383 U.S., at 556] whereby 'the child receives the worst of both worlds....'"

2. There is a possibility, at least, that the jury trial, if required as a matter of constitutional precept, will remake the juvenile proceeding into a fully adversary process and will put an effective end to what has been the idealistic prospect of an intimate, informal protective proceeding.

3. The Task Force Report, although concededly pre-*Gault*, is notable for its not making any recommendation that the jury trial be imposed upon the juvenile court system. This is so despite its vivid description of the system's deficiencies and disappointments. Had the Commission deemed this vital to the integrity of the juvenile process, or to the handling of juveniles, surely a recommendation or suggestion to this effect would have appeared. The intimations, instead, are quite the other way. Task Force Report 38. Further, it expressly recommends against abandonment of the system and against the return of the juvenile to the criminal courts.[6]

4. The Court specifically has recognized by dictum that a jury is not a necessary part even of every criminal process that is fair and equitable. *Duncan v. Louisiana*, 391 U.S., at 149-150, n. 14, and 158.

5. The imposition of the jury trial on the juvenile court system would not strengthen greatly, if at all, the factfinding function, and would, contrarily, provide an attrition of the juvenile court's assumed ability to function in a unique manner. It would not remedy the defects of the system. Meager as has been the hoped-for advance in the juvenile field, the alternative would be regressive, would lose what has been gained, and would tend once again to place the juvenile squarely in the routine of the criminal process.

---

6. "Nevertheless, study of the juvenile courts does not necessarily lead to the conclusion that the time has come to jettison the experiment and remand the disposition of children charged with crime to the criminal courts of the country. As trying as are the problems of the juvenile courts, the problems of the criminal courts, particularly those of the lower courts, which would fall heir to much of the juvenile court jurisdiction, are even graver; and the ideal of separate treatment of children is still worth pursuing. What is required is rather a revised philosophy of the juvenile court based on the recognition that in the past our reach exceeded our grasp. The spirit that animated the juvenile court movement was fed in part by a humanitarian compassion for offenders who were children. That willingness to understand and treat people who threaten public safety and security should be nurtured, not turned aside as hopeless sentimentality, both because it is civilized and because social protection itself demands constant search for alternatives to the crude and limited expedient of condemnation and punishment. But neither should it be allowed to outrun reality. The juvenile court is a court of law, charged like other agencies of criminal justice with protecting the community against threatening conduct. Rehabilitating offenders through individualized handling is one way of providing protection, and appropriately the primary way in dealing with children. But the guiding consideration for a court of law that deals with threatening conduct is nonetheless protection of the community. The juvenile court, like other courts, is therefore obliged to employ all the means at hand, not excluding incapacitation, for achieving that protection. What should distinguish the juvenile from the criminal courts is greater emphasis on rehabilitation, not exclusive preoccupation with it." Task Force Report 9.

6. The juvenile concept held high promise. We are reluctant to say that, despite disappointments of grave dimensions, it still does not hold promise, and we are particularly reluctant to say, as do the Pennsylvania appellants here, that the system cannot accomplish its rehabilitative goals. So much depends on the availability of resources, on the interest and commitment of the public, on willingness to learn, and on understanding as to cause and effect and cure. In this field, as in so many others, one perhaps learns best by doing. We are reluctant to disallow the States to experiment further and to seek in new and different ways the elusive answers to the problems of the young, and we feel that we would be impeding that experimentation by imposing the jury trial. The States, indeed, must go forward. If, in its wisdom, any State feels the jury trial is desirable in all cases, or in certain kinds, there appears to be no impediment to its installing a system embracing that feature. That, however, is the State's privilege and not its obligation.

7. Of course there have been abuses. The Task Force Report has noted them. We refrain from saying at this point that those abuses are of constitutional dimension. They relate to the lack of resources and of dedication rather than to inherent unfairness.

8. There is, of course, nothing to prevent a juvenile court judge, in a particular case where he feels the need, or when the need is demonstrated, from using an advisory jury.

9. "The fact that a practice is followed by a large number of states is not conclusive in a decision as to whether that practice accords with due process, but it is plainly worth considering in determining whether the practice 'offends some principle of justice so rooted in the traditions and conscience of our people as to be ranked as fundamental.' *Snyder v. Massachusetts*, 291 U.S. 97, 105 (1934)." *Leland v. Oregon*, 343 U.S. 790, 798 (1952). It therefore is of more than passing interest that at least 29 States and the District of Columbia by statute deny the juvenile a right to a jury trial in cases such as these.[7] The same result is achieved in other States by judicial decision.[8] In 10 States statutes provide for a jury trial under certain circumstances.[9]

10. Since *Gault* and since *Duncan* the great majority of States, in addition to Pennsylvania and North Carolina, that have faced the issue have concluded that the considerations

---

7. Ala. Code, Tit. 13, 369 (1958); Alaska Stat. 47.10.070 (Supp. 1970); Ariz. Rev. Stat. Ann. 8-229 (1956), see Ariz. Laws, c. 223 (May 19, 1970); Ark. Stat. Ann. 45-206 (1964); Del. Code Ann., Tit. 10, 1175 (Supp. 1970); Fla. Stat. 39.09 (2) (1965); Ga. Code Ann. 24-2420 (Supp. 1970); Hawaii Rev. Stat. 571-41 (1968); Idaho Code 16-1813 (Supp. 1969); Ind. Ann. Stat. 9-3215 (Supp. 1970); Iowa Code 232.27 (1971); Ky. Rev. Stat. 208.060 (1962); La Rev. Stat. 13:1579 (Supp. 1962); Minn. Stat. 260.155 subd. 1 (1969); Miss. Code Ann. 7185-08 (1942); Mo. Rev. Stat. 211.171 (6) (1969) (equity practice controls); Neb. Rev. Stat. 43-206.03 (2) (1968); Nev. Rev. Stat. 62.190 (3) (1968); NJ Stat. Ann. 2A:4-35 (1952); NY. Family Court Act 164 and 165 and Civ. Prac. Law and Rules 4101; N.C. Gen. Stat. 7A-285 (1969); ND. Cent. Code 27-16-18 (1960); Ohio Rev. Code Ann. 2151.35 (Supp. 1970); Ore. Rev. Stat. 419.498 (1) (1968); Pa. Stat. Ann., Tit. 11, 247 (1965); SC. Code Ann. 15-1095.19 (Supp. 1970); Utah Code Ann. 55-10-94 (Supp. 1969); Vt. Stat. Ann., Tit. 33, 651 (a) (Supp. 1970); Wash. Rev. Code Ann. 13.04.030; D.C. Code 16-2316 (a) (Supp. 1971).

8. *In re Daedler*, 194 Cal. 320, 228 P. 467 (1924); *Cinque v. Boyd* 99 Conn. 70, 121 A. 678 (1923); *In re Fletcher*, 251 Md. 520, 248 A. 2d 364 (1968); *Commonwealth v. Page*, 339 Mass. 313, 316, 159 N. E. 2d 82, 85 (1959); *In re Perham*, 104 N. H. 276, 184 A. 2d 449 (1962).

9. Colo. Rev. Stat. Ann. 37-19-24 (Supp. 1965); Kan. Stat. Ann. 38-808 (Supp. 1969); Mich. Comp. Laws 712A.17 (1948); Mont. Rev. Codes Ann. 10-604.1 (Supp. 1969); Okla. Stat. Ann., Tit. 10. 1110 (Supp. 1970); SD. Comp. Laws 26-8-31 (1967); Tex. Civ. Stat., Art. 2338-1, 13 (b) (Supp. 1970); W. Va. Code Ann. 49-5-6 (1966); Wis. Stat. Ann. 48.25 (2) (Supp. 1971): Wyo. Stat. Ann. 14-115.24 (Supp. 1971).

that led to the result in those two cases do not compel trial by jury in the juvenile court. *In re Fucini,* 44 Ill. 2d 305, 255 N. E. 2d 380 (1970); *Bible v. State,* 254 N. E. 2d 319 (1970); *Dryden v. Commonwealth,* 435 S. W. 2d 457 (Ky. 1968); *In re Johnson,* 254 Md. 517, 255 A. 2d 419 (1969); *Hopkins v. Youth Court,* 227 So.2d 282 (Miss. 1969); *In re J. W.,* 106 N. J. Super. 129, 254 A. 2d 334 (1969); *In re D.,* 27 N.Y. 2d 90, 261 N.E. 2d 627 (1970); *In re Agler,* 19 Ohio St. 2d 70, 249 N. E. 2d 808 (1969); *State v. Turner,* 253 Ore. 235, 453 P.2d 910 (1969). See *In re Estes v. Hopp,* 73 Wash. 2d 263, 438 P.2d 205 (1968); *McMullen v. Geiger,* 184 Neb. 581, 169 NW. 2d 431 (1969). To the contrary are *Peyton v. Nord,* 78 N.M. 717, 437 P.2d 716 (1968), and, *semble, Nieves v. United States,* 280 F. Supp. 994 (SDNY 1968).

11. Stopping short of proposing the jury trial for juvenile proceedings are the Uniform Juvenile Court Act, 24 (a), approved in July 1968 by the National Conference of Commissioners on Uniform State Laws: the Standard Juvenile Court Act, Art. V, 19, proposed by the National Council on Crime and Delinquency (see W. Sheridan, Standards for Juvenile and Family Courts 73, Dept. of HEW., Children's Bureau Pub. No. 437-1966); and the Legislative Guide for Drafting Family and Juvenile Court Acts 29 (a) (Dept. of HEW., Children's Bureau Pub. No. 472-1969).

12. If the jury trial were to be injected into the juvenile court system as a matter of right, it would bring with it into that system the traditional delay, the formality, and the clamor of the adversary system and, possibly, the public trial. It is of interest that these very factors were stressed by the District Committee of the Senate when, through Senator Tydings, it recommended, and Congress then approved, as a provision in the District of Columbia Crime Bill, the abolition of the jury trial in the juvenile court. S. Rep. No. 91-620, pp. 13–14 (1969).

13. Finally, the arguments advanced by the juveniles here are, of course, the identical arguments that underlie the demand for the jury trial for criminal proceedings. The arguments necessarily equate the juvenile proceeding—or at least the adjudicative phase of it—with the criminal trial. Whether they should be so equated is our issue. Concern about the inapplicability of exclusionary and other rules of evidence, about the juvenile court judge's possible awareness of the juvenile's prior record and of the contents of the social file; about repeated appearances of the same familiar witnesses in the persons of juvenile and probation officers and social workers—all to the effect that this will create the likelihood of pre-judgment—chooses to ignore, it seems to us, every aspect of fairness, of concern, of sympathy, and of paternal attention that the juvenile court system contemplates.

If the formalities of the criminal adjudicative process are to be superimposed upon the juvenile court system, there is little need for its separate existence. Perhaps that ultimate disillusionment will come one day, but for the moment we are disinclined to give impetus to it.

Affirmed.

CHAPTER 4

DOUBLE JEOPARDY

Introduction

Within a period of just five years, the U.S. Supreme Court had systematically granted due process rights to juveniles (*Kent,* 1966; *Gault,* 1967), clarified the standard of proof that would govern juvenile trials (*Winship,* 1970), and resolved the issue of whether juveniles had a right to a jury trial (*McKeiver,* 1971). The next issue that confronted the Supreme Court concerned another juvenile waiver case (*Breed v. Jones,* 1975). The *Breed* case concerned the prosecution of a juvenile as an adult in a California Superior Court after an adjudicatory proceeding in juvenile court had already been held. The issue before the Court was whether a juvenile court adjudication followed by a waiver to adult court had violated the double jeopardy clause of the Fifth Amendment, as applied to the states through the Fourteenth Amendment. The Court concluded that jeopardy attached when the juvenile court began to hear evidence at the adjudicatory hearing. This holding requires that the waiver hearing take place prior to any adjudicatory hearing. *Breed v. Jones* is significant because it is another example of the Supreme Court applying criminal procedural standards to the juvenile justice system.

Double Jeopardy in Waiver Proceedings

Case Comment

What is the rule of law governing prosecution of a minor in adult court after the child was originally held in jeopardy within the jurisdiction of the juvenile court? In *Breed v. Jones* the Supreme Court determined that further prosecution (after a waiver to adult court) of a boy already found to be a delinquent violated his Fifth and Fourteenth Amendment rights ("tried twice for the same offense"). In reaching its decision, the Court cited the recent trend in juvenile court to provide the delinquent with protection similar to that enjoyed by an adult offender. Though discretionary flexibility may be an important feature of juvenile court, the heavy burden imposed by criminal trial outweighs such consideration. In essence, the decision mandates that waiver procedures be held prior to the adjudicatory hearing.

The *Breed* ruling provides answers on several important waiver issues: (1) *Breed* prohibits trying a child in adult court when there has already been a prior adjudicatory proceeding in the juvenile justice system; (2) probable cause may exist at a transfer hearing, and this does not violate subsequent jeopardy if the child is transferred to the adult court; and (3) because the same evidence is often used in both the transfer hearing and subsequent trial in either the juvenile or adult court, a different judge is often required for the hearing.

Thus, practically speaking, the *Breed* case is extremely important in ensuring due process rights for juveniles. It prevents the state from taking two bites at the apple, which could occur when the state first seeks a juvenile court disposition and is unhappy with the ruling and decides to try again in adult court. Clearly, under Breed the state must choose either juvenile court process or waiver to adult court—it cannot do both.

BREED V. JONES

Supreme Court of the United States, 1975.

421 U.S. 519.

Mr. Chief Justice Burger delivered the opinion of the Court.

We granted certiorari to decide whether the prosecution of respondent as an adult, after Juvenile Court proceedings which resulted in a finding that respondent had violated a criminal statute and a subsequent finding that he was unfit for treatment as a juvenile, violated the Fifth and Fourteenth Amendments to the United States Constitution.

On February 9, 1971, a petition was filed in the Superior Court of California, County of Los Angeles, Juvenile Court, alleging that respondent, then 17 years of age, was a person described by Cal. Welf. & Inst'ns Code 602 (1966),[1] in that, on or about February 8, while armed with a deadly weapon, he had committed acts which, if committed by an adult, would constitute the crime of robbery in violation of Cal. Penal Code 211 (1970). The following day, a detention hearing was held, at the conclusion of which respondent was ordered detained pending a hearing on the petition.[2]

The jurisdictional or adjudicatory hearing was conducted on March 1, pursuant to Cal. Welf. & Inst'ns Code 701 (1966).[3] After taking testimony from two prosecution witnesses and

---

1. As of the date of filing of the petition in this case, Cal. Welf. & Inst'ns Code 602 (1966) provided: "Any person under the age of 21 years who violates any law of this State or of the United States or any ordinance of any city or county of this State defining crime or who, after having been found by the juvenile court to be a person described by Section 601, fails to obey any lawful order of the juvenile court, is within the jurisdiction of the juvenile court, which may adjudge such person to be a ward of the court." An amendment in 1971, not relevant here, lowered the jurisdictional age from 21 to 18. 1971 Cal. Stats. 3766, c. 1748, 66.

2. See Cal. Welf. & Inst'ns Code 632, 635, 636 (1966). The probation officer was required to present a prima facie case that respondent had committed the offense alleged in the petition. *In re William M.*, 3 Cal. 3d 16, 473 P.2d 737 (1970). Respondent was represented by court-appointed counsel at the detention hearing and thereafter.

3. At the time of the hearing, Cal. Welf. & Inst'ns Code 701 (1966) provided: "At the hearing, the court shall first consider only the question whether the minor is a person described by Sections 600, 601, or 602, and for this purpose, any matter or information relevant and material to the circumstances or acts which are alleged to bring him within the jurisdiction of the juvenile court is admissible and may be received in evidence; however, a preponderance of evidence, legally admissible in the trial of criminal cases, must be adduced to support a finding that the minor is a person described by Section 602, and a preponderance of evidence, legally admissible in the trial of civil cases must be adduced to support a finding that the minor is a person described by Sections 600 or 601. When it appears that the minor has made an extrajudicial admission or confession and denies the same at the hearing, the court may continue the hearing for not to exceed seven days to enable the probation officer to subpoena witnesses to attend the hearing to prove the allegations of the petition. If the minor is not represented by counsel at the hearing, it

respondent, the Juvenile Court found that the allegations in the petition were true and that respondent was a person described by 602, and it sustained the petition. The proceedings were continued for a dispositional hearing,[4] pending which the court ordered that respondent remain detained.

At a hearing conducted on March 15, the Juvenile Court indicated its intention to find respondent "not . . . amenable to the care, treatment and training program available through the facilities of the juvenile court" under Cal. Welf. & Inst'ns Code 707 (Supp. 1967).[5] Respondent's counsel orally moved "to continue the matter on the ground of surprise," contending that respondent "was not informed that it was going to be a fitness hearing." The court continued the matter for one week, at which time, having considered the report of the

---

shall be deemed that objections that could have been made to the evidence were made." A 1971 amendment substituted "proof beyond a reasonable doubt supported by evidence" for the language in italics. 1971 Cal. Stats. 1832, c. 934, 1. Respondent does not claim that the standard of proof at the hearing failed to satisfy due process. See *In re Winship*, 397 U.S. 358 (1970); *DeBacker v. Brainard*, 396 U.S. 28, 31 (1969). Hereafter, the 701 hearing will be referred to as the adjudicatory hearing.

4. At the time, Cal. Welf. & Inst'ns Code 702 (Supp. 1968) provided: "After hearing such evidence, the court shall make a finding, noted in the minutes of the court, whether or not the minor is a person described by Sections 600, 601, or 602. If it finds that the minor is not such a person, it shall order that the petition be dismissed and the minor be discharged from any detention or restriction theretofore ordered. If the court finds that the minor is such a person, it shall make and enter its findings and order accordingly and shall then proceed to hear evidence on the question of the proper disposition to be made of the minor. Prior to doing so, it may continue the hearing, if necessary, to receive the social study of the probation officer or to receive other evidence on its own motion or the motion of a parent or guardian for not to exceed 10 judicial days if the minor is detained during such continuance, and if the minor is not detained, it may continue the hearing to a date not later than 30 days after the date of filing of the petition. The court may, for good cause shown continue the hearing for an additional 15 days, if the minor is not detained. The court may make such order for detention of the minor or his release from detention, during the period of the continuance, as is appropriate."

5. At the time, Cal. Welf. & Inst'ns Code 707 (Supp. 1967) provided: "At any time during a hearing upon a petition alleging that a minor is, by reason of violation of any criminal statute or ordinance, a person described in Section 602, when substantial evidence has been adduced to support a finding that the minor was 16 years of age or older at the time of the alleged commission of such offense and that the minor would not be amenable to the care, treatment and training program available through the facilities of the juvenile court, or if, at any time after such hearing, a minor who was 16 years of age or older at the time of the commission of an offense and who was committed therefore by the court to the Youth Authority, is returned to the court by the Youth Authority pursuant to Section 780 or 1737.1, the court may make a finding noted in the minutes of the court that the minor is not a fit and proper subject to be dealt with under this chapter, and the court shall direct the district attorney or other appropriate prosecuting officer to prosecute the person under the applicable criminal statute or ordinance and thereafter dismiss the petition or, if a prosecution has been commenced in another court but has been suspended while juvenile court proceedings are held, shall dismiss the petition and issue its order directing that the other court proceedings resume. "In determining whether the minor is a fit and proper subject to be dealt with under this chapter, the offense, in itself, shall not be sufficient to support a finding that such minor is not a fit and proper subject to be dealt with under the provisions of the Juvenile Court Law. "A denial by the person on whose behalf the petition is brought of any or all of the facts or conclusions set forth therein or of any inference to be drawn therefrom is not, of itself, sufficient to support a finding that such person is not a fit and proper subject to be dealt with under the provisions of the Juvenile Court Law. "The court shall cause the probation officer to investigate and submit a report on the behavioral patterns of the person being considered for unfitness."

probation officer assigned to the case and having heard her testimony, it declared respondent "unfit for treatment as a juvenile,"[6] and ordered that he be prosecuted as an adult.[7]

Thereafter, respondent filed a petition for a writ of habeas corpus in Juvenile Court, raising the same double jeopardy claim now presented. Upon the denial of that petition, respondent sought habeas corpus relief in the California Court of Appeal, Second Appellate District. Although it initially stayed the criminal prosecution pending against respondent, that court denied the petition. *In re Gary J.,* 17 Cal. App. 3d 704, 95 Cal. Rptr. 185 (1971). The Supreme Court of California denied respondent's petition for hearing.

After a preliminary hearing respondent was ordered held for trial in Superior Court, where an information was subsequently filed accusing him of having committed robbery, in violation of Cal. Penal Code 211 (1970), while armed with a deadly weapon, on or about February 8, 1971. Respondent entered a plea of not guilty, and he also pleaded that he had "already been placed once in jeopardy and convicted of the offense charged, by the judgment of the Superior Court of the County of Los Angeles, Juvenile Court, rendered . . . on the 1st day of March, 1971." App. 47. By stipulation, the case was submitted to the court on the transcript of the preliminary hearing. The court found respondent guilty of robbery in the first degree under Cal. Penal Code 211a (1970) and ordered that he be committed to the California Youth Authority.[8] No appeal was taken from the judgment of conviction.

On December 10, 1971, respondent, through his mother as guardian ad litem, filed the instant petition for a writ of habeas corpus in the United States District Court for the Central District of California. In his petition he alleged that his transfer to adult court pursuant to Cal. Welf. & Inst'ns Code 707 and subsequent trial there "placed him in double jeopardy." App. 13. The District Court denied the petition, rejecting respondent's contention that jeopardy attached at his adjudicatory hearing. It concluded that the "distinctions between the preliminary procedures and hearings provided by California law for juveniles and a criminal trial are many and apparent and the effort of [respondent] to relate them is unconvincing," and that "even assuming jeopardy attached during the preliminary juvenile proceedings . . . it is clear that no new jeopardy arose by the juvenile proceeding sending the case to the criminal court." 343 F. Supp. 690, 692 (1972).

The Court of Appeals reversed, concluding that applying double jeopardy protection to juvenile proceedings would not "impede the juvenile courts in carrying out their basic goal of rehabilitating the erring youth," and that the contrary result might "do irreparable harm

---

6. The Juvenile Court noted: "This record I have read is one of the most threatening records I have read about any Minor who has come before me. "We have, as a matter of simple fact, no less than three armed robberies, each with a loaded weapon. The degree of delinquency which that represents, the degree of sophistication which that represents and the degree of impossibility of assistance as a juvenile which that represents, I think is overwhelming . . . ." App. 33.

7. In doing so, the Juvenile Court implicitly rejected respondent's double jeopardy argument, made at both the original 702 hearing and in a memorandum submitted by counsel prior to the resumption of that hearing after the continuance.

8. The authority for the order of commitment derived from Cal. Welf. & Inst'ns Code 1731.5 (Supp. 1971). At the time of the order, Cal. Welf. & Inst'ns Code 1771 (1966) provided: "Every person convicted of a felony and committed to the authority shall be discharged when such person reaches his 25th birthday, unless an order for further detention has been made by the committing court pursuant to Article 6 (commencing with Section 1800) or unless a petition is filed under Article 5 of this chapter. In the event such a petition under Article 5 is filed, the authority shall retain control until the final disposition of the proceeding under Article 5."

to or destroy their confidence in our judicial system." The court therefore held that the Double Jeopardy Clause "is fully applicable to juvenile court proceedings." 497 F.2d 1160, 1165 (CA9 1974).

Turning to the question whether there had been a constitutional violation in this case, the Court of Appeals pointed to the power of the Juvenile Court to "impose severe restrictions upon the juvenile's liberty," ibid., in support of its conclusion that jeopardy attached in respondent's adjudicatory hearing.[9] It rejected petitioner's contention that no new jeopardy attached when respondent was referred to Superior Court and subsequently tried and convicted, finding "continuing jeopardy" principles advanced by petitioner inapplicable. Finally, the Court of Appeals observed that acceptance of petitioner's position would "allow the prosecution to review in advance the accused's defense and, as here, hear him testify about the crime charged," a procedure it found offensive to "our concepts of basic, even-handed fairness." The court therefore held that once jeopardy attached at the adjudicatory hearing, a minor could not be retried as an adult or a juvenile "absent some exception to the double jeopardy prohibition," and that there "was none here." Id., at 1168.

We granted certiorari because of a conflict between Courts of Appeals and the highest courts of a number of States on the issue presented in this case and similar issues and because of the importance of final resolution of the issue to the administration of the juvenile-court system.

I

The parties agree that, following his transfer from Juvenile Court, and as a defendant to a felony information, respondent was entitled to the full protection of the Double Jeopardy Clause of the Fifth Amendment, as applied to the States through the Fourteenth Amendment. See *Benton v. Maryland*, 395 U.S. 784 (1969). In addition, they agree that respondent was put in jeopardy by the proceedings on that information, which resulted in an adjudication that he was guilty of robbery in the first degree and in a sentence of commitment. Finally, there is no dispute that the petition filed in Juvenile Court and the information filed in Superior Court related to the "same offense" within the meaning of the constitutional prohibition. The point of disagreement between the parties, and the question for our decision, is whether, by reason of the proceedings in Juvenile Court, respondent was "twice put in jeopardy."

II

Jeopardy denotes risk. In the constitutional sense, jeopardy describes the risk that is traditionally associated with a criminal prosecution. See *Price v. Georgia*, 398 U.S. 323, 326, 329 (1970); *Serfass v. United States*, 420 U.S. 377, 387–389 (1975). Although the constitutional language, "jeopardy of life or limb," suggests proceedings in which only the most serious penalties can be imposed, the Clause has long been construed to mean something far broader

---

9. In reaching this conclusion, the Court of Appeals also relied on *Fain v. Duff*, 488 F.2d 218 (CA5 1973), cert. pending, No. 73–1768, and *Richard M. v. Superior Court*, 4 Cal. 3d 370, 482 P.2d 664 (1971), and it noted that "California concedes that jeopardy attaches when the juvenile is adjudicated a ward of the court." 497 F.2d, at 1166.

than its literal language. See *Ex parte Lange,* 18 Wall. 163, 170-173 (1874).[10] At the same time, however, we have held that the risk to which the Clause refers is not present in proceedings that are not "essentially criminal." *Helvering v. Mitchell,* 303 U.S. 391, 398 (1938). See *United States ex rel. Marcus v. Hess,* 317 U.S. 537 (1943); *One Lot Emerald Cut Stones v. United States,* 409 U.S. 232 (1972). See also J. Sigler, Double Jeopardy 60-62 (1969).

Although the juvenile-court system had its genesis in the desire to provide a distinctive procedure and setting to deal with the problems of youth, including those manifested by antisocial conduct, our decisions in recent years have recognized that there is a gap between the originally benign conception of the system and its realities. With the exception of *McKeiver v. Pennsylvania,* 403 U.S. 528 (1971), the Court's response to that perception has been to make applicable in juvenile proceedings constitutional guarantees associated with traditional criminal prosecutions. *In re Gault,* 387 U.S. 1 (1967); *In re Winship,* 397 U.S. 358 (1970). In so doing the Court has evinced awareness of the threat which such a process represents to the efforts of the juvenile-court system, functioning in a unique manner, to ameliorate the harshness of criminal justice when applied to youthful offenders. That the system has fallen short of the high expectations of its sponsors in no way detracts from the broad social benefits sought or from those benefits that can survive constitutional scrutiny.

We believe it is simply too late in the day to conclude, as did the District Court in this case, that a juvenile is not put in jeopardy at a proceeding whose object is to determine whether he has committed acts that violate a criminal law and whose potential consequences include both the stigma inherent in such a determination and the deprivation of liberty for many years.[11] For it is clear under our cases that determining the relevance of constitutional policies, like determining the applicability of constitutional rights, in juvenile proceedings, requires that courts eschew "the 'civil' label-of-convenience which has been attached to juvenile proceedings," *In re Gault,* supra, at 50, and that "the juvenile process . . . be candidly appraised." 387 U.S., at 21. See *In re Winship,* supra, at 365-366.

As we have observed, the risk to which the term jeopardy refers is that traditionally associated with "actions intended to authorize criminal punishment to vindicate public justice." *United States ex rel. Marcus v. Hess,* supra, at 548-549. Because of its purpose and potential consequences, and the nature and resources of the State, such a proceeding imposes heavy pressures and burdens—psychological, physical, and financial—on a person charged. The purpose of the Double Jeopardy Clause is to require that he be subject to the experience only once "for the same offense." See *Green v. United States,* 355 U.S. 184, 187(1957); *Price v. Georgia,* 398 U.S., at 331; *United States v. Jorn,* 400 U.S. 470, 479 (1971) (opinion of Harlan, J.).

In *In re Gault,* supra, at 36, this Court concluded that, for purposes of the right to counsel, a "proceeding where the issue is whether the child will be found to be 'delinquent' and

---

10. Distinctions which in other contexts have proved determinative of the constitutional rights of those charged with offenses against public order have not similarly confined the protection of the Double Jeopardy Clause. Compare *Robinson v. Neil,* 409 U.S. 505 (1973), with *Baldwin v. New York,* 399 U.S. 66 (1970), and *Argersinger v. Hamlin,* 407 U.S. 25 (1972). For the details of Robinson's trial for violating a city ordinance, see *Robinson v. Henderson,* 268 F. Supp. 349 (ED Tenn. 1967), aff'd, 391 F.2d 933 (CA6 1968).

11. At the time of respondent's dispositional hearing, permissible dispositions included commitment to the California Youth Authority until he reached the age of 21 years. See Cal. Welf. & Inst'ns Code 607, 731 (1966). Petitioner has conceded that the "adjudicatory hearing is, in every sense, a court trial." Tr. of Oral Arg. 4.

subjected to the loss of his liberty for years is comparable in seriousness to a felony prosecution." See *In re Winship,* supra, at 366. The Court stated that the term "delinquent" had "come to involve only slightly less stigma than the term 'criminal' applied to adults," *In re Gault,* supra, at 24; see *In re Winship,* supra, at 367, and that, for purposes of the privilege against self-incrimination, "commitment is a deprivation of liberty. It is incarceration against one's will, whether it is called 'criminal' or 'civil.'" *In re Gault,* supra, at 50. See 387 U.S., at 27; *In re Winship,* supra, at 367.[12]

Thus, in terms of potential consequences, there is little to distinguish an adjudicatory hearing such as was held in this case from a traditional criminal prosecution. For that reason, it engenders elements of "anxiety and insecurity" in a juvenile, and imposes a "heavy personal strain." See *Green v. United States,* supra, at 187; *United States v. Jorn,* supra, at 479; Snyder, The Impact of the Juvenile Court Hearing on the Child, 17 Crime & Delinquency 180 (1971). And we can expect that, since our decisions implementing fundamental fairness in the juvenile-court system, hearings have been prolonged, and some of the burdens incident to a juvenile's defense increased, as the system has assimilated the process thereby imposed. See Note, Double Jeopardy and the Waiver of Jurisdiction in California's Juvenile Courts, 24 Stan. L. Rev. 874, 902 n. 138 (1972). Cf. Canon & Kolson, Rural Compliance with Gault: Kentucky, A Case Study, 10 J. Fam. L. 300, 320-326 (1971).

We deal here, not with "the formalities of the criminal adjudicative process," *McKeiver v. Pennsylvania,* 403 U.S., at 551 (opinion of BLACKMUN, J.), but with an analysis of an aspect of the juvenile-court system in terms of the kind of risk to which jeopardy refers. Under our decisions we can find no persuasive distinction in that regard between the proceeding conducted in this case pursuant to Cal. Welf. & Inst'ns Code 701 (1966) and a criminal prosecution, each of which is designed "to vindicate [the] very vital interest in enforcement of criminal laws." *United States v. Jorn,* supra, at 479. We therefore conclude that respondent was put in jeopardy at the adjudicatory hearing. Jeopardy attached when respondent was "put to trial before the trier of the facts," 400 U.S., at 479, that is, when the Juvenile Court, as the trier of the facts, began to hear evidence. See *Serfass v. United States,* 420 U.S., at 388.[13]

III

Petitioner argues that, even assuming jeopardy attached at respondent's adjudicatory hearing, the procedure by which he was transferred from Juvenile Court and tried on a felony information in Superior Court did not violate the Double Jeopardy Clause. The argument is supported by two distinct, but in this case overlapping, lines of analysis. First, petitioner reasons that the procedure violated none of the policies of the Double Jeopardy Clause or that,

---

12. Nor does the fact "that the purpose of the commitment is rehabilitative and not punitive . . . change its nature. . . . Regardless of the purposes for which the incarceration is imposed, the fact remains that it is incarceration. The rehabilitative goals of the system are admirable, but they do not change the drastic nature of the action taken. Incarceration of adults is also intended to produce rehabilitation." *Fain v. Duff,* 488 F.2d, at 225. See President's Commission on Law Enforcement and Administration of Justice, Task Force Report: Juvenile Delinquency and Youth Crime 8–9 (1967).

13. The same conclusion was reached by the California Court of Appeal in denying respondent's petition for a writ of habeas corpus. *In re Gary J.,* 17 Cal. App. 3d 704, 710, 95 Cal. Rptr. 185, 189 (1971).

alternatively, it should be upheld by analogy to those cases which permit retrial of an accused who has obtained reversal of a conviction on appeal. Second, pointing to this Court's concern for "the juvenile court's assumed ability to function in a unique manner," *McKeiver v. Pennsylvania,* supra, at 547, petitioner urges that, should we conclude traditional principles "would otherwise bar a transfer to adult court after a delinquency adjudication," we should avoid that result here because it "would diminish the flexibility and informality of juvenile court proceedings without conferring any additional due process benefits upon juveniles charged with delinquent acts."

A

We cannot agree with petitioner that the trial of respondent in Superior Court on an information charging the same offense as that for which he had been tried in Juvenile Court violated none of the policies of the Double Jeopardy Clause. For, even accepting petitioner's premise that respondent "never faced the risk of more than one punishment," we have pointed out that "the Double Jeopardy Clause ... is written in terms of potential or risk of trial and conviction, not punishment." *Price v. Georgia,* 398 U.S., at 329. And we have recently noted:

> "The policy of avoiding multiple trials has been regarded as so important that exceptions to the principle have been only grudgingly allowed. Initially, a new trial was thought to be unavailable after appeal, whether requested by the prosecution or the defendant. ... It was not until 1896 that it was made clear that a defendant could seek a new trial after conviction, even though the Government enjoyed no similar right. ... Following the same policy, the Court has granted the Government the right to retry a defendant after a mistrial only where 'there is a manifest necessity for the act, or the ends of public justice would otherwise be defeated.' *United States v. Perez,* 9 Wheat. 579, 580 (1824)." *United States v. Wilson,* 420 U.S. 332, 343-344 (1975). (Footnote omitted.)

Respondent was subjected to the burden of two trials for the same offense; he was twice put to the task of marshaling his resources against those of the State, twice subjected to the "heavy personal strain" which such an experience represents. *United States v. Jorn,* 400 U.S., at 479. We turn, therefore, to inquire whether either traditional principles or "the juvenile court's assumed ability to function in a unique manner," *McKeiver v. Pennsylvania,* supra, at 547, supports an exception to the "constitutional policy of finality" to which respondent would otherwise be entitled. *United States v. Jorn,* supra, at 479.

B

In denying respondent's petitions for writs of habeas corpus, the California Court of Appeal first, and the United States District Court later, concluded that no new jeopardy arose as a result of his transfer from Juvenile Court and trial in Superior Court. See *In re Gary J.,* 17 Cal. App. 3d, at 710, 95 Cal. Rptr., at 189; 343 F. Supp., at 692. In the view of those courts, the jeopardy that attaches at an adjudicatory hearing continues until there is a final disposition of the case under the adult charge. See also *In re Juvenile,* 364 Mass. 531, 306 N. E. 2d 822 (1974). Cf. *Bryan v. Superior Court,* 7 Cal. 3d 575, 498 P.2d 1079 (1972), cert. denied, 410 U.S. 944 (1973).

The phrase "continuing jeopardy" describes both a concept and a conclusion. As originally articulated by Mr. Justice Holmes in his dissent in *Kepner v. United States,* 195 U.S. 100, 134-137 (1904), the concept has proved an interesting model for comparison with the system of constitutional protection which the Court has in fact derived from the rather ambiguous language and history of the Double Jeopardy Clause. See *United States v. Wilson,* supra, at 351-352. Holmes' view has "never been adopted by a majority of this Court." *United States v. Jenkins,* 420 U.S. 358, 369 (1975).

The conclusion, "continuing jeopardy," as distinguished from the concept, has occasionally been used to explain why an accused who has secured the reversal of a conviction on appeal may be retried for the same offense. See *Green v. United States,* 355 U.S., at 189; *Price v. Georgia,* 398 U.S., at 326; *United States v. Wilson,* supra, at 343-344, n. 11. Probably a more satisfactory explanation lies in analysis of the respective interests involved. See *United States v. Tateo,* 377 U.S. 463, 465-466 (1964); *Price v. Georgia,* supra, at 329 n. 4; *United States v. Wilson,* supra. Similarly, the fact that the proceedings against respondent had not "run their full course," *Price v. Georgia,* supra, at 326, within the contemplation of the California Welfare and Institutions Code, at the time of transfer, does not satisfactorily explain why respondent should be deprived of the constitutional protection against a second trial. If there is to be an exception to that protection in the context of the juvenile-court system, it must be justified by interests of society, reflected in that unique institution, or of juveniles themselves, of sufficient substance to render tolerable the costs and burdens, noted earlier, which the exception will entail in individual cases.

C

The possibility of transfer from juvenile court to a court of general criminal jurisdiction is a matter of great significance to the juvenile. See *Kent v. United States,* 383 U.S. 541 (1966). At the same time, there appears to be widely shared agreement that not all juveniles can benefit from the special features and programs of the juvenile-court system and that a procedure for transfer to an adult court should be available. See, e.g., National Advisory Commission on Criminal Justice Standards and Goals, Courts, Commentary to Standard 14.3, pp. 300–301 (1973). This general agreement is reflected in the fact that an overwhelming majority of jurisdictions permits transfer in certain circumstances.[14] As might be expected, the statutory provisions differ in numerous details. Whatever their differences, however, such transfer provisions represent an attempt to impart to the juvenile-court system the flexibility needed to deal with youthful offenders who cannot benefit from the specialized guidance and treatment contemplated by the system.

We do not agree with petitioner that giving respondent the constitutional protection against multiple trials in this context will diminish flexibility and informality to the extent that those qualities relate uniquely to the goals of the juvenile-court system.[15] We agree that such a holding will require, in most cases, that the transfer decision be made prior to an adjudicatory hearing. To the extent that evidence concerning the alleged offense is considered

---

14. See generally Task Force Report, supra, n. 12, at 24–25. See also Rudstein, Double Jeopardy in Juvenile Proceedings, 14 Wm. & Mary L. Rev. 266, 297–300 (1972); Carr, The Effect of the Double Jeopardy Clause on Juvenile Proceedings, 6 U. Tol. L. Rev. 1, 21–22 (1974).

15. That the flexibility and informality of juvenile proceedings are diminished by the application of due process standards is not open to doubt. Due process standards inevitably produce such an effect, but that tells us no more than that the Constitution imposes burdens on the functioning of government and especially of law enforcement institutions.

relevant,[16] it may be that, in those cases where transfer is considered and rejected, some added burden will be imposed on the juvenile courts by reason of duplicative proceedings. Finally, the nature of the evidence considered at a transfer hearing may in some States require that, if transfer is rejected, a different judge preside at the adjudicatory hearing.[17]

We recognize that juvenile courts, perhaps even more than most courts, suffer from the problems created by spiraling caseloads unaccompanied by enlarged resources and manpower. See President's Commission on Law Enforcement and Administration of Justice, Task Force Report: Juvenile Delinquency and Youth Crime 7–8 (1967). And courts should be reluctant to impose on the juvenile-court system any additional requirements which could so strain its resources as to endanger its unique functions. However, the burdens that petitioner envisions appear to us neither qualitatively nor quantitatively sufficient to justify a departure in this context from the fundamental prohibition against double jeopardy.

A requirement that transfer hearings be held prior to adjudicatory hearings affects not at all the nature of the latter proceedings. More significantly, such a requirement need not affect the quality of decisionmaking at transfer hearings themselves. In *Kent v. United States*, 383 U.S., at 562, the Court held that hearings under the statute there involved "must measure up to the essentials of due process and fair treatment." However, the Court has never attempted to prescribe criteria for, or the nature and quantum of evidence that must support, a decision to transfer a juvenile for trial in adult court. We require only that, whatever the relevant criteria, and whatever the evidence demanded, a State determine whether it wants to treat a juvenile within the juvenile-court system before entering upon a proceeding that may result in an adjudication that he has violated a criminal law and in a substantial deprivation of liberty, rather than subject him to the expense, delay, strain, and embarrassment of two such proceedings.[18]

---

16. Under Cal. Welf. & Inst'ns Code 707 (1972), the governing criterion with respect to transfer, assuming the juvenile is 16 years of age and is charged with a violation of a criminal statute or ordinance, is amenability "to the care, treatment and training program available through the facilities of the juvenile court." The section further provides that neither "the offense, in itself" nor a denial by the juvenile of the facts or conclusions set forth in the petition shall be "sufficient to support a finding that [he] is not a fit and proper subject to be dealt with under the provisions of the Juvenile Court Law." See n. 5, supra. The California Supreme Court has held that the only factor a juvenile court must consider is the juvenile's "behavior pattern as described in the probation officer's report," *Jimmy H. v. Superior Court*, 3 Cal. 3d 709, 714, 478 P.2d 32, 35 (1970), but that it may also consider, inter alia, the nature and circumstances of the alleged offense. See id., at 716, 478 P.2d, at 36. In contrast to California, which does not require any evidentiary showing with respect to the commission of the offense, a number of jurisdictions require a finding of probable cause to believe the juvenile committed the offense before transfer is permitted. See Rudstein, supra, n. 14, at 298–299; Carr, supra, n. 14, at 21–22. In addition, two jurisdictions appear presently to require a finding of delinquency before the transfer of a juvenile to adult court. Ala. Code, Tit. 13, 364 (1959) (see *Rudolph v. State*, 286 Ala. 189, 238 So.2d 542 (1970)); W. Va. Code Ann. 49-5-14 (1966).

17. See, e.g., Fla. Stat. Ann. 39.09 (2) (g) (1974); Tenn. Code. Ann. 37–234 (e) (Supp. 1974); Wyo. Stat. 14-115.38 (c) (Supp. 1973); Uniform Juvenile Court Act 34 (e), approved in July 1968 by the National Conference of Commissioners on Uniform State Laws. See also *Donald L. v. Superior Court*, 7 Cal. 3d 592, 598, 498 P.2d 1098, 1101 (1972).

18. We note that nothing decided today forecloses States from requiring, as a prerequisite to the transfer of a juvenile, substantial evidence that he committed the offense charged, so long as the showing required is not made in an adjudicatory proceeding. See *Collins v. Loisel*, 262 U.S. 426–429 (1923); *Serfass v. United States*, 420 U.S. 377, 391–392 (1975). The instant case is not one in which the judicial determination was simply a finding of, e.g., probable cause. Rather, it was an adjudication that respondent had violated a criminal statute.

Moreover, we are not persuaded that the burdens petitioner envisions would pose a significant problem for the administration of the juvenile-court system. The large number of jurisdictions that presently require that the transfer decision be made prior to an adjudicatory hearing,[19] and the absence of any indication that the juvenile courts in those jurisdictions have not been able to perform their task within that framework, suggest the contrary. The likelihood that in many cases the lack of need or basis for a transfer hearing can be recognized promptly reduces the number of cases in which a commitment of resources is necessary. In addition, we have no reason to believe that the resources available to those who recommend transfer or participate in the process leading to transfer decisions are inadequate to enable them to gather the information relevant to informed decision prior to an adjudicatory hearing. See generally *State v. Halverson,* 192 N. W. 2d 765, 769 (Iowa 1971); Rudstein, Double Jeopardy in Juvenile Proceedings, 14 Wm. & Mary L. Rev. 266, 305–306 (1972); Note, 24 Stan. L. Rev., at 897–899.[20]

To the extent that transfer hearings held prior to adjudication result in some duplication of evidence if transfer is rejected, the burden on juvenile courts will tend to be offset somewhat by the cases in which, because of transfer, no further proceedings in juvenile court are required. Moreover, when transfer has previously been rejected, juveniles may well be more likely to admit the commission of the offense charged, thereby obviating the need for adjudicatory hearings, than if transfer remains a possibility. Finally, we note that those States which presently require a different judge to preside at an adjudicatory hearing if transfer is rejected also permit waiver of that requirement.[21] Where the requirement is not waived, it is difficult to see a substantial strain on judicial resources. See Note, 24 Stan. L. Rev., at 900–901.

Quite apart from our conclusions with respect to the burdens on the juvenile-court system envisioned by petitioner, we are persuaded that transfer hearings prior to adjudication will aid the objectives of that system. What concerns us here is the dilemma that the possibility of transfer after an adjudicatory hearing presents for a juvenile, a dilemma to which the Court of Appeals alluded. See supra, at 527. Because of that possibility, a juvenile, thought to be the beneficiary of special consideration, may in fact suffer substantial disadvantages. If he appears uncooperative, he runs the risk of an adverse adjudication, as well as of an

---

19. See Rudstein, supra, n. 14, at 299–300; Carr, supra, n. 14, at 24, 57–58. See also Uniform Juvenile Court Act 34 (a), (c); Council of Judges of the Nat. Council on Crime and Delinquency, Model Rules for Juvenile Courts, Rule 9 (1969); W. Sheridan, Legislative Guide for Drafting Family and Juvenile Court Acts 27, 31 (a) (Dept. of HEW, Children's Bureau Pub. No. 472-1969). In contrast, apparently only three States presently require that a hearing on the juvenile petition or complaint precede transfer. Ala. Code, Tit. 13, 364 (1959) (see *Rudolph v. State,* supra); Mass. Gen. Laws Ann., c. 119, 61 (1969) (see *In re Juvenile,* 364 Mass. 531, 542, and n. 10, 306 N. E. 2d 822, 829–830, and n. 10 (1974)); W. Va. Code Ann. 49-5-14 (1966).

20. We intimate no views concerning the constitutional validity of transfer following the attachment of jeopardy at an adjudicatory hearing where the information which forms the predicate for the transfer decision could not, by the exercise of due diligence, reasonably have been obtained previously. Cf., e.g., *Illinois v. Somerville,* 410 U.S. 458 (1973).

21. See the statutes cited in n. 16, supra. "The reason for this waiver provision is clear. A juvenile will ordinarily not want to dismiss a judge who has refused to transfer him to a criminal court. There is a risk of having another judge assigned to the case who is not as sympathetic. Moreover, in many cases, a rapport has been established between the judge and the juvenile, and the goal of rehabilitation is well on its way to being met." Brief for National Council of Juvenile Court Judges as Amicus Curiae 38.

unfavorable dispositional recommendation.[22] If, on the other hand, he is cooperative, he runs the risk of prejudicing his chances in adult court if transfer is ordered. We regard a procedure that results in such a dilemma as at odds with the goal that, to the extent fundamental fairness permits, adjudicatory hearings be informal and nonadversary. See *In re Gault,* 387 U.S., at 25-27; *In re Winship,* 397 U.S., at 366–367; *McKeiver v. Pennsylvania,* 403 U.S., at 534, 550. Knowledge of the risk of transfer after an adjudicatory hearing can only undermine the potential for informality and cooperation which was intended to be the hallmark of the juvenile-court system. Rather than concerning themselves with the matter at hand, establishing innocence or seeking a disposition best suited to individual correctional needs, the juvenile and his attorney are pressed into a posture of adversary wariness that is conducive to neither. Cf. Kay & Segal, The Role of the Attorney in Juvenile Court Proceedings: A Non-Polar Approach, 61 Geo. L. J. 1401 (1973); Carr, The Effect of the Double Jeopardy Clause on Juvenile Proceedings, 6 U. Tol. L. Rev. 1, 52-54 (1974).[23]

IV

We hold that the prosecution of respondent in Superior Court, after an adjudicatory proceeding in Juvenile Court, violated the Double Jeopardy Clause of the Fifth Amendment, as applied to the States through the Fourteenth Amendment. The mandate of the Court of Appeals, which was stayed by that court pending our decision, directs the District Court "to issue a writ of habeas corpus directing the state court, within 60 days, to vacate the adult conviction of Jones and either set him free or remand him to the juvenile court for disposition." Since respondent is no longer subject to the jurisdiction of the California Juvenile Court, we vacate the judgment and remand the case to the Court of Appeals for such further proceedings consistent with this opinion as may be appropriate in the circumstances.

So ordered.

---

22. Although denying respondent's petition for a writ of habeas corpus, the judge of the Juvenile Court noted: "If he doesn't open up with a probation officer there is of course the danger that the probation officer will find that he is so uncooperative that he cannot make a recommendation for the kind of treatment you think he really should have and, yet, as the attorney worrying about what might happen a[t] the disposition hearing, you have to advise him to continue to more or less stand upon his constitutional right not to incriminate himself . . . ." App. 38. See Note, Double Jeopardy and the Waiver of Jurisdiction in California's Juvenile Courts, 24 Stan. L. Rev. 874, 902 n. 137 (1972).

23. With respect to the possibility of "making the juvenile proceedings confidential and not being able to be used against the minor," the judge of the Juvenile Court observed: "I must say that doesn't impress me because if the minor admitted something in the Juvenile Court and named his companions nobody is going to eradicate from the minds of the district attorney or other people the information they obtained." App. 41–42.

CHAPTER 5

SELF-INCRIMINATION

Introduction

This chapter deals with the preadjudicatory stage of the juvenile process and the issues surrounding police investigation, custodial interrogation, and arrest. Throughout the 1960s, many U.S. Supreme Court decisions significantly increased constitutional safeguards for the adult offender. During this period, nearly all the provisions of the Bill of Rights were made applicable to the states through the due process clause of the Fourteenth Amendment. Many of these decisions affected the defendant's pretrial rights. *Mapp v. Ohio* (1981), for example, extended the exclusionary rule to state court proceedings.[1] The case of *Escobedo v. Illinois* (1964) held that a state must afford an accused the right to counsel in a police station.[2] In *Miranda v. Arizona* (1966), the Court defined a defendant's Fifth Amendment privilege against self-incrimination when taken into custody and delineated a specific warning that must be read to each and every person before a custodial interrogation so as to warn the individual against self-incrimination.[3]

As a result of these decisions, children have also been granted pretrial protections similar to those of adults. In addition, the landmark juvenile decision of *In re Gault* (1964), although specifically applicable to the trial process, served to extend constitutional guarantees of due process to juveniles at preadjudication proceedings.

When a juvenile engages in delinquent or incorrigible behavior, the police must make a decision to release the child or refer him or her to the juvenile court. This discretionary decision—to release or refer—is based on a police investigation of the total circumstances of a particular offense. The following partial list of factors is generally taken into consideration in making such a decision: (1) type and seriousness of the child's offense; (2) ability of the parents to be of assistance in disciplining the child; (3) history of the child's past contacts with police; (4) degree of cooperation obtained from the child and the parents; and (5) whether the child denies the allegations in the petition and insists upon a court hearing. Cases generally involving person-oriented crimes, as well as serious property offenses, are often referred to court. On the other hand, minor disputes between juveniles, school and neighborhood complaints, petty shoplifting cases, runaways, and ungovernable children are diverted from court action. The police may consult with the juvenile probation staff in making this decision. In adjusting a case, the police may simply release the child at the point of contact on the

---

1. 367 U.S. 643 (1961).
2. 378 U.S. 478 (1964).
3. 385 U.S. 436 (1966).

street, give an official warning and release him or her to the child's parents at the station house or the child's home, or seek to refer the child to a social service program. It is an accepted practice for police today to establish formal alternatives to arrest and to screen out cases from juvenile court action.[4]

When a child is taken into custody by the police, the law of arrest for adults is normally applied. This requires that the police officer made a determination that probable cause exists to believe that a crime may have been committed and that the child may have committed it. Most states do not have specific statutory provisions distinguishing the arrest process for children from that for adults. Some jurisdictions, however, give broad arrest powers to the police in juvenile cases by authorizing officers to make an arrest whenever it is believed that the child falls within the jurisdiction of the juvenile court. Similarly, may states give the police authority to take a child into custody if his or her welfare requires such action. Because of the state's interest in the child, the police generally have more discretion in the investigatory and arrest stages of the juvenile process than in dealing with adult offenders.[5]

Once a juvenile has been taken into custody, he or she has the same constitutional right to be free from unreasonable searches and seizures as an adult. This means that the Fourth Amendment is generally held to be applicable to juvenile proceedings and that illegally seized evidence is inadmissible in a juvenile trial. The legal procedure used to exclude any incriminating evidence is for the child's attorney to make a pretrial motion to suppress the evidence, as is done in the adult criminal process. The courts have held that illegally seized evidence can be excluded on the basis of traditional due process, as exemplified in *Gault*, as well as on Fourth Amendment grounds.

Normally, a child's parents are contacted immediately after he or she is taken into custody. In years past, the police often questioned juveniles without their parents or even an attorney present. Any incriminatory statements or confessions made by juveniles could be placed in evidence at their trial. In 1966, the U.S. Supreme Court, in *Miranda v. Arizona*, placed constitutional limitations on police interrogation procedures with adult offenders. *Miranda* held that an accused in police custody must be given the following warning: (1) that he or she has a right to remain silent; (2) that any statements made can be used against him or her; (3) that he or she has a right to counsel; (4) and that if he or she cannot afford counsel, one will be furnished at public expense. This warning, which represents the adult defendant's Fifth Amendment privilege against self-incrimination in dealing with the police, has been made applicable to children taken into custody.[6] The landmark *Gault* decision further reinforced *Miranda* by giving juveniles similar procedural safeguards at trial proceedings, including the right to counsel, the right to confront witnesses, and the privilege against self-incrimination. These decisions would seem to require that *Miranda* warnings be given to all juvenile offenders who are questioned in custody, if the police intend to admit their statements in a subsequent proceeding. Most states have since incorporated the *Miranda* decision into their juvenile statutes.

One of the most difficult problems involving self-incrimination is whether a juvenile can waive his or her *Miranda* rights. This issue has resulted in considerable litigation. Some

---

4. For an excellent review of early police practices with juveniles, see Donald Black and Albert J. Reiss, Jr., "Police Control of Juveniles." *American Sociological Review* 35:64 (1970).

5. See American Bar Association—Institute of Judicial Administration, *Standards Relating to Police Handling of Juvenile Problems* (Cambridge, MA: Ballinger Press, 1977).

6. See *Haley v. Ohio*, 332 U.S. 596 (1948) and *West v. United States*, 39 F.2d 467 (1968).

courts have concluded that it is not essential for the parent or attorney to be prese...
child to effectively waive his or her rights. The validity of the waiver in this respect
on the totality of the circumstances of a given case. This means that the court must ...ter-
mine if the child has the ability to make a knowing, intelligent, and voluntary waiver. In the
case of *Fare v. Michael C.,* the court ruled that a child's asking to speak to a probation officer was not the equivalent of asking for an attorney; consequently, statements made to the
police absent legal counsel were held to be admissible in court. However, some jurisdictions
will not accept a waiver of the juvenile's *Miranda* rights unless it is made in the presence of
the child's parents or attorney.

Another issue in the early police processing of juvenile offenders is whether the constitutional safeguards established for adult offenders in lineups and other forms of identifica-
tions are applicable to juvenile proceedings. This problem has been dealt with in the adult
case of *United States v. Wade,* in which the Supreme Court held that the accused has a right
to have counsel present at postindictment lineup procedures.[7] Where right to counsel is violated, the pretrial identification is inadmissible. The Supreme Court further clarified this
issue in *Kirby v. Illinois* by holding that the defendant's right to counsel at pretrial identification proceedings attaches only after the complaint or indictment has been issued.[8] Based
on these decisions, juveniles have the same constitutional protections from tainted lineup and
identification procedures as adults. This means that once charged with a delinquent act, the
juvenile has a right to counsel at a police lineup, and if this right is violated, the pretrial identification is to be excluded. Furthermore, the Court in *Stovall v. Denno* has developed a totality of the circumstances test in analyzing the legality of any identification procedure.[9] In
Stovall, the Court held that a lineup or showup that is unnecessarily suggestive and may lead
to misidentification is a denial of the defendants due process rights. The test is also applicable to juvenile cases.

Application of *Miranda* Rights to Juvenile Proceedings

Case Comment

One of the most difficult problems associated with the custodial interrogation of children
has to do with their waiver of *Miranda* rights. Under what circumstances can juvenile offenders knowingly and willingly waive the rights accorded to them by *Miranda v. Arizona*
and discuss their actions with police without the benefit of a lawyer? Is it possible for a
youngster, acting alone, to be mature enough to appreciate the right to remain silent? Are
youth, by virtue of the fact that they are expected to succumb to authority figures, more susceptible to being influenced by police investigators? These are difficult questions.

In *Fare v. Michael C.,* the U.S. Supreme Court ruled that a juvenile's request to speak to
his probation officer was not a *per se* request to remain silent nor was it tantamount to a request for an attorney. As a result, the Court concluded that the child voluntarily and knowingly waived his Fifth Amendment rights and thereby consented to the interrogation.

7. 388 U.S. 218 (1967).
8. 406 U.S. 683 (1972).
9. 388 U.S. 293 (1967).

FARE V. MICHAEL C.

Supreme Court of the United States, 1979.

442 U.S. 707.

Mr. Justice Blackmun delivered the opinion of the Court.

In *Miranda v. Arizona*, 384 U.S. 436 (1966), this Court established certain procedural safeguards designed to protect the rights of an accused, under the Fifth and Fourteenth Amendments, to be free from compelled self-incrimination during custodial interrogation. The Court specified, among other things, that if the accused indicates in any manner that he wishes to remain silent or to consult an attorney, interrogation must cease, and any statement obtained from him during interrogation thereafter may not be admitted against him at his trial. Id., at 444–445, 473–474.

In this case, the State of California, in the person of its acting chief probation officer, attacks the conclusion of the Supreme Court of California that a juvenile's request, made while undergoing custodial interrogation, to see his probation officer is per se an invocation of the juvenile's Fifth Amendment rights as pronounced in *Miranda*.

I

Respondent Michael C. was implicated in the murder of Robert Yeager. The murder occurred during a robbery of the victim's home on January 19, 1976. A small truck registered in the name of respondent's mother was identified as having been near the Yeager home at the time of the killing, and a young man answering respondent's description was seen by witnesses near the truck and near the home shortly before Yeager was murdered.

On the basis of this information, Van Nuys, Cal., police took respondent into custody at approximately 6:30 p. m. on February 4. Respondent then was 16 1/2 years old and on probation to the Juvenile Court. He had been on probation since the age of 12. Approximately one year earlier he had served a term in a youth corrections camp under the supervision of the Juvenile Court. He had a record of several previous offenses, including burglary of guns and purse snatching, stretching back over several years.

Upon respondent's arrival at the Van Nuys station house two police officers began to interrogate him. The officers and respondent were the only persons in the room during the interrogation. The conversation was tape-recorded. One of the officers initiated the interview by informing respondent that he had been brought in for questioning in relation to a murder. The officer fully advised respondent of his *Miranda* rights. The following exchange then occurred, as set out in the opinion of the California Supreme Court, In re Michael C., 21 Cal. 3d 471, 473–474, 579 P.2d 7, 8 (1978) (emphasis added by that court):

"Q. . . . . Do you understand all of these rights as I have explained them to you?

"A. Yeah.

"Q. Okay, do you wish to give up your right to remain silent and talk to us about this murder?

"A. What murder? I don't know about no murder.

"Q. I'll explain to you which one it is if you want to talk to us about it.

"A. Yeah, I might talk to you.

"Q. Do you want to give up your right to have an attorney present here while we talk about it?

"A. Can I have my probation officer here?

"Q. Well I can't get a hold of your probation officer right now. You have the right to an attorney.

"A. How I know you guys won't pull no police officer in and tell me he's an attorney?

"Q. Huh?

"A. How I know you guys won't pull no police officer in and tell me he's an attorney?

"Q. Your probation officer is Mr. Christiansen.

"A. Yeah.

"Q. Well I'm not going to call Mr. Christiansen tonight. There's a good chance we can talk to him later, but I'm not going to call him right now. If you want to talk to us without an attorney present, you can. If you don't want to, you don't have to. But if you want to say something, you can, and if you don't want to say something you don't have to. That's your right. You understand that right?

"A. Yeah.

"Q. Okay, will you talk to us without an attorney present?

"A. Yeah I want to talk to you."

Respondent thereupon proceeded to answer questions put to him by the officers. He made statements and drew sketches that incriminated him in the Yeager murder.

Largely on the basis of respondent's incriminating statements, probation authorities filed a petition in Juvenile Court alleging that respondent had murdered Robert Yeager, in violation of Cal. Penal Code Ann. 187 (West Supp. 1979), and that respondent therefore should be adjudged a ward of the Juvenile Court, pursuant to Cal. Welf. & Inst. Code Ann. 602 (West Supp. 1979).[1] App. 4–5. Respondent thereupon moved to suppress the statements and sketches he gave the police during the interrogation. He alleged that the statements had been obtained in violation of *Miranda* in that his request to see his probation officer at the outset of the questioning constituted an invocation of his Fifth Amendment right to remain silent, just as if he had requested the assistance of an attorney. Accordingly, respondent argued that since the interrogation did not cease until he had a chance to confer with his probation officer, the statements and sketches could not be admitted against him in the Juvenile Court proceedings. In so arguing, respondent relied by analogy on the decision in *People v. Burton*, 6 Cal. 3d 375, 491 P.2d 793 (1971), where the Supreme Court of California had held that a minor's request, made during custodial interrogation, to see his parents constituted an invocation of the minor's Fifth Amendment rights. In support of his suppression motion, respondent called his probation officer, Charles P. Christiansen, as a witness. Christiansen testified that he had instructed respondent that if at any time he had "a concern with his family," or ever had "a police contact," App. 27, he should get in touch with his probation officer immediately. The witness stated that, on a previous occasion, when respondent had had a police contact and had failed to communicate with Christiansen, the probation officer had reprimanded him. Id., at 28. This testimony, respondent argued, indicated that when he asked for his probation officer, he was in fact asserting his right to remain silent in the face of further questioning.

In a ruling from the bench, the court denied the motion to suppress. Id., at 41–42. It held that the question whether respondent had waived his right to remain silent was one of fact

---

1. The petition also alleged that respondent had participated in an attempted armed robbery earlier on the same evening Yeager was murdered. The Juvenile Court, however, held that the evidence was insufficient to support this charge and it was dismissed. App. 6. No issue relating to this second charge is before the Court.

to be determined on a case-by-case basis, and that the facts of this case showed a "clear waiver" by respondent of that right. Id., at 42. The court observed that the transcript of the interrogation revealed that respondent specifically had told the officers that he would talk with them, and that this waiver had come at the outset of the interrogation and not after prolonged questioning. The court noted that respondent was a "16 and a half year old minor who has been through the court system before, has been to [probation] camp, has a probation officer, [and is not] a young, naive minor with no experience with the courts." Ibid. Accordingly, it found that on the facts of the case respondent had waived his Fifth Amendment rights, notwithstanding the request to see his probation officer.[2]

On appeal, the Supreme Court of California took the case by transfer from the California Court of Appeal and, by a divided vote, reversed. In re Michael C., 21 Cal. 3d 471, 579 P.2d 7 (1978). The court held that respondent's "request to see his probation officer at the commencement of interrogation negated any possible willingness on his part to discuss his case with the police [and] thereby invoked his Fifth Amendment privilege." Id., at 474, 579 P.2d, at 8. The court based this conclusion on its view that, because of the juvenile court system's emphasis on the relationship between a probation officer and the probationer, the officer was "a trusted guardian figure who exercises the authority of the state as parens patriae and whose duty it is to implement the protective and rehabilitative powers of the juvenile court." Id., at 476, 579 P.2d, at 10. As a consequence, the court found that a minor's request for his probation officer was the same as a request to see his parents during interrogation, and thus under the rule of Burton constituted an invocation of the minor's Fifth Amendment rights.

The fact that the probation officer also served as a peace officer, and, whenever a proceeding against a juvenile was contemplated, was charged with a duty to file a petition alleging that the minor had committed an offense, did not alter, in the court's view, the fact that the officer in the eyes of the juvenile was a trusted guardian figure to whom the minor normally would turn for help when in trouble with the police. 21 Cal. 3d, at 476, 579 P.2d, at 10. Relying on Burton, the court ruled that it would unduly restrict Miranda to limit its reach in a case involving a minor to a request by the minor for an attorney, since it would be " 'fatuous to assume that a minor in custody will be in a position to call an attorney for assistance and it is unrealistic to attribute no significance to his call for help from the only person to whom he normally looks—a parent or guardian.' " 21 Cal. 3d, at 475–476, 579 P.2d, at 9, quoting People v. Burton, 6 Cal. 3d, at 382, 491 P.2d, at 797–798. The court dismissed the concern expressed by the State that a request for a probation officer could not be distinguished from a request for one's football coach, music teacher, or clergyman on the ground that the proba-

---

2. The California Court of Appeal, in an opinion reported and then vacated, affirmed. In re Michael C., 135 Cal. Rptr. 762 (1977). That court noted that since the Juvenile Court's findings of fact resolved against respondent his contention that the confession had been coerced from him by threats and promises, it would have to "conclude that there was a knowing and intelligent waiver of the minor's Miranda rights unless it can be said that the request to speak to a probation officer was in and of itself sufficient to invoke" respondent's Fifth Amendment privilege. Id., at 765–766 (footnote omitted). It refused to extend the rule of People v. Burton, 6 Cal. 3d 375, 491 P.2d 793 (1971), to include a request for a probation officer, finding it difficult to distinguish such a request from a request to see "one's football coach, music teacher or clergyman." 135 Cal. Rptr., at 766. Even if the Burton rule were applicable, the court held, there was sufficient evidence of an affirmative waiver of his rights by respondent to distinguish Burton, where the California Supreme Court had noted that there was "nothing in the way of affirmative proof that defendant did not intend to assert his privilege." 6 Cal. 3d, at 383, 491 P.2d, at 798.

tion officer, unlike those other figures in the juvenile's life, was charged by statute to represent the interests of the juvenile. 21 Cal. 3d, at 477, 579 P.2d, at 10.

The court accordingly held that the probation officer would act to protect the minor's Fifth Amendment rights in precisely the way an attorney would act if called for by the accused. In so holding, the court found the request for a probation officer to be a per se invocation of Fifth Amendment rights in the same way the request for an attorney was found in *Miranda* to be, regardless of what the interrogation otherwise might reveal. In rejecting a totality-of-the-circumstances inquiry, the court stated:

> "Here, however, we face conduct which, regardless of considerations of capacity, coercion or voluntariness, per se invokes the privilege against self-incrimination. Thus our question turns not on whether the [respondent] had the ability, capacity or willingness to give a knowledgeable waiver, and hence whether he acted voluntarily, but whether, when he called for his probation officer, he exercised his Fifth Amendment privilege. We hold that in doing so he no less invoked the protection against self-incrimination than if he asked for the presence of an attorney." Ibid., 579 P.2d, at 10–11.

See also id., at 478 n. 4, 579 P.2d, at 11 n. 4. The court went on to conclude that since the State had not met its "burden of proving that a minor who requests to see his probation officer does not intend to assert his Fifth Amendment privilege," id., at 478, 579 P.2d, at 11, the trial court should not have admitted the confessions obtained after respondent had requested his probation officer.[3]

---

3. Two justices concurred in the court's opinion and judgment. 21 Cal. 3d, at 478, 579 P.2d, at 11. They expressed concern that a probation officer's public responsibilities would make it difficult for him to offer legal advice to a minor implicated in a crime, and that a minor advised to cooperate with the police, perhaps even to confess, justifiably could complain later "that he had been subjected to a variation of the Mutt-and-Jeff technique criticized in *Miranda:* initial interrogating by overbearing officers, then comforting by a presumably friendly and gentle peace officer in the guise of a probation officer." Id., at 479, 579 P.2d, at 12.

Two justices dissented. Id., at 480, 579 P.2d, at 12. They would have affirmed respondent's conviction on the basis of the finding of the Juvenile Court that, in light of all the circumstances surrounding the interrogation of respondent, there was sufficient affirmative proof that respondent had waived his privilege.

The dissenters pointed out that the opinion of the court was confusing in holding, on the one hand, that the request for a probation officer was per se an invocation of the minor's Fifth Amendment rights, and, on the other, that reversal was required because the State had not carried its burden of proving that respondent, by requesting his probation officer, did not intend thereby to assert his Fifth Amendment privilege. Ibid., 579 P.2d, at 12–13.

There may well be ambiguity in this regard. See id., at 477–478, 579 P.2d, at 11. On the basis of that ambiguity, respondent argues that the California court did not establish a per se rule, but held only that on the facts here respondent's request to see his probation officer constituted an invocation of his Fifth Amendment rights. The decision in *People v. Randall*, 1 Cal. 3d 948, 464 P.2d 114 (1970), upon which the California court relied in both *Burton* and the present case, however, indicates that the court did indeed establish a per se rule in this case. In *Randall*, the court stated that even though a suspect might have invoked his Fifth Amendment rights by asking for counsel or by stating he wished to remain silent, it might be possible that subsequent voluntary statements of the accused, not prompted by custodial interrogation, would be admissible if the State could show that they were the product of the voluntary decision of the accused to waive the rights he had asserted. *People v. Randall*, 1 Cal. 3d, at 956, and n. 7, 464 P.2d, at 119, and n. 7.

Randall thus indicates that the per se language employed by the California Supreme Court in this case is compatible with the finding that the State could have negated the per se effect of the request for a probation officer by showing that, notwithstanding his per se invocation of his rights, respondent later voluntarily decided to waive those rights and volunteer statements. In light of *Randall,* and in light of the strong per se language used by the California Supreme Court in its opinion in this case, see, e.g., 21 Cal. 3d, at 477, 579 P.2d, at 10–11, we think that any ambiguity in that opinion must be resolved in favor of a conclusion that the court did in fact establish a per se rule.

The State of California petitioned this Court for a writ of certiorari. Mr. Justice Rehnquist, as Circuit Justice, stayed the execution of the mandate of the Supreme Court of California. 439 U.S. 1310 (1978). Because the California judgment extending the per se aspects of *Miranda* presents an important question about the reach of that case, we thereafter issued the writ. 439 U.S. 925 (1978).

II

We note at the outset that it is clear that the judgment of the California Supreme Court rests firmly on that court's interpretation of federal law. This Court, however, has not heretofore extended the per se aspects of the *Miranda* safeguards beyond the scope of the holding in the *Miranda* case itself.[4] We therefore must examine the California court's decision to determine whether that court's conclusion so to extend *Miranda* is in harmony with *Miranda*'s underlying principles. For it is clear that "a State may not impose . . . greater restrictions as a matter of federal constitutional law when this Court specifically refrains from imposing them." *Oregon v. Hass,* 420 U.S. 714, 719 (1975) (emphasis in original). See *North Carolina v. Butler,* 441 U.S. 369 (1979).

The rule the Court established in *Miranda* is clear. In order to be able to use statements obtained during custodial interrogation of the accused, the State must warn the accused prior to such questioning of his right to remain silent and of his right to have counsel, retained or appointed, present during interrogation. 384 U.S., at 473. "Once [such] warnings have been given, the subsequent procedure is clear." Ibid.

> "If the individual indicates in any manner, at any time prior to or during questioning, that he wishes to remain silent, the interrogation must cease. At this point he has shown that he intends to exercise his Fifth Amendment privilege; any statement taken after the person invokes his privilege cannot be other than the product of compulsion, subtle or otherwise. . . . If the individual states that he wants an attorney, the interrogation must cease until an attorney is present. At that time, the individual must have an opportunity to confer with the attorney and to have him present during any subsequent questioning. If the individual cannot obtain an attorney and he indicates that he wants one before speaking to police, they must respect his decision to remain silent." Id., at 473–474 (footnote omitted).

Any statements obtained during custodial interrogation conducted in violation of these rules may not be admitted against the accused, at least during the State's case in chief. Id., at 479. Cf. *Harris v. New York,* 401 U.S. 222, 224 (1971).

Whatever the defects, if any, of this relatively rigid requirement that interrogation must cease upon the accused's request for an attorney, *Miranda*'s holding has the virtue of informing police and prosecutors with specificity as to what they may do in conducting cus-

---

4. Indeed, this Court has not yet held that *Miranda* applies with full force to exclude evidence obtained in violation of its proscriptions from consideration in juvenile proceedings, which for certain purposes have been distinguished from formal criminal prosecutions. See *McKeiver v. Pennsylvania,* 403 U.S. 528, 540–541 (1971) (plurality opinion). We do not decide that issue today. In view of our disposition of this case, we assume without deciding that the *Miranda* principles were fully applicable to the present proceedings.

todial interrogation, and of informing courts under what circumstances statements obtained during such interrogation are not admissible. This gain in specificity, which benefits the accused and the State alike, has been thought to outweigh the burdens that the decision in *Miranda* imposes on law enforcement agencies and the courts by requiring the suppression of trustworthy and highly probative evidence even though the confession might be voluntary under traditional Fifth Amendment analysis. See *Michigan v. Tucker,* 417 U.S. 433, 443–446 (1974).

The California court in this case, however, significantly has extended this rule by providing that a request by a juvenile for his probation officer has the same effect as a request for an attorney. Based on the court's belief that the probation officer occupies a position as a trusted guardian figure in the minor's life that would make it normal for the minor to turn to the officer when apprehended by the police, and based as well on the state-law requirement that the officer represent the interest of the juvenile, the California decision found that consultation with a probation officer fulfilled the role for the juvenile that consultation with an attorney does in general, acting as a " 'protective [device] . . . to dispel the compulsion inherent in custodial surroundings.' " 21 Cal. 3d, at 477, 579 P.2d, at 10, quoting *Miranda v. Arizona,* 384 U.S., at 458.

The rule in *Miranda,* however, was based on this Court's perception that the lawyer occupies a critical position in our legal system because of his unique ability to protect the Fifth Amendment rights of a client undergoing custodial interrogation. Because of this special ability of the lawyer to help the client preserve his Fifth Amendment rights once the client becomes enmeshed in the adversary process, the Court found that "the right to have counsel present at the interrogation is indispensable to the protection of the Fifth Amendment privilege under the system" established by the Court. Id., at 469. Moreover, the lawyer's presence helps guard against overreaching by the police and ensures that any statements actually obtained are accurately transcribed for presentation into evidence. Id., at 470.

The *per se* aspect of *Miranda* was thus based on the unique role the lawyer plays in the adversary system of criminal justice in this country. Whether it is a minor or an adult who stands accused, the lawyer is the one person to whom society as a whole looks as the protector of the legal rights of that person in his dealings with the police and the courts. For this reason, the Court fashioned in *Miranda* the rigid rule that an accused's request for an attorney is per se an invocation of his Fifth Amendment rights, requiring that all interrogation cease.

A probation officer is not in the same posture with regard to either the accused or the system of justice as a whole. Often he is not trained in the law, and so is not in a position to advise the accused as to his legal rights. Neither is he a trained advocate, skilled in the representation of the interests of his client before both police and courts. He does not assume the power to act on behalf of his client by virtue of his status as adviser, nor are the communications of the accused to the probation officer shielded by the lawyer-client privilege.

Moreover, the probation officer is the employee of the State which seeks to prosecute the alleged offender. He is a peace officer, and as such is allied, to a greater or lesser extent, with his fellow peace officers. He owes an obligation to the State, notwithstanding the obligation he may also owe the juvenile under his supervision. In most cases, the probation officer is duty bound to report wrongdoing by the juvenile when it comes to his attention, even if by communication from the juvenile himself. Indeed, when this case arose, the probation officer had the responsibility for filing the petition alleging wrongdoing by the juvenile and seeking to have him taken into the custody of the Juvenile Court. It was respondent's probation officer who filed the petition against him, and it is the acting chief of probation for the State of California, a probation officer, who is petitioner in this Court today.[5]

In these circumstances, it cannot be said that the probation officer is able to offer the type of independent advice that an accused would expect from a lawyer retained or assigned to assist him during questioning. Indeed, the probation officer's duty to his employer in many, if not most, cases would conflict sharply with the interests of the juvenile. For where an attorney might well advise his client to remain silent in the face of interrogation by the police, and in doing so would be "exercising [his] good professional judgment ... to protect to the extent of his ability the rights of his client," *Miranda v. Arizona*, 384 U.S., at 480–481, a probation officer would be bound to advise his charge to cooperate with the police. The justices who concurred in the opinion of the California Supreme Court in this case aptly noted: "Where a conflict between the minor and the law arises, the probation officer can be neither neutral nor in the minor's corner." 21 Cal. 3d, at 479, 579 P.2d, at 12. It thus is doubtful that a general rule can be established that a juvenile, in every case, looks to his probation officer as a "trusted guardian figure" rather than as an officer of the court system that imposes punishment.

By the same token, a lawyer is able to protect his client's rights by learning the extent, if any, of the client's involvement in the crime under investigation, and advising his client accordingly. To facilitate this, the law rightly protects the communications between client and attorney from discovery. We doubt, however, that similar protection will be afforded the communications between the probation officer and the minor. Indeed, we doubt that a probation officer, consistent with his responsibilities to the public and his profession, could

---

5. When this case arose, a California statute provided that a proceeding in juvenile court to declare a minor a ward of the court was to be commenced by the filing of a petition by a probation officer. Cal. Welf. & Inst. Code Ann. 650 (West 1972). This provision since has been amended to provide that most such petitions are to be filed by the prosecuting attorney. 1976 Cal. Stats., ch. 1071, 20. Respondent argues that, whatever the status of the probation officer as a peace officer at the time this case arose, the amendment of 650 indicates that in the future a probation officer is not to be viewed as a legal adversary of the accused juvenile. Consequently, respondent believes that any holding of this Court with regard to respondent's 1976 request for a probation officer will be mere dictum with regard to a juvenile's similar request today. Brief for Respondent 9–10, and n. 4.

We disagree. The fact that a California probation officer in 1976 was responsible for initiating a complaint is only one factor in our analysis. The fact remains that a probation officer does not fulfill the role in our system of criminal justice that an attorney does, regardless of whether he acts merely as a counselor or has significant law enforcement duties. And in California, as in many States, the other duties of a probation officer are incompatible with the view that he may act as a counselor to a juvenile accused of crime. The very California statute that imposes upon the probation officer the duty to represent the interests of the juvenile also provides: "It shall be the duty of the probation officer to prepare for every hearing [of criminal charges against a juvenile] a social study of the minor, containing such matters as may be relevant to a proper disposition of the case." Cal. Welf. & Inst. Code Ann. 280 (West Supp. 1979).

Similarly, a probation officer is required, upon the order of the juvenile court or the Youth Authority, to investigate the circumstances surrounding the charge against the minor and to file written reports and recommendations. 281, 284. And a probation officer in California continues to have the powers and authority of a peace officer in connection with any violation of a criminal statute that is discovered by the probation officer in the course of his probation activities. 283; Cal. Penal Code Ann. 830.5 (West 1970). The duties of a peace officer, like the investigative and reporting duties of probation officers, are incompatible with the role of legal adviser to a juvenile accused of crime.

withhold from the police or the courts facts made known to him by the juvenile implicating the juvenile in the crime under investigation.

We thus believe it clear that the probation officer is not in a position to offer the type of legal assistance necessary to protect the Fifth Amendment rights of an accused undergoing custodial interrogation that a lawyer can offer. The Court in *Miranda* recognized that "the attorney plays a vital role in the administration of criminal justice under our Constitution." 384 U.S., at 481. It is this pivotal role of legal counsel that justifies the *per se* rule established in *Miranda,* and that distinguishes the request for counsel from the request for a probation officer, a clergyman, or a close friend. A probation officer simply is not necessary, in the way an attorney is, for the protection of the legal rights of the accused, juvenile or adult. He is significantly handicapped by the position he occupies in the juvenile system from serving as an effective protector of the rights of a juvenile suspected of a crime.

The California Supreme Court, however, found that the close relationship between juveniles and their probation officers compelled the conclusion that a probation officer, for purposes of *Miranda,* was sufficiently like a lawyer to justify extension of the *per se* rule. 21 Cal. 3d, at 476, 579 P.2d, at 10. The fact that a relationship of trust and cooperation between a probation officer and a juvenile might exist, however, does not indicate that the probation officer is capable of rendering effective legal advice sufficient to protect the juvenile's rights during interrogation by the police, or of providing the other services rendered by a lawyer. To find otherwise would be "an extension of the *Miranda* requirements [that] would cut this Court's holding in that case completely loose from its own explicitly stated rationale." *Beckwith v. United States,* 425 U.S. 341, 345 (1976). Such an extension would impose the burdens associated with the rule of *Miranda* on the juvenile justice system and the police without serving the interests that rule was designed simultaneously to protect. If it were otherwise, a juvenile's request for almost anyone he considered trustworthy enough to give him reliable advice would trigger the rigid rule of *Miranda.*

Similarly, the fact that the State has created a statutory duty on the part of the probation officer to protect the interests of the juvenile does not render the probation officer any more capable of rendering legal assistance to the juvenile or of protecting his legal rights, especially in light of the fact that the State has also legislated a duty on the part of the officer to report wrongdoing by the juvenile and serve the ends of the juvenile court system. The State cannot transmute the relationship between probation officer and juvenile offender into the type of relationship between attorney and client that was essential to the holding of *Miranda* simply by legislating an amorphous "duty to advise and care for the juvenile defendant." 21 Cal. 3d, at 477, 579 P.2d, at 10. Though such a statutory duty might serve to distinguish to some degree the probation officer from the coach and the clergyman, it does not justify the extension of *Miranda* to requests to see probation officers. If it did, the State could expand the class of persons covered by the *Miranda* per se rule simply by creating a duty to care for the juvenile on the part of other persons, regardless of whether the logic of *Miranda* would justify that extension.

Nor do we believe that a request by a juvenile to speak with his probation officer constitutes a per se request to remain silent. As indicated, since a probation officer does not fulfill the important role in protecting the rights of the accused juvenile that an attorney plays, we decline to find that the request for the probation officer is tantamount to the request for an attorney. And there is nothing inherent in the request for a probation officer that requires us to find that a juvenile's request to see one necessarily constitutes an expression of the juvenile's right to remain silent. As discussed below, courts may take into account such a request in evaluating whether a juvenile in fact had waived his Fifth Amendment rights before confessing. But in other circumstances such a request might well be consistent with a desire to speak with the police. In the absence of further evidence that the minor intended in the circumstances to invoke his Fifth Amendment rights by such a request, we decline to attach such overwhelming significance to this request.

We hold, therefore, that it was error to find that the request by respondent to speak with his probation officer per se constituted an invocation of respondent's Fifth Amendment right to be free from compelled self-incrimination. It therefore was also error to hold that because the police did not then cease interrogating respondent the statements he made during interrogation should have been suppressed.

III

Miranda further recognized that after the required warnings are given the accused, "[i]f the interrogation continues without the presence of an attorney and a statement is taken, a heavy burden rests on the government to demonstrate that the defendant knowingly and intelligently waived his privilege against self-incrimination and his right to retained or appointed counsel." 384 U.S., at 475. We noted in *North Carolina v. Butler*, 441 U.S., at 373, that the question whether the accused waived his rights "is not one of form, but rather whether the defendant in fact knowingly and voluntarily waived the rights delineated in the *Miranda* case." Thus, the determination whether statements obtained during custodial interrogation are admissible against the accused is to be made upon an inquiry into the totality of the circumstances surrounding the interrogation, to ascertain whether the accused in fact knowingly and voluntarily decided to forgo his rights to remain silent and to have the assistance of counsel. *Miranda v. Arizona*, 384 U.S., at 475–477.

This totality-of-the-circumstances approach is adequate to determine whether there has been a waiver even where interrogation of juveniles is involved. We discern no persuasive reasons why any other approach is required where the question is whether a juvenile has waived his rights, as opposed to whether an adult has done so. The totality approach permits— indeed, it mandates—inquiry into all the circumstances surrounding the interrogation. This includes evaluation of the juvenile's age, experience, education, background, and intelligence, and whether he has the capacity to understand the warnings given him, the nature of his Fifth Amendment rights, and the consequences of waiving those rights. See *North Carolina v. Butler*, supra.

Courts repeatedly must deal with these issues of waiver with regard to a broad variety of constitutional rights. There is no reason to assume that such courts—especially juvenile courts, with their special expertise in this area—will be unable to apply the totality-of-the-circumstances analysis so as to take into account those special concerns that are present when young persons, often with limited experience and education and with immature judgment, are involved. Where the age and experience of a juvenile indicate that his request for his probation officer or his parents is, in fact, an invocation of his right to remain silent, the totality approach will allow the court the necessary flexibility to take this into account in making a waiver determination. At the same time, that approach refrains from imposing rigid restraints on police and courts in dealing with an experienced older juvenile with an extensive prior record who knowingly and intelligently waives his Fifth Amendment rights and voluntarily consents to interrogation.

In this case, we conclude that the California Supreme Court should have determined the issue of waiver on the basis of all the circumstances surrounding the interrogation of respondent. The Juvenile Court found that under this approach, respondent in fact had waived his Fifth Amendment rights and consented to interrogation by the police after his request to see his probation officer was denied. Given its view of the case, of course, the California Supreme Court did not consider this issue, though it did hold that the State had failed to prove that, notwithstanding respondent's request to see his probation officer, respondent had not intended to invoke his Fifth Amendment rights.

We feel that the conclusion of the Juvenile Court was correct. The transcript of the interrogation reveals that the police officers conducting the interrogation took care to ensure that respondent understood his rights. They fully explained to respondent that he was being questioned in connection with a murder. They then informed him of all the rights delineated in *Miranda,* and ascertained that respondent understood those rights. There is no indication in the record that respondent failed to understand what the officers told him. Moreover, after his request to see his probation officer had been denied, and after the police officer once more had explained his rights to him, respondent clearly expressed his willingness to waive his rights and continue the interrogation.

Further, no special factors indicate that respondent was unable to understand the nature of his actions. He was a 16 1/2-year-old juvenile with considerable experience with the police. He had a record of several arrests. He had served time in a youth camp, and he had been on probation for several years. He was under the full-time supervision of probation authorities. There is no indication that he was of insufficient intelligence to understand the rights he was waiving, or what the consequences of that waiver would be. He was not worn down by improper interrogation tactics or lengthy questioning or by trickery or deceit.

On these facts, we think it clear that respondent voluntarily and knowingly waived his Fifth Amendment rights. Respondent argues, however, that any statements he made during interrogation were coerced. Specifically, respondent alleges that the police made threats and promises during the interrogation to pressure him into cooperating in the hope of obtaining leniency for his cooperative attitude. He notes also that he repeatedly told the officers during his interrogation that he wished to stop answering their questions, but that the officers ignored his pleas. He argues further that the record reveals that he was afraid that the police would coerce him, and that this fear caused him to cooperate. He points out that at one point the transcript revealed that he wept during the interrogation.

Review of the entire transcript reveals that respondent's claims of coercion are without merit. As noted, the police took care to inform respondent of his rights and to ensure that he understood them. The officers did not intimidate or threaten respondent in any way. Their questioning was restrained and free from the abuses that so concerned the Court in *Miranda.* See 384 U.S., at 445–455. The police did indeed indicate that a cooperative attitude would be to respondent's benefit, but their remarks in this regard were far from threatening or coercive. And respondent's allegation that he repeatedly asked that the interrogation cease goes too far: at some points he did state that he did not know the answer to a question put to him or that he could not, or would not, answer the question, but these statements were not assertions of his right to remain silent.

IV

We hold, in short, that the California Supreme Court erred in finding that a juvenile's request for his probation officer was a per se invocation of that juvenile's Fifth Amendment rights under *Miranda*. We conclude, rather, that whether the statements obtained during subsequent interrogation of a juvenile who has asked to see his probation officer, but who has not asked to consult an attorney or expressly asserted his right to remain silent, are admissible on the basis of waiver remain a question to be resolved on the totality of the circumstances surrounding the interrogation. On the basis of the record in this case, we hold that the Juvenile Court's findings that respondent voluntarily and knowingly waived his rights and consented to continued interrogation, and that the statements obtained from him were voluntary, were proper, and that the admission of those statements in the proceeding against respondent in Juvenile Court was correct.

The judgment of the Supreme Court of California is reversed, and the case is remanded for further proceedings not inconsistent with this opinion.

It is so ordered.

Mr. Justice Marshall, with whom Mr. Justice Brennan and Mr. Justice Stevens join, dissenting.

In *Miranda v. Arizona*, 384 U.S. 436 (1966), this Court sought to ensure that the inherently coercive pressures of custodial interrogation would not vitiate a suspect's privilege against self-incrimination. Nothing that these pressures "can operate very quickly to overbear the will of one merely made aware of his privilege," id., at 469, the Court held:

> "If [a suspect in custody] indicates in any manner, at any time prior to or during questioning, that he wishes to remain silent, the interrogation must cease. At this point he has shown that he intends to exercise his Fifth Amendment privilege; any statement taken after the person invokes his privilege cannot be other than the product of compulsion, subtle or otherwise.... If the individual states that he wants an attorney, the interrogation must cease until an attorney is present." Id., at 473–474 (footnote omitted).

See also id., at 444–445.

As this Court has consistently recognized, the coerciveness of the custodial setting is of heightened concern where, as here, a juvenile is under investigation. In *Haley v. Ohio*, 332 U.S. 596 (1948), the plurality reasoned that because a 15 1/2-year-old minor was particularly susceptible to overbearing interrogation tactics, the voluntariness of his confession could not "be judged by the more exacting standards of maturity." Id., at 599. The Court reiterated this point in *Gallegos v. Colorado*, 370 U.S. 49, 54 (1962), observing that a 14-year-old suspect could not "be compared with an adult in full possession of his senses and knowledgeable of the consequences of his admissions." The juvenile defendant, in the Court's view, required

> "the aid of more mature judgment as to the steps he should take in the predicament in which he found himself. A lawyer or an adult relative or friend could have given the petitioner the protection which his own immaturity could not." Ibid.

And, in *In re Gault*, 387 U.S. 1, 55 (1967), the Court admonished that "the greatest care must be taken to assure that [a minor's] admission was voluntary."

It is therefore critical in the present context that we construe *Miranda's* prophylactic requirements broadly to accomplish their intended purpose—"dispel[ling] the compulsion inherent in custodial surroundings." 384 U.S., at 458. To effectuate this purpose, the Court must ensure that the "protective device" of legal counsel, id., at 465–466, 469, be readily available, and that any intimation of a desire to preclude questioning be scrupulously honored. Thus, I believe *Miranda* requires that interrogation cease whenever a juvenile requests an adult who is obligated to represent his interests. Such a request, in my judgment, constitutes both an attempt to obtain advice and a general invocation of the right to silence. For, as the California Supreme Court recognized, "'[i]t is fatuous to assume that a minor in custody will be in a position to call an attorney for assistance,'" 21 Cal. 3d 471, 475–476, 579 P.2d 7, 9 (1978), quoting *People v. Burton*, 6 Cal. 3d 375, 382, 491 P.2d 793, 797 (1971), or that he will trust the police to obtain a lawyer for him.[1] A juvenile in these circumstances will likely turn to his parents, or another adult responsible for his welfare, as the only means of securing legal counsel. Moreover, a request for such adult assistance is surely inconsistent with a present desire to speak freely. Requiring a strict verbal formula to invoke the protections of *Miranda* would "protect the knowledgeable accused from stationhouse coercion while abandoning the young person who knows no more than to ask for the . . . person he trusts." *Chaney v. Wainwright*, 561 F.2d 1129, 1134 (CA5 1977) (Goldberg, J., dissenting).

On my reading of *Miranda*, a California juvenile's request for his probation officer should be treated as a per se assertion of Fifth Amendment rights. The California Supreme Court determined that probation officers have a statutory duty to represent minors' interests and, indeed, are "trusted guardian figure[s]" to whom a juvenile would likely turn for assistance. 21 Cal. 3d, at 476, 579 P.2d, at 10. In addition, the court found, probation officers are particularly well suited to assist a juvenile "on such matters as to whether or not he should obtain an attorney" and "how to conduct himself with police." Id., at 476, 477, 579 P.2d, at 10. Hence, a juvenile's request for a probation officer may frequently be an attempt to secure protection from the coercive aspects of custodial questioning.[2]

This Court concludes, however, that because a probation officer has law enforcement duties, juveniles generally would not call upon him to represent their interests, and if they did, would not be well served. Ante, at 721–722. But that conclusion ignores the California

---

1. The facts of the instant case are illustrative. When the police offered to obtain an attorney for respondent, he replied: "How I know you guys won't pull no police officer in and tell me he's an attorney?" Ante, at 710. Significantly, the police made no attempt to allay that concern. See 21 Cal. 3d, at 476 n. 3, 579 P.2d, at 10 n. 3.

2. The Court intimates that construing a request for a probation officer as an invocation of the Fifth Amendment privilege would undermine the specificity of *Miranda's* prophylactic rules. Ante, at 718. Yet the Court concedes that the statutory duty to "advise and care for the juvenile defendant," 21 Cal. 3d, at 477, 579 P.2d, at 10, distinguishes probation officers from other adults, such as coaches and clergymen. Ante, at 723. Since law enforcement officials should be on notice of such legal relationships, they would presumably have no difficulty determining whether a suspect has asserted his Fifth Amendment rights.

Although I agree with my Brother POWELL that, on the facts here, respondent was not "subjected to a fair interrogation free from inherently coercive circumstances," post, at 734, I do not believe a case-by-case approach provides police sufficient guidance, or affords juveniles adequate protection.

Supreme Court's express determination that the officer's responsibility to initiate juvenile proceedings did not negate his function as personal adviser to his wards.[3] I decline to second-guess that court's assessment of state law. See *Murdock v. Memphis*, 20 Wall. 590, 626 (1875); *General Trading Co. v. State Tax Comm'n*, 322 U.S. 335, 337 (1944); *Scripto, Inc. v. Carson*, 362 U.S. 207, 210 (1960).[4] Further, although the majority here speculates that probation officers have a duty to advise cooperation with the police, ante, at 721—a proposition suggested only in the concurring opinion of two justices below, 21 Cal. 3d, at 479, 579 P.2d, at 11–12 (Mosk, J., joined by Bird, C. J., concurring)—respondent's probation officer instructed all his charges "not to go and admit openly to an offense, [but rather] to get some type of advice from . . . parents or a lawyer." App. 30. Absent an explicit statutory provision or judicial holding, the officer's assessment of the obligations imposed by state law is entitled to deference by this Court.

Thus, given the role of probation officers under California law, a juvenile's request to see his officer may reflect a desire for precisely the kind of assistance *Miranda* guarantees an accused before he waives his Fifth Amendment rights. At the very least, such a request signals a desire to remain silent until contact with the officer is made. Because the Court's contrary determination withdraws the safeguards of *Miranda* from those most in need of protection, I respectfully dissent.

Mr. Justice Powell, dissenting.

Although I agree with the Court that the Supreme Court of California misconstrued *Miranda v. Arizona*, 384 U.S. 436 (1966),[1] I would not reverse the California court's judgment. This Court repeatedly has recognized that "the greatest care" must be taken to assure that an alleged confession of a juvenile was voluntary. See, e.g., *In re Gault*, 387 U.S. 1, 55 (1967); *Gallegos v. Colorado*, 370 U.S. 49, 54 (1962); *Haley v. Ohio*, 332 U.S. 596, 599–600 (1948) (plurality opinion). Respondent was a young person, 16 years old at the time of his arrest and the subsequent prolonged interrogation at the station house. Although respondent had had prior brushes with the law, and was under supervision by a probation officer, the taped transcript of his interrogation—as well as his testimony at the suppression hearing—

---

3. In filing the petition and performing the other functions enumerated ante, at 720–721, n. 5, the probation officer must act in the best interests of the minor. See In re Steven C., 9 Cal. App. 3d 255, 264–265, 88 Cal. Rptr. 97, 101–102 (1970).

4. One thing is certain. The California Supreme Court is more familiar with the duties and performance of its probation officers than we are.

Of course, "[i]t is peculiarly within the competence of the highest court of a State to determine that in its jurisdiction the police should be subject to more stringent rules than are required as a federal constitutional minimum." *Oregon v. Hass*, 420 U.S. 714, 728 (1975) (MARSHALL, J., dissenting). See also *People v. Disbrow*, 16 Cal. 3d 101, 545 P.2d 272 (1976) (refusing to follow *Harris v. New York*, 401 U.S. 222 (1971)); Brennan, State Constitutions and the Protection of Individual Rights, 90 Harv. L. Rev. 489 (1977).

1. The California Supreme Court, purporting to apply *Miranda v. Arizona*, stated:

"Here . . . we face conduct which, regardless of considerations of capacity, coercion or voluntariness, per se invokes the privilege against self-incrimination." 21 Cal. 3d 471, 477, 579 P.2d 7, 10 (1978). I agree with the Court's opinion today that *Miranda* cannot be read as support for any such per se rule.

2. The Juvenile Court Judge observed that he had "heard the tapes" of the interrogation and was "aware of the fact that Michael [respondent] was crying at the time he talked to the police officers." App. 53.

demonstrates that he was immature, emotional,[2] and uneducated, and therefore was likely to be vulnerable to the skillful, two-on-one, repetitive style of interrogation to which he was subjected. App. 54–82.

When given *Miranda* warnings and asked whether he desired an attorney, respondent requested permission to "have my probation officer here," a request that was refused. Id., at 55. That officer testified later that he had communicated frequently with respondent, that respondent had serious and "extensive" family problems, and that the officer had instructed respondent to call him immediately "at any time he has a police contact, even if they stop him and talk to him on the street." Id., at 26–31.[3] The reasons given by the probation officer for having so instructed his charge were substantially the same reasons that prompt this Court to examine with special care the circumstances under which a minor's alleged confession was obtained. After stating that respondent had been "going through problems," the officer observed that "many times the kids don't understand what is going on, and what they are supposed to do relative to police. . . ." Id., at 29. This view of the limited understanding of the average 16-year-old was borne out by respondent's question when, during interrogation, he was advised of his right to an attorney: "How I know you guys won't pull no police officer in and tell me he's an attorney?" Id., at 55. It was during this part of the interrogation that the police had denied respondent's request to "have my probation officer here." Ibid.

The police then proceeded, despite respondent's repeated denial of any connection to the murder under investigation, see id., at 56–60, persistently to press interrogation until they extracted a confession. In *In re Gault*, in addressing police interrogation of detained juveniles, the Court stated:

> "If counsel was not present for some permissible reason when an admission was obtained [from a child], the greatest care must be taken to assure that the admission was voluntary, in the sense not only that it was not coerced or suggested, but also that it was not the product of ignorance of rights or of adolescent fantasy, fright or despair." 387 U.S., at 55.

It is clear that the interrogating police did not exercise "the greatest care" to assure that respondent's "admission was voluntary."[4] In the absence of counsel, and having refused to call the probation officer, they nevertheless engaged in protracted interrogation.

Although I view the case as close, I am not satisfied that this particular 16-year-old boy, in this particular situation, was subjected to a fair interrogation free from inherently coercive circumstances. For these reasons, I would affirm the judgment of the Supreme Court of California.

---

3. The Supreme Court of California stated that a "probation officer is an official appointed pursuant to legislative enactment 'to represent the interests' of the juvenile [and] . . . has borne the duty to advise and care for the juvenile defendant." 21 Cal. 3d, at 477, 579 P.2d, at 10.

4. Minors who become embroiled with the law range from the very young up to those on the brink of majority. Some of the older minors become fully "street-wise," hardened criminals, deserving no greater consideration than that properly accorded all persons suspected of crime. Other minors are more of a child than an adult. As the Court indicated in *In re Gault*, 387 U.S. 1 (1967), the facts relevant to the care to be exercised in a particular case vary widely. They include the minor's age, actual maturity, family environment, education, emotional and mental stability, and, of course, any prior record he might have.

Case Comment

The Supreme Court also sought to clarify children's rights when they are interrogated by police in the case of *California v. Prysock*. In *Prysock* the Court was asked to rule on the adequacy of a *Miranda* warning given Randall Prysock, a youthful murder suspect. After reviewing the taped exchange between the police interrogator and the boy, the Court upheld Prysock's conviction when it ruled that even though the *Miranda* warning was given in slightly different terms and out of context, its meaning was plain and easily understandable, even to a juvenile. The Court ruled that the content of the warnings to an accused prior to police interrogation required by *Miranda v. Arizona* need not be a virtual incantation of the precise language contained in the *Miranda* opinion.

Taken together, the *Fare* and *Prysock* cases make it seem indisputable that juveniles are entitled to receive at least the same *Miranda* rights as adults and ought to be entitled to even greater consideration to ensure that they understand their legal rights.

CALIFORNIA V. PRYSOCK

Supreme Court of the United States, 1981.

453 U.S. 355.

PER CURIAM.

This case presents the question whether the warnings given to respondent prior to a recorded conversation with a police officer satisfied the requirements of *Miranda v. Arizona*, 384 U.S. 436 (1966). Although ordinarily this Court would not be inclined to review a case involving application of that precedent to a particular set of facts, see *Fare v. Michael C.*, 439 U.S. 1310, 1314 (1978) (REHNQUIST, J., in chambers, opinion of Court at 442 U.S. 707 (1979)), the opinion of the California Court of Appeal essentially laid down a flat rule requiring that the content of *Miranda* warnings be a virtual incantation of the precise language contained in the *Miranda* opinion. Because such a rigid rule was not mandated by *Miranda* or any other decision of this Court, and is not required to serve the purposes of *Miranda*, we grant the motion of respondent for leave to proceed in forma pauperis and the petition for certiorari and reverse.

On January 30, 1978, Mrs. Donna Iris Erickson was brutally murdered. Later that evening respondent and a co-defendant were apprehended for commission of the offense. Respondent was brought to a substation of the Tulare County Sheriff's Department and advised of his *Miranda* rights. He declined to talk and, since he was a minor, his parents were notified. Respondent's parents arrived and after meeting with them respondent decided to answer police questions. An officer questioned respondent, on tape, with respondent's parents present. The tape reflects that the following warnings were given prior to any questioning:

> "Sgt. Byrd: . . . Mr. Randall James Prysock, earlier today I advised you of your legal rights and at that time you advised me you did not wish to talk to me, is that correct?
>
> "Randall P.: Yeh.
>
> "Sgt. Byrd: And, uh, during, at the first interview your folks were not present, they are now present. I want to go through your legal rights again with you and after each legal right I would like for you to answer whether you understand it or not. . . . Your legal rights. Mr. Prysock,

is [sic] follows: Number One, you have the right to remain silent. This means you don't have to talk to me at all unless you so desire. Do you understand this?

"Randall P.: Yeh.

"Sgt. Byrd: If you give up your right to remain silent, anything you say can and will be used as evidence against you in a court of law. Do you understand this?

"Randall P.: Yes.

"Sgt. Byrd: You have the right to talk to a lawyer before you are questioned, have him present with you while you are being questioned, and all during the questioning. Do you understand this?

"Randall P.: Yes.

"Sgt. Byrd: You also, being a juvenile, you have the right to have your parents present, which they are. Do you understand this?

"Randall P.: Yes.

"Sgt. Byrd: Even if they weren't here, you'd have this right. Do you understand this?

"Randall P.: Yes.

"Sgt. Byrd: You all, uh,—if,—you have the right to have a lawyer appointed to represent you at no cost to yourself. Do you understand this?

"Randall P.: Yes.

"Sgt. Byrd: Now, having all these legal rights in mind, do you wish to talk to me at this time?

"Randall P.: Yes." App. A to Pet. for Cert. i–iii.

At this point, at the request of Mrs. Prysock, a conversation took place with the tape recorder turned off. According to Sgt. Byrd, Mrs. Prysock asked if respondent could still have an attorney at a later time if he gave a statement now without one. Sgt. Byrd assured Mrs. Prysock that respondent would have an attorney when he went to court and that "he could have one at this time if he wished one." Id., at 11.[1]

At trial in the Superior Court of Tulare County the court denied respondent's motion to suppress the taped statement. Respondent was convicted by a jury of first-degree murder with two special circumstances—torture and robbery. Cal. Penal Code Ann. 187, 190.2,

---

1. The tape reflects the following concerning the off-the-record discussion:

"Sgt. Byrd: . . . Okay, Mrs. Prysock, you asked to get off the tape. . . . During that time you asked, decided you wanted some time to think about getting, whether to hire a lawyer or not.

"Mrs. P.: 'Cause I didn't understand it.

"Sgt. Byrd: And you have decided now that you want to go ahead and you do not wish a lawyer present at this time?

"Mrs. P.: That's right.

"Sgt. Byrd: And I have not persuaded you in any way, is that correct?

"Mrs. P.: No, you have not.

"Sgt. Byrd: And, Mr. Prysock is that correct that I have done nothing to persuade you not to, to hire a lawyer or to go on with this?

"Mr. P.: That's right.

"Sgt. Byrd: Okay, everything we're doing here is strictly in accordance with Randall and yourselves, is that correct?

"Mr. P.: That is correct.

"Sgt. Byrd: Okay. Uh, all right, Randy, I can't remember where I left off, I think I asked you, uh, with your legal rights in mind, do you wish to talk to me at this time? This is with everything I told you, all your legal rights, your right to an attorney and your right to remain silent, and all these, I mean do you wish to talk to me at this time about the case?

"Randall P.: Yes." App. A to Pet. for Cert. iii–iv.

12022 (b) (West Supp. 1981). He was also convicted of robbery with the use of a dangerous weapon, 211, 12022 (b), burglary with the use of a deadly weapon, 459, 12022 (b), automobile theft, Cal. Veh. Code Ann. 10851 (West Supp. 1981), escape from a youth facility,
Cal. Welf. & Inst. Code Ann. 871 (West 1972), and destruction of evidence, Cal. Penal Code
Ann. 135 (West 1970).

The Court of Appeal for the Fifth Appellate District reversed respondent's convictions and
ordered a new trial because of what it thought to be error under *Miranda*. App. A to Pet. for
Cert. 4. The Court of Appeal ruled that respondent's recorded incriminating statements,
given with his parents present, had to be excluded from consideration by the jury because
respondent was not properly advised of his right to the services of a free attorney before and
during interrogation. Although respondent was indisputably informed that he had "the right
to talk to a lawyer before you are questioned, have him present with you while you are being
questioned, and all during the questioning," and further informed that he had "the right to
have a lawyer appointed to represent you at no cost to yourself," the Court of Appeal ruled
that these warnings were inadequate because respondent was not explicitly informed of his
right to have an attorney appointed before further questioning. The Court of Appeal stated
that "[o]ne of [*Miranda*'s] virtues is its precise requirements which are so easily met," and
quoted from *Harryman v. Estelle*, 616 F.2d 870, 873-874 (CA5), cert denied, 449 U.S. 860
(1980), that "'the rigidity of the *Miranda* rules and the way in which they are to be applied
was conceived of and continues to be recognized as the decision's greatest strength.'" App. A
to Pet. for Cert. 12. Relying on two previous decisions of the California Court of Appeal,
People v. Bolinski, 260 Cal. App. 2d 705, 67 Cal. Rptr. 347 (1968), and *People v. Stewart*, 267
Cal. App. 2d 366, 73 Cal. Rptr. 484 (1968), the court ruled that the requirements of *Miranda*
were not met in this case.[2] The California Supreme Court denied a petition for hearing, with
two justices dissenting. App. D to Pet. for Cert.

This Court has never indicated that the "rigidity" of *Miranda* extends to the precise formulation of the warnings given a criminal defendant. See, e.g., *United States v. Lamia*, 429
F.2d 373, 375-376 (CA2), cert. denied, 400 U.S. 907 (1970). This Court and others have
stressed as one virtue of *Miranda* the fact that the giving of the warnings obviates the need
for a case-by-case inquiry into the actual voluntariness of the admissions of the accused.
See *Fare v. Michael C.*, 442 U.S., at 718; *Harryman v. Estelle*, supra. Nothing in these observations suggests any desirable rigidity in the form of the required warnings.

Quite the contrary, *Miranda* itself indicated that no talismanic incantation was required
to satisfy its strictures. The Court in that case stated that "[t]he warnings required and the
waiver necessary in accordance with our opinion today are, in the absence of a fully effective equivalent, prerequisites to the admissibility of any statement made by a defendant."
384 U.S., at 476. See also id., at 479. Just last Term in considering when *Miranda* applied we
noted that that decision announced procedural safeguards including "the now familiar
Miranda warnings . . . or their equivalent." *Rhode Island v. Innis*, 446 U.S. 291, 297 (1980).

Other courts considering the precise question presented by this case—whether a criminal defendant was adequately informed of his right to the presence of appointed counsel
prior to and during interrogation—have not required a verbatim recital of the words of the

---

2. Contrary to respondent's suggestion, it is clear that the decision below was based on federal law. The Court
of Appeal stated that it was reversing and ordering a new trial "because of *Miranda* error." Id., at 4.

Miranda opinion but rather have examined the warnings given to determine if the reference to the right to appointed counsel was linked with some future point in time after the police interrogation. In *United States v. Garcia,* 431 F.2d 134 (CA9 1970) (per curiam), for example, the court found inadequate advice to the defendant that she could "have an attorney appointed to represent you when you first appear before the U.S. Commissioner or the Court." *People v. Bolinski,* supra, relied upon by the court below, is a case of this type. Two separate sets of warnings were ruled inadequate. In the first, the defendant was advised that "if he was charged . . . he would be appointed counsel." 260 Cal. App. 2d, at 718, 67 Cal. Rptr., at 355. In the second, the defendant, then in Illinois and about to be moved to California, was advised that "'the court would appoint [an attorney] in Riverside County [, California].'" Id., at 723, 67 Cal. Rptr., at 359. In both instances the reference to appointed counsel was linked to a future point in time after police interrogation, and therefore did not fully advise the suspect of his right to appointed counsel before such interrogation.

Here, in contrast, nothing in the warnings given respondent suggested any limitation on the right to the presence of appointed counsel different from the clearly conveyed rights to a lawyer in general, including the right "to a lawyer before you are questioned . . . while you are being questioned, and all during the questioning." App. A to Pet. for Cert. 9-10; ii. Like *United States v. Noa,* 443 F.2d 144 (CA9 1971), where the warnings given were substantially similar to those given here and defendant's argument was the same as that adopted by the Court of Appeal, "[t]his is not a case in which the defendant was not informed of his right to the presence of an attorney during questioning . . . or in which the offer of an appointed attorney was associated with a future time in court . . . ." Id., at 146.

It is clear that the police in this case fully conveyed to respondent his rights as required by *Miranda.* He was told of his right to have a lawyer present prior to and during interrogation, and his right to have a lawyer appointed at no cost if he could not afford one. These warnings conveyed to respondent his right to have a lawyer appointed if he could not afford one prior to and during interrogation. The Court of Appeal erred in holding that the warnings were inadequate simply because of the order in which they were given.[3]

Because respondent was given the warnings required by *Miranda,* the decision of the California Court of Appeal to the contrary is reversed, and the case is remanded for further proceedings not inconsistent with this opinion.

It is so ordered.

---

3. The dissent, arguing that the Court of Appeal opinion is unfairly criticized as requiring mimicking of *Miranda,* post, at 365–366, ignores substantial portions of the opinion below and substitutes arguments of its own for those articulated by the Court of Appeal. For example, the dissent makes no mention of the lower court's stress on the "precise requirements" of *Miranda* or its "rigidity" in this area, and ignores the portion of the opinion in which the court quotes from *Miranda* and then criticizes the officer for not repeating the exact language in advising respondent of his rights. See App. A to Pet. for Cert. 12-14. The Court of Appeal did conclude that respondent was not advised of his right to appointed counsel prior to and during interrogation, but this was because the officer did not parrot the language of *Miranda.* The more substantive reasons suggested by the dissent are implausible. The reference to "appointed" counsel has never been considered as suggesting that the availability of counsel was postponed, and Mrs. Prysock's off-the-record conversation was occasioned by her fear that waiving the right to counsel at interrogation would occasion a waiver of the right to counsel later in court, App. A to Pet. for Cert. 11, clearly indicating that the officer conveyed the right to counsel at interrogation.

Justice Stevens, with whom Justice Brennan and Justice Marshall join, dissenting.

A juvenile informed by police that he has a right to counsel may understand that right to include one or more of three options: (1) that he has a right to have a lawyer represent him if he or his parents are able and willing to hire one; (2) that, if he cannot afford to hire an attorney, he has a right to have a lawyer represent him without charge at trial, even if his parents are unwilling to spend money on his behalf; or (3) that, if he is unable to afford an attorney, he has a right to consult a lawyer without charge before he decides whether to talk to the police, even if his parents decline to pay for such legal representation.[1] All three of these options are encompassed within the right to counsel possessed by a juvenile charged with a crime. In this case, the first two options were explained to respondent, but the third was not.

In *Miranda v. Arizona*, 384 U.S. 436, this Court held that in order to protect an accused's privilege against self-incrimination, certain procedural safeguards must be employed.

In particular, an individual taken into police custody and subjected to questioning must be given the *Miranda* warnings:

> "He must be warned prior to any questioning that he has the right to remain silent, that anything he says can be used against him in a court of law, that he has the right to the presence of an attorney, and that if he cannot afford an attorney one will be appointed for him prior to any questioning if he so desires." Id., at 479.

See also *Rhode Island v. Innis*, 446 U.S. 291, 297. This formulation makes it clear beyond any doubt that an indigent accused has the right to the presence of an attorney and the right to have that attorney appointed to represent him prior to any questioning. While it is certainly true, as the Court emphasizes today, that the Federal Constitution does not require a "talismanic incantation" of the language of the *Miranda* opinion, ante, at 359, it is also indisputable that it requires that an accused be adequately informed of his right to have counsel appointed prior to any police questioning.

The California Court of Appeal in this case analyzed the warning given respondent, quoted ante, at 356–357, and concluded that he had not been adequately informed of this crucial right. The police sergeant informed respondent that he had the right to have counsel present during questioning and, after a brief interlude, informed him that he had the right to appointed counsel. See ibid. The Court of Appeal concluded that this warning was constitutionally inadequate, not because it deviated from the precise language of *Miranda*, but because

> "[u]nfortunately, the minor was not given the crucial information that the services of the free attorney were available prior to the impending questioning." App. A to Pet. for Cert. 15.[2]

---

1. In his dissenting opinion in *Miranda v. Arizona*, 384 U.S. 436, 504, Justice Harlan accurately summarized the four essential elements of the warning that must be given a person in custody before he is questioned, "namely, that he has a right to remain silent, that anything he says may be used against him, that he has a right to have present an attorney during the questioning, and that if indigent he has a right to a lawyer without charge."

2. According to the Court of Appeal, the principal defect in the warning was that the police sergeant, in a "needless excursion," inserted a discussion of respondent's right to have his parents present between the description of the right to have counsel present during questioning and the description of the right of an indigent to have counsel appointed to represent him. See App. A to Pet. for Cert. 14–15. The subsequent untaped conversation "obfuscated, rather than clarified" the matter. Id., at 15. The warnings given respondent were defective, not because "the

There can be no question that *Miranda* requires, as a matter of federal constitutional law, that an accused effectively be provided with this "crucial information" in some form. The Court's demonstration that the Constitution does not require that the precise language of *Miranda* be recited to an accused simply fails to come to terms with the express finding of the California Court of Appeal that respondent was not given this information. The warning recited by the police sergeant is sufficiently ambiguous on its face to provide adequate support for the California court's finding. That court's conclusion is at least reasonable, and is clearly not so patently erroneous as to warrant summary reversal.

The ambiguity in the warning given respondent is further demonstrated by the colloquy between the police sergeant and respondent's parents that occurred after respondent was told that he had the "right to have a lawyer appointed to represent you at no cost to yourself." Because lawyers are normally "appointed" by judges, and not by law enforcement officers, the reference to appointed counsel could reasonably have been understood to refer to trial counsel.[3] That is what respondent's parents must have assumed, because their ensuing colloquy with the sergeant related to their option "to hire a lawyer."[4]

The judges on the California Court of Appeal and on the California Supreme Court, all of whom are presumably more familiar with the procedures followed by California police officers than we are, concluded that respondent was not adequately informed of his right to have a lawyer present without charge during the questioning. This Court is not at all fair to

---

officer did not parrot the language of *Miranda,*" ante, at 361, n. 3, but because, in the form in which the warnings were given, they failed to convey the essential information required by *Miranda.*

3. The fact that the reference also might have been understood to refer to the appointment of counsel prior to questioning does not undercut the Court of Appeal's conclusion. *Miranda* requires "meaningful advice to the unlettered and unlearned in language which he can comprehend and on which he can knowingly act." *Coyote v. United States,* 380 F.2d 305, 308 (CA10 1967), cert. denied, 389 U.S. 992. Such meaningful advice is not provided by a warning which requires that an accused choose among several reasonable interpretations of the language employed by a police officer in a custodial situation.

4. The Court simply ignores the significance of the references to hiring a lawyer in the colloquy which it quotes ante, at 357-358, n. 1. The colloquy bears repeating:

"Sgt. Byrd: . . . Okay, Mrs. Prysock, you asked to get off the tape. . . . During that time you asked, decided you wanted some time to think about getting, whether to hire a lawyer or not.

"Mrs. P.: 'Cause I didn't understand it.

"Sgt. Byrd: And you have decided now that you want to go ahead and you do not wish a lawyer present at this time?

"Mrs. P.: That's right.

"Sgt. Byrd: And I have not persuaded you in any way, is that correct?

"Mrs. P.: No, you have not.

"Sgt. Byrd: And, Mr. Prysock is that correct that I have done nothing to persuade you not to, to hire a lawyer or to go on with this?

"Mr. P.: That's right.

"Sgt. Byrd: Okay, everything we're doing here is strictly in accordance with Randall and yourselves, is that correct?

"Mr. P.: That is correct.

"Sgt. Byrd: Okay. Uh, all right, Randy, I can't remember where I left off, I think I asked you, uh, with your legal rights in mind, do you wish to talk to me at this time? This is with everything I told you, all your legal rights, your right to an attorney, and your right to remain silent, and all these, I mean do you wish to talk to me at this time about the case?

"Randall P.: Yes." App. A to Pet. for Cert. iii-iv.

those judges when it construes their conscientious appraisal of a somewhat ambiguous record as requiring "a virtual incantation of the precise language contained in the *Miranda* opinion." *Ante*, at 355. It seems clear to me that it is this Court, rather than the state courts, that is guilty of attaching greater importance to the form of the *Miranda* ritual than to the substance of the message it is intended to convey.

I respectfully dissent.

Case Comment

In *Yarborough v. Alvarado*, the Supreme Court was confronted with a case that provided a clear opportunity to clarify whether a juvenile's youth and inexperience requires special attention by police. Alvarado was interrogated by a detective for two hours and finally implicated himself in a felony murder. Alvarado alleged that his confession was inadmissible because he had not been given *Miranda* warnings. The Supreme Court ruled that Alvarado was not in custody for *Miranda* purposes and should have known that he could end the interview at any time and leave.

YARBOROUGH, WARDEN V. ALVARADO

Supreme Court of the United States, 2004.

541 U.S. 652.

Justice Kennedy delivered the opinion of the Court.

Under the Antiterrorism and Effective Death Penalty Act of 1996 (AEDPA), 110 Stat. 1214, a federal court can grant an application for a writ of habeas corpus on behalf of a person held pursuant to a state-court judgment if the state-court adjudication "resulted in a decision that was contrary to, or involved an unreasonable application of, clearly established Federal law, as determined by the Supreme Court of the United States." 28 U.S.C. §2254(d)(1). The United States Court of Appeals for the Ninth Circuit ruled that a state court unreasonably applied clearly established law when it held that the respondent was not in custody for *Miranda* purposes. *Alvarado v. Hickman*, 316 F. 3d 841 (2002). We disagree and reverse.

I

Paul Soto and respondent Michael Alvarado attempted to steal a truck in the parking lot of a shopping mall in Santa Fe Springs, California. Soto and Alvarado were part of a larger group of teenagers at the mall that night. Soto decided to steal the truck, and Alvarado agreed to help. Soto pulled out a .357 Magnum and approached the driver, Francisco Castaneda, who was standing near the truck emptying trash into a dumpster. Soto demanded money and the ignition keys from Castaneda. Alvarado, then five months short of his 18th birthday, approached the passenger side door of the truck and crouched down. When Castaneda refused to comply with Soto's demands, Soto shot Castaneda, killing him. Alvarado then helped hide Soto's gun.

Los Angeles County Sheriff's detective Cheryl Comstock led the investigation into the circumstances of Castaneda's death. About a month after the shooting, Comstock left word at Alvarado's house and also contacted Alvarado's mother at work with the message that she wished to speak with Alvarado. Alvarado's parents brought him to the Pico Rivera Sheriff's Station to be interviewed around lunchtime. They waited in the lobby while Alvarado went with Comstock to be interviewed. Alvarado contends that his parents asked to be present during the interview but were rebuffed.

Comstock brought Alvarado to a small interview room and began interviewing him at about 12:30 p.m. The interview lasted about two hours, and was recorded by Comstock with Alvarado's knowledge. Only Comstock and Alvarado were present. Alvarado was not given a warning under *Miranda v. Arizona*, 384 U.S. 436 (1965). Comstock began the interview by asking Alvarado to recount the events on the night of the shooting. On that night, Alvarado explained, he had been drinking alcohol at a friend's house with some other friends and acquaintances. After a few hours, part of the group went home and the rest walked to a nearby mall to use its public telephones. In Alvarado's initial telling, that was the end of it. The group went back to the friend's home and "just went to bed." App. 101.

Unpersuaded, Comstock pressed on:

> "Q. Okay. We did real good up until this point and everything you've said it's pretty accurate till this point, except for you left out the shooting.
> "A. The shooting?
> "Q. Uh huh, the shooting.
> "A. Well I had never seen no shooting.
> "Q. Well I'm afraid you did.
> "A. I had never seen no shooting.
> "Q. Well I beg to differ with you. I've been told quite the opposite and we have witnesses that are saying quite the opposite.
> "A. That I had seen the shooting?
> "Q. So why don't you take a deep breath, like I told you before, the very best thing is to be honest . . . . You can't have that many people get involved in a murder and expect that some of them aren't going to tell the truth, okay? Now granted if it was maybe one person, you might be able to keep your fingers crossed and say, god I hope he doesn't tell the truth, but the problem is is that they have to tell the truth, okay? Now all I'm simply doing is giving you the opportunity to tell the truth and when we got that many people telling a story and all of a sudden you tell something way far fetched different." *Id.*, at 101-102.

At this point, Alvarado slowly began to change his story. First he acknowledged being present when the carjacking occurred but claimed that he did not know what happened or who had a gun. When he hesitated to say more, Comstock tried to encourage Alvarado to discuss what happened by appealing to his sense of honesty and the need to bring the man who shot Castaneda to justice. See, *e.g., id.*, at 106 ("[W]hat I'm looking for is to see if you'll tell the truth"); *id.*, at 105-106 ("I know it's very difficult when it comes time to 'drop the dime' on somebody[,] . . . [but] if that had been your parent, your mother, or your brother, or your sister, you would darn well want [the killer] to go to jail 'cause no one has the right to take someone's life like that . . ."). Alvarado then admitted he had helped the other man try to steal the truck by standing near the passenger side door. Next he admitted that the other man was Paul Soto, that he knew Soto was armed, and that he had helped hide the gun after the murder. Alvarado explained that he had expected Soto to scare the driver with the gun, but that he did not expect Soto to kill anyone. *Id.*, at 127. Toward the end of the interview, Comstock twice asked Alvarado if he needed to take a break. Alvarado declined. When the interview was over, Comstock returned with Alvarado to the lobby of the sheriff's station where his parents were waiting. Alvarado's father drove him home.

A few months later, the State of California charged Soto and Alvarado with first-degree murder and attempted robbery. Citing *Miranda, supra*, Alvarado moved to suppress his statements from the Comstock interview. The trial court denied the motion on the ground that the interview was noncustodial. App. 196. Alvarado and Soto were tried together, and Alvarado testified in his own defense. He offered an innocent explanation for his conduct, testifying that he happened to be standing in the parking lot of the mall when a gun went off nearby. The government's cross-examination relied on Alvarado's statement to Comstock. Alvarado admitted having made some of the statements but denied others. When Alvarado denied particular statements, the prosecution countered by playing excerpts from the audio recording of the interview.

During cross-examination, Alvarado agreed that the interview with Comstock "was a pretty friendly conversation," *id.*, at 438, that there was "sort of a free flow between [Alvarado] and Detective Comstock," *id.*, at 439, and that Alvarado did not "feel coerced or threatened in any way" during the interview, *(ibid.)* The jury convicted Soto and Alvarado of first-degree murder and attempted robbery. The trial judge later reduced Alvarado's conviction to second-degree murder for his comparatively minor role in the offense. The judge sentenced Soto to life in prison and Alvarado to 15-years-to-life.

On direct appeal, the Second Appellate District Court of Appeal (hereinafter state court) affirmed. *People* v. *Soto*, 74 Cal. App. 4th 1099, 88 Cal. Rptr. 688 (1999) (unpublished in relevant part). The state court rejected Alvarado's contention that his statements to Comstock should have been excluded at trial because no *Miranda* warnings were given. The court ruled Alvarado had not been in custody during the interview, so no warning was required. The state court relied upon the custody test articulated in *Thompson v. Keohane*, 516 U.S. 99, 112 (1995), which requires a court to consider the circumstances surrounding the interrogation and then determine whether a reasonable person would have felt at liberty to leave. The state court reviewed the facts of the Comstock interview and concluded Alvarado was not in custody. App. to Pet. for Cert. C-17. The court emphasized the absence of any intense or aggressive tactics and noted that Comstock had not told Alvarado that he could not leave. The California Supreme Court denied discretionary review.

Alvarado filed a petition for a writ of habeas corpus in the United States District Court for the Central District of California. The District Court agreed with the state court that Alvarado was not in custody for *Miranda* purposes during the interview. *Alvarado v. Hickman*, No. ED CV-00-326-VAP(E) (2000), App. to Pet. for Cert. B1-B10. "At a minimum," the District Court added, the deferential standard of review provided by 28 U.S.C. § 2254(d) foreclosed relief. App. to Pet. for Cert. B-7.

The Court of Appeals for the Ninth Circuit reversed. *Alvarado v. Hickman*, 316 F. 3d 841 (2002). First, the Court of Appeals held that the state court erred in failing to account for Alvarado's youth and inexperience when evaluating whether a reasonable person in his position would have felt free to leave. It noted that this Court has considered a suspect's juvenile status when evaluating the voluntariness of confessions and the waiver of the privilege against self-incrimination. See *id.*, at 843 (citing, *inter alia, Haley v. Ohio,* 332 U.S. 596, 599-601 (1948), and *In re Gault,* 387 U.S. 1, 45 (1967)). The Court of Appeals held that in light of these authorities, Alvarado's age and experience must be a factor in the *Miranda* custody inquiry. 316 F. 3d, at 843. A minor with no criminal record would be more likely to feel coerced by police tactics and conclude he is under arrest than would an experienced adult, the Court of Appeals reasoned. This required extra "safeguards . . . commensurate with the age and circumstances of a juvenile defendant." See *id.*, at 850. According to the Court of Appeals, the effect of Alvarado's age and inexperience was so substantial that it turned the interview into a custodial interrogation.

The Court of Appeals next considered whether Alvarado could obtain relief in light of the deference a federal court must give to a state-court determination on habeas review. The deference required by AEDPA did not bar relief, the Court of Appeals held, because the relevance of juvenile status in Supreme Court case law as a whole compelled the "extension of the principle that juvenile status is relevant" to the context of *Miranda* custody determinations. 316 F. 3d, at 853. In light of the clearly established law considering juvenile status, it was "simply unreasonable to conclude that a reasonable 17-year-old, with no prior history of arrest or police interviews, would have felt that he was at liberty to terminate the interrogation and leave." *Id.*, at 854-855 (internal quotation marks omitted).

We granted certiorari. 539 U. S. 986 (2003).

II

We begin by determining the relevant clearly established law. For purposes of 28 U. S. C. § 2254(d)(1), clearly established law as determined by this Court "refers to the holdings, as opposed to the dicta, of this Court's decisions as of the time of the relevant state-court decision." *Williams v. Taylor,* 529 U.S. 362, 412 (2000). We look for "the governing legal principle or principles set forth by the Supreme Court at the time the state court renders its decision." *Lockyer v. Andrade,* 538 U.S. 62, 71, 72 (2003).

Miranda itself held that preinterrogation warnings are required in the context of custodial interrogations given "the compulsion inherent in custodial surroundings." 384 U.S., at 458. The Court explained that "custodial interrogation" meant "questioning initiated by law enforcement officers after a person has been taken into custody or otherwise deprived of his freedom of action in any significant way." *Id.*, at 444. The *Miranda* decision did not provide the Court with an opportunity to apply that test to a set of facts.

After *Miranda,* the Court first applied the custody test in *Oregon v. Mathiason,* 429 U.S. 492 (1977) *(per curiam).* In *Mathiason,* a police officer contacted the suspect after a burglary victim identified him. The officer arranged to meet the suspect at a nearby police station. At the outset of the questioning, the officer stated his belief that the suspect was involved in the burglary but that he was not under arrest. During the 30-minute interview, the suspect admitted his guilt. He was then allowed to leave. The Court held that the questioning was not custodial because there was "no indication that the questioning took place in a context where [the suspect's] freedom to depart was restricted in any way." *Id.*, at 495. The Court noted that the suspect had come voluntarily to the police station, that he was informed that he was not under arrest, and that he was allowed to leave at the end of the interview. *Ibid.*

In *California v. Beheler,* 463 U.S. 1121 (1983) *(per curiam),* the Court reached the same result in a case with facts similar to those in *Mathiason.* In *Beheler,* the state court had distinguished *Mathiason* based on what it described as differences in the totality of the circumstances. The police interviewed Beheler shortly after the crime occurred; Beheler had been drinking earlier in the day; he was emotionally distraught; he was well known to the police; and he was a parolee who knew it was necessary for him to cooperate with the police. 463 U.S., at 1124-1125. The Court agreed that "the circumstances of each case must certainly influence" the custody determination, but reemphasized that "the ultimate inquiry is simply whether there is a formal arrest or restraint on freedom of movement of the degree associated with a formal arrest." *Id.,* at 1125 (internal quotation marks omitted). The Court found the case indistinguishable from *Mathiason.* It noted that how much the police knew about the suspect and how much time had elapsed after the crime occurred were irrelevant to the custody inquiry. 463 U.S., at 1125.

Our more recent cases instruct that custody must be determined based on a how a reasonable person in the suspect's situation would perceive his circumstances. In *Berkemer v. McCarty,* 468 U.S. 420 (1984), a police officer stopped a suspected drunk driver and asked him some questions. Although the officer reached the decision to arrest the driver at the beginning of the traffic stop, he did not do so until the driver failed a sobriety test and acknowledged that he had been drinking beer and smoking marijuana. The Court held the traffic stop noncustodial despite the officer's intent to arrest because he had not communicated that intent to the driver. "A policeman's unarticulated plan has no bearing on the question whether a suspect was 'in custody' at a particular time," the Court explained. *Id.,* at 442. "[T]he only relevant inquiry is how a reasonable man in the suspect's position would have understood his situation." *Ibid.* In a footnote, the Court cited a New York state case for the view that an objective test was preferable to a subjective test in part because it does not "'place upon the police the burden of anticipating the frailties or idiosyncrasies of every person whom they question.'" *Id.,* at 442, n. 35 (quoting *People v. P.,* 21 N.Y. 2d 1, 9-10, 233 N.E. 2d 255, 260 (1967)).

Stansbury v. California, 511 U.S. 318 (1994) *(per curiam),* confirmed this analytical framework. *Stansbury* explained that "the initial determination of custody depends on the objective circumstances of the interrogation, not on the subjective views harbored by either the interrogating officers or the person being questioned." *Id.,* at 323. Courts must examine "all of the circumstances surrounding the interrogation" and determine "how a reasonable person in the position of the individual being questioned would gauge the breadth of his or her freedom of action." *Id.,* at 322, 325 (internal quotation marks and alteration omitted).

Finally, in *Thompson v. Keohane,* 516 U.S. 99 (1995), the Court offered the following description of the *Miranda* custody test: "Two discrete inquiries are essential to the determination: first, what were the circumstances surrounding the interrogation; and second, given those circumstances, would a reasonable person have felt he or she was not at liberty to terminate the interrogation and leave. Once the scene is set and the players' lines and actions are reconstructed, the court must apply an objective test to resolve the ultimate inquiry: was there a formal arrest or restraint on freedom of movement of the degree associated with a formal arrest." 516 U.S., at 112 (internal quotation marks omitted).

We turn now to the case before us and ask if the state-court adjudication of the claim "involved an unreasonable application" of clearly established law when it concluded that Alvarado was not in custody. 28 U.S.C. § 2254(d)(1). See *Williams,* 529 U.S., at 413 ("Under the 'unreasonable application' clause, a federal habeas court may grant the writ if the state court identifies the correct governing principle from this Court's decisions but unreasonably applies that principle to the facts of the prisoner's case"). The term "unreasonable" is "a common term in the legal world and, accordingly, federal judges are familiar with its meaning." *Id.*, at 410. At the same time, the range of reasonable judgment can depend in part on the nature of the relevant rule. If a legal rule is specific, the range may be narrow. Applications of the rule may be plainly correct or incorrect. Other rules are more general, and their meaning must emerge in application over the course of time. Applying a general standard to a specific case can demand a substantial element of judgment. As a result, evaluating whether a rule application was unreasonable requires considering the rule's specificity. The more general the rule, the more leeway courts have in reaching outcomes in case by case determinations. Cf. *Wright v. West,* 505 U.S. 277, 308-309 (1992) (Kennedy, J., concurring in judgment).

Based on these principles, we conclude that the state court's application of our clearly established law was reasonable. Ignoring the deferential standard of § 2254(d)(1) for the moment, it can be said that fair-minded jurists could disagree over whether Alvarado was in custody. On one hand, certain facts weigh against a finding that Alvarado was in custody. The police did not transport Alvarado to the station or require him to appear at a particular time. Cf. *Mathiason,* 429 U.S., at 495. They did not threaten him or suggest he would be placed under arrest. *Ibid.* Alvarado's parents remained in the lobby during the interview, suggesting that the interview would be brief. See *Berkemer,* 468 U.S., at 441-442. In fact, according to trial counsel for Alvarado, he and his parents were told that the interview was " 'not going to be long.' " App. 186. During the interview, Comstock focused on Soto's crimes rather than Alvarado's. Instead of pressuring Alvarado with the threat of arrest and prosecution, she appealed to his interest in telling the truth and being helpful to a police officer. Cf. *Mathiason,* 429 U.S., at 495. In addition, Comstock twice asked Alvarado if he wanted to take a break. At the end of the interview, Alvarado went home. *Ibid.* All of these objective facts are consistent with an interrogation environment in which a reasonable person would have felt free to terminate the interview and leave. Indeed, a number of the facts echo those of *Mathiason,* a *per curiam* summary reversal in which we found it "clear from these facts" that the suspect was not in custody. *Ibid.*

Other facts point in the opposite direction. Comstock interviewed Alvarado at the police station. The interview lasted two hours, four times longer than the 30-minute interview in *Mathiason.* Unlike the officer in *Mathiason,* Comstock did not tell Alvarado that he was free to leave. Alvarado was brought to the police station by his legal guardians rather than arriving on his own accord, making the extent of his control over his presence unclear. Counsel for Alvarado alleges that Alvarado's parents asked to be present at the interview but were rebuffed, a fact that—if known to Alvarado—might reasonably have led someone in Alvarado's position to feel more restricted than otherwise. These facts weigh in favor of the view that Alvarado was in custody.

These differing indications lead us to hold that the state court's application of our custody standard was reasonable. The Court of Appeals was nowhere close to the mark when it concluded otherwise. Although the question of what an "unreasonable application" of law might be difficult in some cases, it is not difficult here. The custody test is general, and the state court's application of our law fits within the matrix of our prior decisions. We cannot grant relief under AEDPA by conducting our own independent inquiry into whether the state court was correct as a *de novo* matter. "[A] federal habeas court may not issue the writ simply because that court concludes in its independent judgment that the state-court decision applied [the law] incorrectly." *Woodford v. Visciotti*, 537 U.S. 19, 24-25 (2002) *(per curiam)*. Relief is available under § 2254(d)(1) only if the state court's decision is objectively unreasonable. See *Williams, supra*, at 410; *Andrade*, 538 U.S., at 75. Under that standard, relief cannot be granted.

III

The Court of Appeals reached the opposite result by placing considerable reliance on Alvarado's age and inexperience with law enforcement. Our Court has not stated that a suspect's age or experience is relevant to the *Miranda* custody analysis, and counsel for Alvarado did not press the importance of either factor on direct appeal or in habeas proceedings. According to the Court of Appeals, however, our Court's emphasis on juvenile status in other contexts demanded consideration of Alvarado's age and inexperience here. The Court of Appeals viewed the state court's failure to "extend a clearly established legal principle [of the relevance of juvenile status] to a new context" as objectively unreasonable in this case, requiring issuance of the writ. 316 F. 3d, at 853 (quoting *Anthony v. Cambra*, 236 F. 3d 568, 578 (CA9 2000)).

The petitioner contends that if a habeas court must extend a rationale before it can apply to the facts at hand then the rationale cannot be clearly established at the time of the state-court decision. Brief for Petitioner 10-24. See also *Hawkins v. Alabama*, 318 F. 3d 1302, 1306, n. 3 (CA11 2003) (asserting a similar argument). There is force to this argument. Section 2254(d)(1) would be undermined if habeas courts introduced rules not clearly established under the guise of extensions to existing law. Cf. *Teague v. Lane*, 489 U.S. 288 (1989). At the same time, the difference between applying a rule and extending it is not always clear. Certain principles are fundamental enough that when new factual permutations arise, the necessity to apply the earlier rule will be beyond doubt.

This is not such a case, however. Our opinions applying the *Miranda* custody test have not mentioned the suspect's age, much less mandated its consideration. The only indications in the Court's opinions relevant to a suspect's experience with law enforcement have rejected reliance on such factors. See *Beheler*, 463 U.S., at 1125 (rejecting a lower court's view that the defendant's prior interview with the police was relevant to the custody inquiry); *Berkemer, supra*, at 442, n. 35 (citing *People v. P.*, 21 N. Y. 2d, at 9-10, 233 N. E. 2d, at 260, which noted the difficulties of a subjective test that would require police to "'anticipat[e] the frailties or idiosyncrasies of every person whom they question'"); 468 U.S., at 430-432 (describing a suspect's criminal past and police record as a circumstance "unknowable to the police").

There is an important conceptual difference between the *Miranda* custody test and the line of cases from other contexts considering age and experience. The *Miranda* custody inquiry is an objective test. As we stated in *Keohane*, "[o]nce the scene is set and the players' lines and actions are reconstructed, the court must apply an objective test to resolve the ultimate inquiry." 516 U.S., at 112 (internal quotation marks omitted). The objective test furthers "the clarity of [*Miranda*'s] rule," *Berkemer*, 468 U.S., at 430, ensuring that the police do not need "to make guesses as to [the circumstances] at issue before deciding how they may interrogate the suspect." *Id.*, at 431. To be sure, the line between permissible objective facts and impermissible subjective experiences can be indistinct in some cases. It is possible to subsume a subjective factor into an objective test by making the latter more specific in its formulation. Thus the Court of Appeals styled its inquiry as an objective test by considering what a "reasonable 17-year-old, with no prior history of arrest or police interviews" would perceive. 316 F. 3d, at 854-855.

At the same time, the objective *Miranda* custody inquiry could reasonably be viewed as different from doctrinal tests that depend on the actual mindset of a particular suspect, where we do consider a suspect's age and experience. For example, the voluntariness of a statement is often said to depend on whether "the defendant's will was overborne," *Lynumn v. Illinois,* 372 U.S. 528, 534 (1963), a question that logically can depend on "the characteristics of the accused." *Schneckloth v. Bustamonte,* 412 U.S. 218, 226 (1973). The characteristics of the accused can include the suspect's age, education, and intelligence, see *ibid.,* as well as a suspect's prior experience with law enforcement, see *Lynumn, supra,* at 534. In concluding that there was "no principled reason" why such factors should not also apply to the *Miranda* custody inquiry, 316 F. 3d, at 850, the Court of Appeals ignored the argument that the custody inquiry states an objective rule designed to give clear guidance to the police, while consideration of a suspect's individual characteristics—including his age—could be viewed as creating a subjective inquiry. Cf. *Mathiason,* 429 U.S., at 495-496 (noting that facts arguably relevant to whether an environment is coercive may have "nothing to do with whether respondent was in custody for purposes of the *Miranda* rule"). For these reasons, the state court's failure to consider Alvarado's age does not provide a proper basis for finding that the state court's decision was an unreasonable application of clearly established law.

Indeed, reliance on Alvarado's prior history with law enforcement was improper not only under the deferential standard of 28 U.S.C. § 2254(d)(1), but also as a *de novo* matter. In most cases, police officers will not know a suspect's interrogation history. See *Berkemer, supra,* at 430-431. Even if they do, the relationship between a suspect's past experiences and the likelihood a reasonable person with that experience would feel free to leave often will be speculative. True, suspects with prior law enforcement experience may understand police procedures and reasonably feel free to leave unless told otherwise. On the other hand, they may view past as prologue and expect another in a string of arrests. We do not ask police officers to consider these contingent psychological factors when deciding when suspects should be advised of their *Miranda* rights. See *Berkemer, supra,* at 431-432. The inquiry turns too much on the suspect's subjective state of mind and not enough on the "objective circumstances of the interrogation." *Stansbury,* 511 U.S., at 323.

The state court considered the proper factors and reached a reasonable conclusion. The judgment of the Court of Appeals is

Reversed.

Justice Breyer, with whom *Justice Stevens, Justice Souter,* and *Justice Ginsburg* join, dissenting. In my view, Michael Alvarado clearly was "in custody" when the police questioned him (without *Miranda* warnings) about the murder of Francisco Castaneda. To put the question in terms of federal law's well-established legal standards: Would a "reasonable person" in Alvarado's "position" have felt he was "at liberty to terminate the interrogation and leave"? *Thompson v. Keohane,* 516 U.S. 99, 112 (1995); *Stansbury v. California* 511 U.S. 318, 325 (1994) *(per curiam).* A court must answer this question in light of "all of the circumstances surrounding the interrogation." *Id.,* at 322. And the obvious answer here is "no."

I

A

The law in this case asks judges to apply, not arcane or complex legal directives, but ordinary common sense. Would a reasonable person in Alvarado's position have felt free simply to get up and walk out of the small room in the station house at will during his 2-hour police interrogation? I ask the reader to put himself, or herself, in Alvarado's circumstances and then answer that question: Alvarado hears from his parents that he is needed for police questioning. His parents take him to the station. On arrival, a police officer separates him from his parents. His parents ask to come along, but the officer says they may not. App. 185-186. Another officer says, " 'What do we have here; we are going to question a suspect.' " *Id.*, at 189.

The police take Alvarado to a small interrogation room, away from the station's public area. A single officer begins to question him, making clear in the process that the police have evidence that he participated in an attempted carjacking connected with a murder. When he says that he never saw any shooting, the officer suggests that he is lying, while adding that she is "giving [him] the opportunity to tell the truth" and "tak[e] care of [him]self." *Id.*, at 102, 105. Toward the end of the questioning, the officer gives him permission to take a bathroom or water break. After two hours, by which time he has admitted he was involved in the attempted theft, knew about the gun, and helped to hide it, the questioning ends.

What reasonable person in the circumstances—brought to a police station by his parents at police request, put in a small interrogation room, questioned for a solid two hours, and confronted with claims that there is strong evidence that he participated in a serious crime—could have thought to himself, "Well, anytime I want to leave I can just get up and walk out"? If the person harbored any doubts, would he still think he might be free to leave once he recalls that the police officer has just refused to let his parents remain with him during questioning? Would he still think that he, rather than the officer, controls the situation?

There is only one possible answer to these questions. A reasonable person would *not* have thought he was free simply to pick up and leave in the middle of the interrogation. I believe the California courts were clearly wrong to hold the contrary, and the Ninth Circuit was right in concluding that those state courts unreasonably applied clearly established federal law. See 28 U.S.C. § 2254(d)(1).

B

What about the majority's view that "fair-minded jurists could disagree over whether Alvarado was in custody"? *Ante,* at 10. Consider each of the facts it says "weigh against a finding" of custody:

1. "*The police did not transport Alvarado to the station or require him to appear at a particular time.*" *Ibid.* True. His parents brought him to the station at police request. But why does that matter? The relevant question is whether Alvarado came to the station of his own free will or submitted to questioning voluntarily. Cf. *Oregon v. Mathiason,* 429 U.S. 492, 493-495 (1977) *(per curiam); California v. Beheler,* 463 U.S. 1121, 1122-1123 (1983) *(per curiam); Thompson, supra,* at 118 *(Thomas,* J., dissenting). And the involvement of Alvarado's parents suggests *in*voluntary, not voluntary, behavior on Alvarado's part.

2. "*Alvarado's parents remained in the lobby during the interview, suggesting that the interview would be brief. In fact, [Alvarado] and his parents were told that the interview 'was not going*

to be long.'" Ante, at 10-11 (citation omitted). Whatever was communicated to Alvarado *before* the questioning began, the fact is that the interview was not brief, nor, after the first half hour or so, would Alvarado have expected it to be brief. And those are the relevant considerations. See *Berkemer v. McCarty,* 468 U.S. 420, 441 (1984).

3. *"At the end of the interview, Alvarado went home." Ante,* at 11. As the majority acknowledges, our recent case law makes clear that the relevant question is how a reasonable person would have gauged his freedom to leave *during,* not *after,* the interview. See *ante,* at 9 (citing *Stansbury, supra,* at 325).

4. *"During the interview, [Officer] Comstock focused on Soto's crimes rather than Alvarado's." Ante,* at 11. In fact, the police officer characterized Soto as the ringleader, while making clear that she knew Alvarado had participated in the attempted carjacking during which Castaneda was killed. See App. 102-103, 109. Her questioning would have reinforced, not diminished, Alvarado's fear that he was not simply a witness, but also suspected of having been involved in a serious crime. See *Stansbury,* 511 U.S., at 325.

5. *"[The officer did not] pressur[e] Alvarado with the threat of arrest and prosecution . . . [but instead] appealed to his interest in telling the truth and being helpful to a police officer." Ante,* at 11. This factor might be highly significant were the question one of "coercion." But it is not. The question is whether Alvarado would have felt free to terminate the interrogation and leave. In respect to that question, police politeness, while commendable, does not significantly help the majority.

6. *"Comstock twice asked Alvarado if he wanted to take a break." Ibid.* This circumstance, emphasizing the officer's control of Alvarado's movements, makes it *less* likely, not *more* likely, that Alvarado would have thought he was free to leave at will.

The facts to which the majority points make clear what the police did *not* do, for example, come to Alvarado's house, tell him he was under arrest, handcuff him, place him in a locked cell, threaten him, or tell him explicitly that he was not free to leave. But what is important here is what the police *did* do—namely, have Alvarado's parents bring him to the station, put him with a single officer in a small room, keep his parents out, let him know that he was a suspect, and question him for two hours. These latter facts compel a single conclusion: A reasonable person in Alvarado's circumstances would *not* have felt free to terminate the interrogation and leave.

C

What about Alvarado's youth? The fact that Alvarado was 17 helps to show that he was unlikely to have felt free to ignore his parents' request to come to the station. See *Schall v. Martin,* 467 U.S. 253, 265 (1984) (juveniles assumed "to be subject to the control of their parents"). And a 17-year-old is more likely than, say, a 35-year-old, to take a police officer's assertion of authority to keep parents outside the room as an assertion of authority to keep their child inside as well.

The majority suggests that the law might *prevent* a judge from taking account of the fact that Alvarado was 17. See *ante,* at 13-14. I can find nothing in the law that supports that conclusion. Our cases do instruct lower courts to apply a "reasonable person" standard. But the "reasonable person" standard does not require a court to pretend that Alvarado was a 35-year-old with aging parents whose middle-aged children do what their parents ask only out of respect. Nor does it say that a court should pretend that Alvarado was the statistically determined "average person"—a working, married, 35-year-old white female with a high school degree. See U.S. Dept. of Commerce, Bureau of Census, Statistical Abstract of the United States: 2003 (123d ed.).

Rather, the precise legal definition of "reasonable person" may, depending on legal context, appropriately account for certain personal characteristics. In negligence suits, for example, the question is what would a "reasonable person" do " 'under the same or similar circumstances.' " In answering that question, courts enjoy "latitude" and may make "allowance not only for external facts, but sometimes for certain characteristics of the actor himself," including physical disability, youth, or advanced age. W. Keeton, D. Dobbs, R. Keeton, & D. Owen, Prosser and Keeton on Law of Torts § 32, pp. 174–179 (5th ed. 1984); see id., at 179-181; see also Restatement (Third) of Torts § 10, Comment b, pp. 128–130 (Tent. Draft No. 1, Mar. 28, 2001) (all American jurisdictions count a person's childhood as a "relevant circumstance" in negligence determinations). This allowance makes sense in light of the tort standard's recognized purpose: deterrence. Given that purpose, why pretend that a child is an adult or that a blind man can see? See O. Holmes, The Common Law 85–89 (M. Howe ed. 1963).

In the present context, that of *Miranda*'s "in custody" inquiry, the law has introduced the concept of a "reasonable person" to avoid judicial inquiry into subjective states of mind, and to focus the inquiry instead upon objective circumstances that are known to both the officer and the suspect and that are likely relevant to the way a person would understand his situation. See *Stansbury, supra*, at 323-325; *Berkemer*, 468 U.S., at 442, and n. 35. This focus helps to keep *Miranda* a workable rule. See *Berkemer, supra*, at 430-431.

In this case, Alvarado's youth is an objective circumstance that was known to the police. It is not a special quality, but rather a widely shared characteristic that generates common-sense conclusions about behavior and perception. To focus on the circumstance of age in a case like this does not complicate the "in custody" inquiry. And to say that courts should ignore widely shared, objective characteristics, like age, on the ground that only a (large) *minority* of the population possesses them would produce absurd results, the present instance being a case in point. I am not surprised that the majority points to no case suggesting any such limitation. Cf. *Alvarado v. Hickman*, 316 F. 3d 841, 848, 851, n. 5 (CA9 2002) (listing 12 cases from 12 different jurisdictions suggesting the contrary).

Nor am I surprised that the majority makes no real argument at all explaining *why* any court would believe that the objective fact of a suspect's age could *never* be relevant. But see *ante*, at 1 (*O'Connor*, J., concurring) ("There may be cases in which a suspect's age will be relevant to the *Miranda* 'custody' inquiry"). The majority does discuss a suspect's "history with law enforcement," *ante*, at 15—a bright red herring in the present context where Alvarado's youth (an objective fact) simply helps to show (with the help of a legal presumption) that his appearance at the police station was not voluntary. See *supra*, at 5.

II

As I have said, the law in this case is clear. This Court's cases establish that, even if the police do not tell a suspect he is under arrest, do not handcuff him, do not lock him in a cell, and do not threaten him, he may nonetheless reasonably believe he is not free to leave the place of questioning—and thus be in custody for *Miranda* purposes. See *Stansbury*, 511 U.S., at 325-326; *Berkemer, supra*, at 440.

Our cases also make clear that to determine how a suspect would have "gaug[ed]" his "freedom of movement," a court must carefully examine "all of the circumstances surrounding the interrogation," *Stansbury, supra,* at 322, 325 (internal quotation marks omitted), including, for example, how long the interrogation lasted (brief and routine or protracted?), see, *e.g., Berkemer, supra,* at 441; how the suspect came to be questioned (voluntarily or against his will?), see, *e.g., Mathiason,* 429 U.S., at 495; where the questioning took place (at a police station or in public?), see, *e.g., Berkemer, supra,* at 438-439; and what the officer communicated to the individual during the interrogation (that he was a suspect? that he was under arrest? that he was free to leave at will?) see, *e.g., Stansbury, supra,* at 325. In the present case, every one of these factors argues—and argues strongly—that Alvarado was in custody for *Miranda* purposes when the police questioned him.

Common sense, and an understanding of the law's basic purpose in this area, are enough to make clear that Alvarado's age—an objective, widely shared characteristic about which the police plainly knew—is also relevant to the inquiry. Cf. *Kaupp v. Texas,* 538 U.S. 626, 629-631 (2003) *(per curiam).* Unless one is prepared to pretend that Alvarado is someone he is not, a middle-aged gentleman, well-versed in police practices, it seems to me clear that the California courts made a serious mistake. I agree with the Ninth Circuit's similar conclusions. Consequently, I dissent.

CHAPTER 6

DETENTION OF JUVENILES PRIOR TO ADJUDICATION

Introduction

This chapter deals with the issue of juvenile detention and the related issue of right to bail. After a child is taken into custody, regardless of whether the offense involves a delinquent act or merely a status offense like truancy or runaway, it is necessary for the juvenile court to determine whether the child should be released to the parent or guardian or detained in shelter care. In the past, far too many children were routinely placed in detention to await court appearances. At the same time, detention facilities were inadequate, and in many parts of the country, jails were used to detain juvenile offenders. Although this situation may continue to some degree, the thrust in recent years has been to reduce the number of children placed in detention. In practice, upon arrest and after being detained, the child is usually released to the parent or guardian. It is important to note that most jurisdictions require immediate notice to the parents after the child has been arrested. The statutes ordinarily also require a hearing on detention if the initial decision is to keep the child in custody. At a detention hearing, the child has a right to counsel and is generally given other procedural due process safeguards, notably the privilege against self-incrimination and the right to confront and cross-examine witnesses.

Most state juvenile court acts provide criteria that support a decision not to release the child. These criteria include: (1) the need to protect the child, (2) whether the child presents a serious danger to the public, and (3) the likelihood of whether the juvenile will return to court for adjudication. Unlike the adult system, in which the sole criterion for pretrial release is availability for trial, the juvenile may be detained for other reasons, including his or her own protection. Normally, the finding of the judge that the child be detained should be supported by evidence.

If the child is to be detained, the question of bail arises. Here, the statutes and cases vary widely. Some states' statutes allow release on bail for juveniles, while others provide no such statutory procedure. Many states have juvenile code provisions that emphasize the release of the child to the parents as an acceptable substitute to bail. The law is also unclear as to whether juveniles have a state or federal constitutional right to bail. Some courts have found it unnecessary to rule on this issue because liberal statutory release provisions act as an appropriate alternative to the bail process.

Preventitive Detention

Case Comment

Pretrial detention is considered a critical area of juvenile justice since it often involves the incarceration of minors who have not yet been adjudicated as delinquent. In *Sprowal v. Hendrick,* a boy sought release from a detention center via a *habeas corpus* petition. The trial judge had claimed that during the detention hearing, the youth's friends had threatened the court and had based the detention on that fact. The Pennsylvania Supreme Court reversed the decision and ruled that the detention of a child must be based on a lack of parental supervision, a threat of running away, or a need for treatment. In other words, detention cannot be used capriciously.

Preventive detention refers to the practice of keeping a person in custody before trial because of his or her suspected danger to the community.

Most state jurisdictions allow judges to deny bail to adult offenders only in cases involving capital murder or murder, when the offender has jumped bail in the past, or when the offender has committed another offense while on bail. However, every state allows preventive detention of juveniles. The reason for this discrepancy hinges on the legal principle that while adults have a fundamental right to liberty, juveniles have a right to custody and protection. Therefore, it is not unreasonable to detain juveniles for their own protection while awaiting their hearing in a juvenile or family court.

In *Schall v. Martin,* the U.S. Supreme Court upheld the state's right to place juveniles in preventive detention. It held that preventive detention serves the legitimate objective of protecting both the juvenile and society from pretrial crime. Pretrial detention need not be considered punishment merely because the juvenile is eventually released without being adjudicated a delinquent or placed on probation following the determination that he or she was adjudged to be a delinquent offender.

Schall v. Martin established the authority of juvenile court judges to deny youths pretrial release if the juvenile was perceived to be "dangerous." However, the case also established a due process standard for detention hearings that includes notice and a statement of substantial reasons for the detention.

SCHALL V. MARTIN

Supreme Court of the United States, 1984.

467 U.S. 253.

Justice Rehnquist delivered the opinion of the Court.

Section 320.5(3)(b) of the New York Family Court Act [FCA] authorizes pretrial detention of an accused juvenile delinquent based on a finding that there is a "serious risk" that the child "may before the return date commit an act which if committed by an adult would constitute a crime."[1] Appellees brought suit on behalf of a class of all juveniles detained pursuant to that provision.[2] The District Court struck down 320.5(3)(b) as permitting detention without due process of law and ordered the immediate release of all class members. *United States ex rel. Martin v. Strasburg*, 513 F. Supp. 691 (SDNY 1981). The Court of Appeals for the Second Circuit affirmed, holding the provision "unconstitutional as to all juveniles" because the statute is administered in such a way that "the detention period serves as punishment imposed without proof of guilt established according to the requisite constitutional standard." *Martin v. Strasburg*, 689 F.2d 365, 373-374 (1982). We noted probable jurisdiction, 460 U.S. 1079 (1983),[3] and now reverse. We conclude that preventive detention under the FCA serves a legitimate state objective, and that the procedural protections afforded pretrial de-

---

1. New York Jud. Law 320.5 (McKinney 1983) (Family Court Act (hereinafter FCA)) provides, in relevant part:
   (1) "At the initial appearance, the court in its discretion may release the respondent or direct his detention.

   * * * *

   (3) "The court shall not direct detention unless it finds and states the facts and reasons for so finding that unless the respondent is detained;
   "(a) there is a substantial probability that he will not appear in court on the return date; or
   "(b) there is a serious risk that he may before the return date commit an act which if committed by an adult would constitute a crime."

Appellees have only challenged pretrial detention under 320.5(3)(b). Thus, the propriety of detention to ensure that a juvenile appears in court on the return date, pursuant to 320.5(3)(a), is not before the Court.

2. The original challenge was to 739(a)(ii) of the FCA, which, at the time of the commencement of this suit, governed pretrial release or detention of both alleged juvenile delinquents and persons in need of supervision. Effective July 1, 1983, a new Article 3 to the Act governs, inter alia, "all juvenile delinquency actions and proceedings commenced upon or after the effective date thereof and all appeals and other post-judgment proceedings relating or attaching thereto." FCA 301.3(1). Article 7 now applies only to proceedings concerning persons in need of supervision.

Obviously, this Court must "review the judgment below in light of the . . . statute as it now stands, not as it once did." *Hall v. Beals*, 396 U.S. 45, 48 (1969). But since new Article 3 contains a preventive detention section identical to former 739(a)(ii), see FCA 320.5(3), the appeal is not moot. *Brockington v. Rhodes*, 396 U.S. 41, 43 (1969).

3. Although the pretrial detention of the class representatives has long since ended, see infra, at 257-261, this case is not moot for the same reason that the class action in *Gerstein v. Pugh*, 420 U.S. 103, 110, n. 11 (1975), was not mooted by the termination of the claims of the named plaintiffs.

"Pretrial detention is by nature temporary, and it is most unlikely that any given individual could have his constitutional claim decided on appeal before he is either released or convicted. The individual could nonetheless suffer repeated deprivations, and it is certain that other persons similarly situated will be detained under the allegedly unconstitutional procedures. The claim, in short, is one that is distinctly 'capable of repetition, yet evading review.'"

See also *People ex rel. Wayburn v. Schupf*, 39 N.Y. 2d 682, 686-687, 350 N. E. 2d 906, 907-908 (1976).

tainees by the New York statute satisfy the requirements of the Due Process Clause of the Fourteenth Amendment to the United States Constitution.

I

Appellee Gregory Martin was arrested on December 13th, 1977, and charged with first-degree robbery, second-degree assault, and criminal possession of a weapon based on an incident in which he, with two others, allegedly hit a youth on the head with a loaded gun and stole his jacket and sneakers. Martin had possession of the gun when he was arrested. He was 14 years old at the time and, therefore, came within the jurisdiction of New York's Family Court.[4] The incident occurred at 11:30 at night, and Martin lied to the police about where and with whom he lived. He was consequently detained overnight.[5]

A petition of delinquency was filed,[6] and Martin made his "initial appearance" in Family Court on December 14th, accompanied by his grandmother.[7] The Family Court Judge, citing the possession of the loaded weapon, the false address given to the police, and the lateness of the hour, as evidencing a lack of supervision, ordered Martin detained under 320.5(3)(b) (at that time 739(a)(ii); see n. 2, supra). A probable-cause hearing was held five

---

4. In New York, a child over the age of 7 but less than 16 is not considered criminally responsible for his conduct. FCA 301.2(1). If he commits an act that would constitute a crime if committed by an adult, he comes under the exclusive jurisdiction of the Family Court. 302.1(1). That court is charged not with finding guilt and affixing punishment, *In re Bogart*, 45 Misc. 2d 1075, 259 N. Y. S. 2d 351 (1963), but rather with determining and pursuing the needs and best interests of the child insofar as those are consistent with the need for the protection of the community. FCA 301.1. See *In re Craig S.*, 57 App. Div. 2d 761, 394 N.Y.S. 2d 200 (1977). Juvenile proceedings are, thus, civil rather than criminal, although because of the restrictions that may be placed on a juvenile adjudged delinquent, some of the same protections afforded accused adult criminals are also applicable in this context. Cf. FCA 303.1.

5. When a juvenile is arrested, the arresting officer must immediately notify the parent or other person legally responsible for the child's care. FCA 305.2(3). Ordinarily, the child will be released into the custody of his parent or guardian after being issued an "appearance ticket" requiring him to meet with the probation service on a specified day. 307.1(1). See n. 9, infra. If, however, he is charged with a serious crime, one of several designated felonies, see 301.2(8), or if his parent or guardian cannot be reached, the juvenile may be taken directly before the Family Court. 305.2. The Family Court judge will make a preliminary determination as to the jurisdiction of the court, appoint a law guardian for the child, and advise the child of his or her rights, including the right to counsel and the right to remain silent.

Only if, as in Martin's case, the Family Court is not in session and special circumstances exist, such as an inability to notify the parents, will the child be taken directly by the arresting officer to a juvenile detention facility. 305.2(4)(c). If the juvenile is so detained, he must be brought before the Family Court within 72 hours or the next day the court is in session, whichever is sooner. 307.3(4). The propriety of such detention, prior to a juvenile's initial appearance in Family Court, is not at issue in this case. Appellees challenged only judicially ordered detention pursuant to 320.5(3)(b).

6. A delinquency petition, prepared by the "presentment agency," originates delinquency proceedings. FCA 310.1. The petition must contain, inter alia, a precise statement of each crime charged and factual allegations which "clearly apprise" the juvenile of the conduct which is the subject of the accusation. 311.1. A petition is not deemed sufficient unless the allegations of the factual part of the petition, together with those of any supporting depositions which may accompany it, provide reasonable cause to believe that the juvenile committed the crime or crimes charged. 311.2(2). Also, nonhearsay allegations in the petition and supporting deposition must establish, if true, every element of each crime charged and the juvenile's commission thereof. 311.2(3). The sufficiency of a petition may be tested by filing a motion to dismiss under 315.1.

7. The first proceeding in Family Court following the filing of the petition is known as the initial appearance even if the juvenile has already been brought before the court immediately following his arrest. FCA 320.2.

days later, on December 19th, and probable cause was found to exist for all the crimes charged. At the factfinding hearing held December 27th–29th, Martin was found guilty on the robbery and criminal possession charges. He was adjudicated a delinquent and placed on two years' probation.[8] He had been detained pursuant to 320.5(3)(b), between the initial appearance and the completion of the factfinding hearing, for a total of 15 days.

Appellees Luis Rosario and Kenneth Morgan, both age 14, were also ordered detained pending their factfinding hearings. Rosario was charged with attempted first-degree robbery and second-degree assault for an incident in which he, with four others, allegedly tried to rob two men, putting a gun to the head of one of them and beating both about the head with sticks. See Petitioners' Exhibit 2b. At the time of his initial appearance, on March 15th, 1978, Rosario had another delinquency petition pending for knifing a student, and two prior petitions had been adjusted.[9] Probable cause was found on March 21st. On April 11, Rosario was released to his father, and the case was terminated without adjustment on September 25th, 1978.

Kenneth Morgan was charged with attempted robbery and attempted grand larceny for an incident in which he and another boy allegedly tried to steal money from a 14-year-old girl and her brother by threatening to blow their heads off and grabbing them to search their pockets. See Petitioners' Exhibit 3b. Morgan, like Rosario, was on release status on another petition (for robbery and criminal possession of stolen property) at the time of his initial appearance on March 27th, 1978. He had been arrested four previous times, and his mother

---

8. The "factfinding" is the juvenile's analogue of a trial. As in the earlier proceedings, the juvenile has a right to counsel at this hearing. 341.2. See *In re Gault*, 387 U.S. 1 (1967). Evidence may be suppressed on the same grounds as in criminal cases, FCA 330.2, and proof of guilt, based on the record evidence, must be beyond a reasonable doubt, 342.2. See *In re Winship*, 397 U.S. 358 (1970). If guilt is established, the court enters an appropriate order and schedules a dispositional hearing. 345.1.

The dispositional hearing is the final and most important proceeding in the Family Court. If the juvenile has committed a designated felony, the court must order a probation investigation and a diagnostic assessment. 351.1. Any other material and relevant evidence may be offered by the probation agency or the juvenile. Both sides may call and cross-examine witnesses and recommend specific dispositional alternatives. 350.4. The court must find, based on a preponderance of the evidence, 350.3(2), that the juvenile is delinquent and requires supervision, treatment, or confinement. 352.1. Otherwise, the petition is dismissed. Ibid.

If the juvenile is found to be delinquent, then the court enters an order of disposition. Possible alternatives include a conditional discharge; probation for up to two years; nonsecure placement with, perhaps, a relative or the Division for Youth; transfer to the Commissioner of Mental Health; or secure placement. 353.1-353.5. Unless the juvenile committed one of the designated felonies, the court must order the least restrictive available alternative consistent with the needs and best interests of the juvenile and the need for protection of the community. 352.2(2).

9. Every accused juvenile is interviewed by a member of the staff of the Probation Department. This process is known as "probation intake." See Testimony of Mr. Benjamin (Supervisor, New York Dept. of Probation), App. 142. In the course of the interview, which lasts an average of 45 minutes, the probation officer will gather what information he can about the nature of the case, the attitudes of the parties involved, and the child's past history and current family circumstances. Id., at 144, 153. His sources of information are the child, his parent or guardian, the arresting officer, and any records of past contacts between the child and the Family Court. On the basis of this interview, the probation officer may attempt to "adjust," or informally resolve, the case. FCA 308.1(2). Adjustment is a purely voluntary process in which the complaining witness agrees not to press the case further, while the juvenile is given a warning or agrees to counseling sessions or, perhaps, referral to a community agency. 308.1 (Practice Commentary). In cases involving designated felonies or other serious crimes, adjustment is not permitted without written approval of the Family Court. 308.1(4). If a case is not informally adjusted, it is referred to the "presentment agency." See n. 6, supra.

refused to come to court because he had been in trouble so often she did not want him home. A probable-cause hearing was set for March 30th, but was continued until April 4, when it was combined with a factfinding hearing. Morgan was found guilty of harassment and petit larceny and was ordered placed with the Department of Social Services for 18 months. He was detained a total of eight days between his initial appearance and the factfinding hearing.

On December 21st, 1977, while still in preventive detention pending his factfinding hearing, Gregory Martin instituted a habeas corpus class action on behalf of "those persons who are, or during the pendency of this action will be, preventively detained pursuant to" 320.5(3)(b) of the FCA. Rosario and Morgan were subsequently added as additional named plaintiffs. These three class representatives sought a declaratory judgment that 320.5(3)(b) violates the Due Process and Equal Protection Clauses of the Fourteenth Amendment.

In an unpublished opinion, the District Court certified the class. App. 20-32.[10] The court also held that appellees were not required to exhaust their state remedies before resorting to federal habeas because the highest state court had already rejected an identical challenge to the juvenile preventive detention statute. See *People ex rel. Wayburn v. Schupf,* 39 NY. 2d 682, 350 NE. 2d 906 (1976). Exhaustion of state remedies, therefore, would be "an exercise in futility." App. 26.

At trial, appellees offered in evidence the case histories of 34 members of the class, including the three named petitioners. Both parties presented some general statistics on the relation between pretrial detention and ultimate disposition. In addition, there was testimony concerning juvenile proceedings from a number of witnesses, including a legal aid attorney specializing in juvenile cases, a probation supervisor, a child psychologist, and a Family Court Judge. On the basis of this evidence, the District Court rejected the equal protection challenge as "insubstantial,"[11] but agreed with appellees that pretrial detention under the FCA violates due process.[12] The court ordered that "all class members in custody pursuant to Family Court Act Section [320.5(3)(b)] shall be released forthwith." Id., at 93.

---

10. We have never decided whether Federal Rule of Civil Procedure 23, providing for class actions, is applicable to petitions for habeas corpus relief. See *Bell v. Wolfish,* 441 U.S. 520, 527, n. 6 (1979); *Middendorf v. Henry,* 425 U.S. 25, 30 (1976). Although appellants contested the class certification in the District Court, they did not raise the issue on appeal; nor do they urge it here. Again, therefore, we have no occasion to reach the question.

11. The equal protection claim, which was neither raised on appeal nor decided by the Second Circuit, is not before us.

12. The District Court gave three reasons for this conclusion. First, under the FCA, a juvenile may be held in pretrial detention for up to five days without any judicial determination of probable cause. Relying on *Gerstein v. Pugh,* 420 U.S., at 114, the District Court concluded that pretrial detention without a prior adjudication of probable cause is, itself, a per se violation of due process. *United States ex rel. Martin v. Strasburg,* 513 F. Supp. 691, 717 (SDNY 1981).

Second, after a review of the pertinent scholarly literature, the court noted that "no diagnostic tools have as yet been devised which enable even the most highly trained criminologists to predict reliably which juveniles will engage in violent crime." Id., at 708. A fortiori, the court concluded, a Family Court judge cannot make a reliable prediction based on the limited information available to him at the initial appearance. Id., at 712. Moreover, the court felt that the trial record was "replete" with examples of arbitrary and capricious detentions. Id., at 713.

Finally, the court concluded that preventive detention is merely a euphemism for punishment imposed without an adjudication of guilt. The alleged purpose of the detention—to protect society from the juvenile's criminal conduct—is indistinguishable from the purpose of post-trial detention. And given "the inability of trial judges to predict which juveniles will commit crimes," there is no rational connection between the decision to detain and the alleged purpose, even if that purpose were legitimate. Id., at 716.

The Court of Appeals affirmed. After reviewing the trial record, the court opined that "the vast majority of juveniles detained under [320.5(3)(b)] either have their petitions dismissed before an adjudication of delinquency or are released after adjudication." 689 F.2d, at 369. The court concluded from that fact that 320.5(3)(b) "is utilized principally, not for preventive purposes, but to impose punishment for unadjudicated criminal acts." Id., at 372. The early release of so many of those detained contradicts any asserted need for pretrial confinement to protect the community. The court therefore concluded that 320.5(3)(b) must be declared unconstitutional as to all juveniles. Individual litigation would be a practical impossibility because the periods of detention are so short that the litigation is mooted before the merits are determined.[13]

II

There is no doubt that the Due Process Clause is applicable in juvenile proceedings. "The problem," we have stressed, "is to ascertain the precise impact of the due process requirement upon such proceedings." *In re Gault,* 387 U.S. 1, 13–14 (1967). We have held that certain basic constitutional protections enjoyed by adults accused of crimes also apply to juveniles. See id., at 31–57 (notice of charges, right to counsel, privilege against self-incrimination, right to confrontation and cross-examination); *In re Winship,* 397 U.S. 358 (1970) (proof beyond a reasonable doubt); *Breed v. Jones,* 421 U.S. 519 (1975) (double jeopardy). But the Constitution does not mandate elimination of all differences in the treatment of juveniles. See, e.g., *McKeiver v. Pennsylvania,* 403 U.S. 528 (1971) (no right to jury trial). The State has "a parens patriae interest in preserving and promoting the welfare of the child," *Santosky v. Kramer,* 455 U.S. 745, 766 (1982), which makes a juvenile proceeding fundamentally different from an adult criminal trial. We have tried, therefore, to strike a balance—to respect the "informality" and "flexibility" that characterize juvenile proceedings, *In re Winship,* supra, at 366, and yet to ensure that such proceedings comport with the "fundamental fairness" demanded by the Due Process Clause. *Breed v. Jones,* supra, at 531; *McKeiver,* supra, at 543 (plurality opinion).

The statutory provision at issue in these cases, 320.5(3)(b), permits a brief pretrial detention based on a finding of a "serious risk" that an arrested juvenile may commit a crime before his return date. The question before us is whether preventive detention of juveniles pursuant to 320.5(3)(b) is compatible with the "fundamental fairness" required by due process. Two separate inquiries are necessary to answer this question. First, does preventive detention under the New York statute serve a legitimate state objective? See *Bell v. Wolfish,* 441 U.S. 520, 534, n. 15 (1979); *Kennedy v. Mendoza-Martinez,* 372 U.S. 144, 168–169 (1963). And, second, are the procedural safeguards contained in the FCA adequate to authorize the

---

13. Judge Newman concurred separately. He was not convinced that the record supported the majority's statistical conclusions. But he thought that the statute was procedurally infirm because it granted unbridled discretion to Family Court judges to make an inherently uncertain prediction of future criminal behavior. 689 F.2d, at 377.

pretrial detention of at least some juveniles charged with crimes? See *Mathews v. Eldridge,* 424 U.S. 319, 335 (1976); *Gerstein v. Pugh,* 420 U.S. 103, 114 (1975).

A

Preventive detention under the FCA is purportedly designed to protect the child and society from the potential consequences of his criminal acts. *People ex rel. Wayburn v. Schupf,* 39 N. Y. 2d, at 689–690, 350 N. E. 2d, at 910. When making any detention decision, the Family Court judge is specifically directed to consider the needs and best interests of the juvenile as well as the need for the protection of the community. FCA 301.1; *In re Craig S.,* 57 App. Div. 2d 761, 394 N. Y. S. 2d 200 (1977). In *Bell v. Wolfish, supra,* at 534, n. 15, we left open the question whether any governmental objective other than ensuring a detainee's presence at trial may constitutionally justify pretrial detention. As an initial matter, therefore, we must decide whether, in the context of the juvenile system, the combined interest in protecting both the community and the juvenile himself from the consequences of future criminal conduct is sufficient to justify such detention.

The "legitimate and compelling state interest" in protecting the community from crime cannot be doubted. *De Veau v. Braisted,* 363 U.S. 144, 155 (1960). See also *Terry v. Ohio,* 392 U.S. 1, 22 (1968). We have stressed before that crime prevention is "a weighty social objective," *Brown v. Texas,* 443 U.S. 47, 52 (1979), and this interest persists undiluted in the juvenile context. See *In re Gault, supra,* at 20, n. 26. The harm suffered by the victim of a crime is not dependent upon the age of the perpetrator.[14] And the harm to society generally may even be greater in this context given the high rate of recidivism among juveniles. *In re Gault, supra,* at 22.

The juvenile's countervailing interest in freedom from institutional restraints, even for the brief time involved here, is undoubtedly substantial as well. See *In re Gault, supra,* at 27. But that interest must be qualified by the recognition that juveniles, unlike adults, are always in some form of custody. *Lehman v. Lycoming County Children's Services,* 458 U.S. 502, 510–511 (1982); *In re Gault, supra,* at 17. Children, by definition, are not assumed to have the capacity to take care of themselves. They are assumed to be subject to the control of their parents, and if parental control falters, the State must play its part as *parens patriae.* See *State v. Gleason,* 404 A. 2d 573, 580 (Me. 1979); *People ex rel. Wayburn v. Schupf, supra,* at 690, 350 N. E. 2d, at 910; *Baker v. Smith,* 477 S. W. 2d 149, 150–151 (Ky. App. 1971). In this respect, the juvenile's liberty interest may, in appropriate circumstances, be subordinated to the State's "parens patriae interest in preserving and promoting the welfare of the child." *Santosky v. Kramer, supra,* at 766.

The New York Court of Appeals, in upholding the statute at issue here, stressed at some length "the desirability of protecting the juvenile from his own folly." *People ex rel. Wayburn*

---

14. In 1982, juveniles under 16 accounted for 7.5 percent of all arrests for violent crimes, 19.9 percent of all arrests for serious property crime, and 17.3 percent of all arrests for violent and serious property crimes combined. U.S. Dept. of Justice, Federal Bureau of Investigation, Crime in the United States 176–177 (1982) ("violent crimes" include murder, nonnegligent manslaughter, forcible rape, robbery, and aggravated assault; "serious property crimes" include burglary, larceny-theft, motor vehicle theft, and arson).

v. Schupf, supra, at 688–689, 350 NE. 2d, at 909.[15] Society has a legitimate interest in protecting a juvenile from the consequences of his criminal activity—both from potential physical injury which may be suffered when a victim fights back or a policeman attempts to make an arrest and from the downward spiral of criminal activity into which peer pressure may lead the child. See *L. O. W. v. District Court of Arapahoe,* 623 P.2d 1253, 1258–1259 (Colo. 1981); *Morris v. D'Amario,* 416 A. 2d 137, 140 (R. I. 1980). See also *Eddings v. Oklahoma,* 455 U.S. 104, 115 (1982) (minority "is a time and condition of life when a person may be most susceptible to influence and to psychological damage"); *Bellotti v. Baird,* 443 U.S. 622, 635 (1979) (juveniles "often lack the experience, perspective, and judgment to recognize and avoid choices that could be detrimental to them").

The substantiality and legitimacy of the state interests underlying this statute are confirmed by the widespread use and judicial acceptance of preventive detention for juveniles. Every State, as well as the United States in the District of Columbia, permits preventive detention of juveniles accused of crime.[16] A number of model juvenile justice Acts also contain provisions permitting preventive detention.[17] And the courts of eight States, including the

---

15. "Our society recognizes that juveniles in general are in the earlier stages of their emotional growth, that their intellectual development is incomplete, that they have had only limited practical experience, and that their value systems have not yet been clearly identified or firmly adopted. . . .

"For the same reasons that our society does not hold juveniles to an adult standard of responsibility for their conduct, our society may also conclude that there is a greater likelihood that a juvenile charged with delinquency, if released, will commit another criminal act than that an adult charged with crime will do so. To the extent that self-restraint may be expected to constrain adults, it may not be expected to operate with equal force as to juveniles. Because of the possibility of juvenile delinquency treatment and the absence of second-offender sentencing, there will not be the deterrent for the juvenile which confronts the adult. Perhaps more significant is the fact that in consequence of lack of experience and comprehension the juvenile does not view the commission of what are criminal acts in the same perspective as an adult. . . . There is the element of games-manship and the excitement of 'getting away' with something and the powerful inducement of peer pressures. All of these commonly acknowledged factors make the commission of criminal conduct on the part of juveniles in general more likely than in the case of adults." *People ex rel. Wayburn v. Schupf,* 39 N. Y. 2d, at 687-688, 350 N. E. 2d, at 908-909.

16. Ala. Code 12-15-59 (1975); Alaska Stat. Ann. 47.10.140 (1979); Rule 3, Ariz. Juv. Ct. Rules of Proc., Ariz. Rev. Stat. Ann. (Supp. 1983-1984 to vol. 17A); Ark. Stat. Ann. 45-421 (Supp. 1983); Cal. Welf. & Inst. Code Ann. 628 (West Supp. 1984); Colo. Rev. Stat. 19-2-102 (Supp. 1983); Conn. Gen. Stat. 46b-131 (Supp. 1984); Del. Fam. Ct. Rule 60 (1981); D.C. Code 16–2310 (1981); Fla. Stat. 39.032 (Supp. 1984); Ga. Code Ann. 15-11-19 (1982); Haw. Rev. Stat. 571-31.1 (Supp. 1984); Idaho Code 16-1811 (Supp. 1983); Ill. Rev. Stat., ch. 37, 703-4 (1983); Ind. Code 31-6-4-5 (1982); Iowa Code 232.22 (1983); Kan. Stat. Ann. 38-1632 (Supp. 1983); Ky. Rev. Stat. 208.192 (1982); La. Code Juv. Proc. Ann., Art. 40 (West 1983 Pamphlet); Me. Rev. Stat. Ann., Tit. 15, 3203 (1964 and Supp. 1983-1984); Md. Cts. & Jud. Proc. Code Ann. 3–815 (1984); Mass. Gen. Laws Ann., ch. 119, 66 (West Supp. 1983-1984); Mich. Comp. Laws 712A.15 (1979); Minn. Stat. 260.171 (1982); Miss. Code Ann. 43-23-11 (1972); Mo. Juv. Ct. Rule 111.02 (1981); Mont. Code Ann. 41-5-305 (1983); Neb. Rev. Stat. 43-255 (Supp. 1982); Nev. Rev. Stat. 62.140 (1983); N.H. Rev. Stat. Ann. 169B:14 (Supp. 1983); N.J. Stat. Ann. 2A:4-56 (Supp. 1983-1984); N.M. Stat. Ann. 32-1-24 (1981); N. Y. FCA 320.5(3) (McKinney 1983); N.C. Gen. Stat. 7A-574 (Supp. 1983); N.D. Cent. Code 27-20-14 (1974); Ohio Rev. Code Ann. 2151.311 (1976); Okla. Stat., Tit. 10, 1107 (Supp. 1983); Ore. Rev. Stat. 419.573 (1983); 42 Pa. Cons. Stat. 6325 (1982); R. I. Gen. Laws 14-1-20, 14-1-21 (1981); S. C. Code 20-7-600 (Supp. 1983); S. D. Codified Laws 26-8-19.2 (Supp. 1983); Tenn. Code Ann. 37-1-114 (1984); Tex. Fam. Code Ann. 53.02 (1975 and Supp. 1984); Utah Code Ann. 78-3a-30 (Supp. 1983); Vt. Stat. Ann., Tit. 33, 643 (1981); Va. Code 16.1-248 (1982); Wash. Rev. Code 13.40.040 (1983); W. Va. Code 49-5-8 (Supp. 1983); Wis. Stat. 48.208 (1981-1982); Wyo. Stat. 14-6-206 (1977).

17. See U.S. Dept. of Justice, Office of Juvenile Justice and Delinquency Prevention, Standards for the Administration of Juvenile Justice, Report of the National Advisory Committee for Juvenile Justice and Delinquency Prevention

New York Court of Appeals, have upheld their statutes with specific reference to protecting the juvenile and the community from harmful pretrial conduct, including pretrial crime. *L.O.W. v. District Court of Arapahoe*, supra, at 1258–1259; *Morris v. D'Amario*, supra, at 139–140; *State v. Gleason*, 404 A. 2d, at 583; *Pauley v. Gross*, 1 Kan. App. 2d 736, 738–740, 574 P.2d 234, 237–238 (1977); *People ex rel. Wayburn v. Schupf*, 39 N. Y. 2d, at 688–689, 350 N. E. 2d, at 909–910; *Aubrey v. Gadbois*, 50 Cal. App. 3d 470, 472, 123 Cal. Rptr. 365, 366 (1975); *Baker v. Smith*, 477 S. W. 2d, at 150–151; *Commonwealth ex rel. Sprowal v. Hendrick*, 438 Pa. 435, 438–439, 265 A. 2d 348, 349–350 (1970).

"The fact that a practice is followed by a large number of states is not conclusive in a decision as to whether that practice accords with due process, but it is plainly worth considering in determining whether the practice 'offends some principle of justice so rooted in the traditions and conscience of our people as to be ranked as fundamental.' *Snyder v. Massachusetts*, 291 U.S. 97, 105 (1934)." *Leland v. Oregon*, 343 U.S. 790, 798 (1952). In light of the uniform legislative judgment that pretrial detention of juveniles properly promotes the interests both of society and the juvenile, we conclude that the practice serves a legitimate regulatory purpose compatible with the "fundamental fairness" demanded by the Due Process Clause in juvenile proceedings. Cf. *McKeiver v. Pennsylvania*, 403 U.S., at 548 (plurality opinion).[18]

Of course, the mere invocation of a legitimate purpose will not justify particular restrictions and conditions of confinement amounting to punishment. It is axiomatic that "[d]ue process requires that a pretrial detainee not be punished." *Bell v. Wolfish*, 441 U.S., at 535, n. 16. Even given, therefore, that pretrial detention may serve legitimate regulatory purposes, it is still necessary to determine whether the terms and conditions of confinement under 320.5(3)(b) are in fact compatible with those purposes. *Kennedy v. Mendoza-Martinez*, 372 U.S., at 168–169. "A court must decide whether the disability is imposed for the purpose of punishment or whether it is but an incident of some other legitimate governmental purpose." *Bell v. Wolfish*, supra, at 538. Absent a showing of an express intent to punish on the part of the State, that determination generally will turn on "whether an alternative purpose to which [the restriction] may rationally be connected is assignable for it, and whether it

---

294–296 (July 1980); Uniform Juvenile Court Act 14, 9A U. L. A. 22 (1979); Standard Juvenile Court Act, Art. IV, 16, proposed by the National Council on Crime and Delinquency (1959); W. Sheridan, Legislative Guide for Drafting Family and Juvenile Court Acts 20(a)(1) (Dept. of HEW, Children's Bureau, Pub. No. 472-1969); see also Standards for Juvenile and Family Courts 62-63 (Dept. of HEW, Children's Bureau, Pub. No. 437-1966). Cf. Institute of Judicial Administration/American Bar Association Project on Juvenile Justice Standards Relating to Interim Status: The Release Control, and Detention of Accused Juvenile Offenders Between Arrest and Disposition 3.2(B) (Tent. Draft 1977) (detention limited to "reducing the likelihood that the juvenile may inflict serious bodily harm on others during the interim").

18. Appellees argue that some limit must be placed on the categories of crimes that detained juveniles must be accused of having committed or being likely to commit. But the discretion to delimit the categories of crimes justifying detention, like the discretion to define criminal offenses and prescribe punishments, resides wholly with the state legislatures. *Whalen v. United States*, 445 U.S. 684, 689 (1980); *Rochin v. California*, 342 U.S. 165, 168 (1952). See also *Rummel v. Estelle*, 445 U.S. 263, 275 (1980) ("the presence or absence of violence does not always affect the strength of society's interest in deterring a particular crime").

More fundamentally, this sort of attack on a criminal statute must be made on a case-by-case basis. *United States v. Raines*, 362 U.S. 17, 21 (1960). The Court will not sift through the entire class to determine whether the statute was constitutionally applied in each case. And, outside the limited First Amendment context, a criminal statute may not be attacked as overbroad. See *New York v. Ferber*, 458 U.S. 747 (1982).

appears excessive in relation to the alternative purpose assigned [to it]." *Kennedy v. Mendoza-Martinez,* supra, at 168-189. See *Bell v. Wolfish,* supra, at 538; *Flemming v. Nestor,* 363 U.S. 603, 613–614 (1960).

There is no indication in the statute itself that preventive detention is used or intended as a punishment. First of all, the detention is strictly limited in time. If a juvenile is detained at his initial appearance and has denied the charges against him, he is entitled to a probable-cause hearing to be held not more than three days after the conclusion of the initial appearance or four days after the filing of the petition, whichever is sooner. FCA 325.1(2).[19] If the Family Court judge finds probable cause, he must also determine whether continued detention is necessary pursuant to 320.5(3)(b). 325.3(3).

Detained juveniles are also entitled to an expedited factfinding hearing. If the juvenile is charged with one of a limited number of designated felonies, the factfinding hearing must be scheduled to commence not more than 14 days after the conclusion of the initial appearance. 340.1. If the juvenile is charged with a lesser offense, then the factfinding hearing must be held not more than three days after the initial appearance.[20] In the latter case, since the times for the probable-cause hearing and the factfinding hearing coincide, the two hearings are merged.

Thus, the maximum possible detention under 320.5(3)(b) of a youth accused of a serious crime, assuming a 3-day extension of the factfinding hearing for good cause shown, is 17 days. The maximum detention for less serious crimes, again assuming a 3-day extension for good cause shown, is 6 days. These time frames seem suited to the limited purpose of providing the youth with a controlled environment and separating him from improper influences pending the speedy disposition of his case.

The conditions of confinement also appear to reflect the regulatory purposes relied upon by the State. When a juvenile is remanded after his initial appearance, he cannot, absent exceptional circumstances, be sent to a prison or lockup where he would be exposed to adult criminals. FCA 304.1(2). Instead, the child is screened by an "assessment unit" of the Department of Juvenile Justice. Testimony of Mr. Kelly (Deputy Commissioner of Operations, New York City Department of Juvenile Justice), App. 286-287. The assessment unit places the child in either nonsecure or secure detention. Nonsecure detention involves an open facility in the community, a sort of "halfway house," without locks, bars, or security officers where the child receives schooling and counseling and has access to recreational facilities. Id., at 285; Testimony of Mr. Benjamin, id., at 149-150.

Secure detention is more restrictive, but it is still consistent with the regulatory and parens patriae objectives relied upon by the State. Children are assigned to separate dorms based on age, size, and behavior. They wear street clothes provided by the institution and partake in educational and recreational programs and counseling sessions run by trained social workers. Misbehavior is punished by confinement to one's room. See Testimony of Mr. Kelly, id., at 292–297. We cannot conclude from this record that the controlled environment briefly imposed by the State on juveniles in secure pretrial detention "is imposed for the purpose of

---

19. For good cause shown, the court may adjourn the hearing, but for no more than three additional court days. FCA 325.1(3).

20. In either case, the court may adjourn the hearing for not more than three days for good cause shown. FCA 340.1(3). The court must state on the record the reason for any adjournment. 340.1(4).

punishment" rather than as "an incident of some other legitimate governmental purpose." *Bell v. Wolfish,* 441 U.S., at 538.

The Court of Appeals, of course, did conclude that the underlying purpose of 320.5(3)(b) is punitive rather than regulatory. But the court did not dispute that preventive detention might serve legitimate regulatory purposes or that the terms and conditions of pretrial confinement in New York are compatible with those purposes. Rather, the court invalidated a significant aspect of New York's juvenile justice system based solely on some case histories and a statistical study which appeared to show that "the vast majority of juveniles detained under [320.5(3)(b)] either have their petitions dismissed before an adjudication of delinquency or are released after adjudication." 689 F.2d, at 369. The court assumed that dismissal of a petition or failure to confine a juvenile at the dispositional hearing belied the need to detain him prior to factfinding and that, therefore, the pretrial detention constituted punishment. Id., at 373. Since punishment imposed without a prior adjudication of guilt is per se illegitimate, the Court of Appeals concluded that no juveniles could be held pursuant to 320.5(3)(b).

There are some obvious flaws in the statistics and case histories relied upon by the lower court.[21] But even assuming it to be the case that "by far the greater number of juveniles incarcerated under [320.5(3)(b)] will never be confined as a consequence of a disposition imposed after an adjudication of delinquency," 689 F.2d, at 371-372, we find that to be an insufficient ground for upsetting the widely shared legislative judgment that preventive detention serves an important and legitimate function in the juvenile justice system. We are unpersuaded by the Court of Appeals' rather cavalier equation of detentions that do not lead to continued confinement after an adjudication of guilt and "wrongful" or "punitive" pretrial detentions.

Pretrial detention need not be considered punitive merely because a juvenile is subsequently discharged subject to conditions or put on probation. In fact, such actions reinforce the original finding that close supervision of the juvenile is required. Lenient but supervised disposition is in keeping with the Act's purpose to promote the welfare and development of the child.[22] As the New York Court of Appeals noted:

> "It should surprise no one that caution and concern for both the juvenile and society may indicate the more conservation decision to detain at the very outset, whereas the later development of

---

21. For example, as the Court of Appeals itself admits, 689 F.2d, at 369, n. 18, the statistical study on which it relied mingles indiscriminately detentions under 320.5(3)(b) with detentions under 320.5(3)(a). The latter provision applies only to juveniles who are likely not to appear on the return date if not detained, and appellees concede that such juveniles may be lawfully detained. Brief for Appellees 93. Furthermore, the 34 case histories on which the court relied were handpicked by appellees' counsel from over a 3-year period. Compare Petitioners' Exhibit 19a (detention of Geraldo Delgado on March 5, 1976) with Petitioners' Exhibit 35a (detention of James Ancrum on August 19, 1979). The Court of Appeals stated that appellants did not contest the representativeness of these case histories. 689 F.2d, at 369, n. 19. Appellants argue, however, that there was no occasion to contest their representativeness because the case histories were not even offered by appellees as a representative sample, and were not evaluated by appellees' expert statistician or the District Court in that light. See Brief for Appellant in No. 82-1278, pp. 24-25, n.[**]. We need not resolve this controversy.

22. Judge Quinones testified that detention at disposition is considered a "harsh solution." At the dispositional hearing, the Family Court judge usually has "a much more complete picture of the youngster" and tries to tailor the least restrictive dispositional order compatible with that picture. Testimony of Judge Quinones, App. 279-281.

very much more relevant information may prove that while a finding of delinquency was warranted, placement may not be indicated." *People ex rel. Wayburn v. Schupf*, 39 N. Y. 2d, at 690, 350 N.E. 2d, at 910.

Even when a case is terminated prior to factfinding, it does not follow that the decision to detain the juvenile pursuant to 320.5(3)(b) amounted to a due process violation. A delinquency petition may be dismissed for any number of reasons collateral to its merits, such as the failure of a witness to testify. The Family Court judge cannot be expected to anticipate such developments at the initial hearing. He makes his decision based on the information available to him at that time, and the propriety of the decision must be judged in that light. Consequently, the final disposition of a case is "largely irrelevant" to the legality of a pretrial detention. *Baker v. McCollan*, 443 U.S. 137, 145 (1979).

It may be, of course, that in some circumstances detention of a juvenile would not pass constitutional muster. But the validity of those detentions must be determined on a case-by-case basis. Section 320.5(3)(b) is not invalid "on its face" by reason of the ambiguous statistics and case histories relied upon by the court below.[23] We find no justification for the conclusion that, contrary to the express language of the statute and the judgment of the highest state court, 320.5(3)(b) is a punitive rather than a regulatory measure. Preventive detention under the FCA serves the legitimate state objective, held in common with every State in the country, of protecting both the juvenile and society from the hazards of pretrial crime.

B

Given the legitimacy of the State's interest in preventive detention, and the nonpunitive nature of that detention, the remaining question is whether the procedures afforded juveniles detained prior to factfinding provide sufficient protection against erroneous and unnecessary deprivations of liberty. See *Mathews v. Eldridge*, 424 U.S., at 335.[24] In *Gerstein v. Pugh*, 420 U.S., at 114, we held that a judicial determination of probable cause is a prerequisite to any extended restraint on the liberty of an adult accused of crime. We did not, however, mandate a specific timetable. Nor did we require the "full panoply of adversary safeguards—counsel, confrontation, cross-examination, and compulsory process for witnesses." Id., at 119. Instead, we recognized "the desirability of flexibility and experimentation by the States."

---

23. Several amici argue that similar statistics obtain throughout the country. See, e.g., Brief for American Bar Association as Amicus Curiae 23; Brief for Association for Children of New Jersey as Amicus Curiae 8, 11; Brief for Youth Law Center et al. as Amici Curiae 13-14. But even if New York's experience were duplicated on a national scale, that fact would not lead us, as amici urge, to conclude that every State and the United States are illicitly punishing juveniles prior to their trial. On the contrary, if such statistics obtain nationwide, our conclusion is strengthened that the existence of the statistics in these cases is not a sufficient ground for striking down New York's statute. As already noted: "The fact that a practice is followed by a large number of states is not conclusive in a decision as to whether that practice accords with due process, but it is plainly worth considering in determining whether the practice 'offends some principle of justice so rooted in the traditions and conscience of our people as to be ranked as fundamental.' *Snyder v. Massachusetts*, 291 U.S. 97, 105 (1934)." *Leland v. Oregon*, 343 U.S. 790, 798 (1952).

24. Appellees urge the alleged lack of procedural safeguards as an alternative ground for upholding the judgment of the Court of Appeals. Brief for Appellees 62-75. The court itself intimated that it would reach the same result on that ground, 689 F.2d, at 373-374, and Judge Newman, in his concurrence, relied expressly on perceived procedural flaws in the statute. Accordingly, we deem it necessary to consider the question.

Id., at 123. *Gerstein* arose under the Fourth Amendment, but the same concern with "flexibility" and "informality," while yet ensuring adequate predetention procedures, is present in this context. *In re Winship*, 397 U.S., at 366; *Kent v. United States*, 383 U.S. 541, 554 (1966).

In many respects, the FCA provides far more predetention protection for juveniles than we found to be constitutionally required for a probable-cause determination for adults in Gerstein. The initial appearance is informal, but the accused juvenile is given full notice of the charges against him and a complete stenographic record is kept of the hearing. See 513 F. Supp., at 702. The juvenile appears accompanied by his parent or guardian.[25] He is first informed of his rights, including the right to remain silent and the right to be represented by counsel chosen by him or by a law guardian assigned by the court. FCA 320.3. The initial appearance may be adjourned for no longer than 72 hours or until the next court day, whichever is sooner, to enable an appointed law guardian or other counsel to appear before the court. 320.2(3). When his counsel is present, the juvenile is informed of the charges against him and furnished with a copy of the delinquency petition. 320.4(1). A representative from the presentment agency appears in support of the petition.

The nonhearsay allegations in the delinquency petition and supporting depositions must establish probable cause to believe the juvenile committed the offense. Although the Family Court judge is not required to make a finding of probable cause at the initial appearance, the youth may challenge the sufficiency of the petition on that ground. FCA 315.1. Thus, the juvenile may oppose any recommended detention by arguing that there is not probable cause to believe he committed the offense or offenses with which he is charged. If the petition is not dismissed, the juvenile is given an opportunity to admit or deny the charges. 321.1.[26]

At the conclusion of the initial appearance, the presentment agency makes a recommendation regarding detention. A probation officer reports on the juvenile's record, including other prior and current Family Court and probation contacts, as well as relevant information concerning home life, school attendance, and any special medical or developmental problems. He concludes by offering his agency's recommendation on detention. Opposing counsel, the juvenile's parents, and the juvenile himself may all speak on his behalf and challenge any information or recommendation. If the judge does decide to detain the juvenile under 320.5(3)(b), he must state on the record the facts and reasons for the detention.[27]

As noted, a detained juvenile is entitled to a formal, adversarial probable-cause hearing within three days of his initial appearance, with one 3-day extension possible for good cause

---

25. If the juvenile's parent or guardian fails to appear after reasonable and substantial efforts have been made to notify such person, the court must appoint a law guardian for the child. FCA 320.3.

26. If the child chooses to remain silent, he is assumed to deny the charges. FCA 321.1. With the consent of the court and of the presentment agency, the child may admit to a lesser charge. If he wishes to admit to the charges or to a lesser charge, the court must, before accepting the admission, advise the child of his right to a factfinding hearing and of the possible specific dispositional orders that may result from the admission. Ibid. The court must also satisfy itself that the child actually did commit the acts to which he admits. Ibid.

With the consent of the victim or complainant and the juvenile, the court may also refer a case to the probation service for adjustment. If the case is subsequently adjusted, the petition is then dismissed. 320.6.

27. Given that under Gerstein, 420 U.S., at 119-123, a probable-cause hearing may be informal and nonadversarial, a Family Court judge could make a finding of probable cause at the initial appearance. That he is not required to do so does not, under the circumstances, amount to a deprivation of due process. Appellees fail to point to a single example where probable cause was not found after a decision was made to detain the child.

shown.[28] The burden at this hearing is on the presentment agency to call witnesses and offer evidence in support of the charges. 325.2. Testimony is under oath and subject to cross-examination. Ibid. The accused juvenile may call witnesses and offer evidence in his own behalf. If the court finds probable cause, the court must again decide whether continued detention is necessary under 320.5(3)(b). Again, the facts and reasons for the detention must be stated on the record.

In sum, notice, a hearing, and a statement of facts and reasons are given prior to any detention under 320.5(3)(b). A formal probable-cause hearing is then held within a short while thereafter, if the factfinding hearing is not itself scheduled within three days. These flexible procedures have been found constitutionally adequate under the Fourth Amendment, see *Gerstein v. Pugh,* and under the Due Process Clause, see *Kent v. United States,* supra, at 557. Appellees have failed to note any additional procedures that would significantly improve the accuracy of the determination without unduly impinging on the achievement of legitimate state purposes.[29]

Appellees argue, however, that the risk of erroneous and unnecessary detentions is too high despite these procedures because the standard for detention is fatally vague. Detention under 320.5(3)(b) is based on a finding that there is a "serious risk" that the juvenile, if released, would commit a crime prior to his next court appearance. We have already seen that detention of juveniles on that ground serves legitimate regulatory purposes. But appellees claim, and the District Court agreed, that it is virtually impossible to predict future criminal conduct with any degree of accuracy. Moreover, they say, the statutory standard fails to channel the discretion of the Family Court judge by specifying the factors on which he should rely in making that prediction. The procedural protections noted above are thus, in their view, unavailing because the ultimate decision is intrinsically arbitrary and uncontrolled.

Our cases indicate, however, that from a legal point of view there is nothing inherently unattainable about a prediction of future criminal conduct. Such a judgment forms an important element in many decisions,[30] and we have specifically rejected the contention, based

---

28. The Court in Gerstein indicated approval of pretrial detention procedures that supplied a probable-cause hearing within five days of the initial detention. Id., at 124, n. 25. The brief delay in the probable-cause hearing may actually work to the advantage of the juvenile since it gives his counsel, usually appointed at the initial appearance pursuant to FCA 320.2(2), time to prepare.

29. Judge Newman, in his concurrence below, offered a list of statutory improvements. These suggested changes included: limitations on the crimes for which the juvenile has been arrested or which he is likely to commit if released; a determination of the likelihood that the juvenile committed the crime; an assessment of the juvenile's background; and a more specific standard of proof. The first and second of these suggestions have already been considered. See nn. 18 and 27, supra. We need only add to the discussion in n. 18 that there is no indication that delimiting the category of crimes justifying detention would improve the accuracy of the 320.5(3)(b) determination in any respect. The third and fourth suggestions are discussed in text, infra.

30. See *Jurek v. Texas,* 428 U.S. 262, 274-275 (1976) (death sentence imposed by jury); *Greenholtz v. Nebraska Penal Inmates,* 442 U.S. 1, 9-10 (1979) (grant of parole); *Morrissey v. Brewer,* 408 U.S. 471, 480 (1972) (parole revocation).

A prediction of future criminal conduct may also form the basis for an increased sentence under the "dangerous special offender" statute, 18 U.S.C. 3575. Under 3575(f), a "dangerous" offender is defined as an individual for whom "a period of confinement longer than that provided for such [underlying] felony is required for the protection of the public from further criminal conduct by the defendant." The statute has been challenged numerous times on the grounds that the standards is unconstitutionally vague. Every Court of Appeals considering the question has rejected that claim. *United States v. Davis,* 710 F.2d 104, 108-109 (CA3), cert. denied, 464 U.S. 1001 (1983); *United States v. Schell,* 692 F.2d 672, 675-676 (CA10 1982); *United States v. Williamson,* 567 F.2d 610, 613 (CA4

on the same sort of sociological data relied upon by appellees and the District Court, "that it is impossible to predict future behavior and that the question is so vague as to be meaningless." *Jurek v. Texas*, 428 U.S. 262, 274 (1976) (opinion of Stewart, Powell, and Stevens, JJ.); id., at 279 (White, J., concurring in judgment).

We have also recognized that a prediction of future criminal conduct is "an experienced prediction based on a host of variables" which cannot be readily codified. *Greenholtz v. Nebraska Penal Inmates*, 442 U.S. 1, 16 (1979). Judge Quinones of the Family Court testified at trial that he and his colleagues make a determination under 320.5(3)(b) based on numerous factors including the nature and seriousness of the charges; whether the charges are likely to be proved at trial; the juvenile's prior record; the adequacy and effectiveness of his home supervision; his school situation, if known; the time of day of the alleged crime as evidence of its seriousness and a possible lack of parental control; and any special circumstances that might be brought to his attention by the probation officer, the child's attorney, or any parents, relatives, or other responsible persons accompanying the child. Testimony of Judge Quinones, App. 254-267. The decision is based on as much information as can reasonably be obtained at the initial appearance. Ibid.

Given the right to a hearing, to counsel, and to a statement of reasons, there is no reason that the specific factors upon which the Family Court judge might rely must be specified in the statute. As the New York Court of Appeals concluded, *People ex rel. Wayburn v. Schupf*, 39 N.Y. 2d, at 690, 350 N. E. 2d, at 910, "to a very real extent Family Court must exercise a substitute parental control for which there can be no particularized criteria." There is also no reason, we should add, for a federal court to assume that a state court judge will not strive to apply state law as conscientiously as possible. *Sumner v. Mata*, 449 U.S. 539, 549 (1981).

It is worth adding that the Court of Appeals for the Second Circuit was mistaken in its conclusion that "[i]ndividual litigation . . . is a practical impossibility because the periods of detention are so short that the litigation is mooted before the merits are determined." 689 F.2d, at 373. In fact, one of the juveniles in the very case histories upon which the court relied was released from pretrial detention on a writ of habeas corpus issued by the State Supreme Court. New York courts also have adopted a liberal view of the doctrine of "capable of repetition, yet evading review" precisely in order to ensure that pretrial detention orders are not unreviewable. In *People ex rel. Wayburn v. Schupf*, supra, at 686, 350 N. E. 2d, at 908, the court declined to dismiss an appeal from the grant of a writ of habeas corpus despite the technical mootness of the case.

> "Because the situation is likely to recur . . . and the substantial issue may otherwise never be reached (in view of the predictably recurring happenstance that, however expeditiously an appeal might be prosecuted, fact-finding and dispositional hearings normally will have been held and a disposition made before the appeal could reach us), . . . we decline to dismiss [the appeal] on the ground of mootness."

The required statement of facts and reasons justifying the detention and the stenographic record of the initial appearance will provide a basis for the review of individual cases. Pretrial detention orders in New York may be reviewed by writ of habeas corpus brought in

1977); *United States v. Bowdach*, 561 F.2d 1160, 1175 (CA5 1977); *United States v. Neary*, 552 F.2d 1184, 1194 (CA7), cert. denied, 434 U.S. 864 (1977); *United States v. Stewart*, 531 F.2d 326, 336-337 (CA6), cert. denied, 426 U.S. 922 (1976).

State Supreme Court. And the judgment of that court is appealable as of right and may be taken directly to the Court of Appeals if a constitutional question is presented. N. Y. Civ. Prac. Law 5601(b)(2) (McKinney 1978). Permissive appeal from a Family Court order may also be had to the Appellate Division. FCA 365.2. Or a motion for reconsideration may be directed to the Family Court judge. 355.1(1)(b). These post-detention procedures provide a sufficient mechanism for correcting on a case-by-case basis any erroneous detentions ordered under 320.5(3). Such procedures may well flesh out the standards specified in the statute.

III

The dissent would apparently have us strike down New York's preventive detention statute on two grounds: first, because the preventive detention of juveniles constitutes poor public policy, with the balance of harms outweighing any positive benefits either to society or to the juveniles themselves, post, at 290-291, 308, and, second, because the statute could have been better drafted to improve the quality of the decisionmaking process, post, at 304-306. But it is worth recalling that we are neither a legislature charged with formulating public policy nor an American Bar Association committee charged with drafting a model statute. The question before us today is solely whether the preventive detention system chosen by the State of New York and applied by the New York Family Court comports with constitutional standards. Given the regulatory purpose for the detention and the procedural protections that precede its imposition, we conclude that 320.5(3)(b) of the New York FCA is not invalid under the Due Process Clause of the Fourteenth Amendment.

The judgment of the Court of Appeals is Reversed.

CHAPTER 7

JUVENILES AND CAPITAL PUNISHMENT

Introduction

Capital punishment is a very controversial topic. There are few topics in criminal law that engender as much debate as the two fundamental issues surrounding the death penalty: (1) whether it is appropriate for the state to execute anyone; and (2) whether such executions actually serve the general deterrence goals that are often used as the justification for capital punishment. These issues become especially problematic when juveniles are the object of the death penalty. The U.S. Supreme Court only tangentially confronted the issue of age and capital punishment in 1982 in *Eddings v. Oklahoma*.[1] This case did involve a juvenile, a sixteen-year-old boy who killed a highway patrol officer, but *Eddings* is not a juvenile law case. Although Eddings was a juvenile, he was tried in adult court, convicted, and sentenced to death. The Supreme Court overturned the death sentence, not on the basis of age, but rather on the grounds that the trial court had failed to consider the boy's emotional state and troubled childhood as mitigating factors when dispensing the death penalty. The issue of the boy being a sixteen-year-old juvenile was not dispositive—it was only recognized as a legitimate mitigating factor.

Following *Eddings,* the Supreme Court did rule in three cases in which the age of the offender was the critical issue before the Court. In *Thompson v. Oklahoma* (1988) the issue was whether the execution of a juvenile murderer sentenced to death would violate the constitutional prohibition against the infliction of "cruel and unusual punishments" because the juvenile petitioner was only fifteen years old at the time of his offense. *Stanford v. Kentucky* (1989) was decided just one year after *Thompson.* This case involved two juveniles; one was seventeen years and four months old at the time he committed murder in Kentucky, while the second was approximately sixteen years and six months old when he committed murder in Missouri. Each petitioner appealed the death sentence and contended that he had a constitutional right to treatment in the juvenile justice system, and further declared that his age and the possibility that he might be rehabilitated were mitigating factors. While the Court agreed with Thompson and overturned his death sentence, the Court affirmed the death sentences in *Stanford.* Thus, not until the case of *Roper v. Simmons* (2005) did the Supreme Court resolve once and for all the issue of the constitutionality of the death penalty for minors under the age of 18.

---

1. 455 U.S. 104 (1982).

Capital Punishment

Case Comment

In *Thompson v. Oklahoma,* the U.S. Supreme Court was confronted with the question of whether the execution of a fifteen-year-old would violate the Eighth Amendment's prohibition against "cruel and unusual punishments." In 1983, when he was fifteen years old, William Wayne Thompson, in the company of three older males, ambushed his sister's abusive ex-husband at his home. The victim was stabbed multiple times and shot twice. A cement block was tied to the victim's body, and the body was dumped in a river. Thompson's three accomplices, all of whom were over age 18, were convicted and sentenced to death. Thompson was waived to adult court after a hearing requested by the prosecutor and was found guilty and sentenced to death. Neither the facts of the crime nor Thompson's guilt were ever in doubt. Thompson had a history of juvenile offenses, and witnesses from the juvenile justice system testified that he was not amenable to rehabilitation. A psychologist hired by the prosecution evaluated Thompson and testified that Thompson had "antisocial personality disorder," demonstrated a callous disregard for others, and had no capacity for change.

The U.S. Supreme Court reviewed the intent of the Eighth Amendment's prohibition against cruel and unusual punishments and ruled that the execution of a person under the age of 16 was unconstitutional. The Court supported its ruling by noting a nearly universal ban among all relevant state statutes against the execution of persons under the age of 16. The Court explained that such an act would violate the "evolving standards of decency that mark the progress of a maturing society." The effect of *Thompson* was that no one under the age of 16 could face the death penalty in America.

THOMPSON V. OKLAHOMA

Supreme Court of the United States, 1988.

487 U.S. 815.

Justice Stevens announced the judgment of the Court and delivered an opinion in which Justice Brennan, Justice Marshall, and Justice Blackmun join.

Petitioner was convicted of first-degree murder and sentenced to death. The principal question presented is whether the execution of that sentence would violate the constitutional prohibition against the infliction of "cruel and unusual punishments"[1] because petitioner was only 15 years old at the time of his offense.

---

1. The Eighth Amendment provides:

"Excessive bail shall not be required, nor excessive fines imposed, nor cruel and unusual punishments inflicted."

This proscription must be observed by the States as well as the Federal Government. See, e.g., *Robinson v. California,* 370 U.S. 660 (1962).

I

Because there is no claim that the punishment would be excessive if the crime had been committed by an adult, only a brief statement of facts is necessary. In concert with three older persons, petitioner actively participated in the brutal murder of his former brother-in-law in the early morning hours of January 23, 1983. The evidence disclosed that the victim had been shot twice, and that his throat, chest, and abdomen had been cut. He also had multiple bruises and a broken leg. His body had been chained to a concrete block and thrown into a river where it remained for almost four weeks. Each of the four participants was tried separately and each was sentenced to death.

Because petitioner was a "child" as a matter of Oklahoma law,[2] the District Attorney filed a statutory petition, see Okla. Stat., Tit. 10, 1112(b) (1981), seeking an order finding "that said child is competent and had the mental capacity to know and appreciate the wrongfulness of his [conduct]." App. 4. After a hearing, the trial court concluded "that there are virtually no reasonable prospects for rehabilitation of William Wayne Thompson within the juvenile system and that William Wayne Thompson should be held accountable for his acts as if he were an adult and should be certified to stand trial as an adult." Id., at 8.

At the guilt phase of petitioner's trial, the prosecutor introduced three color photographs showing the condition of the victim's body when it was removed from the river. Although the Court of Criminal Appeals held that the use of two of those photographs was error,[3] it concluded that the error was harmless because the evidence of petitioner's guilt was so convincing. However, the prosecutor had also used the photographs in his closing argument during the penalty phase. The Court of Criminal Appeals did not consider whether this display was proper.

At the penalty phase of the trial, the prosecutor asked the jury to find two aggravating circumstances: that the murder was especially heinous, atrocious, or cruel; and that there was a probability that the defendant would commit criminal acts of violence that would constitute a continuing threat to society. The jury found the first, but not the second, and fixed petitioner's punishment at death.

The Court of Criminal Appeals affirmed the conviction and sentence, 724 P.2d 780 (1986), citing its earlier opinion in *Eddings v. State*, 616 P.2d 1159 (1980), rev'd on other grounds, 455 U.S. 104 (1982), for the proposition that "once a minor is certified to stand trial as an adult, he may also, without violating the Constitution, be punished as an adult." 724 P.2d, at 784. We granted certiorari to consider whether a sentence of death is cruel and unusual punishment for a crime committed by a 15-year-old child, as well as whether photographic

---

2. Oklahoma Stat., Tit. 10, 1101(1) (Supp. 1987) provides:

"Child" means any person under eighteen (18) years of age, except for any person sixteen (16) or seventeen (17) years of age who is charged with murder, kidnapping for purposes of extortion, robbery with a dangerous weapon, rape in the first degree, use of a firearm or other offensive weapon while committing a felony, arson in the first degree, burglary with explosives, shooting with intent to kill, manslaughter in the first degree, or nonconsensual sodomy."

3. "The other two color photographs . . . were gruesome. Admitting them into evidence served no purpose other than to inflame the jury. We do not understand why an experienced prosecutor would risk reversal of the whole case by introducing such ghastly, color photographs with so little probative value. We fail to see how they could possibly assist the jury in the determination of defendant's guilt. The trial court's admission of these two photographs was error." 724 P.2d 780, 782–783 (1986).

evidence that a state court deems erroneously admitted but harmless at the guilt phase nevertheless violates a capital defendant's constitutional rights by virtue of its being considered at the penalty phase. 479 U.S. 1084 (1987).

II

The authors of the Eighth Amendment drafted a categorical prohibition against the infliction of cruel and unusual punishments, but they made no attempt to define the contours of that category. They delegated that task to future generations of judges who have been guided by the "evolving standards of decency that mark the progress of a maturing society." *Trop v. Dulles,* 356 U.S. 86, 101 (1958) (plurality opinion) (Warren, C. J.).[4] In performing that task the Court has reviewed the work product of state legislatures and sentencing juries,[5] and has carefully considered the reasons why a civilized society may accept or reject the death penalty in certain types of cases. Thus, in confronting the question whether the youth of the defendant—more specifically, the fact that he was less than 16 years old at the time of his offense—is a sufficient reason for denying the State the power to sentence him to death, we first review relevant legislative enactments,[6] then refer to jury determinations,[7] and finally explain

---

4. That Eighth Amendment jurisprudence must reflect "evolving standards of decency" was settled early this century in the case of *Weems v. United States,* 217 U.S. 349 (1910). The Court held that a sentence of 15 years of hard, enchained labor, plus deprivation of various civil rights and perpetual state surveillance, constituted "cruel and unusual punishment" under the Bill of Rights of the Philippines (then under United States control). Premising its opinion on the synonymity of the Philippine and United States "cruel and unusual punishments" clauses, the Court wrote:

"Time works changes, brings into existence new conditions and purposes. Therefore a principle to be vital must be capable of wider application than the mischief which gives it birth.

. . .

"The [cruel and unusual punishments clause] in the opinion of the learned commentators may be therefore progressive, and is not fastened to the obsolete but may acquire meaning as public opinion becomes enlightened by a humane justice." Id., at 373–374, 378.

See also *Ollman v. Evans,* 242 U.S. App. D.C. 301, 326-327, 750 F.2d 970, 995-996 (1984) (en banc) (Bork, J., concurring):

"Judges given stewardship of a constitutional provision . . . whose core is known but whose outer reach and contours are ill-defined, face the neverending task of discerning the meaning of the provision from one case to the next. There would be little need for judges—and certainly no office for a philosophy of judging—if the boundaries of every constitutional provision were self-evident. They are not. . . . [I]t is the task of the judge in this generation to discern how the framers' values, defined in the context of the world they knew, apply to the world we know. The world changes in which unchanging values find their application. . . .

. . . . .

"We must never hesitate to apply old values to new circumstances . . . . The important thing, the ultimate consideration, is the constitutional freedom that is given into our keeping. A judge who refuses to see new threats to an established constitutional value, and hence provides a crabbed interpretation that robs a provision of its full, fair and reasonable meaning, fails in his judicial duty."

5. See, e.g., *Woodson v. North Carolina,* 428 U.S. 280, 293 (1976) (plurality opinion) (Stewart, Powell, and Stevens, J.J.); *Coker v. Georgia,* 433 U.S. 584, 593-597 (1977) (plurality opinion) (White, J.); *Enmund v. Florida,* 458 U.S. 782, 789-796 (1982); id., at 814 (legislative and jury statistics important in Eighth Amendment adjudication) (O'-Connor, J., dissenting).

6. See *Furman v. Georgia,* 408 U.S. 238, 277-279 (1972) (Court must look to objective signs of how today's society views a particular punishment) (Brennan, J., concurring); *Enmund v. Florida,* 458 U.S., at 789-793.

7. Our capital punishment jurisprudence has consistently recognized that contemporary standards, as reflected by the actions of legislatures and juries, provide an important measure of whether the death penalty is "cruel and unusual." Part of the rationale for this index of constitutional value lies in the very language of the construed clause:

why these indicators of contemporary standards of decency confirm our judgment that such a young person is not capable of acting with the degree of culpability that can justify the ultimate penalty.[8]

III

Justice Powell has repeatedly reminded us of the importance of "the experience of mankind, as well as the long history of our law, recognizing that there are differences which must be accommodated in determining the rights and duties of children as compared with those of adults. Examples of this distinction abound in our law: in contracts, in torts, in criminal law and procedure, in criminal sanctions and rehabilitation, and in the right to vote and to hold office." *Goss v. Lopez,* 419 U.S. 565, 590-591 (1975) (dissenting opinion).[9] Oklahoma recognizes this basic distinction in a number of its statutes. Thus, a minor is not eligible to vote,[10] to sit on a jury,[11] to marry without parental consent,[12] or to purchase alcohol[13] or cigarettes.[14] Like all other States, Oklahoma has developed a juvenile justice system in which most offenders under the age of 18 are not held criminally responsible. Its statutes do provide, however, that a 16- or 17-year-old charged with murder and other serious felonies shall be considered an adult.[15] Other than the special certification procedure that was used to authorize petitioner's trial in this case "as an adult," apparently there are no Oklahoma statutes, either civil or criminal, that treat a person under 16 years of age as anything but a "child."

The line between childhood and adulthood is drawn in different ways by various States. There is, however, complete or near unanimity among all 50 States and the District of

---

whether an action is "unusual" depends, in common usage, upon the frequency of its occurrence or the magnitude of its acceptance.

The focus on the acceptability and regularity of the death penalty's imposition in certain kinds of cases—that is, whether imposing the sanction in such cases comports with contemporary standards of decency as reflected by legislative enactments and jury sentences—is connected to the insistence that statutes permitting its imposition channel the sentencing process toward nonarbitrary results. For both a statutory scheme that fails to guide jury discretion in a meaningful way, and a pattern of legislative enactments or jury sentences revealing a lack of interest on the part of the public in sentencing certain people to death, indicate that contemporary morality is not really ready to permit the regular imposition of the harshest of sanctions in such cases.

8. Thus, in explaining our conclusion that the death penalty may not be imposed for the crime of raping an adult woman, Justice White stated:

"[T]he Constitution contemplates that in the end our own judgment will be brought to bear on the question of the acceptability of the death penalty under the Eighth Amendment." *Coker v. Georgia,* 433 U.S., at 597.

9. See also *New Jersey v. T.L.O.,* 469 U.S. 325, 350, n. 2 (1985) (Powell, J., concurring); *Burger v. Kemp,* 483 U.S. 776 (1987) (Powell, J., dissenting).

10. Okla. Const., Art. 3, 1.

11. Okla. Stat., Tit. 38, 28 (1981), and Okla. Const., Art. 3, 1.

12. Okla. Stat., Tit. 43, 3 (1981).

13. Okla. Stat., Tit. 21, 1215 (1981).

14. Okla. Stat., Tit. 21, 1241 (Supp. 1987). Additionally, minors may not patronize bingo parlors or pool halls unless accompanied by an adult, Okla. Stat., Tit. 21, 995.13, 1103 (1981), pawn property, Okla. Stat., Tit. 59, 1511 (C)(1) (1981), consent to services by health professionals for most medical care, unless married or otherwise emancipated, Okla. Stat., Tit. 63, 2602 (1981), 2601(a) (Supp. 1987), or operate or work at a shooting gallery, Okla. Stat., Tit. 63, 703 (1984), and may disaffirm any contract, except for "necessaries," Okla. Stat., Tit. 15, 19, 20 (1981).

15. See n. 2, supra; cf. *Craig v. Boren,* 429 U.S. 190, 197 (1976).

Columbia[16] in treating a person under 16 as a minor for several important purposes. In no State may a 15-year-old vote or serve on a jury.[17] Further, in all but one State a 15-year-old may not drive without parental consent,[18] and in all but four States a 15-year-old may not marry without parental consent.[19] Additionally, in those States that have legislated on the subject, no one under age 16 may purchase pornographic materials (50 States),[20] and in most States that have some form of legalized gambling, minors are not permitted to participate without parental consent (42 States).[21] Most relevant, however, is the fact that all States have enacted legislation designating the maximum age for juvenile court jurisdiction at no less than 16.[22] All of this legislation is consistent with the experience of mankind, as well as the long history of our law, that the normal 15-year-old is not prepared to assume the full responsibilities of an adult.[23]

---

16. Henceforth, the opinion will refer to the 50 States and the District of Columbia as "States," for sake of simplicity.

17. See Appendices A and B, infra.

18. See Appendix C, infra.

19. See Appendix D, infra.

20. See Appendix E, infra.

21. See Appendix F, infra.

22. S. Davis, *Rights of Juveniles: The Juvenile Justice System,* Appendix B (1987). Thus, every State has adopted "a rebuttable presumption" that a person under 16 "is not mature and responsible enough to be punished as an adult," no matter how minor the offense may be. Post, at 859 (dissenting opinion).

23. The law must often adjust the manner in which it affords rights to those whose status renders them unable to exercise choice freely and rationally. Children, the insane, and those who are irreversibly ill with loss of brain function, for instance, all retain "rights," to be sure, but often such rights are only meaningful as they are exercised by agents acting with the best interests of their principals in mind. See Garvey, Freedom and Choice in Constitutional Law, 94 Harv. L. Rev. 1756 (1981). It is in this way that paternalism bears a beneficent face, paternalism in the sense of a caring, nurturing parent making decisions on behalf of a child who is not quite ready to take on the fully rational and considered task of shaping his or her own life. The assemblage of statutes in the text above, from both Oklahoma and other States, reflects this basic assumption that our society makes about children as a class; we assume that they do not yet act as adults do, and thus we act in their interest by restricting certain choices that we feel they are not yet ready to make with full benefit of the costs and benefits attending such decisions. It would be ironic if these assumptions that we so readily make about children as a class—about their inherent difference from adults in their capacity as agents, as choosers, as shapers of their own lives—were suddenly unavailable in determining whether it is cruel and unusual to treat children the same as adults for purposes of inflicting capital punishment. Thus, informing the judgment of the Court today is the virtue of consistency, for the very assumptions we make about our children when we legislate on their behalf tells us that it is likely cruel, and certainly unusual, to impose on a child a punishment that takes as its predicate the existence of a fully rational, choosing agent, who may be deterred by the harshest of sanctions and toward whom society may legitimately take a retributive stance. As we have observed: "Children, by definition, are not assumed to have the capacity to take care of themselves. They are assumed to be subject to the control of their parents, and if parental control falters, the State must play its part as parens patriae." *Schall v. Martin,* 467 U.S. 253, 265 (1984); see also *May v. Anderson,* 345 U.S. 528, 536 (1953) (Frankfurter, J., concurring) ("Children have a very special place in life which law should reflect. Legal theories . . . lead to fallacious reasoning if uncritically transferred to determination of a State's duty towards children"); *Ginsberg v. New York,* 390 U.S. 629, 649–650 (1968) (Stewart, J., concurring in result) ("[A]t least in some precisely delineated areas, a child . . . is not possessed of that full capacity for individual choice which is the presupposition of First Amendment guarantees. It is only upon such a premise . . . that a State may deprive children of other rights—the right to marry, for example, or the right to vote—deprivations that would be constitutionally intolerable for adults"); *Parham v. J. R.,* 442 U.S. 584, 603 (1979) ("Most children, even in adolescence, simply are not able to make sound judgments concerning many decisions").

Most state legislatures have not expressly confronted the question of establishing a minimum age for imposition of the death penalty.[24] In 14 States, capital punishment is not authorized at all,[25] and in 19 others capital punishment is authorized but no minimum age is

24. Almost every State, and the Federal Government, has set a minimum age at which juveniles accused of committing serious crimes can be waived from juvenile court into criminal court. See Davis, supra, n. 22; 18 U.S.C. 5032 (1982 ed., Supp IV). The dissent's focus on the presence of these waiver ages in jurisdictions that retain the death penalty but that have not expressly set a minimum age for the death sentence, see post, at 867-868, distorts what is truly at issue in this case. Consider the following example: The States of Michigan, Oregon, and Virginia have all determined that a 15-year-old may be waived from juvenile to criminal court when charged with first-degree murder. See Mich. Comp. Laws 712A.4(1) (1979); Ore. Rev. Stat. 419.533(1)(a), (1)(b), (3) (1987); Va. Code 16.1-269(A) (1988). However, in Michigan, that 15-year-old may not be executed—because the State has abolished the death penalty—and, in Oregon, that 15-year-old may not be executed—because the State has abolished the death penalty—and, in Oregon, that 15-year-old may not be executed—because the State has expressly set a minimum age of 18 for executions—but, in Virginia, that 15-year-old may be executed—because the State has a death penalty and has not expressly addressed the issue of minimum age for execution. That these three States have all set a 15-year-old waiver floor for first-degree murder tells us that the States consider 15-year-olds to be old enough to be tried in criminal court for serious crimes (or too old to be dealt with effectively in juvenile court), but tells us nothing about the judgment these States have made regarding the appropriate punishment for such youthful offenders. As a matter of fact, many States in the Union have waiver ages below 16, including many of the States that have either abolished the death penalty or that have set an express minimum age for the death penalty at 16 or higher. See Davis, supra, n. 22. In sum, we believe that the more appropriate measures for determining how the States view the issue of minimum age for the death penalty are those discussed in the text and in n. 29, infra.

25. Alaska (Territory of Alaska, Session Laws, 1957, ch. 132, 23d Sess., an Act abolishing the death penalty for the commission of any crime; see Alaska Stat. Ann. 12.55.015 (1987). "Authorized sentences" do not include the death penalty; 12.55.125, "Sentences of imprisonment for felonies" do not include the death penalty); District of Columbia (*United States v. Lee,* 160 U.S. App. D.C. 118, 122-123, 489 F.2d 1242, 1246-1247 (1973), death penalty unconstitutional in light of *Furman v. Georgia,* 408 U.S. 238 (1972); see D.C. Code 22-2404 (1981), penalty for first-degree murder does not include death); Hawaii (Territory of Hawaii, Regular Session Laws, 1957, Act 282, 28th Leg., an Act relating to the abolishment of capital punishment; see Hawaii Rev. Stat., 706-656 (Supp. 1987), sentence for offense of murder does not include death penalty); Iowa (1965 Iowa Acts, ch. 435, Death Penalty Abolished; see Iowa Code 902.1 (1987), penalties for Class A felonies do not include death); Kansas (*State v. Randol,* 212 Kan. 461, 471, 513 P.2d 248, 256 (1973), death penalty unconstitutional after *Furman v. Georgia,* supra; death penalty still on books, Kan. Stat. Ann. 22-4001-22-4014 (1981); but see 21-3401, first-degree murder is a Class A felony, and 21-4501(a), sentence for a Class A felony does not include death penalty); Maine (1887 Maine Acts, ch. 133, an Act to abolish the death penalty; see Me. Rev. Stat. Ann., Tit. 17-A, 1251, 1152 (1983 and Supp. 1987-1988), authorized sentences for murder do not include death penalty); Massachusetts (*Commonwealth v. Colon-Cruz,* 393 Mass. 150, 470 N. E. 2d 116 (1984), death penalty statute violates State Constitution; death penalty law still on books, Mass. Gen. Laws 279:57–279:71 (1986)); Michigan (Const., Art. 4, 46, "No law shall be enacted providing for the penalty of death"; see Mich. Comp. Laws 750.316 (Supp. 1988-1989), no death penalty provided for first-degree murder); Minnesota (1911 Minn. Laws, ch. 387, providing for life imprisonment and not death as sentence; see Minn. Stat. 609.10 (1986), sentences available do not include death penalty, and 609.185, sentence for first-degree murder is life imprisonment); New York (*People v. Smith,* 63 N.Y. 2d 41, 70-79, 468 N. E. 2d 879, 893-899 (1984), mandatory death penalty for first-degree murder while serving a sentence of life imprisonment unconstitutional after *Woodson v. North Carolina,* 428 U.S. 280 (1976), thus invalidating remainder of New York's death penalty statute; death penalty still on books, N.Y. Penal Law 60.06 (McKinney 1987), providing for death penalty for first-degree murder); North Dakota (N.D. Cent. Code, ch. 12-50 (1985), "The Death Sentence and Execution Thereof," repealed by 1973 N.D. Laws, ch. 116, 41, effective July 1, 1975); Rhode Island (*State v. Cline,* 121 R. I. 299, 397 A. 2d 1309 (1979), mandatory death penalty for any prisoner unconstitutional after *Woodson v. North Carolina,* supra; see R.I. Gen. Laws 11-23-2 (Supp. 1987), penalties for murder do not include death); West Virginia (W. Va. Code 61-11-2 (1984), "Capital punishment abolished"); Wisconsin (1853 Wis. Laws, ch. 103, "An act to provide for the punishment of murder in the first degree, and to abolish the penalty of death"; see Wis. Stat. 939.50(3)(a), 940.01 (1985-1986), first-degree murder is a Class A felony, and the penalty for such felonies is life imprisonment).

expressly stated in the death penalty statute.[26] One might argue on the basis of this body of legislation that there is no chronological age at which the imposition of the death penalty is unconstitutional and that our current standards of decency would still tolerate the execution of 10-year-old children.[27] We think it self-evident that such an argument is unacceptable; indeed, no such argument has been advanced in this case.[28] If, therefore, we accept the premise that some offenders are simply too young to be put to death, it is reasonable to put this group of statutes to one side because they do not focus on the question of where the chronological age line should be drawn.[29] When we confine our attention to the 18 States that have expressly established a minimum age in their death penalty statutes, we find that all of them require that the defendant have attained at least the age of 16 at the time of the capital offense.[30]

---

26. Alabama (see Ala. Code 13A-5-39–13A-5-59, 13A-6-2 (1982 and Supp. 1987)); Arizona (see Ariz. Rev. Stat. Ann. 13-703–13-706, 13-1105 (1978 and Supp. 1987)); Arkansas (see Ark. Code Ann. 5-4-104(b), 5-4-601–5-4-617, 5-10-101, 5-51-201 (1987 and Supp. 1987)); Delaware (see Del. Code Ann., Tit. 11, 636, 4209 (1987)); Florida (see Fla. Stat. 775.082, 782.04(1), 921.141 (1987)); Idaho (see Idaho Code 18-4001–18-4004, 19-2515 (1987)); Louisiana (see La. Rev. Stat. Ann. 14:30(C), 14:113 (West 1986); La. Code Crim. Proc. Ann., Art. 905 et seq. (West 1984 and Supp. 1988)); Mississippi (see Miss. Code Ann. 97-3-21, 97-7-67, 99-19-101–99-19-107 (Supp. 1987)); Missouri (see Mo. Rev. Stat. 565.020, 565.030-565.040 (1986)); Montana (see Mont. Code Ann. 45-5-102, 46-18-301–46-18-310 (1987)); Oklahoma (see Okla. Stat., Tit. 21, 701.10-701.15 (1981 and Supp. 1987)); Pennsylvania (see Pa. Cons. Stat., Tit. 18, 1102(a), Tit. 42, 9711 (1982 and Supp. 1987)); South Carolina (see S.C. Code 16-3-10, 16-3-20 (1985 and Supp. 1987)); South Dakota (see S.D. Codified Laws 22-16-4, 22-16-12, 23A-27A-1–23A-27A-41 (1988)); Utah (see Utah Code Ann. 76-3-206, 76-3-207 (1978 and Supp. 1987)); Vermont (see Vt. Stat. Ann., Tit. 13, 2303, 2403, 7101-7107 (1974 and Supp. 1987)); Virginia (see Va. Code 18.2-31 (1988), 19.2-264.2–19.2-264.5 (1983 and Supp. 1987)); Washington (see Wash. Rev. Code 10.95.010–10.95.900 (1987)); Wyoming (see Wyo. Stat. 6-2-101–6-2-103 (1988)).

27. It is reported that a 10-year-old black child was hanged in Louisiana in 1855 and a Cherokee Indian child of the same age was hanged in Arkansas in 1885. See Streib, Death Penalty for Children: The American Experience with Capital Punishment for Crimes Committed While under Age Eighteen, 36 Okla. L. Rev. 613, 619–620 (1983).

28. See Tr. of Oral Arg. 31 (respondent suggests a minimum age of 14); post, at 872 (dissent agrees that some line exists); post, at 848 (concurrence similarly agrees).

29. One might argue, of course, that petitioner's execution "could theoretically be imposed" in 19 States, see post, at 864 (dissenting opinion), just as execution was permissible above the age of 7 in Blackstone's time. Ibid. This argument would, though, first have to acknowledge that the execution would be impermissible in 32 States. Additionally, 2 of the 19 States that retain a death penalty without setting a minimum age simply do not sentence people to death anymore. Neither South Dakota nor Vermont has imposed a death sentence since our landmark decision in Furman v. Georgia, 408 U.S. 238 (1972). See Greenberg, Capital Punishment as a System, 91 Yale L. J. 908, 929–936 (1982); NAACP Legal Defense and Educational Fund, Inc., Death Row, U.S.A. (1980-1987). (Vermont is frequently counted as a 15th State without a death penalty, since its capital punishment scheme fails to guide jury discretion, see Vt. Stat. Ann., Tit. 13, 7101-7107 (1974), and has not been amended since our decision in Furman v. Georgia, supra, holding similar statutes unconstitutional. South Dakota's statute does provide for jury consideration of aggravating and mitigating factors. See S.D. Codified Laws, ch. 23A-27A (1988)). Thus, if one were to shift the focus from those States that have expressly dealt with the issue of minimum age and toward a general comparison of States whose statutes, facially, would and would not permit petitioner's execution, one would have to acknowledge a 2-to-1 ratio of States in which it is not even "theoretically" possible that Thompson's execution could occur.

30. California (Cal. Penal Code Ann. 190.5 (West 1988)) (age 18); Colorado (Colo. Rev. Stat. 16-11-103(1)(a) (1986)) (age 18); Connecticut (Conn. Gen. Stat. 53a-46a(g)(1) (1985)) (age 18); Georgia (Ga. Code Ann. 17-9-3 (1982)) (age 17); Illinois (Ill. Rev. Stat., ch. 38, 9-1(b) (1987)) (age 18); Indiana (Ind. Code 35-50-2-3 (Supp. 1987)) (age 16); Kentucky (Ky. Rev. Stat. 640.040(1) (1987)) (age 16); Maryland (Md. Ann. Code, Art. 27, 412(f) (1988)) (age 18); Nebraska (Neb. Rev. Stat. 28-105.01 (1985)) (age 18); Nevada (Nev. Rev. Stat. 176.025 (1987)) (age 16); New Hampshire (N. H. Rev. Stat. Ann. 630:5(XIII) (Supp. 1987)) (prohibiting execution of one who was a minor at time of crime) (21-B:1 indicates that age 18 is age of majority, while 630:1(V) provides that no one under age 17 shall be held culpable of a capital offense); New Jersey (N.J. Stat. Ann. 2A:4A-22(a) (1987), 2C:11-3(g) (West Supp.

The conclusion that it would offend civilized standards of decency to execute a person who was less than 16 years old at the time of his or her offense is consistent with the views that have been expressed by respected professional organizations, by other nations that share our Anglo-American heritage, and by the leading members of the Western European community.[31] Thus, the American Bar Association[32] and the American Law Institute[33] have formally expressed their opposition to the death penalty for juveniles. Although the death penalty has not been entirely abolished in the United Kingdom or New Zealand (it has been abolished in Australia, except in the State of New South Wales, where it is available for treason and piracy), in neither of those countries may a juvenile be executed. The death penalty has been abolished in West Germany, France, Portugal, The Netherlands, and all of the Scandinavian countries, and is available only for exceptional crimes such as treason in Canada, Italy, Spain, and Switzerland. Juvenile executions are also prohibited in the Soviet Union.[34]

IV

The second societal factor the Court has examined in determining the acceptability of capital punishment to the American sensibility is the behavior of juries. In fact, the infrequent and haphazard handing out of death sentences by capital juries was a prime factor underlying

---

1988)) (age 18); New Mexico (N.M. Stat. Ann. 28-6-1(A), 31-18-14(A) (1987)) (age 18); North Carolina (N.C. Gen. Stat. 14-17 (Supp. 1987)) (age 17, except death penalty still valid for anyone who commits first-degree murder while serving prison sentence for prior murder or while on escape from such sentence); Ohio (Ohio Rev. Code Ann. 2929.02(A) (1984)) (age 18); Oregon (Ore. Rev. Stat. 161.620, 419.476(1) (1987)) (age 18); Tennessee (Tenn. Code Ann. 37-1-102(3), (4), 37-1-103, 37-1-134(a)(1) (1984 and Supp. 1987)) (age 18); Texas (Tex. Penal Code Ann. 8.07(d) (Supp. 1987-1988)) (age 17).

In addition, the Senate recently passed a bill authorizing the death penalty for certain drug-related killings, with the caveat that "[a] sentence of death shall not be carried out upon a person who is under 18 years of age at the time the crime was committed." S. 2455, 100th Cong., 2d Sess.; 134 Cong. Rec. 14118 (1988).

31. We have previously recognized the relevance of the views of the international community in determining whether a punishment is cruel and unusual. See *Trop v. Dulles,* 356 U.S. 86, 102, and n. 35 (1958); *Coker v. Georgia,* 433 U.S., at 596, n. 10; *Enmund v. Florida,* 458 U.S., at 796–797, n. 22.

32. "Be It Resolved, That the American Bar Association opposes, in principle, the imposition of capital punishment upon any person for any offense committed while under the age of eighteen (18)." American Bar Association, Summary of Action Taken by the House of Delegates 17 (1983 Annual Meeting).

33. "[C]ivilized societies will not tolerate the spectacle of execution of children . . . ." American Law Institute, Model Penal Code 210.6, commentary, p. 133 (Official Draft and Revised Comments 1980).

34. All information regarding foreign death penalty laws is drawn from App. to Brief for Amnesty International as Amicus Curiae A-1–A-9, and from Death Penalty in Various Countries, prepared by members of the staff of the Law Library of the Library of Congress, January 22, 1988 (available in Clerk of Court's case file). See also Children and Young Persons Act, 1933, 23 Geo. 5, ch. 12, 53(1), as amended by the Murder (Abolition of Death Penalty) Act 1965, 1(5), 4 (abolishing death penalty for juvenile offenders in United Kingdom), reprinted in 6 Halsbury's Statutes 55–56 (4th ed. 1985); Crimes Act, 1961, 16, in 1 Reprinted Statutes of New Zealand 650-651 (1979). In addition, three major human rights treaties explicitly prohibit juvenile death penalties. Article 6(5) of the International Covenant on Civil and Political Rights, Annex to G. A. Res. 2200, 21 U.N. GAOR Res. Supp. (No. 16) 53, U.N. Doc. A/6316 (1966) (signed but not ratified by the United States), reprinted in 6 International Legal Material 368, 370 (1967); Article 4(5) of the American Convention on Human Rights, O.A.S. Official Records, OEA/Ser.K/XVI/1.1, Doc. 65, Rev. 1, Corr. 2 (1970) (signed but not ratified by the United States), reprinted in 9 International Legal Material 673, 676 (1970); Article 68 of the Geneva Convention Relative to the Protection of Civilian Persons in Time of War, August 12, 1949, 1955. 6 U.S. T. 3516, 3560, T. I. A. S. No. 3365 (ratified by the United States).

our judgment in *Furman v. Georgia,* 408 U.S. 238 (1972), that the death penalty, as then administered in unguided fashion, was unconstitutional.[35]

While it is not known precisely how many persons have been executed during the 20th century for crimes committed under the age of 16, a scholar has recently compiled a table revealing this number to be between 18 and 20.[36] All of these occurred during the first half of the century, with the last such execution taking place apparently in 1948.[37] In the following year this Court observed that this "whole country has traveled far from the period in which the death sentence was an automatic and commonplace result of convictions . . . ." *Williams v. New York,* 337 U.S. 241, 247 (1949). The road we have traveled during the past four decades—in which thousands of juries have tried murder cases—leads to the unambiguous conclusion that the imposition of the death penalty on a 15-year-old offender is now generally abhorrent to the conscience of the community.

Department of Justice statistics indicate that during the years 1982 through 1986 an average of over 16,000 persons were arrested for willful criminal homicide (murder and nonnegligent manslaughter) each year. Of that group of 82,094 persons, 1,393 were sentenced to death. Only 5 of them, including the petitioner in this case, were less than 16 years old at the time of the offense.[38] Statistics of this kind can, of course, be interpreted in different ways,[39] but they do suggest that these five young offenders have received sentences that are "cruel and unusual in the same way that being struck by lightning is cruel and unusual." *Furman v. Georgia,* 408 U.S., at 309 (Stewart, J., concurring).

V

"Although the judgments of legislatures, juries, and prosecutors weigh heavily in the balance, it is for us ultimately to judge whether the Eighth Amendment permits imposition of the death penalty" on one such as petitioner who committed a heinous murder when he

---

35. See *Furman v. Georgia,* 408 U.S., at 249 (rarity of a sentence leads to an inference of its arbitrary imposition) (Douglas, J., concurring); id., at 274-277 (Eighth Amendment prevents arbitrary death sentences; rarity of death sentences results in an inference of arbitrariness) (Brennan, J., concurring); id., at 299-300 (Brennan, J., concurring); id., at 312 (rarity of imposition indicates arbitrariness; "A penalty with such negligible returns to the State would be patently excessive" and therefore violate the Eighth Amendment) (White, J., concurring); id., at 314 (White, J., concurring); see also *Enmund v. Florida,* 458 U.S., at 794-796 (few juries sentence defendants to death who neither killed nor intended to kill).

36. V. Streib, Death Penalty for Juveniles 190-208 (1987) (compiling information regarding all executions in this country from 1620 through 1986 for crimes committed while under age 18; uncertainty between 18 and 20 because of two persons executed who may have been either 15 or 16 at time of crime).

37. Professor Streib reports that the last execution of a person for a crime committed under age 16 was on January 9, 1948, when Louisiana executed Irvin Mattio, 15 at the time of his crime. Id., at 197.

38. See U.S. Dept. of Justice, Uniform Crime Reports: Crime in the United States 174 (1986); id., at 174 (1985); id., at 172 (1984); id., at 179 (1983); id., at 176 (1982); U.S. Dept. of Justice, Bureau of Justice Statistics Bulletin: Capital Punishment, 1986, p. 4 (1987); id., Capital Punishment 1985, p. 5 (1986); id., Capital Punishment 1984, p. 6 (1985); Streib, supra, n. 36, at 168-169.

39. For example, one might observe that of the 80,233 people arrested for willful criminal homicide who were over the age of 16, 1,388, or 1.7%, received the death sentence, while 5 of the 1,861, or 0.3%, of those under 16 who were arrested for willful criminal homicide received the death penalty.

was only 15 years old. *Enmund v. Florida,* 458 U.S. 782, 797 (1982).[40] In making that judgment, we first ask whether the juvenile's culpability should be measured by the same standard as that of an adult, and then consider whether the application of the death penalty to this class of offenders "measurably contributes" to the social purposes that are served by the death penalty. Id., at 798.

It is generally agreed "that punishment should be directly related to the personal culpability of the criminal defendant." *California v. Brown,* 479 U.S. 538, 545 (1987) (O'Connor, J., concurring). There is also broad agreement on the proposition that adolescents as a class are less mature and responsible than adults. We stressed this difference in explaining the importance of treating the defendant's youth as a mitigating factor in capital cases:

> "But youth is more than a chronological fact. It is a time and condition of life when a person may be most susceptible to influence and to psychological damage. Our history is replete with laws and judicial recognition that minors, especially in their earlier years, generally are less mature and responsible than adults. Particularly 'during the formative years of childhood and adolescence, minors often lack the experience, perspective, and judgment' expected of adults. *Bellotti v. Baird,* 443 U.S. 622, 635 (1979)." *Eddings v. Oklahoma,* 455 U.S. 104, 115–116 (1982) (footnotes omitted).

To add further emphasis to the special mitigating force of youth, Justice Powell quoted the following passage from the 1978 Report of the Twentieth Century Fund Task Force on Sentencing Policy Toward Young Offenders:

> "'[A]dolescents, particularly in the early and middle teen years, are more vulnerable, more impulsive, and less self-disciplined than adults. Crimes committed by youths may be just as harmful to victims as those committed by older persons, but they deserve less punishment because adolescents may have less capacity to control their conduct and to think in long-range terms than adults. Moreover, youth crime as such is not exclusively the offender's fault; offenses by the young also represent a failure of family, school, and the social system, which share responsibility for the development of America's youth.'" 455 U.S., at 115, n. 11.

Thus, the Court has already endorsed the proposition that less culpability should attach to a crime committed by a juvenile than to a comparable crime committed by an adult.[41] The

---

40. That the task of interpreting the great, sweeping clauses of the Constitution ultimately falls to us has been for some time an accepted principle of American jurisprudence. See *Marbury v. Madison,* 1 Cranch 137, 177 (1803) ("It is emphatically the province and duty of the judicial department to say what the law is"). With the Eighth Amendment, whose broad, vague terms do not yield to a mechanical parsing, the method is no different. See, e.g., *Furman v. Georgia,* 408 U.S., at 268-269 (Brennan, J., concurring); *Coker v. Georgia,* 433 U.S., at 598 ("We have the abiding conviction" that the death penalty is an excessive penalty for rape).

41. "[T]he conception of criminal responsibility with which the Juvenile Court operates also provides supporting rationale for its role in crime prevention. The basic philosophy concerning this is that criminal responsibility is absent in the case of misbehaving children.... But, what does it mean to say that a child has no criminal responsibility? ... One thing about this does seem clearly implied, ... and that is an absence of the basis for adult criminal accountability—the exercise of an unfettered free will." S. Fox, The Juvenile Court: Its Context, Problems and Opportunities 11–12 (1967) (publication of the President's Commission on Law Enforcement and Administration of Justice).

basis for this conclusion is too obvious to require extended explanation.[42] Inexperience, less education, and less intelligence make the teenager less able to evaluate the consequences of his or her conduct while at the same time he or she is much more apt to be motivated by mere emotion or peer pressure than is an adult. The reasons why juveniles are not trusted with the privileges and responsibilities of an adult also explain why their irresponsible conduct is not as morally reprehensible as that of an adult.[43]

"The death penalty is said to serve two principal social purposes: retribution and deterrence of capital crimes by prospective offenders." *Gregg v. Georgia*, 428 U.S. 153, 183 (1976) (joint opinion of Stewart, Powell, and Stevens, J. J.). In Gregg we concluded that as "an expression of society's moral outrage at particularly offensive conduct," retribution was not "inconsistent with our respect for the dignity of men." Ibid.[44] Given the lesser culpability of the juvenile offender, the teenager's capacity for growth, and society's fiduciary obligations to its children, this conclusion is simply inapplicable to the execution of a 15-year-old offender.

---

42. A report on a professional evaluation of 14 juveniles condemned to death in the United States, which was accepted for presentation to the American Academy of Child and Adolescent Psychiatry, concluded:
"Adolescence is well recognized as a time of great physiological and psychological stress. Our data indicate that, above and beyond these maturational stresses, homicidal adolescents must cope with brain dysfunction, cognitive limitations, and severe psychopathology. Moreover, they must function in families that are not merely nonsupportive but also violent and brutally abusive. These findings raise questions about the American tradition of considering adolescents to be as responsible as adults for their offenses and of sentencing them to death." Lewis, Pincus, Bard, Richardson, Prichep, Feldman, & Yeager, Neuropsychiatric, Psychoeducational, and Family Characteristics of 14 Juveniles Condemned to Death in the United States 11 (1987).

43. See n. 23, supra; see also, e.g., E. Erikson, Childhood and Society 261–263 (1985) ("In their search for a new sense of continuity and sameness, adolescents have to refight many of the battles of earlier years, even though to do so they must artificially appoint perfectly well-meaning people to play the roles of adversaries"); E. Erikson, Identity: Youth and Crisis 128–135 (1968) (discussing adolescence as a period of "identity confusion," during which youths are "preoccupied with what they appear to be in the eyes of others as compared with what they feel they are"); Gordon, The Tattered Cloak of Immortality, in Adolescence and Death 16, 27 (C. Corr & J. McNeil eds. 1986) ("Risk-taking with body safety is common in the adolescent years, though sky diving, car racing, excessive use of drugs and alcoholic beverages, and other similar activities may not be directly perceived as a kind of flirting with death. In fact, in many ways, this is counterphobic behavior—a challenge to death wherein each survival of risk is a victory over death"); Kastenbaum, Time and Death in Adolescence, in The Meaning of Death 99, 104 (H. Feifel ed. 1959) ("The adolescent lives in an intense present; 'now' is so real to him that past and future seem pallid by comparison. Everything that is important and valuable in life lies either in the immediate life situation or in the rather close future"); Kohlberg, The Development of Children's Orientations Toward a Moral Order, 6 Vita Humana 11, 30 (1963) (studies reveal that "large groups of moral concepts and ways of thought only attain meaning at successively advanced ages and require the extensive background of social experience and cognitive growth represented by the age factor"); Miller, Adolescent Suicide: Etiology and Treatment, 9 Adolescent Psychiatry 327, 329 (S. Feinstein, J. Looney, A. Schwartzberg, & A. Sorosky eds. 1981) (many adolescents possess a "profound conviction of their own omnipotence and immortality. Thus many adolescents may appear to be attempting suicide, but they do not really believe that death will occur"); Streib, supra n. 36, at 3-20, 184-189 ("The difference that separates children from adults for most purposes of the law is children's immature, undeveloped ability to reason in an adult-like manner").

44. We have invalidated death sentences when this significant justification was absent. See *Enmund v. Florida*, 458 U.S., at 800-801 (death penalty for one who neither kills nor intends to kill "does not measurably contribute to the retributive end of ensuring that the criminal gets his just deserts"); *Ford v. Wainwright*, 477 U.S. 399 (1986) (unconstitutional to execute someone when he is insane, in large part because retributive value is so low).

For such a young offender, the deterrence rationale is equally unacceptable.[45] The Department of Justice statistics indicate that about 98% of the arrests for willful homicide involved persons who were over 16 at the time of the offense.[46] Thus, excluding younger persons from the class that is eligible for the death penalty will not diminish the deterrent value of capital punishment for the vast majority of potential offenders. And even with respect to those under 16 years of age, it is obvious that the potential deterrent value of the death sentence is insignificant for two reasons. The likelihood that the teenage offender has made the kind of cost-benefit analysis that attaches any weight to the possibility of execution is so remote as to be virtually nonexistent. And, even if one posits such a cold-blooded calculation by a 15-year-old, it is fanciful to believe that he would be deterred by the knowledge that a small number of persons his age have been executed during the 20th century. In short, we are not persuaded that the imposition of the death penalty for offenses committed by persons under 16 years of age has made, or can be expected to make, any measurable contribution to the goals that capital punishment is intended to achieve. It is, therefore, "nothing more than the purposeless and needless imposition of pain and suffering," *Coker v. Georgia,* 433 U.S., at 592, and thus an unconstitutional punishment.[47]

VI

Petitioner's counsel and various amici curiae have asked us to "draw a line" that would prohibit the execution of any person who was under the age of 18 at the time of the offense. Our task today, however, is to decide the case before us; we do so by concluding that the Eighth and Fourteenth Amendments prohibit the execution of a person who was under 16 years of age at the time of his or her offense.[48]

The judgment of the Court of Criminal Appeals is vacated, and the case is remanded with instructions to enter an appropriate order vacating petitioner's death sentence.

It is so ordered.

---

45. Although we have held that a legislature may base a capital punishment scheme on the goal of deterrence, some Members of the Court have expressed doubts about whether fear of death actually deters crimes in certain instances. See *Lockett v. Ohio,* 438 U.S. 586, 624-628 (1978) (deterrence argument unavailable for one who neither kills nor intends to kill; "doubtful" that prospect of death penalty would deter "individuals from becoming involved in ventures in which death may unintentionally result") (White, J., concurring in judgment); *Spaziano v. Florida,* 468 U.S. 447, 480 (1984) (because of invalidation of mandatory death penalty laws and additional procedural requirements to death penalty laws in which the jury's discretion must be carefully guided, deterrence rationale now rather weak support for capital punishment) (Stevens, J., dissenting); *Enmund v. Florida,* 458 U.S., at 798-800 (unlikely that prospect of death penalty will deter one who neither kills nor intends to kill) (White, J.); *Furman v. Georgia,* 408 U.S., at 301-302 (unverifiable that the death penalty deters more effectively than life imprisonment) (Brennan, J., concurring); id., at 345-355, and nn. 124-125 (deterrence rationale unsupported by the evidence) (Marshall, J., concurring).

46. See United States Department of Justice, Uniform Crime Reports, supra, n. 38 (80,233 of 82,094, or 97.7%).

47. See also *Gregg v. Georgia,* 428 U.S. 153, 183 (1976) ("[T]he sanction imposed cannot be so totally without penological justification that it results in the gratuitous infliction of suffering") (joint opinion of Stewart, Powell, and Stevens, J. J.).

48. Given the Court's disposition of the principal issue, it is unnecessary to resolve the second question presented, namely, whether photographic evidence that a state court deems erroneously admitted but harmless at the guilt phase nevertheless violates a capital defendant's constitutional rights by virtue of its being considered at the penalty phase.

Case Comment

In *Stanford v. Kentucky,* The U.S. Supreme Court was essentially asked to extend its ruling in *Thompson* by increasing the age at which the death penalty was prohibited. The issue before the Court was whether virtually all juvenile murderers (i.e., anyone under the age of 18 at the time of the capital murder) were entitled to the same Eighth Amendment prohibition against the death penalty as juveniles under the age of 16 like Thompson.

Stanford was 17 years old when he was convicted by a Kentucky jury of murder, sodomy, robbery, and the receipt of stolen property. Stanford was sentenced to death under a Kentucky statute that permitted juvenile offenders to receive the death penalty for Class A felonies or capital crimes. Stanford appealed his sentence, and his case was consolidated with that of *Wilkins v. Missouri,* which involved a 16-year-old's appeal of his death sentence following a conviction for murder. Both Stanford and Wilkins alleged that the imposition of the death penalty on offenders as young as themselves violated their constitutional rights.

The Supreme Court held that there was no consensus reflective of an evolving decency standard regarding the imposition of capital punishment on 16- or 17-year-old juveniles. The Court noted that of the 37 states that permit capital punishment, 12 prohibit the death penalty for offenders below the age of 17 while 15 states prohibit capital punishment for 16-year-olds. Further, the Court noted discrepancies in national opinion polls, interest group views, and professional association studies, which indicated a lack of unanimity concerning the acceptability of death sentences for such relatively young offenders. Thus, the age limit established in *Thompson* (under age 16) remained unchanged.

STANFORD V. KENTUCKY

Supreme Court of the United States, 1989.

492 U.S. 361.

Justice Scalia announced the judgment of the Court and delivered the opinion of the Court with respect to Parts I, II, III, and IV-A, in which Rehnquist, C. J., and White, O'Connor, and Kennedy, J. J., joined, and an opinion with respect to Parts IV-B and V, in which Rehnquist, C. J., and White and Kennedy, J. J., joined. O'Connor, J., filed an opinion concurring in part and concurring in the judgment, post, p. 380. Brennan, J., filed a dissenting opinion, in which Marshall, Blackmun, and Stevens, J. J., joined, post, p. 382.

These two consolidated cases require us to decide whether the imposition of capital punishment on an individual for a crime committed at 16 or 17 years of age constitutes cruel and unusual punishment under the Eighth Amendment.

I

The first case, No. 87–5765, involves the shooting death of 20-year-old Barbel Poore in Jefferson County, Kentucky. Petitioner Kevin Stanford committed the murder on January 7, 1981, when he was approximately 17 years and 4 months of age. Stanford and his accomplice repeatedly raped and sodomized Poore during and after their commission of a robbery at a gas station where she worked as an attendant. They then drove her to a secluded area near the station, where Stanford shot her pointblank in the face and then in the back of her head.

The proceeds from the robbery were roughly 300 cartons of cigarettes, two gallons of fuel, and a small amount of cash. A corrections officer testified that petitioner explained the murder as follows: "'[H]e said, I had to shoot her, [she] lived next door to me and she would recognize me. . . . I guess we could have tied her up or something or beat [her up] . . . and tell her if she tells, we would kill her. . . . Then after he said that he started laughing.'" 734 S. W. 2d 781, 788 (Ky. 1987).

After Stanford's arrest, a Kentucky juvenile court conducted hearings to determine whether he should be transferred for trial as an adult under Ky. Rev. Stat. Ann. 208.170 (Michie 1982). That statute provided that juvenile court jurisdiction could be waived and an offender tried as an adult if he was either charged with a Class A felony or capital crime, or was over 16 years of age and charged with a felony. Stressing the seriousness of petitioner's offenses and the unsuccessful attempts of the juvenile system to treat him for numerous instances of past delinquency, the juvenile court found certification for trial as an adult to be in the best interest of petitioner and the community.

Stanford was convicted of murder, first-degree sodomy, first-degree robbery, and receiving stolen property, and was sentenced to death and 45 years in prison. The Kentucky Supreme Court affirmed the death sentence, rejecting Stanford's "deman[d] that he has a constitutional right to treatment." 734 S. W. 2d, at 792. Finding that the record clearly demonstrated that "there was no program or treatment appropriate for the appellant in the juvenile justice system," the court held that the juvenile court did not err in certifying petitioner for trial as an adult. The court also stated that petitioner's "age and the possibility that he might be rehabilitated were mitigating factors appropriately left to the consideration of the jury that tried him." Ibid.

The second case before us today, No. 87–6026, involves the stabbing death of Nancy Allen, a 26-year-old mother of two who was working behind the sales counter of the convenience store she and David Allen owned and operated in Avondale, Missouri. Petitioner Heath Wilkins committed the murder on July 27, 1985, when he was approximately 16 years and 6 months of age. The record reflects that Wilkins' plan was to rob the store and murder "whoever was behind the counter" because "a dead person can't talk." While Wilkins' accomplice, Patrick Stevens, held Allen, Wilkins stabbed her, causing her to fall to the floor. When Stevens had trouble operating the cash register, Allen spoke up to assist him, leading Wilkins to stab her three more times in her chest. Two of these wounds penetrated the victim's heart. When Allen began to beg for her life, Wilkins stabbed her four more times in the neck, opening her carotid artery. After helping themselves to liquor, cigarettes, rolling papers, and approximately $450 in cash and checks, Wilkins and Stevens left Allen to die on the floor.

Because he was roughly six months short of the age of majority for purposes of criminal prosecution, Mo. Rev. Stat. 211.021(1) (1986), Wilkins could not automatically be tried as an adult under Missouri law. Before that could happen, the juvenile court was required to terminate juvenile court jurisdiction and certify Wilkins for trial as an adult under 211.071, which permits individuals between 14 and 17 years of age who have committed felonies to be tried as adults. Relying on the "viciousness, force and violence" of the alleged crime, petitioner's maturity, and the failure of the juvenile justice system to rehabilitate him after previous delinquent acts, the juvenile court made the necessary certification.

Wilkins was charged with first-degree murder, armed criminal action, and carrying a concealed weapon. After the court found him competent, petitioner entered guilty pleas to all charges. A punishment hearing was held, at which both the State and petitioner himself urged imposition of the death sentence. Evidence at the hearing revealed that petitioner had been in and out of juvenile facilities since the age of eight for various acts of burglary, theft, and arson, had attempted to kill his mother by putting insecticide into Tylenol capsules, and had killed several animals in his neighborhood. Although psychiatric testimony indicated that Wilkins had "personality disorders," the witnesses agreed that Wilkins was aware of his actions and could distinguish right from wrong.

Determining that the death penalty was appropriate, the trial court entered the following order:

> "[T]he court finds beyond reasonable doubt that the following aggravating circumstances exist:
>
> "1. The murder in the first degree was committed while the defendant was engaged in the perpetration of the felony of robbery, and
>
> "2. The murder in the first degree involved depravity of mind and that as a result thereof, it was outrageously or wantonly vile, horrible or inhuman." App. in No. 87–6026, p. 77.

On mandatory review of Wilkins' death sentence, the Supreme Court of Missouri affirmed, rejecting the argument that the punishment violated the Eighth Amendment. 736 S. W. 2d 409 (1987).

We granted certiorari in these cases, 488 U.S. 887 (1988) and 487 U.S. 1233 (1988), to decide whether the Eighth Amendment precludes the death penalty for individuals who commit crimes at 16 or 17 years of age.

II

The thrust of both *Wilkins'* and *Stanford's* arguments is that imposition of the death penalty on those who were juveniles when they committed their crimes falls within the Eighth Amendment's prohibition against "cruel and unusual punishments." *Wilkins* would have us define juveniles as individuals 16 years of age and under; *Stanford* would draw the line at 17.

Neither petitioner asserts that his sentence constitutes one of "those modes or acts of punishment that had been considered cruel and unusual at the time that the Bill of Rights was adopted." *Ford v. Wainwright*, 477 U.S. 399, 405 (1986). Nor could they support such a contention. At that time, the common law set the rebuttable presumption of incapacity to commit any felony at the age of 14, and theoretically permitted capital punishment to be imposed on anyone over the age of 7. See 4 W. Blackstone, Commentaries 23–24; 1 M. Hale, Pleas of the Crown 24–29 (1800). See also *In re Gault*, 387 U.S. 1, 16 (1967); Streib, Death Penalty for Children: The American Experience with Capital Punishment for Crimes Committed While Under Age Eighteen, 36 Okla. L. Rev. 613, 614–615 (1983); Kean, The History of the Criminal Liability of Children, 53 L. Q. Rev. 364, 369–370 (1937). In accordance with the standards of this common-law tradition, at least 281 offenders under the age of 18 have been executed in this country, and at least 126 under the age of 17. See V. Streib, Death Penalty for Juveniles 57 (1987).

Thus petitioners are left to argue that their punishment is contrary to the "evolving standards of decency that mark the progress of a maturing society," *Trop v. Dulles*, 356 U.S. 86, 101 (1958) (plurality opinion). They are correct in asserting that this Court has "not confined the prohibition embodied in the Eighth Amendment to 'barbarous' methods that were generally outlawed in the 18th century," but instead has interpreted the Amendment "in a flexible and dynamic manner." *Gregg v. Georgia,* 428 U.S. 153, 171 (1976) (opinion of Stewart, Powell, and Stevens, J. J.). In determining what standards have "evolved," however, we have looked not to our own conceptions of decency, but to those of modern American society as a whole.[1] As we have said, "Eighth Amendment judgments should not be, or appear to be, merely the subjective views of individual Justices; judgment should be informed by objective factors to the maximum possible extent." *Coker v. Georgia,* 433 U.S. 584, 592 (1977) (plurality opinion). See also *Penry v. Lynaugh,* ante, at 331; *Ford v. Wainwright,* supra, at 406; *Enmund v. Florida,* 458 U.S. 782, 788–789 (1982); *Furman v. Georgia,* 408 U.S. 238, 277–279 (1972) (Brennan, J., concurring). This approach is dictated both by the language of the Amendment—which proscribes only those punishments that are both "cruel and unusual"— and by the "deference we owe to the decisions of the state legislatures under our federal system," *Gregg v. Georgia,* supra, at 176.

III

"[F]irst" among the "'objective indicia that reflect the public attitude toward a given sanction'" are statutes passed by society's elected representatives. *McCleskey v. Kemp,* 481 U.S. 279, 300 (1987), quoting *Gregg v. Georgia,* supra, at 173. Of the 37 States whose laws permit capital punishment, 15 decline to impose it upon 16-year-old offenders and 12 decline to impose it on 17-year-old offenders.[2] This does not establish the degree of national consensus

---

1. We emphasize that it is American conceptions of decency that are dispositive, rejecting the contention of petitioners and their various amici (accepted by the dissent, see post, at 389-390) that the sentencing practices of other countries are relevant. While "[t]he practices of other nations, particularly other democracies, can be relevant to determining whether a practice uniform among our people is not merely a historical accident, but rather so 'implicit in the concept of ordered liberty' that it occupies a place not merely in our mores, but, text permitting, in our Constitution as well," *Thompson v. Oklahoma,* 487 U.S. 815, 868-869, n. 4 (1988) (SCALIA, J., dissenting), quoting *Palko v. Connecticut,* 302 U.S. 319, 325 (1937) (Cardozo, J.), they cannot serve to establish the first Eighth Amendment prerequisite, that the practice is accepted among our people.

2. The following States preclude capital punishment of offenders under 18: California (Cal. Penal Code Ann. 190.5 (West 1988)); Colorado (Colo. Rev. Stat. 16-11-103(1)(a) (1986)); Connecticut (Conn. Gen. Stat. 53a-46a(g)(1) (1989)); Illinois (Ill. Rev. Stat., ch. 38, 9-1(b) (1987)); Maryland (Md. Ann. Code, Art. 27, 412(f) (Supp. 1988)); Nebraska (Neb. Rev. Stat. 28-105.01 (1985)); New Hampshire (N.H. Rev. Stat. Ann. 630:5 (XIII) (Supp. 1988)); New Jersey (N.J. Stat. Ann. 2A:4A-22(a) (West 1987) and 2C:11-3(g) (West Supp. 1988)); New Mexico (N.M. Stat. Ann. 28-6-1(A), 31-18-14(A) (1987)); Ohio (Ohio Rev. Code Ann. 2929.02(A) (1987)); Oregon (Ore. Rev. Stat. 161.620 and 419.476(1) (1987)); Tennessee (Tenn. Code Ann. 37-1-102(3), 37-1-102(4), 37-1-103, 37-1-134(a)(1) (1984 and Supp. 1988)). Three more States preclude the death penalty for offenders under 17: Georgia (Ga. Code Ann. 17-9-3 (1982)); North Carolina (N.C. Gen. Stat. 14-17 (Supp. 1988)); Texas (Tex. Penal Code Ann. 8.07(d) (Supp. 1989)).

The dissent takes issue with our failure to include, among those States evidencing a consensus against executing 16- and 17-year-old offenders, the District of Columbia and the 14 States that do not authorize capital punishment. Post, at 384-385. It seems to us, however, that while the number of those jurisdictions bears upon the question whether there is a consensus against capital punishment altogether, it is quite irrelevant to the specific inquiry in this case: whether there is a settled consensus in favor of punishing offenders under 18 differently from those over 18 insofar as capital punishment is concerned. The dissent's position is rather like discerning a national consensus that wagering on cockfights is inhumane by counting within that consensus those States that bar all wagering. The issue in the present case is not whether capital punishment is thought to be desirable but whether persons under 18 are thought to be specially exempt from it. With respect to that inquiry, it is no more logical to say that the capital-punishment laws of those States which prohibit capital punishment (and thus do not address age) support the dissent's position, than it would be to say that the age-of-adult-criminal-responsibility laws of those same States (which do not address capital punishment) support our position.

this Court has previously thought sufficient to label a particular punishment cruel and unusual. In invalidating the death penalty for rape of an adult woman, we stressed that Georgia was the sole jurisdiction that authorized such a punishment. See *Coker v. Georgia*, supra, at 595–596. In striking down capital punishment for participation in a robbery in which an accomplice takes a life, we emphasized that only eight jurisdictions authorized similar punishment. *Enmund v. Florida*, supra, at 792. In finding that the Eighth Amendment precludes execution of the insane and thus requires an adequate hearing on the issue of sanity, we relied upon (in addition to the common-law rule) the fact that "no State in the Union" permitted such punishment. *Ford v. Wainwright*, 477 U.S., at 408. And in striking down a life sentence without parole under a recidivist statute, we stressed that "[i]t appears that [petitioner] was treated more severely than he would have been in any other State." *Solem v. Helm*, 463 U.S. 277, 300 (1983).

Since a majority of the States that permit capital punishment authorize it for crimes committed at age 16 or above,[3] petitioners' cases are more analogous to *Tison v. Arizona*, 481 U.S. 137 (1987), than *Coker, Enmund, Ford*, and *Solem*. In *Tison*, which upheld Arizona's imposition of the death penalty for major participation in a felony with reckless indifference to human life, we noted that only 11 of those jurisdictions imposing capital punishment rejected its use in such circumstances. Id., at 154. As we noted earlier, here the number is 15 for offenders under 17, and 12 for offenders under 18. We think the same conclusion as in *Tison* is required in these cases.

Petitioners make much of the recently enacted federal statute providing capital punishment for certain drug-related offenses, but limiting that punishment to offenders 18 and over. The Anti-Drug Abuse Act of 1988, Pub. L. 100–690, 102 Stat. 4390, 7001(l), 21 U.S.C. 848(l) (1988 ed.). That reliance is entirely misplaced. To begin with, the statute in question does not embody a judgment by the Federal Legislature that no murder is heinous enough to warrant the execution of such a youthful offender, but merely that the narrow class of offense it defines is not. The congressional judgment on the broader question, if apparent at all, is to be found in the law that permits 16- and 17-year-olds (after appropriate findings) to be tried and punished as adults for all federal offenses, including those bearing a capital penalty that is not limited to 18-year-olds.[4] See 18 U.S.C. 5032 (1982 ed., Supp. V). Moreover, even if it were true that no federal statute permitted the execution of persons under 18,

---

3. The dissent again works its statistical magic by refusing to count among the States that authorize capital punishment of 16- and 17-year-old offenders those 19 States that set no minimum age in their death penalty statute, and specifically permit 16- and 17-year-olds to be sentenced as adults. Post, at 385. We think that describing this position is adequate response.

4. See 10 U.S.C. 906a (1982 ed., Supp. V) (peacetime espionage); 918 (murder by persons subject to Uniform Code of Military Justice); 18 U.S.C. 32, 33, and 34 (1982 ed. and Supp. V) (destruction of aircraft, motor vehicles, or related facilities resulting in death); 115(b)(3) (1982 ed., Supp. V) (retaliatory murder of member of immediate family of law enforcement officials) (by cross reference to 1111 (1982 ed. and Supp. V)); 351 (1982 ed. and Supp. V) (murder of Member of Congress, high-ranking executive official, or Supreme Court Justice) (by cross reference to 1111); 794 (1982 ed. and Supp. V) (espionage); 844(f) (1982 ed., Supp. V) (destruction of Government property resulting in death); 1111 (first-degree murder within federal jurisdiction); 1716 (1982 ed. and Supp. V) (mailing of injurious articles resulting in death); 1751 (assassination or kidnapping resulting in death of President or Vice President); 1992 (willful wrecking of train resulting in death); 2113 (1982 ed. and Supp. V) (bank robbery–related murder or kidnapping); 2381 (treason); 49 U.S.C. App. 1472 and 1473 (1982 ed. and Supp. V) (death resulting from aircraft hijacking).

that would not remotely establish—in the face of a substantial number of state statutes to the contrary—a national consensus that such punishment is inhumane, any more than the absence of a federal lottery establishes a national consensus that lotteries are socially harmful. To be sure, the absence of a federal death penalty for 16- or 17-year-olds (if it existed) might be evidence that there is no national consensus in favor of such punishment. It is not the burden of Kentucky and Missouri, however, to establish a national consensus approving what their citizens have voted to do; rather, it is the "heavy burden" of petitioners, *Gregg v. Georgia,* 428 U.S., at 175, to establish a national consensus against it. As far as the primary and most reliable indication of consensus is concerned—the pattern of enacted laws—petitioners have failed to carry that burden.

IV

A

Wilkins and *Stanford* argue, however, that even if the laws themselves do not establish a settled consensus, the application of the laws does. That contemporary society views capital punishment of 16- and 17-year-old offenders as inappropriate is demonstrated, they say, by the reluctance of juries to impose, and prosecutors to seek, such sentences. Petitioners are quite correct that a far smaller number of offenders under 18 than over 18 have been sentenced to death in this country. From 1982 through 1988, for example, out of 2,106 total death sentences, only 15 were imposed on individuals who were 16 or under when they committed their crimes, and only 30 on individuals who were 17 at the time of the crime. See Streib, Imposition of Death Sentences For Juvenile Offenses, January 1, 1982, Through April 1, 1989, p. 2 (paper for Cleveland-Marshall College of Law, April 5, 1989). And it appears that actual executions for crimes committed under age 18 accounted for only about two percent of the total number of executions that occurred between 1642 and 1986. See Streib, Death Penalty for Juveniles, at 55, 57. As *Wilkins* points out, the last execution of a person who committed a crime under 17 years of age occurred in 1959. These statistics, however, carry little significance. Given the undisputed fact that a far smaller percentage of capital crimes are committed by persons under 18 than over 18, the discrepancy in treatment is much less than might seem. Granted, however, that a substantial discrepancy exists, that does not establish the requisite proposition that the death sentence for offenders under 18 is categorically unacceptable to prosecutors and juries. To the contrary, it is not only possible, but overwhelmingly probable, that the very considerations which induce petitioners and their supporters to believe that death should never be imposed on offenders under 18 cause prosecutors and juries to believe that it should rarely be imposed.

B

This last point suggests why there is also no relevance to the laws cited by petitioners and their amici which set 18 or more as the legal age for engaging in various activities, ranging from driving to drinking alcoholic beverages to voting. It is, to begin with, absurd to think that one must be mature enough to drive carefully, to drink responsibly, or to vote intelligently, in order to be mature enough to understand that murdering another human being is profoundly wrong, and to conform one's conduct to that most minimal of all civilized standards. But even if the requisite degrees of maturity were comparable, the age statutes in question would still not be relevant. They do not represent a social judgment that all persons under the designated ages are not responsible enough to drive, to drink, or to vote, but at most a judgment that the vast majority are not. These laws set the appropriate ages for the operation of a system that makes its determinations in gross, and that does not conduct individualized maturity tests for each driver, drinker, or voter. The criminal justice system, however, does provide individualized testing. In the realm of capital punishment in particular, "individualized consideration [is] a constitutional requirement," *Lockett v. Ohio*, 438 U.S. 586, 605 (1978) (opinion of Burger, C. J.) (footnote omitted); see also *Zant v. Stephens*, 462 U.S. 862, 879 (1983) (collecting cases), and one of the individualized mitigating factors that sentencers must be permitted to consider is the defendant's age, see *Eddings v. Oklahoma*, 455 U.S. 104, 115–116 (1982). Twenty-nine States, including both Kentucky and Missouri, have codified this constitutional requirement in laws specifically designating the defendant's age as a mitigating factor in capital cases.[5] Moreover, the determinations required by juvenile transfer statutes to certify a juvenile for trial as an adult ensure individualized consideration of the maturity and moral responsibility of 16- and 17-year-old offenders before they are even held to stand trial as adults.[6] The application of this particularized system to the petitioners can

---

5. See Ala. Code 13A-5-51(7) (1982); Ariz. Rev. Stat. Ann. 13-703(G)(5) (Supp. 1988); Ark. Code Ann. 5-4-605(4) (1987); Cal. Penal Code Ann. 190.3(i) (West 1988); Colo. Rev. Stat. 16-11-103(5)(a) (1986); Conn. Gen. Stat. 53a-46a(g)(1) (1989); Fla. Stat. 921.141(6)(g) (1987); Ind. Code 35-50-2-9(c)(7) (1988); Ky. Rev. Stat. Ann. 532.025(2)(b)(8) (Baldwin 1988); La. Code Crim. Proc. Ann., Art. 905.5(f) (West 1984); Md. Ann. Code, Art. 27, 413(g)(5) (1988); Miss. Code Ann. 99-19-101(6)(g) (Supp. 1988); Mo. Rev. Stat. 565.032(3)(7) (1986); Mont. Code Ann. 46-18-304(7) (1987); Neb. Rev. Stat. 29-2523(2)(d) (1985); Nev. Rev. Stat. 200.035(6) (1987); N.H. Rev. Stat. Ann. 630:5(II)(b)(5) (1986); N.J. Stat. Ann. 2C:11-3(c)(5)(c) (West Supp. 1988); N.M. Stat. Ann. 31-20A-6(I) (1987); N.C. Gen. Stat. 15A-2000(f)(7) (1988); Ohio Rev. Code Ann. 2929.04(B)(4) (1987); Ore. Rev. Stat. 163.150(1)(b)(B) (1987); 42 Pa. Cons. Stat. 9711(e)(4) (1982); S.C. Code 16-3-20(C)(b)(9) (Supp. 1988); Tenn. Code Ann. 39-2-203(j)(7) (1982); Utah Code Ann. 76-3-207 (2)(e) (Supp. 1988); Va. Code 19.2-264.4(B)(v) (1983); Wash. Rev. Code 10.95.070(7) (Supp. 1989); Wyo. Stat. 6-2-102(j)(vii) (1988).

6. The Kentucky statute under which Stanford was certified to be tried as an adult provides in relevant part: "(3) If the court determines that probable cause exists [to believe that a person 16 years old or older committed a felony or that a person under 16 years of age committed a Class A felony or a capital offense], it shall then determine if it is in the best interest of the child and the community to order such a transfer based upon the seriousness of the alleged offense; whether the offense was against person or property, with greater weight being given to offenses against persons; the maturity of the child as determined by his environment; the child's prior record; and the prospects for adequate protection of the public and the likelihood of reasonable rehabilitation of the child by the use of procedures, services, and facilities currently available to the juvenile justice system." Ky. Rev. Stat. Ann. 208.170 (Michie 1982) (repealed effective July 15, 1984).

The Missouri statute under which Wilkins was certified provides that in determining whether to transfer a juvenile the court must consider:
> "(1) The seriousness of the offense alleged and whether the protection of the community requires transfer to the court of general jurisdiction;
> "(2) Whether the offense alleged involved viciousness, force and violence;
> "(3) Whether the offense alleged was against persons or property with greater weight being given to the offense against persons, especially if personal injury resulted;
> "(4) Whether the offense alleged is a part of a repetitive pattern of offenses which indicates that the child may be beyond rehabilitation under the juvenile code;
> "(5) The record and history of the child, including experience with the juvenile justice system, other courts, supervision, commitments to juvenile institutions and other placements;
> "(6) The sophistication and maturity of the child as determined by consideration of his home and environmental situation, emotional condition and pattern of living;
> "(7) The program and facilities available to the juvenile court in considering disposition; and

be declared constitutionally inadequate only if there is a consensus, not that 17 or 18 is the age at which most persons, or even almost all persons, achieve sufficient maturity to be held fully responsible for murder; but that 17 or 18 is the age before which no one can reasonably be held fully responsible. What displays society's views on this latter point are not the ages set forth in the generalized system of driving, drinking, and voting laws cited by petitioners and their amici, but the ages at which the States permit their particularized capital punishment systems to be applied.[7]

V

Having failed to establish a consensus against capital punishment for 16- and 17-year-old offenders through state and federal statutes and the behavior of prosecutors and juries, petitioners seek to demonstrate it through other indicia, including public opinion polls, the views of interest groups, and the positions adopted by various professional associations. We decline the invitation to rest constitutional law upon such uncertain foundations. A revised national consensus so broad, so clear, and so enduring as to justify a permanent prohibition upon all units of democratic government must appear in the operative acts (laws and the application of laws) that the people have approved.

We also reject petitioners' argument that we should invalidate capital punishment of 16- and 17-year-old offenders on the ground that it fails to serve the legitimate goals of penology. According to petitioners, it fails to deter because juveniles, possessing less developed cognitive skills than adults, are less likely to fear death; and it fails to exact just retribution because juveniles, being less mature and responsible, are also less morally blameworthy. In support of these claims, petitioners and their supporting amici marshal an array of socioscientific evidence concerning the psychological and emotional development of 16- and 17-year-olds.

If such evidence could conclusively establish the entire lack of deterrent effect and moral responsibility, resort to the Cruel and Unusual Punishments Clause would be unnecessary; the Equal Protection Clause of the Fourteenth Amendment would invalidate these laws for lack of rational basis. See *Dallas v. Stanglin*, 490 U.S. 19 (1989). But as the adjective "socioscientific" suggests (and insofar as evaluation of moral responsibility is concerned perhaps the adjective "ethicoscientific" would be more apt), it is not demonstrable that no 16-year-old is "adequately responsible" or significantly deterred. It is rational, even if mistaken, to think the contrary. The battle must be fought, then, on the field of the Eighth Amendment; and in that struggle socioscientific, ethicoscientific, or even purely scientific evidence is not an available weapon. The punishment is either "cruel and unusual" (i.e., society has set its face against it) or it is not. The audience for these arguments, in other words, is not this Court

---

"(8) Whether or not the child can benefit from the treatment or rehabilitative programs available to the juvenile court." Mo. Rev. Stat. 211.071(6) (1986).

7. The dissent believes that individualized consideration is no solution, because "the Eighth Amendment requires that a person who lacks that full degree of responsibility for his or her actions associated with adulthood not be sentenced to death," and this absolute cannot be assured if "a juvenile offender's level of responsibility [is] taken into account only along with a host of other factors that the court or jury may decide outweigh that want of responsibility." Post, at 397. But it is equally true that individualized consideration will not absolutely assure immunity from the death penalty to the nonjuvenile who happens to be immature. If individualized consideration is constitutionally inadequate, then, the only logical conclusion is that everyone is exempt from the death penalty.

but the citizenry of the United States. It is they, not we, who must be persuaded. For as we stated earlier, our job is to identify the "evolving standards of decency"; to determine, not what they should be, but what they are. We have no power under the Eighth Amendment to substitute our belief in the scientific evidence for the society's apparent skepticism. In short, we emphatically reject petitioner's suggestion that the issues in this case permit us to apply our "own informed judgment," Brief for Petitioner in No. 87-6026, p. 23, regarding the desirability of permitting the death penalty for crimes by 16- and 17-year-olds.

We reject the dissent's contention that our approach, by "largely return[ing] the task of defining the contours of Eighth Amendment protection to political majorities," leaves "'[c]onstitutional doctrine [to] be formulated by the acts of those institutions which the Constitution is supposed to limit,'" post, at 391, 392 (citation omitted). When this Court cast loose from the historical moorings consisting of the original application of the Eighth Amendment, it did not embark rudderless upon a wide-open sea. Rather, it limited the Amendment's extension to those practices contrary to the "evolving standards of decency that mark the progress of a maturing society," Trop v. Dulles, 356 U.S., at 101 (plurality opinion). It has never been thought that this was a shorthand reference to the preferences of a majority of this Court. By reaching a decision supported neither by constitutional text nor by the demonstrable current standards of our citizens, the dissent displays a failure to appreciate that "those institutions which the Constitution is supposed to limit" include the Court itself. To say, as the dissent says, that "'it is for us ultimately to judge whether the Eighth Amendment permits imposition of the death penalty,'" post, at 391 quoting Enmund v. Florida, 458 U.S., at 797—and to mean that as the dissent means it, i.e., that it is for us to judge, not on the basis of what we perceive the Eighth Amendment originally prohibited, or on the basis of what we perceive the society through its democratic processes now overwhelmingly disapproves, but on the basis of what we think "proportionate" and "measurably contributory to acceptable goals of punishment"—to say and mean that, is to replace judges of the law with a committee of philosopher-kings.

While the dissent is correct that several of our cases have engaged in so-called "proportionality" analysis, examining whether "there is a disproportion 'between the punishment imposed and the defendant's blameworthiness,'" and whether a punishment makes any "measurable contribution to acceptable goals of punishment," see post, at 393, we have never invalidated a punishment on this basis alone. All of our cases condemning a punishment under this mode of analysis also found that the objective indicators of state laws or jury determinations evidenced a societal consensus against that penalty. See Solem v. Helm, 463 U.S., at 299-300; Enmund v. Florida, supra, at 789-796; Coker v. Georgia, 433 U.S., at 593-597 (plurality opinion). In fact, the two methodologies blend into one another, since "proportionality" analysis itself can only be conducted on the basis of the standards set by our own society; the only alternative, once again, would be our personal preferences.

* * * *

We discern neither a historical nor a modern societal consensus forbidding the imposition of capital punishment on any person who murders at 16 or 17 years of age. Accordingly, we conclude that such punishment does not offend the Eighth Amendment's prohibition against cruel and unusual punishment.

The judgments of the Supreme Court of Kentucky and the Supreme Court of Missouri are therefore

Affirmed.

Justice O'Connor, concurring in part and concurring in the judgment.

Last Term, in *Thompson v. Oklahoma,* 487 U.S. 815, 857-858 (1988) (opinion concurring in judgment), I expressed the view that a criminal defendant who would have been tried as a juvenile under state law, but for the granting of a petition waiving juvenile court jurisdiction, may only be executed for a capital offense if the State's capital punishment statute specifies a minimum age at which the commission of a capital crime can lead to an offender's execution and the defendant had reached that minimum age at the time the crime was committed. As a threshold matter, I indicated that such specificity is not necessary to avoid constitutional problems if it is clear that no national consensus forbids the imposition of capital punishment for crimes committed at such an age. Id., at 857. Applying this two-part standard in Thompson, I concluded that Oklahoma's imposition of a death sentence on an individual who was 15 years old at the time he committed a capital offense should be set aside. Applying the same standard today, I conclude that the death sentences for capital murder imposed by Missouri and Kentucky on petitioners Wilkins and Stanford respectively should not be set aside because it is sufficiently clear that no national consensus forbids the imposition of capital punishment on 16- or 17-year-old capital murderers.

In Thompson I noted that "[t]he most salient statistic that bears on this case is that every single American legislature that has expressly set a minimum age for capital punishment has set that age at 16 or above." Id., at 849. It is this difference between Thompson and these cases, more than any other, that convinces me there is no national consensus forbidding the imposition of capital punishment for crimes committed at the age of 16 and older. See ante, at 370-372. As the Court indicates, "a majority of the States that permit capital punishment authorize it for crimes committed at age 16 or above. . . ." Ante, at 371. Three States, including Kentucky, have specifically set the minimum age for capital punishment at 16, see Ind. Code 35-50-2-3(b) (1988); Ky. Rev. Stat. Ann. 640.040(1) (Baldwin 1987); Nev. Rev. Stat. 176.025 (1987), and a fourth, Florida, clearly contemplates the imposition of capital punishment on 16-year-olds in its juvenile transfer statute, see Fla. Stat. 39.02(5)(c) (1987). Under these circumstances, unlike the "peculiar circumstances" at work in *Thompson,* I do not think it necessary to require a state legislature to specify that the commission of a capital crime can lead to the execution of a 16- or 17-year-old offender. Because it is sufficiently clear that today no national consensus forbids the imposition of capital punishment in these circumstances, "the implicit nature of the [Missouri] Legislature's decision [is] not . . . constitutionally problematic." 487 U.S., at 857. This is true, a fortiori, in the case of Kentucky, which has specified 16 as the minimum age for the imposition of the death penalty. The day may come when there is such general legislative rejection of the execution of 16- or 17-year-old capital murderers that a clear national consensus can be said to have developed. Because I do not believe that day has yet arrived, I concur in Parts I, II, III, and IV-A of the Court's opinion, and I concur in its judgment.

I am unable, however, to join the remainder of the plurality's opinion for reasons I stated in Thompson. Part V of the plurality's opinion "emphatically reject[s]," ante, at 378, the suggestion that, beyond an assessment of the specific enactments of American legislatures, there remains a constitutional obligation imposed upon this Court to judge whether the "'nexus between the punishment imposed and the defendant's blameworthiness'" is proportional. Thompson, supra, at 853, quoting *Enmund v. Florida,* 458 U.S. 782, 825 (1982) (O'Connor, J., dissenting). Part IV-B of the plurality's opinion specifically rejects as irrelevant to Eighth Amendment considerations state statutes that distinguish juveniles from adults for a variety of other purposes. In my view, this Court does have a constitutional obligation to conduct proportionality analysis. See *Penry v. Lynaugh,* ante, at 335-340; *Tison v. Arizona,* 481 U.S. 137, 155-158 (1987); *Enmund,* 458 U.S., at 797-801; id., at 825-826 (O'Connor, J., dissenting). In *Thompson* I specifically identified age-based statutory classifications as "relevant to Eighth Amendment proportionality analysis." 487 U.S., at 854 (opinion concurring in judgment). Thus, although I do not believe that these particular cases can be resolved through proportionality analysis, see Thompson, supra, at 853-854, I reject the suggestion that the use of such analysis is improper as a matter of Eighth Amendment jurisprudence. Accordingly, I join all but Parts IV-B and V of Justice Scalia's opinion.

Justice Brennan, with whom Justice Marshall, Justice Blackmun, and Justice Stevens join, dissenting.

I believe that to take the life of a person as punishment for a crime committed when below the age of 18 is cruel and unusual and hence is prohibited by the Eighth Amendment.

The method by which this Court assesses a claim that a punishment is unconstitutional because it is cruel and unusual is established by our precedents, and it bears little resemblance to the method four Members of the Court apply in this case. To be sure, we begin the task of deciding whether a punishment is unconstitutional by reviewing legislative enactments and the work of sentencing juries relating to the punishment in question to determine whether our Nation has set its face against a punishment to an extent that it can be concluded that the punishment offends our "evolving standards of decency." *Trop v. Dulles,* 356 U.S. 86, 101 (1958) (plurality opinion). The Court undertakes such an analysis in this case. Ante, at 370-373. But Justice Scalia, in his plurality opinion on this point, ante, at 374-380, would treat the Eighth Amendment inquiry as complete with this investigation. I agree with Justice O'Connor, ante, at 382, that a more searching inquiry is mandated by our precedents interpreting the Cruel and Unusual Punishments Clause. In my view, that inquiry must in these cases go beyond age-based statutory classifications relating to matters other than capital punishment, cf. ibid. (O'Connor, J., concurring in part and concurring in judgment), and must also encompass what Justice Scalia calls, with evident but misplaced disdain, "ethico-scientific" evidence. Only then can we be in a position to judge, as our cases require, whether a punishment is unconstitutionally excessive, either because it is disproportionate given the culpability of the offender, or because it serves no legitimate penal goal.

I

Our judgment about the constitutionality of a punishment under the Eighth Amendment is informed, though not determined, see infra, at 391, by an examination of contemporary attitudes toward the punishment, as evidenced in the actions of legislatures and of juries. *McCleskey v. Kemp,* 481 U.S. 279, 300 (1987); *Coker v. Georgia,* 433 U.S. 584, 592 (1977) (plurality opinion). The views of organizations with expertise in relevant fields and the choices of governments elsewhere in the world also merit our attention as indicators whether a punishment is acceptable in a civilized society.

A

The Court's discussion of state laws concerning capital sentencing, ante, at 370-372, gives a distorted view of the evidence of contemporary standards that these legislative determinations provide. Currently, 12 of the States whose statutes permit capital punishment specifically mandate that offenders under age 18 not be sentenced to death. Ante, at 370-371, n. 2. When one adds to these 12 States the 15 (including the District of Columbia) in which capital punishment is not authorized at all,[1] it appears that the governments in fully 27 of the States have concluded that no one under 18 should face the death penalty. A further three States explicitly refuse to authorize sentences of death for those who committed their offense when under 17, ante, at 370, n. 2, making a total of 30 States that would not tolerate the execution of petitioner Wilkins. Congress' most recent enactment of a death penalty statute also excludes those under 18. Pub. L. 100-690, 7001(1), 102 Stat. 4390, 21 U.S.C. 848(l) (1988 ed.).

In 19 States that have a death penalty, no minimum age for capital sentences is set in the death penalty statute. See *Thompson v. Oklahoma,* 487 U.S. 815, 826-827, and n. 26 (1988), and n. 1, supra. The notion that these States have consciously authorized the execution of juveniles derives from the congruence in those jurisdictions of laws permitting state courts to hand down death sentences, on the one hand, and, on the other, statutes permitting the transfer of offenders under 18 from the juvenile to state court systems for trial in certain circumstances. See Thompson, supra, at 867-868, and n. 3 (Scalia, J., dissenting). I would not assume, however, in considering how the States stand on the moral issue that underlies the constitutional question with which we are presented, that a legislature that has never specifically considered the issue has made a conscious moral choice to permit the execution of juveniles. See 487 U.S., at 826-827, n. 24 (plurality opinion). On a matter of such moment that most States have expressed an explicit and contrary judgment, the decisions of legislatures that are only implicit, and that lack the "earmarks of careful consideration that we have required for other kinds of decisions leading to the death penalty," id., at 857 (O'Connor, J., concurring in judgment), must count for little. I do not suggest, of course, that laws of these States cut against the constitutionality of the juvenile death penalty—only that accuracy demands that the baseline for our deliberations should be that 27 States refuse to authorize a sentence of death in the circumstances of petitioner Stanford's case, and 30 would not permit Wilkins' execution; that 19 States have not squarely faced the question; and that only the few remaining jurisdictions have explicitly set an age below 18 at which a person may be sentenced to death.

---

1. See *Thompson v. Oklahoma,* 487 U.S. 815, 826 , and n. 25 (1988), listing 14 States. The 15th State to have rejected capital punishment altogether is Vermont. Vermont repealed a statute that had allowed capital punishment for some murders. See Vt. Stat. Ann., Tit. 13, 2303 (1974 and Supp. 1988). The State now provides for the death penalty only for kidnapping with intent to extort money. 2403. Insofar as it permits a sentence of death, 2403 was rendered unconstitutional by our decision in *Furman* v. *Georgia,* 408 U.S. 238 (1972), because Vermont's sentencing scheme does not guide jury discretion, see Vt. Stat. Ann., Tit. 13, 7101-7107 (1974). Vermont's decision not to amend its only law allowing the death penalty in light of *Furman* and its progeny, in combination with its repeal of its statute permitting capital punishment for murder, leads to the conclusion that the State rejects capital punishment.

In addition, South Dakota, though it statutorily provides for a death penalty, has sentenced no one to death since *Furman,* arguably making a 28th State that has abandoned the death penalty.

B

The application of these laws is another indicator the Court agrees to be relevant. The fact that juries have on occasion sentenced a minor to death shows, the Court says, that the death penalty for adolescents is not categorically unacceptable to juries. Ante, at 374. This, of course, is true; but it is not a conclusion that takes Eighth Amendment analysis very far. Just as we have never insisted that a punishment have been rejected unanimously by the States before we may judge it cruel and unusual, so we have never adopted the extraordinary view that a punishment is beyond Eighth Amendment challenge if it is sometimes handed down by a jury. See, e.g., *Enmund v. Florida,* 458 U.S. 782, 792 (1982) (holding the death penalty cruel and unusual punishment for participation in a felony in which an accomplice commits murder, though about a third of American jurisdictions authorized such punishment, and at least six non-triggerman felony murderers had been executed, and three others were on death rows); *Coker v. Georgia,* 433 U.S., at 596-597 (holding capital punishment unconstitutional for the rape of an adult woman, though 72 persons had been executed for rape in this country since 1955, see *Enmund,* supra, at 795, and though Georgia juries handed down six death sentences for rape between 1973 and 1977). *Enmund* and *Coker* amply demonstrate that it is no "requisite" of finding an Eighth Amendment violation that the punishment in issue be "categorically unacceptable to prosecutors and juries," ante, at 374—and, evidently, resort to the Cruel and Unusual Punishments Clause would not be necessary to test a sentence never imposed because categorically unacceptable to juries.

Both in absolute and in relative terms, imposition of the death penalty on adolescents is distinctly unusual. Adolescent offenders make up only a small proportion of the current death-row population: 30 out of a total of 2,186 inmates, or 1.37 percent. NAACP Legal Defense and Educational Fund, Inc. (LDF), Death Row, U.S.A. (Mar. 1, 1989).[2] Eleven minors were sentenced to die in 1982; nine in 1983; six in 1984; five in 1985; seven in 1986; and two in 1987. App. N to Brief for the Office of the Capital Collateral Representative for the State of Florida as Amicus Curiae (hereafter OCCR Brief). Forty-one, or 2.3 percent, of the 1,813 death sentences imposed between January 1, 1982, and June 30, 1988, were for juvenile crimes. Id., at 15, and App. R. And juvenile offenders are significantly less likely to receive the death penalty than adults. During the same period, there were 97,086 arrests of adults for homicide, and 1,772 adult death sentences, or 1.8 percent; and 8,911 arrests of minors for homicide, compared to 41 juvenile death sentences, or 0.5 percent. Ibid., and Apps. Q and R.[3]

The Court speculates that this very small number of capital sentences imposed on adolescents indicates that juries have considered the youth of the offender when determining sentence, and have reserved the punishment for rare cases in which it is nevertheless appropriate. Ante, at 374. The State of Georgia made a very similar and equally conjectural argument in *Coker*—that "as a practical matter juries simply reserve the extreme sanction for extreme cases of rape, and that recent experience . . . does not prove that jurors consider the death

---

2. One person currently on death row for juvenile crimes was sentenced in Maryland, which has since set 18 as the minimum age for its death penalty.

3. Capital sentences for juveniles would presumably be more unusual still were capital juries drawn from a cross section of our society, rather than excluding many who oppose capital punishment, see *Lockhart* v. *McCree,* 476 U.S. 162 (1986)—a fact that renders capital jury sentences a distinctly weighted measure of contemporary standards.

penalty to be a disproportionate punishment for every conceivable instance of rape." 433 U.S., at 597. This Court, however, summarily rejected this claim, noting simply that in the vast majority of cases, Georgia juries had not imposed the death sentence for rape. It is certainly true that in the vast majority of cases, juries have not sentenced juveniles to death, and it seems to me perfectly proper to conclude that a sentence so rarely imposed is "unusual."

C

Further indicators of contemporary standards of decency that should inform our consideration of the Eighth Amendment question are the opinions of respected organizations. *Thompson*, 487 U.S., at 830 (plurality opinion). Where organizations with expertise in a relevant area have given careful consideration to the question of a punishment's appropriateness, there is no reason why that judgment should not be entitled to attention as an indicator of contemporary standards. There is no dearth of opinion from such groups that the state-sanctioned killing of minors is unjustified. A number, indeed, have filed briefs amicus curiae in these cases, in support of petitioners.[4] The American Bar Association has adopted a resolution opposing the imposition of capital punishment upon any person for an offense committed while under age 18,[5] as has the National Council of Juvenile and Family Court Judges.[6] 6 The American Law Institute's Model Penal Code similarly includes a lower age limit of 18 for the death sentence.[7] And the National Commission on Reform of the Federal Criminal Laws also recommended that 18 be the minimum age.[8]

Our cases recognize that objective indicators of contemporary standards of decency in the form of legislation in other countries is also of relevance to Eighth Amendment analysis. *Thompson*, supra, at 830–831; *Enmund*, 458 U.S., at 796 , n. 22; *Coker*, supra, at 596, n. 10; *Trop v. Dulles*, 356 U.S., at 102 , and n. 35. Many countries, of course—over 50, including nearly all in Western Europe—have formally abolished the death penalty, or have limited its

---

4. Briefs for American Bar Association; Child Welfare League of America, National Parents and Teachers Association, National Council on Crime and Delinquency, Children's Defense Fund, National Association of Social Workers, National Black Child Development Institute, National Network of Runaway and Youth Services, National Youth Advocate Program, and American Youth Work Center; American Society for Adolescent Psychiatry and American Orthopsychiatric Association; Defense for Children International—USA; National Legal Aid and Defender Association, and National Association of Criminal Defense Lawyers; Office of Capital Collateral Representative for the State of Florida; and International Human Rights Law Group, as Amici Curiae. See also Briefs for American Baptist Churches, American Friends Service Committee, American Jewish Committee, American Jewish Congress, Christian Church (Disciples of Christ), Mennonite Central Committee, General Conference Mennonite Church, National Council of Churches, General Assembly of the Presbyterian Church, Southern Christian Leadership Conference, Union of American Hebrew Congregations, United Church of Christ Commission for Racial Justice, United Methodist Church General Board of Church and Society, and United States Catholic Conference; West Virginia Council of Churches; and Amnesty International as Amici Curiae.

5. American Bar Association, Summary of Action of the House of Delegates 17 (1983 Annual Meeting).

6. National Council of Juvenile and Family Court Judges, Juvenile and Family Court Newsletter, Vol. 19, No. 1, p. 4 (Oct. 1988).

7. American Law Institute, Model Penal Code 210.6(1)(d) (Proposed Official Draft 1962); American Law Institute, Model Penal Code and Commentaries 210.6, Commentary, p. 133 (1980) ("[C]ivilized societies will not tolerate the spectacle of execution of children").

8. National Commission on Reform of Federal Criminal Laws, Final Report of the Proposed New Federal Criminal Code 3603 (1971).

use to exceptional crimes such as treason. App. to Brief for Amnesty International as Amicus Curiae. Twenty-seven others do not in practice impose the penalty. Ibid. Of the nations that retain capital punishment, a majority—65—prohibit the execution of juveniles. Ibid. Sixty-one countries retain capital punishment and have no statutory provision exempting juveniles, though some of these nations are ratifiers of international treaties that do prohibit the execution of juveniles. Ibid. Since 1979, Amnesty International has recorded only eight executions of offenders under 18 throughout the world, three of these in the United States. The other five executions were carried out in Pakistan, Bangladesh, Rwanda, and Barbados.[9] In addition to national laws, three leading human rights treaties ratified or signed by the United States explicitly prohibit juvenile death penalties.[10] Within the world community, the imposition of the death penalty for juvenile crimes appears to be overwhelmingly disapproved.

D

Together, the rejection of the death penalty for juveniles by a majority of the States, the rarity of the sentence for juveniles, both as an absolute and a comparative matter, the decisions of respected organizations in relevant fields that this punishment is unacceptable, and its rejection generally throughout the world, provide to my mind a strong grounding for the view that it is not constitutionally tolerable that certain States persist in authorizing the execution of adolescent offenders. It is unnecessary, however, to rest a view that the Eighth Amendment prohibits the execution of minors solely upon a judgment as to the meaning to be attached to the evidence of contemporary values outlined above, for the execution of juveniles fails to satisfy two well-established and independent Eighth Amendment requirements—that a punishment not be disproportionate, and that it make a contribution to acceptable goals of punishment.

II

Justice Scalia forthrightly states in his plurality opinion that Eighth Amendment analysis is at an end once legislation and jury verdicts relating to the punishment in question are analyzed as indicators of contemporary values. A majority of the Court rejected this revision-

---

9. Brief for Amnesty International as Amicus Curiae in *Thompson* v. *Oklahoma*, O.T. 1987, No. 86-6169, p. 6.

10. Article 6(5) of the International Covenant on Civil and Political Rights, Annex to G.A. Res. 2200, 21 U.N. GAOR Res. Supp. (No. 16) 53, U.N. Doc. A/6316 (1966) (signed but not ratified by the United States), reprinted in 6 International Legal Material 368, 370 (1967); Article 4(5) of the American Convention on Human Rights, O.A.S. Official Records, OEA/Ser. K/XVI/1.1, Doc. 65, Rev. 1, Corr. 2 (1970) (same), reprinted in 9 International Legal Material 673, 676 (1970); Article 68 of the Geneva Convention Relative to the Protection of Civilian Persons in Time of War, August 12, 1949, 6 U.S. T. 3516, T. I. A. S. No. 3365 (ratified by the United States). See also Resolutions and Decisions of the United Nations Economic and Social Council, Res. 1984/50, U.N. ESCOR Supp. (No. 1), p. 33, U.N. Doc. E/1984/84 (1984) (adopting "safeguards guaranteeing protection of the rights of those facing the death penalty," including the safeguard that "[p]ersons below 18 years of age at the time of the commission of the crime shall not be sentenced to death"), endorsed by the United Nations General Assembly, U.N. GAOR Res. 39/118, U.N. Doc. A/39/51, p. 211, 2, 5 (1985), and adopted by the Seventh United Nations Congress on the Prevention of Crime and the Treatment of Offenders, p. 83, U.N. Doc. A/Conf. 121/22, U.N. Sales No. E.86.IV.1 (1986).

ist view as recently as last Term, see *Thompson,* 487 U.S., at 833–838 (plurality opinion); id., at 853–854 (opinion of O'Connor, J.), and does so again in this case and in *Penry v. Lynaugh,* ante, p. 302. We need not and should not treat this narrow range of factors as determinative of our decision whether a punishment violates the Constitution because it is excessive.

The Court has explicitly stated that "the attitude of state legislatures and sentencing juries do not wholly determine" a controversy arising under the Eighth Amendment, *Coker,* 433 U.S., at 597 (plurality opinion) because "the Constitution contemplates that in the end our own judgment will be brought to bear on the question of the [constitutional] acceptability of" a punishment, ibid. See also id., at 603–604, n. 2 (Powell, J., concurring in judgment) ("[T]he ultimate decision as to the appropriateness of the death penalty under the Eighth Amendment . . . must be decided on the basis of our own judgment in light of the precedents of this Court"); *Enmund,* supra, at 797 ("Although the judgments of legislatures, juries, and prosecutors weigh heavily in the balance, it is for us ultimately to judge whether the Eighth Amendment permits imposition of the death penalty" in a particular class of cases).

Justice Scalia's approach would largely return the task of defining the contours of Eighth Amendment protection to political majorities. But "[t]he very purpose of a Bill of Rights was to withdraw certain subjects from the vicissitudes of political controversy, to place them beyond the reach of majorities and officials and to establish them as legal principles to be applied by the courts. One's right to life, liberty, and property, to free speech, a free press, freedom of worship and assembly, and other fundamental rights may not be submitted to vote; they depend on the outcome of no elections." *West Virginia Board of Education v. Barnette,* 319 U.S. 624, 638 (1943).

Compare ante, at 375–377, with *Whitley v. Albers,* 475 U.S. 312, 318 (1986) ("The language of the Eighth Amendment . . . manifests 'an intention to limit the power of those entrusted with the criminal-law function of government'"). The promise of the Bill of Rights goes unfulfilled when we leave "[c]onstitutional doctrine [to] be formulated by the acts of those institutions which the Constitution is supposed to limit," Radin, The Jurisprudence of Death, 126 U. Pa. L. Rev. 989, 1036 (1978), as is the case under Justice Scalia's positivist approach to the definition of citizens' rights. This Court abandons its proven and proper role in our constitutional system when it hands back to the very majorities the Framers distrusted the power to define the precise scope of protection afforded by the Bill of Rights, rather than bringing its own judgment to bear on that question, after complete analysis.

Despite Justice Scalia's view to the contrary, however, "our cases . . . make clear that public perceptions of standards of decency with respect to criminal sanctions are not conclusive. A penalty also must accord with 'the dignity of man,' which is the 'basic concept underlying the Eighth Amendment.' . . . This means, at least, that the punishment not be 'excessive.' . . . [T]he inquiry into 'excessiveness' has two aspects. First, the punishment must not involve the unnecessary and wanton infliction of pain. . . . Second, the punishment must not be grossly out of proportion to the severity of the crime." *Gregg v. Georgia,* 428 U.S. 153, 173 (1976) (opinion of Stewart, Powell, and Stevens, J. J.).

Thus, in addition to asking whether legislative or jury rejection of a penalty shows that "society has set its face against it," ante, at 378, the Court asks whether "a punishment is 'excessive' and unconstitutional" because there is disproportion "between the punishment imposed and the defendant's blameworthiness," ante, at 382 (opinion of O'Connor, J.), or because it "makes no measurable contribution to acceptable goals of punishment and hence is nothing more than the purposeless and needless imposition of pain and suffering," *Coker,* supra, at 592 (plurality opinion). See, e.g., *Penry,* ante, at 335 (opinion of O'Connor, J.); ante, at 342–343 (Brennan, J., concurring in part and dissenting in part).

III

There can be no doubt at this point in our constitutional history that the Eighth Amendment forbids punishment that is wholly disproportionate to the blameworthiness of the offender. "The constitutional principle of proportionality has been recognized explicitly in this Court for almost a century." *Solem v. Helm,* 463 U.S. 277, 286 (1983). Usually formulated as a requirement that sentences not be "disproportionate to the crime committed," id., at 284; see, e.g., *Weems v. United States,* 217 U.S. 349 (1910); *O'Neil v. Vermont,* 144 U.S. 323, 339–340 (1892) (Field, J., dissenting), the proportionality principle takes account not only of the "injury to the person and to the public" caused by a crime, but also of the "moral depravity" of the offender. *Coker,* supra, at 598. The offender's culpability for his criminal acts—"the degree of the defendant's blameworthiness," Enmund, 458 U.S., at 815 (O'Connor, J., dissenting); see also id., at 798 (opinion of the Court)—is thus of central importance to the constitutionality of the sentence imposed. Indeed, this focus on a defendant's blameworthiness runs throughout our constitutional jurisprudence relating to capital sentencing. See, e.g., *Booth v. Maryland,* 482 U.S. 496, 502 (1987) (striking down state statute requiring consideration by sentencer of evidence other than defendant's record and characteristics and the circumstances of the crime, which had no "bearing on the defendant's 'personal responsibility and moral guilt'"); *California v. Brown,* 479 U.S. 538, 545 (1987) (an "emphasis on culpability in sentencing decisions has long been reflected in Anglo-American jurisprudence. . . . Lockett and Eddings reflect the belief that punishment should be directly related to the personal culpability of the criminal defendant") (O'Connor, J., concurring).

Proportionality analysis requires that we compare "the gravity of the offense," understood to include not only the injury caused, but also the defendant's culpability, with "the harshness of the penalty." *Solem,* supra, at 292. In my view, juveniles so generally lack the degree of responsibility for their crimes that is a predicate for the constitutional imposition of the death penalty that the Eighth Amendment forbids that they receive that punishment.

A

Legislative determinations distinguishing juveniles from adults abound. These age-based classifications reveal much about how our society regards juveniles as a class, and about societal beliefs regarding adolescent levels of responsibility. See *Thompson,* 487 U.S., at 823–825 (plurality opinion).

The participation of juveniles in a substantial number of activities open to adults is either barred completely or significantly restricted by legislation. All States but two have a uniform age of majority, and have set that age at 18 or above. OCCR Brief, App. A. No State has lowered its voting age below 18. Id., App. C; see *Thompson,* supra, at 839, App. A. Nor does any State permit a person under 18 to serve on a jury. OCCR Brief, App. B; see *Thompson,* supra, at 840, App. B. Only four States ever permit persons below 18 to marry without parental consent. OCCR Brief, App. D; see *Thompson,* supra, at 843, App. D. Thirty-seven States have specific enactments requiring that a patient have attained 18 before she may validly consent to medical treatment. OCCR Brief, App. E. Thirty-four States require parental consent before a person below 18 may drive a motor car. Id., App. F; see *Thompson,* supra, at 842, App. C. Legislation in 42 States prohibits those under 18 from purchasing pornographic materials. OCCR Brief, App. G; see *Thompson,* supra, at 845, App. E. Where gambling is legal, adolescents under 18 are generally not permitted to participate in it, in some or all of its forms. OCCR Brief, App. H; see *Thompson,* supra, at 847, App. F. In these and a host of other ways, minors are treated differently from adults in our laws, which reflects the simple truth derived from communal experience that juveniles as a class have not the level of maturation and responsibility that we presume in adults and consider desirable for full participation in the rights and duties of modern life.

"The reasons why juveniles are not trusted with the privileges and responsibilities of an adult also explain why their irresponsible conduct is not as morally reprehensible as that of an adult." *Thompson,* supra, at 835 (plurality opinion). Adolescents "are more vulnerable, more impulsive, and less self-disciplined than adults," and are without the same "capacity to control their conduct and to think in long-range terms." Twentieth Century Fund Task Force on Sentencing Policy Toward Young Offenders, Confronting Youth Crime 7 (1978) (hereafter Task Force). They are particularly impressionable and subject to peer pressure, see *Eddings v. Oklahoma,* 455 U.S. 104, 115 (1982), and prone to "experiment, risk-taking and bravado," Task Force 3. They lack "experience, perspective, and judgment." *Bellotti v. Baird,* 443 U.S. 622, 635 (1979). See generally *Thompson,* supra, at 43–44, n. 43; Brief for American Society for Adolescent Psychiatry et al. as Amici Curiae (reviewing scientific evidence). Moreover, the very paternalism that our society shows toward youths and the dependency it forces upon them mean that society bears a responsibility for the actions of juveniles that it does not for the actions of adults who are at least theoretically free to make their own choices: "youth crime . . . is not exclusively the offender's fault; offenses by the young represent a failure of family, school, and the social system, which share responsibility for the development of America's youth." Task Force 7.

To be sure, the development of cognitive and reasoning abilities and of empathy, the acquisition of experience upon which these abilities operate and upon which the capacity to make sound value judgments depends, and in general the process of maturation into a self-directed individual fully responsible for his or her actions, occur by degrees. See, e.g., G. Manaster, Adolescent Development and the Life Tasks (1977). But the factors discussed above indicate that 18 is the dividing line that society has generally drawn, the point at which it is thought reasonable to assume that persons have an ability to make, and a duty to bear responsibility for their, judgments. Insofar as age 18 is a necessarily arbitrary social choice as a point at which to acknowledge a person's maturity and responsibility, given the different developmental rates of individuals, it is in fact "a conservative estimate of the dividing line between adolescence and adulthood. Many of the psychological and emotional changes that an adolescent experiences in maturing do not actually occur until the early 20s." Brief for American Society for Adolescent Psychiatry et al. as Amici Curiae 4 (citing social scientific studies).

B

There may be exceptional individuals who mature more quickly than their peers, and who might be considered fully responsible for their actions prior to the age of 18, despite their lack of the experience upon which judgment depends.[11] In my view, however, it is not sufficient to accommodate the facts about juveniles that an individual youth's culpability may be taken into account in the decision to transfer him or her from the juvenile to the adult court system for trial, or that a capital sentencing jury is instructed to consider youth and other mitigating factors. I believe that the Eighth Amendment requires that a person who lacks that full degree of responsibility for his or her actions associated with adulthood not be sentenced to death. Hence it is constitutionally inadequate that a juvenile offender's level of responsibility be taken into account only along with a host of other factors that the court or jury may decide outweigh that want of responsibility.

Immaturity that constitutionally should operate as a bar to a disproportionate death sentence does not guarantee that a minor will not be transferred for trial to the adult court system. Rather, the most important considerations in the decision to transfer a juvenile offender are the seriousness of the offense, the extent of prior delinquency, and the response to prior treatment within the juvenile justice system. National Institute for Juvenile Justice and Delinquency, United States Dept. of Justice, Major Issues in Juvenile Justice Information and Training, Youth in Adult Courts: Between Two Worlds 211 (1982). Psychological, intellectual, and other personal characteristics of juvenile offenders receive little attention at the transfer stage, and cannot account for differences between those transferred and those who remain in the juvenile court system. See Solway, Hays, Schreiner, & Cansler, Clinical Study of Youths Petitioned for Certification as Adults, 46 Psychological Rep. 1067 (1980). Nor is an adolescent's lack of full culpability isolated at the sentencing stage as a factor that determinatively bars a death sentence. A jury is free to weigh a juvenile offender's youth and lack of full responsibility against the heinousness of the crime and other aggravating factors—and, finding the aggravating factors weightier, to sentence even the most immature of 16- or 17-year olds to be killed. By no stretch of the imagination, then, are the transfer and sentencing decisions designed to isolate those juvenile offenders who are exceptionally mature and responsible, and who thus stand out from their peers as a class.

It is thus unsurprising that individualized consideration at transfer and sentencing has not in fact ensured that juvenile offenders lacking an adult's culpability are not sentenced to die. Quite the contrary. Adolescents on death row appear typically to have a battery of psychological, emotional, and other problems going to their likely capacity for judgment and level of blameworthiness. A recent diagnostic evaluation of all 14 juveniles on death rows in four States is instructive. Lewis et al., Neuropsychiatric, Psychoeducational, and Family Characteristics of 14 Juveniles Condemned to Death in the United States, 145 Am. J. Psychiatry 584 (1988). Seven of the adolescents sentenced to die were psychotic when evaluated, or had been so diagnosed in earlier childhood; four others had histories consistent with diagnoses of severe mood disorders; and the remaining three experienced periodic paranoid episodes,

---

11. Delinquent juveniles are unlikely to be among these few. Instead, they will typically be among those persons for whom society's presumption of a capacity for mature judgment at 18 is much too generous. See, e.g., Scharf, Law and the Child's Evolving Legal Conscience, in Advances in Law and Child Development, 16 (R. Sprague ed. 1982) (discussing study of delinquents aged 15 to 17, suggesting that the group's mean moral maturity level was below that of average middle-class 10- to 12-year-olds).

during which they would assault perceived enemies. Id., at 585, and Table 3. Eight had suffered severe head injuries during childhood, id., at 585, and Table 1, and nine suffered from neurological abnormalities, id., at 585, and Table 2. Psychoeducational testing showed that only 2 of these death-row inmates had IQ scores above 90 (that is, in the normal range)—and both individuals suffered from psychiatric disorders—while 10 offenders showed impaired abstract reasoning on at least some tests. Id., at 585-586, and Tables 3 and 4. All but two of the adolescents had been physically abused, and five sexually abused. Id., at 586-587, and Table 5. Within the families of these children, violence, alcoholism, drug abuse, and psychiatric disorders were commonplace. Id., at 587, and Table 5.

The cases under consideration today certainly do not suggest that individualized consideration at transfer and sentencing ensure that only exceptionally mature juveniles, as blameworthy for their crimes as an adult, are sentenced to death. Transferring jurisdiction over Kevin Stanford to Circuit Court, the Juvenile Division of the Jefferson, Kentucky, District Court nevertheless found that Stanford, who was 17 at the time of his crime, "has a low internalization of the values and morals of society and lacks social skills. That he does possess an institutionalized personality and has, in effect, because of his chaotic family life and lack of treatment, become socialized in delinquent behavior. That he is emotionally immature and could be amenable to treatment if properly done on a long term basis of psychotherap[eu]tic intervention and reality based therapy for socialization and drug therapy in a residential facility." App. in No. 87-5765, p. 9.

At the penalty phase of Stanford's trial, witnesses testified that Stanford, who lived with various relatives, had used drugs from the age of about 13, and that his drug use had caused changes in his personality and behavior. Record in No. 87-5765, pp. 1383–1392, 1432. Stanford had been placed at times in juvenile treatment facilities, and a witness who had assessed him upon his admission to an employment skills project found that he lacked age-appropriate social interaction skills; had a history of drug abuse; and wanted for family support or supervision. Id., at 1408; see also id., at 1440–1442.

Heath Wilkins was 16 when he committed the crime for which Missouri intends to kill him. The juvenile court, in ordering him transferred for trial to adult court, focused upon the viciousness of Wilkins' crime, the juvenile system's inability to rehabilitate him in the 17 months of juvenile confinement available, and the need to protect the public, though it also mentioned that Wilkins was, in its view, "an experienced person, and mature in his appearance and habits." App. in No. 87-6026, p. 5. The Circuit Court found Wilkins competent to stand trial.[12] 12 Record in No. 87-6026, p. 42. Wilkins then waived counsel, with the avowed

---

12. Two psychological reports were prepared concerning Wilkins when the issue of his competency to stand trial arose. Neither suggests that Wilkins was exceptionally mature for his age. One found his intellectual functioning "within the average range," App. in No. 87-6026, p. 10, and his "[h]igher order processes," such as reasoning and judgment, to be "within the approximate normal range," id., at 11. The other concluded:

"[Wilkins'] capacity to manage and control affect is tenuous and inconsistent, leaving him a subject to impulsive actions as well as arbitrary and capricious thinking which is prone to skirt over details, and considerations for logical systematic thought. He is intolerant of intense affects such as anxiety, depression, or anger, in that such feelings are overwhelming, interfere with his ability to think clearly, and gives rise to impulsive action. He is vulnerable to massive infusions of intense rage which leads to spasms of destructive action. His rage co-mingles with a profound depressive experience generated by an excruciating sense of lonely alienation whereby he experiences both himself and other people as being lifeless and empty. . . ." He barely experiences ties to others or emp[athe]tic attunement . . . ." Id., at 22.

intention of pleading guilty and seeking the death penalty, id., at 42, 55, and the Circuit Court accepted the waiver, id., at 84, and later Wilkins' guilty plea, id., at 144–145. Wilkins was not represented by counsel at sentencing. See id., at 188–190. Presenting no mitigating evidence, he told the court he would prefer the death penalty to life in prison, id., at 186–187—"[o]ne I fear, the other one I don't," id., at 295—and after hearing evidence from the State, the Court sentenced Wilkins to die. Wilkins took no steps to appeal and objected to an amicus' efforts on his behalf. The Missouri Supreme Court, however, ordered an evaluation to determine whether Wilkins was competent to waive his right to appellate counsel. Concluding that Wilkins was incompetent to waive his rights,[13] the state-appointed forensic psychiatrist found that [492 u.s. 361, 401] Wilkins "suffers from a mental disorder" that affects his "reasoning and impairs his behavior." App. in No. 87-6026, p. 74. It would be incredible to suppose, given this psychiatrist's conclusion and his summary of Wilkins' past, set out in the margin,[14] that Missouri's transfer and sentencing schemes had operated to identify in Wilkins a 16-year old mature and culpable beyond his years.

---

13. Wilkins was diagnosed as being of a "Conduct Disorder, Undersocialized-Aggressive Type," with a borderline personality disorder that left him with "difficulty in establishing a pattern of predictable response to stressful situations vacillating between aggression towards others or self-destructive activity." Id., at 67-68. He had been "exhibiting bizarre behavior, paranoid ideation, and idiosyncratic thinking" since 1982. Id., at 68.

14. The state-appointed psychiatrist summarized Wilkins' past in his report:

"Mr. Wilkins . . . was raised in a rather poor socioeconomic environment [and] reportedly had extremely chaotic upbringing during his childhood. He was physically abused by his mother, sometimes the beatings would last for two hours. . . . As a child, he started robbing houses for knives and money and loved to set fires. Mr. Wilkins' mother worked at night and slept during the day, thus the children were left alone at night by themselves. He claims that he was started on drugs by his uncle [at age six; see id., at 67]. Apparently he used to shoot BB guns at passing cars. Mr. Wilkins indicated that his mother's boyfriend had a quick temper and that he hated him. He also started disliking his mother, not only because she punished [him], but also because she stood up for her boyfriend who was unkind towards [him]. He then decided to poison his mother and boyfriend by placing rat poison in Tylenol capsules. They were informed by his brother about the situation. They secretly emptied the capsules and made him eat them. He was afraid of death and attempted vomiting by placing [his] fingers in his throat. Then he ended up getting a beating from his mother and boyfriend. At the age of ten, Mr. Wilkins was evaluated at Tri-County Mental Health Center and Western Missouri Mental Health Center. He stayed there for a period of six months. He was then sent to Butterfield Youth's Home and then to East Range, a residential facility for boys. He started using drugs quite heavily. . . . He also started drinking hard liquor. . .

"At Butterfield, he was very angry at the teachers because they considered him to be 'dumb.' He showed rather strange behavior there. When he became depressed he would dance with a net over his head. On another occasion he cut his wrist and claimed to have had frequent thoughts of suicide. Prior to going to Butterfield, he had jumped off a bridge but the car swerved before he was hit. At Butterfield, he attempted to overdose with alcohol and drugs and another time with antipsychotic medication, Mellaril. Mr. Wilkins was placed on Mellaril because he was 'too active.' He stayed at . . . Butterfield . . . for three and one half years between the ages of 10 through 13 1/2. After that, he was transferred to Crittenton Center since it was closer to his mother's residence. He stayed there only for four or five months and was then kicked out. The court gave him permission to go home on probation. At this time his mother had started seeing another boyfriend and Mr. Wilkins apparently liked him. He continued the usage of alcohol and drugs while at school, continued to break into houses stealing money, jewelry, and knives, and generally stole money to spend at the arcade. On one occasion he ran away to Southern California. He was introduced to amphetamines there and spent all his money. . . . After his return [home, he] was charged with a stolen knife and was sent to [a] Detention Center. . . . At age 15, he was sent to the Northwest Regional Youth Services in Kansas City. There, an attempt at prescribing Thorazine (major tranquilizer) was made. After this, Mr. Wilkins was placed in a foster home. He ran away from the foster home . . . . Beginning in May of 1985 he lived on the streets. . . .
. . . .'Records from Butterfield . . . indicated that Mr. Wilkins' natural father was committed to a mental in-

C

Juveniles very generally lack that degree of blameworthiness that is, in my view, a constitutional prerequisite for the imposition of capital punishment under our precedents concerning the Eighth Amendment proportionality principle. The individualized consideration of an offender's youth and culpability at the transfer stage and at sentencing has not operated to ensure that the only offenders under 18 singled out for the ultimate penalty are exceptional individuals whose level of responsibility is more developed than that of their peers. In that circumstance, I believe that the same categorical assumption that juveniles as a class are insufficiently mature to be regarded as fully responsible that we make in so many other areas is appropriately made in determining whether minors may be subjected to the death penalty. As we noted in *Thompson,* 487 U.S., at 825-826, n. 23, it would be ironic if the assumptions we so readily make about minors as a class were suddenly unavailable in conducting proportionality analysis. I would hold that the Eighth Amendment prohibits the execution of any person for a crime committed below the age of 18.

IV

Under a second strand of Eighth Amendment inquiry into whether a particular sentence is excessive and hence unconstitutional, we ask whether the sentence makes a measurable contribution to acceptable goals of punishment. *Thompson,* supra, at 833; *Enmund v. Florida,* 458 U.S., at 798; *Coker v. Georgia,* 433 U.S., at 592; *Gregg v. Georgia,* 428 U.S., at 173. The two "principal social purposes" of capital punishment are said to be "retribution and the deterrence of capital crimes by prospective offenders." *Gregg,* supra, at 183; see *Enmund,* 458 U.S., at 798. Unless the death penalty applied to persons for offenses committed under 18 measurably contributes to one of these goals, the Eighth Amendment prohibits it. See ibid.

"[R]etribution as a justification for executing [offenders] very much depends on the degree of [their] culpability." Id., at 800. I have explained in Part III, supra, why I believe juveniles lack the culpability that makes a crime so extreme that it may warrant, according to this Court's cases, the death penalty; and why we should treat juveniles as a class as exempt from the ultimate penalty. These same considerations persuade me that executing juveniles "does not measurably contribute to the retributive end of ensuring that the criminal gets his just deserts." Id., at 801. See *Thompson,* supra, at 836-837. A punishment that fails the Eighth Amendment test of proportionality because disproportionate to the offender's blameworthiness by definition is not justly deserved.

---

stitution in Arkansas, and there was considerable amount of physical abuse that existed in the family.... In the educational testing, he gave rather unusual responses. For example, when asked the reasons why we need policemen, he replied, 'To get rid of people like me.' He also revealed plans to blow up a large building in Kansas City [and] made bizarre derogatory sexual comments towards women prior to visits with his mother. He had episodes of hyperventilation and passed out by fainting or chest squeezing.... On one occasion in September of 1981, he put gasoline into a toilet and set fire to it, causing an explosion. Mr. Wilkins' brother was diagnosed to be suffering from schizophrenia when he was admitted along with Mr. Wilkins in 1982 at Crittenton Center. Mr. Wilkins was often noticed to be fantasizing about outer space and supernatural powers. In the fall of 1982, [the Crittenton psychiatrist] recommended placement on Mellaril because of a 'disoriented thinking pattern and high anxiety.' In 1983, his condition started deteriorating.... His final diagnoses in November of 1983 when he was discharged from Crittenton were Borderline Personality and Passive-Aggressive Personality. Psychological testing at Crittenton indicated isolated episodes of paranoid functioning." Id., at 57–61.

Nor does the execution of juvenile offenders measurably contribute to the goal of deterrence. Excluding juveniles from the class of persons eligible to receive the death penalty will have little effect on any deterrent value capital punishment may have for potential offenders who are over 18: these adult offenders may of course remain eligible for a death sentence. The potential deterrent effect of juvenile executions on adolescent offenders is also insignificant. The deterrent value of capital punishment rests "on the assumption that we are rational beings who always think before we act, and then base our actions on a careful calculation of the gains and losses involved." Gardiner, The Purposes of Criminal Punishment, 21 Mod. L. Rev. 117, 122 (1958). As the plurality noted in *Thompson,* supra, at 837, "[t]he likelihood that the teenage offender has made the kind of cost-benefit analysis that attaches any weight to the possibility of execution is so remote as to be virtually nonexistent." First, juveniles "have less capacity . . . to think in long-range terms than adults," Task Force 7, and their careful weighing of a distant, uncertain, and indeed highly unlikely consequence prior to action is most improbable.[15] In addition, juveniles have little fear of death, because they have "a profound conviction of their own omnipotence and immortality." Miller, Adolescent Suicide: Etiology and Treatment, in 9 Adolescent Psychiatry 327, 329 (S. Feinstein, J. Looney, A. Schwartzberg, & A. Sorosky eds. 1981). See also, e.g., Gordon, The Tattered Cloak of Immortality, in Adolescence and Death 16, 27 (C. Corr & J. McNeil eds. 1986) (noting prevalence of adolescent risk taking); Brief for American Society for Adolescent Psychiatry et al. as Amici Curiae 5-6 (citing research). Because imposition of the death penalty on persons for offenses committed under the age of 18 makes no measurable contribution to the goals of either retribution or deterrence, it is "nothing more than the purposeless and needless imposition of pain and suffering," *Coker,* supra, at 592, and is thus excessive and unconstitutional.

V

There are strong indications that the execution of juvenile offenders violates contemporary standards of decency: a majority of States decline to permit juveniles to be sentenced to death; imposition of the sentence upon minors is very unusual even in those States that permit it; and respected organizations with expertise in relevant areas regard the execution of juveniles as unacceptable, as does international opinion. These indicators serve to confirm in my view my conclusion that the Eighth Amendment prohibits the execution of persons for offenses they committed while below the age of 18, because the death penalty is disproportionate when applied to such young offenders and fails measurably to serve the goals of capital punishment. I dissent.

Case Comment

In the case of *Roper v. Simmons,* the U.S. Supreme Court finally resolved the question of the minimum age at which persons convicted of murder could receive the death penalty. Simply, the Supreme Court noted that, in the sixteen years since *Stanford,* standards of decency

---

15. See, e.g., Kastenbaum, Time and Death in Adolescence, in The Meaning of Death 99, 104 (H. Feifel ed. 1959). Among the conclusions Kastenbaum drew from his study were that "[t]he adolescent lives in an intense present; 'now' is so real to him that both past and future seem pallid by comparison. Everything that is important and valuable in life lies either in the immediate life situation or in the rather close future." Ibid.

had evolved so that executing minors is now considered cruel and unusual punisl
is prohibited by the Eighth Amendment. The Court noted a consensus against tl
death penalty among state legislatures, and its own determination that the death penalty is
a disproportionate punishment for minors. The Court also pointed to "overwhelming" international opinion against executing juveniles. The effect of *Roper v. Simmons* is that no
person who is under the age of 18 at the time of the commission of a capital crime may be
sentenced to death.

ROPER V. SIMMONS

Supreme Court of the United States, 2005.

543 U.S. 551.

Justice Kennedy delivered the opinion of the Court.

This case requires us to address, for the second time in a decade and a half, whether it is
permissible under the Eighth and Fourteenth Amendments to the Constitution of the United
States to execute a juvenile offender who was older than 15 but younger than 18 when he committed a capital crime. In *Stanford v. Kentucky,* 492 U.S. 361 (1989), a divided Court rejected
the proposition that the Constitution bars capital punishment for juvenile offenders in this
age group. We reconsider the question.

I

At the age of 17, when he was still a junior in high school, Christopher Simmons, the respondent here, committed murder. About nine months later, after he had turned 18, he was
tried and sentenced to death. There is little doubt that Simmons was the instigator of the
crime. Before its commission Simmons said he wanted to murder someone. In chilling, callous terms he talked about his plan, discussing it for the most part with two friends, Charles
Benjamin and John Tessmer, then aged 15 and 16 respectively. Simmons proposed to commit burglary and murder by breaking and entering, tying up a victim, and throwing the victim off a bridge. Simmons assured his friends they could "get away with it" because they
were minors.

The three met at about 2 a.m. on the night of the murder, but Tessmer left before the
other two set out. (The State later charged Tessmer with conspiracy, but dropped the charge
in exchange for his testimony against Simmons.) Simmons and Benjamin entered the home
of the victim, Shirley Crook, after reaching through an open window and unlocking the
back door. Simmons turned on a hallway light. Awakened, Mrs. Crook called out, "Who's
there?" In response Simmons entered Mrs. Crook's bedroom, where he recognized her from
a previous car accident involving them both. Simmons later admitted this confirmed his resolve to murder her.

Using duct tape to cover her eyes and mouth and bind her hands, the two perpetrators
put Mrs. Crook in her minivan and drove to a state park. They reinforced the bindings, covered her head with a towel, and walked her to a railroad trestle spanning the Meramec River.
There they tied her hands and feet together with electrical wire, wrapped her whole face in
duct tape and threw her from the bridge, drowning her in the waters below.

By the afternoon of September 9, Steven Crook had returned home from an overnight trip, found his bedroom in disarray, and reported his wife missing. On the same afternoon fishermen recovered the victim's body from the river. Simmons, meanwhile, was bragging about the killing, telling friends he had killed a woman "because the bitch seen my face."

The next day, after receiving information of Simmons' involvement, police arrested him at his high school and took him to the police station in Fenton, Missouri. They read him his *Miranda* rights. Simmons waived his right to an attorney and agreed to answer questions. After less than two hours of interrogation, Simmons confessed to the murder and agreed to perform a videotaped reenactment at the crime scene.

The State charged Simmons with burglary, kidnapping, stealing, and murder in the first degree. As Simmons was 17 at the time of the crime, he was outside the criminal jurisdiction of Missouri's juvenile court system. See Mo. Rev. Stat. §§ 211.021 (2000) and 211.031 (Supp. 2003). He was tried as an adult. At trial the State introduced Simmons' confession and the videotaped reenactment of the crime, along with testimony that Simmons discussed the crime in advance and bragged about it later. The defense called no witnesses in the guilt phase. The jury having returned a verdict of murder, the trial proceeded to the penalty phase.

The State sought the death penalty. As aggravating factors, the State submitted that the murder was committed for the purpose of receiving money; was committed for the purpose of avoiding, interfering with, or preventing lawful arrest of the defendant; and involved depravity of mind and was outrageously and wantonly vile, horrible, and inhuman. The State called Shirley Crook's husband, daughter, and two sisters, who presented moving evidence of the devastation her death had brought to their lives.

In mitigation Simmons' attorneys first called an officer of the Missouri juvenile justice system, who testified that Simmons had no prior convictions and that no previous charges had been filed against him. Simmons' mother, father, two younger half brothers, a neighbor, and a friend took the stand to tell the jurors of the close relationships they had formed with Simmons and to plead for mercy on his behalf. Simmons' mother, in particular, testified to the responsibility Simmons demonstrated in taking care of his two younger half brothers and of his grandmother and to his capacity to show love for them.

During closing arguments, both the prosecutor and defense counsel addressed Simmons' age, which the trial judge had instructed the jurors they could consider as a mitigating factor. Defense counsel reminded the jurors that juveniles of Simmons' age cannot drink, serve on juries, or even see certain movies, because "the legislatures have wisely decided that individuals of a certain age aren't responsible enough." Defense counsel argued that Simmons' age should make "a huge difference to [the jurors] in deciding just exactly what sort of punishment to make." In rebuttal, the prosecutor gave the following response: "Age, he says. Think about age. Seventeen years old. Isn't that scary? Doesn't that scare you? Mitigating? Quite the contrary I submit. Quite the contrary."

The jury recommended the death penalty after finding the State had proved each of the three aggravating factors submitted to it. Accepting the jury's recommendation, the trial judge imposed the death penalty.

Simmons obtained new counsel, who moved in the trial court to set aside the conviction and sentence. One argument was that Simmons had received ineffective assistance at trial. To support this contention, the new counsel called as witnesses Simmons' trial attorney, Simmons' friends and neighbors, and clinical psychologists who had evaluated him.

Part of the submission was that Simmons was "very immature," "very impulsive," and "very susceptible to being manipulated or influenced." The experts testified about Simmons' background including a difficult home environment and dramatic changes in behavior, accompanied by poor school performance in adolescence. Simmons was absent from home for long periods, spending time using alcohol and drugs with other teenagers or young adults. The contention by Simmons' postconviction counsel was that these matters should have been established in the sentencing proceeding.

The trial court found no constitutional violation by reason of ineffective assistance of counsel and denied the motion for postconviction relief. In a consolidated appeal from Simmons' conviction and sentence, and from the denial of postconviction relief, the Missouri Supreme Court affirmed. *State v. Simmons*, 944 S.W. 2d 165, 169 (en banc), cert. denied, 522 U.S. 953 (1997). The federal courts denied Simmons' petition for a writ of habeas corpus. *Simmons v. Bowersox*, 235 F. 3d 1124, 1127 (CA8), cert. denied, 534 U.S. 924 (2001).

After these proceedings in Simmons' case had run their course, this Court held that the Eighth and Fourteenth Amendments prohibit the execution of a mentally retarded person. *Atkins v. Virginia*, 536 U.S. 304 (2002). Simmons filed a new petition for state postconviction relief, arguing that the reasoning of *Atkins* established that the Constitution prohibits the execution of a juvenile who was under 18 when the crime was committed.

The Missouri Supreme Court agreed. *State ex rel. Simmons v. Roper*, 112 S. W. 3d 397 (2003) (en banc). It held that since *Stanford*, "a national consensus has developed against the execution of juvenile offenders, as demonstrated by the fact that eighteen states now bar such executions for juveniles, that twelve other states bar executions altogether, that no state has lowered its age of execution below 18 since *Stanford*, that five states have legislatively or by case law raised or established the minimum age at 18, and that the imposition of the juvenile death penalty has become truly unusual over the last decade." 112 S. W. 3d, at 399.

On this reasoning it set aside Simmons' death sentence and resentenced him to "life imprisonment without eligibility for probation, parole, or release except by act of the Governor." *Id.*, at 413.

We granted certiorari, 540 U.S. 1160 (2004), and now affirm.

II

The Eighth Amendment provides: "Excessive bail shall not be required, nor excessive fines imposed, nor cruel and unusual punishments inflicted." The provision is applicable to the States through the Fourteenth Amendment. *Furman v. Georgia*, 408 U.S. 238, 239 (1972) (*per curiam*); *Robinson v. California*, 370 U.S. 660, 666-667 (1962); *Louisiana ex rel. Francis v. Resweber*, 329 U.S. 459, 463 (1947) (plurality opinion). As the Court explained in *Atkins*, the Eighth Amendment guarantees individuals the right not to be subjected to excessive sanctions. The right flows from the basic "'precept of justice that punishment for crime should be graduated and proportioned to [the] offense.'" 536 U.S., at 311 (quoting *Weems v. United States*, 217 U.S. 349, 367 (1910)). By protecting even those convicted of heinous crimes, the Eighth Amendment reaffirms the duty of the government to respect the dignity of all persons.

The prohibition against "cruel and unusual punishments," like other expansive language in the Constitution, must be interpreted according to its text, by considering history, tradition, and precedent, and with due regard for its purpose and function in the constitutional design. To implement this framework we have established the propriety and affirmed the necessity of referring to "the evolving standards of decency that mark the progress of a maturing society" to determine which punishments are so disproportionate as to be cruel and unusual. *Trop v. Dulles,* 356 U.S. 86, 100-101 (1958) (plurality opinion).

In *Thompson* v. *Oklahoma,* 487 U.S. 815 (1988), a plurality of the Court determined that our standards of decency do not permit the execution of any offender under the age of 16 at the time of the crime. *Id.,* at 818-838 (opinion of Stevens, J., joined by Brennan, Marshall, and Blackmun, J. J.). The plurality opinion explained that no death penalty State that had given express consideration to a minimum age for the death penalty had set the age lower than 16. *Id.,* at 826-829. The plurality also observed that "[t]he conclusion that it would offend civilized standards of decency to execute a person who was less than 16 years old at the time of his or her offense is consistent with the views that have been expressed by respected professional organizations, by other nations that share our Anglo-American heritage, and by the leading members of the Western European community." *Id.,* at 830. The opinion further noted that juries imposed the death penalty on offenders under 16 with exceeding rarity; the last execution of an offender for a crime committed under the age of 16 had been carried out in 1948, 40 years prior. *Id.,* at 832-833.

Bringing its independent judgment to bear on the permissibility of the death penalty for a 15-year-old offender, the *Thompson* plurality stressed that "[t]he reasons why juveniles are not trusted with the privileges and responsibilities of an adult also explain why their irresponsible conduct is not as morally reprehensible as that of an adult." *Id.,* at 835. According to the plurality, the lesser culpability of offenders under 16 made the death penalty inappropriate as a form of retribution, while the low likelihood that offenders under 16 engaged in "the kind of cost-benefit analysis that attaches any weight to the possibility of execution" made the death penalty ineffective as a means of deterrence. *Id.,* at 836-838. With Justice O'Connor concurring in the judgment on narrower grounds, *id.,* at 848-859, the Court set aside the death sentence that had been imposed on the 15-year-old offender.

The next year, in *Stanford v. Kentucky,* 492 U.S. 361 (1989), the Court, over a dissenting opinion joined by four Justices, referred to contemporary standards of decency in this country and concluded the Eighth and Fourteenth Amendments did not proscribe the execution of juvenile offenders over 15 but under 18. The Court noted that 22 of the 37 death penalty States permitted the death penalty for 16-year-old offenders, and, among these 37 States, 25 permitted it for 17-year-old offenders. These numbers, in the Court's view, indicated there was no national consensus "sufficient to label a particular punishment cruel and unusual." *Id.,* at 370-371. A plurality of the Court also "emphatically reject[ed]" the suggestion that the Court should bring its own judgment to bear on the acceptability of the juvenile death penalty. *Id.,* at 377-378 (opinion of Scalia, J., joined by Rehnquist, C. J., and White and Kennedy, J. J.); see also *id.,* at 382 (O'Connor, J., concurring in part and concurring in judgment) (criticizing the plurality's refusal "to judge whether the 'nexus between the punishment imposed and the defendant's blameworthiness' is proportional").

The same day the Court decided *Stanford,* it held that the Eighth Amendment did not mandate a categorical exemption from the death penalty for the mentally retarded. *Penry v. Lynaugh,* 492 U.S. 302 (1989). In reaching this conclusion it stressed that only two States had enacted laws banning the imposition of the death penalty on a mentally retarded person convicted of a capital offense. *Id.*, at 334. According to the Court, "the two state statutes prohibiting execution of the mentally retarded, even when added to the 14 States that have rejected capital punishment completely, [did] not provide sufficient evidence at present of a national consensus." *Ibid.*

Three Terms ago the subject was reconsidered in *Atkins.* We held that standards of decency have evolved since *Penry* and now demonstrate that the execution of the mentally retarded is cruel and unusual punishment. The Court noted objective indicia of society's standards, as expressed in legislative enactments and state practice with respect to executions of the mentally retarded. When *Atkins* was decided only a minority of States permitted the practice, and even in those States it was rare. 536 U.S., at 314-315. On the basis of these indicia the Court determined that executing mentally retarded offenders "has become truly unusual, and it is fair to say that a national consensus has developed against it." *Id.*, at 316.

The inquiry into our society's evolving standards of decency did not end there. The *Atkins* Court neither repeated nor relied upon the statement in *Stanford* that the Court's independent judgment has no bearing on the acceptability of a particular punishment under the Eighth Amendment. Instead we returned to the rule, established in decisions predating *Stanford*, that "'the Constitution contemplates that in the end our own judgment will be brought to bear on the question of the acceptability of the death penalty under the Eighth Amendment.'" 536 U.S., at 312 (quoting *Coker v. Georgia*, 433 U.S. 584, 597 (1977) (plurality opinion)). Mental retardation, the Court said, diminishes personal culpability even if the offender can distinguish right from wrong. 536 U.S., at 318. The impairments of mentally retarded offenders make it less defensible to impose the death penalty as retribution for past crimes and less likely that the death penalty will have a real deterrent effect. *Id.*, at 319-320. Based on these considerations and on the finding of national consensus against executing the mentally retarded, the Court ruled that the death penalty constitutes an excessive sanction for the entire category of mentally retarded offenders, and that the Eighth Amendment "'places a substantive restriction on the State's power to take the life' of a mentally retarded offender." *Id.*, at 321 (quoting *Ford v. Wainwright*, 477 U.S. 399, 405 (1986)).

Just as the *Atkins* Court reconsidered the issue decided in *Penry*, we now reconsider the issue decided in *Stanford.* The beginning point is a review of objective indicia of consensus, as expressed in particular by the enactments of legislatures that have addressed the question. This data gives us essential instruction. We then must determine, in the exercise of our own independent judgment, whether the death penalty is a disproportionate punishment for juveniles.

III

A

The evidence of national consensus against the death penalty for juveniles is similar, and in some respects parallel, to the evidence *Atkins* held sufficient to demonstrate a national consensus against the death penalty for the mentally retarded. When *Atkins* was decided, 30 States prohibited the death penalty for the mentally retarded. This number comprised 12 that had abandoned the death penalty altogether, and 18 that maintained it but excluded the mentally retarded from its reach. 536 U.S., at 313-315. By a similar calculation in this case, 30 States prohibit the juvenile death penalty, comprising 12 that have rejected the death penalty altogether and 18 that maintain it but, by express provision or judicial interpretation, exclude juveniles from its reach. See Appendix A, *infra. Atkins* emphasized that even in the 20 States without formal prohibition, the practice of executing the mentally retarded was infrequent. Since *Penry*, only five States had executed offenders known to have an IQ under 70. 536 U.S., at 316. In the present case, too, even in the 20 States without a formal prohibition on executing juveniles, the practice is infrequent. Since *Stanford*, six States have executed prisoners for crimes committed as juveniles. In the past 10 years, only three have done so: Oklahoma, Texas, and Virginia. See V. Streib, The Juvenile Death Penalty Today: Death Sentences and Executions for Juvenile Crimes, January 1, 1973–December 31 2004, No. 76, p. 4 (2005), available at http://www.law.onu.edu/faculty/streib/documents/ JuvDeathDec2004.pdf (last updated Jan. 31, 2005) (as visited Feb. 25, 2005, and available in the Clerk of Court's case file). In December 2003 the Governor of Kentucky decided to spare the life of Kevin Stanford, and commuted his sentence to one of life imprisonment without parole, with the declaration that "'[w]e ought not be executing people who, legally, were children.'" *Lexington Herald Leader,* Dec. 9, 2003, p. B3, 2003 WL 65043346. By this act the Governor ensured Kentucky would not add itself to the list of States that have executed juveniles within the last 10 years even by the execution of the very defendant whose death sentence the Court had upheld in *Stanford v. Kentucky.*

There is, to be sure, at least one difference between the evidence of consensus in *Atkins* and in this case. Impressive in *Atkins* was the rate of abolition of the death penalty for the mentally retarded. Sixteen States that permitted the execution of the mentally retarded at the time of *Penry* had prohibited the practice by the time we heard *Atkins.* By contrast, the rate of change in reducing the incidence of the juvenile death penalty, or in taking specific steps to abolish it, has been slower. Five States that allowed the juvenile death penalty at the time of *Stanford* have abandoned it in the intervening 15 years—four through legislative enactments and one through judicial decision. Streib, *supra,* at 5, 7; *State v. Furman,* 122 Wash. 2d 400, 858 P.2d 1092 (1993) (en banc).

Though less dramatic than the change from *Penry* to *Atkins* ("telling," to borrow the word *Atkins* used to describe this difference, 536 U.S., at 315, n. 18), we still consider the change from *Stanford* to this case to be significant. As noted in *Atkins,* with respect to the States that had abandoned the death penalty for the mentally retarded since *Penry,* "[i]t is not so much the number of these States that is significant, but the consistency of the direction of change." 536 U.S., at 315. In particular we found it significant that, in the wake of *Penry,* no State that had already prohibited the execution of the mentally retarded had passed legislation to reinstate the penalty. 536 U.S., at 315–316. The number of States that have abandoned capital punishment for juvenile offenders since *Stanford* is smaller than the number of States that abandoned capital punishment for the mentally retarded after *Penry;* yet we think the same consistency of direction of change has been demonstrated. Since *Stanford,* no State that previously prohibited capital punishment for juveniles has reinstated it. This fact, coupled with the trend toward abolition of the juvenile death penalty, carries special force in light of the general popularity of anticrime legislation, *Atkins, supra,* at 315, and in light of the particular trend in recent years toward cracking down on juvenile crime in other respects, see H. Snyder & M. Sickmund, National Center for Juvenile Justice, Juvenile Offenders and Victims: 1999 National Report 89, 133 (Sept. 1999); Scott & Grisso, The Evolution of Adolescence: A Developmental Perspective on Juvenile Justice Reform, 88 J. Crim. L. & C. 137, 148

(1997). Any difference between this case and *Atkins* with respect to the pace of abolition is thus counterbalanced by the consistent direction of the change.

The slower pace of abolition of the juvenile death penalty over the past 15 years, moreover, may have a simple explanation. When we heard *Penry*, only two death penalty States had already prohibited the execution of the mentally retarded. When we heard *Stanford*, by contrast, 12 death penalty States had already prohibited the execution of any juvenile under 18, and 15 had prohibited the execution of any juvenile under 17. If anything, this shows that the impropriety of executing juveniles between 16 and 18 years of age gained wide recognition earlier than the impropriety of executing the mentally retarded. In the words of the Missouri Supreme Court: "It would be the ultimate in irony if the very fact that the inappropriateness of the death penalty for juveniles was broadly recognized sooner than it was recognized for the mentally retarded were to become a reason to continue the execution of juveniles now that the execution of the mentally retarded has been barred." 112 S. W. 3d, at 408, n. 10.

Petitioner cannot show national consensus in favor of capital punishment for juveniles but still resists the conclusion that any consensus exists against it. Petitioner supports this position with, in particular, the observation that when the Senate ratified the International Covenant on Civil and Political Rights (ICCPR), Dec. 19, 1966, 999 U.N.T.S. 171 (entered into force Mar. 23, 1976), it did so subject to the President's proposed reservation regarding Article 6(5) of that treaty, which prohibits capital punishment for juveniles. Brief for Petitioner 27. This reservation at best provides only faint support for petitioner's argument. First, the reservation was passed in 1992; since then, five States have abandoned capital punishment for juveniles. Second, Congress considered the issue when enacting the Federal Death Penalty Act in 1994, and determined that the death penalty should not extend to juveniles. See 18 U.S.C. § 3591. The reservation to Article 6(5) of the ICCPR provides minimal evidence that there is not now a national consensus against juvenile executions.

As in *Atkins*, the objective indicia of consensus in this case—the rejection of the juvenile death penalty in the majority of States; the infrequency of its use even where it remains on the books; and the consistency in the trend toward abolition of the practice—provide sufficient evidence that today our society views juveniles, in the words *Atkins* used respecting the mentally retarded, as "categorically less culpable than the average criminal." 536 U.S., at 316.

B

A majority of States have rejected the imposition of the death penalty on juvenile offenders under 18, and we now hold this is required by the Eighth Amendment. Because the death penalty is the most severe punishment, the Eighth Amendment applies to it with special force. *Thompson*, 487 U.S., at 856 (O'Connor, J., concurring in judgment). Capital punishment must be limited to those offenders who commit "a narrow category of the most serious crimes" and whose extreme culpability makes them "the most deserving of execution." *Atkins, supra*, at 319. This principle is implemented throughout the capital sentencing process. States must give narrow and precise definition to the aggravating factors that can result in a capital sentence. *Godfrey v. Georgia*, 446 U.S. 420, 428–429 (1980) (plurality opinion). In any capital case a defendant has wide latitude to raise as a mitigating factor "any aspect of [his or her] character or record and any of the circumstances of the offense that the defendant proffers as a basis for a sentence less than death." *Lockett v. Ohio*, 438 U.S. 586, 604 (1978) (plurality opinion); *Eddings v. Oklahoma,* 455 U.S. 104, 110-112 (1982); see also *Johnson v. Texas,* 509 U.S. 350, 359-362 (1993) (summarizing the Court's jurisprudence after *Furman v. Georgia,* 408 U.S. 238 (1972) *(per curiam),* with respect to a sentencer's consideration of aggravating and mitigating factors). There are a number of crimes that beyond question are severe in absolute terms, yet the death penalty may not be imposed for their commission. *Coker v. Georgia,* 433 U.S. 584 (1977) (rape of an adult woman); *Enmund v. Florida,* 458 U.S. 782 (1982) (felony murder where defendant did not kill, attempt to kill, or intend to kill). The death penalty may not be imposed on certain classes of offenders, such as juveniles under 16, the insane, and the mentally retarded, no matter how heinous the crime. *Thompson v. Oklahoma, supra; Ford v. Wainwright,* 477 U.S. 399 (1986); *Atkins, supra.* These rules vindicate the underlying principle that the death penalty is reserved for a narrow category of crimes and offenders.

Three general differences between juveniles under 18 and adults demonstrate that juvenile offenders cannot with reliability be classified among the worst offenders. First, as any parent knows and as the scientific and sociological studies respondent and his *amici* cite tend to confirm, "[a] lack of maturity and an underdeveloped sense of responsibility are found in youth more often than in adults and are more understandable among the young. These qualities often result in impetuous and ill-considered actions and decisions." *Johnson, supra,* at 367; see also *Eddings, supra,* at 115-116 ("Even the normal 16-year-old customarily lacks the maturity of an adult"). It has been noted that "adolescents are overrepresented statistically in virtually every category of reckless behavior." Arnett, Reckless Behavior in Adolescence: A Developmental Perspective, 12 Developmental Review 339 (1992). In recognition of the comparative immaturity and irresponsibility of juveniles, almost every State prohibits those under 18 years of age from voting, serving on juries, or marrying without parental consent. See Appendixes B–D, *infra.*

The second area of difference is that juveniles are more vulnerable or susceptible to negative influences and outside pressures, including peer pressure. *Eddings, supra,* at 115 ("[Y]outh is more than a chronological fact. It is a time and condition of life when a person may be most susceptible to influence and to psychological damage"). This is explained in part by the prevailing circumstance that juveniles have less control, or less experience with control, over their own environment. See Steinberg & Scott, Less Guilty by Reason of Adolescence: Developmental Immaturity, Diminished Responsibility, and the Juvenile Death Penalty, 58 Am. Psychologist 1009, 1014 (2003) (hereinafter Steinberg & Scott) ("[A]s legal minors, [juveniles] lack the freedom that adults have to extricate themselves from a criminogenic setting").

The third broad difference is that the character of a juvenile is not as well formed as that of an adult. The personality traits of juveniles are more transitory, less fixed. See generally E. Erikson, Identity: Youth and Crisis (1968).

These differences render suspect any conclusion that a juvenile falls among the worst offenders. The susceptibility of juveniles to immature and irresponsible behavior means "their irresponsible conduct is not as morally reprehensible as that of an adult." *Thompson, supra,* at 835 (plurality opinion). Their own vulnerability and comparative lack of control over their immediate surroundings mean juveniles have a greater claim than adults to be forgiven for failing to escape negative influences in their whole environment. See *Stanford,* 492 U.S., at 395 (Brennan, J., dissenting). The reality that juveniles still struggle to define their identity means it is less supportable to conclude that even a heinous crime committed by a juvenile is evidence of irretrievably depraved character. From a moral standpoint it would be misguided to equate the failings of a minor with those of an adult, for a greater possibility exists that a minor's character deficiencies will be reformed. Indeed, "[t]he relevance of youth as a mitigating factor derives from the fact that the signature qualities of youth are transient; as individuals mature, the impetuousness and recklessness that may dominate in younger years can subside." *Johnson, supra,* at 368; see also Steinberg & Scott 1014 ("For most teens, [risky or antisocial] behaviors are fleeting; they cease with maturity as individual identity becomes settled. Only a relatively small proportion of adolescents who experiment in risky or illegal activities develop entrenched patterns of problem behavior that persist into adulthood").

In *Thompson,* a plurality of the Court recognized the import of these characteristics with respect to juveniles under 16, and relied on them to hold that the Eighth Amendment prohibited the imposition of the death penalty on juveniles below that age. 487 U.S., at 833-838. We conclude the same reasoning applies to all juvenile offenders under 18.

Once the diminished culpability of juveniles is recognized, it is evident that the penological justifications for the death penalty apply to them with lesser force than to adults. We have held there are two distinct social purposes served by the death penalty: "'retribution and deterrence of capital crimes by prospective offenders.'" *Atkins,* 536 U.S., at 319 (quoting *Gregg v. Georgia,* 428 U.S. 153, 183 (1976) (joint opinion of Stewart, Powell, and Stevens, J. J.)). As for retribution, we remarked in *Atkins* that "[i]f the culpability of the average murderer is insufficient to justify the most extreme sanction available to the State, the lesser culpability of the mentally retarded offender surely does not merit that form of retribution." 536 U.S., at 319. The same conclusions follow from the lesser culpability of the juvenile offender. Whether viewed as an attempt to express the community's moral outrage or as an attempt to right the balance for the wrong to the victim, the case for retribution is not as strong with a minor as with an adult. Retribution is not proportional if the law's most severe penalty is imposed on one whose culpability or blameworthiness is diminished, to a substantial degree, by reason of youth and immaturity.

As for deterrence, it is unclear whether the death penalty has a significant or even measurable deterrent effect on juveniles, as counsel for the petitioner acknowledged at oral argument. Tr. of Oral Arg. 48. In general we leave to legislatures the assessment of the efficacy of various criminal penalty schemes, see *Harmelin v. Michigan,* 501 U.S. 957, 998–999 (1991) (Kennedy, J., concurring in part and concurring in judgment). Here, however, the absence of evidence of deterrent effect is of special concern because the same characteristics that render juveniles less culpable than adults suggest as well that juveniles will be less susceptible to deterrence. In particular, as the plurality observed in *Thompson,* "[t]he likelihood that the teenage offender has made the kind of cost-benefit analysis that attaches any weight to the possibility of execution is so remote as to be virtually nonexistent." 487 U.S., at 837. To the extent the juvenile death penalty might have residual deterrent effect, it is worth noting that the punishment of life imprisonment without the possibility of parole is itself a severe sanction, in particular for a young person.

In concluding that neither retribution nor deterrence provides adequate justification for imposing the death penalty on juvenile offenders, we cannot deny or overlook the brutal crimes too many juvenile offenders have committed. See Brief for Alabama et al. as *Amici Curiae.* Certainly it can be argued, although we by no means concede the point, that a rare case might arise in which a juvenile offender has sufficient psychological maturity, and at the same time demonstrates sufficient depravity, to merit a sentence of death. Indeed, this possibility is the linchpin of one contention pressed by petitioner and his *amici*. They assert that even assuming the truth of the observations we have made about juveniles' diminished culpability in general, jurors nonetheless should be allowed to consider mitigating arguments related to youth on a case-by-case basis, and in some cases to impose the death penalty if justified. A central feature of death penalty sentencing is a particular assessment of the circumstances of the crime and the characteristics of the offender. The system is designed to consider both aggravating and mitigating circumstances, including youth, in every case. Given this Court's own insistence on individualized consideration, petitioner maintains that it is both arbitrary and unnecessary to adopt a categorical rule barring imposition of the death penalty on any offender under 18 years of age.

We disagree. The differences between juvenile and adult offenders are too marked and well understood to risk allowing a youthful person to receive the death penalty despite insufficient culpability. An unacceptable likelihood exists that the brutality or cold-blooded nature of any particular crime would overpower mitigating arguments based on youth as a matter of course, even where the juvenile offender's objective immaturity, vulnerability, and lack of true depravity should require a sentence less severe than death. In some cases a defendant's youth may even be counted against him. In this very case, as we noted above, the prosecutor argued Simmons' youth was aggravating rather than mitigating. *Supra*, at 4. While this sort of overreaching could be corrected by a particular rule to ensure that the mitigating force of youth is not overlooked, that would not address our larger concerns.

It is difficult even for expert psychologists to differentiate between the juvenile offender whose crime reflects unfortunate yet transient immaturity, and the rare juvenile offender whose crime reflects irreparable corruption. See Steinberg & Scott 1014-1016. As we understand it, this difficulty underlies the rule forbidding psychiatrists from diagnosing any patient under 18 as having antisocial personality disorder, a disorder also referred to as psychopathy or sociopathy, and which is characterized by callousness, cynicism, and contempt for the feelings, rights, and suffering of others. American Psychiatric Association, Diagnostic and Statistical Manual of Mental Disorders 701–706 (4th ed. text rev. 2000); see also Steinberg & Scott 1015. If trained psychiatrists with the advantage of clinical testing and observation refrain, despite diagnostic expertise, from assessing any juvenile under 18 as having antisocial personality disorder, we conclude that States should refrain from asking jurors to issue a far graver condemnation—that a juvenile offender merits the death penalty. When a juvenile offender commits a heinous crime, the State can exact forfeiture of some of the most basic liberties, but the State cannot extinguish his life and his potential to attain a mature understanding of his own humanity.

Drawing the line at 18 years of age is subject, of course, to the objections always raised against categorical rules. The qualities that distinguish juveniles from adults do not disappear when an individual turns 18. By the same token, some under 18 have already attained a level of maturity some adults will never reach. For the reasons we have discussed, however, a line must be drawn. The plurality opinion in *Thompson* drew the line at 16. In the intervening years the *Thompson* plurality's conclusion that offenders under 16 may not be executed has not been challenged. The logic of *Thompson* extends to those who are under 18. The age of 18 is the point where society draws the line for many purposes between childhood and adulthood. It is, we conclude, the age at which the line for death eligibility ought to rest.

These considerations mean *Stanford v. Kentucky* should be deemed no longer controlling on this issue. To the extent *Stanford* was based on review of the objective indicia of consensus that obtained in 1989, 492 U.S., at 370-371, it suffices to note that those indicia have changed. *Supra,* at 10-13. It should be observed, furthermore, that the *Stanford* Court should have considered those States that had abandoned the death penalty altogether as part of the consensus against the juvenile death penalty, 492 U.S., at 370, n. 2; a State's decision to bar the death penalty altogether of necessity demonstrates a judgment that the death penalty is inappropriate for all offenders, including juveniles. Last, to the extent *Stanford* was based on a rejection of the idea that this Court is required to bring its independent judgment to bear on the proportionality of the death penalty for a particular class of crimes or offenders, *id.,* at 377-378 (plurality opinion), it suffices to note that this rejection was inconsistent with prior Eighth Amendment decisions, *Thompson,* 487 U.S., at 833-838 (plurality opinion); *Enmund,* 458 U.S., at 797; *Coker,* 433 U.S., at 597 (plurality opinion). It is also inconsistent with the premises of our recent decision in *Atkins.* 536 U.S., at 312-313, 317-321.

In holding that the death penalty cannot be imposed upon juvenile offenders, we take into account the circumstance that some States have relied on *Stanford* in seeking the death penalty against juvenile offenders. This consideration, however, does not outweigh our conclusion that *Stanford* should no longer control in those few pending cases or in those yet to arise.

IV

Our determination that the death penalty is disproportionate punishment for offenders under 18 finds confirmation in the stark reality that the United States is the only country in the world that continues to give official sanction to the juvenile death penalty. This reality does not become controlling, for the task of interpreting the Eighth Amendment remains our responsibility. Yet at least from the time of the Court's decision in *Trop,* the Court has referred to the laws of other countries and to international authorities as instructive for its interpretation of the Eighth Amendment's prohibition of "cruel and unusual punishments." 356 U.S., at 102-103 (plurality opinion) ("The civilized nations of the world are in virtual unanimity that statelessness is not to be imposed as punishment for crime"); see also *Atkins, supra,* at 317, n. 21 (recognizing that "within the world community, the imposition of the death penalty for crimes committed by mentally retarded offenders is overwhelmingly disapproved"); *Thompson, supra,* at 830-831, and n. 31 (plurality opinion) (noting the abolition of the juvenile death penalty "by other nations that share our Anglo-American heritage, and by the leading members of the Western European community," and observing that "[w]e have previously recognized the relevance of the views of the international community in determining whether a punishment is cruel and unusual"); *Enmund, supra,* at 796-797, n. 22 (observing that "the doctrine of felony murder has been abolished in England and India, severely restricted in Canada and a number of other Commonwealth countries, and is unknown in continental Europe"); *Coker, supra,* at 596, n. 10 (plurality opinion) ("It is . . . not irrelevant here that out of 60 major nations in the world surveyed in 1965, only 3 retained the death penalty for rape where death did not ensue").

As respondent and a number of *amici* emphasize, Article 37 of the United Nations Convention on the Rights of the Child, which every country in the world has ratified save for the United States and Somalia, contains an express prohibition on capital punishment for crimes committed by juveniles under 18. United Nations Convention on the Rights of the Child, Art. 37, Nov. 20, 1989, 1577 U.N.T.S. 3, 28 I.L.M. 1448, 1468-1470 (entered into force Sept. 2, 1990); Brief for Respondent 48; Brief for European Union et al. as *Amici Curiae* 12-13; Brief for President James Earl Carter, Jr., et al. as *Amici Curiae* 9; Brief for Former U.S. Diplomats Morton Abramowitz et al. as *Amici Curiae* 7; Brief for Human Rights Committee of the Bar of England and Wales et al. as *Amici Curiae* 13-14. No ratifying country has entered a reservation to the provision prohibiting the execution of juvenile offenders. Parallel prohibitions are contained in other significant international covenants. See ICCPR, Art. 6(5), 999 U.N.T.S., at 175 (prohibiting capital punishment for anyone under 18 at the time of offense) (signed and ratified by the United States subject to a reservation regarding Article 6(5), as noted, *supra*, at 13); American Convention on Human Rights: Pact of San José, Costa Rica, Art. 4(5), Nov. 22, 1969, 1144 U.N.T.S. 146 (entered into force July 19, 1978) (same); African Charter on the Rights and Welfare of the Child, Art. 5(3), OAU Doc. CAB/LEG/24.9/49 (1990) (entered into force Nov. 29, 1999) (same).

Respondent and his *amici* have submitted, and petitioner does not contest, that only seven countries other than the United States have executed juvenile offenders since 1990: Iran, Pakistan, Saudi Arabia, Yemen, Nigeria, the Democratic Republic of Congo, and China. Since then each of these countries has either abolished capital punishment for juveniles or made public disavowal of the practice. Brief for Respondent 49-50. In sum, it is fair to say that the United States now stands alone in a world that has turned its face against the juvenile death penalty.

Though the international covenants prohibiting the juvenile death penalty are of more recent date, it is instructive to note that the United Kingdom abolished the juvenile death penalty before these covenants came into being. The United Kingdom's experience bears particular relevance here in light of the historic ties between our countries and in light of the Eighth Amendment's own origins. The Amendment was modeled on a parallel provision in the English Declaration of Rights of 1689, which provided: "[E]xcessive Bail ought not to be required nor excessive Fines imposed; nor cruel and unusuall Punishments inflicted." 1 W. & M., ch. 2, § 10, in 3 Eng. Stat. at Large 441 (1770); see also *Trop, supra,* at 100 (plurality opinion). As of now, the United Kingdom has abolished the death penalty in its entirety; but, decades before it took this step, it recognized the disproportionate nature of the juvenile death penalty; and it abolished that penalty as a separate matter. In 1930 an official committee recommended that the minimum age for execution be raised to 21. House of Commons Report from the Select Committee on Capital Punishment (1930), 193, p. 44. Parliament then enacted the Children and Young Person's Act of 1933, 23 Geo. 5, ch. 12, which prevented execution of those aged 18 at the date of the sentence. And in 1948, Parliament enacted the Criminal Justice Act, 11 & 12 Geo. 6, ch. 58, prohibiting the execution of any person under 18 at the time of the offense. In the 56 years that have passed since the United Kingdom abolished the juvenile death penalty, the weight of authority against it there, and in the international community, has become well established.

It is proper that we acknowledge the overwhelming weight of international opinion against the juvenile death penalty, resting in large part on the understanding that the instability and emotional imbalance of young people may often be a factor in the crime. See Brief for Human Rights Committee of the Bar of England and Wales et al. as *Amici Curiae* 10-11. The opinion of the world community, while not controlling our outcome, does provide respected and significant confirmation for our own conclusions.

Over time, from one generation to the next, the Constitution has come to earn the high respect and even, as Madison dared to hope, the veneration of the American people. See The Federalist No. 49, p. 314 (C. Rossiter ed. 1961). The document sets forth, and rests upon, innovative principles original to the American experience, such as federalism; a proven balance in political mechanisms through separation of powers; specific guarantees for the accused in criminal cases; and broad provisions to secure individual freedom and preserve human dignity. These doctrines and guarantees are central to the American experience and remain essential to our present-day self-definition and national identity. Not the least of the reasons we honor the Constitution, then, is because we know it to be our own. It does not lessen our fidelity to the Constitution or our pride in its origins to acknowledge that the express affirmation of certain fundamental rights by other nations and peoples simply underscores the centrality of those same rights within our own heritage of freedom.

* * * *

The Eighth and Fourteenth Amendments forbid imposition of the death penalty on offenders who were under the age of 18 when their crimes were committed. The judgment of the Missouri Supreme Court setting aside the sentence of death imposed upon Christopher Simmons is affirmed.

It is so ordered.

Juveniles and the Educational System

CHAPTER 8

PRAYER IN SCHOOL

Introduction

The issue of prayer in school exemplifies the conflicts and tensions that can arise when the courts are forced to rule in cases involving the "separation of church and state." Government sponsored religion is regulated by the First Amendment to the U.S. Constituiton, which reads

> Congress shall make no law respecting an establishment of religion, or prohibiting the free exercise thereof; or abridging the freedom of speech, or of the press; or the right of the people peaceably to assemble, and to petition the Government for a redress of grievances.

Since public education is an institution regulated by the government and supported by public funds, and since education is mandatory, thus making children in public school a captive audience, shouldn't schools be neutral on the issue of religion? Public schools exist to educate, not to proselytize nor endorse nor promote religious principles. Thus, does making prayer an official part of the school day amount to government coercion even when the prayers recited as part of class routine are allegedly "voluntary"?

The intent of the framers of the Constitution through the First Amendment was to recognize that religion is private, while government activity is public so it is entirely appropriate and necessary that these two should not mix. Clearly, there is a special need for schools to remain neutral on the topic of religion. Public schools exist to educate all children, whether Christian, Catholic, Baptist, Muslim, Quaker, atheist, Buddhist, Jewish, agnostic, and so on. Schools are supported by taxpayers and should be free from religious observances and symbols. Although it would seem that the intent of the First Amendment is very clear, the U.S. Supreme Court has been confronted with several cases concerning school prayer. These cases—*Engel v. Vitale* (1962), *Abington School District v. Shempp* (1963), and *Santa Fe Independent School District v. Doe* (2000)—span a period of about forty years and demonstrate the persistence of the school prayer issue.

Prayer in Schools

Case Comment

The case of *Engel v. Vitale* concerns the fact that, in the late 1950s, the New York Board of Regents published a "Statement on Moral and Spiritual Training in the Schools" and it included a prayer to be recited by public school students: "Almighty God, we acknowledge our dependence upon Thee, and we beg Thy blessings upon us, our parents, our teachers and our Country." The Board of Education of Union Free School District No. 9 of New Hyde Park, New York, instructed its school principal to have the Regents' prayer recited by the students "aloud by each class in the presence of a teacher at the beginning of each school day." The parents of ten pupils, who were enrolled in this school district, launched a lawsuit in New York State Court. They asserted that the prayer conflicted with their beliefs, religions, or religious practices and those of their children and based their case on the First Amendment to the U.S. Constitution, which requires that "Congress shall make no law respecting an establishment of religion." The state court rejected the parents' claim and ruled that the prayer was constitutional as long as the school did not compel any student to join in the prayer over their parents' objection. The New York Court of Appeals sustained this ruling. The parents then appealed to the U.S. Supreme Court. If the Supreme Court agreed with the parents, then state-mandated prayer in public schools would be unconstitutional everywhere in the United States. If the Supreme Court ruled decisively against the parents, then it would discourage future lawsuits against this form of school prayer.

Although the Board of Education argued that (1) the prayer was so generally worded that it was different from ordinary prayers; (2) it was based on the country's "spiritual heritage;" (3) no student was compelled to recite the prayer; and (4) neither teachers nor any school authority shall comment on participation or nonparticipation, the Supreme Court upheld the claim of the parents and ruled that the Regents' prayer was unconstitutional. The Court ruled that daily classroom invocation of God's blessings as prescribed in the Regents' prayer is a religious activity, and under the First Amendment, governments cannot compose official prayers for any group of the American people to recite as a part of a religious program carried on by government.

ENGEL V. VITALE

Supreme Court of the United States, 1962.

370 U.S. 421.

Mr. Justice Black delivered the opinion of the Court.

The respondent Board of Education of Union Free School District No. 9, New Hyde Park, New York, acting in its official capacity under state law, directed the School District's principal to cause the following prayer to be said aloud by each class in the presence of a teacher at the beginning of each school day:

"Almighty God, we acknowledge our dependence upon Thee, and we beg Thy blessings upon us, our parents, our teachers and our Country."

This daily procedure was adopted on the recommendation of the State Board of Regents, a governmental agency created by the State Constitution to which the New York Legislature has granted broad supervisory, executive, and legislative powers over the State's public school system.[1] These state officials composed the prayer which they recommended and published as a part of their "Statement on Moral and Spiritual Training in the Schools," saying: "We believe that this Statement will be subscribed to by all men and women of good will, and we call upon all of them to aid in giving life to our program."

Shortly after the practice of reciting the Regents' prayer was adopted by the School District, the parents of ten pupils brought this action in a New York State Court insisting that use of this official prayer in the public schools was contrary to the beliefs, religions, or religious practices of both themselves and their children. Among other things, these parents challenged the constitutionality of both the state law authorizing the School District to direct the use of prayer in public schools and the School District's regulation ordering the recitation of this particular prayer on the ground that these actions of official governmental agencies violate that part of the First Amendment of the Federal Constitution which commands that "Congress shall make no law respecting an establishment of religion"—a command which was "made applicable to the State of New York by the Fourteenth Amendment of the said Constitution." The New York Court of Appeals, over the dissents of Judges Dye and Fuld, sustained an order of the lower state courts which had upheld the power of New York to use the Regents' prayer as a part of the daily procedures of its public schools so long as the schools did not compel any pupil to join in the prayer over his or his parents' objection.[2] We granted certiorari to review this important decision involving rights protected by the First and Fourteenth Amendments.[3]

We think that by using its public school system to encourage recitation of the Regents' prayer, the State of New York has adopted a practice wholly inconsistent with the Establishment Clause. There can, of course, be no doubt that New York's program of daily classroom invocation of God's blessings as prescribed in the Regents' prayer is a religious activity. It is

---

1. See New York Constitution, Art. V, 4; New York Education Law, 101, 120 et seq., 202, 214–219, 224, 245 et seq., 704, and 801 et seq.

2. 10 N.Y. 2d 174, 176 N.E. 2d 579. The trial court's opinion, which is reported at 18 Misc. 2d 659, 191 N.Y.S. 2d 453, had made it clear that the Board of Education must set up some sort of procedures to protect those who objected to reciting the prayer: "This is not to say that the rights accorded petitioners and their children under the 'free exercise' clause do not mandate safeguards against such embarrassments and pressures. It is enough on this score, however, that regulations, such as were adopted by New York City's Board of Education in connection with its released time program, be adopted, making clear that neither teachers nor any other school authority may comment on participation or nonparticipation in the exercise nor suggest or require that any posture or language be used or dress be worn or be not used or not worn. Nonparticipation may take the form either of remaining silent during the exercise, or if the parent or child so desires, of being excused entirely from the exercise. Such regulations must also make provision for those nonparticipants who are to be excused from the prayer exercise. The exact provision to be made is a matter for decision by the board, rather than the court, within the framework of constitutional requirements. Within that framework would fall a provision that prayer participants proceed to a common assembly while nonparticipants attend other rooms, or that nonparticipants be permitted to arrive at school a few minutes late or to attend separate opening exercises, or any other method which treats with equality both participants and nonparticipants." 18 Misc. 2d, at 696, 191 N.Y.S. 2d, at 492–493. See also the opinion of the Appellate Division affirming that of the trial court, reported at 11 App. Div. 2d 340, 206 N.Y.S. 2d 183.

3. 368 U.S. 924.

a solemn avowal of divine faith and supplication for the blessings of the Almighty. The nature of such a prayer has always been religious, none of the respondents has denied this and the trial court expressly so found:

> "The religious nature of prayer was recognized by Jefferson and has been concurred in by theological writers, the United States Supreme Court and State courts and administrative officials, including New York's Commissioner of Education. A committee of the New York Legislature has agreed.
>
> "The Board of Regents as amicus curiae, the respondents and intervenors all concede the religious nature of prayer, but seek to distinguish this prayer because it is based on our spiritual heritage. . . ."[4]

The petitioners contend among other things that the state laws requiring or permitting use of the Regents' prayer must be struck down as a violation of the Establishment Clause because that prayer was composed by governmental officials as a part of a governmental program to further religious beliefs. For this reason, petitioners argue, the State's use of the Regents' prayer in its public school system breaches the constitutional wall of separation between Church and State. We agree with that contention since we think that the constitutional prohibition against laws respecting an establishment of religion must at least mean that in this country it is no part of the business of government to compose official prayers for any group of the American people to recite as a part of a religious program carried on by government.

It is a matter of history that this very practice of establishing governmentally composed prayers for religious services was one of the reasons which caused many of our early colonists to leave England and seek religious freedom in America. The Book of Common Prayer, which was created under governmental direction and which was approved by Acts of Parliament in 1548 and 1549,[5] set out in minute detail the accepted form and content of prayer and other religious ceremonies to be used in the established, tax-supported Church of England.[6] The controversies over the Book and what should be its content repeatedly threatened to disrupt the peace of that country as the accepted forms of prayer in the established church changed with the views of the particular ruler that happened to be in control at the time.[7] Powerful groups representing some of the varying religious views of the people strug-

---

4. 18 Misc. 2d, at 671–672, 191 N.Y.S. 2d, at 468–469.

5. 2 & 3 Edward VI, c. 1, entitled "An Act for Uniformity of Service and Administration of the Sacraments throughout the Realm"; 3 & 4 Edward VI, c. 10, entitled "An Act for the abolishing and putting away of divers Books and Images."

6. The provisions of the various versions of the Book of Common Prayer are set out in broad outline in the *Encyclopedia Britannica*, Vol. 18 (1957 ed.), pp. 420–423. For a more complete description, see Pullan, *The History of the Book of Common Prayer* (1900).

7. The first major revision of the Book of Common Prayer was made in 1552 during the reign of Edward VI. 5 & 6 Edward VI, c. 1. In 1553, Edward VI died and was succeeded by Mary, who abolished the Book of Common Prayer entirely. 1 Mary, c. 2. But upon the accession of Elizabeth in 1558, the Book was restored with important alterations from the form it had been given by Edward VI. 1 Elizabeth, c. 2. The resentment to this amended form of the Book was kept firmly under control during the reign of Elizabeth but, upon her death in 1603, a petition signed by more than 1,000 Puritan ministers was presented to King James 1 asking for further alterations in the Book. Some alterations were made and the Book retained substantially this form until it was completely suppressed again in 1645 as a result of the successful Puritan Revolution. Shortly after the restoration in 1660 of Charles II, the Book was again reintroduced, 13 & 14 Charles II, c. 4, and again with alterations. Rather than accept this form of the Book

gled among themselves to impress their particular views upon the Government and obtain amendments of the Book more suitable to their respective notions of how religious services should be conducted in order that the official religious establishment would advance their particular religious beliefs.[8] Other groups, lacking the necessary political power to influence the Government on the matter, decided to leave England and its established church and seek freedom in America from England's governmentally ordained and supported religion.

It is an unfortunate fact of history that when some of the very groups which had most strenuously opposed the established Church of England found themselves sufficiently in control of colonial governments in this country to write their own prayers into law, they passed laws making their own religion the official religion of their respective colonies.[9] Indeed, as late as the time of the Revolutionary War, there were established churches in at least eight of the thirteen former colonies and established religions in at least four of the other five.[10] But the successful Revolution against English political domination was shortly followed by intense opposition to the practice of establishing religion by law. This opposition crystallized rapidly into an effective political force in Virginia where the minority religious groups such as Presbyterians, Lutherans, Quakers and Baptists had gained such strength that the adherents to the established Episcopal Church were actually a minority themselves. In 1785–1786, those opposed to the established Church, led by James Madison and Thomas Jefferson, who, though themselves not members of any of these dissenting religious groups, opposed all religious establishments by law on grounds of principle, obtained the enactment of the famous "Virginia Bill for Religious Liberty" by which all religious groups were

---

some 2,000 Puritan ministers vacated their benefices. See generally Pullan, The History of the Book of Common Prayer (1900), pp. vii–xvi; Encyclopaedia Britannica (1957 ed.), Vol. 18, pp. 421–422.

8. For example, the Puritans twice attempted to modify the Book of Common Prayer and once attempted to destroy it. The story of their struggle to modify the Book in the reign of Charles I is vividly summarized in Pullan, History of the Book of Common Prayer, at p. xiii: "The King actively supported those members of the Church of England who were anxious to vindicate its Catholic character and maintain the ceremonial which Elizabeth had approved. Laud, Archbishop of Canterbury, was the leader of this school. Equally resolute in his opposition to the distinctive tenets of Rome and of Geneva, he enjoyed the hatred of both Jesuit and Calvinist. He helped the Scottish bishops, who had made large concessions to the uncouth habits of Presbyterian worship, to draw up a Book of Common Prayer for Scotland. It contained a Communion Office resembling that of the book of 1549. It came into use in 1637, and met with a bitter and barbarous opposition. The vigour of the Scottish Protestants strengthened the hands of their English sympathisers. Laud and Charles were executed, Episcopacy was abolished, the use of the Book of Common Prayer was prohibited."

9. For a description of some of the laws enacted by early theocratic governments in New England, see Parrington, Main Currents in American Thought (1930), Vol. 1, pp. 5–50; Whipple, Our Ancient Liberties (1927), pp. 63–78; Wertenbaker, The Puritan Oligarchy (1947).

10. The Church of England was the established church of at least five colonies: Maryland, Virginia, North Carolina, South Carolina and Georgia. There seems to be some controversy as to whether that church was officially established in New York and New Jersey but there is no doubt that it received substantial support from those States. See Cobb, The Rise of Religious Liberty in America (1902), pp. 338, 408. In Massachusetts, New Hampshire and Connecticut, the Congregationalist Church was officially established. In Pennsylvania and Delaware, all Christian sects were treated equally in most situations but Catholics were discriminated against in some respects. See generally Cobb, The Rise of Religious Liberty in America (1902). In Rhode Island all Protestants enjoyed equal privileges but it is not clear whether Catholics were allowed to vote. Compare Fiske, The Critical Period in American History (1899), p. 76 with Cobb, The Rise of Religious Liberty in America (1902), pp. 437–438.

placed on an equal footing so far as the State was concerned.[11] Similar though less far-reaching legislation was being considered and passed in other States.[12]

By the time of the adoption of the Constitution, our history shows that there was a widespread awareness among many Americans of the dangers of a union of Church and State. These people knew, some of them from bitter personal experience, that one of the greatest dangers to the freedom of the individual to worship in his own way lay in the Government's placing its official stamp of approval upon one particular kind of prayer or one particular form of religious services. They knew the anguish, hardship and bitter strife that could come when zealous religious groups struggled with one another to obtain the Government's stamp of approval from each King, Queen, or Protector that came to temporary power. The Constitution was intended to avert a part of this danger by leaving the government of this country in the hands of the people rather than in the hands of any monarch. But this safeguard was not enough. Our Founders were no more willing to let the content of their prayers and their privilege of praying whenever they pleased be influenced by the ballot box than they were to let these vital matters of personal conscience depend upon the succession of monarchs. The First Amendment was added to the Constitution to stand as a guarantee that neither the power nor the prestige of the Federal Government would be used to control, support or influence the kinds of prayer the American people can say—that the people's religious must not be subjected to the pressures of government for change each time a new political administration is elected to office. Under that Amendment's prohibition against governmental establishment of religion, as reinforced by the provisions of the Fourteenth Amendment, government in this country, be it state or federal, is without power to prescribe by law any particular form of prayer which is to be used as an official prayer in carrying on any program of governmentally sponsored religious activity.

There can be no doubt that New York's state prayer program officially establishes the religious beliefs embodied in the Regents' prayer. The respondents' argument to the contrary, which is largely based upon the contention that the Regents' prayer is "non-denominational" and the fact that the program, as modified and approved by state courts, does not require all pupils to recite the prayer but permits those who wish to do so to remain silent or be excused from the room, ignores the essential nature of the program's constitutional defects. Neither the fact that the prayer may be denominationally neutral nor the fact that its observance on the part of the students is voluntary can serve to free it from the limitations of the Establishment Clause, as it might from the Free Exercise Clause, of the First Amendment, both of which are operative against the States by virtue of the Fourteenth Amendment. Although these two clauses may in certain instances overlap, they forbid two quite different kinds of

---

11. 12 Hening, Statutes of Virginia (1823), 84, entitled "An act for establishing religious freedom." The story of the events surrounding the enactment of this law was reviewed in *Everson v. Board of Education*, 330 U.S. 1, both by the Court, at pp. 11–13, and in the dissenting opinion of Mr. Justice Rutledge, at pp. 33–42. See also Fiske, The Critical Period in American History (1899), pp. 78–82; James, The Struggle for Religious Liberty in Virginia (1900); Thom, The Struggle for Religious Freedom in Virginia: The Baptists (1900); Cobb, The Rise of Religious Liberty in America (1902), pp. 74–115, 482–499.

12. See Cobb, The Rise of Religious Liberty in America (1902), pp. 482–509.

governmental encroachment upon religious freedom. The Establishment Clause, unlike the Free Exercise Clause, does not depend upon any showing of direct governmental compulsion and is violated by the enactment of laws which establish an official religion whether those laws operate directly to coerce nonobserving individuals or not. This is not to say, of course, that laws officially prescribing a particular form of religious worship do not involve coercion of such individuals. When the power, prestige and financial support of government is placed behind a particular religious belief, the indirect coercive pressure upon religious minorities to conform to the prevailing officially approved religion is plain. But the purposes underlying the Establishment Clause go much further than that. Its first and most immediate purpose rested on the belief that a union of government and religion tends to destroy government and to degrade religion. The history of governmentally established religion, both in England and in this country, showed that whenever government had allied itself with one particular form of religion, the inevitable result had been that it had incurred the hatred, disrespect and even contempt of those who held contrary beliefs.[13] That same history showed that many people had lost their respect for any religion that had relied upon the support of government to spread its faith.[14] The Establishment Clause thus stands as an expression of principle on the part of the Founders of our Constitution that religion is too personal, too sacred, too holy, to permit its "unhallowed perversion" by a civil magistrate.[15] Another purpose of the Establishment Clause rested upon an awareness of the historical fact that governmentally established religions and religious persecutions go hand in hand.[16] The Founders knew that only a few years after the Book of Common Prayer became the only accepted form of religious services in the established Church of England, an Act of Uniformity was passed to compel all Englishmen to attend those services and to make it a criminal offense to conduct

---

13. "[A]ttempts to enforce by legal sanctions, acts obnoxious to so great a proportion of Citizens, tend to enervate the laws in general, and to slacken the bands of Society. If it be difficult to execute any law which is not generally deemed necessary or salutary, what must be the case where it is deemed invalid and dangerous? and what may be the effect of so striking an example of impotency in the Government, on its general authority." Memorial and Remonstrance against Religious Assessments, II Writings of Madison 183, 190.

14. "It is moreover to weaken in those who profess this Religion a pious confidence in its innate excellence, and the patronage of its Author; and to foster in those who still reject it, a suspicion that its friends are too conscious of its fallacies, to trust it to its own merits. . . . [E]xperience witnesseth that ecclesiastical establishments, instead of maintaining the purity and efficacy of Religion, have had a contrary operation. During almost fifteen centuries, has the legal establishment of Christianity been on trial. What have been its fruits? More or less in all places, pride and indolence in the Clergy; ignorance and servility in the laity; in both, superstition, bigotry and persecution. Enquire of the Teachers of Christianity for the ages in which it appeared in its greatest lustre; those of every sect, point to the ages prior to its incorporation with Civil policy." Id., at 187.

15. Memorial and Remonstrance against Religious Assessments, II Writings of Madison, at 187.

16. "[T]he proposed establishment is a departure from that generous policy, which, offering an asylum to the persecuted and oppressed of every Nation and Religion, promised a lustre to our country, and an accession to the number of its citizens. What a melancholy mark is the Bill of sudden degeneracy? Instead of holding forth an asylum to the persecuted, it is itself a signal of persecution. . . . Distant as it may be, in its present form, from the Inquisition it differs from it only in degree. The one is the first step, the other the last in the career of intolerance. The magnanimous sufferer under this cruel scourge in foreign Regions, must view the Bill as a Beacon on our Coast, warning him to seek some other haven, where liberty and philanthropy in their due extent may offer a more certain repose from his troubles." Id., at 188.

or attend religious gatherings of any other kind[17]—a law which was consistently flouted by dissenting religious groups in England and which contributed to widespread persecutions of people like John Bunyan who persisted in holding "unlawful [religious] meetings . . . to the great disturbance and distraction of the good subjects of this kingdom. . . ."[18] And they knew that similar persecutions had received the sanction of law in several of the colonies in this country soon after the establishment of official religions in those colonies.[19] It was in large part to get completely away from this sort of systematic religious persecution that the Founders brought into being our Nation, our Constitution, and our Bill of Rights with its prohibition against any governmental establishment of religion. The New York laws officially prescribing the Regents' prayer are inconsistent both with the purposes of the Establishment Clause and with the Establishment Clause itself.

It has been argued that to apply the Constitution in such a way as to prohibit state laws respecting an establishment of religious services in public schools is to indicate a hostility toward religion or toward prayer. Nothing, of course, could be more wrong. The history of man is inseparable from the history of religion. And perhaps it is not too much to say that since the beginning of that history many people have devoutly believed that "More things are wrought by prayer than this world dreams of." It was doubtless largely due to men who believed this that there grew up a sentiment that caused men to leave the cross-currents of officially established state religions and religious persecution in Europe and come to this country filled with the hope that they could find a place in which they could pray when they pleased to the God of their faith in the language they chose.[20] And there were men of this same

---

17. 5 & 6 Edward VI, c. 1, entitled "An Act for the Uniformity of Service and Administration of Sacraments throughout the Realm." This Act was repealed during the reign of Mary but revived upon the accession of Elizabeth. See note 7, supra. The reasons which led to the enactment of this statute were set out in its preamble: "Where there hath been a very godly Order set forth by the Authority of Parliament, for Common Prayer and Administration of the Sacraments to be used in the Mother Tongue within the Church of England, agreeable to the Word of God and the Primitive Church, very comfortable to all good People desiring to live in Christian Conversation, and most profitable to the Estate of this Realm, upon the which the Mercy, Favour and Blessing of Almighty God is in no wise so readily and plenteously poured as by Common Prayers, due using of the Sacraments, and often preaching of the Gospel, with the Devotion of the Hearers: (1) And yet this notwithstanding, a great Number of People in divers Parts of this Realm, following their own Sensuality, and living either without Knowledge or due Fear of God, do wilfully and damnably before Almighty God abstain and refuse to come to their Parish Churches and other Places where Common Prayer, Administration of the Sacraments, and Preaching of the Word of God, is used upon Sundays and other Days ordained to be Holydays."

18. Bunyan's own account of his trial is set forth in A Relation of the Imprisonment of Mr. John Bunyan, reprinted in Grace Abounding and The Pilgrim's Progress (Brown ed. 1907), at 103–132.

19. For a vivid account of some of these persecutions, see Wertenbaker, The Puritan Oligarchy (1947).

20. Perhaps the best example of the sort of men who came to this country for precisely that reason is Roger Williams, the founder of Rhode Island, who has been described as "the truest Christian amongst many who sincerely desired to be Christian." Parrington, Main Currents in American Thought (1930), Vol. 1, at p. 74. Williams, who was one of the earliest exponents of the doctrine of separation of church and state, believed that separation was necessary in order to protect the church from the danger of destruction which he thought inevitably flowed from control by even the best-intentioned civil authorities: "The unknowing zeale of Constantine and other Emperours, did more hurt to Christ Jesus his Crowne and Kingdome, then the raging fury of the most bloody Neroes. In the persecutions of the later, Christians were sweet and fragrant, like spice pounded and beaten in morters: But those good Emperours, persecuting some erroneous persons, Arrius, & c. and advancing the professours of some Truths of Christ (for there was no small number of Truths lost in those times) and maintaining their Religion by the materiall Sword, I say by this meanes Christianity was ecclipsed, and the Professors of it fell asleep . . . ." Williams,

faith in the power of prayer who led the fight for adoption of our Constitution and also for our Bill of Rights with the very guarantees of religious freedom that forbid the sort of governmental activity which New York has attempted here. These men knew that the First Amendment, which tried to put an end to governmental control of religion and of prayer, was not written to destroy either. They knew rather that it was written to quiet well-justified fears which nearly all of them felt arising out of an awareness that governments of the past had shackled men's tongues to make them speak only the religious thoughts that government wanted them to speak and to pray only to the God that government wanted them to pray to. It is neither sacrilegious nor antireligious to say that each separate government in this country should stay out of the business of writing or sanctioning official prayers and leave that purely religious function to the people themselves and to those the people choose to look to for religious guidance.[21]

It is true that New York's establishment of its Regents' prayer as an officially approved religious doctrine of that State does not amount to a total establishment of one particular religious sect to the exclusion of all others—that, indeed, the governmental endorsement of that prayer seems relatively insignificant when compared to the governmental encroachments upon religion which were commonplace 200 years ago. To those who may subscribe to the view that because the Regents' official prayer is so brief and general there can be no danger to religious freedom in its governmental establishment, however, it may be appropriate to say in the words of James Madison, the author of the First Amendment:

> "[I]t is proper to take alarm at the first experiment on our liberties. . . . Who does not see that the same authority which can establish Christianity, in exclusion of all other Religions, may establish with the same ease any particular sect of Christians, in exclusion of all other Sects? That the same authority which can force a citizen to contribute three pence only of his property for the support of any one establishment, may force him to conform to any other establishment in all cases whatsoever?"[22]

The judgment of the Court of Appeals of New York is reversed and the cause remanded for further proceedings not inconsistent with this opinion.

Reversed and remanded.

The Bloudy Tenent, of Persecution, for cause of Conscience, discussed in A Conference between Truth and Peace (London, 1644), reprinted in Narragansett Club Publications, Vol. III, p. 184. To Williams, it was no part of the business or competence of a civil magistrate to interfere in religious matters: "[W]hat imprudence and indiscretion is it in the most common affaires of Life, to conceive that Emperours, Kings and Rulers of the earth must not only be qualified with politicall and state abilities to make and execute such Civill Lawes which may concerne the common rights, peace and safety (which is worke and businesse, load and burthen enough for the ablest shoulders in the Commonweal) but also furnished with such Spirituall and heavenly abilities to governe the Spirituall and Christian Commonweale . . . ." Id., at 366. See also id., at 136–137.

21. There is of course nothing in the decision reached here that is inconsistent with the fact that school children and others are officially encouraged to express love for our country by reciting historical documents such as the Declaration of Independence which contain references to the Deity or by singing officially espoused anthems which include the composer's professions of faith in a Supreme Being, or with the fact that there are many manifestations in our public life of belief in God. Such patriotic or ceremonial occasions bear no true resemblance to the unquestioned religious exercise that the State of New York has sponsored in this instance.

22. Memorial and Remonstrance against Religious Assessments, II Writings of Madison 183, at 185–186.

Mr. Justice Frankfurter took no part in the decision of this case.

Mr. Justice White took no part in the consideration or decision of this case.

Case Comment

The case of *Abington School Dist. v. Schempp* was decided just one year after the *Engel* case. The case involved a Pennsylvania statute that required that ten verses from the Holy Bible shall be read at the opening of each public school on each school day. The Supreme Court followed its precedent from *Engel* and ruled that, because of the prohibition of the First Amendment against the enactment by Congress of any law "respecting an establishment of religion," which is made applicable to the States by the Fourteenth Amendment, no state law or school board may require that passages from the Bible be read or that the Lord's Prayer be recited in the public schools of a State at the beginning of each school day—even if individual students may be excused from attending or participating in such exercises upon written request of their parents.

ABINGTON SCHOOL DIST. V. SCHEMPP

Supreme Court of the United States, 1963.

374 U.S. 203.

Mr. Justice Clark delivered the opinion of the Court.

Once again we are called upon to consider the scope of the provision of the First Amendment to the United States Constitution which declares that "Congress shall make no law respecting an establishment of religion, or prohibiting the free exercise thereof . . . ." These companion cases present the issues in the context of state action requiring that schools begin each day with readings from the Bible. While raising the basic questions under slightly different factual situations, the cases permit of joint treatment. In light of the history of the First Amendment and of our cases interpreting and applying its requirements, we hold that the practices at issue and the laws requiring them are unconstitutional under the Establishment Clause, as applied to the States through the Fourteenth Amendment.

I

The Facts in Each Case: No. 142. The Commonwealth of Pennsylvania by law, 24 Pa. Stat. 15–1516, as amended, Pub. Law 1928 (Supp. 1960) Dec. 17, 1959, requires that "At least ten verses from the Holy Bible shall be read, without comment, at the opening of each public school on each school day. Any child shall be excused from such Bible reading, or attending such Bible reading, upon the written request of his parent or guardian." The Schempp family, husband and wife and two of their three children, brought suit to enjoin enforcement of the statute, contending that their rights under the Fourteenth Amendment to the Constitution of the United States are, have been, and will continue to be violated unless this statute be declared unconstitutional as violative of these provisions of the First Amendment. They sought to enjoin the appellant school district, wherein the Schempp children attend school, and its officers and the Superintendent of Public Instruction of the Commonwealth from continuing to conduct such readings and recitation of the Lord's Prayer in the public schools of the district pursuant to the statute. A three-judge statutory District Court for the Eastern District of Pennsylvania held that the statute is violative of the Establishment Clause of the First Amendment as applied to the States by the Due Process Clause of the Fourteenth Amendment and directed that appropriate injunctive relief issue. 201 F. Supp. 815.[1] On appeal by the District, its officials and the Superintendent, under 28 U.S.C. 1253, we noted probable jurisdiction. 371 U.S. 807.

The appellees Edward Lewis Schempp, his wife Sidney, and their children, Roger and Donna, are of the Unitarian faith and are members of the Unitarian church in Germantown, Philadelphia, Pennsylvania, where they, as well as another son, Ellory, regularly attend religious services. The latter was originally a party but having graduated from the school system pendente lite was voluntarily dismissed from the action. The other children attend the Abington Senior High School, which is a public school operated by appellant district.

On each school day at the Abington Senior High School between 8:15 and 8:30 a.m., while the pupils are attending their home rooms or advisory sections, opening exercises are conducted pursuant to the statute. The exercises are broadcast into each room in the school building through an intercommunications system and are conducted under the supervision of a teacher by students attending the school's radio and television workshop. Selected students from this course gather each morning in the school's workshop studio for the exercises, which include readings by one of the students of 10 verses of the Holy Bible, broadcast to each room in the building. This is followed by the recitation of the Lord's Prayer, likewise over the intercommunications system, but also by the students in the various classrooms, who are asked to stand and join in repeating the prayer in unison. The exercises are closed with the flag salute and such pertinent announcements as are of interest to the students. Participation in the opening exercises, as directed by the statute, is voluntary. The student reading the verses from the Bible may select the passages and read from any version he chooses, although the only copies furnished by the school are the King James version, copies of which were circulated to each teacher by the school district. During the period in which the exercises have been conducted the King James, the Douay and the Revised Standard versions of the Bible have been used, as well as the Jewish Holy Scriptures. There are no prefatory statements, no questions asked or solicited, no comments or explanations made and no interpretations given at or during the exercises. The students and parents are advised that the student may absent himself from the classroom or, should he elect to remain, not participate in the exercises.

It appears from the record that in schools not having an intercommunications system the Bible reading and the recitation of the Lord's Prayer were conducted by the home-room teacher,[2] who chose the text of the verses and read them herself or had students read them

---

1. The action was brought in 1958, prior to the 1959 amendment of 15–1516 authorizing a child's nonattendance at the exercises upon parental request. The three-judge court held the statute and the practices complained of unconstitutional under both the Establishment Clause and the Free Exercise Clause. 177 F. Supp. 398. Pending appeal to this Court by the school district, the statute was so amended, and we vacated the judgment and remanded for further proceedings. 364 U.S. 298. The same three-judge court granted appellees' motion to amend the pleadings, 195 F. Supp. 518, held a hearing on the amended pleadings and rendered the judgment, 201 F. Supp. 815, from which appeal is now taken.

2. The statute as amended imposes no penalty upon a teacher refusing to obey its mandate. However, it remains to be seen whether one refusing could have his contract of employment terminated for "wilful violation of the school laws." 24 Pa. Stat. (Supp. 1960) 11–1122.

in rotation or by volunteers. This was followed by a standing recitation of the Lord's Prayer, together with the Pledge of Allegiance to the Flag by the class in unison and a closing announcement of routine school items of interest.

At the first trial Edward Schempp and the children testified as to specific religious doctrines purveyed by a literal reading of the Bible "which were contrary to the religious beliefs which they held and to their familial teaching." 177 F. Supp. 398, 400. The children testified that all of the doctrines to which they referred were read to them at various times as part of the exercises. Edward Schempp testified at the second trial that he had considered having Roger and Donna excused from attendance at the exercises but decided against it for several reasons, including his belief that the children's relationships with their teachers and classmates would be adversely affected.[3]

Expert testimony was introduced by both appellants and appellees at the first trial, which testimony was summarized by the trial court as follows:

"Dr. Solomon Grayzel testified that there were marked differences between the Jewish Holy Scriptures and the Christian Holy Bible, the most obvious of which was the absence of the New Testament in the Jewish Holy Scriptures. Dr. Grayzel testified that portions of the New Testament were offensive to Jewish tradition and that, from the standpoint of Jewish faith, the concept of Jesus Christ as the Son of God was 'practically blasphemous.' He cited instances in the New Testament which, assertedly, were not only sectarian in nature but tended to bring the Jews into ridicule or scorn. Dr. Grayzel gave as his expert opinion that such material from the New Testament could be explained to Jewish children in such a way as to do no harm to them. But if portions of the New Testament were read without explanation, they could be, and in his specific experience with children Dr. Grayzel observed, had been, psychologically harmful to the child and had caused a divisive force within the social media of the school.

"Dr. Grayzel also testified that there was significant difference in attitude with regard to the respective Books of the Jewish and Christian Religions in that Judaism attaches no special significance to the reading of the Bible per se and that the Jewish Holy Scriptures are source materials to be studied. But Dr. Grayzel did state that many portions of the New, as well as of the Old, Testament contained passages of great literary and moral value.

"Dr. Luther A. Weigle, an expert witness for the defense, testified in some detail as to the reasons for and the methods employed in developing the King James and the Revised Standard Versions of the Bible. On direct examination, Dr. Weigle stated that the Bible was non-sectarian. He later stated that the phrase 'non-sectarian' meant to him non-sectarian within the Christian

---

3. The trial court summarized his testimony as follows:
"Edward Schempp, the children's father, testified that after careful consideration he had decided that he should not have Roger or Donna excused from attendance at these morning ceremonies. Among his reasons were the following. He said that he thought his children would be 'labeled as "odd balls"' before their teachers and classmates every school day; that children, like Roger's and Donna's classmates, were liable 'to lump all particular religious difference[s] or religious objections [together] as "atheism"' and that today the word 'atheism' is often connected with 'atheistic communism,' and has 'very bad' connotations, such as 'un-American' or 'anti-Red,' with overtones of possible immorality. Mr. Schempp pointed out that due to the events of the morning exercises following in rapid succession, the Bible reading, the Lord's Prayer, the Flag Salute, and the announcements, excusing his children from the Bible reading would mean that probably they would miss hearing the announcements so important to children. He testified also that if Roger and Donna were excused from Bible reading they would have to stand in the hall outside their 'homeroom' and that this carried with it the imputation of punishment for bad conduct." 201 F. Supp., at 818.

faiths. Dr. Weigle stated that his definition of the Holy Bible would include the Jewish Holy Scriptures, but also stated that the 'Holy Bible' would not be complete without the New Testament. He stated that the New Testament 'conveyed the message of Christians.' In his opinion, reading of the Holy Scriptures to the exclusion of the New Testament would be a sectarian practice. Dr. Weigle stated that the Bible was of great moral, historical and literary value. This is conceded by all the parties and is also the view of the court." 177 F. Supp. 398, 401–402.

The trial court, in striking down the practices and the statute requiring them, made specific findings of fact that the children's attendance at Abington Senior High School is compulsory and that the practice of reading 10 verses from the Bible is also compelled by law. It also found that:

> "The reading of the verses, even without comment, possesses a devotional and religious character and constitutes in effect a religious observance. The devotional and religious nature of the morning exercises is made all the more apparent by the fact that the Bible reading is followed immediately by a recital in unison by the pupils of the Lord's Prayer. The fact that some pupils, or theoretically all pupils, might be excused from attendance at the exercises does not mitigate the obligatory nature of the ceremony for . . . Section 1516 . . . unequivocally requires the exercises to be held every school day in every school in the Commonwealth. The exercises are held in the school buildings and perforce are conducted by and under the authority of the local school authorities and during school sessions. Since the statute requires the reading of the 'Holy Bible,' a Christian document, the practice . . . prefers the Christian religion. The record demonstrates that it was the intention of . . . the Commonwealth . . . to introduce a religious ceremony into the public schools of the Commonwealth." 201 F. Supp., at 819.

No. 119. In 1905 the Board of School Commissioners of Baltimore City adopted a rule pursuant to Art. 77, 202 of the Annotated Code of Maryland. The rule provided for the holding of opening exercises in the schools of the city, consisting primarily of the "reading, without comment, of a chapter in the Holy Bible and/or the use of the Lord's Prayer." The petitioners, Mrs. Madalyn Murray and her son, William J. Murray III, are both professed atheists. Following unsuccessful attempts to have the respondent school board rescind the rule, this suit was filed for mandamus to compel its rescission and cancellation. It was alleged that William was a student in a public school of the city and Mrs. Murray, his mother, was a taxpayer therein; that it was the practice under the rule to have a reading on each school morning from the King James version of the Bible; that at petitioners' insistence the rule was amended[4] to permit children to be excused from the exercise on request of the parent and that William had been excused pursuant thereto; that nevertheless the rule as amended was in violation of the petitioners' rights "to freedom of religion under the First and Fourteenth Amendments" and in violation of "the principle of separation between church and

---

4. The rule as amended provides as follows:
"Opening Exercises. Each school, either collectively or in classes, shall be opened by the reading, without comment, of a chapter in the Holy Bible and/or the use of the Lord's Prayer. The Douay version may be used by those pupils who prefer it. Appropriate patriotic exercises should be held as a part of the general opening exercise of the school or class. Any child shall be excused from participating in the opening exercises or from attending the opening exercises upon the written request of his parent or guardian."

state, contained therein. . . ." The petition particularized the petitioners' atheistic beliefs and stated that the rule, as practiced, violated their rights

> "in that it threatens their religious liberty by placing a premium on belief as against non-belief and subjects their freedom of conscience to the rule of the majority; it pronounces belief in God as the source of all moral and spiritual values, equating these values with religious values, and thereby renders sinister, alien and suspect the beliefs and ideals of your Petitioners, promoting doubt and question of their morality, good citizenship and good faith."

The respondents demurred and the trial court, recognizing that the demurrer admitted all facts well pleaded, sustained it without leave to amend. The Maryland Court of Appeals affirmed, the majority of four justices holding the exercise not in violation of the First and Fourteenth Amendments, with three justices dissenting. 228 Md. 239, 179 A. 2d 698. We granted certiorari. 371 U.S. 809.

II

It is true that religion has been closely identified with our history and government. As we said in *Engel v. Vitale*, 370 U.S. 421, 434 (1962), "The history of man is inseparable from the history of religion. And . . . since the beginning of that history many people have devoutly believed that 'More things are wrought by prayer than this world dreams of.'" In *Zorach v. Clauson*, 343 U.S. 306, 313 (1952), we gave specific recognition to the proposition that "[w]e are a religious people whose institutions presuppose a Supreme Being." The fact that the Founding Fathers believed devotedly that there was a God and that the unalienable rights of man were rooted in Him is clearly evidenced in their writings, from the Mayflower Compact to the Constitution itself. This background is evidenced today in our public life through the continuance in our oaths of office from the Presidency to the Alderman of the final supplication, "So help me God." Likewise each House of the Congress provides through its Chaplain an opening prayer, and the sessions of this Court are declared open by the crier in a short ceremony, the final phrase of which invokes the grace of God. Again, there are such manifestations in our military forces, where those of our citizens who are under the restrictions of military service wish to engage in voluntary worship. Indeed, only last year an official survey of the country indicated that 64% of our people have church membership, Bureau of the Census, U.S. Department of Commerce, Statistical Abstract of the United States (83d ed. 1962), 48, while less than 3% profess no religion whatever. Id., at p. 46. It can be truly said, therefore, that today, as in the beginning, our national life reflects a religious people who, in the words of Madison, are "earnestly praying, as . . . in duty bound, that the Supreme Lawgiver of the Universe . . . guide them into every measure which may be worthy of his [blessing . . . .]" Memorial and Remonstrance Against Religious Assessments, quoted in *Everson v. Board of Education*, 330 U.S. 1, 71–72 (1947) (Appendix to dissenting opinion of Rutledge, J.).

This is not to say, however, that religion has been so identified with our history and government that religious freedom is not likewise as strongly imbedded in our public and private life. Nothing but the most telling of personal experiences in religious persecution suffered by our forebears, see *Everson v. Board of Education*, supra, at 8–11, could have planted our belief in liberty of religious opinion any more deeply in our heritage. It is true that this liberty frequently was not realized by the colonists, but this is readily accountable by their close ties to the Mother Country.[5] However, the views of Madison and Jefferson, preceded by Roger Williams,[6] came to be incorporated not only in the Federal Constitution but likewise in those of most of our States. This freedom to worship was indispensable in a country whose people came from the four quarters of the earth and brought with them a diversity of religious opinion. Today authorities list 83 separate religious bodies, each with membership exceeding 50,000, existing among our people, as well as innumerable smaller groups. Bureau of the Census. op. cit., supra, at 46–47.

III

Almost a hundred years ago in *Minor v. Board of Education of Cincinnati*,[7] Judge Alphonso Taft, father of the revered Chief Justice, in an unpublished opinion stated the ideal of our people as to religious freedom as one of

"absolute equality before the law, of all religious opinions and sects . . . .

. . . . .

"The government is neutral, and, while protecting all, it prefers none, and it disparages none."

Before examining this "neutral" position in which the Establishment and Free Exercise Clauses of the First Amendment place our Government it is well that we discuss the reach of the Amendment under the cases of this Court.

First, this Court has decisively settled that the First Amendment's mandate that "Congress shall make no law respecting an establishment of religion, or prohibiting the free exercise thereof" has been made wholly applicable to the States by the Fourteenth Amendment. Twenty-three years ago in *Cantwell v. Connecticut*, 310 U.S. 296, 303 (1940), this Court, through Mr. Justice Roberts, said:

"The fundamental concept of liberty embodied in that [Fourteenth] Amendment embraces the liberties guaranteed by the First Amendment. The First Amendment declares that Congress shall make no law respecting an establishment of religion or prohibiting the free exercise thereof. The

---

5. There were established churches in at least eight of the original colonies, and various degrees of religious support in others as late as the Revolutionary War. See *Engel v. Vitale*, supra, at 428, n. 10.

6. "There goes many a ship to sea, with many hundred souls in one ship, whose weal and woe is common, and is a true picture of a commonwealth, or human combination, or society. It hath fallen out sometimes, that both Papists and Protestants, Jews and Turks, may be embarked in one ship; upon which supposal, I affirm that all the liberty of conscience I ever pleaded for, turns upon these two hinges, that none of the Papists, Protestants, Jews, or Turks be forced to come to the ship's prayers or worship, nor compelled from their own particular prayers or worship, if they practice any."

7. Superior Court of Cincinnati, February 1870. The opinion is not reported but is published under the title, The Bible in the Common Schools (Cincinnati: Robert Clarke & Co. 1870). Judge Taft's views, expressed in dissent, prevailed on appeal. See *Board of Education of Cincinnati v. Minor*, 23 Ohio St. 211, 253 (1872), in which the Ohio Supreme Court held that:

"The great bulk of human affairs and human interests is left by any free government to individual enterprise and individual action. Religion is eminently one of these interests, lying outside the true and legitimate province of government."

Fourteenth Amendment has rendered the legislatures of the states as incompetent as Congress to enact such laws . . . ."[8]

In a series of cases since *Cantwell* the Court has repeatedly reaffirmed that doctrine, and we do so now. *Murdock v. Pennsylvania,* 319 U.S. 105, 108 (1943); *Everson v. Board of Education,* supra; *Illinois ex rel. McCollum v. Board of Education,* 333 U.S. 203, 210–211 (1948); *Zorach v. Clauson,* supra; *McGowan v. Maryland,* 366 U.S. 420 (1961); *Torcaso v. Watkins,* 367 U.S. 488 (1961); and *Engel v. Vitale,* supra.

Second, this Court has rejected unequivocally the contention that the Establishment Clause forbids only governmental preference of one religion over another. Almost 20 years ago in Everson, supra, at 15, the Court said that "[n]either a state nor the Federal Government can set up a church. Neither can pass laws which aid one religion, aid all religions, or prefer one religion over another." And Mr. Justice Jackson, dissenting, agreed:

"There is no answer to the proposition . . . that the effect of the religious freedom Amendment to our Constitution was to take every form of propagation of religion out of the realm of things which could directly or indirectly be made public business and thereby be supported in whole or in part at taxpayers' expense. . . . This freedom was first in the Bill of Rights because it was first in the forefathers' minds; it was set forth in absolute terms, and its strength is its rigidity." Id., at 26.

Further, Mr. Justice Rutledge, joined by Justices Frankfurter, Jackson and Burton, declared:

"The [First] Amendment's purpose was not to strike merely at the official establishment of a single sect, creed or religion, outlawing only a formal relation such as had prevailed in England and some of the colonies. Necessarily it was to uproot all such relationships. But the object was broader than separating church and state in this narrow sense. It was to create a complete and permanent separation of the spheres of religious activity and civil authority by comprehensively forbidding every form of public aid or support for religion." Id., at 31–32.

The same conclusion has been firmly maintained ever since that time, see *Illinois ex rel. McCollum,* supra, at pp. 210–211; *McGowan v. Maryland,* supra, at 442–443; *Torcaso v. Watkins,* supra, at 492–493, 495, and we reaffirm it now.

While none of the parties to either of these cases has questioned these basic conclusions of the Court, both of which have been long established, recognized and consistently reaffirmed, others continue to question their history, logic and efficacy. Such contentions, in the light of the consistent interpretation in cases of this Court, seem entirely untenable and of value only as academic exercises.

IV

The interrelationship of the Establishment and the Free Exercise Clauses was first touched upon by Mr. Justice Roberts for the Court in *Cantwell v. Connecticut,* supra, at 303–304, where it was said that their "inhibition of legislation" had

---

8. Application to the States of other clauses of the First Amendment obtained even before Cantwell. Almost 40 years ago in the opinion of the Court in *Gitlow v. New York,* 268 U.S. 652, 666 (1925), Mr. Justice Sanford said: "For present purposes we may and do assume that freedom of speech and of the press—which are protected by the First Amendment from abridgment by Congress—are among the fundamental personal rights and 'liberties' protected by the due process clause of the Fourteenth Amendment from impairment by the States."

"a double aspect. On the one hand, it forestalls compulsion by law of the acceptance of any creed or the practice of any form of worship. Freedom of conscience and freedom to adhere to such religious organization or form of worship as the individual may choose cannot be restricted by law. On the other hand, it safeguards the free exercise of the chosen form of religion. Thus the Amendment embraces two concepts—freedom to believe and freedom to act. The first is absolute but, in the nature of things, the second cannot be."

A half dozen years later in *Everson v. Board of Education,* supra, at 14–15, this Court, through Mr. Justice Black, stated that the "scope of the First Amendment . . . was designed forever to suppress" the establishment of religion or the prohibition of the free exercise thereof. In short, the Court held that the Amendment

"requires the state to be a neutral in its relations with groups of religious believers and non-believers; it does not require the state to be their adversary. State power is no more to be used so as to handicap religions than it is to favor them." Id., at 18.

And Mr. Justice Jackson, in dissent, declared that public schools are organized

"on the premise that secular education can be isolated from all religious teaching so that the school can inculcate all needed temporal knowledge and also maintain a strict and lofty neutrality as to religion. The assumption is that after the individual has been instructed in worldly wisdom he will be better fitted to choose his religion." Id., at 23–24.

Moreover, all of the four dissenters, speaking through Mr. Justice Rutledge, agreed that

"Our constitutional policy . . . does not deny the value or the necessity for religious training, teaching or observance. Rather it secures their free exercise. But to that end it does deny that the state can undertake or sustain them in any form or degree. For this reason the sphere of religious activity, as distinguished from the secular intellectual liberties, has been given the twofold protection and, as the state cannot forbid, neither can it perform or aid in performing the religious function. The dual prohibition makes that function altogether private." Id., at 52.

Only one year later the Court was asked to reconsider and repudiate the doctrine of these cases in *McCollum v. Board of Education.* It was argued that "historically the First Amendment was intended to forbid only government preference of one religion over another. . . . In addition they ask that we distinguish or overrule our holding in the Everson case that the Fourteenth Amendment made the 'establishment of religion' clause of the First Amendment applicable as a prohibition against the States." 333 U.S., at 211. The Court, with Mr. Justice Reed alone dissenting, was unable to "accept either of these contentions." Ibid. Mr. Justice Frankfurter, joined by Justices Jackson, Rutledge and Burton, wrote a very comprehensive and scholarly concurrence in which he said that "[s]eparation is a requirement to abstain from fusing functions of Government and of religious sects, not merely to treat them all equally." Id., at 227. Continuing, he stated that:

"the Constitution . . . prohibited the Government common to all from becoming embroiled, however innocently, in the destructive religious conflicts of which the history of even this country records some dark pages." Id., at 228.

In 1952 in *Zorach v. Clauson,* supra, Mr. Justice Douglas for the Court reiterated:

> "There cannot be the slightest doubt that the First Amendment reflects the philosophy that Church and State should be separated. And so far as interference with the 'free exercise' of religion and an 'establishment' of religion are concerned, the separation must be complete and unequivocal. The First Amendment within the scope of its coverage permits no exception; the prohibition is absolute. The First Amendment, however, does not say that in every and all respects there shall be a separation of Church and State. Rather, it studiously defines the manner, the specific ways, in which there shall be no concert or union or dependency one on the other. That is the common sense of the matter." 343 U.S., at 312.

And then in 1961 in *McGowan v. Maryland* and in *Torcaso v. Watkins* each of these cases was discussed and approved. Chief Justice Warren in *McGowan,* for a unanimous Court on this point, said:

> "But, the First Amendment, in its final form, did not simply bar a congressional enactment establishing a church; it forbade all laws respecting an establishment of religion. Thus, this Court has given the Amendment a 'broad interpretation . . . in the light of its history and the evils it was designed forever to suppress. . . .'" 366 U.S., at 441–442.

And Mr. Justice Black for the Court in Torcaso, without dissent but with Justices Frankfurter and Harlan concurring in the result, used this language:

> "We repeat and again reaffirm that neither a State nor the Federal Government can constitutionally force a person 'to profess a belief or disbelief in any religion.' Neither can constitutionally pass laws or impose requirements which aid all religions as against non-believers, and neither can aid those religions based on a belief in the existence of God as against those religions founded on different beliefs." 367 U.S., at 495.

Finally, in *Engel v. Vitale,* only last year, these principles were so universally recognized that the Court, without the citation of a single case and over the sole dissent of Mr. Justice Stewart, reaffirmed them. The Court found the 22-word prayer used in "New York's program of daily classroom invocation of God's blessings as prescribed in the Regents' prayer . . . [to be] a religious activity." 370 U.S., at 424. It held that "it is no part of the business of government to compose official prayers for any group of the American people to recite as a part of a religious program carried on by government." Id., at 425. In discussing the reach of the Establishment and Free Exercise Clauses of the First Amendment the Court said:

> "Although these two clauses may in certain instances overlap, they forbid two quite different kinds of governmental encroachment upon religious freedom. The Establishment Clause, unlike the Free Exercise Clause, does not depend upon any showing of direct governmental compulsion and is violated by the enactment of laws which establish an official religion whether those laws operate directly to coerce non-observing individuals or not. This is not to say, of course, that laws officially prescribing a particular form of religious worship do not involve coercion of such individuals. When the power, prestige and financial support of government is placed behind a particular religious belief, the indirect coercive pressure upon religious minorities to conform to the prevailing officially approved religion is plain." Id., at 430–431.

And in further elaboration the Court found that the "first and most immediate purpose [of the Establishment Clause] rested on the belief that a union of government and religion tends to destroy government and to degrade religion." Id., at 431. When government, the Court said, allies itself with one particular form of religion, the inevitable result is that it incurs "the hatred, disrespect and even contempt of those who held contrary beliefs." Ibid.

V

The wholesome "neutrality" of which this Court's cases speak thus stems from a recognition of the teachings of history that powerful sects or groups might bring about a fusion of governmental and religious functions or a concert or dependency of one upon the other to the end that official support of the State or Federal Government would be placed behind the tenets of one or of all orthodoxies. This the Establishment Clause prohibits. And a further reason for neutrality is found in the Free Exercise Clause, which recognizes the value of religious training, teaching and observance and, more particularly, the right of every person to freely choose his own course with reference thereto, free of any compulsion from the state. This the Free Exercise Clause guarantees. Thus, as we have seen, the two clauses may overlap. As we have indicated, the Establishment Clause has been directly considered by this Court eight times in the past score of years and, with only one Justice dissenting on the point, it has consistently held that the clause withdrew all legislative power respecting religious belief or the expression thereof. The test may be stated as follows: what are the purpose and the primary effect of the enactment? If either is the advancement or inhibition of religion then the enactment exceeds the scope of legislative power as circumscribed by the Constitution. That is to say that to withstand the strictures of the Establishment Clause there must be a secular legislative purpose and a primary effect that neither advances nor inhibits religion. *Everson v. Board of Education,* supra; *McGowan v. Maryland,* supra, at 442. The Free Exercise Clause, likewise considered many times here, withdraws from legislative power, state and federal, the exertion of any restraint on the free exercise of religion. Its purpose is to secure religious liberty in the individual by prohibiting any invasions thereof by civil authority. Hence it is necessary in a free exercise case for one to show the coercive effect of the enactment as it operates against him in the practice of his religion. The distinction between the two clauses is apparent—a violation of the Free Exercise Clause is predicated on coercion while the Establishment Clause violation need not be so attended.

Applying the Establishment Clause principles to the cases at bar we find that the States are requiring the selection and reading at the opening of the school day of verses from the Holy Bible and the recitation of the Lord's Prayer by the students in unison. These exercises are prescribed as part of the curricular activities of students who are required by law to attend school. They are held in the school buildings under the supervision and with the participation of teachers employed in those schools. None of these factors, other than compulsory school attendance, was present in the program upheld in *Zorach v. Clauson.* The trial court in No. 142 has found that such an opening exercise is a religious ceremony and was intended by the State to be so. We agree with the trial court's finding as to the religious character of the exercises. Given that finding, the exercises and the law requiring them are in violation of the Establishment Clause.

There is no such specific finding as to the religious character of the exercises in No. 119, and the State contends (as does the State in No. 142) that the program is an effort to extend its benefits to all public school children without regard to their religious belief. Included within its secular purposes, it says, are the promotion of moral values, the contradiction to the materialistic trends of our times, the perpetuation of our institutions and the teaching of literature. The case came up on demurrer, of course, to a petition which alleged that the uniform practice under the rule had been to read from the King James version of the Bible and that the exercise was sectarian. The short answer, therefore, is that the religious character of the exercise was admitted by the State. But even if its purpose is not strictly religious, it is sought to be accomplished through readings, without comment, from the Bible. Surely the place of the Bible as an instrument of religion cannot be gainsaid, and the State's recognition of the pervading religious character of the ceremony is evident from the rule's specific permission of the alternative use of the Catholic Douay version as well as the recent amendment permitting nonattendance at the exercises. None of these factors is consistent with the contention that the Bible is here used either as an instrument for nonreligious moral inspiration or as a reference for the teaching of secular subjects.

The conclusion follows that in both cases the laws require religious exercises and such exercises are being conducted in direct violation of the rights of the appellees and petitioners.[9] Nor are these required exercises mitigated by the fact that individual students may absent themselves upon parental request, for that fact furnishes no defense to a claim of unconstitutionality under the Establishment Clause. See *Engel v. Vitale,* supra, at 430. Further, it is no defense to urge that the religious practices here may be relatively minor encroachments on the First Amendment. The breach of neutrality that is today a trickling stream may all too soon become a raging torrent and, in the words of *Madison,* "it is proper to take alarm at the first experiment on our liberties." Memorial and Remonstrance Against Religious Assessments, quoted in *Everson,* supra, at 65.

It is insisted that unless these religious exercises are permitted a "religion of secularism" is established in the schools. We agree of course that the State may not establish a "religion of secularism" in the sense of affirmatively opposing or showing hostility to religion, thus "preferring those who believe in no religion over those who do believe." *Zorach v. Clauson,* supra, at 314. We do not agree, however, that this decision in any sense has that effect. In addition, it might well be said that one's education is not complete without a study of comparative religion or the history of religion and its relationship to the advancement of civilization. It certainly may be said that the Bible is worthy of study for its literary and historic qualities. Nothing we have said here indicates that such study of the Bible or of religion, when presented objectively as part of a secular program of education, may not be effected consistently with the First Amendment. But the exercises here do not fall into those categories. They are reli-

---

9. It goes without saying that the laws and practices involved here can be challenged only by persons having standing to complain. But the requirements for standing to challenge state action under the Establishment Clause, unlike those relating to the Free Exercise Clause, do not include proof that particular religious freedoms are infringed. *McGowan v. Maryland,* supra, at 429–430. The parties here are school children and their parents, who are directly affected by the laws and practices against which their complaints are directed. These interests surely suffice to give the parties standing to complain. See *Engel v. Vitale,* supra. Cf. *McCollum v. Board of Education,* supra; *Everson v. Board of Education,* supra. Compare *Doremus v. Board of Education,* 342 U.S. 429 (1952), which involved the same substantive issues presented here. The appeal was there dismissed upon the graduation of the school child involved and because of the appellants' failure to establish standing as taxpayers.

gious exercises, required by the States in violation of the command of the First Amendment that the Government maintain strict neutrality, neither aiding nor opposing religion.

Finally, we cannot accept that the concept of neutrality, which does not permit a State to require a religious exercise even with the consent of the majority of those affected, collides with the majority's right to free exercise of religion.[10] While the Free Exercise Clause clearly prohibits the use of state action to deny the rights of free exercise to anyone, it has never meant that a majority could use the machinery of the State to practice its beliefs. Such a contention was effectively answered by Mr. Justice Jackson for the Court in *West Virginia Board of Education v. Barnette*, 319 U.S. 624, 638 (1943):

> "The very purpose of a Bill of Rights was to withdraw certain subjects from the vicissitudes of political controversy, to place them beyond the reach of majorities and officials and to establish them as legal principles to be applied by the courts. One's right to . . . freedom of worship . . . and other fundamental rights may not be submitted to vote; they depend on the outcome of no elections."

The place of religion in our society is an exalted one, achieved through a long tradition of reliance on the home, the church and the inviolable citadel of the individual heart and mind. We have come to recognize through bitter experience that it is not within the power of government to invade that citadel, whether its purpose or effect be to aid or oppose, to advance or retard. In the relationship between man and religion, the State is firmly committed to a position of neutrality. Though the application of that rule requires interpretation of a delicate sort, the rule itself is clearly and concisely stated in the words of the First Amendment. Applying that rule to the facts of these cases, we affirm the judgment in No. 142. In No. 119, the judgment is reversed and the cause remanded to the Maryland Court of Appeals for further proceedings consistent with this opinion.

It is so ordered.

Case Comment

The case of *Santa Fe Independent School District v. Doe* (2000) is the most recent case involving school prayer to come before the Supreme Court. The legal issues in the case posed an interesting situation for the Court to resolve. Prior to 1995, a student elected as Santa Fe High School's student council chaplain delivered a prayer over the public address system before each home varsity football game. A group of Mormon and Catholic students, alumni, and their mothers filed suit challenging this practice and others under the Establishment Clause of the First Amendment. While the suit was pending, the school district adopted a different policy, which authorized two student elections, the first to determine whether "invocations" should be delivered at games, and the second to select the spokesperson to deliver them. After the students held elections authorizing such prayers and selecting a spokesperson, the District Court entered an order modifying the policy to permit only nonsectarian,

---

10. We are not of course presented with and therefore do not pass upon a situation such as military service, where the Government regulates the temporal and geographic environment of individuals to a point that, unless it permits voluntary religious services to be conducted with the use of government facilities, military personnel would be unable to engage in the practice of their faiths.

nonproselytizing prayer. The Fifth Circuit held that, even as modified by the District Court, the football prayer policy was invalid.

The Supreme Court held that a policy permitting student-led, student-initiated prayer at football games violates the Establishment Clause and based its ruling on a number of factors: (1) The Constitution guarantees that government may not coerce anyone to support or participate in religion or its exercise, or otherwise act in a way that establishes a state religion or religious faith, or tends to do so; and (2) the argument that there is no coercion here because attendance at an extracurricular event, unlike a graduation ceremony, is voluntary, is unpersuasive because for some students—such as cheerleaders, members of the band, and the team members themselves—attendance at football games is mandated, sometimes for class credit.

SANTA FE INDEPENDENT SCHOOL DISTRICT V. DOE

Supreme Court of the United States, 2000.

530 U.S. 290

Justice Stevens delivered the opinion of the Court.

Prior to 1995, the Santa Fe High School student who occupied the school's elective office of student council chaplain delivered a prayer over the public address system before each varsity football game for the entire season. This practice, along with others, was challenged in District Court as a violation of the Establishment Clause of the First Amendment. While these proceedings were pending in the District Court, the school district adopted a different policy that permits, but does not require, prayer initiated and led by a student at all home games. The District Court entered an order modifying that policy to permit only nonsectarian, nonproselytizing prayer. The Court of Appeals held that, even as modified by the District Court, the football prayer policy was invalid. We granted the school district's petition for certiorari to review that holding.

I

The Santa Fe Independent School District (District) is a political subdivision of the State of Texas, responsible for the education of more than 4,000 students in a small community in the southern part of the State. The District includes the Santa Fe High School, two primary schools, an intermediate school and the junior high school. Respondents are two sets of current or former students and their respective mothers. One family is Mormon and the other is Catholic. The District Court permitted respondents (Does) to litigate anonymously to protect them from intimidation or harassment.[1]

---

1. A decision, the Fifth Circuit Court of Appeals noted, that many District officials "apparently neither agreed with nor particularly respected." 168 F. 3d 806, 809, n. 1 (CA5 1999). About a month after the complaint was filed, the District Court entered an order that provided, in part: "[A]ny further attempt on the part of District or school administration, officials, counsellors, teachers, employees or servants of the School District, parents, students or anyone else, overtly or covertly to ferret out the identities of the Plaintiffs in this cause, by means of bogus petitions, questionnaires, individual interrogation, or downright 'snooping', will cease immediately. ANYONE TAKING ANY ACTION ON SCHOOL PROPERTY, DURING SCHOOL HOURS, OR WITH SCHOOL RESOURCES OR APPROVAL FOR PURPOSES OF ATTEMPTING TO ELICIT THE NAMES OR IDENTITIES OF THE PLAINTIFFS IN THIS CAUSE OF ACTION, BY OR ON BEHALF OF ANY OF THESE INDIVIDUALS, WILL FACE THE

Respondents commenced this action in April 1995 and moved for a temporary restraining order to prevent the District from violating the Establishment Clause at the imminent graduation exercises. In their complaint the Does alleged that the District had engaged in several proselytizing practices, such as promoting attendance at a Baptist revival meeting, encouraging membership in religious clubs, chastising children who held minority religious beliefs, and distributing Gideon Bibles on school premises. They also alleged that the District allowed students to read Christian invocations and benedictions from the stage at graduation ceremonies,[2] and to deliver overtly Christian prayers over the public address system at home football games.

On May 10, 1995, the District Court entered an interim order addressing a number of different issues.[3] With respect to the impending graduation, the order provided that "nondenominational prayer" consisting of "an invocation and/or benediction" could be presented by a senior student or students selected by members of the graduating class. The text of the prayer was to be determined by the students, without scrutiny or preapproval by school officials. References to particular religious figures "such as Mohammed, Jesus, Buddha, or the like" would be permitted "as long as the general thrust of the prayer is nonproselytizing." App. 32.

In response to that portion of the order, the District adopted a series of policies over several months dealing with prayer at school functions. The policies enacted in May and July for graduation ceremonies provided the format for the August and October policies for football games. The May policy provided:

> "'The board has chosen to permit the graduating senior class, with the advice and counsel of the senior class principal or designee, to elect by secret ballot to choose whether an invocation and benediction shall be part of the graduation exercise. If so chosen the class shall elect by secret ballot, from a list of student volunteers, students to deliver nonsectarian, nonproselytizing invocations and benedictions for the purpose of solemnizing their graduation ceremonies.'" 168 F.3d 806, 811 (CA5 1999) (emphasis deleted).

HARSHEST POSSIBLE CONTEMPT SANCTIONS FROM THIS COURT, AND MAY ADDITIONALLY FACE CRIMINAL LIABILITY. The Court wants these proceedings addressed on their merits, and not on the basis of intimidation or harassment of the participants on either side." App. 34-35.

2. At the 1994 graduation ceremony the senior class president delivered this invocation:

"Please bow your heads.

"Dear heavenly Father, thank you for allowing us to gather here safely tonight. We thank you for the wonderful year you have allowed us to spend together as students of Santa Fe. We thank you for our teachers who have devoted many hours to each of us. Thank you, Lord, for our parents and may each one receive the special blessing. We pray also for a blessing and guidance as each student moves forward in the future. Lord, bless this ceremony and give us all a safe journey home. In Jesus' name we pray." Id., at 19.

3. For example, it prohibited school officials from endorsing or participating in the baccalaureate ceremony sponsored by the Santa Fe Ministerial Alliance, and ordered the District to establish policies to deal with "manifest First Amendment infractions of teachers, counsellors, or other District or school officials or personnel, such as ridiculing, berating or holding up for inappropriate scrutiny or examination the beliefs of any individual students. Similarly, the School District will establish or clarify existing procedures for excluding overt or covert sectarian and proselytizing religious teaching, such as the use of blatantly denominational religious terms in spelling lessons, denominational religious songs and poems in English or choir classes, denominational religious stories and parables in grammar lessons and the like, while at the same time allowing for frank and open discussion of moral, religious, and societal views and beliefs, which are non-denominational and non-judgmental." Id., at 34.

The parties stipulated that after this policy was adopted, "the senior class held an election to determine whether to have an invocation and benediction at the commencement [and that the] class voted, by secret ballot, to include prayer at the high school graduation." App. 52. In a second vote the class elected two seniors to deliver the invocation and benediction.[4]

In July, the District enacted another policy eliminating the requirement that invocations and benedictions be "nonsectarian and nonproselytising," but also providing that if the District were to be enjoined from enforcing that policy, the May policy would automatically become effective.

The August policy, which was titled "Prayer at Football Games," was similar to the July policy for graduations. It also authorized two student elections, the first to determine whether "invocations" should be delivered, and the second to select the spokesperson to deliver them. Like the July policy, it contained two parts, an initial statement that omitted any requirement that the content of the invocation be "nonsectarian and nonproselytising," and a fall-back provision that automatically added that limitation if the preferred policy should be enjoined. On August 31, 1995, according to the parties' stipulation, "the district's high school students voted to determine whether a student would deliver prayer at varsity football games . . . . The students chose to allow a student to say a prayer at football games." *Id.,* at 65. A week later, in a separate election, they selected a student "to deliver the prayer at varsity football games." *Id.,* at 66.

The final policy (October policy) is essentially the same as the August policy, though it omits the word "prayer" from its title, and refers to "messages" and "statements" as well as "invocations."[5] It is the validity of that policy that is before us.[6]

---

4. The student giving the invocation thanked the Lord for keeping the class safe through 12 years of school and for gracing their lives with two special people and closed: "Lord, we ask that You keep Your hand upon us during this ceremony and to help us keep You in our hearts through the rest of our lives. In God's name we pray. Amen." *Id.,* at 53. The student benediction was similar in content and closed: "Lord, we ask for Your protection as we depart to our next destination and watch over us as we go our separate ways. Grant each of us a safe trip and keep us secure throughout the night. In Your name we pray. Amen." *Id.,* at 54.

5. Despite these changes, the school did not conduct another election, under the October policy, to supersede the results of the August policy election.

6. It provides:

"STUDENT ACTIVITIES:

"PRE-GAME CEREMONIES AT FOOTBALL GAMES

"The board has chosen to permit students to deliver a brief invocation and/or message to be delivered during the pre-game ceremonies of home varsity football games to solemnize the event, to promote good sportsmanship and student safety, and to establish the appropriate environment for the competition.

"Upon advice and direction of the high school principal, each spring, the high school student council shall conduct an election, by the high school student body, by secret ballot, to determine whether such a statement or invocation will be a part of the pre-game ceremonies and if so, shall elect a student, from a list of student volunteers, to deliver the statement or invocation. The student volunteer who is selected by his or her classmates may decide what message and/or invocation to deliver, consistent with the goals and purposes of this policy.

"If the District is enjoined by a court order from the enforcement of this policy, then and only then will the following policy automatically become the applicable policy of the school district.

"The board has chosen to permit students to deliver a brief invocation and/or message to be delivered during the pre-game ceremonies of home varsity football games to solemnize the event, to promote good sportsmanship and student safety, and to establish the appropriate environment for the competition.

"Upon advice and direction of the high school principal, each spring, the high school student council shall conduct an election, by the high school student body, by secret ballot, to determine whether such a message

The District Court did enter an order precluding enforcement of the first, open-ended policy. Relying on our decision in *Lee v. Weisman*, 505 U.S. 577 (1992), it held that the school's "action must not 'coerce anyone to support or participate in' a religious exercise." App. to Pet. for Cert. E7. Applying that test, it concluded that the graduation prayers appealed "to distinctively Christian beliefs,"[7] and that delivering a prayer "over the school's public address system prior to each football and baseball game coerces student participation in religious events."[8] Both parties appealed, the District contending that the enjoined portion of the October policy was permissible and the Does contending that both alternatives violated the Establishment Clause. The Court of Appeals majority agreed with the Does.

The decision of the Court of Appeals followed Fifth Circuit precedent that had announced two rules. In *Jones v. Clear Creek Independent School Dist.*, 977 F. 2d 963 (1992), that court held that student-led prayer that was approved by a vote of the students and was nonsectarian and nonproselytizing was permissible at high school graduation ceremonies. On the other hand, in later cases the Fifth Circuit made it clear that the *Clear Creek* rule applied only to high school graduations and that school-encouraged prayer was constitutionally impermissible at school-related sporting events. Thus, in *Doe v. Duncanville Independent School Dist.*, 70 F.3d 402 (1995), it had described a high school graduation as "a significant, once in-a-lifetime event" to be contrasted with athletic events in "a setting that is far less solemn and extraordinary." *Id.*, at 406-407.[9]

In its opinion in this case, the Court of Appeals explained:

> "The controlling feature here is the same as in *Duncanville*: The prayers are to be delivered *at football games*—hardly the sober type of annual event that can be appropriately solemnized with prayer. The distinction to which [the District] points is simply one without difference. Regardless of whether the prayers are selected by vote or spontaneously initiated at these frequently-recurring, informal, school-sponsored events, school officials are present and have the authority to stop the prayers. Thus, as we indicated in *Duncanville*, our decision in *Clear Creek II* hinged on the singular context and singularly serious nature of a graduation ceremony. Outside that nurturing context, a Clear Creek Prayer Policy cannot survive. We therefore reverse the district court's holding that [the District's] alternative Clear Creek Prayer Policy can be extended to football games, irrespective of the presence of the nonsectarian, nonproselytizing restrictions." 168 F. 3d, at 823.

The dissenting judge rejected the majority's distinction between graduation ceremonies and football games. In his opinion the District's October policy created a limited public

---

or invocation will be a part of the pre-game ceremonies and if so, shall elect a student, from a list of student volunteers, to deliver the statement or invocation. The student volunteer who is selected by his or her classmates may decide what statement or invocation to deliver, consistent with the goals and purposes of this policy. Any message and/or invocation delivered by a student must be nonsectarian and nonproselytizing." *Id.*, at 104-105.

7. "The graduation prayers at issue in the instant case, in contrast, are infused with explicit references to Jesus Christ and otherwise appeal to distinctively Christian beliefs. The Court accordingly finds that use of these prayers during graduation ceremonies, considered in light of the overall manner in which they were delivered, violated the Establishment Clause." App. to Pet. for Cert. E8.

8. *Id.*, at E8-E9.

9. Because the dissent overlooks this case, it incorrectly assumes that a "prayer-only policy" at football games was permissible in the Fifth Circuit. See *post*, at 6-7.

forum that had a secular purpose[10] and provided neutral accommodation of noncoerced, private, religious speech.[11]

We granted the District's petition for certiorari, limited to the following question: "Whether petitioner's policy permitting student-led, student-initiated prayer at football games violates the Establishment Clause." 528 U.S. 1002 (1999). We conclude, as did the Court of Appeals, that it does.

II

The first Clause in the First Amendment to the Federal Constitution provides that "Congress shall make no law respecting an establishment of religion, or prohibiting the free exercise thereof." The Fourteenth Amendment imposes those substantive limitations on the legislative power of the States and their political subdivisions. *Wallace v. Jaffree*, 472 U.S. 38, 49–50 (1985). In *Lee v. Weisman*, 505 U.S. 577 (1992), we held that a prayer delivered by a rabbi at a middle school graduation ceremony violated that Clause. Although this case involves student prayer at a different type of school function, our analysis is properly guided by the principles that we endorsed in *Lee*.

As we held in that case:

"The principle that government may accommodate the free exercise of religion does not supersede the fundamental limitations imposed by the Establishment Clause. It is beyond dispute that, at a minimum, the Constitution guarantees that government may not coerce anyone to support or participate in religion or its exercise, or otherwise act in a way which 'establishes a [state] religion or religious faith, or tends to do so.'" *Id.*, at 587 (citations omitted) (quoting *Lynch v. Donnelly*, 465 U.S. 668, 678 (1984)).

In this case the District first argues that this principle is inapplicable to its October policy because the messages are private student speech, not public speech. It reminds us that "there is a crucial difference between *government* speech endorsing religion, which the Establishment Clause forbids, and *private* speech endorsing religion, which the Free Speech and Free Exercise Clauses protect." *Board of Ed. of Westside Community Schools (Dist. 66) v. Mergens*, 496 U.S. 226, 250 (1990) (opinion of O'Connor, J.). We certainly agree with that distinction, but we are not persuaded that the pregame invocations should be regarded as "private speech."

---

10. "There are in fact several secular reasons for allowing a brief, serious message before football games—some of which [the District] has listed in its policy. At sporting events, messages and/or invocations can promote, among other things, honest and fair play, clean competition, individual challenge to be one's best, importance of team work, and many more goals that the majority could conceive would it only pause to do so.

"Having again relinquished all editorial control, [the District] has created a limited public forum for the students to give brief statements or prayers concerning the value of those goals and the methods for achieving them." 168 F. 3d, at 835.

11. "The majority fails to realize that what is at issue in this *facial challenge* to this school policy is the neutral accommodation of non-coerced, private, religious speech, which allows students, selected by students, to express their personal viewpoints. The state is not involved. The school board has neither scripted, supervised, endorsed, suggested, nor edited these personal viewpoints. Yet the majority imposes a judicial curse upon sectarian religious speech." *Id.*, at 836.

These invocations are authorized by a government policy and take place on government property at government-sponsored school-related events. Of course, not every message delivered under such circumstances is the government's own. We have held, for example, that an individual's contribution to a government-created forum was not government speech. See *Rosenberger v. Rector and Visitors of Univ. of Va.*, 515 U.S. 819 (1995). Although the District relies heavily on *Rosenberger* and similar cases involving such forums,[12] it is clear that the pregame ceremony is not the type of forum discussed in those cases.[13] The Santa Fe school officials simply do not "evince either 'by policy or by practice,' any intent to open the [pregame ceremony] to 'indiscriminate use,' . . . by the student body generally." *Hazelwood School Dist. v. Kuhlmeier*, 484 U.S. 260, 270 (1988) (quoting *Perry Ed. Assn. v. Perry Local Educators' Assn.*, 460 U.S. 37, 47 (1983)). Rather, the school allows only one student, the same student for the entire season, to give the invocation. The statement or invocation, moreover, is subject to particular regulations that confine the content and topic of the student's message, see *infra*, at 14-15, 17. By comparison, in *Perry* we rejected a claim that the school had created a limited public forum in its school mail system despite the fact that it had allowed far more speakers to address a much broader range of topics than the policy at issue here.[14] As we concluded in *Perry*, "selective access does not transform government property into a public forum." 460 U.S., at 47.

Granting only one student access to the stage at a time does not, of course, necessarily preclude a finding that a school has created a limited public forum. Here, however, Santa Fe's student election system ensures that only those messages deemed "appropriate" under the District's policy may be delivered. That is, the majoritarian process implemented by the District guarantees, by definition, that minority candidates will never prevail and that their views will be effectively silenced.

Recently, in *Board of Regents of Univ. of Wis. System v. Southworth*, 529 U.S. ____ (2000), we explained why student elections that determine, by majority vote, which expressive activities shall receive or not receive school benefits are constitutionally problematic:

"To the extent the referendum substitutes majority determinations for viewpoint neutrality it would undermine the constitutional protection the program requires. The whole theory of viewpoint neutrality is that minority views are treated with the same respect as are majority views. Access to a public forum, for instance, does not depend upon majoritarian consent. That principle is controlling here." *Id.*, at _____ (slip op., at 16-17).

---

12. See, *e.g.*, Brief for Petitioner 44-48, citing *Rosenberger*, 515 U.S., 819 (limited public forum); *Widmar v. Vincent*, 454 U.S. 263 (1981) (limited public forum); *Capitol Square Review and Advisory Bd. v. Pinette*, 515 U.S. 753(1995) (traditional public forum); *Lamb's Chapel v. Center Moriches Union Free School Dist.*, 508 U.S. 384 (1993) (limited public forum). Although the District relies on these public forum cases, it does not actually argue that the pregame ceremony constitutes such a forum.

13. A conclusion that the District had created a public forum would help shed light on whether the resulting speech is public or private, but we also note that we have never held the mere creation of a public forum shields the government entity from scrutiny under the Establishment Clause. See, *e.g.*, *Pinette*, 515 U.S., at 772 (O'Connor, J., concurring in part and concurring in judgment) ("I see no necessity to carve out . . . an exception to the endorsement test for the public forum context").

14. The school's internal mail system in *Perry* was open to various private organizations such as "[l]ocal parochial schools, church groups, YMCA's, and Cub Scout units." 460 U.S., at 39, n. 2.

Like the student referendum for funding in *Southworth,* this student election does nothing to protect minority views but rather places the students who hold such views at the mercy of the majority.[15] Because "fundamental rights may not be submitted to vote; they depend on the outcome of no elections," *West Virginia Bd. of Ed. v. Barnette,* 319 U.S. 624, 638 (1943), the District's elections are insufficient safeguards of diverse student speech.

In *Lee,* the school district made the related argument that its policy of endorsing only "civic or nonsectarian" prayer was acceptable because it minimized the intrusion on the audience as a whole. We rejected that claim by explaining that such a majoritarian policy "does not lessen the offense or isolation to the objectors. At best it narrows their number, at worst increases their sense of isolation and affront." 505 U.S., at 594. Similarly, while Santa Fe's majoritarian election might ensure that *most* of the students are represented, it does nothing to protect the minority; indeed, it likely serves to intensify their offense.

Moreover, the District has failed to divorce itself from the religious content in the invocations. It has not succeeded in doing so, either by claiming that its policy is "'one of neutrality rather than endorsement'"[16] or by characterizing the individual student as the "circuit-breaker"[17] in the process. Contrary to the District's repeated assertions that it has adopted a "hands-off" approach to the pregame invocation, the realities of the situation plainly reveal that its policy involves both perceived and actual endorsement of religion. In this case, as we found in *Lee,* the "degree of school involvement" makes it clear that the pregame prayers bear "the imprint of the State and thus put school-age children who objected in an untenable position." 505 U.S., at 590.

The District has attempted to disentangle itself from the religious messages by developing the two-step student election process. The text of the October policy, however, exposes the extent of the school's entanglement. The elections take place at all only because the school "board *has chosen to permit* students to deliver a brief invocation and/or message." App. 104 (emphasis added). The elections thus "shall" be conducted "by the high school student council" and "[u]pon advice and direction of the high school principal." *Id.,* at 104-105. The decision whether to deliver a message is first made by majority vote of the entire student body, followed by a choice of the speaker in a separate, similar majority election. Even though the particular words used by the speaker are not determined by those votes, the policy mandates that the "statement or invocation" be "consistent with the goals and purposes of this policy," which are "to solemnize the event, to promote good sportsmanship and student safety, and to establish the appropriate environment for the competition." *Ibid.*

In addition to involving the school in the selection of the speaker, the policy, by its terms, invites and encourages religious messages. The policy itself states that the purpose of the message is "to solemnize the event." A religious message is the most obvious method of solem-

---

15. If instead of a choice between an invocation and no pregame message, the first election determined whether a political speech should be made, and the second election determined whether the speaker should be a Democrat or a Republican, it would be rather clear that the public address system was being used to deliver a partisan message reflecting the viewpoint of the majority rather than a random statement by a private individual.

The fact that the District's policy provides for the election of the speaker only after the majority has voted on her message identifies an obvious distinction between this case and the typical election of a "student body president, or even a newly elected prom king or queen." *Post,* at 5.

16. Brief for Petitioner 19 (quoting *Board of Ed. of Westside Community Schools (Dist. 66) Mergens,* 496 U.S. 226, 248 (1990) (plurality opinion)).

17. Tr. of Oral Arg. 7.

nizing an event. Moreover, the requirements that the message "promote good citizenship" and "establish the appropriate environment for competition" further narrow the types of message deemed appropriate, suggesting that a solemn, yet nonreligious, message, such as commentary on United States foreign policy, would be prohibited.[18] Indeed, the only type of message that is expressly endorsed in the text is an "invocation"—a term that primarily describes an appeal for divine assistance.[19] In fact, as used in the past at Santa Fe High School, an "invocation" has always entailed a focused religious message. Thus, the expressed purposes of the policy encourage the selection of a religious message, and that is precisely how the students understand the policy. The results of the elections described in the parties' stipulation[20] make it clear that the students understood that the central question before them was whether prayer should be a part of the pregame ceremony.[21] We recognize the important role that public worship plays in many communities, as well as the sincere desire to include public prayer as a part of various occasions so as to mark those occasions' significance. But such religious activity in public schools, as elsewhere, must comport with the First Amendment.

The actual or perceived endorsement of the message, moreover, is established by factors beyond just the text of the policy. Once the student speaker is selected and the message composed, the invocation is then delivered to a large audience assembled as part of a regularly scheduled, school-sponsored function conducted on school property. The message is broadcast over the school's public address system, which remains subject to the control of school officials. It is fair to assume that the pregame ceremony is clothed in the traditional indicia of school sporting events, which generally include not just the team, but also cheerleaders and band members dressed in uniforms sporting the school name and mascot. The school's name is likely written in large print across the field and on banners and flags. The crowd will certainly include many who display the school colors and insignia on their school T-shirts, jackets, or hats and who may also be waving signs displaying the school name. It is in a setting such as this that "[t]he board has chosen to permit" the elected student to rise and give the "statement or invocation."

In this context the members of the listening audience must perceive the pregame message as a public expression of the views of the majority of the student body delivered with the approval of the school administration. In cases involving state participation in a religious activity, one of the relevant questions is "whether an objective observer, acquainted with the text, legislative history, and implementation of the statute, would perceive it as a state endorsement of prayer in public schools." *Wallace*, 472 U.S., at 73, 76 (*O'Connor, J.*, concurring

---

18. *The Chief Justice*'s hypothetical of the student body president asked by the school to introduce a guest speaker with a biography of her accomplishments, see *post*, at 9 (dissenting opinion), obviously would pose no problems under the Establishment Clause.

19. See, *e.g.*, Webster's Third New International Dictionary 1190 (1993) (defining "invocation" as "a prayer of entreaty that is usu[ally] a call for the divine presence and is offered at the beginning of a meeting or service of worship").

20. See *supra*, at 4-5, and n. 4;

21. Even if the plain language of the October policy were facially neutral, "the Establishment Clause forbids a State to hide behind the application of formally neutral criteria and remain studiously oblivious to the effects of its actions." *Capitol Square Review and Advisory Bd. v. Pinette*, 515 U.S., at 777 (*O'Connor, J.*, concurring in part and concurring in judgment); see also *Church of Lukumi Babalu Aye, Inc. v. Hialeah*, 508 U.S. 520, 534-535 (1993) (making the same point in the Free Exercise context).

in judgment); see also *Capital Square Review and Advisory Bd. v. Pinette*, 515 U.S. 753, 777 (1995) (*O'Connor, J.,* concurring in part and concurring in judgment). Regardless of the listener's support for, or objection to, the message, an objective Santa Fe High School student will unquestionably perceive the inevitable pregame prayer as stamped with her school's seal of approval.

The text and history of this policy, moreover, reinforce our objective student's perception that the prayer is, in actuality, encouraged by the school. When a governmental entity professes a secular purpose for an arguably religious policy, the government's characterization is, of course, entitled to some deference. But it is nonetheless the duty of the courts to "distinguis[h] a sham secular purpose from a sincere one." *Wallace*, 472 U.S., at 75 (*O'Connor, J.,* concurring in judgment).

According to the District, the secular purposes of the policy are to "foste[r] free expression of private persons ... as well [as to] solemniz[e] sporting events, promot[e] good sportsmanship and student safety, and establis[h] an appropriate environment for competition." Brief for Petitioner 14. We note, however, that the District's approval of only one specific kind of message, an "invocation," is not necessary to further any of these purposes. Additionally, the fact that only one student is permitted to give a content-limited message suggests that this policy does little to "foste[r] free expression." Furthermore, regardless of whether one considers a sporting event an appropriate occasion for solemnity, the use of an invocation to foster such solemnity is impermissible when, in actuality, it constitutes prayer sponsored by the school. And it is unclear what type of message would be both appropriately "solemnizing" under the District's policy and yet non-religious.

Most striking to us is the evolution of the current policy from the long-sanctioned office of "Student Chaplain" to the candidly titled "Prayer at Football Games" regulation. This history indicates that the District intended to preserve the practice of prayer before football games. The conclusion that the District viewed the October policy simply as a continuation of the previous policies is dramatically illustrated by the fact that the school did not conduct a new election, pursuant to the current policy, to replace the results of the previous election, which occurred under the former policy. Given these observations, and in light of the school's history of regular delivery of a student-led prayer at athletic events, it is reasonable to infer that the specific purpose of the policy was to preserve a popular "state-sponsored religious practice." *Lee*, 505 U.S., at 596.

School sponsorship of a religious message is impermissible because it sends the ancillary message to members of the audience who are nonadherants "that they are outsiders, not full members of the political community, and an accompanying message to adherants that they are insiders, favored members of the political community." *Lynch v. Donnelly*, 465 U.S., at 688 (1984) (*O'Connor, J.,* concurring). The delivery of such a message—over the school's public address system, by a speaker representing the student body, under the supervision of school faculty, and pursuant to a school policy that explicitly and implicitly encourages public prayer—is not properly characterized as "private" speech.

III

The District next argues that its football policy is distinguishable from the graduation prayer in *Lee* because it does not coerce students to participate in religious observances. Its argument has two parts: first, that there is no impermissible government coercion because the pregame messages are the product of student choices; and second, that there is really no co-ercion at all because attendance at an extracurricular event, unlike a graduation ceremony, is voluntary.

The reasons just discussed explaining why the alleged "circuit-breaker" mechanism of the dual elections and student speaker do not turn public speech into private speech also demonstrate why these mechanisms do not insulate the school from the coercive element of the final message. In fact, this aspect of the District's argument exposes anew the concerns that are created by the majoritarian election system. The parties' stipulation clearly states that the issue resolved in the first election was "whether a student would deliver prayer at var-sity football games," App. 65, and the controversy in this case demonstrates that the views of the students are not unanimous on that issue.

One of the purposes served by the Establishment Clause is to remove debate over this kind of issue from governmental supervision or control. We explained in *Lee* that the "preserva-tion and transmission of religious beliefs and worship is a responsibility and a choice com-mitted to the private sphere." 505 U.S., at 589. The two student elections authorized by the policy, coupled with the debates that presumably must precede each, impermissibly invade that private sphere. The election mechanism, when considered in light of the history in which the policy in question evolved, reflects a device the District put in place that determines whether religious messages will be delivered at home football games. The mechanism encourages di-visiveness along religious lines in a public school setting, a result at odds with the Establish-ment Clause. Although it is true that the ultimate choice of student speaker is "attributable to the students," Brief for Petitioner 40, the District's decision to hold the constitutionally problematic election is clearly "a choice attributable to the State," *Lee,* 505 U.S., at 587.

The District further argues that attendance at the commencement ceremonies at issue in *Lee* "differs dramatically" from attendance at high school football games, which it contends "are of no more than passing interest to many students" and are "decidedly extracurricular," thus dissipating any coercion. Brief for Petitioner 41. Attendance at a high school football game, unlike showing up for class, is certainly not required in order to receive a diploma. Moreover, we may assume that the District is correct in arguing that the informal pressure to attend an athletic event is not as strong as a senior's desire to attend her own graduation ceremony.

There are some students, however, such as cheerleaders, members of the band, and, of course, the team members themselves, for whom seasonal commitments mandate their at-tendance, sometimes for class credit. The District also minimizes the importance to many students of attending and participating in extracurricular activities as part of a complete educational experience. As we noted in *Lee*, "[l]aw reaches past formalism." 505 U.S., at 595. To assert that high school students do not feel immense social pressure, or have a truly gen-uine desire, to be involved in the extracurricular event that is American high school football is "formalistic in the extreme." *Ibid.* We stressed in *Lee* the obvious observation that "ado-lescents are often susceptible to pressure from their peers towards conformity, and that the influence is strongest in matters of social convention." *Id.,* at 593. High school home foot-ball games are traditional gatherings of a school community; they bring together students and faculty as well as friends and family from years present and past to root for a common cause. Undoubtedly, the games are not important to some students, and they voluntarily choose not to attend. For many others, however, the choice between whether to attend these games or to risk facing a personally offensive religious ritual is in no practical sense an easy one. The Constitution, moreover, demands that the school may not force this difficult choice upon these students for "[i]t is a tenet of the First Amendment that the State cannot require one of its citizens to forfeit his or her rights and benefits as the price of resisting conformance to state-sponsored religious practice." *Id.,* at 596.

Even if we regard every high school student's decision to attend a home football game as purely voluntary, we are nevertheless persuaded that the delivery of a pregame prayer has the improper effect of coercing those present to participate in an act of religious worship. For "the government may no more use social pressure to enforce orthodoxy than it may use more direct means." *Id.,* at 594. As in *Lee,* "[w]hat to most believers may seem nothing more than a reasonable request that the nonbeliever respect their religious practices, in a school context may appear to the nonbeliever or dissenter to be an attempt to employ the machinery of the State to enforce a religious orthodoxy." *Id.,* at 592. The constitutional command will not permit the District "to exact religious conformity from a student as the price" of joining her classmates at a varsity football game.[22]

The Religion Clauses of the First Amendment prevent the government from making any law respecting the establishment of religion or prohibiting the free exercise thereof. By no means do these commands impose a prohibition on all religious activity in our public schools. See, e.g., *Lamb's Chapel v. Center Moriches Union Free School Dist.,* 508 U.S. 384, 395 (1993); *Board of Ed. of Westside Community Schools (Dist. 66) v. Mergens,* 496 U.S. 226 (1990); *Wallace v. Jaffree,* 472 U.S. 38, 59 (1985). Indeed, the common purpose of the Religion Clauses "is to secure religious liberty." *Engel v. Vitale,* 370 U.S. 421, 430 (1962). Thus, nothing in the Constitution as interpreted by this Court prohibits any public school student from voluntarily praying at any time before, during, or after the schoolday. But the religious liberty protected by the Constitution is abridged when the State affirmatively sponsors the particular religious practice of prayer.

IV

Finally, the District argues repeatedly that the Does have made a premature facial challenge to the October policy that necessarily must fail. The District emphasizes, quite correctly, that until a student actually delivers a solemnizing message under the latest version of the policy, there can be no certainty that any of the statements or invocations will be religious. Thus, it concludes, the October policy necessarily survives a facial challenge.

This argument, however, assumes that we are concerned only with the serious constitutional injury that occurs when a student is forced to participate in an act of religious worship because she chooses to attend a school event. But the Constitution also requires that we keep in mind "the myriad, subtle ways in which Establishment Clause values can be eroded,"

---

22. "We think the Government's position that this interest suffices to force students to choose between compliance or forfeiture demonstrates fundamental inconsistency in its argumentation. It fails to acknowledge that what for many of Deborah's classmates and their parents was a spiritual imperative was for Daniel and Deborah Weisman religious conformance compelled by the State. While in some societies the wishes of the majority might prevail, the Establishment Clause of the First Amendment is addressed to this contingency and rejects the balance urged upon us. The Constitution forbids the State to exact religious conformity from a student as the price of attending her own high school graduation. This is the calculus the Constitution commands." *Lee,* 505 U.S., at 595-596.

Lynch, 465 U.S., at 694 (*O'Connor, J.,* concurring), and that we guard against other different, yet equally important, constitutional injuries. One is the mere passage by the District of a policy that has the purpose and perception of government establishment of religion. Another is the implementation of a governmental electoral process that subjects the issue of prayer to a majoritarian vote.

The District argues that the facial challenge must fail because "Santa Fe's Football Policy cannot be invalidated on the basis of some 'possibility or even likelihood' of an unconstitutional application." Brief for Petitioner 17 (quoting *Bowen v. Kendrick,* 487 U.S. 589, 613 (1988)). Our Establishment Clause cases involving facial challenges, however, have not focused solely on the possible applications of the statute, but rather have considered whether the statute has an unconstitutional purpose. Writing for the Court in *Bowen, The Chief Justice* concluded that "[a]s in previous cases involving facial challenges on Establishment Clause grounds, *e.g., Edwards v. Aguillard,* [482 U.S. 578 (1987)]; *Mueller v. Allen,* 463 U.S. 388 (1983), we assess the constitutionality of an enactment by reference to the three factors first articulated in *Lemon v. Kurtzman,* 403 U.S. 602, 612 (1971) ..., which guides '[t]he general nature of our inquiry in this area,' *Mueller v. Allen, supra,* at 394." 487 U.S., at 602. Under the *Lemon* standard, a court must invalidate a statute if it lacks "a secular legislative purpose." *Lemon v. Kurtzman,* 403 U.S. 602, 612 (1971). It is therefore proper, as part of this facial challenge, for us to examine the purpose of the October policy.

As discussed, *supra,* at 14-15, 17, the text of the October policy alone reveals that it has an unconstitutional purpose. The plain language of the policy clearly spells out the extent of school involvement in both the election of the speaker and the content of the message. Additionally, the text of the October policy specifies only one, clearly preferred message—that of Santa Fe's traditional religious "invocation." Finally, the extremely selective access of the policy and other content restrictions confirm that it is not a content-neutral regulation that creates a limited public forum for the expression of student speech. Our examination, however, need not stop at an analysis of the text of the policy.

This case comes to us as the latest step in developing litigation brought as a challenge to institutional practices that unquestionably violated the Establishment Clause. One of those practices was the District's long-established tradition of sanctioning student-led prayer at varsity football games. The narrow question before us is whether implementation of the October policy insulates the continuation of such prayers from constitutional scrutiny. It does not. Our inquiry into this question not only can, but must, include an examination of the circumstances surrounding its enactment. Whether a government activity violates the Establishment Clause is "in large part a legal question to be answered on the basis of judicial interpretation of social facts. ... Every government practice must be judged in its unique circumstances. ..." *Lynch,* 465 U.S., at 693-694 (*O'Connor, J.,* concurring). Our discussion in the previous sections, *supra,* at 15-18, demonstrates that in this case the District's direct involvement with school prayer exceeds constitutional limits.

The District, nevertheless, asks us to pretend that we do not recognize what every Santa Fe High School student understands clearly—that this policy is about prayer. The District further asks us to accept what is obviously untrue: that these messages are necessary to "solemnize" a football game and that this single-student, year-long position is essential to the protection of student speech. We refuse to turn a blind eye to the context in which this policy arose, and that context quells any doubt that this policy was implemented with the purpose of endorsing school prayer.

Therefore, the simple enactment of this policy, with the purpose and perception of school endorsement of student prayer, was a constitutional violation. We need not wait for the inevitable to confirm and magnify the constitutional injury. In *Wallace,* for example, we invalidated Alabama's as yet unimplemented and voluntary "moment of silence" statute based on our conclusion that it was enacted "for the sole purpose of expressing the State's endorsement of prayer activities for one minute at the beginning of each school day." 472 U.S., at 60; see also *Church of Lukumi Babalu Aye, Inc. v. Hialeah,* 508 U.S. 520, 532 (1993). Therefore, even if no Santa Fe High School student were ever to offer a religious message, the October policy fails a facial challenge because the attempt by the District to encourage prayer is also at issue. Government efforts to endorse religion cannot evade constitutional reproach based solely on the remote possibility that those attempts may fail.

This policy likewise does not survive a facial challenge because it impermissibly imposes upon the student body a majoritarian election on the issue of prayer. Through its election scheme, the District has established a governmental electoral mechanism that turns the school into a forum for religious debate. It further empowers the student body majority with the authority to subject students of minority views to constitutionally improper messages. The award of that power alone, regardless of the students' ultimate use of it, is not acceptable.[23] Like the referendum in *Board of Regents of Univ. of Wis. System v. Southworth,* 529 U.S. (2000), the election mechanism established by the District undermines the essential protection of minority viewpoints. Such a system encourages divisiveness along religious lines and threatens the imposition of coercion upon those students not desiring to participate in a religious exercise. Simply by establishing this school-related procedure, which entrusts the inherently nongovernmental subject of religion to a majoritarian vote, a constitutional violation has occurred.[24] No further injury is required for the policy to fail a facial challenge.

To properly examine this policy on its face, we "must be deemed aware of the history and context of the community and forum," *Pinette,* 515 U.S., at 780 (*O'Connor, J.,* concurring in part and concurring in judgment). Our examination of those circumstances above leads to the conclusion that this policy does not provide the District with the constitutional safe harbor it sought. The policy is invalid on its face because it establishes an improper majoritarian election on religion, and unquestionably has the purpose and creates the perception of encouraging the delivery of prayer at a series of important school events.

The judgment of the Court of Appeals is, accordingly, affirmed.

It is so ordered.

---

23. *The Chief Justice* accuses us of "essentially invalidat[ing] all student elections," see *post,* at 5. This is obvious hyperbole. We have concluded that the resulting religious message under this policy would be attributable to the school, not just the student, see *supra,* at 9-18. For this reason, we now hold only that the District's decision to allow the student majority to control whether students of minority views are subjected to a school-sponsored prayer violates the Establishment Clause.

24. *The Chief Justice* contends that we have "misconstrue[d] the nature . . . [of] the policy as being an election on 'prayer' and 'religion,' " see *post,* at 3-4. We therefore reiterate that the District has stipulated to the facts that the most recent election was held "to determine whether a student would deliver *prayer* at varsity football games," that the "students chose to allow a student to say a *prayer* at football games," and that a second election was then held "to determine which student would deliver the *prayer.*" App. 65-66 (emphases added). Furthermore, the policy was titled "*Prayer* at Football Games." *Id.,* at 99 (emphasis added). Although the District has since eliminated the word "prayer" from the policy, it apparently viewed that change as sufficiently minor as to make holding a new election unnecessary.

CHAPTER 9

FREE SPEECH

Introduction

In addition to prayer in schools, the U.S. Supreme Court has been confronted with another First Amendment issue conserning the rights of children in a school setting to free speech. The principle of free expression is so fundamental to an open society that the right to freedom of expression is protected by the First Amendment. There are few people who would disagree that the government should never be allowed to stifle the free speech of American citizens. The debate, of course, concerns whether all speech should be protected. Thus, for example, should the First Amendment protect flag burning, hate speech, pornography, or even the offensive lyrics of modern music? The issues then are (1) whether some forms of speech should be prohibited; or (2) perhaps in certain settings not all speech is protected. Consequently, the issue arises whether public school students should be entitled to the same free speech rights when school authorities deem that certain speech, whether active or passive, jeopardizes the smooth functioning of the school system.

Free Speech at School

Case Comment

Tinker v. Des Moines School District (1969) was the first major U.S. Supreme Court case dealing with free speech in a public school setting. In this particular case the issue concerned "passive speech" because the expression was not associated with the actual speeking of words. The case involved students who wore black armbands to school to protest the Vietnam War in defiance of a school policy prohibiting such behavior. After having been suspended, the students filed a civil rights action that was dismissed by the district court and affirmed by the appellate court. However, the U.S. Supreme Court reversed the lower court decisions, ruling that neither students nor teachers shed their constitutional rights to freedom of speech or expression at the schoolhouse gate.

The *Tinker* case is significant because it recognizes the child's right to free speech in a public school system. *Tinker* established two things: (1) A child is entitled to free speech in school under the First Amendment of the U.S. Constitution; and (2) the test to determine whether the child has gone beyond proper speech is whether he or she materially and substantially interferes with the requirements of appropriate discipline in the operation of the school.

TINKER V. DES MOINES SCHOOL DISTRICT

Supreme Court of the United States, 1969.

393 U.S. 503.

Mr. Justice Fortas delivered the opinion of the Court.

Petitioner John F. Tinker, 15 years old, and petitioner Christopher Eckhardt, 16 years old, attended high schools in Des Moines, Iowa. Petitioner Mary Beth Tinker, John's sister, was a 13-year-old student in junior high school.

In December 1965, a group of adults and students in Des Moines held a meeting at the Eckhardt home. The group determined to publicize their objections to the hostilities in Vietnam and their support for a truce by wearing black armbands during the holiday season and by fasting on December 16 and New Year's Eve. Petitioners and their parents had previously engaged in similar activities, and they decided to participate in the program.

The principals of the Des Moines schools became aware of the plan to wear armbands. On December 14, 1965, they met and adopted a policy that any student wearing an armband to school would be asked to remove it, and if he refused he would be suspended until he returned without the armband. Petitioners were aware of the regulation that the school authorities adopted. On December 16, Mary Beth and Christopher wore black armbands to their schools. John Tinker wore his armband the next day. They were all sent home and suspended from school until they would come back without their armbands. They did not return to school until after the planned period for wearing armbands had expired—that is, until after New Year's Day.

This complaint was filed in the United States District Court by petitioners, through their fathers, under 1983 of Title 42 of the United States Code. It prayed for an injunction restraining the respondent school officials and the respondent members of the board of directors of the school district from disciplining the petitioners, and it sought nominal damages. After an evidentiary hearing the District Court dismissed the complaint. It upheld the constitutionality of the school authorities' action on the ground that it was reasonable in order to prevent disturbance of school discipline. 258 F. Supp. 971 (1966). The court referred to but expressly declined to follow the Fifth Circuit's holding in a similar case that the wearing of symbols like the armbands cannot be prohibited unless it "materially and substantially interfere[s] with the requirements of appropriate discipline in the operation of the school." *Burnside v. Byars*, 363 F.2d 744, 749 (1966).[1]

On appeal, the Court of Appeals for the Eighth Circuit considered the case en banc. The court was equally divided, and the District Court's decision was accordingly affirmed, without opinion. 383 F.2d 988 (1967). We granted certiorari. 390 U.S. 942 (1968).

---

1. In Burnside, the Fifth Circuit ordered that high school authorities be enjoined from enforcing a regulation forbidding students to wear "freedom buttons." It is instructive that in *Blackwell v. Issaquena County Board of Education*, 363 F.2d 749 (1966), the same panel on the same day reached the opposite result on different facts. It declined to enjoin enforcement of such a regulation in another high school where the students wearing freedom buttons harassed students who did not wear them and created much disturbance.

I

The District Court recognized that the wearing of an armband for the purpose of expressing certain views is the type of symbolic act that is within the Free Speech Clause of the First Amendment. See *West Virginia v. Barnette,* 319 U.S. 624 (1943); *Stromberg v. California,* 283 U.S. 359 (1931). Cf. *Thornhill v. Alabama,* 310 U.S. 88 (1940); *Edwards v. South Carolina,* 372 U.S. 229 (1963); *Brown v. Louisiana,* 383 U.S. 131 (1966). As we shall discuss, the wearing of armbands in the circumstances of this case was entirely divorced from actually or potentially disruptive conduct by those participating in it. It was closely akin to "pure speech" which, we have repeatedly held, is entitled to comprehensive protection under the First Amendment. Cf. *Cox v. Louisiana,* 379 U.S. 536, 555 (1965); *Adderley v. Florida,* 385 U.S. 39 (1966).

First Amendment rights, applied in light of the special characteristics of the school environment, are available to teachers and students. It can hardly be argued that either students or teachers shed their constitutional rights to freedom of speech or expression at the schoolhouse gate. This has been the unmistakable holding of this Court for almost 50 years. In *Meyer v. Nebraska,* 262 U.S. 390 (1923), and *Bartels v. Iowa,* 262 U.S. 404 (1923), this Court, in opinions by Mr. Justice McReynolds, held that the Due Process Clause of the Fourteenth Amendment prevents States from forbidding the teaching of a foreign language to young students. Statutes to this effect, the Court held, unconstitutionally interfere with the liberty of teacher, student, and parent.[2] See also *Pierce v. Society of Sisters,* 268 U.S. 510 (1925); *West Virginia v. Barnette,* 319 U.S. 624 (1943); *McCollum v. Board of Education,* 333 U.S. 203 (1948); *Wieman v. Updegraff,* 344 U.S. 183, 195 (1952) (concurring opinion); *Sweezy v. New Hampshire,* 354 U.S. 234 (1957); *Shelton v. Tucker,* 364 U.S. 479, 487 (1960); *Engel v. Vitale,* 370 U.S. 421 (1962); *Keyishian v. Board of Regents,* 385 U.S. 589, 603 (1967); *Epperson v. Arkansas,* ante, p. 97 (1968).

In *West Virginia v. Barnette,* supra, this Court held that under the First Amendment, the student in public school may not be compelled to salute the flag. Speaking through Mr. Justice Jackson, the Court said:

> "The Fourteenth Amendment, as now applied to the States, protects the citizen against the State itself and all of its creatures—Boards of Education not excepted. These have, of course, important, delicate, and highly discretionary functions, but none that they may not perform within the limits of the Bill of Rights. That they are educating the young for citizenship is reason for scrupulous protection of Constitutional freedoms of the individual, if we are not to strangle the free mind at

---

2. *Hamilton v. Regents of Univ. of Cal.,* 293 U.S. 245 (1934), is sometimes cited for the broad proposition that the State may attach conditions to attendance at a state university that require individuals to violate their religious convictions. The case involved dismissal of members of a religious denomination from a land grant college for refusal to participate in military training. Narrowly viewed, the case turns upon the Court's conclusion that merely requiring a student to participate in school training in military "science" could not conflict with his constitutionally protected freedom of conscience. The decision cannot be taken as establishing that the State may impose and enforce any conditions that it chooses upon attendance at public institutions of learning, however violative they may be of fundamental constitutional guarantees. See, e.g., *West Virginia v. Barnette,* 319 U.S. 624 (1943); *Dixon v. Alabama State Board of Education,* 294 F.2d 150 (C.A. 5th Cir. 1961); *Knight v. State Board of Education,* 200 F. Supp. 174 (D.C. M.D. Tenn. 1961); *Dickey v. Alabama State Board of Education,* 273 F. Supp. 613 (D.C. M.D. Ala. 1967). See also Note, Unconstitutional Conditions, 73 Harv. L. Rev. 1595 (1960); Note, Academic Freedom, 81 Harv. L. Rev. 1045 (1968).

its source and teach youth to discount important principles of our government as mere platitudes." 319 U.S., at 637.

On the other hand, the Court has repeatedly emphasized the need for affirming the comprehensive authority of the States and of school officials, consistent with fundamental constitutional safeguards, to prescribe and control conduct in the schools. See *Epperson v. Arkansas*, supra, at 104; *Meyer v. Nebraska*, supra, at 402. Our problem lies in the area where students in the exercise of First Amendment rights collide with the rules of the school authorities.

II

The problem posed by the present case does not relate to regulation of the length of skirts or the type of clothing, to hair style, or deportment. Cf. *Ferrell v. Dallas Independent School District*, 392 F.2d 697 (1968); *Pugsley v. Sellmeyer*, 158 Ark. 247, 250 S. W. 538 (1923). It does not concern aggressive, disruptive action or even group demonstrations. Our problem involves direct, primary First Amendment rights akin to "pure speech."

The school officials banned and sought to punish petitioners for a silent, passive expression of opinion, unaccompanied by any disorder or disturbance on the part of petitioners. There is here no evidence whatever of petitioners' interference, actual or nascent, with the schools' work or of collision with the rights of other students to be secure and to be let alone. Accordingly, this case does not concern speech or action that intrudes upon the work of the schools or the rights of other students.

Only a few of the 18,000 students in the school system wore the black armbands. Only five students were suspended for wearing them. There is no indication that the work of the schools or any class was disrupted. Outside the classrooms, a few students made hostile remarks to the children wearing armbands, but there were no threats or acts of violence on school premises.

The District Court concluded that the action of the school authorities was reasonable because it was based upon their fear of a disturbance from the wearing of the armbands. But, in our system, undifferentiated fear or apprehension of disturbance is not enough to overcome the right to freedom of expression. Any departure from absolute regimentation may cause trouble. Any variation from the majority's opinion may inspire fear. Any word spoken, in class, in the lunchroom, or on the campus, that deviates from the views of another person may start an argument or cause a disturbance. But our Constitution says we must take this risk, *Terminiello v. Chicago*, 337 U.S. 1 (1949); and our history says that it is this sort of hazardous freedom—this kind of openness—that is the basis of our national strength and of the independence and vigor of Americans who grow up and live in this relatively permissive, often disputatious, society.

In order for the State in the person of school officials to justify prohibition of a particular expression of opinion, it must be able to show that its action was caused by something more than a mere desire to avoid the discomfort and unpleasantness that always accompany an unpopular viewpoint. Certainly where there is no finding and no showing that engaging in the forbidden conduct would "materially and substantially interfere with the requirements of appropriate discipline in the operation of the school," the prohibition cannot be sustained. *Burnside v. Byars*, supra, at 749.

In the present case, the District Court made no such finding, and our independent examination of the record fails to yield evidence that the school authorities had reason to anticipate that the wearing of the armbands would substantially interfere with the work of the school or impinge upon the rights of other students. Even an official memorandum prepared after the suspension that listed the reasons for the ban on wearing the armbands made no reference to the anticipation of such disruption.[3]

On the contrary, the action of the school authorities appears to have been based upon an urgent wish to avoid the controversy which might result from the expression, even by the silent symbol of armbands, of opposition to this Nation's part in the conflagration in Vietnam.[4] It is revealing, in this respect, that the meeting at which the school principals decided to issue the contested regulation was called in response to a student's statement to the journalism teacher in one of the schools that he wanted to write an article on Vietnam and have it published in the school paper. (The student was dissuaded.[5])

It is also relevant that the school authorities did not purport to prohibit the wearing of all symbols of political or controversial significance. The record shows that students in some of the schools wore buttons relating to national political campaigns, and some even wore the Iron Cross, traditionally a symbol of Nazism. The order prohibiting the wearing of armbands did not extend to these. Instead, a particular symbol—black armbands worn to exhibit opposition to this Nation's involvement in Vietnam—was singled out for prohibition. Clearly, the prohibition of expression of one particular opinion, at least without evidence that it is necessary to avoid material and substantial interference with schoolwork or discipline, is not constitutionally permissible.

In our system, state-operated schools may not be enclaves of totalitarianism. School officials do not possess absolute authority over their students. Students in school as well as out of school are "persons" under our Constitution. They are possessed of fundamental

---

3. The only suggestions of fear of disorder in the report are these:

"A former student of one of our high schools was killed in Viet Nam. Some of his friends are still in school and it was felt that if any kind of a demonstration existed, it might evolve into something which would be difficult to control."

"Students at one of the high schools were heard to say they would wear arm bands of other colors if the black bands prevailed."

Moreover, the testimony of school authorities at trial indicates that it was not fear of disruption that motivated the regulation prohibiting the armbands; the regulation was directed against "the principle of the demonstration" itself. School authorities simply felt that "the schools are no place for demonstrations," and if the students "didn't like the way our elected officials were handling things, it should be handled with the ballot box and not in the halls of our public schools."

4. The District Court found that the school authorities, in prohibiting black armbands, were influenced by the fact that "[t]he Viet Nam war and the involvement of the United States therein has been the subject of a major controversy for some time. When the arm band regulation involved herein was promulgated, debate over the Viet Nam war had become vehement in many localities. A protest march against the war had been recently held in Washington, D.C. A wave of draft card burning incidents protesting the war had swept the country. At that time two highly publicized draft card burning cases were pending in this Court. Both individuals supporting the war and those opposing it were quite vocal in expressing their views." 258 F. Supp., at 972–973.

5. After the principals' meeting, the director of secondary education and the principal of the high school informed the student that the principals were opposed to publication of his article. They reported that "we felt that it was a very friendly conversation, although we did not feel that we had convinced the student that our decision was a just one."

rights which the State must respect, just as they themselves must respect their obligations to the State. In our system, students may not be regarded as closed-circuit recipients of only that which the State chooses to communicate. They may not be confined to the expression of those sentiments that are officially approved. In the absence of a specific showing of constitutionally valid reasons to regulate their speech, students are entitled to freedom of expression of their views. As Judge Gewin, speaking for the Fifth Circuit, said, school officials cannot suppress "expressions of feelings with which they do not wish to contend." *Burnside v. Byars*, supra, at 749.

In *Meyer v. Nebraska*, supra, at 402, Mr. Justice McReynolds expressed this Nation's repudiation of the principle that a State might so conduct its schools as to "foster a homogeneous people." He said:

"In order to submerge the individual and develop ideal citizens, Sparta assembled the males at seven into barracks and intrusted their subsequent education and training to official guardians. Although such measures have been deliberately approved by men of great genius, their ideas touching the relation between individual and State were wholly different from those upon which our institutions rest; and it hardly will be affirmed that any legislature could impose such restrictions upon the people of a State without doing violence to both letter and spirit of the Constitution."

This principle has been repeated by this Court on numerous occasions during the intervening years. In *Keyishian v. Board of Regents,* 385 U.S. 589, 603, Mr. Justice Brennan, speaking for the Court, said:

"'The vigilant protection of constitutional freedoms is nowhere more vital than in the community of American schools.' *Shelton v. Tucker* at 487. The classroom is peculiarly the 'marketplace of ideas.' The Nation's future depends upon leaders trained through wide exposure to that robust exchange of ideas which discovers truth 'out of a multitude of tongues, [rather] than through any kind of authoritative selection.'"

The principle of these cases is not confined to the supervised and ordained discussion which takes place in the classroom. The principal use to which the schools are dedicated is to accommodate students during prescribed hours for the purpose of certain types of activities. Among those activities is personal intercommunication among the students.[6] This is not only an inevitable part of the process of attending school; it is also an important part of the educational process. A student's rights, therefore, do not embrace merely the classroom hours. When he is in the cafeteria, or on the playing field, or on the campus during the authorized hours, he may express his opinions, even on controversial subjects like the conflict in Vietnam, if he does so without "materially and substantially interfer[ing] with the requirements of appropriate discipline in the operation of the school" and without colliding with the rights of others. *Burnside v. Byars*, supra, at 749. But conduct by the student, in class

---

6. In *Hammond v. South Carolina State College,* 272 F. Supp. 947 (D.C. S.C. 1967), District Judge Hemphill had before him a case involving a meeting on campus of 300 students to express their views on school practices. He pointed out that a school is not like a hospital or a jail enclosure. Cf. *Cox v. Louisiana,* 379 U.S. 536 (1965); *Adderley v. Florida,* 385 U.S. 39 (1966). It is a public place, and its dedication to specific uses does not imply that the constitutional rights of persons entitled to be there are to be gauged as if the premises were purely private property. Cf. *Edwards v. South Carolina,* 372 U.S. 229 (1963); *Brown v. Louisiana,* 383 U.S. 131 (1966).

or out of it, which for any reason—whether it stems from time, place, or type of behavior—materially disrupts classwork or involves substantial disorder or invasion of the rights of others is, of course, not immunized by the constitutional guarantee of freedom of speech. Cf. *Blackwell v. Issaquena County Board of Education*, 363 F.2d 749 (C.A. 5th Cir. 1966).

Under our Constitution, free speech is not a right that is given only to be so circumscribed that it exists in principle but not in fact. Freedom of expression would not truly exist if the right could be exercised only in an area that a benevolent government has provided as a safe haven for crackpots. The Constitution says that Congress (and the States) may not abridge the right to free speech. This provision means what it says. We properly read it to permit reasonable regulation of speech-connected activities in carefully restricted circumstances. But we do not confine the permissible exercise of First Amendment rights to a telephone booth or the four corners of a pamphlet, or to supervised and ordained discussion in a school classroom.

If a regulation were adopted by school officials forbidding discussion of the Vietnam conflict, or the expression by any student of opposition to it anywhere on school property except as part of a prescribed classroom exercise, it would be obvious that the regulation would violate the constitutional rights of students, at least if it could not be justified by a showing that the students' activities would materially and substantially disrupt the work and discipline of the school. Cf. *Hammond v. South Carolina State College*, 272 F. Supp. 947 (D.C. S.C. 1967) (orderly protest meeting on state college campus); *Dickey v. Alabama State Board of Education*, 273 F. Supp. 613 (D.C. M.D. Ala. 1967) (expulsion of student editor of college newspaper). In the circumstances of the present case, the prohibition of the silent, passive "witness of the armbands," as one of the children called it, is no less offensive to the Constitution's guarantees.

As we have discussed, the record does not demonstrate any facts which might reasonably have led school authorities to forecast substantial disruption of or material interference with school activities, and no disturbances or disorders on the school premises in fact occurred. These petitioners merely went about their ordained rounds in school. Their deviation consisted only in wearing on their sleeve a band of black cloth, not more than two inches wide. They wore it to exhibit their disapproval of the Vietnam hostilities and their advocacy of a truce, to make their views known, and, by their example, to influence others to adopt them. They neither interrupted school activities nor sought to intrude in the school affairs or the lives of others. They caused discussion outside of the classrooms, but no interference with work and no disorder. In the circumstances, our Constitution does not permit officials of the State to deny their form of expression.

We express no opinion as to the form of relief which should be granted, this being a matter for the lower courts to determine. We reverse and remand for further proceedings consistent with this opinion.

Reversed and remanded.

Case Comment

The concept of free speech articulated in *Tinker* can be contrasted with the "active speech" issue raised in *Hazlewood School District v. Kuhlmeier*. In *Kuhlmeier*, three student staff members of a high school newspaper filed suit against the local school board contending that their First Amendment rights were violated by the principal's censorship of articles in the student newspaper. The Supreme Court ruled that that the school newspaper was not a public forum and that school officials could act to impose reasonable limitations on what students could print in a school-sponsored publication. The Supreme Court also ruled that the First Amendment rights of students in the public schools are not automatically coextensive with the rights of adults in other settings, and must be applied in light of the special characteristics of the school environment. A school need not tolerate student speech that is inconsistent with its basic educational mission, even though the government could not censor similar speech outside the school.

HAZLEWOOD SCHOOL DISTRICT V. KUHLMEIER

Supreme Court of the United States, 1988.

484 U.S. 260.

Justice White delivered the opinion of the Court.

This case concerns the extent to which educators may exercise editorial control over the contents of a high school newspaper produced as part of the school's journalism curriculum.

I

Petitioners are the Hazelwood School District in St. Louis County, Missouri; various school officials; Robert Eugene Reynolds, the principal of Hazelwood East High School; and Howard Emerson, a teacher in the school district. Respondents are three former Hazelwood East students who were staff members of *Spectrum,* the school newspaper. They contend that school officials violated their First Amendment rights by deleting two pages of articles from the May 13, 1983, issue of *Spectrum.*

Spectrum was written and edited by the Journalism II class at Hazelwood East. The newspaper was published every three weeks or so during the 1982–1983 school year. More than 4,500 copies of the newspaper were distributed during that year to students, school personnel, and members of the community.

The Board of Education allocated funds from its annual budget for the printing of *Spectrum.* These funds were supplemented by proceeds from sales of the newspaper. The printing expenses during the 1982–1983 school year totaled $4,668.50; revenue from sales was $1,166.84. The other costs associated with the newspaper—such as supplies, textbooks, and a portion of the journalism teacher's salary—were borne entirely by the Board. The Journalism II course was taught by Robert Stergos for most of the 1982–1983 academic year. Stergos left Hazelwood East to take a job in private industry on April 29, 1983, when the May 13 edition of *Spectrum* was nearing completion, and petitioner Emerson took his place as newspaper adviser for the remaining weeks of the term.

The practice at Hazelwood East during the spring 1983 semester was for the journalism teacher to submit page proofs of each *Spectrum* issue to Principal Reynolds for his review prior to publication. On May 10, Emerson delivered the proofs of the May 13 edition to Reynolds, who objected to two of the articles scheduled to appear in that edition. One of the stories described three Hazelwood East students' experiences with pregnancy; the other discussed the impact of divorce on students at the school.

Reynolds was concerned that, although the pregnancy story used false names "to keep the identity of these girls a secret," the pregnant students still might be identifiable from the text. He also believed that the article's references to sexual activity and birth control were inappropriate for some of the younger students at the school. In addition, Reynolds was concerned that a student identified by name in the divorce story had complained that her father "wasn't spending enough time with my mom, my sister and I" prior to the divorce, "was always out of town on business or out late playing cards with the guys," and "always argued about everything" with her mother. App. to Pet. for Cert. 38. Reynolds believed that the student's parents should have been given an opportunity to respond to these remarks or to consent to their publication. He was unaware that Emerson had deleted the student's name from the final version of the article.

Reynolds believed that there was no time to make the necessary changes in the stories before the scheduled press run and that the newspaper would not appear before the end of the school year if printing were delayed to any significant extent. He concluded that his only options under the circumstances were to publish a four-page newspaper instead of the planned six-page newspaper, eliminating the two pages on which the offending stories appeared, or to publish no newspaper at all. Accordingly, he directed Emerson to withhold from publication the two pages containing the stories on pregnancy and divorce.[1] He informed his superiors of the decision, and they concurred.

Respondents subsequently commenced this action in the United States District Court for the Eastern District of Missouri seeking a declaration that their First Amendment rights had been violated, injunctive relief, and monetary damages. After a bench trial, the District Court denied an injunction, holding that no First Amendment violation had occurred. 607 F. Supp. 1450 (1985).

The District Court concluded that school officials may impose restraints on students' speech in activities that are "'an integral part of the school's educational function'"— including the publication of a school-sponsored newspaper by a journalism class—so long as their decision has "'a substantial and reasonable basis.'" Id., at 1466 (quoting *Frasca v. Andrews*, 463 F. Supp. 1043, 1052 (EDNY 1979)). The court found that Principal Reynolds' concern that the pregnant student's anonymity would be lost and their privacy invaded was "legitimate and reasonable," given "the small number of pregnant students at Hazelwood East and several identifying characteristics that were disclosed in the article." 607 F. Supp., at 1466. The court held that Reynolds' action was also justified "to avoid the impression that [the school] endorses the sexual norms of the subjects" and to shield younger students from exposure to unsuitable material. Ibid. The deletion of the article on divorce was seen by the court as a reasonable response to the invasion of privacy concerns raised by the named student's remarks. Because the article did not indicate that the student's parents had been offered an opportunity to respond to her allegations, said the court, there was cause for "serious doubt that the article complied with the rules of fairness which are standard in the field of journalism and which were covered in the textbook used in the Journalism II class." Id., at

---

1. The two pages deleted from the newspaper also contained articles on teenage marriage, runaways, and juvenile delinquents, as well as a general article on teenage pregnancy. Reynolds testified that he had no objection to these articles and that they were deleted only because they appeared on the same pages as the two objectionable articles.

1467. Furthermore, the court concluded that Reynolds was justified in deleting two full pages of the newspaper, instead of deleting only the pregnancy and divorce stories or requiring that those stories be modified to address his concerns, based on his "reasonable belief that he had to make an immediate decision and that there was no time to make modifications to the articles in question." Id., at 1466.

The Court of Appeals for the Eighth Circuit reversed. 795 F.2d 1368 (1986). The court held at the outset that *Spectrum* was not only "a part of the school adopted curriculum," id., at 1373, but also a public forum, because the newspaper was "intended to be and operated as a conduit for student viewpoint." Id., at 1372. The court then concluded that *Spectrum*'s status as a public forum precluded school officials from censoring its contents except when "'necessary to avoid material and substantial interference with school work or discipline . . . or the rights of others.'" Id., at 1374 (quoting *Tinker v. Des Moines Independent Community School Dist.,* 393 U.S. 503, 511 (1969)).

The Court of Appeals found "no evidence in the record that the principal could have reasonably forecast that the censored articles or any materials in the censored articles would have materially disrupted classwork or given rise to substantial disorder in the school." 795 F.2d, at 1375. School officials were entitled to censor the articles on the ground that they invaded the rights of others, according to the court, only if publication of the articles could have resulted in tort liability to the school. The court concluded that no tort action for libel or invasion of privacy could have been maintained against the school by the subjects of the two articles or by their families. Accordingly, the court held that school officials had violated respondents' First Amendment rights by deleting the two pages of the newspaper.

We granted certiorari, 479 U.S. 1053 (1987), and we now reverse.

II

Students in the public schools do not "shed their constitutional rights to freedom of speech or expression at the schoolhouse gate." *Tinker,* supra, at 506. They cannot be punished merely for expressing their personal views on the school premises—whether "in the cafeteria, or on the playing field, or on the campus during the authorized hours," 393 U.S., at 512–513—unless school authorities have reason to believe that such expression will "substantially interfere with the work of the school or impinge upon the rights of other students." Id., at 509.

We have nonetheless recognized that the First Amendment rights of students in the public schools "are not automatically coextensive with the rights of adults in other settings," *Bethel School District No. 403 v. Fraser,* 478 U.S. 675, 682 (1986), and must be "applied in light of the special characteristics of the school environment." *Tinker,* supra, at 506; cf. *New Jersey v. T.L.O.,* 469 U.S. 325, 341–343 (1985). A school need not tolerate student speech that is inconsistent with its "basic educational mission," *Fraser,* supra, at 685, even though the government could not censor similar speech outside the school. Accordingly, we held in *Fraser* that a student could be disciplined for having delivered a speech that was "sexually explicit" but not legally obscene at an official school assembly, because the school was entitled to "disassociate itself" from the speech in a manner that would demonstrate to others that such vulgarity is "wholly inconsistent with the 'fundamental values' of public school education." 478 U.S., at 685–686. We thus recognized that "[t]he determination of what manner of speech in the classroom or in school assembly is inappropriate properly rests with the school board," id., at 683, rather than with the federal courts. It is in this context that respondents' First Amendment claims must be considered.

A

We deal first with the question whether *Spectrum* may appropriately be characterized as a forum for public expression. The public schools do not possess all of the attributes of streets, parks, and other traditional public forums that "time out of mind, have been used for purposes of assembly, communicating thoughts between citizens, and discussing public questions." *Hague v. CIO,* 307 U.S. 496, 515 (1939). Cf. *Widmar v. Vincent,* 454 U.S. 263, 267–268, n. 5 (1981). Hence, school facilities may be deemed to be public forums only if school authorities have "by policy or by practice" opened those facilities "for indiscriminate use by the general public," *Perry Education Assn. v. Perry Local Educators' Assn.,* 460 U.S. 37, 47 (1983), or by some segment of the public, such as student organizations. Id., at 46, n. 7 (citing *Widmar v. Vincent*). If the facilities have instead been reserved for other intended purposes, "communicative or otherwise," then no public forum has been created, and school officials may impose reasonable restrictions on the speech of students, teachers, and other members of the school community. 460 U.S., at 46, n. 7. "The government does not create a public forum by inaction or by permitting limited discourse, but only by intentionally opening a nontraditional forum for public discourse." *Cornelius v. NAACP Legal Defense & Educational Fund, Inc.,* 473 U.S. 788, 802 (1985).

The policy of school officials toward *Spectrum* was reflected in Hazelwood School Board Policy 348.51 and the Hazelwood East Curriculum Guide. Board Policy 348.51 provided that "[s]chool sponsored publications are developed within the adopted curriculum and its educational implications in regular classroom activities." App. 22. The Hazelwood East Curriculum Guide described the Journalism II course as a "laboratory situation in which the students publish the school newspaper applying skills they have learned in Journalism I." Id., at 11. The lessons that were to be learned from the Journalism II course, according to the Curriculum Guide, included development of journalistic skills under deadline pressure, "the legal, moral, and ethical restrictions imposed upon journalists within the school community," and "responsibility and acceptance of criticism for articles of opinion." Ibid. Journalism II was taught by a faculty member during regular class hours. Students received grades and academic credit for their performance in the course.

School officials did not deviate in practice from their policy that production of *Spectrum* was to be part of the educational curriculum and a "regular classroom activit[y]." The District Court found that Robert Stergos, the journalism teacher during most of the 1982–1983 school year, "both had the authority to exercise and in fact exercised a great deal of control over *Spectrum.*" 607 F. Supp., at 1453. For example, Stergos selected the editors of the newspaper, scheduled publication dates, decided the number of pages for each issue, assigned story ideas to class members, advised students on the development of their stories, reviewed the use of quotations, edited stories, selected and edited the letters to the editor, and dealt with the printing company. Many of these decisions were made without consultation with the Journalism II students. The District Court thus found it "clear that Mr. Stergos was the final authority with respect to almost every aspect of the production and publication of

Spectrum, including its content." Ibid. Moreover, after each *Spectrum* issue had been finally approved by Stergos or his successor, the issue still had to be reviewed by Principal Reynolds prior to publication. Respondents' assertion that they had believed that they could publish "practically anything" in *Spectrum* was therefore dismissed by the District Court as simply "not credible." Id., at 1456. These factual findings are amply supported by the record, and were not rejected as clearly erroneous by the Court of Appeals.

The evidence relied upon by the Court of Appeals in finding *Spectrum* to be a public forum, see 795 F.2d, at 1372-1373, is equivocal at best. For example, Board Policy 348.51, which stated in part that "[s]chool sponsored student publications will not restrict free expression or diverse viewpoints within the rules of responsible journalism," also stated that such publications were "developed within the adopted curriculum and its educational implications." App. 22. One might reasonably infer from the full text of Policy 348.51 that school officials retained ultimate control over what constituted "responsible journalism" in a school-sponsored newspaper. Although the Statement of Policy published in the September 14, 1982, issue of *Spectrum* declared that "*Spectrum,* as a student-press publication, accepts all rights implied by the First Amendment," this statement, understood in the context of the paper's role in the school's curriculum, suggests at most that the administration will not interfere with the students' exercise of those First Amendment rights that attend the publication of a school-sponsored newspaper. It does not reflect an intent to expand those rights by converting a curricular newspaper into a public forum.[2] Finally, that students were permitted to exercise some authority over the contents of *Spectrum* was fully consistent with the Curriculum Guide objective of teaching the Journalism II students "leadership responsibilities as issue and page editors." App. 11. A decision to teach leadership skills in the context of a classroom activity hardly implies a decision to relinquish school control over that activity. In sum, the evidence relied upon by the Court of Appeals fails to demonstrate the "clear intent to create a public forum," *Cornelius,* 473 U.S., at 802, that existed in cases in which we found public forums to have been created. See id., at 802–803 (citing *Widmar v. Vincent,* 454 U.S., at 267; *Madison School District v. Wisconsin Employment Relations Comm'n,* 429 U.S. 167, 174, n. 6 (1976); *Southeastern Promotions, Ltd. v. Conrad,* 420 U.S. 546, 555 (1975)). School officials did not evince either "by policy or by practice," Perry Education Assn., 460 U.S., at 47, any intent to open the pages of *Spectrum* to "indiscriminate use," ibid., by its student reporters and editors, or by the student body generally. Instead, they "reserve[d] the forum for its intended purpos[e]," id., at 46, as a supervised learning experience for journalism students. Accordingly, school officials were entitled to regulate the contents of *Spectrum* in any reasonable manner. Ibid. It is this standard, rather than our decision in *Tinker,* that governs this case.

---

2. The Statement also cited *Tinker v. Des Moines Independent Community School Dist.,* 393 U.S. 503 (1969), for the proposition that "[o]nly speech that 'materially and substantially interferes with the requirements of appropriate discipline' can be found unacceptable and therefore be prohibited." App. 26. This portion of the Statement does not, of course, even accurately reflect our holding in *Tinker.* Furthermore, the Statement nowhere expressly extended the *Tinker* standard to the news and feature articles contained in a school-sponsored newspaper. The dissent apparently finds as a fact that the Statement was published annually in *Spectrum;* however, the District Court was unable to conclude that the Statement appeared on more than one occasion. In any event, even if the Statement says what the dissent believes that it says, the evidence that school officials never intended to designate *Spectrum* as a public forum remains overwhelming.

B

The question whether the First Amendment requires a school to tolerate particular student speech—the question that we addressed in *Tinker*—is different from the question whether the First Amendment requires a school affirmatively to promote particular student speech. The former question addresses educators' ability to silence a student's personal expression that happens to occur on the school premises. The latter question concerns educators' authority over school-sponsored publications, theatrical productions, and other expressive activities that students, parents, and members of the public might reasonably perceive to bear the imprimatur of the school. These activities may fairly be characterized as part of the school curriculum, whether or not they occur in a traditional classroom setting, so long as they are supervised by faculty members and designed to impart particular knowledge or skills to student participants and audiences.[3]

Educators are entitled to exercise greater control over this second form of student expression to assure that participants learn whatever lessons the activity is designed to teach, that readers or listeners are not exposed to material that may be inappropriate for their level of maturity, and that the views of the individual speaker are not erroneously attributed to the school. Hence, a school may in its capacity as publisher of a school newspaper or producer of a school play "disassociate itself," *Fraser,* 478 U.S., at 685, not only from speech that would "substantially interfere with [its] work . . . or impinge upon the rights of other students," *Tinker,* 393 U.S., at 509, but also from speech that is, for example, ungrammatical, poorly written, inadequately researched, biased or prejudiced, vulgar or profane, or unsuitable for immature audiences.[4] A school must be able to set high standards for the student speech that is disseminated under its auspices—standards that may be higher than those demanded by some newspaper publishers or theatrical producers in the "real" world—and may refuse to disseminate student speech that does not meet those standards. In addition, a school must be able to take into account the emotional maturity of the intended audience in determining whether to disseminate student speech on potentially sensitive topics, which might range from the existence of Santa Claus in an elementary school setting to the particulars of teenage sexual activity in a high school setting. A school must also retain the authority to refuse to sponsor student speech that might reasonably be perceived to advocate drug or alcohol use, irresponsible sex, or conduct otherwise inconsistent with "the shared values of a civilized social order," *Fraser,* supra, at 683, or to associate the school with any position other than neutrality on matters of political controversy. Otherwise, the schools would be unduly constrained

---

3. The distinction that we draw between speech that is sponsored by the school and speech that is not is fully consistent with *Papish v. University of Missouri Board of Curators,* 410 U.S. 667 (1973) (per curiam), which involved an off-campus "underground" newspaper that school officials merely had allowed to be sold on a state university campus.

4. The dissent perceives no difference between the First Amendment analysis applied in *Tinker* and that applied in *Fraser.* We disagree. The decision in *Fraser* rested on the "vulgar," "lewd," and "plainly offensive" character of a speech delivered at an official school assembly rather than on any propensity of the speech to "materially disrup[t] classwork or involv[e] substantial disorder or invasion of the rights of others." 393 U.S., at 513. Indeed, the *Fraser* Court cited as "especially relevant" a portion of Justice Black's dissenting opinion in *Tinker* "'disclaim[ing] any purpose . . . to hold that the Federal Constitution compels the teachers, parents, and elected school officials to surrender control of the American public school system to public school students.'" 478 U.S., at 686 (quoting 393 U.S., at 526). Of course, Justice Black's observations are equally relevant to the instant case.

from fulfilling their role as "a principal instrument in awakening the child to cultural values, in preparing him for later professional training, and in helping him to adjust normally to his environment." *Brown v. Board of Education,* 347 U.S. 483, 493 (1954).

Accordingly, we conclude that the standard articulated in *Tinker* for determining when a school may punish student expression need not also be the standard for determining when a school may refuse to lend its name and resources to the dissemination of student expression.[5] Instead, we hold that educators do not offend the First Amendment by exercising editorial control over the style and content of student speech in school-sponsored expressive activities so long as their actions are reasonably related to legitimate pedagogical concerns.[6]

This standard is consistent with our oft-expressed view that the education of the Nation's youth is primarily the responsibility of parents, teachers, and state and local school officials, and not of federal judges. See, e.g., *Board of Education of Hendrick Hudson Central School Dist. v. Rowley,* 458 U.S. 176, 208 (1982); *Wood v. Strickland,* 420 U.S. 308, 326 (1975); *Epperson v. Arkansas,* 393 U.S. 97, 104 (1968). It is only when the decision to censor a school-sponsored publication, theatrical production, or other vehicle of student expression has no valid educational purpose that the First Amendment is so "directly and sharply implicate[d]," ibid., as to require judicial intervention to protect students' constitutional rights.[7]

III

We also conclude that Principal Reynolds acted reasonably in requiring the deletion from the May 13 issue of *Spectrum* of the pregnancy article, the divorce article, and the remaining articles that were to appear on the same pages of the newspaper.

The initial paragraph of the pregnancy article declared that "[a]ll names have been changed to keep the identity of these girls a secret." The principal concluded that the students' anonymity was not adequately protected, however, given the other identifying information in the article and the small number of pregnant students at the school. Indeed, a teacher at the school credibly testified that she could positively identify at least one of the girls and possibly all three. It is likely that many students at Hazelwood East would have been at least

---

5. We therefore need not decide whether the Court of Appeals correctly construed *Tinker* as precluding school officials from censoring student speech to avoid "invasion of the rights of others," 393 U.S., at 513, except where that speech could result in tort liability to the school.

6. We reject respondents' suggestion that school officials be permitted to exercise prepublication control over school-sponsored publications only pursuant to specific written regulations. To require such regulations in the context of a curricular activity could unduly constrain the ability of educators to educate. We need not now decide whether such regulations are required before school officials may censor publications not sponsored by the school that students seek to distribute on school grounds. See *Baughman v. Freienmuth,* 478 F.2d 1345 (CA4 1973); *Shanley v. Northeast Independent School Dist.,* Bexar Cty., Tex., 462 F.2d 960 (CA5 1972); *Eisner v. Stamford Board of Education,* 440 F.2d 803 (CA2 1971).

7. A number of lower federal courts have similarly recognized that educators' decisions with regard to the content of school-sponsored newspapers, dramatic productions, and other expressive activities are entitled to substantial deference. See, e.g., *Nicholson v. Board of Education, Torrance Unified School Dist.,* 682 F.2d 858 (CA9 1982); *Seyfried v. Walton,* 668 F.2d 214 (CA3 1981); *Trachtman v. Anker,* 563 F.2d 512 (CA2 1977), cert. denied, 435 U.S. 925 (1978); *Frasca v. Andrews,* 463 F. Supp. 1043 (EDNY 1979). We need not now decide whether the same degree of deference is appropriate with respect to school-sponsored expressive activities at the college and university level.

as successful in identifying the girls. Reynolds therefore could reasonably have feared that the article violated whatever pledge of anonymity had been given to the pregnant students. In addition, he could reasonably have been concerned that the article was not sufficiently sensitive to the privacy interests of the students' boyfriends and parents, who were discussed in the article but who were given no opportunity to consent to its publication or to offer a response. The article did not contain graphic accounts of sexual activity. The girls did comment in the article, however, concerning their sexual histories and their use or nonuse of birth control. It was not unreasonable for the principal to have concluded that such frank talk was inappropriate in a school-sponsored publication distributed to 14-year-old freshmen and presumably taken home to be read by students' even younger brothers and sisters.

The student who was quoted by name in the version of the divorce article seen by Principal Reynolds made comments sharply critical of her father. The principal could reasonably have concluded that an individual publicly identified as an inattentive parent—indeed, as one who chose "playing cards with the guys" over home and family—was entitled to an opportunity to defend himself as a matter of journalistic fairness. These concerns were shared by both of *Spectrum*'s faculty advisers for the 1982–1983 school year, who testified that they would not have allowed the article to be printed without deletion of the student's name.[8]

Principal Reynolds testified credibly at trial that, at the time that he reviewed the proofs of the May 13 issue during an extended telephone conversation with Emerson, he believed that there was no time to make any changes in the articles, and that the newspaper had to be printed immediately or not at all. It is true that Reynolds did not verify whether the necessary modifications could still have been made in the articles, and that Emerson did not volunteer the information that printing could be delayed until the changes were made. We nonetheless agree with the District Court that the decision to excise the two pages containing the problematic articles was reasonable given the particular circumstances of this case. These circumstances included the very recent replacement of Stergos by Emerson, who may not have been entirely familiar with *Spectrum* editorial and production procedures, and the pressure felt by Reynolds to make an immediate decision so that students would not be deprived of the newspaper altogether. In sum, we cannot reject as unreasonable Principal Reynolds' conclusion that neither the pregnancy article nor the divorce article was suitable for publication in *Spectrum*. Reynolds could reasonably have concluded that the students who had written and edited these articles had not sufficiently mastered those portions of the Journalism II curriculum that pertained to the treatment of controversial issues and personal attacks, the need to protect the privacy of individuals whose most intimate concerns are to be revealed in the newspaper, and "the legal, moral, and ethical restrictions imposed

---

8. The reasonableness of Principal Reynolds' concerns about the two articles was further substantiated by the trial testimony of Martin Duggan, a former editorial page editor of the *St. Louis Globe Democrat* and a former college journalism instructor and newspaper adviser. Duggan testified that the divorce story did not meet journalistic standards of fairness and balance because the father was not given an opportunity to respond, and that the pregnancy story was not appropriate for publication in a high school newspaper because it was unduly intrusive into the privacy of the girls, their parents, and their boyfriends. The District Court found Duggan to be "an objective and independent witness" whose testimony was entitled to significant weight. 607 F. Supp. 1450, 1461 (ED Mo. 1985).

upon journalists within [a] school community" that includes adolescent subjects and readers. Finally, we conclude that the principal's decision to delete two pages of *Spectrum*, rather than to delete only the offending articles or to require that they be modified, was reasonable under the circumstances as he understood them. Accordingly, no violation of First Amendment rights occurred.[9]

The judgment of the Court of Appeals for the Eighth Circuit is therefore
Reversed.

Justice Brennan, with whom Justice Marshall and Justice Blackmun join, dissenting.

When the young men and women of Hazelwood East High School registered for Journalism II, they expected a civics lesson. *Spectrum*, the newspaper they were to publish, "was not just a class exercise in which students learned to prepare papers and hone writing skills, it was a ... forum established to give students an opportunity to express their views while gaining an appreciation of their rights and responsibilities under the First Amendment to the United States Constitution. ..." 795 F.2d 1368, 1373 (CA8 1986). "[A]t the beginning of each school year," id., at 1372, the student journalists published a Statement of Policy—tacitly approved each year by school authorities—announcing their expectation that "*Spectrum*, as a student-press publication, accepts all rights implied by the First Amendment. ... Only speech that 'materially and substantially interferes with the requirements of appropriate discipline' can be found unacceptable and therefore prohibited." App. 26 (quoting *Tinker v. Des Moines Independent Community School Dist.*, 393 U.S. 503, 513 (1969)).[1] The school board itself affirmatively guaranteed the students of Journalism II an atmosphere conducive to fostering such an appreciation and exercising the full panoply of rights associated with a free student press. "School sponsored student publications," it vowed, "will not restrict free expression or diverse viewpoints within the rules of responsible journalism." App. 22 (Board Policy 348.51).

This case arose when the Hazelwood East administration breached its own promise, dashing its students' expectations. The school principal, without prior consultation or explanation, excised six articles—comprising two full pages—of the May 13, 1983, issue of *Spectrum*. He did so not because any of the articles would "materially and substantially interfere with the requirements of appropriate discipline," but simply because he considered two of the six "inappropriate, personal, sensitive, and unsuitable" for student consumption. 795 F.2d, at 1371. In my view the principal broke more than just a promise. He violated the First Amendment's prohibitions against censorship of any student expression that neither disrupts classwork nor invades the rights of others, and against any censorship that is not narrowly tailored to serve its purpose.

---

9. It is likely that the approach urged by the dissent would as a practical matter have far more deleterious consequences for the student press than does the approach that we adopt today. The dissent correctly acknowledges "[t]he State's prerogative to dissolve the student newspaper entirely." Post, at 287. It is likely that many public schools would do just that rather than open their newspapers to all student expression that does not threaten "materia[l] disrup[tion of] classwork" or violation of "rights that are protected by law," post, at 289, regardless of how sexually explicit, racially intemperate, or personally insulting that expression otherwise might be.

1. The Court suggests that the passage quoted in the text did not "exten[d] the *Tinker* standard to the news and feature articles contained in a school-sponsored newspaper" because the passage did not expressly mention them. Ante, at 269, n. 2. It is hard to imagine why the Court (or anyone else) might expect a passage that applies categorically to "a student-press publication," composed almost exclusively of "news and feature articles," to mention those categories expressly. Understandably, neither court below so limited the passage.

I

Public education serves vital national interests in preparing the Nation's youth for life in our increasingly complex society and for the duties of citizenship in our democratic Republic. See *Brown v. Board of Education*, 347 U.S. 483, 493 (1954). The public school conveys to our young the information and tools required not merely to survive in, but to contribute to, civilized society. It also inculcates in tomorrow's leaders the "fundamental values necessary to the maintenance of a democratic political system. . . ." *Ambach v. Norwick*, 441 U.S. 68, 77 (1979). All the while, the public educator nurtures students' social and moral development by transmitting to them an official dogma of "'community values.'" *Board of Education v. Pico*, 457 U.S. 853, 864 (1982) (plurality opinion) (citation omitted).

The public educator's task is weighty and delicate indeed. It demands particularized and supremely subjective choices among diverse curricula, moral values, and political stances to teach or inculcate in students, and among various methodologies for doing so. Accordingly, we have traditionally reserved the "daily operation of school systems" to the States and their local school boards. *Epperson v. Arkansas*, 393 U.S. 97, 104 (1968); see *Board of Education v. Pico*, supra, at 863–864. We have not, however, hesitated to intervene where their decisions run afoul of the Constitution. See e.g., *Edwards v. Aguillard*, 482 U.S. 578 (1987) (striking state statute that forbade teaching of evolution in public school unless accompanied by instruction on theory of "creation science"); *Board of Education v. Pico*, supra (school board may not remove books from library shelves merely because it disapproves of ideas they express); *Epperson v. Arkansas*, supra (striking state-law prohibition against teaching Darwinian theory of evolution in public school); *West Virginia Board of Education v. Barnette*, 319 U.S. 624 (1943) (public school may not compel student to salute flag); *Meyer v. Nebraska*, 262 U.S. 390 (1923) (state law prohibiting the teaching of foreign languages in public or private schools is unconstitutional).

Free student expression undoubtedly sometimes interferes with the effectiveness of the school's pedagogical functions. Some brands of student expression do so by directly preventing the school from pursuing its pedagogical mission: The young polemic who stands on a soapbox during calculus class to deliver an eloquent political diatribe interferes with the legitimate teaching of calculus. And the student who delivers a lewd endorsement of a student-government candidate might so extremely distract an impressionable high school audience as to interfere with the orderly operation of the school. See *Bethel School Dist. No. 403 v. Fraser*, 478 U.S. 675 (1986). Other student speech, however, frustrates the school's legitimate pedagogical purposes merely by expressing a message that conflicts with the school's, without directly interfering with the school's expression of its message: A student who responds to a political science teacher's question with the retort, "socialism is good," subverts the school's inculcation of the message that capitalism is better. Even the maverick who sits in class passively sporting a symbol of protest against a government policy, cf. *Tinker v. Des Moines Independent Community School Dist.*, 393 U.S. 503 (1969), or the gossip who sits in the student commons swapping stories of sexual escapade could readily muddle a clear official message condoning the government policy or condemning teenage sex. Likewise, the student newspaper that, like *Spectrum*, conveys a moral position at odds with the school's official stance might subvert the administration's legitimate inculcation of its own perception of community values.

If mere incompatibility with the school's pedagogical message were a constitutionally sufficient justification for the suppression of student speech, school officials could censor each of the students or student organizations in the foregoing hypotheticals, converting our public schools into "enclaves of totalitarianism," id., at 511, that "strangle the free mind at its source," *West Virginia Board of Education v. Barnette,* supra, at 637. The First Amendment permits no such blanket censorship authority. While the "constitutional rights of students in public school are not automatically coextensive with the rights of adults in other settings," *Fraser,* supra, at 682, students in the public schools do not "shed their constitutional rights to freedom of speech or expression at the schoolhouse gate," *Tinker,* supra, at 506. Just as the public on the street corner must, in the interest of fostering "enlightened opinion," *Cantwell v. Connecticut,* 310 U.S. 296, 310 (1940), tolerate speech that "tempt[s] [the listener] to throw [the speaker] off the street," id., at 309, public educators must accommodate some student expression even if it offends them or offers views or values that contradict those the school wishes to inculcate.

In *Tinker,* this Court struck the balance. We held that official censorship of student expression—there the suspension of several students until they removed their armbands protesting the Vietnam war—is unconstitutional unless the speech "materially disrupts classwork or involves substantial disorder or invasion of the rights of others. . . ." 393 U.S., at 513. School officials may not suppress "silent, passive expression of opinion, unaccompanied by any disorder or disturbance on the part of" the speaker. Id., at 508. The "mere desire to avoid the discomfort and unpleasantness that always accompany an unpopular viewpoint," id., at 509, or an unsavory subject, *Fraser,* supra, at 688-689 (Brennan, J., concurring in judgment), does not justify official suppression of student speech in the high school.

This Court applied the *Tinker* test just a Term ago in *Fraser,* supra, upholding an official decision to discipline a student for delivering a lewd speech in support of a student-government candidate. The Court today casts no doubt on *Tinker's* vitality. Instead it erects a taxonomy of school censorship, concluding that *Tinker* applies to one category and not another. On the one hand is censorship "to silence a student's personal expression that happens to occur on the school premises." Ante, at 271. On the other hand is censorship of expression that arises in the context of "school-sponsored . . . expressive activities that students, parents, and members of the public might reasonably perceive to bear the imprimatur of the school." Ibid.

The Court does not, for it cannot, purport to discern from our precedents the distinction it creates. One could, I suppose, readily characterize the students' symbolic speech in *Tinker* as "personal expression that happens to [have] occur[red] on school premises," although *Tinker* did not even hint that the personal nature of the speech was of any (much less dispositive) relevance. But that same description could not by any stretch of the imagination fit Fraser's speech. He did not just "happen" to deliver his lewd speech to an ad hoc gathering on the playground. As the second paragraph of *Fraser* evinces, if ever a forum for student expression was "school-sponsored," Fraser's was:

> "Fraser . . . delivered a speech nominating a fellow student for student elective office. Approximately 600 high school students . . . attended the assembly. Students were required to attend the assembly or to report to the study hall. The assembly was part of a school-sponsored educational program in self-government." *Fraser,* 478 U.S., at 677.

Yet, from the first sentence of its analysis, see id., at 680, *Fraser* faithfully applied *Tinker*. Nor has this Court ever intimated a distinction between personal and school-sponsored speech in any other context. Particularly telling is this Court's heavy reliance on *Tinker* in two cases of First Amendment infringement on state college campuses. See *Papish v. University of Missouri Board of Curators,* 410 U.S. 667, 671, n. 6 (1973) (per curiam); *Healy v. James,* 408 U.S. 169, 180, 189, and n. 18, 191 (1972). One involved the expulsion of a student for lewd expression in a newspaper that she sold on campus pursuant to university authorization, see *Papish,* supra, at 667–668, and the other involved the denial of university recognition and concomitant benefits to a political student organization, see *Healy,* supra, at 174, 176, 181–182. Tracking *Tinker's* analysis, the Court found each act of suppression unconstitutional. In neither case did this Court suggest the distinction, which the Court today finds dispositive, between school-sponsored and incidental student expression.

II

Even if we were writing on a clean slate, I would reject the Court's rationale for abandoning *Tinker* in this case. The Court offers no more than an obscure tangle of three excuses to afford educators "greater control" over school-sponsored speech than the *Tinker* test would permit: the public educator's prerogative to control curriculum; the pedagogical interest in shielding the high school audience from objectionable viewpoints and sensitive topics; and the school's need to dissociate itself from student expression. Ante, at 271. None of the excuses, once disentangled, supports the distinction that the Court draws. *Tinker* fully addresses the first concern; the second is illegitimate; and the third is readily achievable through less oppressive means.

A

The Court is certainly correct that the First Amendment permits educators "to assure that participants learn whatever lessons the activity is designed to teach. . . ." Ante, at 271. That is, however, the essence of the *Tinker* test, not an excuse to abandon it. Under *Tinker,* school officials may censor only such student speech as would "materially disrup[t]" a legitimate curricular function. Manifestly, student speech is more likely to disrupt a curricular function when it arises in the context of a curricular activity—one that "is designed to teach" something—than when it arises in the context of a noncurricular activity. Thus, under *Tinker,* the school may constitutionally punish the budding political orator if he disrupts calculus class but not if he holds his tongue for the cafeteria. See *Consolidated Edison Co. v. Public Service Comm'n of New York,* 447 U.S. 530, 544–545 (1980) (Stevens, J., concurring in judgment). That is not because some more stringent standard applies in the curricular context. (After all, this Court applied the same standard whether the students in *Tinker* wore their armbands to the "classroom" or the "cafeteria." 393 U.S., at 512.) It is because student speech in the noncurricular context is less likely to disrupt materially any legitimate pedagogical purpose.

I fully agree with the Court that the First Amendment should afford an educator the prerogative not to sponsor the publication of a newspaper article that is "ungrammatical, poorly written, inadequately researched, biased or prejudiced," or that falls short of the "high standards for . . . student speech that is disseminated under [the school's] auspices. . . ." Ante, at 271–272. But we need not abandon *Tinker* to reach that conclusion; we need only apply it.

The enumerated criteria reflect the skills that the curricular newspaper "is designed to teach." The educator may, under *Tinker,* constitutionally "censor" poor grammar, writing, or research because to reward such expression would "[materially disrupt]" the newspaper's curricular purpose.

The same cannot be said of official censorship designed to shield the audience or dissociate the sponsor from the expression. Censorship so motivated might well serve (although, as I demonstrate infra, at 285–289, cannot legitimately serve) some other school purpose. But it in no way furthers the curricular purposes of a student newspaper, unless one believes that the purpose of the school newspaper is to teach students that the press ought never report bad news, express unpopular views, or print a thought that might upset its sponsors. Unsurprisingly, Hazelwood East claims no such pedagogical purpose.

The Court relies on bits of testimony to portray the principal's conduct as a pedagogical lesson to Journalism II students who "had not sufficiently mastered those portions of the . . . curriculum that pertained to the treatment of controversial issues and personal attacks, the need to protect the privacy of individuals . . . , and 'the legal, moral, and ethical restrictions imposed upon journalists. . . .'" Ante, at 276. In that regard, the Court attempts to justify censorship of the article on teenage pregnancy on the basis of the principal's judgment that (1) "the [pregnant] students' anonymity was not adequately protected," despite the article's use of aliases; and (2) the judgment that "the article was not sufficiently sensitive to the privacy interests of the students' boyfriends and parents. . . ." Ante, at 274. Similarly, the Court finds in the principal's decision to censor the divorce article a journalistic lesson that the author should have given the father of one student an "opportunity to defend himself" against her charge that (in the Court's words) he "chose 'playing cards with the guys' over home and family. . . ." Ante, at 275.

But the principal never consulted the students before censoring their work. "[T]hey learned of the deletions when the paper was released. . . ." 795 F.2d, at 1371. Further, he explained the deletions only in the broadest of generalities. In one meeting called at the behest of seven protesting *Spectrum* staff members (presumably a fraction of the full class), he characterized the articles as "'too sensitive' for 'our immature audience of readers,'" 607 F. Supp. 1450, 1459 (ED Mo. 1985), and in a later meeting he deemed them simply "inappropriate, personal, sensitive and unsuitable for the newspaper," ibid. The Court's supposition that the principal intended (or the protesters understood) those generalities as a lesson on the nuances of journalistic responsibility is utterly incredible. If he did, a fact that neither the District Court nor the Court of Appeals found, the lesson was lost on all but the psychic *Spectrum* staffer.

B

The Court's second excuse for deviating from precedent is the school's interest in shielding an impressionable high school audience from material whose substance is "unsuitable for immature audiences." Ante, at 271 (footnote omitted). Specifically, the majority decrees that we must afford educators authority to shield high school students from exposure to "potentially sensitive topics" (like "the particulars of teenage sexual activity") or unacceptable social viewpoints (like the advocacy of "irresponsible se[x] or conduct otherwise inconsistent with 'the shared values of a civilized social order'") through school-sponsored student activities. Ante, at 272 (citation omitted).

Tinker teaches us that the state educator's undeniable, and undeniably vital, mandate to inculcate moral and political values is not a general warrant to act as "thought police" stifling discussion of all but state-approved topics and advocacy of all but the official position. See also *Epperson v. Arkansas,* 393 U.S. 97 (1968); *Meyer v. Nebraska,* 262 U.S. 390 (1923). Otherwise educators could transform students into "closed-circuit recipients of only that which the State chooses to communicate," *Tinker,* 393 U.S., at 511, and cast a perverse and impermissible "pall of orthodoxy over the classroom," *Keyishian v. Board of Regents,* 385 U.S. 589, 603 (1967). Thus, the State cannot constitutionally prohibit its high school students from recounting in the locker room "the particulars of [their] teen-age sexual activity," nor even from advocating "irresponsible se[x]" or other presumed abominations of "the shared values of a civilized social order." Even in its capacity as educator the State may not assume an Orwellian "guardianship of the public mind," *Thomas v. Collins,* 323 U.S. 516, 545 (1945) (Jackson, J., concurring).

The mere fact of school sponsorship does not, as the Court suggests, license such thought control in the high school, whether through school suppression of disfavored viewpoints or through official assessment of topic sensitivity.[2] The former would constitute unabashed and unconstitutional viewpoint discrimination, see *Board of Education v. Pico,* 457 U.S., at 878–879 (Blackmun, J., concurring in part and concurring in judgment), as well as an impermissible infringement of the students' "right to receive information and ideas,'" id., at 867 (plurality opinion) (citations omitted); see *First National Bank v. Bellotti,* 435 U.S. 765, 783 (1978).[3] Just as a school board may not purge its state-funded library of all books that "offen[d] [its] social, political and moral tastes,'" 457 U.S., at 858–859 (plurality opinion) (citation omitted), school officials may not, out of like motivation, discriminatorily excise objectionable ideas from a student publication. The State's prerogative to dissolve the student newspaper entirely (or to limit its subject matter) no more entitles it to dictate which viewpoints students may express on its pages, than the State's prerogative to close down the schoolhouse entitles it to prohibit the nondisruptive expression of antiwar sentiment within its gates.

---

2. The Court quotes language in *Bethel School Dist. No. 403 v. Fraser,* 478 U.S. 675 (1986), for the proposition that "[t]he determination of what manner of speech in the classroom or in school assembly is inappropriate properly rests with the school board.'" Ante, at 267 (quoting 478 U.S., at 683). As the discussion immediately preceding that quotation makes clear, however, the Court was referring only to the appropriateness of the manner in which the message is conveyed, not of the message's content. See, e.g., *Fraser,* 478 U.S., at 683 ("[T]he 'fundamental values necessary to the maintenance of a democratic political system' disfavor the use of terms of debate highly offensive or highly threatening to others"). In fact, the *Fraser* Court coupled its first mention of "society's . . . interest in teaching students the boundaries of socially appropriate behavior," with an acknowledgment of "[t]he undoubted freedom to advocate unpopular and controversial views in schools and classrooms," id., at 681. See also id., at 689 (Brennan, J., concurring in judgment) ("Nor does this case involve an attempt by school officials to ban written materials they consider 'inappropriate' for high school students" (citation omitted)).

3. Petitioners themselves concede that "[c]ontrol over access'" to *Spectrum* is permissible only if "the distinctions drawn . . . are viewpoint neutral.'" Brief for Petitioners 32 (quoting *Cornelius v. NAACP Legal Defense & Educational Fund, Inc.,* 473 U.S. 788, 806 (1985)).

Official censorship of student speech on the ground that it addresses "potentially sensitive topics" is, for related reasons, equally impermissible. I would not begrudge an educator the authority to limit the substantive scope of a school-sponsored publication to a certain, objectively definable topic, such as literary criticism, school sports, or an overview of the school year. Unlike those determinate limitations, "potential topic sensitivity" is a vaporous nonstandard—like "'public welfare, peace, safety, health, decency, good order, morals or convenience,'" *Shuttlesworth v. Birmingham,* 394 U.S. 147, 150 (1969), or "'general welfare of citizens,'" *Staub v. Baxley,* 355 U.S. 313, 322 (1958)—that invites manipulation to achieve ends that cannot permissibly be achieved through blatant viewpoint discrimination and chills student speech to which school officials might not object. In part because of those dangers, this Court has consistently condemned any scheme allowing a state official boundless discretion in licensing speech from a particular forum. See, e.g., *Shuttlesworth v. Birmingham,* supra, at 150–151, and n. 2; *Cox v. Louisiana,* 379 U.S. 536, 557–558 (1965); *Staub v. Baxley,* supra, at 322–324.

The case before us aptly illustrates how readily school officials (and courts) can camouflage viewpoint discrimination as the "mere" protection of students from sensitive topics. Among the grounds that the Court advances to uphold the principal's censorship of one of the articles was the potential sensitivity of "teenage sexual activity." Ante, at 272. Yet the District Court specifically found that the principal "did not, as a matter of principle, oppose discussion of said topi[c] in *Spectrum*." 607 F. Supp., at 1467. That much is also clear from the same principal's approval of the "squeal law" article on the same page, dealing forthrightly with "teenage sexuality," "the use of contraceptives by teenagers," and "teenage pregnancy," App. 4–5. If topic sensitivity were the true basis of the principal's decision, the two articles should have been equally objectionable. It is much more likely that the objectionable article was objectionable because of the viewpoint it expressed: It might have been read (as the majority apparently does) to advocate "irresponsible sex." See ante, at 272.

C

The sole concomitant of school sponsorship that might conceivably justify the distinction that the Court draws between sponsored and nonsponsored student expression is the risk "that the views of the individual speaker [might be] erroneously attributed to the school." Ante, at 271. Of course, the risk of erroneous attribution inheres in any student expression, including "personal expression" that, like the armbands in *Tinker,* "happens to occur on the school premises," ante, at 271. Nevertheless, the majority is certainly correct that indicia of school sponsorship increase the likelihood of such attribution, and that state educators may therefore have a legitimate interest in dissociating themselves from student speech.

But "'[e]ven though the governmental purpose be legitimate and substantial, that purpose cannot be pursued by means that broadly stifle fundamental personal liberties when the end can be more narrowly achieved.'" *Keyishian v. Board of Regents,* 385 U.S., at 602 (quoting *Shelton v. Tucker,* 364 U.S. 479, 488 (1960)). Dissociative means short of censorship are available to the school. It could, for example, require the student activity to publish a disclaimer, such as the "Statement of Policy" that *Spectrum* published each school year announcing that "[a]ll . . . editorials appearing in this newspaper reflect the opinions of the *Spectrum* staff, which are not necessarily shared by the administrators or faculty of Hazelwood East," App. 26; or it could simply issue its own response clarifying the official position on the matter and explaining why the student position is wrong. Yet, without so much as acknowledging the less oppressive alternatives, the Court approves of brutal censorship.

III

Since the censorship served no legitimate pedagogical purpose, it cannot by any stretch of the imagination have been designed to prevent "materia[l] disrup[tion of] classwork," *Tinker*, 393 U.S., at 513. Nor did the censorship fall within the category that *Tinker* described as necessary to prevent student expression from "inva[ding] the rights of others," ibid. If that term is to have any content, it must be limited to rights that are protected by law. "Any yardstick less exacting than [that] could result in school officials curtailing speech at the slightest fear of disturbance," 795 F.2d, at 1376, a prospect that would be completely at odds with this Court's pronouncement that the "undifferentiated fear or apprehension of disturbance is not enough [even in the public school context] to overcome the right to freedom of expression." *Tinker,* supra, at 508. And, as the Court of Appeals correctly reasoned, whatever journalistic impropriety these articles may have contained, they could not conceivably be tortious, much less criminal. See 795 F.2d, at 1375–1376.

Finally, even if the majority were correct that the principal could constitutionally have censored the objectionable material, I would emphatically object to the brutal manner in which he did so. Where "[t]he separation of legitimate from illegitimate speech calls for more sensitive tools" *Speiser v. Randall,* 357 U.S. 513, 525 (1958); see *Keyishian v. Board of Regents,* supra, at 602, the principal used a paper shredder. He objected to some material in two articles, but excised six entire articles. He did not so much as inquire into obvious alternatives, such as precise deletions or additions (one of which had already been made), rearranging the layout, or delaying publication. Such unthinking contempt for individual rights is intolerable from any state official. It is particularly insidious from one to whom the public entrusts the task of inculcating in its youth an appreciation for the cherished democratic liberties that our Constitution guarantees.

IV

The Court opens its analysis in this case by purporting to reaffirm Tinker's time-tested proposition that public school students "do not 'shed their constitutional rights to freedom of speech or expression at the schoolhouse gate.'" Ante, at 266 (quoting *Tinker*, supra, at 506). That is an ironic introduction to an opinion that denudes high school students of much of the First Amendment protection that *Tinker* itself prescribed. Instead of "teach[ing] children to respect the diversity of ideas that is fundamental to the American system," *Board of Education v. Pico*, 457 U.S., at 880 (Blackmun, J., concurring in part and concurring in judgment), and "that our Constitution is a living reality, not parchment preserved under glass," *Shanley v. Northeast Independent School Dist.*, Bexar Cty., Tex., 462 F.2d 960, 972 (CA5 1972), the Court today "teach[es] youth to discount important principles of our government as mere platitudes." *West Virginia Board of Education v. Barnette,* 319 U.S., at 637. The young men and women of Hazelwood East expected a civics lesson, but not the one the Court teaches them today.

I dissent.

CHAPTER 10

SCHOOL DISCIPLINE

Introduction

The third major aspect surrounding the relationship between a child and the educational system concerns the procedures by which school authorities can inflict discipline on students for infractions of school regulations. We have seen in the *Kent* and *Gault* decisions that the Supreme Court had initiated the due process movement for juveniles by ruling that children are indeed entitled to due process rights when they appear in juvenile court for violations of the law. The Court was especially concerned in these two cases that, when juveniles risk being transferred to adult court or face a disposition in juvenile court that could result in a loss of liberty, fundamental fairness must apply in the process and methods by which juvenile courts dispose of such matters. Yet the issue in this chapter is the extent to which school authorities, and not a juvenile court, are expected to apply the same type of due process standards when children are being disciplined by school officials and are at risk for a range of sanctions, from nothing more serious than suspension, expulsion, or some other penalty to corporal punishment.

Due Process in School Discipinary Proceedings

Case Comment

In *Goss v. Lopez*, the Supreme Court formulated the procedural guidelines for evaluating the constitutionality of school disciplinary procedures. *Goss* was a class action suit brought by Ohio public school students who had been suspended from school for up to ten days without a hearing. The lower court had ruled that the students had been denied due process under the Fourteenth Amendment to the U.S. Constitution. On appeal, the school officials argued that no due process existed where there was no constitutional right to a public education.

The Supreme Court, however, affirmed the lower court by concluding that the students had been deprived of their right to "liberty and property," and thus, minimal due process was required. Since the state had extended the right to an education to students, the state may not withdraw that right on grounds of misconduct, absent fundamentally fair procedures to determine whether the misconduct has occurred, and must recognize a student's legitimate entitlement to a public education as a property interest that is protected by the Due Process

Clause. The Court further ruled that, at a minimum, students facing suspension from school require notice and an opportunity to be heard. The Court did not believe that such a hearing included the right to counsel or a right to confront or cross-examine witnesses.

GOSS V. LOPEZ

Supreme Court of the United States, 1975.

419 U.S. 565.

Mr. Justice White delivered the opinion of the Court.

This appeal by various administrators of the Columbus, Ohio, Public School System (CPSS) challenges the judgment of a three-judge federal court, declaring that appellees—various high school students in the CPSS—were denied due process of law contrary to the command of the Fourteenth Amendment in that they were temporarily suspended from their high schools without a hearing either prior to suspension or within a reasonable time thereafter, and enjoining the administrators to remove all references to such suspensions from the students' records.

I

Ohio law, Rev. Code Ann. 3313.64 (1972), provides for free education to all children between the ages of six and 21. Section 3313.66 of the Code empowers the principal of an Ohio public school to suspend a pupil for misconduct for up to 10 days or to expel him. In either case, he must notify the student's parents within 24 hours and state the reasons for his action. A pupil who is expelled, or his parents, may appeal the decision to the Board of Education and in connection therewith shall be permitted to be heard at the board meeting. The Board may reinstate the pupil following the hearing. No similar procedure is provided in 3313.66 or any other provision of state law for a suspended student. Aside from a regulation tracking the statute, at the time of the imposition of the suspensions in this case the CPSS itself had not issued any written procedure applicable to suspensions.[1] Nor, so far as the

---

1. At the time of the events involved in this case, the only administrative regulation on this subject was 1010.04 of the Administrative Guide of the Columbus Public Schools, which provided: "Pupils may be suspended or expelled from school in accordance with the provisions of Section 3313.66 of the Revised Code." Subsequent to the events involved in this lawsuit, the Department of Pupil Personnel of the CPSS issued three memoranda relating to suspension procedures, dated August 16, 1971, February 21, 1973, and July 10, 1973, respectively. The first two are substantially similar to each other and require no factfinding hearing at any time in connection with a suspension. The third, which was apparently in effect when this case was argued, places upon the principal the obligation to "investigate" "before commencing suspension procedures"; and provides as part of the procedures that the principal shall discuss the case with the pupil, so that the pupil may "be heard with respect to the alleged offense," unless the pupil is "unavailable" for such a discussion or "unwilling" to participate in it. The suspensions involved in this case occurred, and records thereof were made, prior to the effective date of these memoranda. The District Court's judgment, including its expunction order, turns on the propriety of the procedures existing at the time the suspensions were ordered and by which they were imposed.

record reflects, had any of the individual high schools involved in this case.[2] Each, however, had formally or informally described the conduct for which suspension could be imposed.

The nine named appellees, each of whom alleged that he or she had been suspended from public high school in Columbus for up to 10 days without a hearing pursuant to 3313.66, filed an action under 42 U.S.C. 1983 against the Columbus Board of Education and various administrators of the CPSS. The complaint sought a declaration that 3313.66 was unconstitutional in that it permitted public school administrators to deprive plaintiffs of their rights to an education without a hearing of any kind, in violation of the procedural due process component of the Fourteenth Amendment. It also sought to enjoin the public school officials from issuing future suspensions pursuant to 3313.66 and to require them to remove references to the past suspensions from the records of the students in question.[3]

The proof below established that the suspensions arose out of a period of widespread student unrest in the CPSS during February and March 1971. Six of the named plaintiffs, Rudolph Sutton, Tyrone Washington, Susan Cooper, Deborah Fox, Clarence Byars, and Bruce Harris, were students at the Marion-Franklin High School and were each suspended for 10 days[4] on account of disruptive or disobedient conduct committed in the presence of the school administrator who ordered the suspension. One of these, Tyrone Washington, was among a group of students demonstrating in the school auditorium while a class was being conducted there. He was ordered by the school principal to leave, refused to do so, and was suspended. Rudolph Sutton, in the presence of the principal, physically attacked a police officer who was attempting to remove Tyrone Washington from the auditorium. He was immediately suspended. The other four Marion-Franklin students were suspended for similar conduct. None was given a hearing to determine the operative facts underlying the suspension, but each, together with his or her parents, was offered the opportunity to attend a conference, subsequent to the effective date of the suspension, to discuss the student's future.

Two named plaintiffs, Dwight Lopez and Betty Crome, were students at the Central High School and McGuffey Junior High School, respectively. The former was suspended in connection with a disturbance in the lunchroom which involved some physical damage to school

---

2. According to the testimony of Phillip Fulton, the principal of one of the high schools involved in this case, there was an informal procedure applicable at the Marion-Franklin High School. It provided that in the routine case of misconduct, occurring in the presence of a teacher, the teacher would describe the misconduct on a form provided for that purpose and would send the student, with the form, to the principal's office. There, the principal would obtain the student's version of the story, and, if it conflicted with the teacher's written version, would send for the teacher to obtain the teacher's oral version—apparently in the presence of the student. Mr. Fulton testified that, if a discrepancy still existed, the teacher's version would be believed and the principal would arrive at a disciplinary decision based on it.

3. The plaintiffs sought to bring the action on behalf of all students of the Columbus Public Schools suspended on or after February 1971, and a class action was declared accordingly. Since the complaint sought to restrain the "enforcement" and "operation" of a state statute "by restraining the action of any officer of such state in the enforcement or execution of such statute," a three-judge court was requested pursuant to 28 U.S.C. 2281 and convened. The students also alleged that the conduct for which they could be suspended was not adequately defined by Ohio law. This vagueness and overbreadth argument was rejected by the court below and the students have not appealed from this part of the court's decision. ◆

4. Fox was given two separate 10-day suspensions for misconduct occurring on two separate occasions—the second following immediately upon her return to school. In addition to his suspension, Sutton was transferred to another school.

property.[5] Lopez testified that at least 75 other students were suspended from his school on the same day. He also testified below that he was not a party to the destructive conduct but was instead an innocent bystander. Because no one from the school testified with regard to this incident, there is no evidence in the record indicating the official basis for concluding otherwise. Lopez never had a hearing.

Betty Crome was present at a demonstration at a high school other than the one she was attending. There she was arrested together with others, taken to the police station, and released without being formally charged. Before she went to school on the following day, she was notified that she had been suspended for a 10-day period. Because no one from the school testified with respect to this incident, the record does not disclose how the McGuffey Junior High School principal went about making the decision to suspend Crome, nor does it disclose on what information the decision was based. It is clear from the record that no hearing was ever held. There was no testimony with respect to the suspension of the ninth named plaintiff, Carl Smith. The school files were also silent as to his suspension, although as to some, but not all, of the other named plaintiffs the files contained either direct references to their suspensions or copies of letters sent to their parents advising them of the suspension.

On the basis of this evidence, the three-judge court declared that plaintiffs were denied due process of law because they were "suspended without hearing prior to suspension or within a reasonable time thereafter," and that Ohio Rev. Code Ann. 3313.66 (1972) and regulations issued pursuant thereto were unconstitutional in permitting such suspensions.[6] It was ordered that all references to plaintiffs' suspensions be removed from school files.

Although not imposing upon the Ohio school administrators any particular disciplinary procedures and leaving them "free to adopt regulations providing for fair suspension procedures which are consonant with the educational goals of their schools and reflective of the characteristics of their school and locality," the District Court declared that there were "minimum requirements of notice and a hearing prior to suspension, except in emergency situations." In explication, the court stated that relevant case authority would: (1) permit "[i]mmediate removal of a student whose conduct disrupts the academic atmosphere of the school, endangers fellow students, teachers or school officials, or damages property"; (2) require notice of suspension proceedings to be sent to the student's parents within 24 hours of the decision to conduct them; and (3) require a hearing to be held, with the student present, within 72 hours of his removal. Finally, the court stated that, with respect to the nature of the hearing, the relevant cases required that statements in support of the charge be produced, that the student and others be permitted to make statements in defense or mitigation, and that the school need not permit attendance by counsel.

The defendant school administrators have appealed the three-judge court's decision. Because the order below granted plaintiffs' request for an injunction—ordering defendants to

---

5. Lopez was actually absent from school, following his suspension, for over 20 days. This seems to have occurred because of a misunderstanding as to the length of the suspension. A letter sent to Lopez after he had been out for over 10 days purports to assume that, being over compulsory school age, he was voluntarily staying away. Upon asserting that this was not the case, Lopez was transferred to another school.

6. In its judgment, the court stated that the statute is unconstitutional in that it provides "for suspension . . . without first affording the student due process of law." However, the language of the judgment must be read in light of the language in the opinion which expressly contemplates that under some circumstances students may properly be removed from school before a hearing is held, so long as the hearing follows promptly.

expunge their records—this Court has jurisdiction of the appeal pursuant to 28 U.S.C. 1253. We affirm.

II

At the outset, appellants contend that because there is no constitutional right to an education at public expense, the Due Process Clause does not protect against expulsions from the public school system. This position misconceives the nature of the issue and is refuted by prior decisions. The Fourteenth Amendment forbids the State to deprive any person of life, liberty, or property without due process of law. Protected interests in property are normally "not created by the Constitution. Rather, they are created and their dimensions are defined" by an independent source such as state statutes or rules entitling the citizen to certain benefits. *Board of Regents v. Roth,* 408 U.S. 564, 577 (1972).

Accordingly, a state employee who under state law, or rules promulgated by state officials, has a legitimate claim of entitlement to continued employment absent sufficient cause for discharge may demand the procedural protections of due process. *Connell v. Higginbotham,* 403 U.S. 207 (1971); *Wieman v. Updegraff,* 344 U.S. 183, 191–192 (1952); *Arnett v. Kennedy,* 416 U.S. 134, 164 (Powell, J., concurring), 171 (White, J., concurring and dissenting) (1974). So may welfare recipients who have statutory rights to welfare as long as they maintain the specified qualifications. *Goldberg v. Kelly,* 397 U.S. 254 (1970). *Morrissey v. Brewer,* 408 U.S. 471 (1972), applied the limitations of the Due Process Clause to governmental decisions to revoke parole, although a parolee has no constitutional right to that status. In like vein was *Wolff v. McDonnell,* 418 U.S. 539 (1974), where the procedural protections of the Due Process Clause were triggered by official cancellation of a prisoner's good-time credits accumulated under state law, although those benefits were not mandated by the Constitution.

Here, on the basis of state law, appellees plainly had legitimate claims of entitlement to a public education. Ohio Rev. Code Ann. 3313.48 and 3313.64 (1972 and Supp. 1973) direct local authorities to provide a free education to all residents between five and 21 years of age, and a compulsory-attendance law requires attendance for a school year of not less than 32 weeks. Ohio Rev. Code Ann. 3321.04 (1972). It is true that 3313.66 of the Code permits school principals to suspend students for up to 10 days; but suspensions may not be imposed without any grounds whatsoever. All of the schools had their own rules specifying the grounds for expulsion or suspension. Having chosen to extend the right to an education to people of appellees' class generally, Ohio may not withdraw that right on grounds of misconduct, absent fundamentally fair procedures to determine whether the misconduct has occurred. *Arnett v. Kennedy,* supra, at 164 (Powell, J., concurring), 171 (White, J., concurring and dissenting), 206 (Marshall, J., dissenting).

Although Ohio may not be constitutionally obligated to establish and maintain a public school system, it has nevertheless done so and has required its children to attend. Those young people do not "shed their constitutional rights" at the schoolhouse door. *Tinker v. Des Moines School Dist.,* 393 U.S. 503, 506 (1969). "The Fourteenth Amendment, as now applied to the States, protects the citizen against the State itself and all of its creatures—Boards of Education not excepted." *West Virginia Board of Education v. Barnette,* 319 U.S. 624, 637 (1943). The authority possessed by the State to prescribe and enforce standards of conduct in its schools although concededly very broad, must be exercised consistently with constitutional safeguards. Among other things, the State is constrained to recognize a student's legitimate entitlement to a public education as a property interest which is protected by the Due Process Clause and which may not be taken away for misconduct without adherence to the minimum procedures required by that Clause.

The Due Process Clause also forbids arbitrary deprivations of liberty. "Where a person's good name, reputation, honor, or integrity is at stake because of what the government is doing to him," the minimal requirements of the Clause must be satisfied. *Wisconsin v. Constantineau,* 400 U.S. 433, 437 (1971); *Board of Regents v. Roth,* supra, at 573. School authorities here suspended appellees from school for periods of up to 10 days based on charges of misconduct. If sustained and recorded, those charges could seriously damage the students' standing with their fellow pupils and their teachers as well as interfere with later opportunities for higher education and employment.[7] It is apparent that the claimed right of the State to determine unilaterally and without process whether that misconduct has occurred immediately collides with the requirements of the Constitution.

Appellants proceed to argue that even if there is a right to a public education protected by the Due Process Clause generally, the Clause comes into play only when the State subjects a student to a "severe detriment or grievous loss." The loss of 10 days, it is said, is neither severe nor grievous and the Due Process Clause is therefore of no relevance. Appellants' argument is again refuted by our prior decisions; for in determining "whether due process requirements apply in the first place, we must look not to the 'weight' but to the nature of the interest at stake." *Board of Regents v. Roth,* supra, at 570–571. Appellees were excluded from school only temporarily, it is true, but the length and consequent severity of a deprivation, while another factor to weigh in determining the appropriate form of hearing, "is not decisive of the basic right" to a hearing of some kind. *Fuentes v. Shevin,* 407 U.S. 67, 86 (1972). The Court's view has been that as long as a property deprivation is not de minimis, its gravity is irrelevant to the question whether account must be taken of the Due Process Clause. *Sniadach v. Family Finance Corp.,* 395 U.S. 337, 342 (1969) (Harlan, J., concurring); *Boddie v. Connecticut,* 401 U.S. 371, 378–379 (1971); *Board of Regents v. Roth,* supra, at 570 n. 8. A 10-day suspension from school is not de minimis in our view and may not be imposed in complete disregard of the Due Process Clause.

A short suspension is, of course, a far milder deprivation than expulsion. But, "education is perhaps the most important function of state and local governments," *Brown v. Board of Education,* 347 U.S. 483, 493 (1954), and the total exclusion from the educational process

---

7. Appellees assert in their brief that four of 12 randomly selected Ohio colleges specifically inquire of the high school of every applicant for admission whether the applicant has ever been suspended. Brief for Appellees 34–35 and n. 40. Appellees also contend that many employers request similar information. Ibid. Congress has recently enacted legislation limiting access to information contained in the files of a school receiving federal funds. Section 513 of the Education Amendments of 1974, Pub. L. 93-380, 88 Stat. 571, 20 U.S.C. 1232g (1970 ed., Supp. IV), adding 438 to the General Education Provisions Act. That section would preclude release of "verified reports of serious or recurrent behavior patterns" to employers without written consent of the student's parents. While subsection (b) (1) (B) permits release of such information to "other schools . . . in which the student intends to enroll," it does so only upon condition that the parent be advised of the release of the information and be given an opportunity at a hearing to challenge the content of the information to insure against inclusion of inaccurate or misleading information. The statute does not expressly state whether the parent can contest the underlying basis for a suspension, the fact of which is contained in the student's school record.

for more than a trivial period, and certainly if the suspension is for 10 days, is a serious event in the life of the suspended child. Neither the property interest in educational benefits temporarily denied nor the liberty interest in reputation, which is also implicated, is so insubstantial that suspensions may constitutionally be imposed by any procedure the school chooses, no matter how arbitrary.[8]

III

"Once it is determined that due process applies, the question remains what process is due." *Morrissey v. Brewer*, 408 U.S., at 481. We turn to that question, fully realizing as our cases regularly do that the interpretation and application of the Due Process Clause are intensely practical matters and that "[t]he very nature of due process negates any concept of inflexi-

---

8. Since the landmark decision of the Court of Appeals for the Fifth Circuit in *Dixon v. Alabama State Board of Education*, 294 F.2d 150, cert. denied, 368 U.S. 930 (1961), the lower federal courts have uniformly held the Due Process Clause applicable to decisions made by tax-supported educational institutions to remove a student from the institution long enough for the removal to be classified as an expulsion. *Hagopian v. Knowlton*, 470 F.2d 201, 211 (CA2 1972); *Wasson v. Trowbridge*, 382 F.2d 807, 812 (CA2 1967); *Esteban v. Central Missouri State College*, 415 F.2d 1077, 1089 (CA8 1969), cert. denied, 398 U.S. 965 (1970); *Vought v. Van Buren Public Schools*, 306 F. Supp. 1388 (ED Mich. 1969); *Whitfield v. Simpson*, 312 F. Supp. 889 (ED Ill. 1970); *Fielder v. Board of Education of School District of Winnebago, Neb.*, 346 F. Supp. 722, 729 (Neb. 1972); *DeJesus v. Penberthy*, 344 F. Supp. 70, 74 (Conn. 1972); *Soglin v. Kauffman*, 295 F. Supp. 978, 994 (WD Wis. 1968), aff'd, 418 F.2d 163 (CA7 1969); *Stricklin v. Regents of University of Wisconsin*, 297 F. Supp. 416, 420 (WD Wis. 1969), appeal dismissed, 420 F.2d 1257 (CA7 1970); *Buck v. Carter*, 308 F. Supp. 1246 (WD Wis. 1970); General Order on Judicial Standards of Procedure and Substance in Review of Student Discipline in Tax Supported Institutions of Higher Education, 45 F. R. D. 133, 147–148 (WD Mo. 1968) (en banc). The lower courts have been less uniform, however, on the question whether removal from school for some shorter period may ever be so trivial a deprivation as to require no process, and, if so, how short the removal must be to qualify. Courts of Appeals have held or assumed the Due Process Clause applicable to long suspensions, *Pervis v. LaMarque Ind. School Dist.*, 466 F.2d 1054 (CA5 1972); to indefinite suspensions, *Sullivan v. Houston Ind. School Dist.*, 475 F.2d 1071 (CA5), cert. denied, 414 U.S. 1032 (1973); to the addition of a 30-day suspension to a 10-day suspension, *Williams v. Dade County School Board*, 441 F.2d 299 (CA5 1971); to a 10-day suspension, *Black Students of North Fort Myers Jr.–Sr. High School v. Williams*, 470 F.2d 957 (CA5 1972); to "mild" suspensions, *Farrell v. Joel*, 437 F.2d 160 (CA2 1971), and *Tate v. Board of Education*, 453 F.2d 975 (CA8 1972); and to a three-day suspension, *Shanley v. Northeast Ind. School Dist., Bexar County, Texas*, 462 F.2d 960, 967 n. 4 (CA5 1972); but inapplicable to a seven-day suspension, *Linwood v. Board of Ed. of City of Peoria*, 463 F.2d 763 (CA7), cert. denied, 409 U.S. 1027 (1972); to a three-day suspension, *Dunn v. Tyler Ind. School Dist.*, 460 F.2d 137 (CA5 1972); to a suspension for not "more than a few days," *Murray v. West Baton Rouge Parish School Board*, 472 F.2d 438 (CA5 1973); and to all suspensions no matter how short, *Black Coalition v. Portland School District No. 1*, 484 F.2d 1040 (CA9 1973). The Federal District Courts have held the Due Process Clause applicable to an interim suspension pending expulsion proceedings in *Stricklin v. Regents of University of Wisconsin*, supra, and *Buck v. Carter*, supra; to a 10-day suspension, *Banks v. Board of Public Instruction of Dade County*, 314 F. Supp. 285 (SD Fla. 1970), vacated, 401 U.S. 988 (1971) (for entry of a fresh decree so that a timely appeal might be taken to the Court of Appeals), aff'd, 450 F.2d 1103 (CA5 1971); to suspensions of under five days, *Vail v. Board of Education of Portsmouth School Dist.*, 354 F. Supp. 592 (NH 1973); and to all suspensions, *Mills v. Board of Education of the Dist. of Columbia*, 348 F. Supp. 866 (DC 1972), and *Givens v. Poe*, 346 F. Supp. 202 (WDNC 1972); but inapplicable to suspensions of 25 days, *Hernandez v. School District Number One, Denver, Colorado*, 315 F. Supp. 289 (Colo. 1970); to suspensions of 10 days, *Baker v. Downey City Board of Education*, 307 F. Supp. 517 (CD Cal. 1969); and to suspensions of eight days, *Hatter v. Los Angeles City High School District*, 310 F. Supp. 1309 (CD Cal. 1970), rev'd on other grounds, 452 F.2d 673 (CA9 1971). In the cases holding no process necessary in connection with short suspensions, it is not always clear whether the court viewed the Due Process Clause as inapplicable, or simply felt that the process received was "due" even in the absence of some kind of hearing procedure.

ble procedures universally applicable to every imaginable situation." *Cafeteria Workers v. McElroy*, 367 U.S. 886, 895 (1961). We are also mindful of our own admonition: "Judicial interposition in the operation of the public school system of the Nation raises problems requiring care and restraint. . . . By and large, public education in our Nation is committed to the control of state and local authorities." *Epperson v. Arkansas*, 393 U.S. 97, 104 (1968).

There are certain bench marks to guide us, however. *Mullane v. Central Hanover Trust Co.*, 339 U.S. 306 (1950), a case often invoked by later opinions, said that "[m]any controversies have raged about the cryptic and abstract words of the Due Process Clause but there can be no doubt that at a minimum they require that deprivation of life, liberty or property by adjudication be preceded by notice and opportunity for hearing appropriate to the nature of the case." Id., at 313. "The fundamental requisite of due process of law is the opportunity to be heard," *Grannis v. Ordean*, 234 U.S. 385, 394 (1914), a right that "has little reality or worth unless one is informed that the matter is pending and can choose for himself whether to . . . contest." *Mullane v. Central Hanover Trust Co.*, supra, at 314. See also *Armstrong v. Manzo*, 380 U.S. 545, 550 (1965); *Anti-Fascist Committee v. McGrath*, 341 U.S. 123, 168–169 (1951) (Frankfurter, J., concurring). At the very minimum, therefore, students facing suspension and the consequent interference with a protected property interest must be given some kind of notice and afforded some kind of hearing. "Parties whose rights are to be affected are entitled to be heard; and in order that they may enjoy that right they must first be notified." *Baldwin v. Hale*, 1 Wall. 223, 233 (1864).

It also appears from our cases that the timing and content of the notice and the nature of the hearing will depend on appropriate accommodation of the competing interests involved. *Cafeteria Workers v. McElroy*, supra, at 895; *Morrissey v. Brewer*, supra, at 481. The student's interest is to avoid unfair or mistaken exclusion from the educational process, with all of its unfortunate consequences. The Due Process Clause will not shield him from suspensions properly imposed, but it disserves both his interest and the interest of the State if his suspension is in fact unwarranted. The concern would be mostly academic if the disciplinary process were a totally accurate, unerring process, never mistaken and never unfair. Unfortunately, that is not the case, and no one suggests that it is. Disciplinarians, although proceeding in utmost good faith, frequently act on the reports and advice of others; and the controlling facts and the nature of the conduct under challenge are often disputed. The risk of error is not at all trivial, and it should be guarded against if that may be done without prohibitive cost or interference with the educational process.

The difficulty is that our schools are vast and complex. Some modicum of discipline and order is essential if the educational function is to be performed. Events calling for discipline are frequent occurrences and sometimes require immediate, effective action. Suspension is considered not only to be a necessary tool to maintain order but a valuable educational device. The prospect of imposing elaborate hearing requirements in every suspension case is viewed with great concern, and many school authorities may well prefer the untrammeled power to act unilaterally, unhampered by rules about notice and hearing. But it would be a strange disciplinary system in an educational institution if no communication was sought by the disciplinarian with the student in an effort to inform him of his dereliction and to let him tell his side of the story in order to make sure that an injustice is not done. "[F]airness can rarely be obtained by secret, onesided determination of facts decisive of rights. . . ." "Secrecy is not congenial to truth-seeking and self-righteousness gives too slender an assurance of rightness. No better instrument has been devised for arriving at truth than to give a person in jeopardy of serious loss notice of the case against him and opportunity to meet it." *Anti-Fascist Committee v. McGrath,* supra, at 170, 171–172 (Frankfurter, J., concurring).[9]

We do not believe that school authorities must be totally free from notice and hearing requirements if their schools are to operate with acceptable efficiency. Students facing temporary suspension have interests qualifying for protection of the Due Process Clause, and due process requires, in connection with a suspension of 10 days or less, that the student be given oral or written notice of the charges against him and, if he denies them, an explanation of the evidence the authorities have and an opportunity to present his side of the story. The Clause requires at least these rudimentary precautions against unfair or mistaken findings of misconduct and arbitrary exclusion from school.[10]

There need be no delay between the time "notice" is given and the time of the hearing. In the great majority of cases the disciplinarian may informally discuss the alleged misconduct with the student minutes after it has occurred. We hold only that, in being given an opportunity to explain his version of the facts at this discussion, the student first be told what he is accused of doing and what the basis of the accusation is. Lower courts which have addressed the question of the nature of the procedures required in short suspension cases have reached the same conclusion. *Tate v. Board of Education,* 453 F.2d 975, 979 (CA8 1972); *Vail v. Board of Education,* 354 F. Supp. 592, 603 (NH 1973). Since the hearing may occur almost immediately following the misconduct, it follows that as a general rule notice and hearing should precede removal of the student from school. We agree with the District Court, however, that there are recurring situations in which prior notice and hearing cannot be insisted upon. Students whose presence poses a continuing danger to persons or property or

---

9. The facts involved in this case illustrate the point. Betty Crome was suspended for conduct which did not occur on school grounds, and for which mass arrests were made—hardly guaranteeing careful individualized factfinding by the police or by the school principal. She claims to have been involved in no misconduct. However, she was suspended for 10 days without ever being told what she was accused of doing or being given an opportunity to explain her presence among those arrested. Similarly, Dwight Lopez was suspended, along with many others, in connection with a disturbance in the lunchroom. Lopez says he was not one of those in the lunchroom who was involved. However, he was never told the basis for the principal's belief that he was involved, nor was he ever given an opportunity to explain his presence in the lunchroom. The school principals who suspended Crome and Lopez may have been correct on the merits, but it is inconsistent with the Due Process Clause to have made the decision that misconduct had occurred without at some meaningful time giving Crome or Lopez an opportunity to persuade the principals otherwise. We recognize that both suspensions were imposed during a time of great difficulty for the school administrations involved. At least in Lopez' case there may have been an immediate need to send home everyone in the lunchroom in order to preserve school order and property; and the administrative burden of providing 75 "hearings" of any kind is considerable. However, neither factor justifies a disciplinary suspension without at any time gathering facts relating to Lopez specifically, confronting him with them and giving him an opportunity to explain.

10. Appellants point to the fact that some process is provided under Ohio law by way of judicial review. Ohio Rev. Code Ann. 2506.01 (Supp. 1973). Appellants do not cite any case in which this general administrative review statute has been used to appeal from a disciplinary decision by a school official. If it be assumed that it could be so used, it is for two reasons insufficient to save inadequate procedures at the school level. First, although new proof may be offered in a 2501.06 proceeding, *Shaker Coventry Corp. v. Shaker Heights Planning Comm'n,* 18 Ohio Op. 2d 272, 176 N. E. 2d 332 (1961), the proceeding is not de novo. *In re Locke,* 33 Ohio App. 2d 177, 294 N. E. 2d 230 (1972). Thus the decision by the school—even if made upon inadequate procedures—is entitled to weight in the court proceeding. Second, without a demonstration to the contrary, we must assume that delay will attend any 2501.06 proceeding, that the suspension will not be stayed pending hearing, and that the student meanwhile will irreparably lose his educational benefits.

an ongoing threat of disrupting the academic process may be immediately removed from school. In such cases, the necessary notice and rudimentary hearing should follow as soon as practicable, as the District Court indicated.

In holding as we do, we do not believe that we have imposed procedures on school disciplinarians which are inappropriate in a classroom setting. Instead we have imposed requirements which are, if anything, less than a fair-minded school principal would impose upon himself in order to avoid unfair suspensions. Indeed, according to the testimony of the principal of Marion-Franklin High School, that school had an informal procedure, remarkably similar to that which we now require, applicable to suspensions generally but which was not followed in this case. Similarly, according to the most recent memorandum applicable to the entire CPSS, see n. 1, supra, school principals in the CPSS are now required by local rule to provide at least as much as the constitutional minimum which we have described.

We stop short of construing the Due Process Clause to require, countrywide, that hearings in connection with short suspensions must afford the student the opportunity to secure counsel, to confront and cross-examine witnesses supporting the charge, or to call his own witnesses to verify his version of the incident. Brief disciplinary suspensions are almost countless. To impose in each such case even truncated trial-type procedures might well overwhelm administrative facilities in many places and, by diverting resources, cost more than it would save in educational effectiveness. Moreover, further formalizing the suspension process and escalating its formality and adversary nature may not only make it too costly as a regular disciplinary tool but also destroy its effectiveness as part of the teaching process.

On the other hand, requiring effective notice and informal hearing permitting the student to give his version of the events will provide a meaningful hedge against erroneous action. At least the disciplinarian will be alerted to the existence of disputes about facts and arguments about cause and effect. He may then determine himself to summon the accuser, permit cross-examination, and allow the student to present his own witnesses. In more difficult cases, he may permit counsel. In any event, his discretion will be more informed and we think the risk of error substantially reduced.

Requiring that there be at least an informal give-and-take between student and disciplinarian, preferably prior to the suspension, will add little to the factfinding function where the disciplinarian himself has witnessed the conduct forming the basis for the charge. But things are not always as they seem to be, and the student will at least have the opportunity to characterize his conduct and put it in what he deems the proper context.

We should also make it clear that we have addressed ourselves solely to the short suspension, not exceeding 10 days. Longer suspensions or expulsions for the remainder of the school term, or permanently, may require more formal procedures. Nor do we put aside the possibility that in unusual situations, although involving only a short suspension, something more than the rudimentary procedures will be required.

IV

The District Court found each of the suspensions involved here to have occurred without a hearing, either before or after the suspension, and that each suspension was therefore invalid and the statute unconstitutional insofar as it permits such suspensions without notice or hearing. Accordingly, the judgment is

Affirmed.

Due Process in Corporal Punishment

Case Comment

In the case of *Ingraham v. Wright*, the U.S. Supreme Court was confronted by a follow-up case to *Goss v. Lopez* that involved the constitutionality of corporal punishment as a means of school discipline. The case concerned James Ingraham, a fourteen-year-old eighth grader attending Drew Junior High School in Dade County, Florida. On October 6, 1970, a number of students, including James, were apparently too slow in leaving the stage of the school auditorium when asked to do so by a teacher. The school principal, Willie J. Wright, Jr., brought James and the other tardy students to his office to be paddled. But when Ingraham protested and claimed his innocence, Lemmie Deliford, the assistant principal, and Solomon Barnes, an assistant to the principal, were called in and the students were paddled. The students brought suit in federal court arguing that the paddling was "cruel and unusual punishment" and that students should have a right to be heard before physical punishment is given. They lost their case in both the lower court and the Court of Appeals, and then appealed to the Supreme Court.

In comparison to *Goss v. Lopez*, in which juveniles were accorded due process rights, the ruling in *Ingraham* determined that public school students could be paddled without first receiving a hearing. The Court's opinion concluded that the Eighth Amendment's ban on "cruel and unusual punishment" had always been applied to punishment of convicted criminals and was not applicable to noncriminal contexts, such as school discipline. Further, the Court noted that there was a low incidence of abuse of corporal punishment and that common law safeguards already exist thus there was minimal risk of for violating a student's substantive. In reaching its decision, the Court was concerned that the imposition of administrative safeguards might reduce the risk marginally, but would also entail a significant intrusion into an area of primary educational responsibility. The Court was apparently mistaken in its belief that corporal punishment in school would continue to reflect low incidence. Statistics from the United States Department of Education indicate that there were approximately 300,000 children who were subjected to corporal punishment in the 2002–2003 school year.[1] While this is a decline from the 1.5 million cases of corporal punishment in the year after the *Ingraham* ruling, a figure such as 300,000 cannot be considered minimal.[2] The decline is apparently due to the fact that more and more states are instituting bans on corporal punishment voluntarily. Although twenty-eight states and the District of Columbia have done so, there are twenty-two states in which corporal punishment of school children is legal.[3]

---

1. U.S. Department of Education, Office for Civil Rights, 2005. *2002 Elementary and Secondary School Civil Rights Compliance Report.* Washington, D.C.: Unites States Government printing Office.
2. Center for Effective Discipline, http://www.stophitting.com.
3. Ibid.

INGRAHAM V. WRIGHT

Supreme Court of the United States, 1977.

430 U.S. 651.

Mr. Justice Powell delivered the opinion of the Court.

This case presents questions concerning the use of corporal punishment in public schools: First, whether the paddling of students as a means of maintaining school discipline constitutes cruel and unusual punishment in violation of the Eighth Amendment; and, second, to the extent that paddling is constitutionally permissible, whether the Due Process Clause of the Fourteenth Amendment requires prior notice and an opportunity to be heard.

I

Petitioners James Ingraham and Roosevelt Andrews filed the complaint in this case on January 7, 1971, in the United States District Court for the Southern District of Florida.[1] At the time both were enrolled in the Charles R. Drew Junior High School in Dade County, Fla., Ingraham in the eighth grade and Andrews in the ninth. The complaint contained three counts, each alleging a separate cause of action for deprivation of constitutional rights, under 42 U.S.C. 1981–1988. Counts one and two were individual actions for damages by Ingraham and Andrews based on paddling incidents that allegedly occurred in October 1970 at Drew Junior High School. Count three was a class action for declaratory and injunctive relief filed on behalf of all students in the Dade County schools.[2] Named as defendants in all counts were respondents Willie J. Wright (principal at Drew Junior High School), Lemmie Deliford (an assistant principal), Solomon Barnes (an assistant to the principal), and Edward L. Whigham (superintendent of the Dade County School System).[3]

Petitioners presented their evidence at a week-long trial before the District Court. At the close of petitioners' case, respondents moved for dismissal of count three "on the ground that upon the facts and the law the plaintiff has shown no right to relief," Fed. Rule Civ. Proc. 41 (b), and for a ruling that the evidence would be insufficient to go to a jury on counts one and two.[4] The District Court granted the motion as to all three counts, and dismissed the complaint without hearing evidence on behalf of the school authorities. App. 142–150.

---

1. As Ingraham and Andrews were minors, the complaint was filed in the names of Eloise Ingraham, James' mother, and Willie Everett, Roosevelt's father.

2. The District Court certified the class, under Fed. Rules Civ. Proc. 23 (b) (2) and (c) (1), as follows: "'All students of the Dade County School system who are subject to the corporal punishment policies issued by the Defendant, Dade County School Board....'" App. 17. One student was specifically excepted from the class by request.

3. The complaint also named the Dade County School Board as a defendant, but the Court of Appeals held that the Board was not amenable to suit under 42 U.S.C. 1981–1988 and dismissed the suit against the Board for want of jurisdiction. 525 F.2d 909, 912 (CA5 1976). This aspect of the Court of Appeals' judgment is not before us.

4. Petitioners had waived their right to jury trial on the claims for damages in counts one and two, but respondents had not. The District Court proceeded initially to hear evidence only on count three, the claim for injunctive relief. At the close of petitioners' case, however, the parties agreed that the evidence offered on count three (together with certain stipulated testimony) would be considered, for purposes of a motion for directed verdict, as if it had also been offered on counts one and two. It was understood that respondents could reassert a right to jury trial if the motion were denied. App. 142.

Petitioners' evidence may be summarized briefly. In the 1970–1971 school year many of the 237 schools in Dade County used corporal punishment as a means of maintaining discipline pursuant to Florida legislation and a local School Board regulation.[5] The statute then in effect authorized limited corporal punishment by negative inference, proscribing punishment which was "degrading or unduly severe" or which was inflicted without prior consultation with the principal or the teacher in charge of the school. Fla. Stat. Ann. 232.27 (1961).[6] The regulation, Dade County School Board Policy 5144, contained explicit directions and limitations.[7] The authorized punishment consisted of paddling the recalcitrant student on the buttocks with a flat wooden paddle measuring less than two feet long, three to four inches wide, and about one-half inch thick. The normal punishment was limited to one to five "licks" or blows with the paddle and resulted in no apparent physical injury to the student. School authorities viewed corporal punishment as a less drastic means of discipline than suspension or expulsion. Contrary to the procedural requirements of the statute and

---

5. The evidence does not show how many of the schools actually employed corporal punishment as a means of maintaining discipline. The authorization of the practice by the School Board extended to 231 of the schools in the 1970–1971 school year, but at least 10 of those schools did not administer corporal punishment as a matter of school policy. Id., at 137–139.

6. In the 1970–1971 school year, 232.27 provided: "Each teacher or other member of the staff of any school shall assume such authority for the control of pupils as may be assigned to him by the principal and shall keep good order in the classroom and in other places in which he is assigned to be in charge of pupils, but he shall not inflict corporal punishment before consulting the principal or teacher in charge of the school, and in no case shall such punishment be degrading or unduly severe in its nature. . . ." Effective July 1, 1976, the Florida Legislature amended the law governing corporal punishment. Section 232.27 now reads: "Subject to law and to the rules of the district school board, each teacher or other member of the staff of any school shall have such authority for the control and discipline of students as may be assigned to him by the principal or his designated representative and shall keep good order in the classroom and in other places in which he is assigned to be in charge of students. If a teacher feels that corporal punishment is necessary, at least the following procedures shall be followed: "(1) The use of corporal punishment shall be approved in principle by the principal before it is used, but approval is not necessary for each specific instance in which it is used. (2) A teacher or principal may administer corporal punishment only in the presence of another adult who is informed beforehand, and in the student's presence, of the reason for the punishment. (3) A teacher or principal who has administered punishment shall, upon request, provide the pupil's parent or guardian with a written explanation of the reason for the punishment and the name of the other [adult] who was present." Fla. Stat. Ann. 232.27 (1977) (codifier's notation omitted). Corporal punishment is now defined as "the moderate use of physical force or physical contact by a teacher or principal as may be necessary to maintain discipline or to enforce school rules." 228.041 (28). The local school boards are expressly authorized to adopt rules governing student conduct and discipline and are directed to make available codes of student conduct. 230.23 (6). Teachers and principals are given immunity from civil and criminal liability for enforcing disciplinary rules, "[e]xcept in the case of excessive force or cruel and unusual punishment . . . ." 232.275.

7. In the 1970–1971 school year, Policy 5144 authorized corporal punishment where the failure of other means of seeking cooperation from the student made its use necessary. The regulation specified that the principal should determine the necessity for corporal punishment, that the student should understand the seriousness of the offense and the reason for the punishment, and that the punishment should be administered in the presence of another adult in circumstances not calculated to hold the student up to shame or ridicule. The regulation cautioned against using corporal punishment against a student under psychological or medical treatment, and warned that the person administering the punishment "must realize his own personal liabilities" in any case of physical injury. App. 15. While this litigation was pending in the District Court, the Dade County School Board amended Policy 5144 to standardize the size of the paddles used in accordance with the description in the text, to proscribe striking a child with a paddle elsewhere than on the buttocks, to limit the permissible number of "licks" (five for elementary and intermediate grades and seven for junior and senior grades), and to require a contemporaneous explanation of the need for the punishment to the student and a subsequent notification to the parents. App. 126–128.

regulation, teachers often paddled students on their own authority without first consulting the principal.[8]

Petitioners focused on Drew Junior High School, the school in which both Ingraham and Andrews were enrolled in the fall of 1970. In an apparent reference to Drew, the District Court found that "[t]he instances of punishment which could be characterized as severe, accepting the students' testimony as credible, took place in one junior high school." App. 147. The evidence, consisting mainly of the testimony of 16 students, suggests that the regime at Drew was exceptionally harsh. The testimony of Ingraham and Andrews, in support of their individual claims for damages, is illustrative. Because he was slow to respond to his teacher's instructions, Ingraham was subjected to more than 20 licks with a paddle while being held over a table in the principal's office. The paddling was so severe that he suffered a hematoma[9] requiring medical attention and keeping him out of school for several days.[10] Andrews was paddled several times for minor infractions. On two occasions he was struck on his arms, once depriving him of the full use of his arm for a week.[11]

The District Court made no findings on the credibility of the students' testimony. Rather, assuming their testimony to be credible, the court found no constitutional basis for relief. With respect to count three, the class action, the court concluded that the punishment authorized and practiced generally in the county schools violated no constitutional right. Id., at 143, 149. With respect to counts one and two, the individual damages actions, the court concluded that while corporal punishment could in some cases violate the Eighth Amendment, in this case a jury could not lawfully find "the elements of severity, arbitrary infliction, unacceptability in terms of contemporary standards, or gross disproportion which are necessary to bring 'punishment' to the constitutional level of 'cruel and unusual punishment.'" Id., at 143.

A panel of the Court of Appeals voted to reverse. 498 F.2d 248 (CA5 1974). The panel concluded that the punishment was so severe and oppressive as to violate the Eighth and Fourteenth Amendments, and that the procedures outlined in Policy 5144 failed to satisfy the requirements of the Due Process Clause. Upon rehearing, the en banc court rejected these conclusions and affirmed the judgment of the District Court. 525 F.2d 909 (1976). The full court held that the Due Process Clause did not require notice or an opportunity to be heard:

> "In essence, we refuse to set forth, as constitutionally mandated, procedural standards for an activity which is not substantial enough, on a constitutional level, to justify the time and effort which would have to be expended by the school in adhering to those procedures or to justify further interference by federal courts into the internal affairs of public schools." Id., at 919.

---

8. 498 F.2d 248, 255, and n. 7 (1974) (original panel opinion), vacated on rehearing, 525 F.2d 909 (1976); App. 48, 138, 146; Exhibits 14, 15.

9. Stedman's Medical Dictionary (23d ed. 1976) defines "hematoma" as "[a] localized mass of extravasated blood that is relatively or completely confined within an organ or tissue . . . ; the blood is usually clotted (or partly clotted), and, depending on how long it has been there, may manifest various degrees of organization and decolorization."

10. App. 3–4, 18–20, 68–85, 129–136.

11. Id., at 4–5, 104–113. The similar experiences of several other students at Drew, to which they individually testified in the District Court, are summarized in the original panel opinion in the Court of Appeals, 498 F.2d, at 257–259.

The court also rejected the petitioners' substantive contentions. The Eighth Amendment, in the court's view, was simply inapplicable to corporal punishment in public schools. Stressing the likelihood of civil and criminal liability in state law, if petitioners' evidence were believed, the court held that "[t]he administration of corporal punishment in public schools, whether or not excessively administered, does not come within the scope of Eighth Amendment protection." Id., at 915. Nor was there any substantive violation of the Due Process Clause. The court noted that "[p]addling of recalcitrant children has long been an accepted method of promoting good behavior and instilling notions of responsibility and decorum into the mischievous heads of school children." Id., at 917. The court refused to examine instances of punishment individually:

"We think it a misuse of our judicial power to determine, for example, whether a teacher has acted arbitrarily in paddling a particular child for certain behavior or whether in a particular instance of misconduct five licks would have been a more appropriate punishment than ten licks...." Ibid.

We granted certiorari, limited to the questions of cruel and unusual punishment and procedural due process. 425 U.S. 990.[12]

II

In addressing the scope of the Eighth Amendment's prohibition on cruel and unusual punishment, this Court has found it useful to refer to "[t]raditional common-law concepts," *Powell v. Texas*, 392 U.S. 514, 535 (1968) (plurality opinion), and to the "attitude[s] which our society has traditionally taken." Id., at 531. So, too, in defining the requirements of procedural due process under the Fifth and Fourteenth Amendments, the Court has been attuned to what "has always been the law of the land," *United States v. Barnett*, 376 U.S. 681, 692 (1964), and to "traditional ideas of fair procedure." *Greene v. McElroy*, 360 U.S. 474, 508 (1959). We therefore begin by examining the way in which our traditions and our laws have responded to the use of corporal punishment in public schools.

The use of corporal punishment in this country as a means of disciplining schoolchildren dates back to the colonial period.[13] It has survived the transformation of primary and secondary education from the colonials' reliance on optional private arrangements to our present system of compulsory education and dependence on public schools.[14] Despite the general

---

12. We denied review of a third question presented in the petition for certiorari: "Is the infliction of severe corporal punishment upon public school students arbitrary, capricious and unrelated to achieving any legitimate educational purpose and therefore violative of the Due Process Clause of the Fourteenth Amendment?" Pet. for Cert. 2.

13. See H. Falk, *Corporal Punishment* 11–48 (1941); N. Edwards & H. Richey, *The School in the American Social Order* 115–116 (1947).

14. Public and compulsory education existed in New England before the Revolution, see id., at 50–68, 78–81, 97–113, but the demand for free public schools as we now know them did not gain momentum in the country as a whole until the mid-1800s, and it was not until 1918 that compulsory school attendance laws were in force in all the States. See *Brown v. Board of Education*, 347 U.S. 483, 489 n. 4 (1954), citing Cubberley, Public Education in the United States 408–423, 563–565 (1934 ed.); cf. *Wisconsin v. Yoder*, 406 U.S. 205, 226, and n. 15 (1972).

abandonment of corporal punishment as a means of punishing criminal offenders,[15] the practice continues to play a role in the public education of schoolchildren in most parts of the country.[16] Professional and public opinion is sharply divided on the practice,[17] and has been for more than a century.[18] Yet we can discern no trend toward its elimination.

At common law a single principle has governed the use of corporal punishment since before the American Revolution: Teachers may impose reasonable but not excessive force to discipline a child.[19] Blackstone catalogued among the "absolute rights of individuals" the right "to security from the corporal insults of menaces, assaults, beating, and wounding," 1 W. Blackstone, Commentaries 134, but he did not regard it a "corporal insult" for a teacher to inflict "moderate correction" on a child in his care. To the extent that force was "necessary to answer the purposes for which [the teacher] is employed," Blackstone viewed it as "justifiable or lawful." Id., at 453; 3 id., at 120. The basic doctrine has not changed. The prevalent rule in this country today privileges such force as a teacher or administrator "reasonably believes to be necessary for [the child's] proper control, training, or education." Restatement (Second) of Torts 147 (2) (1965); see id., 153 (2). To the extent that the force is excessive or unreasonable, the educator in virtually all States is subject to possible civil and criminal liability.[20]

Although the early cases viewed the authority of the teacher as deriving from the parents,[21] the concept of parental delegation has been replaced by the view—more consonant with compulsory education laws—that the State itself may impose such corporal punishment as is reasonably necessary "for the proper education of the child and for the maintenance of group discipline." 1 F. Harper & F. James, Law of Torts 3.20, p. 292 (1956).[22] All of the circumstances are to be taken into account in determining whether the punishment is reasonable in a particular case. Among the most important considerations are the seriousness of

---

15. See *Jackson v. Bishop*, 404 F.2d 571, 580 (CA8 1968); Falk, supra, at 85–88.

16. See K. Larson & M. Karpas, Effective Secondary School Discipline 146 (1963); A. Reitman, J. Follman, & E. Ladd, Corporal Punishment in the Public Schools 2–5 (ACLU Report 1972).

17. For samplings of scholarly opinion on the use of corporal punishment in the schools, see F. Reardon & R. Reynolds, Corporal Punishment in Pennsylvania 1–2, 34 (1975); National Education Association, Report of the Task Force on Corporal Punishment (1972); K. James, Corporal Punishment in the Public Schools 8–16 (1963). Opinion surveys taken since 1970 have consistently shown a majority of teachers and of the general public favoring moderate use of corporal punishment in the lower grades. See *Reardon & Reynolds*, supra, at 2, 23–26; Delaware Department of Public Instruction, Report on the Corporal Punishment Survey 48 (1974); Reitman, Follman, & Ladd, supra, at 34–35; National Education Association, supra, at 7.

18. See Falk, supra, 66–69; cf. *Cooper v. McJunkin*, 4 Ind. 290 (1853).

19. See 1 F. Harper & F. James, Law of Torts 3.20, pp. 288–292 (1956); Proehl, Tort Liability of Teachers, 12 Vand. L. Rev. 723, 734–738 (1959); W. Prosser, Law of Torts 136–137 (4th ed. 1971).

20. See cases cited n. 28, infra. The criminal codes of many States include provisions explicitly recognizing the teacher's common-law privilege to inflict reasonable corporal punishment. E.g., Ariz. Rev. Stat. Ann. 13–246 (A) (1) (1956); Conn. Gen. Stat. 53a-18 (1977); Neb. Rev. Stat. 28–840 (2) (1975); N.Y. Penal Law 35.10 (McKinney 1975 and Supp. 1976); Ore. Rev. Stat. 161.205 (1) (1975).

21. See Proehl, supra, at 726, and n. 13.

22. Today, corporal punishment in school is conditioned on parental approval only in California. Cal. Educ. Code 49001 (West Supp. 1977). Cf. *Morrow v. Wood*, 35 Wis. 59 (1874). This Court has held in a summary affirmance that parental approval of corporal punishment is not constitutionally required. *Baker v. Owen*, 423 U.S. 907 (1975), aff'g 395 F. Supp. 294 (MDNC).

the offense, the attitude and past behavior of the child, the nature and severity of the punishment, the age and strength of the child, and the availability of less severe but equally effective means of discipline. Id., at 290–291; Restatement (Second) of Torts 150, Comments c–e, p. 268 (1965).

Of the 23 States that have addressed the problem through legislation, 21 have authorized the moderate use of corporal punishment in public schools.[23] Of these States only a few have elaborated on the common-law test of reasonableness, typically providing for approval or notification of the child's parents,[24] or for infliction of punishment only by the principal[25] or in the presence of an adult witness.[26] Only two States, Massachusetts and New Jersey, have prohibited all corporal punishment in their public schools.[27] Where the legislatures have not acted, the state courts have uniformly preserved the common-law rule permitting teachers to use reasonable force in disciplining children in their charge.[28]

Against this background of historical and contemporary approval of reasonable corporal punishment, we turn to the constitutional questions before us.

III

The Eighth Amendment provides: "Excessive bail shall not be required, nor excessive fines imposed, nor cruel and unusual punishments inflicted." Bail, fines, and punishment traditionally have been associated with the criminal process, and by subjecting the three to parallel limitations the text of the Amendment suggests an intention to limit the power of those entrusted with the criminal-law function of government. An examination of the history of the Amendment and the decisions of this Court construing the proscription against cruel and unusual punishment confirms that it was designed to protect those convicted of crimes. We adhere to this long-standing limitation and hold that the Eighth Amendment does not apply to the paddling of children as a means of maintaining discipline in public schools.

---

23. Cal. Educ. Code 49000-49001 (West Supp. 1977); Del. Code Ann., Tit. 14, 701 (Supp. 1976); Fla. Stat. Ann. 232.27 (1977); Ga. Code Ann. 32-835, 32-836 (1976); Haw. Rev. Stat. 298-16 (1975 Supp.), 703-309 (2) (Spec. Pamphlet 1975); Ill. Ann. Stat., c. 122, 24-24, 34-84a (1977 Supp.); Ind. Code Ann. 20-8.1-5-2 (1975); Md. Ann. Code, Art. 77, 98B (1975) (in specified counties); Mich. Comp. Laws Ann., 340.756 (1970); Mont. Rev. Codes Ann. 75-6109 (1971); Nev. Rev. Stat. 392.465 (1973); N.C. Gen. Stat. 115-146 (1975); Ohio Rev. Code Ann. 3319.41 (1972); Okla. Stat. Ann., Tit. 70, 6-114 (1972); Pa. Stat. Ann., Tit. 24, 13-1317 (Supp. 1976); S.C. Code 59-63-260 (1977); S.D. Compiled Laws Ann. 13-32-2 (1975); Vt. Stat. Ann., Tit. 16, 1161 (Supp. 1976); Va. Code Ann. 22-231.1 (1973); W. Va. Code, 18A-5-1 (1977); Wyo. Stat. 21.1-64 (Supp. 1975).

24. Cal. Educ. Code 49001 (West Supp. 1977) (requiring prior parental approval in writing); Fla. Stat. Ann. 232.27 (3) (1977) (requiring a written explanation on request); Mont. Rev. Codes Ann. 75-6109 (1971) (requiring prior parental notification).

25. Md. Ann. Code, Art. 77, 98B (1975).

26. Fla. Stat. Ann. 232.27 (1977); Haw. Rev. Stats. 298-16 (1975 Supp.); Mont. Rev. Codes Ann. 75-6109 (1971).

27. Mass. Gen. Laws Ann., c. 71, 37G (Supp. 1976); N.J. Stat. Ann. 18A: 6-1 (1968).

28. E.g., *Suits v. Glover,* 260 Ala. 449, 71 So.2d 49 (1954); *La Frentz v. Gallagher,* 105 Ariz. 255, 462 P.2d 804 (1969); *Berry v. Arnold School Dist.,* 199 Ark. 1118, 137 S. W. 2d 256 (1940); Andreozzi v. Rubano, 145 Conn. 280, 141 A. 2d 639 (1958); *Tinkham v. Kole,* 252 Iowa 1303, 110 N. W. 2d 258 (1961); *Carr v. Wright,* 423 S. W. 2d 521 (Ky. 1968); Christman v. Hickman, 225 Mo. App. 828, 37 S. W. 2d 672 (1931); *Simms v. School Dist. No. 1,* 13 Ore. App. 119, 508 P.2d 236 (1973); *Marlar v. Bill,* 181 Tenn. 100, 178 S. W. 2d 634 (1944); *Prendergast v. Masterson,* 196 S. W. 246 (Tex. Civ. App. 1917). See generally sources cited n. 19, supra.

A

The history of the Eighth Amendment is well known.[29] The text was taken, almost verbatim, from a provision of the Virginia Declaration of Rights of 1776, which in turn derived from the English Bill of Rights of 1689. The English version, adopted after the accession of William and Mary, was intended to curb the excesses of English judges under the reign of James II. Historians have viewed the English provision as a reaction either to the "Bloody Assize," the treason trials conducted by Chief Justice Jeffreys in 1685 after the abortive rebellion of the Duke of Monmouth,[30] or to the perjury prosecution of Titus Oates in the same year.[31] In either case, the exclusive concern of the English version was the conduct of judges in enforcing the criminal law. The original draft introduced in the House of Commons provided:[32]

> "The requiring excessive bail of persons committed in criminal cases and imposing excessive fines, and illegal punishments, to be prevented."

Although the reference to "criminal cases" was eliminated from the final draft, the preservation of a similar reference in the preamble[33] indicates that the deletion was without substantive significance. Thus, Blackstone treated each of the provision's three prohibitions as bearing only on criminal proceedings and judgments.[34]

The Americans who adopted the language of this part of the English Bill of Rights in framing their own State and Federal Constitutions 100 years later feared the imposition of torture and other cruel punishments not only by judges acting beyond their lawful authority, but also by legislatures engaged in making the laws by which judicial authority would be measured. *Weems v. United States,* 217 U.S. 349, 371–373 (1910). Indeed, the principal concern of the American Framers appears to have been with the legislative definition of crimes and punishments. *In re Kemmler,* 136 U.S. 436, 446–447 (1890); *Furman v. Georgia,* 408 U.S. 238, 263 (1972) (Brennan, J., concurring). But if the American provision was intended to restrain government more broadly than its English model, the subject to which it was intended to apply—the criminal process—was the same.

At the time of its ratification, the original Constitution was criticized in the Massachusetts and Virginia Conventions for its failure to provide any protection for persons convicted

---

29. See *Gregg v. Georgia,* 428 U.S. 153, 168–173 (1976) (joint opinion of Stewart, Powell, and Stevens, JJ.) (hereinafter joint opinion); *Furman v. Georgia,* 408 U.S. 238, 316-328 (1972) (MARSHALL, J., concurring); Granucci, "Nor Cruel and Unusual Punishments Inflicted:" The Original Meaning, 57 Calif. L. Rev. 839 (1969).

30. See I. Brant, The Bill of Rights 155 (1965).

31. See Granucci, supra, at 852–860.

32. Id., at 855.

33. The preamble reads in part: "WHEREAS the late King James the Second, by the assistance of divers evil counsellors, judges, and ministers employed by him, did endeavor to subvert and extirpate . . . the laws and liberties of this kingdom. . . . 10. And excessive bail hath been required of persons committed in criminal cases, to elude the benefit of the laws made for the liberty of the subjects. 11. And excessive fines have been imposed; and illegal and cruel punishments inflicted. . . ." R. Perry & J. Cooper, Sources of Our Liberties 245–246 (1959).

34. 4 W. Blackstone, Commentaries *297 (bail), *379 (fines and other punishments).

of crimes.[35] This criticism provided the impetus for inclusion of the Eighth Amendment in the Bill of Rights. When the Eighth Amendment was debated in the First Congress, it was met by the objection that the Cruel and Unusual Punishments Clause might have the effect of outlawing what were then the common criminal punishments of hanging, whipping, and earcropping. 1 Annals of Cong. 754 (1789). The objection was not heeded, "precisely because the legislature would otherwise have had the unfettered power to prescribe punishments for crimes." *Furman v. Georgia,* supra, at 263.

B

In light of this history, it is not surprising to find that every decision of this Court considering whether a punishment is "cruel and unusual" within the meaning of the Eighth and Fourteenth Amendments has dealt with a criminal punishment. See *Estelle v. Gamble,* 429 U.S. 97 (1976) (incarceration without medical care); *Gregg v. Georgia,* 428 U.S. 153 (1976) (execution for murder); *Furman v. Georgia,* supra (execution for murder); *Powell v. Texas,* 392 U.S. 514 (1968) (plurality opinion) ($20 fine for public drunkenness); *Robinson v. California,* 370 U.S. 660 (1962) (incarceration as a criminal for addiction to narcotics); *Trop v. Dulles,* 356 U.S. 86 (1958) (plurality opinion) (expatriation for desertion); *Louisiana ex rel. Francis v. Resweber,* 329 U.S. 459 (1947) (execution by electrocution after a failed first attempt); *Weems v. United States,* supra (15 years' imprisonment and other penalties for falsifying an official document); *Howard v. Fleming,* 191 U.S. 126 (1903) (10 years' imprisonment for conspiracy to defraud); *In re Kemmler,* supra (execution by electrocution); *Wilkerson v. Utah,* 99 U.S. 130 (1879) (execution by firing squad); *Pervear v. Commonwealth,* 5 Wall. 475 (1867) (fine and imprisonment at hard labor for bootlegging).

These decisions recognize that the Cruel and Unusual Punishments Clause circumscribes the criminal process in three ways: First, it limits the kinds of punishment that can be imposed on those convicted of crimes, e.g., *Estelle v. Gamble* supra; *Trop v. Dulles,* supra; second, it proscribes punishment grossly disproportionate to the severity of the crime, e.g., *Weems v. United States,* supra; and third, it imposes substantive limits on what can be made criminal and punished as such, e.g., *Robinson v. California,* supra. We have recognized the last limitation as one to be applied sparingly. "The primary purpose of [the Cruel and Unusual Punishments Clause] has always been considered, and properly so, to be directed at the method or kind of punishment imposed for the violation of criminal statutes. . . ." *Powell v. Texas,* supra, at 531–532 (plurality opinion).

In the few cases where the Court has had occasion to confront claims that impositions outside the criminal process constituted cruel and unusual punishment, it has had no difficulty finding the Eighth Amendment inapplicable. Thus, in *Fong Yue Ting v. United States,* 149 U.S. 698 (1893), the Court held the Eighth Amendment inapplicable to the deportation of aliens on

---

35. Abraham Holmes of Massachusetts complained specifically of the absence of a provision restraining Congress in its power to determine "what kind of punishments shall be inflicted on persons convicted of crimes." 2 J. Elliot, Debates on the Federal Constitution 111 (1876). Patrick Henry was of the same mind: "What says our [Virginia] bill of rights?—'that excessive bail ought not to be required, nor excessive fines imposed, nor cruel and unusual punishments inflicted.' Are you not, therefore, now calling on those gentlemen who are to compose Congress, to prescribe trials and define punishments without this control? Will they find sentiments there similar to this bill of rights? You let them loose; you do more—you depart from the genius of your country. . . ." 3 id., at 447.

the ground that "deportation is not a punishment for crime." Id., at 730; see *Mahler v. Eby,* 264 U.S. 32 (1924); *Bugajewitz v. Adams,* 228 U.S. 585 (1913). And in *Uphaus v. Wyman,* 360 U.S. 72 (1959), the Court sustained a judgment of civil contempt, resulting in incarceration pending compliance with a subpoena, against a claim that the judgment imposed cruel and unusual punishment. It was emphasized that the case involved "'essentially a civil remedy designed for the benefit of other parties . . . exercised for centuries to secure compliance with judicial decrees.'" Id., at 81, quoting *Green v. United States,* 356 U.S. 165, 197 (1958) (dissenting opinion).[36]

C

Petitioners acknowledge that the original design of the Cruel and Unusual Punishments Clause was to limit criminal punishments, but urge nonetheless that the prohibition should be extended to ban the paddling of schoolchildren. Observing that the Framers of the Eighth Amendment could not have envisioned our present system of public and compulsory education, with its opportunities for noncriminal punishments, petitioners contend that extension of the prohibition against cruel punishments is necessary lest we afford greater protection to criminals than to schoolchildren. It would be anomalous, they say, if schoolchildren could be beaten without constitutional redress, while hardened criminals suffering the same beatings at the hands of their jailers might have a valid claim under the Eighth Amendment. See *Jackson v. Bishop,* 404 F.2d 571 (CA8 1968); cf. *Estelle v. Gamble,* supra. Whatever force this logic may have in other settings,[37] we find it an inadequate basis for wrenching the Eighth Amendment from its historical context and extending it to traditional disciplinary practices in the public schools.

The prisoner and the schoolchild stand in wholly different circumstances, separated by the harsh facts of criminal conviction and incarceration. The prisoner's conviction entitles the State to classify him as a "criminal," and his incarceration deprives him of the freedom "to be with family and friends and to form the other enduring attachments of normal life." *Morrissey v. Brewer,* 408 U.S. 471, 482 (1972); see *Meachum v. Fano,* 427 U.S. 215, 224–225 (1976). Prison brutality, as the Court of Appeals observed in this case, is "part of the total punishment to which the individual is being subjected for his crime and, as such, is a proper subject for Eighth Amendment scrutiny." 525 F.2d, at 915.[38] Even so, the protection afforded

---

36. In urging us to extend the Eighth Amendment to ban school paddlings, petitioners rely on the many decisions in which this Court has held that the prohibition against "cruel and unusual" punishments is not "'fastened to the obsolete but may acquire meaning as public opinion becomes enlightened by a humane justice.'" *Gregg v. Georgia,* 428 U.S., at 171 (joint opinion); see, e.g., *Trop v. Dulles,* 356 U.S., 86, 100–101 (1958) (plurality opinion); *Weems v. United States,* 217 U.S. 349, 373, 378 (1910). This reliance is misplaced. Our Eighth Amendment decisions have referred to "evolving standards of decency," *Trop v. Dulles,* supra, at 101, only in determining whether criminal punishments are "cruel and unusual" under the Amendment.

37. Some punishments, though not labeled "criminal" by the State, may be sufficiently analogous to criminal punishments in the circumstances in which they are administered to justify application of the Eighth Amendment. Cf. *In re Gault,* 387 U.S. 1 (1967). We have no occasion in this case, for example, to consider whether or under what circumstances persons involuntarily confined in mental or juvenile institutions can claim the protection of the Eighth Amendment.

38. Judge Friendly similarly has observed that the Cruel and Unusual Punishments Clause "can fairly be deemed to be applicable to the manner in which an otherwise constitutional sentence . . . is carried out by an executioner, see *Louisiana ex rel. Francis v. Resweber,* 329 U.S. 459 . . . (1947), or to cover conditions of confinement which may make intolerable an otherwise constitutional term of imprisonment." *Johnson v. Glick,* 481 F.2d 1028, 1032 (CA2), cert. denied, 414 U.S. 1033 (1973) (citation omitted).

by the Eighth Amendment is limited. After incarceration, only the "'unnecessary and wanton infliction of pain,'" *Estelle v. Gamble,* 429 U.S., at 103, quoting *Gregg v. Georgia,* 428 U.S., at 173, constitutes cruel and unusual punishment forbidden by the Eighth Amendment.

The schoolchild has little need for the protection of the Eighth Amendment. Though attendance may not always be voluntary, the public school remains an open institution. Except perhaps when very young, the child is not physically restrained from leaving school during school hours; and at the end of the school day, the child is invariably free to return home. Even while at school, the child brings with him the support of family and friends and is rarely apart from teachers and other pupils who may witness and protest any instances of mistreatment.

The openness of the public school and its supervision by the community afford significant safeguards against the kinds of abuses from which the Eighth Amendment protects the prisoner. In virtually every community where corporal punishment is permitted in the schools, these safeguards are reinforced by the legal constraints of the common law. Public school teachers and administrators are privileged at common law to inflict only such corporal punishment as is reasonably necessary for the proper education and discipline of the child; any punishment going beyond the privilege may result in both civil and criminal liability. See Part II, supra. As long as the schools are open to public scrutiny, there is no reason to believe that the common-law constraints will not effectively remedy and deter excesses such as those alleged in this case.[39]

We conclude that when public school teachers or administrators impose disciplinary corporal punishment, the Eighth Amendment is inapplicable. The pertinent constitutional question is whether the imposition is consonant with the requirements of due process.[40]

---

39. Putting history aside as irrelevant, the dissenting opinion of Mr. Justice White argues that a "purposive analysis" should control the reach of the Eighth Amendment. Post, at 686–688. There is no support whatever for this approach in the decisions of this Court. Although an imposition must be "punishment" for the Cruel and Unusual Punishments Clause to apply, the Court has never held that all punishments are subject to Eighth Amendment scrutiny. See n. 40, infra. The applicability of the Eighth Amendment always has turned on its original meaning, as demonstrated by its historical derivation. See *Gregg v. Georgia,* 428 U.S., at 169–173 (joint opinion); *Furman v. Georgia,* 408 U.S., at 315–328 (Marshall, J., concurring). The dissenting opinion warns that as a consequence of our decision today, teachers may "cut off a child's ear for being late to class." Post, at 684. This rhetoric bears no relation to reality or to the issues presented in this case. The laws of virtually every State forbid the excessive physical punishment of schoolchildren. Yet the logic of the dissent would make the judgment of which disciplinary punishments are reasonable and which are excessive a matter of constitutional principle in every case, to be decided ultimately by this Court. The hazards of such a broad reading of the Eighth Amendment are clear. "It is always time to say that this Nation is too large, too complex and composed of too great a diversity of peoples for any one of us to have the wisdom to establish the rules by which local Americans must govern their local affairs. The constitutional rule we are urged to adopt is not merely revolutionary—it departs from the ancient faith based on the premise that experience in making local laws by local people themselves is by far the safest guide for a nation like ours to follow." *Powell v. Texas,* 392 U.S. 514, 547–548 (1968) (opinion of Black, J.).

40. Eighth Amendment scrutiny is appropriate only after the State has complied with the constitutional guarantees traditionally associated with criminal prosecutions. See *United States v. Lovett,* 328 U.S. 303, 317–318 (1946). Thus, in *Trop v. Dulles,* 356 U.S. 86 (1958), the plurality appropriately took the view that denationalization was an impermissible punishment for wartime desertion under the Eighth Amendment, because desertion already had been established at a criminal trial. But in *Kennedy v. Mendoza-Martinez,* 372 U.S. 144 (1963), where the Court considered denationalization as a punishment for evading the draft, the Court refused to reach the Eighth Amendment issue, holding instead that the punishment could be imposed only through the criminal process. Id., at 162–167, 186, and n. 43. As these cases demonstrate, the State does not acquire the power to punish with which the Eighth Amendment is concerned until after it has secured a formal adjudication of guilt in accordance with due

IV

The Fourteenth Amendment prohibits any state deprivation of life, liberty, or property without due process of law. Application of this prohibition requires the familiar two-stage analysis: We must first ask whether the asserted individual interest are encompassed within the Fourteenth Amendment's protection of "life, liberty or property"; if protected interests are implicated, we then must decide what procedures constitute "due process of law." *Morrissey v. Brewer,* 408 U.S., at 481; *Board of Regents v. Roth,* 408 U.S. 564, 569–572 (1972). See Friendly, Some Kind of Hearing, 123 *U. Pa. L. Rev.* 1267 (1975). Following that analysis here, we find that corporal punishment in public schools implicates a constitutionally protected liberty interest, but we hold that the traditional common-law remedies are fully adequate to afford due process.

A

"[T]he range of interests protected by procedural due process is not infinite." *Board of Regents v. Roth,* supra, at 570. We have repeatedly rejected "the notion that any grievous loss visited upon a person by the State is sufficient to invoke the procedural protections of the Due Process Clause." *Meachum v. Fano,* 427 U.S., at 224. Due process is required only when a decision of the State implicates an interest within the protection of the Fourteenth Amendment. And "to determine whether due process requirements apply in the first place, we must look not to the 'weight' but to the nature of the interest at stake." *Roth,* supra, at 570–571.

The Due Process Clause of the Fifth Amendment, later incorporated into the Fourteenth, was intended to give Americans at least the protection against governmental power that they had enjoyed as Englishmen against the power of the Crown. The liberty preserved from deprivation without due process included the right "generally to enjoy those privileges long recognized at common law as essential to the orderly pursuit of happiness by free men." *Meyer v. Nebraska,* 262 U.S. 390, 399 (1923); see *Dent v. West Virginia,* 129 U.S. 114, 123–124 (1889). Among the historic liberties so protected was a right to be free from, and to obtain judicial relief for, unjustified intrusions on personal security.[41]

While the contours of this historic liberty interest in the context of our federal system of government have not been defined precisely,[42] they always have been thought to encompass

---

process of law. Where the State seeks to impose punishment without such an adjudication, the pertinent constitutional guarantee is the Due Process Clause of the Fourteenth Amendment.

41. See 1 W. Blackstone, Commentaries *134. Under the 39th Article of the Magna Carta, an individual could not be deprived of this right of personal security "except by the legal judgment of his peers or by the law of the land." *Perry & Cooper,* supra, n. 33, at 17. By subsequent enactments of Parliament during the time of Edward III, the right was protected from deprivation except "by due process of law." See Shattuck, The True Meaning of the Term "Liberty," 4 *Harv. L. Rev.* 365, 372–373 (1891).

42. See, e.g., *Skinner v. Oklahoma,* 316 U.S. 535, 541 (1942) (sterilization); *Jacobson v. Massachusetts,* 197 U.S. 11 (1905) (vaccination); *Union Pacific R. Co. v. Botsford,* 141 U.S. 250, 251–252 (1891) (physical examinations); cf. *ICC v. Brimson,* 154 U.S. 447, 479 (1894). The right of personal security is also protected by the Fourth Amendment, which was made applicable to the States through the Fourteenth because its protection was viewed as "implicit in 'the concept of ordered liberty' . . . enshrined in the history and the basic constitutional documents of English-speaking peoples." *Wolf v. Colorado,* 338 U.S. 25, 27–28 (1949). It has been said of the Fourth Amendment that its "overriding function . . . is to protect personal privacy and dignity against unwarranted intrusion by the State." *Schmerber v. California,* 384 U.S. 757, 767 (1966). But the principal concern of that Amendment's prohibition against unreasonable searches and seizures is with intrusions on privacy in the course of criminal investigations. See *Whalen v. Roe,* 429 U.S. 589, 604 n. 32 (1977). Petitioners do not contend that the Fourth Amendment applies, according to its terms, to corporal punishment in public school.

freedom from bodily restraint and punishment. See *Rochin v. California,* 342 U.S. 165 (1952). It is fundamental that the state cannot hold and physically punish an individual except in accordance with due process of law.

This constitutionally protected liberty interest is at stake in this case. There is, of course, a de minimis level of imposition with which the Constitution is not concerned. But at least where school authorities, acting under color of state law, deliberately decide to punish a child for misconduct by restraining the child and inflicting appreciable physical pain, we hold that Fourteenth Amendment liberty interests are implicated.[43]

B

"[T]he question remains what process is due." *Morrissey v. Brewer,* supra, at 481. Were it not for the common-law privilege permitting teachers to inflict reasonable corporal punishment on children in their care, and the availability of the traditional remedies for abuse, the case for requiring advance procedural safeguards would be strong indeed.[44] But here we deal with a punishment—paddling—within that tradition, and the question is whether the common-law remedies are adequate to afford due process.

"'[D]ue process,' unlike some legal rules, is not a technical conception with a fixed content unrelated to time, place and circumstances. . . . Representing a profound attitude of fairness . . . 'due process' is compounded of history, reason, the past course of decisions, and stout confidence in the strength of the democratic faith which we profess. . . ." *Anti-Fascist Comm. v. McGrath,* 341 U.S. 123, 162–163 (1951) (Frankfurter, J., concurring).

Whether in this case the common-law remedies for excessive corporal punishment constitute due process of law must turn on an analysis of the competing interests at stake, viewed against the background of "history, reason, [and] the past course of decisions." The analysis requires consideration of three distinct factors: "First, the private interest that will be affected. . . ; second, the risk of an erroneous deprivation of such interest . . . and the probable value, if any, of additional or substitute procedural safeguards; and finally, the [state] interest, including the function involved and the fiscal and administrative burdens that the additional or substitute procedural requirement would entail." *Mathews v. Eldridge,* 424 U.S. 319, 335 (1976). Cf. *Arnett v. Kennedy,* 416 U.S. 134, 167–168 (1974) (Powell, J., concurring).

1

Because it is rooted in history, the child's liberty interest in avoiding corporal punishment while in the care of public school authorities is subject to historical limitations. Under the common

---

43. Unlike *Goss v. Lopez,* 419 U.S. 565 (1975), this case does not involve the state-created property interest in public education. The purpose of corporal punishment is to correct a child's behavior without interrupting his education. That corporal punishment may, in a rare case, have the unintended effect of temporarily removing a child from school affords no basis for concluding that the practice itself deprives students of property protected by the Fourteenth Amendment. Nor does this case involve any state-created interest in liberty going beyond the Fourteenth Amendment's protection of freedom from bodily restraint and corporal punishment. Cf. *Meachum v. Fano,* 427 U.S. 215, 225–227 (1976).

44. If the common-law privilege to inflict reasonable corporal punishment in school were inapplicable, it is doubtful whether any procedure short of a trial in a criminal or juvenile court could satisfy the requirements of procedural due process for the imposition of such punishment. See *United States v. Lovett,* 328 U.S., at 317–318; cf. *Breed v. Jones,* 421 U.S. 519, 528–529 (1975).

law, an invasion of personal security gave rise to a right to recover damages in a subsequent judicial proceeding. 3 W. Blackstone, Commentaries *120–121. But the right of recovery was qualified by the concept of justification. Thus, there could be no recovery against a teacher who gave only "moderate correction" to a child. Id., at *120. To the extent that the force used was reasonable in light of its purpose, it was not wrongful, but rather "justifiable or lawful." Ibid.

The concept that reasonable corporal punishment in school is justifiable continues to be recognized in the laws of most States. See Part II, supra. It represents "the balance struck by this country," *Poe v. Ullman,* 367 U.S. 497, 542 (1961) (Harlan, J., dissenting), between the child's interest in personal security and the traditional view that some limited corporal punishment may be necessary in the course of a child's education. Under that longstanding accommodation of interests, there can be no deprivation of substantive rights as long as disciplinary corporal punishment is within the limits of the common-law privilege.

This is not to say that the child's interest in procedural safeguards is insubstantial. The school disciplinary process is not "a totally accurate, unerring process, never mistaken and never unfair. . . ." *Goss v. Lopez,* 419 U.S. 565, 579–580 (1975). In any deliberate infliction of corporal punishment on a child who is restrained for that purpose, there is some risk that the intrusion on the child's liberty will be unjustified and therefore unlawful. In these circumstances the child has a strong interest in procedural safeguards that minimize the risk of wrongful punishment and provide for the resolution of disputed questions of justification.

We turn now to a consideration of the safeguards that are available under applicable Florida law.

2

Florida has continued to recognize, and indeed has strengthened by statute, the common-law right of a child not to be subjected to excessive corporal punishment in school. Under Florida law the teacher and principal of the school decide in the first instance whether corporal punishment is reasonably necessary under the circumstances in order to discipline a child who has misbehaved. But they must exercise prudence and restraint. For Florida has preserved the traditional judicial proceedings for determining whether the punishment was justified. If the punishment inflicted is later found to have been excessive—not reasonably believed at the time to be necessary for the child's discipline or training—the school authorities inflicting it may be held liable in damages to the child and, if malice is shown, they may be subject to criminal penalties.[45]

---

45. See supra, at 655–657, 661. The statutory prohibition against "degrading" or unnecessarily "severe" corporal punishment in former 232.27 has been construed as a statement of the common-law principle. See 1937 Op. Fla. Atty. Gen., Biennial Report of the Atty. Gen. 169 (1937–1938); cf. 1957 Op. Fla. Atty. Gen., Biennial Report of the Atty. Gen. 7, 8 (1957–1958). Florida Stat. Ann. 827.03 (3) (1976) makes malicious punishment of a child a felony. Both the District Court, App. 144, and the Court of Appeals, 525 F.2d, at 915, expressed the view that the common-law tort remedy was available to the petitioners in this case. And petitioners conceded in this Court that a teacher who inflicts excessive punishment on a child may be held both civilly and criminally liable under Florida law. Brief for Petitioners 33 n. 11, 34; Tr. of Oral Arg. 17, 52–53. In view of the statutory adoption of the common-law rule, and the unanimity of the parties and the courts below, the doubts expressed in Mr. Justice White's dissenting opinion as to the availability of tort remedies in Florida can only be viewed as chimerical. The dissent makes much of the fact that no Florida court has ever "recognized" a damages remedy for unreasonable corporal punishment. Post, at 694 n. 11, 700. But the absence of reported Florida decisions hardly suggests that no remedy is available. Rather, it merely confirms the commonsense judgment that excessive corporal punishment is exceedingly rare in the public schools.

Although students have testified in this case to specific instances of abuse, there is every reason to believe that such mistreatment is an aberration. The uncontradicted evidence suggests that corporal punishment in the Dade County schools was, "[w]ith the exception of a few cases, . . . unremarkable in physical severity." App. 147. Moreover, because paddlings are usually inflicted in response to conduct directly observed by teachers in their presence, the risk that a child will be paddled without cause is typically insignificant. In the ordinary case, a disciplinary paddling neither threatens seriously to violate any substantive rights nor condemns the child "to suffer grievous loss of any kind." *Anti-Fascist Comm. v. McGrath,* 341 U.S., at 168 (Frankfurter, J., concurring).

In those cases where severe punishment is contemplated, the available civil and criminal sanctions for abuse—considered in light of the openness of the school environment—afford significant protection against unjustified corporal punishment. See supra, at 670. Teachers and school authorities are unlikely to inflict corporal punishment unnecessarily or excessively when a possible consequence of doing so is the institution of civil or criminal proceedings against them.[46]

It still may be argued, of course, that the child's liberty interest would be better protected if the common-law remedies were supplemented by the administrative safeguards of prior notice and a hearing. We have found frequently that some kind of prior hearing is necessary to guard against arbitrary impositions on interests protected by the Fourteenth Amendment. See, e.g., *Board of Regents v. Roth,* 408 U.S., at 569–570; *Wolff v. McDonnell,* 418 U.S. 539, 557–558 (1974); cf. Friendly, 123 *U. Pa. L. Rev.,* at 1275–1277. But where the State has preserved what "has always been the law of the land," *United States v. Barnett,* 376 U.S. 681 (1964), the case for administrative safeguards is significantly less compelling.[47]

There is a relevant analogy in the criminal law. Although the Fourth Amendment specifically proscribes "seizure" of a person without probable cause, the risk that police will act unreasonably in arresting a suspect is not thought to require an advance determination of the facts. In *United States v. Watson,* 423 U.S. 411 (1976), we reaffirmed the traditional

---

46. The low incidence of abuse, and the availability of established judicial remedies in the event of abuse, distinguish this case from *Goss v. Lopez,* 419 U.S. 565 (1975). The Ohio law struck down in *Goss* provided for suspensions from public school of up to 10 days without "any written procedure applicable to suspensions." Id., at 567. Although Ohio law provided generally for administrative review, Ohio Rev. Code Ann. 2506.01 (Supp. 1973), the Court assumed that the short suspensions would not be stayed pending review, with the result that the review proceeding could serve neither a deterrent nor a remedial function. 419 U.S., at 581 n. 10. In these circumstances, the Court held the law authorizing suspensions unconstitutional for failure to require "that there be at least an informal give-and-take between student and disciplinarian, preferably prior to the suspension. . . ." Id., at 584. The subsequent civil and criminal proceedings available in this case may be viewed as affording substantially greater protection to the child than the informal conference mandated by *Goss.*

47. "[P]rior hearings might well be dispensed with in many circumstances in which the state's conduct, if not adequately justified, would constitute a common-law tort. This would leave the injured plaintiff in precisely the same posture as a common-law plaintiff, and this procedural consequence would be quite harmonious with the substantive view that the fourteenth amendment encompasses the same liberties as those protected by the common law." Monaghan, Of "Liberty" and "Property," 62 *Cornell L. Rev.* 405, 431 (1977) (footnote omitted). See *Bonner v. Coughlin,* 517 F.2d 1311, 1319 (CA7 1975), modified en banc, 545 F.2d 565 (1976), cert. pending, No. 76-6204. We have no occasion in this case, see supra, at 659, and n. 12, to decide whether or under what circumstances corporal punishment of a public school child may give rise to an independent federal cause of action to vindicate substantive rights under the Due Process Clause.

common-law rule that police officers may make warrantless public arrests on probable cause. Although we observed that an advance determination of probable cause by a magistrate would be desirable, we declined "to transform this judicial preference into a constitutional rule when the judgment of the Nation and Congress has for so long been to authorize warrantless public arrests on probable cause. . . ." Id., at 423; see id., at 429 (Powell, J., concurring). Despite the distinct possibility that a police officer may improperly assess the facts and thus unconstitutionally deprive an individual of liberty, we declined to depart from the traditional rule by which the officer's perception is subjected to judicial scrutiny only after the fact.[48] There is no more reason to depart from tradition and require advance procedural safeguards for intrusions on personal security to which the Fourth Amendment does not apply.

3

But even if the need for advance procedural safeguards were clear, the question would remain whether the incremental benefit could justify the cost. Acceptance of petitioners' claims would work a transformation in the law governing corporal punishment in Florida and most other States. Given the impracticability of formulating a rule of procedural due process that varies with the severity of the particular imposition,[49] the prior hearing petitioners seek would have to precede any paddling, however moderate or trivial.

Such a universal constitutional requirement would significantly burden the use of corporal punishment as a disciplinary measure. Hearings—even informal hearings—require time, personnel, and a diversion of attention from normal school pursuits. School authorities may well choose to abandon corporal punishment rather than incur the burdens of complying with the procedural requirements. Teachers, properly concerned with maintaining authority in the classroom, may well prefer to rely on other disciplinary measures—which they may view as less effective—rather than confront the possible disruption that prior notice and a hearing may entail.[50] Paradoxically, such an alteration of disciplinary policy is most likely to occur in the ordinary case where the contemplated punishment is well within the common-law privilege.[51]

Elimination or curtailment of corporal punishment would be welcomed by many as a societal advance. But when such a policy choice may result from this Court's determination of an asserted right to due process, rather than from the normal processes of community

---

48. See also *Terry v. Ohio*, 392 U.S. 1 (1968). The reasonableness of a warrantless public arrest may be subjected to subsequent judicial scrutiny in a civil action against the law enforcement officer or in a suppression hearing to determine whether any evidence seized in the arrest may be used in a criminal trial.

49. "[P]rocedural due process rules are shaped by the risk of error inherent in the truthfinding process as applied to the generality of cases, not the rare exceptions. . . ." *Mathews v. Eldridge*, 424 U.S. 319, 344 (1976).

50. If a prior hearing, with the inevitable attendant publicity within the school, resulted in rejection of the teacher's recommendation, the consequent impairment of the teacher's ability to maintain discipline in the classroom would not be insubstantial.

51. The effect of interposing prior procedural safeguards may well be to make the punishment more severe by increasing the anxiety of the child. For this reason, the school authorities in Dade County found it desirable that the punishment be inflicted as soon as possible after the infraction. App. 48–49.

debate and legislative action, the societal costs cannot be dismissed as insubstantial.[52] We are reviewing here a legislative judgment, rooted in history and reaffirmed in the laws of many States, that corporal punishment serves important educational interests. This judgment must be viewed in light of the disciplinary problems common-place in the schools. As noted in *Goss v. Lopez*, 419 U.S., at 580: "Events calling for discipline are frequent occurrences and sometimes require immediate, effective action."[53] Assessment of the need for, and the appropriate means of maintaining, school discipline is committed generally to the discretion of school authorities subject to state law. "[T]he Court has repeatedly emphasized the need for affirming the comprehensive authority of the States and of school officials, consistent with fundamental constitutional safeguards, to prescribe and control conduct in the schools." *Tinker v. Des Moines School Dist.*, 393 U.S. 503, 507 (1969).[54]

"At some point the benefit of an additional safeguard to the individual affected . . . and to society in terms of increased assurance that the action is just, may be outweighed by the cost." *Mathews v. Eldridge*, 424 U.S., at 348. We think that point has been reached in this case. In view of the low incidence of abuse, the openness of our schools, and the common-law safeguards that already exist, the risk of error that may result in violation of a schoolchild's substantive rights can only be regarded as minimal. Imposing additional administrative safeguards as a constitutional requirement might reduce that risk marginally, but would also entail a significant intrusion into an area of primary educational responsibility. We conclude that the Due Process Clause does not require notice and a hearing prior to the imposition of corporal punishment in the public schools, as that practice is authorized and limited by the common law.[55]

---

52. "It may be true that procedural regularity in disciplinary proceedings promotes a sense of institutional rapport and open communication, a perception of fair treatment, and provides the offender and his fellow students a showcase of democracy at work. But . . . [r]espect for democratic institutions will equally dissipate if they are thought too ineffectual to provide their students an environment of order in which the educational process may go forward. . . . ." *Wilkinson, Goss v. Lopez*: The Supreme Court as School Superintendent, 1975 Sup. Ct. Rev. 25, 71–72.

53. The seriousness of the disciplinary problems in the Nation's public schools has been documented in a recent congressional report, Senate Committee on the Judiciary, Subcommittee to Investigate Juvenile Page 430 U.S. 651, 682 Delinquency, Challenge for the Third Century: Education in a Safe Environment—Final Report on the Nature and Prevention of School Violence and Vandalism, 95th Cong., 1st Sess. (Comm. Print 1977).

54. The need to maintain order in a trial courtroom raises similar problems. In that context, this Court has recognized the power of the trial judge "to punish summarily and without notice or hearing contemptuous conduct committed in his presence and observed by him." *Taylor v. Hayes*, 418 U.S. 488, 497 (1974), citing *Ex parte Terry*, 128 U.S. 289 (1888). The punishment so imposed may be as severe as six months in prison. See *Codispoti v. Pennsylvania*, 418 U.S. 506, 513–515 (1974); cf. *Muniz v. Hoffman*, 422 U.S. 454, 475–476 (1975).

55. Mr. Justice White's dissenting opinion offers no manageable standards for determining what process is due in any particular case. The dissent apparently would require, as a general rule, only "an informal give-and-take between student and disciplinarian." Post, at 693. But the dissent would depart from these "minimal procedures"—requiring even witnesses, counsel, and cross-examination—in cases where the punishment reaches some undefined level of severity. Post, at 700 n. 18. School authorities are left to guess at the degree of punishment that will require more than an "informal give-and-take" and at the additional process that may be constitutionally required. The impracticality of such an approach is self-evident, and illustrates the hazards of ignoring the traditional solution of the common law. We agree with the dissent that the *Goss* procedures will often be, "if anything, less than a fair-minded school principal would impose upon himself." Post, at 700, quoting *Goss*, 419 U.S., at 583. But before this Court invokes the Constitution to impose a procedural requirement, it should be reasonably certain that the effect will be to afford protection appropriate to the constitutional interests at stake. The dissenting opinion's reading of the Constitution suggests no such beneficial result and, indeed, invites a lowering of existing constitutional standards.

V

Petitioners cannot prevail on either of the theories before us in this case. The Eighth Amendment's prohibition against cruel and unusual punishment is inapplicable to school paddlings, and the Fourteenth Amendment's requirement of procedural due process is satisfied by Florida's preservation of common-law constraints and remedies. We therefore agree with the Court of Appeals that petitioners' evidence affords no basis for injunctive relief, and that petitioners cannot recover damages on the basis of any Eighth Amendment or procedural due process violation.

Affirmed.

Mr. Justice White, with whom Mr. Justice Brennan, Mr. Justice Marshall, and Mr. Justice Stevens join, dissenting.

Today the Court holds that corporal punishment in public schools, no matter how severe, can never be the subject of the protections afforded by the Eighth Amendment. It also holds that students in the public school systems are not constitutionally entitled to a hearing of any sort before beatings can be inflicted on them. Because I believe that these holdings are inconsistent with the prior decisions of this Court and are contrary to a reasoned analysis of the constitutional provisions involved, I respectfully dissent.

I

A

The Eighth Amendment places a flat prohibition against the infliction of "cruel and unusual punishments." This reflects a societal judgment that there are some punishments that are so barbaric and inhumane that we will not permit them to be imposed on anyone, no matter how opprobrious the offense. See *Robinson v. California,* 370 U.S. 660, 676 (1962) (Douglas, J., concurring). If there are some punishments that are so barbaric that they may not be imposed for the commission of crimes, designated by our social system as the most thoroughly reprehensible acts an individual can commit, then, a fortiori, similar punishments may not be imposed on persons for less culpable acts, such as breaches of school discipline. Thus, if it is constitutionally impermissible to cut off someone's ear for the commission of murder, it must be unconstitutional to cut off a child's ear for being late to class.[1] Although there

---

1. There is little reason to fear that if the Eighth Amendment is held to apply at all to corporal punishment of schoolchildren, all paddlings, however moderate, would be prohibited. *Jackson v. Bishop,* 404 F.2d 571 (CA8 1968), held that any paddling or flogging of prisoners, convicted of crime and serving prison terms, violated the cruel and unusual punishment ban of the Eighth Amendment. But aside from the fact that *Bishop* has never been embraced by this Court, the theory of that case was not that bodily punishments are intrinsically barbaric or excessively severe but that paddling of prisoners is "degrading to the punisher and to the punished alike." Id., at 580. That approach may be acceptable in the criminal justice system, but it has little if any relevance to corporal punishment in the schools, for it can hardly be said that the use of moderate paddlings in the discipline of children is inconsistent with the country's evolving standards of decency. On the other hand, when punishment involves a cruel, severe beating or chopping off an ear, something more than merely the dignity of the individual is involved. Whenever a given criminal punishment is "cruel and unusual" because it is inhumane or barbaric, I can think of no reason why it would be any less inhumane or barbaric when inflicted on a schoolchild, as punishment for classroom misconduct. The issue in this case is whether spankings inflicted on public school children for breaking school rules is "punishment," not whether such punishment is "cruel and unusual." If the Eighth Amendment does not bar moderate spanking in public schools, it is because moderate spanking is not "cruel and unusual," not because it is not "punishment" as the majority suggests.

were no ears cut off in this case, the record reveals beatings so severe that if they were inflicted on a hardened criminal for the commission of a serious crime, they might not pass constitutional muster.

Nevertheless, the majority holds that the Eighth Amendment "was designed to protect [only] those convicted of crimes," ante, at 664, relying on a vague and inconclusive recitation of the history of the Amendment. Yet the constitutional prohibition is against cruel and unusual punishments; nowhere is that prohibition limited or modified by the language of the Constitution. Certainly, the fact that the Framers did not choose to insert the word "criminal" into the language of the Eighth Amendment is strong evidence that the Amendment was designed to prohibit all inhumane or barbaric punishments, no matter what the nature of the offense for which the punishment is imposed.

No one can deny that spanking of schoolchildren is "punishment" under any reasonable reading of the word, for the similarities between spanking in public schools and other forms of punishment are too obvious to ignore. Like other forms of punishment, spanking of schoolchildren involves an institutionalized response to the violation of some official rule or regulation proscribing certain conduct and is imposed for the purpose of rehabilitating the offender, deterring the offender and others like him from committing the violation in the future, and inflicting some measure of social retribution for the harm that has been done.

B

We are fortunate that in our society punishments that are severe enough to raise a doubt as to their constitutional validity are ordinarily not imposed without first affording the accused the full panoply of procedural safeguards provided by the criminal process.[2] The effect has been that "every decision of this Court considering whether a punishment is 'cruel and unusual' within the meaning of the Eighth and Fourteenth Amendments has dealt with a criminal punishment." Ante, at 666. The Court would have us believe from this fact that there is a recognized distinction between criminal and noncriminal punishment for purposes of the Eighth Amendment. This is plainly wrong. "[E]ven a clear legislative classification of a statute as 'non-penal' would not alter the fundamental nature of a plainly penal statute." Trop v. Dulles, 356 U.S. 86, 95 (1958) (plurality opinion). The relevant inquiry is not whether the offense for which a punishment is inflicted has been labeled as criminal, but whether the purpose of the deprivation is among those ordinarily associated with punishment, such as retribution, rehabilitation, or deterrence.[3] Id., at 96. Cf. Kennedy v. Mendoza-Martinez, 372 U.S. 144 (1963).

---

2. By no means is it suggested that just because spanking of schoolchildren is "punishment" within the meaning of the Cruel and Unusual Punishments Clause, the school disciplinary process is in any way "criminal" and therefore subject to the full panoply of criminal procedural guarantees. See Part II, infra. Ordinarily, the conduct for which schoolchildren are punished is not sufficiently opprobrious to be called "criminal" in our society, and even violations of school disciplinary rules that might also constitute a crime, see infra, at 688, are not subject to the criminal process. See Baxter v. Palmigiano, 425 U.S. 308 (1976), where the Court held that persons who violate prison disciplinary rules are not entitled to the full panoply of criminal procedural safeguards, even if the rule violation might also constitute a crime.

3. The majority cites Trop as one of the cases that "dealt with a criminal punishment" but neglects to follow the analysis mandated by that decision. In Trop the petitioner was convicted of desertion by a military court-martial and sentenced to three years at hard labor, forfeiture of all pay and allowances, and a dishonorable discharge. After he was punished for the offense he committed, petitioner's application for a passport was turned down. Petitioner

If this purposive approach were followed in the present case, it would be clear that spanking in the Florida public schools is punishment within the meaning of the Eighth Amendment. The District Court found that "[c]orporal punishment is one of a variety of measures employed in the school system for the correction of pupil behavior and the preservation of order." App. 146. Behavior correction and preservation of order are purposes ordinarily associated with punishment.

Without even mentioning the purposive analysis applied in the prior decisions of this Court, the majority adopts a rule that turns on the label given to the offense for which the punishment is inflicted. Thus, the record in this case reveals that one student at Drew Junior High School received 50 licks with a paddle for allegedly making an obscene telephone call. Brief for Petitioners 13. The majority holds that the Eighth Amendment does not prohibit such punishment since it was only inflicted for a breach of school discipline. However, that same conduct is punishable as a misdemeanor under Florida law, Fla. Stat. Ann. 365.16 (Supp. 1977), and there can be little doubt that if that same "punishment" had been inflicted by an officer of the state courts for violation of 365.16, it would have had to satisfy the requirements of the Eighth Amendment.

C

In fact, as the Court recognizes, the Eighth Amendment has never been confined to criminal punishments.[4] Nevertheless, the majority adheres to its view that any protections afforded by the Eighth Amendment must have something to do with criminals, and it would therefore confine any exceptions to its general rule that only criminal punishments are covered by the Eighth Amendment to abuses inflicted on prisoners. Thus, if a prisoner is beaten

---

was told that he had been deprived of the "rights of citizenship" under 401 (g) of the Nationality Act of 1940 because he had been dishonorably discharged from the Armed Forces. The plurality took the view that denationalization in this context was cruel and unusual punishment prohibited by the Eighth Amendment. The majority would have us believe that the determinative factor in *Trop* was that the petitioner had been convicted of desertion; yet there is no suggestion in *Trop* that the disposition of the military court-martial had anything to do with the decision in that case. Instead, while recognizing that the Eighth Amendment extends only to punishments that are penal in nature, the plurality adopted a purposive approach for determining when punishment is penal. "In deciding whether or not a law is penal, this Court has generally based its determination upon the purpose of the statute. If the statute imposes a disability for the purposes of punishment—that is, to reprimand the wrongdoer, to deter others, etc.—it has been considered penal. But a statute has been considered nonpenal if it imposes a disability, not to punish, but to accomplish some other legitimate governmental purpose." 356 U.S., at 96 (footnotes omitted). Although the quoted passage is taken from the plurality opinion of Mr. Chief Justice Warren, joined by three other Justices, Mr. Justice Brennan, in a concurring opinion, adopted a similar approach in concluding that 401 (g) was beyond the power of Congress to enact.

4. Ante, at 669. In *Estelle v. Gamble*, 429 U.S. 97 (1976), a case decided this Term, the Court held that "deliberate indifference to the medical needs of prisoners" by prison officials constitutes cruel and unusual punishment prohibited by the Eighth Amendment. Such deliberate indifference to a prisoner's medical needs clearly is not punishment inflicted for the commission of a crime; it is merely misconduct by a prison official. Similarly, the Eighth Circuit has held that whipping a prisoner with a strap in order to maintain discipline is prohibited by the Eighth Amendment. *Jackson v. Bishop*, 404 F.2d 571 (1968) (Blackmun, J.). See also *Knecht v. Gillman*, 488 F.2d 1136, 1139–1140 (CA8 1973) (injection of vomit-inducing drugs as part of aversion therapy held to be cruel and unusual); *Vann v. Scott*, 467 F.2d 1235, 1240–1241 (CA7 1972) (Stevens, J.) (Eighth Amendment protects runaway children against cruel and inhumane treatment, regardless of whether such treatment is labeled "rehabilitation" or "punishment").

mercilessly for a breach of discipline, he is entitled to the protection of the Eighth Amendment, while a schoolchild who commits the same breach of discipline and is similarly beaten is simply not covered.

The purported explanation of this anomaly is the assertion that schoolchildren have no need for the Eighth Amendment. We are told that schools are open institutions, subject to constant public scrutiny; that schoolchildren have adequate remedies under state law;[5] and that prisoners suffer the social stigma of being labeled as criminals. How any of these policy considerations got into the Constitution is difficult to discern, for the Court has never considered any of these factors in determining the scope of the Eighth Amendment.[6]

The essence of the majority's argument is that schoolchildren do not need Eighth Amendment protection because corporal punishment is less subject to abuse in the public schools than it is in the prison system.[7] However, it cannot be reasonably suggested that just because cruel and unusual punishments may occur less frequently under public scrutiny, they will not occur at all. The mere fact that a public flogging or a public execution would be available for all to see would not render the punishment constitutional if it were otherwise impermissible. Similarly, the majority would not suggest that a prisoner who is placed in a minimum-security prison and permitted to go home to his family on the weekends should be any less entitled to Eighth Amendment protections than his counterpart in a maximum-security prison. In short, if a punishment is so barbaric and inhumane that it goes beyond the tolerance of a civilized society, its openness to public scrutiny should have nothing to do with its constitutional validity.

Nor is it an adequate answer that schoolchildren may have other state and constitutional remedies available to them. Even assuming that the remedies available to public school students are adequate under Florida law,[8] the availability of state remedies has never been determinative of the coverage or of the protections afforded by the Eighth Amendment. The reason is obvious. The fact that a person may have a state-law cause of action against a pub-

---

5. By finding that bodily punishment invades a constitutionally protected liberty interest within the meaning of the Due Process Clause, the majority suggests that the Clause might also afford a remedy for excessive spanking independently of the Eighth Amendment. If this were the case, the Court's present thesis would have little practical significance. If rather than holding that the Due Process Clause affords a remedy by way of the express commands of the Eighth Amendment, the majority would recognize a cause of action under 42 U.S.C. 1983 for a deprivation of "liberty" flowing from an excessive paddling, the Court's opinion is merely a lengthy word of advice with respect to the drafting of civil complaints. Petitioners in this case did raise the substantive due process issue in their petition for certiorari, ante, at 659 n. 12, but consideration of that question was foreclosed by our limited grant of certiorari. If it is probable that schoolchildren would be entitled to protection under some theory of substantive due process, the Court should not now affirm the judgment below, but should amend the grant of certiorari and set this case for reargument.

6. In support of its policy considerations, the only cases from this Court cited by the majority are *Morrissey v. Brewer*, 408 U.S. 471 (1972), and *Meachum v. Fano*, 427 U.S. 215 (1976), both cases involving prisoners' rights to procedural due process.

7. There is no evidence in the record that corporal punishment has been abused in the prison systems more often than in the public schools. Indeed, corporal punishment is seldom authorized in state prisons. See *Jackson v. Bishop*, supra, at 580, where Mr. Justice (then Judge) Blackmun noted: "[O]nly two states still permit the use of the strap [in prisons]. Thus almost uniformly has it been abolished." By relying on its own view of the nature of these two public institutions, without any evidence being heard on the question below, the majority today predicates a constitutional principle on mere armchair speculation.

8. There is some doubt that the state-law remedies available to public school children are adequate. See n. 11, infra.

lic official who tortures him with a thumbscrew for the commission of an antisocial act has nothing to do with the fact that such official conduct is cruel and unusual punishment prohibited by the Eighth Amendment. Indeed, the majority's view was implicitly rejected this Term in *Estelle v. Gamble*, 429 U.S. 97 (1976), when the Court held that failure to provide for the medical needs of prisoners could constitute cruel and unusual punishment even though a medical malpractice remedy in tort was available to prisoners under state law. Id., at 107 n. 15.

D

By holding that the Eighth Amendment protects only criminals, the majority adopts the view that one is entitled to the protections afforded by the Eighth Amendment only if he is punished for acts that are sufficiently opprobrious for society to make them "criminal." This is a curious holding in view of the fact that the more culpable the offender the more likely it is that the punishment will not be disproportionate to the offense, and consequently, the less likely it is that the punishment will be cruel and unusual.[9] Conversely, a public school student who is spanked for a mere breach of discipline may sometimes have a strong argument that the punishment does not fit the offense, depending upon the severity of the beating, and therefore that it is cruel and unusual. Yet the majority would afford the student no protection no matter how inhumane and barbaric the punishment inflicted on him might be.

The issue presented in this phase of the case is limited to whether corporal punishment in public schools can ever be prohibited by the Eighth Amendment. I am therefore not suggesting that spanking in the public schools is in every instance prohibited by the Eighth Amendment. My own view is that it is not. I only take issue with the extreme view of the majority that corporal punishment in public schools, no matter how barbaric, inhumane, or severe, is never limited by the Eighth Amendment. Where corporal punishment becomes so severe as to be unacceptable in a civilized society, I can see no reason that it should become any more acceptable just because it is inflicted on children in the public schools.

II

The majority concedes that corporal punishment in the public schools implicates an interest protected by the Due Process Clause—the liberty interest of the student to be free from "bodily restraint and punishment" involving "appreciable physical pain" inflicted by persons acting under color of state law. Ante, at 674. The question remaining, as the majority recognizes, is what process is due.

The reason that the Constitution requires a State to provide "due process of law" when it punishes an individual for misconduct is to protect the individual from erroneous or mistaken punishment that the State would not have inflicted had it found the facts in a more reliable way. See, e.g., *Mathews v. Eldridge*, 424 U.S. 319, 335, 344 (1976). In *Goss v. Lopez*, 419 U.S. 565 (1975), the Court applied this principle to the school disciplinary process, holding that a student must be given an informal opportunity to be heard before he is finally suspended from public school.

---

9. For a penalty to be consistent with the Eighth Amendment "the punishment must not be grossly out of proportion to the severity of the crime." *Gregg v. Georgia*, 428 U.S. 153, 173 (1976) (joint opinion of Stewart, Powell, and Stevens, JJ.).

"Disciplinarians, although proceeding in utmost good faith, frequently act on the reports and advice of others; and the controlling facts and the nature of the conduct under challenge are often disputed. The risk of error is not at all trivial, and it should be guarded against if that may be done without prohibitive cost or interference with the educational process." Id., at 580.

To guard against this risk of punishing an innocent child, the Due Process Clause requires, not an "elaborate hearing" before a neutral party, but simply "an informal give-and-take between student and disciplinarian" which gives the student "an opportunity to explain his version of the facts." Id., at 580, 582, 584.

The Court now holds that these "rudimentary precautions against unfair or mistaken findings of misconduct," id., at 581, are not required if the student is punished with "appreciable physical pain" rather than with a suspension, even though both punishments deprive the student of a constitutionally protected interest. Although the respondent school authorities provide absolutely no process to the student before the punishment is finally inflicted, the majority concludes that the student is nonetheless given due process because he can later sue the teacher and recover damages if the punishment was "excessive."

This tort action is utterly inadequate to protect against erroneous infliction of punishment for two reasons.[10] First, under Florida law, a student punished for an act he did not commit cannot recover damages from a teacher "proceeding in utmost good faith . . . on the reports and advice of others," supra, at 692; the student has no remedy at all for punishment imposed on the basis of mistaken facts, at least as long as the punishment was reasonable from the point of view of the disciplinarian, uninformed by any prior hearing.[11] The "traditional

---

10. Here, as in *Goss v. Lopez*, 419 U.S. 565, 580–581, n. 9 (1975), the record suggests that there may be a substantial risk of error in the discipline administered by respondent school authorities. Respondents concede that some of the petitioners who were punished "denied misconduct" and that "in some cases the punishments may have been mistaken. . . ." Brief for Respondents 60–61. The Court of Appeals panel below noted numerous instances of students punished despite claims of innocence, 498 F.2d 248, 256–258 (CA5 1974), and was "particularly disturbed by the testimony that whole classes of students were corporally punished for the misconduct of a few." Id., at 268 n. 36. To the extent that the majority focuses on the incidence of and remedies for unduly severe punishments, it fails to address petitioners' claim that procedural safeguards are required to reduce the risk of punishments that are simply mistaken.

11. The majority's assurances to the contrary, it is unclear to me whether and to what extent Florida law provides a damages action against school officials for excessive corporal punishment. Giving the majority the benefit of every doubt, I think it is fair to say that the most a student punished on the basis of mistaken allegations of misconduct can hope for in Florida is a recovery for unreasonable or bad-faith error. But I strongly suspect that even this remedy is not available. Although the majority does not cite a single case decided under Florida law that recognizes a student's right to sue a school official to recover damages for excessive punishment, I am willing to assume that such a tort action does exist in Florida. I nevertheless have serious doubts about whether it would ever provide a recovery to a student simply because he was punished for an offense he did not commit. All the cases in other jurisdictions cited by the majority, ante, at 663 n. 28, involved allegations of punishment disproportionate to the misconduct with which the student was charged; none of the decisions even suggest that a student could recover by showing that the teacher incorrectly imposed punishment for something the student had not done. The majority appears to agree that the damages remedy is available only in cases of punishment unreasonable in light of the misconduct charged. It states: "In those cases where severe punishment is contemplated, the available civil and criminal sanctions for abuse . . . afford significant protection against unjustified corporal punishment." Ante, at 678. Even if the common-law remedy for excessive punishment extends to punishment that is "excessive" only in the sense that it is imposed on the basis of mistaken facts, the school authorities are still protected from personal liability by common-law immunity. (They are protected by statutory immunity for liability for enforcing disciplinary rules "[e]xcept in the case of excessive force or cruel and unusual punishment." Fla. Stat. Ann. 232.275 (1976).) At a minimum, this immunity would protect school officials from damages liability for reasonable mistakes made in good

common-law remedies" on which the majority relies, ante, at 672, thus do nothing to protect the student from the danger that concerned the Court in *Goss*—the risk of reasonable, good-faith mistake in the school disciplinary process.

Second, and more important, even if the student could sue for good-faith error in the infliction of punishment, the lawsuit occurs after the punishment has been finally imposed. The infliction of physical pain is final and irreparable; it cannot be undone in a subsequent proceeding. There is every reason to require, as the Court did in *Goss*, a few minutes of "informal give-and-take between student and disciplinarian" as a "meaningful hedge" against the erroneous infliction of irreparable injury. 419 U.S., at 583-584.[12]

The majority's conclusion that a damages remedy for excessive corporal punishment affords adequate process rests on the novel theory that the State may punish an individual without giving him any opportunity to present his side of the story, as long as he can later recover damages from a state official if he is innocent. The logic of this theory would permit a State that punished speeding with a one-day jail sentence to make a driver serve his sentence first without a trial and then sue to recover damages for wrongful imprisonment.[13] Similarly, the State could finally take away a prisoner's good-time credits for alleged disciplinary infractions and require him to bring a damages suit after he was eventually released.

---

faith. "Although there have been differing emphases and formulations of the common-law immunity of public school officials in cases of student expulsion or suspension, state courts have generally recognized that such officers should be protected from tort liability under state law for all goodfaith, nonmalicious action taken to fulfill their official duties." *Wood v. Strickland*, 420 U.S. 308, 318 (1975) (adopting this rule for 1983 suits involving school discipline) (footnote omitted); see id., at 318 n. 9 (citing state cases). Florida has applied this rule to a police officer's determination of probable cause to arrest; the officer is not liable in damages for an arrest not based on probable cause if the officer reasonably believed that probable cause existed. *Miami v. Albro*, 120 So.2d 23, 26 (Fla. Dist. Ct. App. 1960); cf. *Middleton v. Fort Walton Beach*, 113 So.2d 431 (Fla. Dist. Ct. App. 1959) (police officer would be personally liable for intentional tort of making an arrest pursuant to warrant he knew to be void); *Wilson v. O'Neal*, 118 So.2d 101 (Fla. Dist. Ct. App. 1960) (law enforcement officer not liable in damages for obtaining an arrest warrant on the basis of an incorrect identification). There is every reason to think that the Florida courts would apply a similar immunity standard in a hypothetical damages suit against a school disciplinarian. A final limitation on the student's damages remedy under Florida law is that the student can recover only from the personal assets of the official; the school board's treasury is absolutely protected by sovereign immunity from damages for the torts of its agents. *Buck v. McLean*, 115 So.2d 764 (Fla. Dist. Ct. App. 1959). A teacher's limited resources may deter the jury from awarding, or prevent the student from collecting, the full amount of damages to which he is entitled. Cf. *Bonner v. Coughlin*, 517 F.2d 1311, 1319 n. 23 (CA7 1975), modified en banc, 545 F.2d 565 (1976), cert. pending, No. 76-6204 (state-law remedy affords due process where no sovereign or official immunity bars tort suit for negligence by prison guard).

12. Cf. *G.M. Leasing Corp. v. United States*, 429 U.S. 338, 351–359 (1977). The Court there held that, in levying on a taxpayer's assets pursuant to a jeopardy assessment, revenue agents must obtain a warrant before searching the taxpayer's office but not before seizing his property in a manner that involves no invasion of privacy. *G.M. Leasing* thus reflects the principle that the case for advance procedural safeguards (such as a magistrate's determination of probable cause) is more compelling when the Government finally inflicts an injury that cannot be repaired in a subsequent judicial proceeding (invasion of privacy) than when it inflicts a temporary injury which can be undone (seizure of property). The infliction of bodily punishment, like the invasion of privacy, presents this most compelling case for advance procedural safeguards.

13. To the extent that the majority attempts to find "a relevant analogy in the criminal law"—warrantless arrests on probable cause—to its holding here, ante, at 679–680 (and see infra, at 697–699), it has chosen the wrong analogy. If the majority forthrightly applied its present due process analysis to the area of criminal prosecutions, the police officer not only could arrest a suspect without a warrant but also could convict the suspect without a trial and sentence him to a short jail term. The accused would get his due process in a tort suit for false imprisonment.

There is no authority for this theory, nor does the majority purport to find any,[14] in the procedural due process decisions of this Court. Those cases have "consistently held that some kind of hearing is required at some time before a person is finally deprived of his property interests . . . [and that] a person's liberty is equally protected. . . ." *Wolff v. McDonnell*, 418 U.S. 539, 557–558 (1974).

The majority attempts to support its novel theory by drawing an analogy to warrantless arrests on probable cause, which the Court has held reasonable under the Fourth Amendment. *United States v. Watson*, 423 U.S. 411 (1976). This analogy fails for two reasons. First, the particular requirements of the Fourth Amendment, rooted in the "ancient common-law rule[s]" regulating police practices, id., at 418, must be understood in the context of the criminal justice system for which that Amendment was explicitly tailored. Thus in *Gerstein v. Pugh*, 420 U.S. 103 (1975), the Court, speaking through Mr. Justice Powell, rejected the argument that procedural protections required in *Goss* and other due process cases should be afforded to a criminal suspect arrested without a warrant.

> "The Fourth Amendment was tailored explicitly for the criminal justice system, and its balance between individual and public interests always has been thought to define the 'process that is due' for seizures of person or property in criminal cases, including the detention of suspects pending trial. . . . Moreover, the Fourth Amendment probable cause determination is in fact only the first stage of an elaborate system, unique in jurisprudence, designed to safeguard the rights of those accused of criminal conduct. The relatively simple civil procedures (e.g., prior interview with school principal before suspension) presented in the [procedural due process] cases cited in the concurring opinion are inapposite and irrelevant in the wholly different context of the criminal justice system." Id., at 125 n. 27.

While a case dealing with warrantless arrests is perhaps not altogether "inapposite and irrelevant in the wholly different context" of the school disciplinary process, such a case is far weaker authority than procedural due process cases such as *Goss v. Lopez*, 419 U.S. 565 (1975), that deal with deprivations of liberty outside the criminal context.

Second, contrary to the majority's suggestion, ante, at 680 n. 48, the reason that the Court has upheld warrantless arrests on probable cause is not because the police officer's assessment of the facts "may be subjected to subsequent judicial scrutiny in a civil action against the law enforcement officer or in a suppression hearing. . . ." The reason that the Court has up-

---

14. For the proposition that the need for a prior hearing is "significantly less compelling" where the State has preserved "common-law remedies," ante, at 679, 678, the majority cites only one case, *Bonner v. Coughlin*, supra, dismissing an allegation by a prisoner that prison guards acting under color of state law had deprived him of property without due process of law by negligently failing to close the door of his cell after a search, with the foreseeable consequence that his trial transcript was stolen. The panel held that the right to recover under state law for the negligence of state employees provided the prisoner with due process of law. The decision is distinguishable from the instant case on two grounds. First, recovery was not barred by sovereign or official immunity, and the state remedy ensured that the prisoner would be "made whole for any loss of property." 517 F.2d, at 1319, and n. 23. Cf. *Regional Rail Reorganization Act Cases*, 419 U.S. 102, 156 (1974). The point here, of course, is that the student cannot be made whole for the infliction of wrongful punishment. Second, the State cannot hold a pre-deprivation hearing where it does not intend to inflict the deprivation; the best it can do to protect the individual from an unauthorized and inadvertent act is to provide a damages remedy. 517 F.2d, at 1319 n. 25. Here the deprivation is intentional and a prior hearing altogether feasible.

held arrests without warrants is that they are the "first stage of an elaborate system" of procedural protections, *Gerstein v. Pugh,* supra, at 125 n. 27, and that the State is not free to continue the deprivation beyond this first stage without procedures. The Constitution requires the State to provide "a fair and reliable determination of probable cause" by a judicial officer prior to the imposition of "any significant pretrial restraint of liberty" other than "a brief period of detention to take the administrative steps incident to [a warrantless] arrest." Id., at 114, 125. (Footnote omitted). This "practical compromise" is made necessary because "requiring a magistrate's review of the factual justification prior to any arrest . . . would constitute an intolerable handicap for legitimate law enforcement," id., at 113; but it is the probable-cause determination prior to any significant period of pretrial incarceration, rather than a damages action or suppression hearing, that affords the suspect due process.

There is, in short, no basis in logic or authority for the majority's suggestion that an action to recover damages for excessive corporal punishment "afford[s] substantially greater protection to the child than the informal conference mandated by *Goss.*"[15] The majority purports to follow the settled principle that what process is due depends on "'the risk of an erroneous deprivation of [the protected] interest . . . and the probable value, if any, of additional or *substitute procedural safeguards*'";[16] it recognizes, as did *Goss,* the risk of error in the school disciplinary process[17] and concedes that "the child has a strong interest in procedural safeguards that minimize the risk of wrongful punishment . . . ," ante, at 676; but it somehow concludes that this risk is adequately reduced by a damages remedy that never has been recognized by a Florida court, that leaves unprotected the innocent student punished by mistake, and that allows the State to punish first and hear the student's version of events later. I cannot agree.

The majority emphasizes, as did the dissenters in *Goss,* that even the "rudimentary precautions" required by that decision would impose some burden on the school disciplinary process. But those costs are no greater if the student is paddled rather than suspended; the risk of error in the punishment is no smaller; and the fear of "a significant intrusion" into the disciplinary process, ante, at 682 (cf. *Goss,* supra, at 585 (Powell, J., dissenting)), is just as exaggerated. The disciplinarian need only take a few minutes to give the student "notice of the charges against him and, if he denies them, an explanation of the evidence the authorities have and an opportunity to present his side of the story." 419 U.S., at 581. In this context the Constitution requires, "if anything, less than a fair-minded school principal would impose upon himself" in order to avoid injustice.[18] Id., at 583.

---

15. Ante, at 678 n. 46.

16. Ante, at 675, quoting *Mathews v. Eldridge,* 424 U.S. 319, 335 (1976).

17. Ante, at 676, quoting *Goss,* 419 U.S., at 579–580. Elsewhere in its opinion the majority asserts that the risk of error is "typically insignificant" because "paddlings are usually inflicted in response to conduct directly observed by teachers in their presence." Ante, at 677–678. But it cites no finding or evidence in the record for this assertion, and there is no such restriction in the statute or regulations authorizing corporal punishment. See ante, at 655 n. 6, 656 n. 7. Indeed, the panel below noted specific instances in which students were punished by an assistant to the principal who was not present when the alleged offenses were committed. 498 F.2d, at 257, 259.

18. My view here expressed that the minimal procedures of *Goss* are required for any corporal punishment implicating the student's liberty interest is, of course, not meant to imply that this minimum would be constitutionally sufficient no matter how severe the punishment inflicted. The Court made this reservation explicit in *Goss* by suggesting that more elaborate procedures such as witnesses, counsel, and cross-examination might well be required for suspensions longer than the 10-day maximum involved in that case. 419 U.S., at 583–584. A similar caveat is appropriate here.

I would reverse the judgment below.

Mr. Justice Stevens, dissenting.

Mr. Justice White's analysis of the Eighth Amendment issue is, I believe, unanswerable. I am also persuaded that his analysis of the procedural due process issue is correct. Notwithstanding my disagreement with the Court's holding on the latter question, my respect for Mr. Justice Powell's reasoning in Part IV-B of his opinion for the Court prompts these comments.

The constitutional prohibition of state deprivations of life, liberty, or property without due process of law does not, by its express language, require that a hearing be provided before any deprivation may occur. To be sure, the timing of the process may be a critical element in determining its adequacy—that is, in deciding what process is due in a particular context. Generally, adequate notice and a fair opportunity to be heard in advance of any deprivation of a constitutionally protected interest are essential. The Court has recognized, however, that the wording of the command that there shall be no deprivation "without" due process of law is consistent with the conclusion that a postdeprivation remedy is sometimes constitutionally sufficient.[1]

When only an invasion of a property interest is involved, there is a greater likelihood that a damages award will make a person completely whole than when an invasion of the individual's interest in freedom from bodily restraint and punishment has occurred. In the property context, therefore, frequently a postdeprivation state remedy may be all the process that the Fourteenth Amendment requires. It may also be true—although I do not express an opinion on the point—that an adequate state remedy for defamation may satisfy the due process requirement when a State has impaired an individual's interest in his reputation. On that hypothesis, the Court's analysis today gives rise to the thought that *Paul v. Davis,* 424 U.S. 693, may have been correctly decided on an incorrect rationale. Perhaps the Court will one day agree with Mr. Justice Brennan's appraisal of the importance of the constitutional interest at stake in id., at 720–723, 734 (dissenting opinion), and nevertheless conclude that an adequate state remedy may prevent every state-inflicted injury to a person's reputation from violating 42 U.S.C. 1983.[2]

---

1. *Calero-Toledo v. Pearson Yacht Leasing Co.,* 416 U.S. 663; *Fuentes v. Shevin,* 407 U.S. 67, 82, 90–92; *Ewing v. Mytinger & Casselberry,* 339 U.S. 594, 598–600; *Phillips v. Commissioner,* 283 U.S. 589, 595–599; *Lawton v. Steele,* 152 U.S. 133, 140–142; cf. *Gerstein v. Pugh,* 420 U.S. 103, 113–114.

2. Cf. *Bonner v. Coughlin,* 517 F.2d 1311, 1318–1320 (CA7 1975), modified en banc, 545 F.2d 565 (1976), cert. pending, No. 76-6204; see also Judge Swygert's thoughtful opinion, id., at 569–578.

CHAPTER 11

SEARCH AND SEIZURE

Introduction

One of the most unique and difficult search and seizure problems peculiar to juveniles is whether a search of a child's possessions—or of the child—by a school official on school grounds is constitutionally valid. The U.S. Supreme Court case of *New Jersey v. T. L. O.* decided that the search of a student, without permission by a school official acting as a governmental agent, was valid where the student was suspected of violating the law. Future court decisions regarding the validity of school searches will probably be decided on the basis of the reasonableness of the search; who conducts it; whether the search is of a person, place, or possession; and whether any statutes or school regulations govern such actions.

Search and Seizure at School

Case Comment

Education officials often assume quasi-police powers over children in school. School officials may search students in order to determine whether they are in possession of contraband such as drugs or weapons, search student's lockers and desks, and even question them about illegal activities. Such actions are comparable to the acts of law enforcement officials, certainly in terms of the consequences for the student. In *New Jersey v. T. L. O.*, the U.S. Supreme Court held that a school official had the authority to search the purse of a student, even though no warrant was issued and there was not probable cause that a crime had been committed; there was only the suspicion that T. L. O. had violated school rules.

This important case involves an assistant principal's search of the purse of a fourteen-year-old student observed smoking a cigarette in a school lavatory. The search was prompted when the principal found cigarette rolling papers as the pack of cigarettes was removed from the purse. A further search revealed marijuana and several items indicating that T. L. O. was selling marijuana; as a result, T. L. O. was adjudicated as a delinquent. The Supreme Court held that the Fourth Amendment protections against unreasonable searches and seizures apply to students but further ruled that the need to maintain an orderly educational environment modified the usual Fourth Amendment requirements of warrants and probable cause. The Court relaxed the usual probable cause standard and found the search to be reasonable. It declared that the school's right to maintain discipline on school grounds allowed it to search a student and his or her possessions as a safety precaution. Thus the

Court that had guarded the warrant requirement and its exceptions in the past now permitted a warrantless search in schools, based on the lesser standard of "reasonable suspicion," and established the concept of "reasonableness" in dealing with school searches.

NEW JERSEY V. T. L. O

Supreme Court of the United States, 1985.

469 U.S. 325.

Justice White delivered the opinion of the Court.

We granted certiorari in this case to examine the appropriateness of the exclusionary rule as a remedy for searches carried out in violation of the Fourth Amendment by public school authorities. Our consideration of the proper application of the Fourth Amendment to the public schools, however, has led us to conclude that the search that gave rise to the case now before us did not violate the Fourth Amendment. Accordingly, we here address only the questions of the proper standard for assessing the legality of searches conducted by public school officials and the application of that standard to the facts of this case.

I

On March 7, 1980, a teacher at Piscataway High School in Middlesex County, N.J., discovered two girls smoking in a lavatory. One of the two girls was the respondent T. L. O., who at that time was a 14-year-old high school freshman. Because smoking in the lavatory was a violation of a school rule, the teacher took the two girls to the Principal's office, where they met with Assistant Vice Principal Theodore Choplick. In response to questioning by Mr. Choplick, T. L. O.'s companion admitted that she had violated the rule. T. L. O., however, denied that she had been smoking in the lavatory and claimed that she did not smoke at all.

Mr. Choplick asked T. L. O. to come into his private office and demanded to see her purse. Opening the purse, he found a pack of cigarettes, which he removed from the purse and held before T. L. O. as he accused her of having lied to him. As he reached into the purse for the cigarettes, Mr. Choplick also noticed a package of cigarette rolling papers. In his experience, possession of rolling papers by high school students was closely associated with the use of marihuana. Suspecting that a closer examination of the purse might yield further evidence of drug use, Mr. Choplick proceeded to search the purse thoroughly. The search revealed a small amount of marihuana, a pipe, a number of empty plastic bags, a substantial quantity of money in one-dollar bills, an index card that appeared to be a list of students who owed T. L. O. money, and two letters that implicated T. L. O. in marihuana dealing.

Mr. Choplick notified T. L. O.'s mother and the police, and turned the evidence of drug dealing over to the police. At the request of the police, T. L. O.'s mother took her daughter to police headquarters, where T. L. O. confessed that she had been selling marihuana at the high school. On the basis of the confession and the evidence seized by Mr. Choplick, the State brought delinquency charges against T. L. O. in the Juvenile and Domestic Relations Court of Middlesex County.[1] Contending that Mr. Choplick's search of her purse violated

---

1. T. L. O. also received a 3-day suspension from school for smoking cigarettes in a nonsmoking area and a 7-day suspension for possession of marihuana. On T. L. O.'s motion, the Superior Court of New Jersey, Chancery

the Fourth Amendment, T. L. O. moved to suppress the evidence found in her purse as well as her confession, which, she argued, was tainted by the allegedly unlawful search. The Juvenile Court denied the motion to suppress. *State ex rel. T. L. O.*, 178 N.J. Super. 329, 428 A. 2d 1327 (1980). Although the court concluded that the Fourth Amendment did apply to searches carried out by school officials, it held that

> "a school official may properly conduct a search of a student's person if the official has a reasonable suspicion that a crime has been or is in the process of being committed, or reasonable cause to believe that the search is necessary to maintain school discipline or enforce school policies." Id., at 341, 428 A. 2d, at 1333.

Applying this standard, the court concluded that the search conducted by Mr. Choplick was a reasonable one. The initial decision to open the purse was justified by Mr. Choplick's well-founded suspicion that T. L. O. had violated the rule forbidding smoking in the lavatory. Once the purse was open, evidence of marihuana violations was in plain view, and Mr. Choplick was entitled to conduct a thorough search to determine the nature and extent of T. L. O.'s drug-related activities. Id., at 343, 428 A. 2d, at 1334. Having denied the motion to suppress, the court on March 23, 1981, found T. L. O. to be a delinquent and on January 8, 1982, sentenced her to a year's probation.

On appeal from the final judgment of the Juvenile Court, a divided Appellate Division affirmed the trial court's finding that there had been no Fourth Amendment violation, but vacated the adjudication of delinquency and remanded for a determination whether T. L. O. had knowingly and voluntarily waived her Fifth Amendment rights before confessing. *State ex rel. T. L. O.*, 185 N.J. Super. 279, 448 A. 2d 493 (1982). T. L. O. appealed the Fourth Amendment ruling, and the Supreme Court of New Jersey reversed the judgment of the Appellate Division and ordered the suppression of the evidence found in T. L. O.'s purse. *State ex rel. T. L. O.*, 94 N.J. 331, 463 A. 2d 934 (1983).

The New Jersey Supreme Court agreed with the lower courts that the Fourth Amendment applies to searches conducted by school officials. The court also rejected the State of New Jersey's argument that the exclusionary rule should not be employed to prevent the use in juvenile proceedings of evidence unlawfully seized by school officials. Declining to consider whether applying the rule to the fruits of searches by school officials would have any deterrent value, the court held simply that the precedents of this Court establish that "if an official search violates constitutional rights, the evidence is not admissible in criminal proceedings." Id., at 341, 463 A. 2d, at 939 (footnote omitted).

With respect to the question of the legality of the search before it, the court agreed with the Juvenile Court that a warrantless search by a school official does not violate the Fourth Amendment so long as the official "has reasonable grounds to believe that a student possesses evidence of illegal activity or activity that would interfere with school discipline and order." Id., at 346, 463 A. 2d, at 941-942. However, the court, with two justices dissenting, sharply disagreed with the Juvenile Court's conclusion that the search of the purse was reasonable.

Division, set aside the 7-day suspension on the ground that it was based on evidence seized in violation of the Fourth Amendment. *T. L. O. v. Piscataway Bd. of Ed.*, No. C. 2865-79 (Super. Ct. N.J., Ch. Div., Mar. 31, 1980). The Board of Education apparently did not appeal the decision of the Chancery Division.

According to the majority, the contents of T. L. O.'s purse had no bearing on the accusation against T. L. O., for possession of cigarettes (as opposed to smoking them in the lavatory) did not violate school rules, and a mere desire for evidence that would impeach T. L. O.'s claim that she did not smoke cigarettes could not justify the search. Moreover, even if a reasonable suspicion that T. L. O. had cigarettes in her purse would justify a search, Mr. Choplick had no such suspicion, as no one had furnished him with any specific information that there were cigarettes in the purse. Finally, leaving aside the question whether Mr. Choplick was justified in opening the purse, the court held that the evidence of drug use that he saw inside did not justify the extensive "rummaging" through T. L. O.'s papers and effects that followed. Id., at 347, 463 A. 2d, at 942-943.

We granted the State of New Jersey's petition for certiorari. 464 U.S. 991 (1983). Although the State had argued in the Supreme Court of New Jersey that the search of T. L. O.'s purse did not violate the Fourth Amendment, the petition for certiorari raised only the question whether the exclusionary rule should operate to bar consideration in juvenile delinquency proceedings of evidence unlawfully seized by a school official without the involvement of law enforcement officers. When this case was first argued last Term, the State conceded for the purpose of argument that the standard devised by the New Jersey Supreme Court for determining the legality of school searches was appropriate and that the court had correctly applied that standard; the State contended only that the remedial purposes of the exclusionary rule were not well served by applying it to searches conducted by public authorities not primarily engaged in law enforcement.

Although we originally granted certiorari to decide the issue of the appropriate remedy in juvenile court proceedings for unlawful school searches, our doubts regarding the wisdom of deciding that question in isolation from the broader question of what limits, if any, the Fourth Amendment places on the activities of school authorities prompted us to order reargument on that question.[2] Having heard argument on the legality of the search of T. L. O.'s purse, we are satisfied that the search did not violate the Fourth Amendment.[3]

---

2. State and federal courts considering these questions have struggled to accommodate the interests protected by the Fourth Amendment and the interest of the States in providing a safe environment conducive to education in the public schools. Some courts have resolved the tension between these interests by giving full force to one or the other side of the balance. Thus, in a number of cases courts have held that school officials conducting in-school searches of students are private parties acting in loco parentis and are therefore not subject to the constraints of the Fourth Amendment. See, e.g., *D. R. C. v. State*, 646 P. 2d 252 (Alaska App. 1982); *In re G.*, 11 Cal. App. 3d 1193, 90 Cal. Rptr. 361 (1970); *In re Donaldson*, 269 Cal. App. 2d 509, 75 Cal. Rptr. 220 (1969); *R. C. M. v. State*, 660 S. W. 2d 552 (Tex. App. 1983); *Mercer v. State*, 450 S. W. 2d 715 (Tex. Civ. App. 1970). At least one court has held, on the other hand, that the Fourth Amendment applies in full to in-school searches by school officials and that a search conducted without probable cause is unreasonable, see *State v. Mora*, 307 So. 2d 317 (La.), vacated, 423 U.S. 809 (1975), on remand, 330 So. 2d 900 (La. 1976); others have held or suggested that the probable-cause standard is applicable at least where the police are involved in a search, see *M. v. Board of Ed. Ball-Chatham Community Unit School Dist.* No. 5, 429 F. Supp. 288, 292 (SD Ill. 1977); *Picha v. Wielgos*, 410 F. Supp. 1214, 1219-1221 (ND Ill. 1976); *State v. Young*, 234 Ga. 488, 498, 216 S. E. 2d 586, 594 (1975); or where the search is highly intrusive, see *M. M. v. Anker*, 607 F.2d 588, 589 (CA2 1979).

The majority of courts that have addressed the issue of the Fourth Amendment in the schools have, like the Supreme Court of New Jersey in this case, reached a middle position: the Fourth Amendment applies to searches conducted by school authorities, but the special needs of the school environment require assessment of the legality of such searches against a standard less exacting than that of probable cause. These courts have, by and large, upheld warrantless searches by school authorities provided that they are supported by a reasonable suspicion that the search will uncover evidence of an infraction of school disciplinary rules or a violation of the law. See, e.g.,

II

In determining whether the search at issue in this case violated the Fourth Amendment, we are faced initially with the question whether that Amendment's prohibition on unreasonable searches and seizures applies to searches conducted by public school officials. We hold that it does.

It is now beyond dispute that "the Federal Constitution, by virtue of the Fourteenth Amendment, prohibits unreasonable searches and seizures by state officers." *Elkins v. United States,* 364 U.S. 206, 213 (1960); accord, *Mapp v. Ohio,* 367 U.S. 643 (1961); *Wolf v. Colorado,* 338 U.S. 25 (1949). Equally indisputable is the proposition that the Fourteenth Amendment protects the rights of students against encroachment by public school officials:

> "The Fourteenth Amendment, as now applied to the States, protects the citizen against the State itself and all of its creatures—Boards of Education not excepted. These have, of course, important, delicate, and highly discretionary functions, but none that they may not perform within the limits of the Bill of Rights. That they are educating the young for citizenship is reason for scrupulous protection of Constitutional freedoms of the individual, if we are not to strangle the free mind at its source and teach youth to discount important principles of our government as mere platitudes." *West Virginia State Bd. of Ed. v. Barnette,* 319 U.S. 624, 637 (1943).

These two propositions—that the Fourth Amendment applies to the States through the Fourteenth Amendment, and that the actions of public school officials are subject to the limits placed on state action by the Fourteenth Amendment—might appear sufficient to answer the suggestion that the Fourth Amendment does not proscribe unreasonable searches by school officials. On reargument, however, the State of New Jersey has argued that the history of the Fourth Amendment indicates that the Amendment was intended to regulate only searches and seizures carried out by law enforcement officers; accordingly, although public

---

Tarter v. Raybuck, No. 83-3174 (CA6, Aug. 31, 1984); *Bilbrey v. Brown,* 738 F.2d 1462 (CA9 1984); *Horton v. Goose Creek Independent School Dist.,* 690 F. 2d 470 (CA5 1982); *Bellnier v. Lund,* 438 F. Supp. 47 (NDNY 1977); *M. v. Board of Ed. Ball-Chatham Community Unit School Dist.* No. 5, supra; *In re W.,* 29 Cal. App. 3d 777, 105 Cal. Rptr. 775 (1973); *State v. Baccino,* 282 A. 2d 869 (Del. Super. 1971); *State v. D. T. W.,* 425 So. 2d 1383 (Fla. App. 1983); *State v. Young,* supra; *In re J. A.,* 85 Ill. App. 3d 567, 406 N. E. 2d 958 (1980); *People v. Ward,* 62 Mich. App. 46, 233 N. W. 2d 180 (1975); *Doe v. State,* 88 N.M. 347, 540 P. 2d 827 (App. 1975); *People v. D.,* 34 N.Y. 2d 483, 315 N. E. 2d 466 (1974); *State v. McKinnon,* 88 Wash. 2d 75, 558 P. 2d 781 (1977); *In re L. L.,* 90 Wis. 2d 585, 280 N. W. 2d 343 (App. 1979).

Although few have considered the matter, courts have also split over whether the exclusionary rule is an appropriate remedy for Fourth Amendment violations committed by school authorities. The Georgia courts have held that although the Fourth Amendment applies to the schools, the exclusionary rule does not. See, e.g., *State v. Young,* supra; *State v. Lamb,* 137 Ga. App. 437, 224 S. E. 2d 51 (1976). Other jurisdictions have applied the rule to exclude the fruits of unlawful school searches from criminal trials and delinquency proceedings. See *State v. Mora,* supra; *People v. D.,* supra.

3. In holding that the search of T. L. O.'s purse did not violate the Fourth Amendment, we do not implicitly determine that the exclusionary rule applies to the fruits of unlawful searches conducted by school authorities. The question whether evidence should be excluded from a criminal proceeding involves two discrete inquiries: whether the evidence was seized in violation of the Fourth Amendment, and whether the exclusionary rule is the appropriate remedy for the violation. Neither question is logically antecedent to the other, for a negative answer to either question is sufficient to dispose of the case. Thus, our determination that the search at issue in this case did not violate the Fourth Amendment implies no particular resolution of the question of the applicability of the exclusionary rule.

school officials are concededly state agents for purposes of the Fourteenth Amendment, the Fourth Amendment creates no rights enforceable against them.[4]

It may well be true that the evil toward which the Fourth Amendment was primarily directed was the resurrection of the pre-Revolutionary practice of using general warrants or "writs of assistance" to authorize searches for contraband by officers of the Crown. See *United States v. Chadwick,* 433 U.S. 1, 7-8 (1977); *Boyd v. United States,* 116 U.S. 616, 624–629 (1886). But this Court has never limited the Amendment's prohibition on unreasonable searches and seizures to operations conducted by the police. Rather, the Court has long spoken of the Fourth Amendment's strictures as restraints imposed upon "governmental action"— that is, "upon the activities of sovereign authority." *Burdeau v. McDowell,* 256 U.S. 465, 475 (1921). Accordingly, we have held the Fourth Amendment applicable to the activities of civil as well as criminal authorities: building inspectors, see *Camara v. Municipal Court,* 387 U.S. 523, 528 (1967), Occupational Safety and Health Act inspectors, see *Marshall v. Barlow's, Inc.,* 436 U.S. 307, 312–313 (1978), and even firemen entering privately owned premises to battle a fire, see *Michigan v. Tyler,* 436 U.S. 499, 506 (1978), are all subject to the restraints imposed by the Fourth Amendment. As we observed in *Camara v. Municipal Court,* supra, "[t]he basic purpose of this Amendment, as recognized in countless decisions of this Court, is to safeguard the privacy and security of individuals against arbitrary invasions by governmental officials." 387 U.S., at 528. Because the individual's interest in privacy and personal security "suffers whether the government's motivation is to investigate violations of criminal laws or breaches of other statutory or regulatory standards," *Marshall v. Barlow's, Inc.,* supra, at 312–313, it would be "anomalous to say that the individual and his private property are fully protected by the Fourth Amendment only when the individual is suspected of criminal behavior." *Camara v. Municipal Court,* supra, at 530.

Notwithstanding the general applicability of the Fourth Amendment to the activities of civil authorities, a few courts have concluded that school officials are exempt from the dictates of the Fourth Amendment by virtue of the special nature of their authority over schoolchildren. See, e.g., *R. C. M. v. State,* 660 S. W. 2d 552 (Tex. App. 1983). Teachers and school administrators, it is said, act in loco parentis in their dealings with students: their authority is that of the parent, not the State, and is therefore not subject to the limits of the Fourth Amendment. Ibid.

Such reasoning is in tension with contemporary reality and the teachings of this Court. We have held school officials subject to the commands of the First Amendment, see *Tinker v. Des Moines Independent Community School District,* 393 U.S. 503 (1969), and the Due Process Clause of the Fourteenth Amendment, see *Goss v. Lopez,* 419 U.S. 565 (1975). If school authorities are state actors for purposes of the constitutional guarantees of freedom of expression and due process, it is difficult to understand why they should be deemed to be exercising parental rather than public authority when conducting searches of their students. More generally, the Court has recognized that "the concept of parental delegation" as a source of school authority is not entirely "consonant with compulsory education laws." *Ingraham*

---

4. Cf. *Ingraham v. Wright,* 430 U.S. 651 (1977) (holding that the Eighth Amendment's prohibition of cruel and unusual punishment applies only to punishments imposed after criminal convictions and hence does not apply to the punishment of schoolchildren by public school officials).

v. Wright, 430 U.S. 651, 662 (1977). Today's public school officials do not merely exercise authority voluntarily conferred on them by individual parents; rather, they act in furtherance of publicly mandated educational and disciplinary policies. See, e.g., the opinion in *State ex rel. T. L. O.,* 94 N.J., at 343, 463 A. 2d, at 934, 940, describing the New Jersey statutes regulating school disciplinary policies and establishing the authority of school officials over their students. In carrying out searches and other disciplinary functions pursuant to such policies, school officials act as representatives of the State, not merely as surrogates for the parents, and they cannot claim the parents' immunity from the strictures of the Fourth Amendment.

III

To hold that the Fourth Amendment applies to searches conducted by school authorities is only to begin the inquiry into the standards governing such searches. Although the underlying command of the Fourth Amendment is always that searches and seizures be reasonable, what is reasonable depends on the context within which a search takes place. The determination of the standard of reasonableness governing any specific class of searches requires "balancing the need to search against the invasion which the search entails." *Camara v. Municipal Court,* supra, at 536–537. On one side of the balance are arrayed the individual's legitimate expectations of privacy and personal security; on the other, the government's need for effective methods to deal with breaches of public order.

We have recognized that even a limited search of the person is a substantial invasion of privacy. *Terry v. Ohio,* 392 U.S. 1, 24–25 (1967). We have also recognized that searches of closed items of personal luggage are intrusions on protected privacy interests, for "the Fourth Amendment provides protection to the owner of every container that conceals its contents from plain view." *United States v. Ross,* 456 U.S. 798, 822–823 (1982). A search of a child's person or of a closed purse or other bag carried on her person,[5] no less than a similar search carried out on an adult, is undoubtedly a severe violation of subjective expectations of privacy.

Of course, the Fourth Amendment does not protect subjective expectations of privacy that are unreasonable or otherwise "illegitimate." See, e.g., *Hudson v. Palmer,* 468 U.S. 517 (1984); *Rawlings v. Kentucky,* 448 U.S. 98 (1980). To receive the protection of the Fourth Amendment, an expectation of privacy must be one that society is "prepared to recognize as legitimate." *Hudson v. Palmer,* supra, at 526. The State of New Jersey has argued that because of the pervasive supervision to which children in the schools are necessarily subject, a child has virtually no legitimate expectation of privacy in articles of personal property "unnecessarily"

---

5. We do not address the question, not presented by this case, whether a schoolchild has a legitimate expectation of privacy in lockers, desks, or other school property provided for the storage of school supplies. Nor do we express any opinion on the standards (if any) governing searches of such areas by school officials or by other public authorities acting at the request of school officials. Compare *Zamora v. Pomeroy,* 639 F. 2d 662, 670 (CA10 1981) ("Inasmuch as the school had assumed joint control of the locker it cannot be successfully maintained that the school did not have a right to inspect it"), and *People v. Overton,* 24 N.Y. 2d 522, 249 N. E. 2d 366 (1969) (school administrators have power to consent to search of a student's locker), with *State v. Engerud,* 94 N.J. 331, 348, 463 A. 2d 934, 943 (1983) ("We are satisfied that in the context of this case the student had an expectation of privacy in the contents of his locker. . . . For the four years of high school, the school locker is a home away from home. In it the student stores the kind of personal 'effects' protected by the Fourth Amendment").

carried into a school. This argument has two factual premises: (1) the fundamental incompatibility of expectations of privacy with the maintenance of a sound educational environment; and (2) the minimal interest of the child in bringing any items of personal property into the school. Both premises are severely flawed.

Although this Court may take notice of the difficulty of maintaining discipline in the public schools today, the situation is not so dire that students in the schools may claim no legitimate expectations of privacy. We have recently recognized that the need to maintain order in a prison is such that prisoners retain no legitimate expectations of privacy in their cells, but it goes almost without saying that "[t]he prisoner and the schoolchild stand in wholly different circumstances, separated by the harsh facts of criminal conviction and incarceration." *Ingraham v. Wright,* supra, at 669. We are not yet ready to hold that the schools and the prisons need be equated for purposes of the Fourth Amendment.

Nor does the State's suggestion that children have no legitimate need to bring personal property into the schools seem well anchored in reality. Students at a minimum must bring to school not only the supplies needed for their studies, but also keys, money, and the necessaries of personal hygiene and grooming. In addition, students may carry on their persons or in purses or wallets such nondisruptive yet highly personal items as photographs, letters, and diaries. Finally, students may have perfectly legitimate reasons to carry with them articles of property needed in connection with extracurricular or recreational activities. In short, schoolchildren may find it necessary to carry with them a variety of legitimate, noncontraband items, and there is no reason to conclude that they have necessarily waived all rights to privacy in such items merely by bringing them onto school grounds.

Against the child's interest in privacy must be set the substantial interest of teachers and administrators in maintaining discipline in the classroom and on school grounds. Maintaining order in the classroom has never been easy, but in recent years, school disorder has often taken particularly ugly forms: drug use and violent crime in the schools have become major social problems. See generally 1 NIE, U.S. Dept. of Health, Education and Welfare, Violent Schools—Safe Schools: The Safe School Study Report to the Congress (1978). Even in schools that have been spared the most severe disciplinary problems, the preservation of order and a proper educational environment requires close supervision of schoolchildren, as well as the enforcement of rules against conduct that would be perfectly permissible if undertaken by an adult. "Events calling for discipline are frequent occurrences and sometimes require immediate, effective action." *Goss v. Lopez,* 419 U.S., at 580. Accordingly, we have recognized that maintaining security and order in the schools requires a certain degree of flexibility in school disciplinary procedures, and we have respected the value of preserving the informality of the student-teacher relationship. See id., at 582-583; *Ingraham v. Wright,* 430 U.S., at 680–682.

How, then, should we strike the balance between the schoolchild's legitimate expectations of privacy and the school's equally legitimate need to maintain an environment in which learning can take place? It is evident that the school setting requires some easing of the restrictions to which searches by public authorities are ordinarily subject. The warrant requirement, in particular, is unsuited to the school environment: requiring a teacher to obtain a warrant before searching a child suspected of an infraction of school rules (or of the criminal law) would unduly interfere with the maintenance of the swift and informal disciplinary procedures needed in the schools. Just as we have in other cases dispensed with the warrant requirement when "the burden of obtaining a warrant is likely to frustrate the governmental purpose behind the search," *Camara v. Municipal Court,* 387 U.S., at 532–533, we hold today that school officials need not obtain a warrant before searching a student who is under their authority.

The school setting also requires some modification of the level of suspicion of illicit activity needed to justify a search. Ordinarily, a search—even one that may permissibly be carried out without a warrant—must be based upon "probable cause" to believe that a violation of the law has occurred. See, e.g., *Almeida-Sanchez v. United States,* 413 U.S. 266, 273 (1973); *Sibron v. New York,* 392 U.S. 40, 62–66 (1968). However, "probable cause" is not an irreducible requirement of a valid search. The fundamental command of the Fourth Amendment is that searches and seizures be reasonable, and although "both the concept of probable cause and the requirement of a warrant bear on the reasonableness of a search, . . . in certain limited circumstances neither is required." *Almeida-Sanchez v. United States,* supra, at 277 (POWELL, J., concurring). Thus, we have in a number of cases recognized the legality of searches and seizures based on suspicions that, although "reasonable," do not rise to the level of probable cause. See, e.g., *Terry v. Ohio,* 392 U.S. 1 (1968); United *States v. Brignoni-Ponce,* 422 U.S. 873, 881 (1975); *Delaware v. Prouse,* 440 U.S. 648, 654–655 (1979); *United States v. Martinez-Fuerte,* 428 U.S. 543 (1976); cf. *Camara v. Municipal Court,* supra, at 534–539. Where a careful balancing of governmental and private interests suggests that the public interest is best served by a Fourth Amendment standard of reasonableness that stops short of probable cause, we have not hesitated to adopt such a standard.

We join the majority of courts that have examined this issue[6] in concluding that the accommodation of the privacy interests of schoolchildren with the substantial need of teachers and administrators for freedom to maintain order in the schools does not require strict adherence to the requirement that searches be based on probable cause to believe that the subject of the search has violated or is violating the law. Rather, the legality of a search of a student should depend simply on the reasonableness, under all the circumstances, of the search. Determining the reasonableness of any search involves a twofold inquiry: first, one must consider "whether the . . . action was justified at its inception," *Terry v. Ohio,* 392 U.S., at 20; second, one must determine whether the search as actually conducted "was reasonably related in scope to the circumstances which justified the interference in the first place," ibid. Under ordinary circumstances, a search of a student by a teacher or other school official[7] will be "justified at its inception" when there are reasonable grounds for suspecting that the search will turn up evidence that the student has violated or is violating either the law or the

---

6. See cases cited in n. 2, supra.

7. We here consider only searches carried out by school authorities acting alone and on their own authority. This case does not present the question of the appropriate standard for assessing the legality of searches conducted by school officials in conjunction with or at the behest of law enforcement agencies, and we express no opinion on that question. Cf. *Picha v. Wielgos,* 410 F. Supp. 1214, 1219–1221 (ND Ill. 1976) (holding probable cause standard applicable to searches involving the police).

rules of the school.[8] Such a search will be permissible in its scope when the measures adopted are reasonably related to the objectives of the search and not excessively intrusive in light of the age and sex of the student and the nature of the infraction.[9]

This standard will, we trust, neither unduly burden the efforts of school authorities to maintain order in their schools nor authorize unrestrained intrusions upon the privacy of schoolchildren. By focusing attention on the question of reasonableness, the standard will spare teachers and school administrators the necessity of schooling themselves in the niceties of probable cause and permit them to regulate their conduct according to the dictates of reason and common sense. At the same time, the reasonableness standard should ensure that the interests of students will be invaded no more than is necessary to achieve the legitimate end of preserving order in the schools.

IV

There remains the question of the legality of the search in this case. We recognize that the "reasonable grounds" standard applied by the New Jersey Supreme Court in its consideration of this question is not substantially different from the standard that we have adopted today. Nonetheless, we believe that the New Jersey court's application of that standard to strike down the search of T. L. O.'s purse reflects a somewhat crabbed notion of reasonableness. Our review of the facts surrounding the search leads us to conclude that the search was in no sense unreasonable for Fourth Amendment purposes.[10]

---

8. We do not decide whether individualized suspicion is an essential element of the reasonableness standard we adopt for searches by school authorities. In other contexts, however, we have held that although "some quantum of individualized suspicion is usually a prerequisite to a constitutional search or seizure[,] . . . the Fourth Amendment imposes no irreducible requirement of such suspicion." *United States v. Martinez-Fuerte,* 428 U.S. 543, 560–561 (1976). See also *Camara v. Municipal Court,* 387 U.S. 523 (1967). Exceptions to the requirement of individualized suspicion are generally appropriate only where the privacy interests implicated by a search are minimal and where "other safeguards" are available "to assure that the individual's reasonable expectation of privacy is not 'subject to the discretion of the official in the field.'" *Delaware v. Prouse,* 440 U.S. 648, 654–655 (1979) (citation omitted). Because the search of T. L. O.'s purse was based upon an individualized suspicion that she had violated school rules, see infra, at 343–347, we need not consider the circumstances that might justify school authorities in conducting searches unsupported by individualized suspicion.

9. Our reference to the nature of the infraction is not intended as an endorsement of JUSTICE STEVENS' suggestion that some rules regarding student conduct are by nature too "trivial" to justify a search based upon reasonable suspicion. See post, at 377–382. We are unwilling to adopt a standard under which the legality of a search is dependent upon a judge's evaluation of the relative importance of various school rules. The maintenance of discipline in the schools requires not only that students be restrained from assaulting one another, abusing drugs and alcohol, and committing other crimes, but also that students conform themselves to the standards of conduct prescribed by school authorities. We have "repeatedly emphasized the need for affirming the comprehensive authority of the States and of school officials, consistent with fundamental constitutional safeguards, to prescribe and control conduct in the schools." *Tinker v. Des Moines Independent Community School District,* 393 U.S. 503, 507 (1969). The promulgation of a rule forbidding specified conduct presumably reflects a judgment on the part of school officials that such conduct is destructive of school order or of a proper educational environment. Absent any suggestion that the rule violates some substantive constitutional guarantee, the courts should, as a general matter, defer to that judgment and refrain from attempting to distinguish between rules that are important to the preservation of order in the schools and rules that are not.

10. Of course, New Jersey may insist on a more demanding standard under its own Constitution or statutes. In that case, its courts would not purport to be applying the Fourth Amendment when they invalidate a search.

The incident that gave rise to this case actually involved two separate searches, with the first—the search for cigarettes—providing the suspicion that gave rise to the second—the search for marihuana. Although it is the fruits of the second search that are at issue here, the validity of the search for marijuana must depend on the reasonableness of the initial search for cigarettes, as there would have been no reason to suspect that T. L. O. possessed marijuana had the first search not taken place. Accordingly, it is to the search for cigarettes that we first turn our attention.

The New Jersey Supreme Court pointed to two grounds for its holding that the search for cigarettes was unreasonable. First, the court observed that possession of cigarettes was not in itself illegal or a violation of school rules. Because the contents of T. L. O.'s purse would therefore have "no direct bearing on the infraction" of which she was accused (smoking in a lavatory where smoking was prohibited), there was no reason to search her purse.[11] Second, even assuming that a search of T. L. O.'s purse might under some circumstances be reasonable in light of the accusation made against T. L. O., the New Jersey court concluded that Mr. Choplick in this particular case had no reasonable grounds to suspect that T. L. O. had cigarettes in her purse. At best, according to the court, Mr. Choplick had "a good hunch." 94 N.J., at 347, 463 A. 2d, at 942.

Both these conclusions are implausible. T. L. O. had been accused of smoking, and had denied the accusation in the strongest possible terms when she stated that she did not smoke at all. Surely it cannot be said that under these circumstances, T. L. O.'s possession of cigarettes would be irrelevant to the charges against her or to her response to those charges. T. L. O.'s possession of cigarettes, once it was discovered, would both corroborate the report that she had been smoking and undermine the credibility of her defense to the charge of smoking. To be sure, the discovery of the cigarettes would not prove that T. L. O. had been smoking in the lavatory; nor would it, strictly speaking, necessarily be inconsistent with her claim that she did not smoke at all. But it is universally recognized that evidence, to be relevant to an inquiry, need not conclusively prove the ultimate fact in issue, but only have "any tendency to make the existence of any fact that is of consequence to the determination of the action more probable or less probable than it would be without the evidence." Fed. Rule Evid. 401. The relevance of T. L. O.'s possession of cigarettes to the question whether she had been smoking and to the credibility of her denial that she smoked supplied the necessary "nexus" between the item searched for and the infraction under investigation. See *Warden v. Hayden*, 387 U.S. 294, 306-307 (1967). Thus, if Mr. Choplick in fact had a reasonable suspicion that T. L. O. had cigarettes in her purse, the search was justified despite the fact that the cigarettes, if found, would constitute "mere evidence" of a violation. Ibid.

---

11. Justice Stevens interprets these statements as a holding that enforcement of the school's smoking regulations was not sufficiently related to the goal of maintaining discipline or order in the school to justify a search under the standard adopted by the New Jersey court. See post, at 382–384. We do not agree that this is an accurate characterization of the New Jersey Supreme Court's opinion. The New Jersey court did not hold that the school's smoking rules were unrelated to the goal of maintaining discipline or order, nor did it suggest that a search that would produce evidence bearing directly on an accusation that a student had violated the smoking rules would be impermissible under the court's reasonable-suspicion standard; rather, the court concluded that any evidence a search of T. L. O.'s purse was likely to produce would not have a sufficiently direct bearing on the infraction to justify a search—a conclusion with which we cannot agree for the reasons set forth infra, at 345. Justice Stevens' suggestion that the New Jersey Supreme Court's decision rested on the perceived triviality of the smoking infraction appears to be a reflection of his own views rather than those of the New Jersey court.

Of course, the New Jersey Supreme Court also held that Mr. Choplick had no reasonable suspicion that the purse would contain cigarettes. This conclusion is puzzling. A teacher had reported that T. L. O. was smoking in the lavatory. Certainly this report gave Mr. Choplick reason to suspect that T. L. O. was carrying cigarettes with her; and if she did have cigarettes, her purse was the obvious place in which to find them. Mr. Choplick's suspicion that there were cigarettes in the purse was not an "inchoate and unparticularized suspicion or 'hunch,'" *Terry v. Ohio,* 392 U.S., at 27; rather, it was the sort of "common-sense conclusio[n] about human behavior" upon which "practical people"—including government officials—are entitled to rely. *United States v. Cortez,* 449 U.S. 411, 418 (1981). Of course, even if the teacher's report were true, T. L. O. might not have had a pack of cigarettes with her; she might have borrowed a cigarette from someone else or have been sharing a cigarette with another student. But the requirement of reasonable suspicion is not a requirement of absolute certainty: "sufficient probability, not certainty, is the touchstone of reasonableness under the Fourth Amendment. . . ." *Hill v. California,* 401 U.S. 797, 804 (1971). Because the hypothesis that T. L. O. was carrying cigarettes in her purse was itself not unreasonable, it is irrelevant that other hypotheses were also consistent with the teacher's accusation. Accordingly, it cannot be said that Mr. Choplick acted unreasonably when he examined T. L. O.'s purse to see if it contained cigarettes.[12]

Our conclusion that Mr. Choplick's decision to open T. L. O.'s purse was reasonable brings us to the question of the further search for marijuana once the pack of cigarettes was located. The suspicion upon which the search for marijuana was founded was provided when Mr. Choplick observed a package of rolling papers in the purse as he removed the pack of cigarettes. Although T. L. O. does not dispute the reasonableness of Mr. Choplick's belief that the rolling papers indicated the presence of marijuana, she does contend that the scope of the search Mr. Choplick conducted exceeded permissible bounds when he seized and read certain letters that implicated T. L. O. in drug dealing. This argument, too, is unpersuasive. The discovery of the rolling papers concededly gave rise to a reasonable suspicion that T. L. O. was carrying marijuana as well as cigarettes in her purse. This suspicion justified further exploration of T. L. O.'s purse, which turned up more evidence of drug-related activities: a pipe, a number of plastic bags of the type commonly used to store marijuana, a small quantity of marijuana, and a fairly substantial amount of money. Under these circumstances, it was not unreasonable to extend the search to a separate zippered compartment of the purse;

---

12. T. L. O. contends that even if it was reasonable for Mr. Choplick to open her purse to look for cigarettes, it was not reasonable for him to reach in and take the cigarettes out of her purse once he found them. Had he not removed the cigarettes from the purse, she asserts, he would not have observed the rolling papers that suggested the presence of marijuana, and the search for marijuana could not have taken place. T. L. O.'s argument is based on the fact that the cigarettes were not "contraband," as no school rule forbade her to have them. Thus, according to T. L. O., the cigarettes were not subject to seizure or confiscation by school authorities, and Mr. Choplick was not entitled to take them out of T. L. O.'s purse regardless of whether he was entitled to peer into the purse to see if they were there. Such hairsplitting argumentation has no place in an inquiry addressed to the issue of reasonableness. If Mr. Choplick could permissibly search T. L. O.'s purse for cigarettes, it hardly seems reasonable to suggest that his natural reaction to finding them—picking them up—could be a constitutional violation. We find that neither in opening the purse nor in reaching into it to remove the cigarettes did Mr. Choplick violate the Fourth Amendment.

and when a search of that compartment revealed an index card containing a list of "people who owe me money" as well as two letters, the inference that T. L. O. was involved in mari-huana trafficking was substantial enough to justify Mr. Choplick in examining the letters to determine whether they contained any further evidence. In short, we cannot conclude that the search for marihuana was unreasonable in any respect.

Because the search resulting in the discovery of the evidence of marihuana dealing by T. L. O. was reasonable, the New Jersey Supreme Court's decision to exclude that evidence from T. L. O.'s juvenile delinquency proceedings on Fourth Amendment grounds was erro-neous. Accordingly, the judgment of the Supreme Court of New Jersey is

Reversed.

Justice Brennan, with whom Justice Marshall joins, concurring in part and dissenting in part. I fully agree with Part II of the Court's opinion. Teachers, like all other government of-ficials, must conform their conduct to the Fourth Amendment's protections of personal pri-vacy and personal security. As Justice Stevens points out, post, at 373–374, 385–386, this principle is of particular importance when applied to schoolteachers, for children learn as much by example as by exposition. It would be incongruous and futile to charge teachers with the task of embuing their students with an understanding of our system of constitutional democracy, while at the same time immunizing those same teachers from the need to respect constitutional protections. See *Board of Education v. Pico,* 457 U.S. 853, 864–865 (1982) (plu-rality opinion); *West Virginia State Board of Education v. Barnette,* 319 U.S. 624, 637 (1943).

I do not, however, otherwise join the Court's opinion. Today's decision sanctions school officials to conduct fullscale searches on a "reasonableness" standard whose only definite content is that it is not the same test as the "probable cause" standard found in the text of the Fourth Amendment. In adopting this unclear, unprecedented, and unnecessary departure from generally applicable Fourth Amendment standards, the Court carves out a broad ex-ception to standards that this Court has developed over years of considering Fourth Amend-ment problems. Its decision is supported neither by precedent nor even by a fair application of the "balancing test" it proclaims in this very opinion.

I

Three basic principles underly this Court's Fourth Amendment jurisprudence. First, war-rantless searches are per se unreasonable, subject only to a few specifically delineated and well-recognized exceptions. See, e.g., *Katz v. United States,* 389 U.S. 347, 357 (1967); accord, *Welsh v. Wisconsin,* 466 U.S. 740, 748–749 (1984); *United States v. Place,* 462 U.S. 696, 701 (1983); *Steagald v. United States,* 451 U.S. 204, 211–212 (1981); *Mincey v. Arizona,* 437 U.S. 385 (1978); *Terry v. Ohio,* 392 U.S. 1, 20 (1968); *Johnson v. United States,* 333 U.S. 10, 13–14 (1948). Second, full-scale searches—whether conducted in accordance with the warrant re-quirement or pursuant to one of its exceptions—are "reasonable" in Fourth Amendment terms only on a showing of probable cause to believe that a crime has been committed and that evidence of the crime will be found in the place to be searched. *Beck v. Ohio,* 379 U.S. 89, 91 (1964); *Wong Sun v. United States,* 371 U.S. 471, 479 (1963); *Brinegar v. United States,* 338 U.S. 160, 175–176 (1949). Third, categories of intrusions that are substantially less in-trusive than full-scale searches or seizures may be justifiable in accordance with a balancing test even absent a warrant or probable cause, provided that the balancing test used gives sufficient weight to the privacy interests that will be infringed. *Dunaway v. New York*, 442 U.S. 200, 210 (1979); *Terry v. Ohio,* supra.

Assistant Vice Principal Choplick's thorough excavation of T. L. O.'s purse was undoubtedly a serious intrusion on her privacy. Unlike the searches in *Terry v. Ohio,* supra, or *Adams v. Williams*, 407 U.S. 143 (1972), the search at issue here encompassed a detailed and minute examination of respondent's pocketbook, in which the contents of private papers and letters were thoroughly scrutinized.[1] Wisely, neither petitioner nor the Court today attempts to justify the search of T. L. O.'s pocketbook as a minimally intrusive search in the *Terry* line. To be faithful to the Court's settled doctrine, the inquiry therefore must focus on the warrant and probable-cause requirements.

A

I agree that schoolteachers or principals, when not acting as agents of law enforcement authorities, generally may conduct a search of their students' belongings without first obtaining a warrant. To agree with the Court on this point is to say that school searches may justifiably be held to that extent to constitute an exception to the Fourth Amendment's warrant requirement. Such an exception, however, is not to be justified, as the Court apparently holds, by assessing net social value through application of an unguided "balancing test" in which "the individual's legitimate expectations of privacy and personal security" are weighed against "the government's need for effective methods to deal with breaches of public order." Ante, at 337. The Warrant Clause is something more than an exhortation to this Court to maximize social welfare as we see fit. It requires that the authorities must obtain a warrant before conducting a full-scale search. The undifferentiated governmental interest in law enforcement is insufficient to justify an exception to the warrant requirement. Rather, some special governmental interest beyond the need merely to apprehend lawbreakers is necessary to justify a categorical exception to the warrant requirement. For the most part, special governmental needs sufficient to override the warrant requirement flow from "exigency"—that is, from the press of time that makes obtaining a warrant either impossible or hopelessly infeasible. See *United States v. Place,* supra, at 701–702; *Mincey v. Arizona,* supra, at 393–394; *Johnson v. United States,* supra, at 15. Only after finding an extraordinary governmental interest of this kind do we—or ought we—engage in a balancing test to determine if a warrant should nonetheless be required.[2]

To require a showing of some extraordinary governmental interest before dispensing with the warrant requirement is not to undervalue society's need to apprehend violators of the criminal law. To be sure, forcing law enforcement personnel to obtain a warrant before en-

---

1. A purse typically contains items of highly personal nature. Especially for shy or sensitive adolescents, it could prove extremely embarrassing for a teacher or principal to rummage through its contents, which could include notes from friends, fragments of love poems, caricatures of school authorities, and items of personal hygiene.

2. Administrative search cases involving inspection schemes have recognized that "if inspection is to be effective and serve as a credible deterrent, unannounced, even frequent, inspections are essential. In this context, the prerequisite of a warrant could easily frustrate inspection . . . ." *United States v. Biswell,* 406 U.S. 311, 316 (1972); accord, *Donovan v. Dewey,* 452 U.S. 594, 603 (1981). Cf. *Marshall v. Barlow's, Inc.,* 436 U.S. 307 (1978) (holding that a warrant is nonetheless necessary in some administrative search contexts).

gaging in a search will predictably deter the police from conducting some searches that they would otherwise like to conduct. But this is not an unintended result of the Fourth Amendment's protection of privacy; rather, it is the very purpose for which the Amendment was thought necessary. Only where the governmental interests at stake exceed those implicated in any ordinary law enforcement context—that is, only where there is some extraordinary governmental interest involved—is it legitimate to engage in a balancing test to determine whether a warrant is indeed necessary.

In this case, such extraordinary governmental interests do exist and are sufficient to justify an exception to the warrant requirement. Students are necessarily confined for most of the schoolday in close proximity to each other and to the school staff. I agree with the Court that we can take judicial notice of the serious problems of drugs and violence that plague our schools. As Justice Blackmun notes, teachers must not merely "maintain an environment conducive to learning" among children who "are inclined to test the outer boundaries of acceptable conduct," but must also "protect the very safety of students and school personnel." Ante, at 352–353. A teacher or principal could neither carry out essential teaching functions nor adequately protect students' safety if required to wait for a warrant before conducting a necessary search.

B

I emphatically disagree with the Court's decision to cast aside the constitutional probable-cause standard when assessing the constitutional validity of a schoolhouse search. The Court's decision jettisons the probable-cause standard—the only standard that finds support in the text of the Fourth Amendment—on the basis of its Rohrschach-like "balancing test." Use of such a "balancing test" to determine the standard for evaluating the validity of a full-scale search represents a sizable innovation in Fourth Amendment analysis. This innovation finds support neither in precedent nor policy and portends a dangerous weakening of the purpose of the Fourth Amendment to protect the privacy and security of our citizens. Moreover, even if this Court's historic understanding of the Fourth Amendment were mistaken and a balancing test of some kind were appropriate, any such test that gave adequate weight to the privacy and security interests protected by the Fourth Amendment would not reach the preordained result the Court's conclusory analysis reaches today. Therefore, because I believe that the balancing test used by the Court today is flawed both in its inception and in its execution, I respectfully dissent.

1

An unbroken line of cases in this Court have held that probable cause is a prerequisite for a full-scale search. In *Carroll v. United States*, 267 U.S. 132, 149 (1925), the Court held that "[o]n reason and authority the true rule is that if the search and seizure . . . are made upon probable cause . . . the search and seizure are valid." Under our past decisions probable cause—which exists where "the facts and circumstances within [the officials'] knowledge and of which they had reasonably trustworthy information [are] sufficient in themselves to warrant a man of reasonable caution in the belief" that a criminal offense had occurred and the evidence would be found in the suspected place, id., at 162—is the constitutional minimum for justifying a full-scale search, regardless of whether it is conducted pursuant to a warrant or, as in Carroll, within one of the exceptions to the warrant requirement. *Henry v. United States,* 361 U.S. 98, 104 (1959) (Carroll "merely relaxed the requirements for a warrant on grounds of practicality," but "did not dispense with the need for probable cause"); accord, *Chambers v. Maroney,* 399 U.S. 42, 51 (1970) ("In enforcing the Fourth Amendment's prohibition against unreasonable searches and seizures, the Court has insisted upon probable cause as a minimum requirement for a reasonable search permitted by the Constitution").[3]

Our holdings that probable cause is a prerequisite to a full-scale search are based on the relationship between the two Clauses of the Fourth Amendment. The first Clause ("The right of the people to be secure in their persons, houses, papers and effects, against unreasonable searches and seizures, shall not be violated . . .") states the purpose of the Amendment and its coverage. The second Clause (". . . and no Warrants shall issue but upon probable cause . . .") gives content to the word "unreasonable" in the first Clause. "For all but . . . narrowly defined intrusions, the requisite 'balancing' has been performed in centuries of precedent and is embodied in the principle that seizures are 'reasonable' only if supported by probable cause." *Dunaway v. New York,* 442 U.S., at 214.

I therefore fully agree with the Court that "the underlying command of the Fourth Amendment is always that searches and seizures be reasonable." Ante, at 337. But this "underlying command" is not directly interpreted in each category of cases by some amorphous "balancing test." Rather, the provisions of the Warrant Clause—a warrant and probable cause—provide the yardstick against which official searches and seizures are to be measured. The Fourth Amendment neither requires nor authorizes the conceptual free-for-all that ensues when an unguided balancing test is used to assess specific categories of searches. If the search in question is more than a minimally intrusive *Terry* stop, the constitutional probable-cause standard determines its validity.

To be sure, the Court recognizes that probable cause "ordinarily" is required to justify a full-scale search and that the existence of probable cause "bears on" the validity of the search. Ante, at 340–341. Yet the Court fails to cite any case in which a full-scale intrusion upon privacy interests has been justified on less than probable cause. The line of cases begun by *Terry v. Ohio,* 392 U.S. 1 (1968), provides no support, for they applied a balancing test only in the context of minimally intrusive searches that served crucial law enforcement interests. The search in *Terry* itself, for instance, was a "limited search of the outer clothing." Id., at 30. The type of border stop at issue in *United States v. Brignoni-Ponce,* 422 U.S. 873, 880 (1975), usually "consume[d] no more than a minute"; the Court explicitly noted that "any further detention . . . must be based on consent or probable cause." Id., at 882. See also *United States v. Hensley,* ante, at 224 (momentary stop); *United States v. Place,* 462 U.S., at 706–707 (brief detention of luggage for canine "sniff"); *Pennsylvania v. Mimms,* 434 U.S. 106 (1977) (per

---

3. In fact, despite the somewhat diminished expectation of privacy that this Court has recognized in the automobile context, see South *Dakota v. Opperman,* 428 U.S. 364, 367–368 (1976), we have required probable cause even to justify a warrantless automobile search, see *United States v. Ortiz,* 422 U.S. 891, 896 (1975) ("A search, even of an automobile, is a substantial invasion of privacy. To protect that privacy from official arbitrariness, the Court always has regarded probable cause as the minimum requirement for a lawful search") (footnote omitted); *Chambers v. Maroney,* 399 U.S., at 51.

curiam) (brief frisk after stop for traffic violation); *United States v. Martinez-Fuerte*, 428 U.S. 543, 560 (1976) (characterizing intrusion as "minimal"); *Adams v. Williams*, 407 U.S. 143 (1972) (stop and frisk). In short, all of these cases involved "'seizures' so substantially less intrusive than arrests that the general rule requiring probable cause to make Fourth Amendment 'seizures' reasonable could be replaced by a balancing test." *Dunaway*, supra, at 210.

Nor do the "administrative search" cases provide any comfort for the Court. In *Camara v. Municipal Court*, 387 U.S. 523 (1967), the Court held that the probable-cause standard governed even administrative searches. Although the *Camara* Court recognized that probable-cause standards themselves may have to be somewhat modified to take into account the special nature of administrative searches, the Court did so only after noting that "because [housing code] inspections are neither personal in nature nor aimed at the discovery of evidence of crime, they involve a relatively limited invasion of the urban citizen's privacy." Id., at 537. Subsequent administrative search cases have similarly recognized that such searches intrude upon areas whose owners harbor a significantly decreased expectation of privacy, see, e.g., *Donovan v. Dewey*, 452 U.S. 594, 598–599 (1981), thus circumscribing the injury to Fourth Amendment interests caused by the search.

Considerations of the deepest significance for the freedom of our citizens counsel strict adherence to the principle that no search may be conducted where the official is not in possession of probable cause—that is, where the official does not know of "facts and circumstances [that] warrant a prudent man in believing that the offense has been committed." *Henry v. United States*, 361 U.S., at 102; see also id., at 100–101 (discussing history of probable-cause standard). The Fourth Amendment was designed not merely to protect against official intrusions whose social utility was less as measured by some "balancing test" than its intrusion on individual privacy; it was designed in addition to grant the individual a zone of privacy whose protections could be breached only where the "reasonable" requirements of the probable-cause standard were met. Moved by whatever momentary evil has aroused their fears, officials—perhaps even supported by a majority of citizens—may be tempted to conduct searches that sacrifice the liberty of each citizen to assuage the perceived evil.[4] But the Fourth Amendment rests on the principle that a true balance between the individual and society depends on the recognition of "the right to be let alone—the most comprehensive of rights and the right most valued by civilized men." *Olmstead v. United States*, 277 U.S. 438, 478 (1928) (Brandeis, J., dissenting). That right protects the privacy and security of the individual unless the authorities can cross a specific threshold of need, designated by the term "probable cause." I cannot agree with the Court's assertions today that a "balancing test" can replace the constitutional threshold with one that is more convenient for those enforcing the laws but less protective of the citizens' liberty; the Fourth Amendment's protections should not be defaced by "a balancing process that overwhelms the individual's protection against unwarranted official intrusion by a governmental interest said to justify the search and seizure." *United States v. Martinez-Fuerte*, supra, at 570 (Brennan, J., dissenting).

---

4. As Justice Stewart said in *Coolidge v. New Hampshire*, 403 U.S. 443, 455 (1971): "In times of unrest, whether caused by crime or racial conflict or fear of internal subversion, this basic law and the values that it represents may appear unrealistic or 'extravagant' to some. But the values were those of the authors of our fundamental constitutional concepts."

2

I thus do not accept the majority's premise that "[t]o hold that the Fourth Amendment applies to searches conducted by school authorities is only to begin the inquiry into the standards governing such searches." Ante, at 337. For me, the finding that the Fourth Amendment applies, coupled with the observation that what is at issue is a full-scale search, is the end of the inquiry. But even if I believed that a "balancing test" appropriately replaces the judgment of the Framers of the Fourth Amendment, I would nonetheless object to the cursory and shortsighted "test" that the Court employs to justify its predictable weakening of Fourth Amendment protections. In particular, the test employed by the Court vastly overstates the social costs that a probable-cause standard entails and, though it plausibly articulates the serious privacy interests at stake, inexplicably fails to accord them adequate weight in striking the balance.

The Court begins to articulate its "balancing test" by observing that "the government's need for effective methods to deal with breaches of public order" is to be weighed on one side of the balance. Ibid. Of course, this is not correct. It is not the government's need for effective enforcement methods that should weigh in the balance, for ordinary Fourth Amendment standards—including probable cause—may well permit methods for maintaining the public order that are perfectly effective. If that were the case, the governmental interest in having effective standards would carry no weight at all as a justification for departing from the probable-cause standard. Rather, it is the costs of applying probable cause as opposed to applying some lesser standard that should be weighed on the government's side.[5]

In order to tote up the costs of applying the probable-cause standard, it is thus necessary first to take into account the nature and content of that standard, and the likelihood that it would hamper achievement of the goal—vital not just to "teachers and administrators," see ante, at 339—of maintaining an effective educational setting in the public schools. The seminal statement concerning the nature of the probable-cause standard is found in *Carroll v. United States*, 267 U.S. 132 (1925). Carroll held that law enforcement authorities have probable cause to search where "the facts and circumstances within their knowledge and of which they had reasonably trustworthy information [are] sufficient in themselves to warrant a man of reasonable caution in the belief" that a criminal offense had occurred. Id., at 162. In *Brinegar v. United States*, 338 U.S. 160 (1949), the Court amplified this requirement, holding that probable cause depends upon "the factual and practical considerations of everyday life on which reasonable and prudent men, not legal technicians, act." Id., at 175.

Two Terms ago, in *Illinois v. Gates*, 462 U.S. 213 (1983), this Court expounded at some length its view of the probable-cause standard. Among the adjectives used to describe the standard were "practical," "fluid," "flexible," "easily applied," and "nontechnical." See id., at 232,

---

5. I speak of the "government's side" only because it is the terminology used by the Court. In my view, this terminology itself is seriously misleading. The government is charged with protecting the privacy and security of the citizen, just as it is charged with apprehending those who violate the criminal law. Consequently, the government has no legitimate interest in conducting a search that unduly intrudes on the privacy and security of the citizen. The balance is not between the rights of the government and the rights of the citizen, but between opposing conceptions of the constitutionally legitimate means of carrying out the government's varied responsibilities.

236, 239. The probable-cause standard was to be seen as a "common-sense" test whose application depended on an evaluation of the "totality of the circumstances." Id., at 238.

Ignoring what *Gates* took such great pains to emphasize, the Court today holds that a new "reasonableness" standard is appropriate because it "will spare teachers and school administrators the necessity of schooling themselves in the niceties of probable cause and permit them to regulate their conduct according to the dictates of reason and common sense." Ante, at 343. I had never thought that our pre-*Gates* understanding of probable cause defied either reason or common sense. But after *Gates*, I would have thought that there could be no doubt that this "nontechnical," "practical," and "easily applied" concept was eminently serviceable in a context like a school, where teachers require the flexibility to respond quickly and decisively to emergencies.

A consideration of the likely operation of the probable-cause standard reinforces this conclusion. Discussing the issue of school searches, Professor LaFave has noted that the cases that have reached the appellate courts "strongly suggest that in most instances the evidence of wrongdoing prompting teachers or principals to conduct searches is sufficiently detailed and specific to meet the traditional probable cause test." W. LaFave, Search and Seizure 10.11, pp. 459–460 (1978).[6] The problems that have caused this Court difficulty in interpreting the probable-cause standard have largely involved informants, see, e.g., *Illinois v. Gates,* supra; *Spinelli v. United States,* 393 U.S. 410 (1969); *Aguilar v. Texas,* 378 U.S. 108 (1964); *Draper v. United States,* 358 U.S. 307 (1959). However, three factors make it likely that problems involving informants will not make it difficult for teachers and school administrators to make probable-cause decisions. This Court's decision in *Gates* applying a "totality of the circumstances" test to determine whether an informant's tip can constitute probable cause renders the test easy for teachers to apply. The fact that students and teachers interact daily in the school building makes it more likely that teachers will get to know students who supply information; the problem of informants who remain anonymous even to the teachers—and who are therefore unavailable for verification or further questioning—is unlikely to arise. Finally, teachers can observe the behavior of students under suspicion to corroborate any doubtful tips they do receive.

As compared with the relative ease with which teachers can apply the probable-cause standard, the amorphous "reasonableness under all the circumstances" standard freshly coined by the Court today will likely spawn increased litigation and greater uncertainty among teachers and administrators. Of course, as this Court should know, an essential purpose of developing and articulating legal norms is to enable individuals to conform their conduct to those norms. A school system conscientiously attempting to obey the Fourth Amendment's dictates under a probable-cause standard could, for example, consult decisions and other legal materials and prepare a booklet expounding the rough outlines of the concept. Such a booklet could be distributed to teachers to provide them with guidance as to when a search may be lawfully conducted. I cannot but believe that the same school system faced with interpreting what is permitted under the Court's new "reasonableness" standard would be hopelessly adrift as to when a search may be permissible. The sad result of this

---

6. It should be noted that Professor LaFave reached this conclusion in 1978, before this Court's decision in *Gates* made clear the "flexibility" of the probable-cause concept.

uncertainty may well be that some teachers will be reluctant to conduct searches that are fully permissible and even necessary under the constitutional probable-cause standard, while others may intrude arbitrarily and unjustifiably on the privacy of students.[7]

One further point should be taken into account when considering the desirability of replacing the constitutional probable-cause standard. The question facing the Court is not whether the probable-cause standard should be replaced by a test of "reasonableness under all the circumstances." Rather, it is whether traditional Fourth Amendment standards should recede before the Court's new standard. Thus, although the Court today paints with a broad brush and holds its undefined "reasonableness" standard applicable to all school searches, I would approach the question with considerably more reserve. I would not think it necessary to develop a single standard to govern all school searches, any more than traditional Fourth Amendment law applies even the probable-cause standard to all searches and seizures. For instance, just as police officers may conduct a brief stop and frisk on something less than probable cause, so too should teachers be permitted the same flexibility. A teacher or administrator who had reasonable suspicion that a student was carrying a gun would no doubt have authority under ordinary Fourth Amendment doctrine to conduct a limited search of the student to determine whether the threat was genuine. The "costs" of applying the traditional probable-cause standard must therefore be discounted by the fact that, where additional flexibility is necessary and where the intrusion is minor, traditional Fourth Amendment jurisprudence itself displaces probable cause when it determines the validity of a search.

A legitimate balancing test whose function was something more substantial than reaching a predetermined conclusion acceptable to this Court's impressions of what authority teachers need would therefore reach rather a different result than that reached by the Court today. On one side of the balance would be the costs of applying traditional Fourth Amendment standards—the "practical" and "flexible" probable-cause standard where a full-scale intrusion is sought, a lesser standard in situations where the intrusion is much less severe and the need for greater authority compelling. Whatever costs were toted up on this side would have to be discounted by the costs of applying an unprecedented and ill-defined "reasonableness under all the circumstances" test that will leave teachers and administrators uncertain as to their authority and will encourage excessive fact-based litigation.

On the other side of the balance would be the serious privacy interests of the student, interests that the Court admirably articulates in its opinion, ante, at 337–339, but which the Court's new ambiguous standard places in serious jeopardy. I have no doubt that a fair as-

---

7. A comparison of the language of the standard ("reasonableness under all the circumstances") with the traditional language of probable cause ("facts sufficient to warrant a person of reasonable caution in believing that a crime had been committed and the evidence would be found in the designated place") suggests that the Court's new standard may turn out to be probable cause under a new guise. If so, the additional uncertainty caused by this Court's innovation is surely unjustifiable; it would be naive to expect that the addition of this extra dose of uncertainty would do anything other than "burden the efforts of school authorities to maintain order in their schools," ante, at 342. If, on the other hand, the new standard permits searches of students in instances when probable cause is absent—instances, according to this Court's consistent formulations, when a person of reasonable caution would not think it likely that a violation existed or that evidence of that violation would be found—the new standard is genuinely objectionable and impossible to square with the premise that our citizens have the right to be free from arbitrary intrusions on their privacy.

sessment of the two sides of the balance would necessarily reach the same conclusion that, as I have argued above, the Fourth Amendment's language compels—that school searches like that conducted in this case are valid only if supported by probable cause.

II

Applying the constitutional probable-cause standard to the facts of this case, I would find that Mr. Choplick's search violated T. L. O.'s Fourth Amendment rights. After escorting T. L. O. into his private office, Mr. Choplick demanded to see her purse. He then opened the purse to find evidence of whether she had been smoking in the bathroom. When he opened the purse, he discovered the pack of cigarettes. At this point, his search for evidence of the smoking violation was complete.

Mr. Choplick then noticed, below the cigarettes, a pack of cigarette rolling papers. Believing that such papers were "associated," see ante, at 328, with the use of marihuana, he proceeded to conduct a detailed examination of the contents of her purse, in which he found some marihuana, a pipe, some money, an index card, and some private letters indicating that T. L. O. had sold marihuana to other students. The State sought to introduce this latter material in evidence at a criminal proceeding, and the issue before the Court is whether it should have been suppressed.

On my view of the case, we need not decide whether the initial search conducted by Mr. Choplick—the search for evidence of the smoking violation that was completed when Mr. Choplick found the pack of cigarettes—was valid. For Mr. Choplick at that point did not have probable cause to continue to rummage through T. L. O.'s purse. Mr. Choplick's suspicion of marihuana possession at this time was based solely on the presence of the package of cigarette papers. The mere presence without more of such a staple item of commerce is insufficient to warrant a person of reasonable caution in inferring both that T. L. O. had violated the law by possessing marihuana and that evidence of that violation would be found in her purse. Just as a police officer could not obtain a warrant to search a home based solely on his claim that he had seen a package of cigarette papers in that home, Mr. Choplick was not entitled to search possibly the most private possessions of T. L. O. based on the mere presence of a package of cigarette papers. Therefore, the fruits of this illegal search must be excluded and the judgment of the New Jersey Supreme Court affirmed.

III

In the past several Terms, this Court has produced a succession of Fourth Amendment opinions in which "balancing tests" have been applied to resolve various questions concerning the proper scope of official searches. The Court has begun to apply a "balancing test" to determine whether a particular category of searches intrudes upon expectations of privacy that merit Fourth Amendment protection. See *Hudson v. Palmer*, 468 U.S. 517, 527 (1984) ("Determining whether an expectation of privacy is 'legitimate' or 'reasonable' necessarily entails a balancing of interests"). It applies a "balancing test" to determine whether a warrant is necessary to conduct a search. See ante, at 340; *United States v. Martinez-Fuerte*, 428 U.S., at 564–566. In today's opinion, it employs a "balancing test" to determine what standard should govern the constitutionality of a given category of searches. See ante, at 340-341. Should a search turn out to be unreasonable after application of all of these "balancing tests," the Court then applies an additional "balancing test" to decide whether the evidence resulting from the search must be excluded. See *United States v. Leon,* 468 U.S. 897 (1984).

All of these "balancing tests" amount to brief nods by the Court in the direction of a neutral utilitarian calculus while the Court in fact engages in an unanalyzed exercise of judicial will. Perhaps this doctrinally destructive nihilism is merely a convenient umbrella under which a majority that cannot agree on a genuine rationale can conceal its differences. Compare ante, p. 327 (White, J., delivering the opinion of the Court), with ante, p. 348 (Powell, J., joined by O'Connor, J., concurring), and ante, p. 351 (Blackmun, J., concurring in judgment). And it may be that the real force underlying today's decision is the belief that the Court purports to reject—the belief that the unique role served by the schools justifies an exception to the Fourth Amendment on their behalf. If so, the methodology of today's decision may turn out to have as little influence in future cases as will its result, and the Court's departure from traditional Fourth Amendment doctrine will be confined to the schools.

On my view, the presence of the word "unreasonable" in the text of the Fourth Amendment does not grant a shifting majority of this Court the authority to answer all Fourth Amendment questions by consulting its momentary vision of the social good. Full-scale searches unaccompanied by probable cause violate the Fourth Amendment. I do not pretend that our traditional Fourth Amendment doctrine automatically answers all of the difficult legal questions that occasionally arise. I do contend, however, that this Court has an obligation to provide some coherent framework to resolve such questions on the basis of more than a conclusory recitation of the results of a "balancing test." The Fourth Amendment itself supplies that framework and, because the Court today fails to heed its message, I must respectfully dissent.

Justice Stevens, with whom Justice Marshall joins, and with whom Justice Brennan joins as to Part I, concurring in part and dissenting in part.

Assistant Vice Principal Choplick searched T. L. O.'s purse for evidence that she was smoking in the girls' restroom. Because T. L. O.'s suspected misconduct was not illegal and did not pose a serious threat to school discipline, the New Jersey Supreme Court held that Choplick's search of her purse was an unreasonable invasion of her privacy and that the evidence which he seized could not be used against her in criminal proceedings. The New Jersey court's holding was a careful response to the case it was required to decide.

The State of New Jersey sought review in this Court, first arguing that the exclusionary rule is wholly inapplicable to searches conducted by school officials, and then contending that the Fourth Amendment itself provides no protection at all to the student's privacy. The Court has accepted neither of these frontal assaults on the Fourth Amendment. It has, however, seized upon this "no smoking" case to announce "the proper standard" that should govern searches by school officials who are confronted with disciplinary problems far more severe than smoking in the restroom. Although I join Part II of the Court's opinion, I continue to believe that the Court has unnecessarily and inappropriately reached out to decide a constitutional question. See 468 U.S. 1214 (1984) (Stevens, J., dissenting from reargument order). More importantly, I fear that the concerns that motivated the Court's activism have produced a holding that will permit school administrators to search students suspected of violating only the most trivial school regulations and guidelines for behavior.

I

The question the Court decides today—whether Mr. Choplick's search of T. L. O.'s purse violated the Fourth Amendment—was not raised by the State's petition for writ of certiorari. That petition only raised one question: "Whether the Fourth Amendment's exclusionary rule applies to searches made by public school officials and teachers in school."[1] The State quite properly declined to submit the former question because "[it] did not wish to present what might appear to be solely a factual dispute to this Court."[2] Since this Court has twice had the threshold question argued, I believe that it should expressly consider the merits of the New Jersey Supreme Court's ruling that the exclusionary rule applies.

The New Jersey Supreme Court's holding on this question is plainly correct. As the state court noted, this case does not involve the use of evidence in a school disciplinary proceeding; the juvenile proceedings brought against T. L. O. involved a charge that would have been a criminal offense if committed by an adult.[3] Accordingly, the exclusionary rule issue decided by that court and later presented to this Court concerned only the use in a criminal proceeding of evidence obtained in a search conducted by a public school administrator.

Having confined the issue to the law enforcement context, the New Jersey court then reasoned that this Court's cases have made it quite clear that the exclusionary rule is equally applicable "whether the public official who illegally obtained the evidence was a municipal inspector, *See v. Seattle,* 387 U.S. 541 1967; *Camara [v. Municipal Court],* 387 U.S. 523 1967; a firefighter, *Michigan v. Tyler,* 436 U.S. 499, 506 1978 or a school administrator or law enforcement official."[4] It correctly concluded "that if an official search violates constitutional rights, the evidence is not admissible in criminal proceedings."[5]

When a defendant in a criminal proceeding alleges that she was the victim of an illegal search by a school administrator, the application of the exclusionary rule is a simple corollary of the principle that "all evidence obtained by searches and seizures in violation of the Constitution is, by that same authority, inadmissible in a state court." *Mapp v. Ohio,* 367 U.S. 643, 655 (1961). The practical basis for this principle is, in part, its deterrent effect, see id., at 656, and as a general matter it is tolerably clear to me, as it has been to the Court, that the existence of an exclusionary remedy does deter the authorities from violating the Fourth Amendment by sharply reducing their incentive to do so.[6] In the case of evidence obtained in school searches, the "overall educative effect"[7] of the exclusionary rule adds important symbolic force to this utilitarian judgment.

Justice Brandeis was both a great student and a great teacher. It was he who wrote:

"Our Government is the potent, the omnipresent teacher. For good or for ill, it teaches the whole people by its example. Crime is contagious. If the Government becomes a lawbreaker, it breeds

---

1. Pet. for Cert. i.

2. Supplemental Brief for Petitioner 6.

3. *State ex rel. T. L. O.,* 94 N.J. 331, 337, nn. 1 and 2, 342, n. 5, 463 A. 2d 934, 937, nn. 1 and 2, 939, n. 5 (1983).

4. Id., at 341, 463 A. 2d, at 939.

5. Id., at 341–342, 463 A. 2d, at 939.

6. See, e.g., *Stone v. Powell,* 428 U.S. 465, 492 (1976); *United States v. Janis,* 428 U.S. 433, 453 (1976); *United States v. Calandra,* 414 U.S. 338, 347–348 (1974); *Alderman v. United States,* 394 U.S. 165, 174–175 (1969).

7. *Stone v. Powell,* 428 U.S., at 493.

contempt for law; it invites every man to become a law unto himself; it invites anarchy." *Olmstead v. United States,* 277 U.S. 438, 485 (1928) (dissenting opinion).

Those of us who revere the flag and the ideals for which it stands believe in the power of symbols. We cannot ignore that rules of law also have a symbolic power that may vastly exceed their utility.

Schools are places where we inculcate the values essential to the meaningful exercise of rights and responsibilities by a self-governing citizenry.[8] If the Nation's students can be convicted through the use of arbitrary methods destructive of personal liberty, they cannot help but feel that they have been dealt with unfairly.[9] The application of the exclusionary rule in criminal proceedings arising from illegal school searches makes an important statement to young people that "our society attaches serious consequences to a violation of constitutional rights,"[10] and that this is a principle of "liberty and justice for all."[11]

Thus, the simple and correct answer to the question presented by the State's petition for certiorari would have required affirmance of a state court's judgment suppressing evidence. That result would have been dramatically out of character for a Court that not only grants prosecutors relief from suppression orders with distressing regularity,[12] but also is prone to rely on grounds not advanced by the parties in order to protect evidence from exclusion.[13] In characteristic disregard of the doctrine of judicial restraint, the Court avoided that result

---

8. See *Board of Education v. Pico,* 457 U.S. 853, 864–865 (1982) (Brennan, J., joined by Marshall and Stevens, J. J.); id., at 876, 880 (Blackmun, J., concurring in part and concurring in judgment); *Plyler v. Doe,* 457 U.S. 202, 221 (1982); *Ambach v. Norwick,* 441 U.S. 68, 76 (1979); *Tinker v. Des Moines Independent Community School Dist.,* 393 U.S. 503, 507, 511–513 (1969); *Brown v. Board of Education,* 347 U.S. 483, 493 (1954); *West Virginia State Board of Education v. Barnette,* 319 U.S. 624, 637 (1943).

9. Cf. *In re Gault,* 387 U.S. 1, 26 –27 (1967). Justice Brennan has written of an analogous case:

"We do not know what class petitioner was attending when the police and dogs burst in, but the lesson the school authorities taught her that day will undoubtedly make a greater impression than the one her teacher had hoped to convey. I would grant certiorari to teach petitioner another lesson: that the Fourth Amendment protects '[t]he right of the people to be secure in their persons, houses, papers, and effects, against unreasonable searches and seizures' .... Schools cannot expect their students to learn the lessons of good citizenship when the school authorities themselves disregard the fundamental principles underpinning our constitutional freedoms." *Doe v. Renfrow,* 451 U.S. 1022, 1027–1028 (1981) (dissenting from denial of certiorari).

10. *Stone v. Powell,* 428 U.S., at 492.

11. 36 U.S.C. 172 (pledge of allegiance to the flag).

12. A brief review of the Fourth Amendment cases involving criminal prosecutions since the October Term, 1982, supports the proposition. Compare *Florida v. Rodriguez,* ante, p. 1 (per curiam); *United States v. Leon,* 468 U.S. 897 (1984); *Massachusetts v. Sheppard,* 468 U.S. 981 (1984); *Segura v. United States,* 468 U.S. 796 (1984); *United States v. Karo,* 468 U.S. 705 (1984); *Oliver v. United States,* 466 U.S. 170 (1984); *United States v. Jacobsen,* 466 U.S. 109 (1984); *Massachusetts v. Upton,* 466 U.S. 727 (1984) (per curiam); *Florida v. Meyers,* 466 U.S. 380 (1984) (per curiam); *Michigan v. Long,* 463 U.S. 1032 (1983); *Illinois v. Andreas,* 463 U.S. 765 (1983); *Illinois v. Lafayette,* 462 U.S. 640 (1983); *United States v. Villamonte-Marquez,* 462 U.S. 579 (1983); *Illinois v. Gates,* 462 U.S. 213 (1983); *Texas v. Brown,* 460 U.S. 730 (1983); *United States v. Knotts,* 460 U.S. 276 (1983); *Illinois v. Batchelder,* 463 U.S. 1112 (1983) (per curiam); *Cardwell v. Taylor,* 461 U.S. 571 (1983) (per curiam), with *Thompson v. Louisiana,* ante, p. 17 (per curiam); *Welsh v. Wisconsin,* 466 U.S. 740 (1984); *Michigan v. Clifford,* 464 U.S. 287 (1984); *United States v. Place,* 462 U.S. 696 (1983); *Florida v. Royer,* 460 U.S. 491 (1983).

13. E.g., *United States v. Karo,* 468 U.S., at 719–721; see also *Segura v. United States,* 468 U.S., at 805–813 (opinion of Burger, C. J., joined by O'Connor, J.); cf. *Illinois v. Gates,* 459 U.S. 1028 (1982) (Stevens, J., dissenting from reargument order, joined by Brennan and Marshall, J. J.)

in this case by ordering reargument and directing the parties to address a constitutional question that the parties, with good reason, had not asked the Court to decide. Because judicial activism undermines the Court's power to perform its central mission in a legitimate way, 1 dissented from the reargument order. See 468 U.S. 1214 (1984). I have not modified the views expressed in that dissent, but since the majority has brought the question before us, I shall explain why I believe the Court has misapplied the standard of reasonableness embodied in the Fourth Amendment.

II

The search of a young woman's purse by a school administrator is a serious invasion of her legitimate expectations of privacy. A purse "is a common repository for one's personal effects and therefore is inevitably associated with the expectation of privacy." *Arkansas v. Sanders*, 442 U.S. 753, 762 (1979). Although such expectations must sometimes yield to the legitimate requirements of government, in assessing the constitutionality of a warrantless search, our decision must be guided by the language of the Fourth Amendment: "The right of the people to be secure in their persons, houses, papers and effects, against unreasonable searches and seizures, shall not be violated. . . ." In order to evaluate the reasonableness of such searches, "it is necessary 'first to focus upon the governmental interest which allegedly justifies official intrusion upon the constitutionally protected interests of the private citizen,' for there is 'no ready test for determining reasonableness other than by balancing the need to search [or size] against the invasion which the search [or seizure] entails.'" *Terry v. Ohio*, 392 U.S. 1, 20-21 (1968) (quoting *Camara v. Municipal Court*, 387 U.S. 523, 528, 534–537, (1967)).[14]

The "limited search for weapons" in *Terry* was justified by the "immediate interest of the police officer in taking steps to assure himself that the person with whom he is dealing is not armed with a weapon that could unexpectedly and fatally be used against him." 392 U.S., at 23, 25. When viewed from the institutional perspective, "the substantial need of teachers and administrators for freedom to maintain order in the schools," ante, at 341 (majority opinion), is no less acute. Violent, unlawful, or seriously disruptive conduct is fundamentally inconsistent with the principal function of teaching institutions which is to educate young people and prepare them for citizenship.[15] When such conduct occurs amidst a sizable group of impressionable young people, it creates an explosive atmosphere that requires a prompt and effective response.

Thus, warrantless searches of students by school administrators are reasonable when undertaken for those purposes. But the majority's statement of the standard for evaluating the reasonableness of such searches is not suitably adapted to that end. The majority holds that

---

14. See also *United States v. Brigoni-Ponce*, 422 U.S. 873, 881–882 (1975); *United States v. Martinez-Fuerte*, 428 U.S. 543, 567 (1976).

15. Cf. ante, at 353 (Blackmun, J., concurring in judgment) ("The special need for an immediate response to behavior that threatens either the safety of schoolchildren and teachers or the educational process itself justifies the Court in excepting school searches from the warrant and probable-cause requirement"); ante, at 350 (Powell, J., concurring, joined by O'Connor, J.) ("Without first establishing discipline and maintaining order, teachers cannot begin to educate their students").

"a search of a student by a teacher or other school official will be 'justified at its inception' when there are reasonable grounds for suspecting that the search will turn up evidence that the student has violated or is violating either the law or the rules of the school." Ante, at 341–342. This standard will permit teachers and school administrators to search students when they suspect that the search will reveal evidence of even the most trivial school regulation or precatory guideline for student behavior. The Court's standard for deciding whether a search is justified "at its inception" treats all violations of the rules of the school as though they were fungible. For the Court, a search for curlers and sunglasses in order to enforce the school dress code[16] is apparently just as important as a search for evidence of heroin addiction or violent gang activity. The majority, however, does not contend that school administrators have a compelling need to search students in order to achieve optimum enforcement of minor school regulations.[17] To the contrary, when minor violations are involved, there is every indication that the informal school disciplinary process, with only minimum requirements of due process,[18] can function effectively without the power to search for enough evidence to prove a criminal case. In arguing that teachers and school administrators need the power to search students based on a lessened standard, the United States as amicus curiae relies heavily on empirical evidence of a contemporary crisis of violence and unlawful behavior that is seriously undermining the process of education in American schools.[19] A standard better attuned to this concern would permit teachers and school administrators to search a student when they have reason to believe that the search will uncover evidence that the student is violating the law or engaging in conduct that is seriously disruptive of school order, or the educational process.

This standard is properly directed at "[t]he sole justification for the [warrantless] search."[20] In addition, a standard that varies the extent of the permissible intrusion with the gravity of the suspected offense is also more consistent with common-law experience and this Court's

---

16. Parent-Student Handbook of Piscataway [N.J.] H. S. (1979), Record Doc. S-1, p. 7. A brief survey of school rule books reveals that, under the majority's approach, teachers and school administrators may also search students to enforce school rules regulating: (i) secret societies; (ii) students driving to school; (iii) parking and use of parking lots during school hours; (iv) smoking on campus; (v) the direction of traffic in the hallways; (vi) student presence in the hallways during class hours without a pass; (vii) profanity; (viii) school attendance of interscholastic athletes on the day of a game, meet or match; (ix) cafeteria use and cleanup; (x) eating lunch off-campus; and (xi) unauthorized absence. See id., at 7–18; Student Handbook of South Windsor [Conn.] H. S. (1984); Fairfax County [Va.] Public Schools, Student Responsibilities and Rights (1980); Student Handbook of Chantilly [Va.] H. S. (1984).

17. Cf. *Camara v. Municipal Court,* 387 U.S. 523, 535–536 (1967) ("There is unanimous agreement among those most familiar with this field that the only effective way to seek universal compliance with the minimum standards required by municipal codes is through routine periodic inspections of all structures. . . . [I]f the probable cause standard . . . is adopted, . . . the reasonable goals of code enforcement will be dealt a crushing blow").

18. See *Goss v. Lopez,* 419 U.S. 565, 583–584 (1975).

19. "The sad truth is that many classrooms across the country are not temples of learning teaching the lessons of good will, civility, and wisdom that are central to the fabric of American life. To the contrary, many schools are in such a state of disorder that not only is the educational atmosphere polluted, but the very safety of students and teachers is imperiled." Brief for United States as Amicus Curiae 23.

See also Brief for National Education Association as Amicus Curiae 21 ("If a suspected violation of a rule threatens to disrupt the school or threatens to harm students, school officials should be free to search for evidence of it").

20. *Terry v. Ohio,* 392 U.S. 1, 29 (1968); *United States v. Brignoni-Ponce,* 422 U.S., at 881–882.

precedent. Criminal law has traditionally recognized a distinction between essentially regulatory offenses and serious violations of the peace, and graduated the response of the criminal justice system depending on the character of the violation.[21] The application of a similar distinction in evaluating the reasonableness of warrantless searches and seizures "is not a novel idea." *Welsh v. Wisconsin,* 466 U.S. 740, 750 (1984).[22]

In Welsh, police officers arrived at the scene of a traffic accident and obtained information indicating that the driver of the automobile involved was guilty of a first offense of driving while intoxicated—a civil violation with a maximum fine of $200. The driver had left the scene of the accident, and the officers followed the suspect to his home where they arrested him without a warrant. Absent exigent circumstances, the warrantless invasion of the home was a clear violation of *Payton v. New York,* 445 U.S. 573 (1980). In holding that the warrantless arrest for the "noncriminal, traffic offense" in Welsh was unconstitutional, the Court noted that "application of the exigent-circumstances exception in the context of a home entry should rarely be sanctioned when there is probable cause to believe that only a minor offense . . . has been committed." 466 U.S., at 753.

The logic of distinguishing between minor and serious offenses in evaluating the reasonableness of school searches is almost too clear for argument. In order to justify the serious intrusion on the persons and privacy of young people that New Jersey asks this Court to approve, the State must identify "some real immediate and serious consequences." *McDonald v. United States,* 335 U.S. 451, 460 (1948) (Jackson, J., concurring, joined by Frankfurter, J.).[23] While school administrators have entirely legitimate reasons for adopting school reg-

---

21. Throughout the criminal law this dichotomy has been expressed by classifying crimes as misdemeanors or felonies, malum prohibitum or malum in se, crimes that do not involve moral turpitude or those that do, and major or petty offenses. See generally W. LaFave, Handbook on Criminal Law 6 (1972).

Some codes of student behavior also provide a system of graduated response by distinguishing between violent, unlawful, or seriously disruptive conduct, and conduct that will only warrant serious sanctions when the student engages in repetitive offenses. See, e.g., Parent-Student Handbook of Piscataway [N.J.] H. S. (1979), Record Doc. S-1, pp. 15–16; Student Handbook of South Windsor [Conn.] H. S. E (1984); Rules of the Board of Education of the District of Columbia, Ch. IV, 431.1–.10 (1982). Indeed, at Piscataway High School a violation of smoking regulations that is "[a] student's first offense will result in assignment of up to three (3) days of after school classes concerning hazards of smoking." Record Doc. S-1, supra, at 15.

22. In *Goss v. Lopez,* 419 U.S., at 582–583 (emphasis added), the Court noted that similar considerations require some variance in the requirements of due process in the school disciplinary context:

"[A]s a general rule notice and hearing should precede removal of the student from school. We agree . . . , however, that there are recurring situations in which prior notice and hearing cannot be insisted upon. Students whose presence poses a continuing danger to persons or property or an ongoing threat of disrupting the academic process may be immediately removed from school. In such cases the necessary notice and rudimentary hearing should follow as soon as practicable. . . ."

23. In *McDonald* police officers made a warrantless search of the office of an illegal "numbers" operation. Justice Jackson rejected the view that the search could be supported by exigent circumstances:

"Even if one were to conclude that urgent circumstances might justify a forced entry without a warrant, no such emergency was present in this case. . . . Whether there is reasonable necessity for a search without waiting to obtain a warrant certainly depends somewhat upon the gravity of the offense thought to be in progress as well as the hazards of the method of attempting to reach it. . . . [The defendant's] criminal operation, while a shabby swindle that the police are quite right in suppressing, was not one which endangered life or limb or the peace and good order of the community. . . ." 335 U.S., at 459–460.

ulations and guidelines for student behavior, the authorization of searches to enforce them "displays a shocking lack of all sense of proportion." Id., 459.[24]

The majority offers weak deference to these principles of balance and decency by announcing that school searches will only be reasonable in scope "when the measures adopted are reasonably related to the objectives of the search and not excessively intrusive in light of the age and sex of the student and the nature of the infraction." Ante, at 342 (emphasis added). The majority offers no explanation why a two-part standard is necessary to evaluate the reasonableness of the ordinary school search. Significantly, in the balance of its opinion the Court pretermits any discussion of the nature of T. L. O.'s infraction of the "no smoking" rule.

The "rider" to the Court's standard for evaluating the reasonableness of the initial intrusion apparently is the Court's perception that its standard is overly generous and does not, by itself, achieve a fair balance between the administrator's right to search and the student's reasonable expectations of privacy. The Court's standard for evaluating the "scope" of reasonable school searches is obviously designed to prohibit physically intrusive searches of students by persons of the opposite sex for relatively minor offenses. The Court's effort to establish a standard that is, at once, clear enough to allow searches to be upheld in nearly every case, and flexible enough to prohibit obviously unreasonable intrusions of young adults' privacy only creates uncertainty in the extent of its resolve to prohibit the latter. Moreover, the majority's application of its standard in this case—to permit a male administrator to rummage through the purse of a female high school student in order to obtain evidence that she was smoking in a bathroom—raises grave doubts in my mind whether its effort will be effective.[25] Unlike the Court, I believe the nature of the suspected infraction is a matter of first importance in deciding whether any invasion of privacy is permissible.

III

The Court embraces the standard applied by the New Jersey Supreme Court as equivalent to its own, and then deprecates the state court's application of the standard as reflecting "a somewhat crabbed notion of reasonableness." Ante, at 343. There is no mystery, however, in the state court's finding that the search in this case was unconstitutional; the decision below

---

24. While a policeman who sees a person smoking in an elevator in violation of a city ordinance may conduct a full-blown search for evidence of the smoking violation in the unlikely event of a custodial arrest, *United States v. Robinson,* 414 U.S. 218, 236 (1973); *Gustafson v. Florida,* 414 U.S. 260, 265–266 (1973), it is more doubtful whether a search of this kind would be reasonable if the officer only planned to issue a citation to the offender and depart, see Robinson, 414 U.S., at 236, n. 6. In any case, the majority offers no rationale supporting its conclusion that a student detained by school officials for questioning, on reasonable suspicion that she has violated a school rule, is entitled to no more protection under the Fourth Amendment than a criminal suspect under custodial arrest.

25. One thing is clear under any standard—the shocking strip searches that are described in some cases have no place in the schoolhouse. See *Doe v. Renfrow,* 631 F. 2d 91, 92–93 (CA7 1980) ("It does not require a constitutional scholar to conclude that a nude search of a 13-year-old child is an invasion of constitutional rights of some magnitude"), cert. denied, 451 U.S. 1022 (1981); *Bellnier v. Lund,* 438 F. Supp. 47 (NDNY 1977); *People v. D.,* 34 N.Y. 2d 483, 315 N. E. 2d 466 (1974); *M. J. v. State,* 399 So. 2d 996 (Fla. App. 1981). To the extent that deeply intrusive searches are ever reasonable outside the custodial context, it surely must only be to prevent imminent, and serious harm.

was not based on a manipulation of reasonable suspicion, but on the trivial character of the activity that promoted the official search. The New Jersey Supreme Court wrote:

> "We are satisfied that when a school official has reasonable grounds to believe that a student possesses evidence of illegal activity or activity that would interfere with school discipline and order, the school official has the right to conduct a reasonable search for such evidence.
>
> "In determining whether the school official has reasonable grounds, courts should consider 'the child's age, history, and school record, the prevalence and seriousness of the problem in the school to which the search was directed, the exigency to make the search without delay, and the probative value and reliability of the information used as a justification for the search.'"[26]

The emphasized language in the state court's opinion focuses on the character of the rule infraction that is to be the object of the search.

In the view of the state court, there is a quite obvious and material difference between a search for evidence relating to violent or disruptive activity, and a search for evidence of a smoking rule violation. This distinction does not imply that a no-smoking rule is a matter of minor importance. Rather, like a rule that prohibits a student from being tardy, its occasional violation in a context that poses no threat of disrupting school order and discipline offers no reason to believe that an immediate search is necessary to avoid unlawful conduct, violence, or a serious impairment of the educational process.

A correct understanding of the New Jersey court's standard explains why that court concluded in T. L. O.'s case that "the assistant principal did not have reasonable grounds to believe that the student was concealing in her purse evidence of criminal activity or evidence of activity that would seriously interfere with school discipline or order."[27] The importance of the nature of the rule infraction to the New Jersey Supreme Court's holding is evident from its brief explanation of the principal basis for its decision:

> "A student has an expectation of privacy in the contents of her purse. Mere possession of cigarettes did not violate school rule or policy, since the school allowed smoking in designated areas. The contents of the handbag had no direct bearing on the infraction.
>
> "The assistant principal's desire, legal in itself, to gather evidence to impeach the student's credibility at a hearing on the disciplinary infraction does not validate the search."[28]

Like the New Jersey Supreme Court, I would view this case differently if the Assistant Vice Principal had reason to believe T. L. O.'s purse contained evidence of criminal activity,

---

26. 94 N.J., at 346, 463 A. 2d, at 941–942 (quoting *State v. McKinnon*, 88 Wash. 2d 75, 81, 558 P. 2d 781, 784 (1977)) (emphasis added).

27. 94 N. J., at 347, 463 A. 2d, at 942.

28. Ibid. The court added:

"Moreover, there were not reasonable grounds to believe that the purse contained cigarettes, if they were the object of the search. No one had furnished information to that effect to the school official. He had, at best, a good hunch. No doubt good hunches would unearth much more evidence of crime on the persons of students and citizens as a whole. But more is required to sustain a search." Id., at 347, 463 A. 2d, at 942–943.

It is this portion of the New Jersey Supreme Court's reasoning—a portion that was not necessary to its holding—to which this Court makes its principal response. See ante, at 345–346.

or of an activity that would seriously disrupt school discipline. There was, however, absolutely no basis for any such assumption—not even a "hunch."

In this case, Mr. Choplick overreacted to what appeared to be nothing more than a minor infraction—a rule prohibiting smoking in the bathroom of the freshmen's and sophomores' building.[29] It is, of course, true that he actually found evidence of serious wrongdoing by T. L. O., but no one claims that the prior search may be justified by his unexpected discovery. As far as the smoking infraction is concerned, the search for cigarettes merely tended to corroborate a teacher's eyewitness account of T. L. O.'s violation of a minor regulation designed to channel student smoking behavior into designated locations. Because this conduct was neither unlawful nor significantly disruptive of school order or the educational process, the invasion of privacy associated with the forcible opening of T. L. O.'s purse was entirely unjustified at its inception.

A review of the sampling of school search cases relied on by the Court demonstrates how different this case is from those in which there was indeed a valid justification for intruding on a student's privacy. In most of them the student was suspected of a criminal violation;[30] in the remainder either violence or substantial disruption of school order or the integrity of the academic process was at stake.[31] Few involved matters as trivial as the no-smoking rule violated by T. L. O.[32] The rule the Court adopts today is so open-ended that it may make the Fourth Amendment virtually meaningless in the school context. Although I agree that school administrators must have broad latitude to maintain order and discipline in our classrooms, that authority is not unlimited.

IV

The schoolroom is the first opportunity most citizens have to experience the power of government. Through it passes every citizen and public official, from schoolteachers to policemen and prison guards. The values they learn there, they take with them in life. One of our most cherished ideals is the one contained in the Fourth Amendment: that the government may not intrude on the personal privacy of its citizens without a warrant or compelling cir-

---

29. See Parent-Student Handbook of Piscataway [N.J.] H. S. 15, 18 (1979), Record Doc. S-1. See also Tr. of Mar. 31, 1980, Hearing 13–14.

30. See, e.g., *Tarter v. Raybuck*, 742 F. 2d 977 (CA6 1984) (search for marihuana); *M. v. Board of Education Ball-Chatham Community Unit School Dist. No. 5*, 429 F. Supp. 288 (SD Ill. 1977) (drugs and large amount of money); *D. R. C. v. State*, 646 P.2d 252 (Alaska App. 1982) (stolen money); *In re W.*, 29 Cal. App. 3d 777, 105 Cal. Rptr. 775 (1973) (marihuana); *In re G.*, 11 Cal. App. 3d 1193, 90 Cal. Rptr. 361 (1970) (amphetamine pills); *In re Donaldson*, 269 Cal. App. 2d 509, 75 Cal. Rptr. 220 (1969) (methedrine pills); *State v. Baccino*, 282 A. 2d 869 (Del. Super. 1971) (drugs); *State v. D. T. W.*, 425 So. 2d 1383 (Fla. App. 1983) (drugs); *In re J. A.*, 85 Ill. App. 3d 567, 406 N. E. 2d 958 (1980) (marihuana); *People v. Ward*, 62 Mich. App. 46, 233 N. W. 2d 180 (1975) (drug pills); *Mercer v. State*, 450 S. W. 2d 715 (Tex. Civ. App. 1970) (marihuana); *State v. McKinnon*, 88 Wash. 2d 75, 558 P. 2d 781 (1977) ("speed").

31. See, e.g., *In re L. L.*, 90 Wis. 2d 585, 280 N. W. 2d 343 (App. 1979) (search for knife or razor blade); *R. C. M. v. State*, 660 S. W. 2d 552 (Tex. App. 1983) (student with bloodshot eyes wandering halls in violation of school rule requiring students to remain in examination room or at home during midterm examinations).

32. See, e.g., *State v. Young*, 234 Ga. 488, 216 S. E. 2d 586 (three students searched when they made furtive gestures and displayed obvious consciousness of guilt), cert. denied, 423 U.S. 1039 (1975); *Doe v. State*, 88 N.M. 347, 540 P. 2d 827 (1975) (student searched for pipe when a teacher saw him using it to violate smoking regulations).

cumstance. The Court's decision today is a curious moral for the Nation's youth. Although the search of T. L. O.'s purse does not trouble today's majority, I submit that we are not dealing with "matters relatively trivial to the welfare of the Nation. There are village tyrants as well as village Hampdens, but none who acts under color of law is beyond reach of the Constitution." West *Virginia State Board of Education v. Barnette,* 319 U.S. 624, 638 (1943).

I respectfully dissent.

CHAPTER 12

DRUG TESTING

Introduction

The problem of drug use/abuse in America has affected nearly all age groups, but the problem has been especially acute among young people. One of the leading studies has been *Monitoring the Future,* a research project at the University of Michigan sponsored by the National Institute on Drug Abuse (NIDA). According to the study, drug use among teenagers has shown disturbing trends over the past twenty to thirty years.[1] As of 1975, the year the study began, young people have reported extraordinary levels of illicit drug use. By 1975, the majority of teenagers (55 percent) had used an illicit drug by the time they left high school. The percentage rose to two-thirds (66 percent) by 1981 and then declined steadily to a low point of about 41 percent in 1992. The prevalence statictic began rising again and reached 50 percent again in 1995, the year of the first court case that we discuss in this chapter.

While it certainly provokes little disagreement that drug abuse among teenagers is a serious problem, there is surely controversy about the appropriate methods by which such abuse could be prevented. There have been a number of federal government–sponsored efforts like the Drug Abuse Resistance Education (DARE) program,[2] and numerous media campaigns sponsored by the Office of National Drug Control Strategy.[3] At the local level, one of the most controversial policies that has been implemented is the random drug testing of students. School districts became so concerned about drug use that drug testing was mandated first for student athletes, and then later for any student who wished to participate in extracurricular activites. In 1995 the U.S. Supreme Court was first asked to rule on the constitutionality of student drug testing.

Drug Testing

Case Comment

The case of *Vernonia School District 47J v. Acton* (1995) involves a rural Oregon school district where school officials became so disturbed by an increase in drug use by students that they mandated random urinalysis drug testing for those who wished to participate in school-

---

1. Johnston, L. D., O'Malley, P. M., & Bachman, J. G. (2000). *Monitoring the Future national survey results on adolescent drug use: Overview of key findings, 1999* (NIH Publication No. 00-4690). Bethesda, MD: National Institute on Drug Abuse, 48 pp.

2. See http://www.dare.com/

3. See http://www.whitehousedrugpolicy.gov/

sponsored athletics. It is interesting, and certainly disputable, that athletes were the first group targeted because they were perceived to have greater problems with drug use than the student population as a whole.

James Acton wanted to play football, but was denied the right to participate when he and his parents refused to sign the required urinalysis consent form. They filed suit and were unsuccessful in the district court, but succeeded in their challenge in the court of appeals. The Supreme Court granted certiorari and upheld the constitutionality of the school policy. The Court reiterated the *T. L. O.* holding that public school searches fall within the "special needs" exception to the warrant and probable cause requirements of the Fourth Amendment. Also, as in *T. L. O.*, the Court used a balancing test to determine the reasonableness of the search by weighing the severity of the intrusion on students' privacy interests against the legitimate government interest in deterring the use of drugs by students.

The Court based its ruling on the fact that students had a lower expectation of privacy compared to adults, and participation in athletics was voluntary and subjected the athletes to even lower expectations than other students because they shared locker rooms and other facilities with fellow athletes. Further, the Court noted that the character of the intrusion was minimal because the drug testing took place while the students were fully clothed and monitors only observed the boys' backs and merely listened to the sounds of urination with both boys and girls. The Court also weighed the nature and immediacy of the concern and the efficacy for meeting it and found that there was a compelling state interest for the school district's program in light of the significant threat of illegal drugs in the schools.

VERNONIA V. ACTON

Supreme Court of the United States, 1995.

515 U.S. 646

Justice Scalia delivered the opinion of the Court.

The Student Athlete Drug Policy adopted by School District 47J in the town of Vernonia, Oregon, authorizes random urinalysis drug testing of students who participate in the District's school athletics programs. We granted certiorari to decide whether this violates the Fourth and Fourteenth Amendments to the United States Constitution.

I

A

Petitioner Vernonia School District 47J (District) operates one high school and three grade schools in the logging community of Vernonia, Oregon. As elsewhere in small-town America, school sports play a prominent role in the town's life, and student athletes are admired in their schools and in the community.

Drugs had not been a major problem in Vernonia schools. In the mid-to-late 1980's, however, teachers and administrators observed a sharp increase in drug use. Students began to speak out about their attraction to the drug culture, and to boast that there was nothing the school could do about it. Along with more drugs came more disciplinary problems. Between 1988 and 1989 the number of disciplinary referrals in Vernonia schools rose to more than twice the number reported in the early 1980's, and several students were suspended. Students became increasingly rude during class; outbursts of profane language became common.

Not only were student athletes included among the drug users but, as the District Court found, athletes were the leaders of the drug culture. 796 F. Supp. 1354, 1357 (D. Ore. 1992). This caused the District's administrators particular concern, since drug use increases the risk of sports-related injury. Expert testimony at the trial confirmed the deleterious effects of drugs on motivation, memory, judgment, reaction, coordination, and performance. The high school football and wrestling coach witnessed a severe sternum injury suffered by a wrestler, and various omissions of safety procedures and misexecutions by football players, all attributable in his belief to the effects of drug use.

Initially, the District responded to the drug problem by offering special classes, speakers, and presentations designed to deter drug use. It even brought in a specially trained dog to detect drugs, but the drug problem persisted. According to the District Court:

> "[T]he administration was at its wits end and . . . a large segment of the student body, particularly those involved in interscholastic athletics, was in a state of rebellion. Disciplinary problems had reached 'epidemic proportions.' The coincidence of an almost three-fold increase in classroom disruptions and disciplinary reports along with the staff's direct observations of students using drugs or glamorizing drug and alcohol use led the administration to the inescapable conclusion that the rebellion was being fueled by alcohol and drug abuse as well as the student's misperceptions about the drug culture." Ibid.

At that point, District officials began considering a drug-testing program. They held a parent "input night" to discuss the proposed Student Athlete Drug Policy (Policy), and the parents in attendance gave their unanimous approval. The school board approved the Policy for implementation in the fall of 1989. Its expressed purpose is to prevent student athletes from using drugs, to protect their health and safety, and to provide drug users with assistance programs.

B

The Policy applies to all students participating in interscholastic athletics. Students wishing to play sports must sign a form consenting to the testing and must obtain the written consent of their parents. Athletes are tested at the beginning of the season for their sport. In addition, once each week of the season the names of the athletes are placed in a "pool" from which a student, with the supervision of two adults, blindly draws the names of 10% of the athletes for random testing. Those selected are notified and tested that same day, if possible.

The student to be tested completes a specimen control form which bears an assigned number. Prescription medications that the student is taking must be identified by providing a copy of the prescription or a doctor's authorization. The student then enters an empty locker room accompanied by an adult monitor of the same sex. Each boy selected produces a sample at a urinal, remaining fully clothed with his back to the monitor, who stands approximately 12 to 15 feet behind the student. Monitors may (though do not always) watch the student while he produces the sample, and they listen for normal sounds of urination. Girls produce samples in an enclosed bathroom stall, so that they can be heard but not observed. After the sample is produced, it is given to the monitor, who checks it for temperature and tampering and then transfers it to a vial.

The samples are sent to an independent laboratory, which routinely tests them for amphetamines, cocaine, and marijuana. Other drugs, such as LSD, may be screened at the request of the District, but the identity of a particular student does not determine which drugs will be tested. The laboratory's procedures are 99.94% accurate. The District follows strict procedures regarding the chain of custody and access to test results. The laboratory does not know the identity of the students whose samples it tests. It is authorized to mail written test reports only to the superintendent and to provide test results to District personnel by telephone only after the requesting official recites a code confirming his authority. Only the superintendent, principals, vice-principals, and athletic directors have access to test results, and the results are not kept for more than one year.

If a sample tests positive, a second test is administered as soon as possible to confirm the result. If the second test is negative, no further action is taken. If the second test is positive, the athlete's parents are notified, and the school principal convenes a meeting with the student and his parents, at which the student is given the option of (1) participating for six weeks in an assistance program that includes weekly urinalysis, or (2) suffering suspension from athletics for the remainder of the current season and the next athletic season. The student is then retested prior to the start of the next athletic season for which he or she is eligible. The Policy states that a second offense results in automatic imposition of option (2); a third offense in suspension for the remainder of the current season and the next two athletic seasons.

C

In the fall of 1991, respondent James Acton, then a seventh-grader, signed up to play football at one of the District's grade schools. He was denied participation, however, because he and his parents refused to sign the testing consent forms. The Actons filed suit, seeking declaratory and injunctive relief from enforcement of the Policy on the grounds that it violated the Fourth and Fourteenth Amendments to the United States Constitution and Article I, 9, of the Oregon Constitution. After a bench trial, the District Court entered an order denying the claims on the merits and dismissing the action. 796 F. Supp., at 1355. The United States Court of Appeals for the Ninth Circuit reversed, holding that the Policy violated both the Fourth and Fourteenth Amendments and Article I, 9, of the Oregon Constitution. 23 F.3d 1514 (1994). We granted certiorari. 513 U.S. (1994).

II

The Fourth Amendment to the United States Constitution provides that the Federal Government shall not violate "[t]he right of the people to be secure in their persons, houses, papers, and effects, against unreasonable searches and seizures. . . ." We have held that the Fourteenth Amendment extends this constitutional guarantee to searches and seizures by state officers, *Elkins v. United States,* 364 U.S. 206, 213 (1960), including public school officials, *New Jersey v. T. L. O.,* 469 U.S. 325, 336–337 (1985). In *Skinner v. Railway Labor Executives' Assn.,* 489 U.S. 602, 617 (1989), we held that state-compelled collection and testing of urine, such as that required by the Student Athlete Drug Policy, constitutes a "search" subject to the demands of the Fourth Amendment. See also *Treasury Employees v. Von Raab,* 489 U.S. 656, 665 (1989).

As the text of the Fourth Amendment indicates, the ultimate measure of the constitutionality of a governmental search is "reasonableness." At least in a case such as this, where there was no clear practice, either approving or disapproving the type of search at issue, at the time the constitutional provision was enacted,[1] whether a particular search meets the reasonableness standard "'is judged by balancing its intrusion on the individual's Fourth Amendment interests against its promotion of legitimate governmental interests.'" *Skinner, supra,* at 619 (quoting *Delaware v. Prouse,* 440 U.S. 648, 654 (1979)). Where a search is undertaken by law enforcement officials to discover evidence of criminal wrongdoing, this Court has said that reasonableness generally requires the obtaining of a judicial warrant, *Skinner, supra,* at 619. Warrants cannot be issued, of course, without the showing of probable cause required by the Warrant Clause. But a warrant is not required to establish the reasonableness of all government searches; and when a warrant is not required (and the Warrant Clause therefore not applicable), probable cause is not invariably required either. A search unsupported by probable cause can be constitutional, we have said, "when special needs, beyond the normal need for law enforcement, make the warrant and probable-cause requirement impracticable." *Griffin v. Wisconsin,* 483 U.S. 868, 873 (1987) (internal quotation marks omitted).

We have found such "special needs" to exist in the public-school context. There, the warrant requirement "would unduly interfere with the maintenance of the swift and informal disciplinary procedures [that are] needed," and "strict adherence to the requirement that searches be based upon probable cause" would undercut "the substantial need of teachers and administrators for freedom to maintain order in the schools." *T. L. O., supra,* at 340, 341. The school search we approved in *T. L. O.,* while not based on probable cause, was based on individualized suspicion of wrongdoing. As we explicitly acknowledged, however, "'the Fourth Amendment imposes no irreducible requirement of such suspicion,'" id., at 342, n. 8 (quoting *United States v. Martinez-Fuerte,* 428 U.S. 543, 560–561 (1976)). We have upheld suspicionless searches and seizures to conduct drug testing of railroad personnel involved in train accidents, see *Skinner, supra;* to conduct random drug testing of federal customs officers who carry arms or are involved in drug interdiction, see *Von Raab, supra;* and to maintain automobile checkpoints looking for illegal immigrants and contraband, *Martinez-Fuerte, supra,* and drunk drivers, *Michigan Dept. of State Police v. Sitz,* 496 U.S. 444 (1990).

III

The first factor to be considered is the nature of the privacy interest upon which the search here at issue intrudes. The Fourth Amendment does not protect all subjective expectations of privacy, but only those that society recognizes as "legitimate." *T. L. O.,* 469 U.S., at 338. What expectations are legitimate varies, of course, with context, id., at 337, depending, for example, upon whether the individual asserting the privacy interest is at home, at work, in a car, or in a public park. In addition, the legitimacy of certain privacy expectations vis-a-vis the State may depend upon the individual's legal relationship with the State. For example, in

---

1. Not until 1852 did Massachusetts, the pioneer in the "common school" movement, enact a compulsory school-attendance law, and as late as the 1870's only 14 States had such laws. R. Butts, Public Education in the United States From Revolution to Reform 102–103 (1978); 1 Children and Youth in America 467–468 (R. Bremner ed. 1970). The drug problem, and the technology of drug testing, are of course even more recent.

Griffin, supra, we held that, although a "probationer's home, like anyone else's, is protected by the Fourth Amendmen[t]," the supervisory relationship between probationer and State justifies "a degree of impingement upon [a probationer's] privacy that would not be constitutional if applied to the public at large." 483 U.S., at 873, 875. Central, in our view, to the present case is the fact that the subjects of the Policy are (1) children, who (2) have been committed to the temporary custody of the State as schoolmaster.

Traditionally at common law, and still today, unemancipated minors lack some of the most fundamental rights of self-determination—including even the right of liberty in its narrow sense, i.e., the right to come and go at will. They are subject, even as to their physical freedom, to the control of their parents or guardians. See 59 Am. Jur. 2d 10 (1987). When parents place minor children in private schools for their education, the teachers and administrators of those schools stand in loco parentis over the children entrusted to them. In fact, the tutor or schoolmaster is the very prototype of that status. As Blackstone describes it, a parent "may . . . delegate part of his parental authority, during his life, to the tutor or schoolmaster of his child; who is then in loco parentis, and has such a portion of the power of the parent committed to his charge, viz. that of restraint and correction, as may be necessary to answer the purposes for which he is employed." 1 W. Blackstone, Commentaries on the Laws of England 441 (1769).

In *T. L. O.* we rejected the notion that public schools, like private schools, exercise only parental power over their students, which of course is not subject to constitutional constraints. *T. L. O.,* 469 U.S., at 336. Such a view of things, we said, "is not entirely 'consonant with compulsory education laws,'" ibid. (quoting *Ingraham v. Wright,* 430 U.S. 651, 662 (1977)), and is inconsistent with our prior decisions treating school officials as state actors for purposes of the Due Process and Free Speech Clauses, *T. L. O.,* supra, at 336. But while denying that the State's power over schoolchildren is formally no more than the delegated power of their parents, *T. L. O.* did not deny, but indeed emphasized, that the nature of that power is custodial and tutelary, permitting a degree of supervision and control that could not be exercised over free adults. "[A] proper educational environment requires close supervision of schoolchildren, as well as the enforcement of rules against conduct that would be perfectly permissible if undertaken by an adult." 469 U.S., at 339. While we do not, of course, suggest that public schools as a general matter have such a degree of control over children as to give rise to a constitutional "duty to protect," see *DeShaney v. Winnebago County Dept. of Social Servs.,* 489 U.S. 189, 200 (1989), we have acknowledged that for many purposes "school authorities ac[t] in loco parentis," *Bethel School Dist. No. 403 v. Fraser,* 478 U.S. 675, 684 (1986), with the power and indeed the duty to "inculcate the habits and manners of civility," id., at 681 (internal quotation marks omitted). Thus, while children assuredly do not "shed their constitutional rights . . . at the schoolhouse gate," *Tinker v. Des Moines Independent Community School Dist.,* 393 U.S. 503, 506 (1969), the nature of those rights is what is appropriate for children in school. See, e.g., *Goss v. Lopez,* 419 U.S. 565, 581-582 (1975) (due process for a student challenging disciplinary suspension requires only that the teacher "informally discuss the alleged misconduct with the student minutes after it has occurred"); *Fraser,* supra, at 683 ("[I]t is a highly appropriate function of public school education to prohibit the use of vulgar and offensive terms in public discourse"); *Hazlewood School Dist. v. Kuhlmeier,* 484 U.S. 260, 273 (1988) (public school authorities may censor school-sponsored publications, so long as the censorship is "reasonably related to legitimate pedagogical concerns"); *Ingraham,* supra, at 682 ("[I]mposing additional administrative safeguards [upon corporal punishment] ... would ... entail a significant intrusion into an area of primary educational responsibility").

Fourth Amendment rights, no less than First and Fourteenth Amendment rights, are different in public schools than elsewhere; the "reasonableness" inquiry cannot disregard the schools' custodial and tutelary responsibility for children. For their own good and that of their classmates, public school children are routinely required to submit to various physical examinations, and to be vaccinated against various diseases. According to the American Academy of Pediatrics, most public schools "provide vision and hearing screening and dental and dermatological checks. . . . Others also mandate scoliosis screening at appropriate grade levels." Committee on School Health, American Academy of Pediatrics, School Health: A Guide for Health Professionals 2 (1987). In the 1991–1992 school year, all 50 States required public-school students to be vaccinated against diphtheria, measles, rubella, and polio. U.S. Dept. of Health & Human Services, Public Health Service, Centers for Disease Control, State Immunization Requirements 1991–1992, p. 1. Particularly with regard to medical examinations and procedures, therefore, "students within the school environment have a lesser expectation of privacy than members of the population generally." *T. L. O.*, 469 U.S., at 348 (Powell, J., concurring).

Legitimate privacy expectations are even less with regard to student athletes. School sports are not for the bashful. They require "suiting up" before each practice or event, and showering and changing afterwards. Public school locker rooms, the usual sites for these activities, are not notable for the privacy they afford. The locker rooms in Vernonia are typical: no individual dressing rooms are provided; shower heads are lined up along a wall, unseparated by any sort of partition or curtain; not even all the toilet stalls have doors. As the United States Court of Appeals for the Seventh Circuit has noted, there is "an element of 'communal undress' inherent in athletic participation," *Schaill by Kross v. Tippecanoe County School Corp.*, 864 F.2d 1309, 1318 (1988).

There is an additional respect in which school athletes have a reduced expectation of privacy. By choosing to "go out for the team," they voluntarily subject themselves to a degree of regulation even higher than that imposed on students generally. In Vernonia's public schools, they must submit to a preseason physical exam (James testified that his included the giving of a urine sample, App. 17), they must acquire adequate insurance coverage or sign an insurance waiver, maintain a minimum grade point average, and comply with any "rules of conduct, dress, training hours and related matters as may be established for each sport by the head coach and athletic director with the principal's approval." Record, Exh. 2, p. 30, 8. Somewhat like adults who choose to participate in a "closely regulated industry," students who voluntarily participate in school athletics have reason to expect intrusions upon normal rights and privileges, including privacy. See *Skinner*, 489 U.S., at 627; *United States v. Biswell*, 406 U.S. 311, 316 (1972).

IV

Having considered the scope of the legitimate expectation of privacy at issue here, we turn next to the character of the intrusion that is complained of. We recognized in *Skinner* that collecting the samples for urinalysis intrudes upon "an excretory function traditionally shielded by great privacy." *Skinner*, 489 U.S., at 626. We noted, however, that the degree of intrusion depends upon the manner in which production of the urine sample is monitored.

Ibid. Under the District's Policy, male students produce samples at a urinal along a wall. They remain fully clothed and are only observed from behind, if at all. Female students produce samples in an enclosed stall, with a female monitor standing outside listening only for sounds of tampering. These conditions are nearly identical to those typically encountered in public restrooms, which men, women, and especially school children use daily. Under such conditions, the privacy interests compromised by the process of obtaining the urine sample are in our view negligible. The other privacy-invasive aspect of urinalysis is, of course, the information it discloses concerning the state of the subject's body, and the materials he has ingested. In this regard it is significant that the tests at issue here look only for drugs, and not for whether the student is, for example, epileptic, pregnant, or diabetic. See *Skinner,* supra, at 617. Moreover, the drugs for which the samples are screened are standard, and do not vary according to the identity of the student. And finally, the results of the tests are disclosed only to a limited class of school personnel who have a need to know; and they are not turned over to law enforcement authorities or used for any internal disciplinary function. 796 F. Supp., at 1364; see also 23 F.3d, at 1521.[2]

Respondents argue, however, that the District's Policy is in fact more intrusive than this suggests, because it requires the students, if they are to avoid sanctions for a falsely positive test, to identify in advance prescription medications they are taking. We agree that this raises some cause for concern. In *Von Raab,* we flagged as one of the salutary features of the Customs Service drug-testing program the fact that employees were not required to disclose medical information unless they tested positive, and, even then, the information was supplied to a licensed physician rather than to the Government employer. See *Von Raab,* 489 U.S., at 672–673, n. 2. On the other hand, we have never indicated that requiring advance disclosure of medications is per se unreasonable. Indeed, in Skinner we held that it was not "a significant invasion of privacy." *Skinner,* 489 U.S., at 626, n. 7. It can be argued that, in Skinner, the disclosure went only to the medical personnel taking the sample, and the Government personnel analyzing it, see id., at 609, but see id., at 610 (railroad personnel responsible for forwarding the sample, and presumably accompanying information, to the Government's testing lab); and that disclosure to teachers and coaches—to persons who personally know the student—is a greater invasion of privacy. Assuming for the sake of argument that both those propositions are true, we do not believe they establish a difference that respondents are entitled to rely on here.

The General Authorization Form that respondents refused to sign, which refusal was the basis for James's exclusion from the sports program, said only (in relevant part): "I . . . authorize the Vernonia School District to conduct a test on a urine specimen which I provide

---

2. Despite the fact that, like routine school physicals and vaccinations which the dissent apparently finds unobjectionable even though they "are both blanket searches of a sort," post, at 18—the search here is undertaken for prophylactic and distinctly nonpunitive purposes (protecting student athletes from injury, and deterring drug use in the student population), see 796 F. Supp., at 1363—the dissent would nonetheless lump this search together with "evidentiary" searches, which generally require probable cause, see supra, at 6, because, from the student's perspective, the test may be "regarded" or "understood" as punishment, post, at 18–19. In light of the District Court's findings regarding the purposes and consequences of the testing, any such perception is by definition an irrational one, which is protected nowhere else in the law. In any event, our point is not, as the dissent apparently believes, post, at 18, that since student vaccinations and physical exams are constitutionally reasonable, student drug testing must be so as well; but rather that, by reason of those prevalent practices, public schoolchildren in general, and student athletes in particular, have a diminished expectation of privacy. See supra, at 10.

to test for drugs and/or alcohol use. I also authorize the release of information concerning the results of such a test to the Vernonia School District and to the parents and/or guardians of the student." App. 10–11. While the practice of the District seems to have been to have a school official take medication information from the student at the time of the test, see App. 29, 42, that practice is not set forth in, or required by, the Policy, which says simply: "Student athletes who . . . are or have been taking prescription medication must provide verification (either by a copy of the prescription or by doctor's authorization) prior to being tested." App. 8. It may well be that, if and when James was selected for random testing at a time that he was taking medication, the School District would have permitted him to provide the requested information in a confidential manner—for example, in a sealed envelope delivered to the testing lab. Nothing in the Policy contradicts that, and when respondents choose, in effect, to challenge the Policy on its face, we will not assume the worst. Accordingly, we reach the same conclusion as in Skinner: that the invasion of privacy was not significant.

V

Finally, we turn to consider the nature and immediacy of the governmental concern at issue here, and the efficacy of this means for meeting it. In both *Skinner* and *Von Raab*, we characterized the government interest motivating the search as "compelling." *Skinner*, supra, at 628 (interest in preventing railway accidents); *Von Raab*, supra, at 670 (interest in insuring fitness of customs officials to interdict drugs and handle firearms). Relying on these cases, the District Court held that because the District's program also called for drug testing in the absence of individualized suspicion, the District "must demonstrate a 'compelling need' for the program." 796 F. Supp., at 1363. The Court of Appeals appears to have agreed with this view. See 23 F.3d, at 1526. It is a mistake, however, to think that the phrase "compelling state interest," in the Fourth Amendment context, describes a fixed, minimum quantum of governmental concern, so that one can dispose of a case by answering in isolation the question: Is there a compelling state interest here? Rather, the phrase describes an interest which appears important enough to justify the particular search at hand, in light of other factors which show the search to be relatively intrusive upon a genuine expectation of privacy. Whether that relatively high degree of government concern is necessary in this case or not, we think it is met.

   That the nature of the concern is important—indeed, perhaps compelling can hardly be doubted. Deterring drug use by our Nation's schoolchildren is at least as important as enhancing efficient enforcement of the Nation's laws against the importation of drugs, which was the governmental concern in *Von Raab*, supra, at 668, or deterring drug use by engineers and trainmen, which was the governmental concern in *Skinner*, supra, at 628. School years are the time when the physical, psychological, and addictive effects of drugs are most severe. "Maturing nervous systems are more critically impaired by intoxicants than mature ones are; childhood losses in learning are lifelong and profound"; "children grow chemically dependent more quickly than adults, and their record of recovery is depressingly poor." Hawley, The Bumpy Road to Drug-Free Schools, 72 Phi Delta Kappan 310, 314 (1990). See also Estroff, Schwartz, & Hoffmann, Adolescent Cocaine Abuse: Addictive Potential, Behavioral and Psychiatric Effects, 28 Clinical Pediatrics 550 (Dec. 1989); Kandel, Davies, Karus, & Yamaguchi, The Consequences in Young Adulthood of Adolescent Drug Involvement, 43

Arch. Gen. Psychiatry 746 (Aug. 1986). And of course the effects of a drug-infested school are visited not just upon the users, but upon the entire student body and faculty, as the educational process is disrupted. In the present case, moreover, the necessity for the State to act is magnified by the fact that this evil is being visited not just upon individuals at large, but upon children for whom it has undertaken a special responsibility of care and direction. Finally, it must not be lost sight of that this program is directed more narrowly to drug use by school athletes, where the risk of immediate physical harm to the drug user or those with whom he is playing his sport is particularly high. Apart from psychological effects, which include impairment of judgment, slow reaction time, and a lessening of the perception of pain, the particular drugs screened by the District's Policy have been demonstrated to pose substantial physical risks to athletes. Amphetamines produce an "artificially induced heart rate increase, [p]eripheral vasoconstriction, [b]lood pressure increase, and [m]asking of the normal fatigue response," making them a "very dangerous drug when used during exercise of any type." Hawkins, Drugs and Other Ingesta: Effects on Athletic Performance, in H. Appenzeller, Managing Sports and Risk Management Strategies 90, 90–91 (1993). Marijuana causes "[i]rregular blood pressure responses during changes in body position," "[r]eduction in the oxygen-carrying capacity of the blood," and "[i]nhibition of the normal sweating responses resulting in increased body temperature." Id., at 94. Cocaine produces "[v]asoconstriction[,] [e]levated blood pressure," and "[p]ossible coronary artery spasms and myocardial infarction." Ibid.

As for the immediacy of the District's concerns: We are not inclined to question—indeed, we could not possibly find clearly erroneous—the District Court's conclusion that "a large segment of the student body, particularly those involved in interscholastic athletics, was in a state of rebellion," that "[d]isciplinary actions had reached 'epidemic proportions,'" and that "the rebellion was being fueled by alcohol and drug abuse as well as by the student's misperceptions about the drug culture." 796 F. Supp., at 1357. That is an immediate crisis of greater proportions than existed in *Skinner,* where we upheld the Government's drug testing program based on findings of drug use by railroad employees nationwide, without proof that a problem existed on the particular railroads whose employees were subject to the test. See *Skinner,* 489 U.S., at 607. And of much greater proportions than existed in *Von Raab,* where there was no documented history of drug use by any customs officials. See *Von Raab,* 489 U.S., at 673; id., at 683 (Scalia, J., dissenting).

As to the efficacy of this means for addressing the problem: It seems to us self-evident that a drug problem largely fueled by the "role model" effect of athletes' drug use, and of particular danger to athletes, is effectively addressed by making sure that athletes do not use drugs. Respondents argue that a "less intrusive means to the same end" was available, namely, "drug testing on suspicion of drug use." Brief for Respondents 45–46. We have repeatedly refused to declare that only the "least intrusive" search practicable can be reasonable under the Fourth Amendment. *Skinner,* supra, at 629, n. 9 (collecting cases). Respondents' alternative entails substantial difficulties—if it is indeed practicable at all. It may be impracticable, for one thing, simply because the parents who are willing to accept random drug testing for athletes are not willing to accept accusatory drug testing for all students, which transforms the process into a badge of shame. Respondents' proposal brings the risk that teachers will impose testing arbitrarily upon troublesome but not drug-likely students. It generates the expense of defending lawsuits that charge such arbitrary imposition, or that simply demand greater process before accusatory drug testing is imposed. And not least of all, it adds to the ever-expanding diversionary duties of schoolteachers the new function of spotting and bringing to account drug abuse, a task for which they are ill prepared, and which is not readily compatible with their vocation. Cf. *Skinner*, supra, at 628 (quoting 50 Fed. Reg. 31526 (1985)) (a drug impaired individual "will seldom display any outward 'signs detectable by the lay person or, in many cases, even the physician.'"); *Goss*, 419 U.S., at 594 (Powell, J., dissenting) ("There is an ongoing relationship, one in which the teacher must occupy many roles—educator, adviser, friend, and, at times, parent-substitute. It is rarely adversary in nature . . .") (footnote omitted). In many respects, we think, testing based on "suspicion" of drug use would not be better, but worse.[3]

VI

Taking into account all the factors we have considered above—the decreased expectation of privacy, the relative unobtrusiveness of the search, and the severity of the need met by the search—we conclude Vernonia's Policy is reasonable and hence constitutional.

We caution against the assumption that suspicionless drug testing will readily pass constitutional muster in other contexts. The most significant element in this case is the first we discussed: that the Policy was undertaken in furtherance of the government's responsibilities, under a public school system, as guardian and tutor of children entrusted to its care.[4] Just as when the government conducts a search in its capacity as employer (a warrantless search of an absent employee's desk to obtain an urgently needed file, for example), the relevant question is whether that intrusion upon privacy is one that a reasonable employer might engage in, see *O'Connor v. Ortega*, 480 U.S. 709 (1987); so also when the government acts as guardian and tutor the relevant question is whether the search is one that a reasonable guardian and tutor might undertake. Given the findings of need made by the District Court, we conclude that in the present case it is.

We may note that the primary guardians of Vernonia's schoolchildren appear to agree. The record shows no objection to this districtwide program by any parents other than the couple before us here—even though, as we have described, a public meeting was held to obtain

---

3. There is no basis for the dissent's insinuation that in upholding the District's Policy we are equating the Fourth Amendment status of schoolchildren and prisoners, who, the dissent asserts, may have what it calls the "categorical protection" of "a strong preference for an individualized suspicion requirement," post, at 16. The case on which it relies for that proposition, *Bell v. Wolfish*, 441 U.S. 520 (1979), displays no stronger a preference for individualized suspicion than we do today. It reiterates the proposition on which we rely, that "'elaborate less-restrictive-alternative arguments could raise insuperable barriers to the exercise of virtually all search-and-seizure powers.'" *Wolfish*, supra, at 559, n. 40 (quoting *United States v. Martinez-Fuerte*, 428 U.S. 543, 556–557, n. 12 (1976)). Even *Wolfish*'s arguendo "assum[ption] that the existence of less intrusive alternatives is relevant to the determination of the reasonableness of the particular search method at issue," id., does not support the dissent, for the opinion ultimately rejected the hypothesized alternative (as we do) on the ground that it would impair other policies important to the institution. See id., at 560, n. 40 (monitoring of visits instead of conducting body searches would destroy "the confidentiality and intimacy that these visits are intended to afford").

4. The dissent devotes a few meager paragraphs of its 21 pages to this central aspect of the testing program, see post, at 15–16, in the course of which it shows none of the interest in the original meaning of the Fourth Amendment displayed elsewhere in the opinion, see post, at 3–6. Of course at the time of the framing, as well as at the time of the adoption of the Fourteenth Amendment, children had substantially fewer "rights" than legislatures and courts confer upon them today. See 1 D. Kramer, Legal Rights of Children 1.02, p. 9 (2d ed. 1994); Wald, Children's Rights: A Framework for Analysis, 12 U. C. D. L. Rev. 255, 256 (1979).

parents' views. We find insufficient basis to contradict the judgment of Vernonia's parents, its school board, and the District Court, as to what was reasonably in the interest of these children under the circumstances.

* * * *

The Ninth Circuit held that Vernonia's Policy not only violated the Fourth Amendment, but also, by reason of that violation, contravened Article I, § 9 of the Oregon Constitution. Our conclusion that the former holding was in error means that the latter holding rested on a flawed premise. We therefore vacate the judgment, and remand the case to the Court of Appeals for further proceedings consistent with this opinion.

It is so ordered.

Justice O'Connor, with whom Justice Stevens and Justice Souter join, dissenting.

The population of our Nation's public schools, grades 7 through 12, numbers around 18 million. See U.S. Dept. of Education, National Center for Education Statistics, Digest of Education Statistics 58 (1994) (Table 43). By the reasoning of today's decision, the millions of these students who participate in interscholastic sports, an overwhelming majority of whom have given school officials no reason whatsoever to suspect they use drugs at school, are open to an intrusive bodily search.

In justifying this result, the Court dispenses with a requirement of individualized suspicion on considered policy grounds. First, it explains that precisely because every student athlete is being tested, there is no concern that school officials might act arbitrarily in choosing who to test. Second, a broad-based search regime, the Court reasons, dilutes the accusatory nature of the search. In making these policy arguments, of course, the Court sidesteps powerful, countervailing privacy concerns. Blanket searches, because they can involve "thousands or millions" of searches, "pos[e] a greater threat to liberty" than do suspicion-based ones, which "affec[t] one person at a time," *Illinois v. Krull,* 480 U.S. 340, 365 (1987) (O'CONNOR, J., dissenting). Searches based on individualized suspicion also afford potential targets considerable control over whether they will, in fact, be searched because a person can avoid such a search by not acting in an objectively suspicious way. And given that the surest way to avoid acting suspiciously is to avoid the underlying wrongdoing, the costs of such a regime, one would think, are minimal.

But whether a blanket search is "better," ante, at 18, than a regime based on individualized suspicion is not a debate in which we should engage. In my view, it is not open to judges or government officials to decide on policy grounds which is better and which is worse. For most of our constitutional history, mass, suspicionless searches have been generally considered per se unreasonable within the meaning of the Fourth Amendment. And we have allowed exceptions in recent years only where it has been clear that a suspicion-based regime would be ineffectual. Because that is not the case here, I dissent.

I

A

In *Carroll v. United States,* 267 U.S. 132 (1925), the Court explained that "[t]he Fourth Amendment does not denounce all searches or seizures, but only such as are unreasonable." Id., at 147. Applying this standard, the Court first held that a search of a car was not unreasonable merely because it was warrantless; because obtaining a warrant is impractical for an easily movable object such as a car, the Court explained, a warrant is not required. The Court also held, however, that a warrantless car search was unreasonable unless supported by some level of individualized suspicion, namely probable cause. Significantly, the Court did not base its conclusion on the express probable cause requirement contained in the Warrant Clause, which, as just noted, the Court found inapplicable. Rather, the Court rested its views on "what was deemed an unreasonable search and seizure when [the Fourth Amendment] was adopted" and "[what] will conserve public interests as well as the interests and rights of individual citizens." Id., at 149. With respect to the "rights of individual citizens," the Court eventually offered the simple yet powerful intuition that "those lawfully within the country, entitled to use the public highways, have a right to free passage without interruption or search unless there is known to a competent official authorized to search, probable cause for believing that their vehicles are carrying contraband or illegal merchandise." Id., at 154.

More important for the purposes of this case, the Court clearly indicated that evenhanded treatment was no substitute for the individualized suspicion requirement:

> "It would be intolerable and unreasonable if a prohibition agent were authorized to stop every au-
> tomobile on the chance of finding liquor and thus subject all persons lawfully using the highways
> to the inconvenience and indignity of such a search." Id., at 153–154.

The *Carroll* Court's view that blanket searches are "intolerable and unreasonable" is well-grounded in history. As recently confirmed in one of the most exhaustive analyses of the original meaning of the Fourth Amendment ever undertaken, see W. Cuddihy, The Fourth Amendment: Origins and Original Meaning (1990) (Ph.D. Dissertation at Claremont Graduate School) (hereinafter Cuddihy), what the Framers of the Fourth Amendment most strongly opposed, with limited exceptions wholly inapplicable here, were general searches—that is, searches by general warrant, by writ of assistance, by broad statute, or by any other similar authority. See id., at 1402, 1499, 1555; see also Clancy, The Role of Individualized Suspicion in Assessing the Reasonableness of Searches and Seizures, 25 Mem. St. U. L. Rev. 483, 528 (1994); Maclin, When the Cure for the Fourth Amendment Is Worse Than the Disease, 68 S. Cal. L. Rev. 1, 9–12 (1994); L. Levy, Original Intent and the Framers' Constitution 221–246 (1988). Although, ironically, such warrants, writs, and statutes typically required individualized suspicion, see, e.g., Cuddihy 1140 ("Typical of the American warrants of 1761–76 was Starke's 'tobacco' warrant, which commanded its bearer to 'enter any suspected Houses'"), such requirements were subjective and largely unenforceable. Accordingly, these various forms of authority led in practice to "virtually unrestrained," and hence "general," searches. J. Landynski, Search and Seizure and the Supreme Court 20 (1966). To be sure, the Fourth Amendment, in the Warrant Clause, prohibits by name only searches by general warrants. But that was only because the abuses of the general warrant were particularly vivid in the minds of the Framers' generation, Cuddihy 1554–1560, and not because the Framers viewed other kinds of general searches as any less unreasonable. "Prohibition of the general warrant was part of a larger scheme to extinguish general searches categorically." Id., at 1499.

More important, there is no indication in the historical materials that the Framers' opposition to general searches stemmed solely from the fact that they allowed officials to single out individuals for arbitrary reasons, and thus that officials could render them reasonable simply by making sure to extend their search to every house in a given area or to every person in a given group. See *Delaware v. Prouse*, 440 U.S. 648, 664 (1979) (Rehnquist, J., dissenting) (referring to this as the "'misery loves company'" theory of the Fourth Amendment). On the contrary, although general searches were typically arbitrary, they were not invariably so. Some general searches, for example, were of the arguably evenhanded "door-to-door" kind. Cuddihy 1091; see also id., at 377, 1502, 1557. Indeed, Cuddihy's descriptions of a few blanket searches suggests they may have been considered more worrisome than the typical general search. See id., at 575 ("One type of warrant [between 1700 and 1760] went beyond a general search, in which the searcher entered and inspected suspicious places, by requiring him to search entire categories of places whether he suspected them or not"); id., at 478 ("During the exigencies of Queen Anne's War, two colonies even authorized searches in 1706 that extended to entire geographic areas, not just to suspicious houses in a district, as conventional general warrants allowed").

Perhaps most telling of all, as reflected in the text of the Warrant Clause, the particular way the Framers chose to curb the abuses of general warrants—and by implication, all general searches—was not to impose a novel "evenhandedness" requirement; it was to retain the individualized suspicion requirement contained in the typical general warrant, but to make that requirement meaningful and enforceable, for instance, by raising the required level of individualized suspicion to objective probable cause. See U.S. Const., Amdt. 4. So, for example, when the same Congress that proposed the Fourth Amendment authorized duty collectors to search for concealed goods subject to import duties, specific warrants were required for searches on land; but even for searches at sea, where warrants were impractical and thus not required, Congress nonetheless limited officials to searching only those ships and vessels "in which [a collector] shall have reason to suspect any goods, wares or merchandise subject to duty shall be concealed." The Collection Act of July 31, 1789, 24, 1 Stat. 43 (emphasis added); see also Cuddihy 1490–1491 ("The Collection Act of 1789 was [the] most significant [of all early search statutes], for it identified the techniques of search and seizure that the framers of the amendment believed reasonable while they were framing it"). Not surprisingly, the *Carroll* Court relied on this statute and other subsequent ones like it in arriving at its views. See *Carroll*, 267 U.S., at 150-151, 154; cf. *Clancy*, supra, at 489 ("While the plain language of the Amendment does not mandate individualized suspicion as a necessary component of all searches and seizures, the historical record demonstrates that the framers believed that individualized suspicion was an inherent quality of reasonable searches and seizures").

True, not all searches around the time the Fourth Amendment was adopted required individualized suspicion—although most did. A search incident to arrest was an obvious example of one that did not, see Cuddihy 1518, but even those searches shared the essential characteristics that distinguish suspicion-based searches from abusive general searches: they only "affec[t] one person at a time," *Krull*, 480 U.S., at 365 (O'Connor, J., dissenting), and they are generally avoidable by refraining from wrongdoing. See supra, at 1-2. Protection of privacy, not evenhandedness, was then and is now the touchstone of the Fourth Amendment.

The view that mass, suspicionless searches, however evenhanded, are generally unreasonable remains inviolate in the criminal law enforcement context, see *Ybarra v. Illinois*, 444 U.S. 85 (1979) (invalidating evenhanded, nonaccusatory patdown for weapons of all patrons in a tavern in which there was probable cause to think drug dealing was going on), at least where the search is more than minimally intrusive, see *Michigan Dept. of State Police v. Sitz,* 496 U.S. 444 (1990) (upholding the brief and easily avoidable detention, for purposes of observing signs of intoxication, of all motorists approaching a roadblock). It is worth noting in this regard that state-compelled, state-monitored collection and testing of urine, while perhaps not the most intrusive of searches, see, e.g., *Bell v. Wolfish,* 441 U.S. 520, 558–560 (1979) (visual body cavity searches), is still "particularly destructive of privacy and offensive to personal dignity." *Treasury Employees v. Von Raab,* 489 U.S. 656, 680 (1989) (Scalia, J., dissenting); see also ante, at 11; *Skinner v. Railway Labor Executives' Assn.,* 489 U.S. 602, 617 (1989). We have not hesitated to treat monitored bowel movements as highly intrusive (even in the special border search context), compare *United States v. Martinez-Fuerte,* 428 U.S. 543 (1976) (brief interrogative stops of all motorists crossing certain border checkpoint reasonable without individualized suspicion), with *United States v. Montoya de Hernandez,* 473 U.S. 531 (1985) (monitored bowel movement of border crossers reasonable only upon reasonable suspicion of alimentary canal smuggling), and it is not easy to draw a distinction. See Fried, Privacy, 77 Yale L. J. 475, 487 (1968) ("[I]n our culture the excretory functions are shielded by more or less absolute privacy"). And certainly monitored urination combined with urine testing is more intrusive than some personal searches we have said trigger Fourth Amendment protections in the past. See, e.g., *Cupp v. Murphy,* 412 U.S. 291, 295 (1973) (Stewart, J.) (characterizing the scraping of dirt from under a person's fingernails as a "'severe, though brief, intrusion upon cherished personal security'"). Finally, the collection and testing of urine is, of course, a search of a person, one of only four categories of suspect searches the Constitution mentions by name. See U.S. Const., Amdt. 4 (listing "persons, houses, papers, and effects"); cf. Cuddihy 835, 1518, 1552, n. 394 (indicating long history of outrage at personal searches before 1789).

Thus, it remains the law that the police cannot, say, subject to drug testing every person entering or leaving a certain drug-ridden neighborhood in order to find evidence of crime. 3 W. LaFave, Search and Seizure 9.5(b), pp. 551–553 (2d ed. 1987) (hereinafter LaFave). And this is true even though it is hard to think of a more compelling government interest than the need to fight the scourge of drugs on our streets and in our neighborhoods. Nor could it be otherwise, for if being evenhanded were enough to justify evaluating a search regime under an open-ended balancing test, the Warrant Clause, which presupposes that there is some category of searches for which individualized suspicion is non-negotiable, see 2 LaFave 4.1, at 118, would be a dead letter.

Outside the criminal context, however, in response to the exigencies of modern life, our cases have upheld several evenhanded blanket searches, including some that are more than minimally intrusive, after balancing the invasion of privacy against the government's strong need. Most of these cases, of course, are distinguishable insofar as they involved searches either not of a personally intrusive nature, such as searches of closely regulated businesses, see, e.g., *New York v. Burger,* 482 U.S. 691, 699-703 (1987); cf. Cuddihy 1501 ("Even the states with the strongest constitutional restrictions on general searches had long exposed commercial establishments to warrantless inspection"), or arising in unique contexts such as prisons, see, e.g., *Wolfish,* supra, at 558–560 (visual body cavity searches of prisoners following contact visits); cf. Cuddihy 1516–1519, 1552–1553 (indicating that searches incident to arrest and prisoner searches were the only common personal searches at time of founding). This certainly explains why Justice Scalia, in his dissent in our recent *Von Raab* decision, found it significant that "[u]ntil today this Court had upheld a bodily search separate from arrest and without individualized suspicion of wrong-doing only with respect to prison inmates, relying upon the uniquely dangerous nature of that environment." *Von Raab,* supra, at 680 (citation omitted).

In any event, in many of the cases that can be distinguished on the grounds suggested above and, more important, in all of the cases that cannot, see, e.g., *Skinner,* supra (blanket drug testing scheme); *Von Raab,* supra (same); cf. *Camara v. Municipal Court of San Francisco,* 387 U.S. 523 (1967) (area-wide searches of private residences), we upheld the suspicionless search only after first recognizing the Fourth Amendment's longstanding preference for a suspicion-based search regime, and then pointing to sound reasons why such a regime would likely be ineffectual under the unusual circumstances presented. In *Skinner,* for example, we stated outright that "'some quantum of individualized suspicion'" is "usually required" under the Fourth Amendment, *Skinner,* supra, at 624, quoting *Martinez-Fuerte,* 428 U.S., at 560, and we built the requirement into the test we announced: "In limited circumstances, where the privacy interests implicated by the search are minimal, and where an important governmental interest furthered by the intrusion would be placed in jeopardy by a requirement of individualized suspicion, a search may be reasonable despite the absence of such suspicion." Ibid. The obvious negative implication of this reasoning is that, if such an individualized suspicion requirement would not place the government's objectives in jeopardy, the requirement should not be forsaken. See also *Von Raab,* supra, at 665–666.

Accordingly, we upheld the suspicionless regime at issue in *Skinner* on the firm understanding that a requirement of individualized suspicion for testing train operators for drug or alcohol impairment following serious train accidents would be unworkable because "the scene of a serious rail accident is chaotic." *Skinner,* 489 U.S., at 631. (Of course, it could be plausibly argued that the fact that testing occurred only after train operators were involved in serious train accidents amounted to an individualized suspicion requirement in all but name, in light of the record evidence of a strong link between serious train accidents and drug and alcohol use.) We have performed a similar inquiry in the other cases as well. See *Von Raab,* supra, at 674 (suspicion requirement for searches of customs officials for drug impairment impractical because "not feasible to subject [such] employees and their work product to the kind of day-to-day scrutiny that is the norm in more traditional office environments"); *Camara,* supra, at 537 (suspicion requirement for searches of homes for safety code violations impractical because conditions such as "faulty wiring" not observable from outside of house); see also *Wolfish,* 441 U.S., at 559, n. 40 (suspicion requirement for searches of prisoners for smuggling following contact visits impractical because observation necessary to gain suspicion would cause "obvious disruption of the confidentiality and intimacy that these visits are intended to afford"); *Martinez-Fuerte,* supra, at 557 ("A requirement that stops on major routes inland always be based on reasonable suspicion would be impractical because the flow of traffic tends to be too heavy to allow the particularized study of a given car that would enable it to be identified as a possible carrier of illegal aliens"); *United States v. Edwards,* 498 F.2d 496, 500 (CA2 1974) (Friendly, J.) (suspicion-based searches of airport passengers' carry-on luggage impractical because of the great number of plane travelers and "conceded inapplicability" of the profile method of detecting hijackers).

Moreover, an individualized suspicion requirement was often impractical in these cases because they involved situations in which even one undetected instance of wrongdoing could have injurious consequences for a great number of people. See, e.g., *Camara,* supra, at 535 (even one safety code violation can cause "fires and epidemics [that] ravage large urban areas"); *Skinner,* supra, at 628 (even one drug- or alcohol-impaired train operator can lead to the "disastrous consequences" of a train wreck, such as "great human loss"); *Von Raab,* supra, at 670, 674, 677 (even one customs official caught up in drugs can, by virtue of impairment, susceptibility to bribes, or indifference, result in the noninterdiction of a "sizable drug shipmen[t]," which eventually injures the lives of thousands, or to a breach of "national security"); *Edwards,* supra, at 500 (even one hijacked airplane can destroy "'hundreds of human lives and millions of dollars of property'").

B

The instant case stands in marked contrast. One searches today's majority opinion in vain for recognition that history and precedent establish that individualized suspicion is "usually required" under the Fourth Amendment (regardless of whether a warrant and probable cause are also required) and that, in the area of intrusive personal searches, the only recognized exception is for situations in which a suspicion-based scheme would be likely ineffectual. See supra, at 9–10. Far from acknowledging anything special about individualized suspicion, the Court treats a suspicion-based regime as if it were just any run-of-the-mill, less intrusive alternative—that is, an alternative that officials may bypass if the lesser intrusion, in their reasonable estimation, is outweighed by policy concerns unrelated to practicability.

As an initial matter, I have serious doubts whether the Court is right that the District reasonably found that the lesser intrusion of a suspicion-based testing program outweighed its genuine concerns for the adversarial nature of such a program, and for its abuses. See ante, at 17–18. For one thing, there are significant safeguards against abuses. The fear that a suspicion-based regime will lead to the testing of "troublesome but not drug-likely" students, id., at 17, for example, ignores that the required level of suspicion in the school context is objectively reasonable suspicion. In this respect, the facts of our decision in *New Jersey v. T. L. O.,* 469 U.S. 325 (1985), should be reassuring. There, we found reasonable suspicion to search a ninth-grade girl's purse for cigarettes after a teacher caught the girl smoking in the bathroom with a companion who admitted it. See id., at 328, 345–346. Moreover, any distress arising from what turns out to be a false accusation can be minimized by keeping the entire process confidential.

For another thing, the District's concern for the adversarial nature of a suspicion-based regime (which appears to extend even to those who are rightly accused) seems to ignore the fact that such a regime would not exist in a vacuum. Schools already have adversarial, disciplinary schemes that require teachers and administrators in many areas besides drug use to investigate student wrongdoing (often by means of accusatory searches); to make determinations about whether the wrongdoing occurred; and to impose punishment. To such a scheme, suspicion-based drug testing would be only a minor addition. The District's own elaborate disciplinary scheme is reflected in its handbook, which, among other things, lists the following disciplinary "problem areas" carrying serious sanctions: "DEFIANCE OF AUTHORITY," "DISORDERLY OR DISRUPTIVE CONDUCT INCLUDING FOUL LANGUAGE," "AUTOMOBILE USE OR MISUSE," "FORGERY OR LYING," "GAMBLING," "THEFT," "TOBACCO," "MISCHIEF," "VANDALISM," "RECKLESSLY ENDANGERING,"

"MENACING OR HARASSMENT," "ASSAULT," "FIGHTING," "WEAPONS," "EXTORTION," "EXPLOSIVE DEVICES," and "ARSON." Record, Exh. 2, p. 11; see also id., at 20–21 (listing rules regulating dress and grooming, public displays of affection, and the wearing of hats inside); cf. id., at 8 ("RESPONSIBILITIES OF SCHOOLS" include "To develop and distribute to parents and students reasonable rules and regulations governing student behavior and attendance" and "To provide fair and reasonable standards of conduct and to enforce those standards through appropriate disciplinary action"). The high number of disciplinary referrals in the record in this case illustrates the District's robust scheme in action.

In addition to overstating its concerns with a suspicion-based program, the District seems to have understated the extent to which such a program is less intrusive of students' privacy. By invading the privacy of a few students rather than many (nationwide, of thousands rather than millions), and by giving potential search targets substantial control over whether they will, in fact, be searched, a suspicion-based scheme is significantly less intrusive.

In any event, whether the Court is right that the District reasonably weighed the lesser intrusion of a suspicion-based scheme against its policy concerns is beside the point. As stated, a suspicion-based search regime is not just any less intrusive alternative; the individualized suspicion requirement has a legal pedigree as old as the Fourth Amendment itself, and it may not be easily cast aside in the name of policy concerns. It may only be forsaken, our cases in the personal search context have established, if a suspicion-based regime would likely be ineffectual. But having misconstrued the fundamental role of the individualized suspicion requirement in Fourth Amendment analysis, the Court never seriously engages the practicality of such a requirement in the instant case. And that failure is crucial because nowhere is it less clear that an individualized suspicion requirement would be ineffectual than in the school context. In most schools, the entire pool of potential search targets—students— is under constant supervision by teachers and administrators and coaches, be it in classrooms, hallways, or locker rooms. See *T. L. O.*, 469 U.S., at 339 ("[A] proper educational environment requires close supervision of schoolchildren").

The record here indicates that the Vernonia schools are no exception. The great irony of this case is that most (though not all) of the evidence the District introduced to justify its suspicionless drug-testing program consisted of first- or second-hand stories of particular, identifiable students acting in ways that plainly gave rise to reasonable suspicion of in-school drug use—and thus that would have justified a drug-related search under our *T. L. O.* decision. See id., at 340–342 (warrant and probable cause not required for school searches; reasonable suspicion sufficient). Small groups of students, for example, were observed by a teacher "passing joints back and forth" across the street at a restaurant before school and during school hours. Tr. 67 (Apr. 29, 1992). Another group was caught skipping school and using drugs at one of the students' houses. See id., at 93–94. Several students actually admitted their drug use to school officials (some of them being caught with marijuana pipes). See id., at 24. One student presented himself to his teacher as "clearly obviously inebriated" and had to be sent home. Id., at 68. Still another was observed dancing and singing at the top of his voice in the back of the classroom; when the teacher asked what was going on, he replied, "Well, I'm just high on life." Id., at 89–90. To take a final example, on a certain road trip, the school wrestling coach smelled marijuana smoke in a hotel room occupied by four wrestlers, see id., at 110–112, an observation that (after some questioning) would probably have given him reasonable suspicion to test one or all of them. Cf. 4 LaFave 10.11(b), at 169 ("[I]n most instances the evidence of wrongdoing prompting teachers or principals to conduct searches is sufficiently detailed and specific to meet the traditional probable cause test").

In light of all this evidence of drug use by particular students, there is a substantial basis for concluding that a vigorous regime of suspicion-based testing (for which the District appears already to have rules in place, see Record, Exh. 2, at 14, 17) would have gone a long way toward solving Vernonia's school drug problem while preserving the Fourth Amendment rights of James Acton and others like him. And were there any doubt about such a conclusion, it is removed by indications in the record that suspicion-based testing could have been supplemented by an equally vigorous campaign to have Vernonia's parents encourage their children to submit to the District's voluntary drug testing program. See id., at 32 (describing the voluntary program); ante, at 19 (noting widespread parental support for drug testing). In these circumstances, the Fourth Amendment dictates that a mass, suspicionless search regime is categorically unreasonable.

I recognize that a suspicion-based scheme, even where reasonably effective in controlling in-school drug use, may not be as effective as a mass, suspicionless testing regime. In one sense, that is obviously true just as it is obviously true that suspicion-based law enforcement is not as effective as mass, suspicionless enforcement might be. "But there is nothing new in the realization" that Fourth Amendment protections come with a price. *Arizona v. Hicks,* 480 U.S. 321, 329 (1987). Indeed, the price we pay is higher in the criminal context, given that police do not closely observe the entire class of potential search targets (all citizens in the area) and must ordinarily adhere to the rigid requirements of a warrant and probable cause.

The principal counterargument to all this, central to the Court's opinion, is that the Fourth Amendment is more lenient with respect to school searches. That is no doubt correct, for, as the Court explains, ante, at 8–10, schools have traditionally had special guardian-like responsibilities for children that necessitate a degree of constitutional leeway. This principle explains the considerable Fourth Amendment leeway we gave school officials in *T. L. O.* In that case, we held that children at school do not enjoy two of the Fourth Amendment's traditional categorical protections against unreasonable searches and seizures: the warrant requirement and the probable cause requirement. See *T. L. O.,* 469 U.S., at 337–343. And this was true even though the same children enjoy such protections "in a nonschool setting." Id., at 348 (Powell, J., concurring).

The instant case, however, asks whether the Fourth Amendment is even more lenient than that, i.e., whether it is so lenient that students may be deprived of the Fourth Amendment's only remaining, and most basic, categorical protection: its strong preference for an individualized suspicion requirement, with its accompanying antipathy toward personally intrusive, blanket searches of mostly innocent people. It is not at all clear that people in prison lack this categorical protection, see *Wolfish,* 441 U.S., at 558–560 (upholding certain suspicionless searches of prison inmates); but cf. supra, at 10 (indicating why suspicion requirement was impractical in *Wolfish*), and we have said "we are not yet ready to hold that the schools and the prisons need be equated for purposes of the Fourth Amendment." *T. L. O.,* supra, at 338–339. Thus, if we are to mean what we often proclaim—that students do not "shed their constitutional rights . . . at the schoolhouse gate," *Tinker v. Des Moines Independent Community School Dist.,* 393 U.S. 503, 506 (1969)—the answer must plainly be no.[1]

---

1. The Court says I pay short shrift to the original meaning of the Fourth Amendment as it relates to searches of public school children. See ante, at 19, n. 4. As an initial matter, the historical materials on what the Framers

For the contrary position, the Court relies on cases such as *T. L. O., Ingraham v. Wright*, 430 U.S. 651 (1977), and *Goss v. Lopez*, 419 U.S. 565 (1975). See ante, at 8–10. But I find the Court's reliance on these cases ironic. If anything, they affirm that schools have substantial constitutional leeway in carrying out their traditional mission of responding to particularized wrongdoing. See *T. L. O.*, supra (leeway in investigating particularized wrongdoing); Ingraham, supra (leeway in punishing particularized wrongdoing); *Goss*, supra (leeway in choosing procedures by which particularized wrongdoing is punished).

By contrast, intrusive, blanket searches of school children, most of whom are innocent, for evidence of serious wrongdoing are not part of any traditional school function of which I am aware. Indeed, many schools, like many parents, prefer to trust their children unless given reason to do otherwise. As James Acton's father said on the witness stand, "[suspicionless testing] sends a message to children that are trying to be responsible citizens . . . that they have to prove that they're innocent. . . , and I think that kind of sets a bad tone for citizenship." Tr. 9 (Apr. 29, 1992).

I find unpersuasive the Court's reliance, ante, at 10, on the widespread practice of physical examinations and vaccinations, which are both blanket searches of a sort. Of course, for these practices to have any Fourth Amendment significance, the Court has to assume that these physical exams and vaccinations are typically "required" to a similar extent that urine testing and collection is required in the instant case, i.e., that they are required regardless of parental objection and that some meaningful sanction attaches to the failure to submit. In any event, without forming any particular view of such searches, it is worth noting that a suspicion requirement for vaccinations is not merely impractical; it is nonsensical, for vaccinations are not searches for anything in particular and so there is nothing about which to be suspicious. Nor is this saying anything new; it is the same theory on which, in part, we have repeatedly upheld certain inventory searches. See, e.g., *South Dakota v. Opperman*, 428 U.S. 364, 370, n. 5 (1976) ("The probable-cause approach is unhelpful when analysis centers upon the reasonableness of routine administrative caretaking functions"). As for physical examinations, the practicability of a suspicion requirement is highly doubtful because the conditions for which these physical exams ordinarily search, such as latent heart conditions, do not manifest themselves in observable behavior the way school drug use does. See supra, at 14.

It might also be noted that physical exams (and of course vaccinations) are not searches for conditions that reflect wrongdoing on the part of the student, and so are wholly nonaccusatory and have no consequences that can be regarded as punitive. These facts may explain the absence of Fourth Amendment challenges to such searches. By contrast, although

---

thought of official searches of children, let alone of public school children (the concept of which did not exist at the time, see id., at 6, n. 1), are extremely scarce. Perhaps because of this, the Court does not itself offer an account of the original meaning, but rather resorts to the general proposition that children had fewer recognized rights at the time of the framing than they do today. But that proposition seems uniquely unhelpful in the present case, for although children may have had fewer rights against the private schoolmaster at the time of the framing than they have against public school officials today, parents plainly had greater rights then than now. At the time of the framing, for example, the fact that a child's parents refused to authorize a private schoolmaster's search of the child would probably have rendered any such search unlawful; after all, at common law, the source of the schoolmaster's authority over a child was a delegation of the parent's authority. See id., at 8. Today, of course, the fact that a child's parents refuse to authorize a public school search of the child—as James Acton's parents refused here—is of little constitutional moment. Cf. *Ingraham v. Wright*, 430 U.S. 651, 662, n. 22 (1977) ("parental approval of corporal punishment is not constitutionally required").

I agree with the Court that the accusatory nature of the District's testing program is diluted by making it a blanket one, any testing program that searches for conditions plainly reflecting serious wrongdoing can never be made wholly nonaccusatory from the student's perspective, the motives for the program notwithstanding; and for the same reason, the substantial consequences that can flow from a positive test, such as suspension from sports, are invariably—and quite reasonably—understood as punishment. The best proof that the District's testing program is to some extent accusatory can be found in James Acton's own explanation on the witness stand as to why he did not want to submit to drug testing: "Because I feel that they have no reason to think I was taking drugs." Tr. 13 (Apr. 29, 1992). It is hard to think of a manner of explanation that resonates more intensely in our Fourth Amendment tradition than this.

II

I do not believe that suspicionless drug testing is justified on these facts. But even if I agreed that some such testing were reasonable here, I see two other Fourth Amendment flaws in the District's program.[2] First, and most serious, there is virtually no evidence in the record of a drug problem at the Washington Grade School, which includes the 7th and 8th grades, and which Acton attended when this litigation began. This is not surprising, given that, of the four witnesses who testified to drug-related incidents, three were teachers and/or coaches at the high school, see Tr. 65; id., at 86; id., at 99, and the fourth, though the principal of the grade school at the time of the litigation, had been employed as principal of the high school during the years leading up to (and beyond) the implementation of the drug testing policy. See id., at 17. The only evidence of a grade school drug problem that my review of the record uncovered is a "guarantee" by the late-arriving grade school principal that "our problems we've had in '88 and '89 didn't start at the high school level. They started in the elementary school." Id., at 43. But I would hope that a single assertion of this sort would not serve as an adequate basis on which to uphold mass, suspicionless drug testing of two entire grades of student-athletes—in *Vernonia* and, by the Court's reasoning, in other school districts as well. Perhaps there is a drug problem at the grade school, but one would not know it from this record. At the least, then, I would insist that the parties and the District Court address this issue on remand.

Second, even as to the high school, I find unreasonable the school's choice of student athletes as the class to subject to suspicionless testing—a choice that appears to have been driven more by a belief in what would pass constitutional muster, see id., at 45–47 (indicating that the original program was targeted at students involved in any extracurricular activity), than by a belief in what was required to meet the District's principal disciplinary concern. Reading the full record in this case, as well as the District Court's authoritative summary of it, 796 F. Supp. 1354, 1356–1357 (Ore. 1992), it seems quite obvious that the true driving force behind the District's adoption of its drug testing program was the need to combat the rise in drug-related disorder and disruption in its classrooms and around campus. I mean no criticism of the strength of that interest. On the contrary, where the record demonstrates the ex-

---

2. Because I agree with the Court that we may assume the District's program allows students to confine the advanced disclosure of highly personal prescription medications to the testing lab, see ante, at 13–14, I also agree that *Skinner* controls this aspect of the case, and so do not count the disclosure requirement among the program's flaws.

istence of such a problem, that interest seems self-evidently compelling. "Without first establishing discipline and maintaining order, teachers cannot begin to educate their students." *T. L. O.,* 469 U.S., at 350 (Powell, J., concurring). And the record in this case surely demonstrates there was a drug-related discipline problem in *Vernonia* of "'epidemic proportions.'" 796 F. Supp., at 1357. The evidence of a drug-related sports injury problem at *Vernonia,* by contrast, was considerably weaker.

On this record, then, it seems to me that the far more reasonable choice would have been to focus on the class of students found to have violated published school rules against severe disruption in class and around campus, see Record, Exh. 2, at 9, 11—disruption that had a strong nexus to drug use, as the District established at trial. Such a choice would share two of the virtues of a suspicion-based regime: testing dramatically fewer students, tens as against hundreds, and giving students control, through their behavior, over the likelihood that they would be tested. Moreover, there would be a reduced concern for the accusatory nature of the search, because the Court's feared "badge of shame," ante, at 17, would already exist, due to the antecedent accusation and finding of severe disruption. In a lesser known aspect of *Skinner,* we upheld an analogous testing scheme with little hesitation. See *Skinner,* 489 U.S., at 611 (describing "'Authorization to Test for Cause'" scheme, according to which train operators would be tested "in the event of certain specific rule violations, including noncompliance with a signal and excessive speeding").

III

It cannot be too often stated that the greatest threats to our constitutional freedoms come in times of crisis. But we must also stay mindful that not all government responses to such times are hysterical overreactions; some crises are quite real, and when they are, they serve precisely as the compelling state interest that we have said may justify a measured intrusion on constitutional rights. The only way for judges to mediate these conflicting impulses is to do what they should do anyway: stay close to the record in each case that appears before them, and make their judgments based on that alone. Having reviewed the record here, I cannot avoid the conclusion that the District's suspicionless policy of testing all student-athletes sweeps too broadly, and too imprecisely, to be reasonable under the Fourth Amendment.

Case Comment

Seven years after *Vernonia,* the U.S. Supreme Court was confronted by another case dealing with student drug testing. The case of *Board of Education of Independent School District of Pottawatomie v. Earls* concerned a "Student Activities Drug Testing Policy" adopted by the Tecumseh, Oklahoma, School District that required all middle and high school students to consent to urinalysis testing for drugs in order to participate in any extracurricular activity. The petitioners argued that such a policy violates the Fourth Amendment. The District Court had granted the Pottawatomie School District summary judgment, but the Tenth Circuit reversed, holding that the Policy violated the Fourth Amendment and concluded that before imposing a suspicionless drug testing program a school must demonstrate some identifiable drug abuse problem among a sufficient number of those tested, such that testing that group will actually redress its drug problem. The court then held that the School District had failed to demonstrate such a problem among Tecumseh students participating in competitive extracurricular activities.

The Supreme Court ruled that the drug testing policy was a reasonable means of furthering the School District's important interest in preventing and deterring drug use among its school children and did not violate the Fourth Amendment. In so ruling, the Court found that in a public school context, a search may be reasonable when supported by "special needs" beyond the normal need for law enforcement. The Court merely reiterated its *Vernonia* ruling by finding (1) that the students affected by the drug testing policy have a limited expectation of privacy; (2) that the invasion of students' privacy is not significant, given the minimally intrusive nature of the sample collection and the limited uses to which the test results are put; and (3) that, considering the nature and immediacy of the government's concerns and the efficacy of the Policy in meeting them, the drug testing policy effectively serves the School District's interest in protecting its students' safety and health. Preventing drug use by schoolchildren is an important governmental concern.

BOARD OF EDUCATION OF INDEPENDENT SCHOOL DISTRICT OF POTTAWATOMIE V. EARLS

Supreme Court of the United States, 2002.

536 U.S. 822

Justice Thomas delivered the opinion of the Court.

The Student Activities Drug Testing Policy implemented by the Board of Education of Independent School District No. 92 of Pottawatomie County (School District) requires all students who participate in competitive extracurricular activities to submit to drug testing. Because this Policy reasonably serves the School District's important interest in detecting and preventing drug use among its students, we hold that it is constitutional.

I

The city of Tecumseh, Oklahoma, is a rural community located approximately 40 miles southeast of Oklahoma City. The School District administers all Tecumseh public schools. In the fall of 1998, the School District adopted the Student Activities Drug Testing Policy (Policy), which requires all middle and high school students to consent to drug testing in order to participate in any extracurricular activity. In practice, the Policy has been applied only to competitive extracurricular activities sanctioned by the Oklahoma Secondary Schools Activities Association, such as the Academic Team, Future Farmers of America, Future Homemakers of America, band, choir, pom pon, cheerleading, and athletics. Under the Policy, students are required to take a drug test before participating in an extracurricular activity, must submit to random drug testing while participating in that activity, and must agree to be tested at any time upon reasonable suspicion. The urinalysis tests are designed to detect only the use of illegal drugs, including amphetamines, marijuana, cocaine, opiates, and barbituates, not medical conditions or the presence of authorized prescription medications.

At the time of their suit, both respondents attended Tecumseh High School. Respondent Lindsay Earls was a member of the show choir, the marching band, the Academic Team, and the National Honor Society. Respondent Daniel James sought to participate in the Academic Team.[1] Together with their parents, Earls and James brought a 42 U.S.C. § 1983 action against the School District, challenging the Policy both on its face and as applied to their participation in extracurricular activities.[2] They alleged that the Policy violates the Fourth Amendment as incorporated by the Fourteenth Amendment and requested injunctive and declarative relief. They also argued that the School District failed to identify a special need for testing students who participate in extracurricular activities, and that the "Drug Testing Policy neither addresses a proven problem nor promises to bring any benefit to students or the school." App. 9.

Applying the principles articulated in *Vernonia School Dist. 47J v. Acton,* 515 U.S. 646 (1995), in which we upheld the suspicionless drug testing of school athletes, the United States District Court for the Western District of Oklahoma rejected respondents' claim that the Policy was unconstitutional and granted summary judgment to the School District. The court noted that "special needs" exist in the public school context and that, although the School District did "not show a drug problem of epidemic proportions," there was a history of drug abuse starting in 1970 that presented "legitimate cause for concern." 115 F. Supp. 2d 1281, 1287 (2000). The District Court also held that the Policy was effective because "[i]t can scarcely be disputed that the drug problem among the student body is effectively addressed by making sure that the large number of students participating in competitive, extracurricular activities do not use drugs." *Id.,* at 1295.

The United States Court of Appeals for the Tenth Circuit reversed, holding that the Policy violated the Fourth Amendment. The Court of Appeals agreed with the District Court that the Policy must be evaluated in the "unique environment of the school setting," but reached a different conclusion as to the Policy's constitutionality. 242 F. 3d 1264, 1270 (2001). Before imposing a suspicionless drug testing program, the Court of Appeals concluded that a school "must demonstrate that there is some identifiable drug abuse problem among a sufficient number of those subject to the testing, such that testing that group of students will actually redress its drug problem." *Id.,* at 1278. The Court of Appeals then held that because the School District failed to demonstrate such a problem existed among Tecumseh students participating in competitive extracurricular activities, the Policy was unconstitutional. We granted certiorari, 534 U.S. 1015 (2001), and now reverse.

II

The Fourth Amendment to the United States Constitution protects "[t]he right of the people to be secure in their persons, houses, papers, and effects, against unreasonable searches and seizures." Searches by public school officials, such as the collection of urine samples,

---

1. The District Court noted that the School District's allegations concerning Daniel James called his standing to sue into question because his failing grades made him ineligible to participate in any interscholastic competition. See 115 F. Supp. 2d 1281, 1282, n. 1 (WD Okla. 2000). The court noted, however, that the dispute need not be resolved because Lindsay Earls had standing, and therefore the court was required to address the constitutionality of the drug testing policy. See *ibid.* Because we are likewise satisfied that Earls has standing, we need not address whether James also has standing.

2. The respondents did not challenge the Policy either as it applies to athletes or as it provides for drug testing upon reasonable, individualized suspicion. See App. 28.

implicate Fourth Amendment interests. See *Vernonia, supra,* at 652; cf. *New Jersey v. T. L. O.,* 469 U.S. 325, 334 (1985). We must therefore review the School District's Policy for "reasonableness," which is the touchstone of the constitutionality of a governmental search.

In the criminal context, reasonableness usually requires a showing of probable cause. See, e.g., *Skinner v. Railway Labor Executives' Assn.,* 489 U.S. 602, 619 (1989). The probable-cause standard, however, "is peculiarly related to criminal investigations" and may be unsuited to determining the reasonableness of administrative searches where the "Government seeks to *prevent* the development of hazardous conditions." *Treasury Employees v. Von Raab,* 489 U.S. 656, 667–668 (1989) (internal quotation marks and citations omitted) (collecting cases). The Court has also held that a warrant and finding of probable cause are unnecessary in the public school context because such requirements "'would unduly interfere with the maintenance of the swift and informal disciplinary procedures [that are] needed.'" *Vernonia, supra,* at 653 (quoting *T. L. O., supra,* at 340–341).

Given that the School District's Policy is not in any way related to the conduct of criminal investigations, see Part II-B, *infra,* respondents do not contend that the School District requires probable cause before testing students for drug use. Respondents instead argue that drug testing must be based at least on some level of individualized suspicion. See Brief for Respondents 12-14. It is true that we generally determine the reasonableness of a search by balancing the nature of the intrusion on the individual's privacy against the promotion of legitimate governmental interests. See *Delaware v. Prouse,* 440 U.S. 648, 654 (1979). But we have long held that "the Fourth Amendment imposes no irreducible requirement of [individualized] suspicion." *United States v. Martinez-Fuerte,* 428 U.S. 543, 561 (1976). "[I]n certain limited circumstances, the Government's need to discover such latent or hidden conditions, or to prevent their development, is sufficiently compelling to justify the intrusion on privacy entailed by conducting such searches without any measure of individualized suspicion." *Von Raab, supra,* at 668; see also *Skinner, supra,* at 624. Therefore, in the context of safety and administrative regulations, a search unsupported by probable cause may be reasonable "when 'special needs, beyond the normal need for law enforcement, make the warrant and probable-cause requirement impracticable.'" *Griffin v. Wisconsin,* 483 U.S. 868, 873 (1987) (quoting *T. L. O., supra,* at 351 (Blackmun, J., concurring in judgment)); see also *Vernonia, supra,* at 653; *Skinner, supra,* at 619.

Significantly, this Court has previously held that "special needs" inhere in the public school context. See *Vernonia, supra,* at 653; *T. L. O., supra,* at 339–340. While schoolchildren do not shed their constitutional rights when they enter the schoolhouse, see *Tinker v. Des Moines Independent Community School Dist.,* 393 U.S. 503, 506 (1969), "Fourth Amendment rights . . . are different in public schools than elsewhere; the 'reasonableness' inquiry cannot disregard the schools' custodial and tutelary responsibility for children." *Vernonia, supra,* at 656. In particular, a finding of individualized suspicion may not be necessary when a school conducts drug testing.

In *Vernonia,* this Court held that the suspicionless drug testing of athletes was constitutional. The Court, however, did not simply authorize all school drug testing, but rather conducted a fact-specific balancing of the intrusion on the children's Fourth Amendment rights against the promotion of legitimate governmental interests. See 515 U.S., at 652–653. Applying the principles of *Vernonia* to the somewhat different facts of this case, we conclude that Tecumseh's Policy is also constitutional.

A

We first consider the nature of the privacy interest allegedly compromised by the drug testing. See *id.*, at 654. As in *Vernonia*, the context of the public school environment serves as the backdrop for the analysis of the privacy interest at stake and the reasonableness of the drug testing policy in general. See *ibid.* ("Central . . . is the fact that the subjects of the Policy are (1) children, who (2) have been committed to the temporary custody of the State as schoolmaster"); see also *id.*, at 665 ("The most significant element in this case is the first we discussed: that the Policy was undertaken in furtherance of the government's responsibilities, under a public school system, as guardian and tutor of children entrusted to its care"); *ibid.* ("[W]hen the government acts as guardian and tutor the relevant question is whether the search is one that a reasonable guardian and tutor might undertake").

A student's privacy interest is limited in a public school environment where the State is responsible for maintaining discipline, health, and safety. Schoolchildren are routinely required to submit to physical examinations and vaccinations against disease. See *id.*, at 656. Securing order in the school environment sometimes requires that students be subjected to greater controls than those appropriate for adults. See *T. L. O., supra*, at 350 (Powell, J., concurring) ("Without first establishing discipline and maintaining order, teachers cannot begin to educate their students. And apart from education, the school has the obligation to protect pupils from mistreatment by other children, and also to protect teachers themselves from violence by the few students whose conduct in recent years has prompted national concern").

Respondents argue that because children participating in nonathletic extracurricular activities are not subject to regular physicals and communal undress, they have a stronger expectation of privacy than the athletes tested in *Vernonia*. See Brief for Respondents 18–20. This distinction, however, was not essential to our decision in *Vernonia*, which depended primarily upon the school's custodial responsibility and authority.[3]

In any event, students who participate in competitive extracurricular activities voluntarily subject themselves to many of the same intrusions on their privacy as do athletes.[4] Some of these clubs and activities require occasional off-campus travel and communal undress. All of them have their own rules and requirements for participating students that do not apply to the student body as a whole. 115 F. Supp. 2d, at 1289–1290. For example, each of the competitive extracurricular activities governed by the Policy must abide by the rules of the Oklahoma Secondary Schools Activities Association, and a faculty sponsor monitors the students

---

3. Justice Ginsburg argues that *Vernonia School Dist. 47J v. Acton,* 515 U.S. 646 (1995), depended on the fact that the drug testing program applied only to student athletes. But even the passage cited by the dissent manifests the supplemental nature of this factor, as the Court in *Vernonia* stated that "[l]egitimate privacy expectations are *even less* with regard to student athletes." See *post*, at 5 (citing *Vernonia*, 515 U.S., at 657) (emphasis added). In upholding the drug testing program in *Vernonia*, we considered the school context "[c]entral" and "[t]he most significant element." 515 U.S., at 654, 665. This hefty weight on the side of the school's balance applies with similar force in this case even though we undertake a separate balancing with regard to this particular program.

4. Justice Ginsburg's observations with regard to extracurricular activities apply with equal force to athletics. See *post*, at 4 ("Participation in such [extracurricular] activities is a key component of school life, essential in reality for students applying to college, and, for all participants, a significant contributor to the breadth and quality of the educational experience").

for compliance with the various rules dictated by the clubs and activities. See *id.*, at 1290. This regulation of extracurricular activities further diminishes the expectation of privacy among schoolchildren. Cf. *Vernonia, supra,* at 657 ("Somewhat like adults who choose to participate in a closely regulated industry, students who voluntarily participate in school athletics have reason to expect intrusions upon normal rights and privileges, including privacy" (internal quotation marks omitted)). We therefore conclude that the students affected by this Policy have a limited expectation of privacy.

B

Next, we consider the character of the intrusion imposed by the Policy. See *Vernonia, supra,* at 658. Urination is "an excretory function traditionally shielded by great privacy." *Skinner,* 489 U.S., at 626. But the "degree of intrusion" on one's privacy caused by collecting a urine sample "depends upon the manner in which production of the urine sample is monitored." *Vernonia, supra,* at 658.

Under the Policy, a faculty monitor waits outside the closed restroom stall for the student to produce a sample and must "listen for the normal sounds of urination in order to guard against tampered specimens and to insure an accurate chain of custody." App. 199. The monitor then pours the sample into two bottles that are sealed and placed into a mailing pouch along with a consent form signed by the student. This procedure is virtually identical to that reviewed in *Vernonia,* except that it additionally protects privacy by allowing male students to produce their samples behind a closed stall. Given that we considered the method of collection in *Vernonia* a "negligible" intrusion, 515 U.S., at 658, the method here is even less problematic.

In addition, the Policy clearly requires that the test results be kept in confidential files separate from a student's other educational records and released to school personnel only on a "need to know" basis. Respondents nonetheless contend that the intrusion on students' privacy is significant because the Policy fails to protect effectively against the disclosure of confidential information and, specifically, that the school "has been careless in protecting that information: for example, the Choir teacher looked at students' prescription drug lists and left them where other students could see them." Brief for Respondents 24. But the choir teacher is someone with a "need to know," because during off-campus trips she needs to know what medications are taken by her students. Even before the Policy was enacted the choir teacher had access to this information. See App. 132. In any event, there is no allegation that any other student did see such information. This one example of alleged carelessness hardly increases the character of the intrusion.

Moreover, the test results are not turned over to any law enforcement authority. Nor do the test results here lead to the imposition of discipline or have any academic consequences. Cf. *Vernonia, supra,* at 658, and n. 2. Rather, the only consequence of a failed drug test is to limit the student's privilege of participating in extracurricular activities. Indeed, a student may test positive for drugs twice and still be allowed to participate in extracurricular activities. After the first positive test, the school contacts the student's parent or guardian for a meeting. The student may continue to participate in the activity if within five days of the meeting the student shows proof of receiving drug counseling and submits to a second drug test in two weeks. For the second positive test, the student is suspended from participation in all extracurricular activities for 14 days, must complete four hours of substance abuse counseling, and must submit to monthly drug tests. Only after a third positive test will the student be suspended from participating in any extracurricular activity for the remainder of the school year, or 88 school days, whichever is longer. See App. 201–202.

Given the minimally intrusive nature of the sample collection and the limited uses to which the test results are put, we conclude that the invasion of students' privacy is not significant.

C

Finally, this Court must consider the nature and immediacy of the government's concerns and the efficacy of the Policy in meeting them. See *Vernonia,* 515 U.S., at 660. This Court has already articulated in detail the importance of the governmental concern in preventing drug use by schoolchildren. See *id.,* at 661–662. The drug abuse problem among our Nation's youth has hardly abated since *Vernonia* was decided in 1995. In fact, evidence suggests that it has only grown worse.[5] As in *Vernonia,* "the necessity for the State to act is magnified by the fact that this evil is being visited not just upon individuals at large, but upon children for whom it has undertaken a special responsibility of care and direction." *Id.,* at 662. The health and safety risks identified in *Vernonia* apply with equal force to Tecumseh's children. Indeed, the nationwide drug epidemic makes the war against drugs a pressing concern in every school.

Additionally, the School District in this case has presented specific evidence of drug use at Tecumseh schools. Teachers testified that they had seen students who appeared to be under the influence of drugs and that they had heard students speaking openly about using drugs. See, e.g., App. 72 (deposition of Dean Rogers); *id.,* at 115 (deposition of Sheila Evans). A drug dog found marijuana cigarettes near the school parking lot. Police officers once found drugs or drug paraphernalia in a car driven by a Future Farmers of America member. And the school board president reported that people in the community were calling the board to discuss the "drug situation." See 115 F. Supp. 2d, at 1285–1286. We decline to second-guess the finding of the District Court that "[v]iewing the evidence as a whole, it cannot be reasonably disputed that the [School District] was faced with a 'drug problem' when it adopted the Policy." *Id.,* at 1287.

Respondents consider the proffered evidence insufficient and argue that there is no "real and immediate interest" to justify a policy of drug testing nonathletes. Brief for Respondents 32. We have recognized, however, that "[a] demonstrated problem of drug abuse . . . [is] not in all cases necessary to the validity of a testing regime," but that some showing does "shore up an assertion of special need for a suspicionless general search program." *Chandler v. Miller,* 520 U.S. 305, 319 (1997). The School District has provided sufficient evidence to shore up the need for its drug testing program.

Furthermore, this Court has not required a particularized or pervasive drug problem before allowing the government to conduct suspicionless drug testing. For instance, in *Von Raab* the Court upheld the drug testing of customs officials on a purely preventive basis, without any documented history of drug use by such officials. See 489 U.S., at 673. In response

---

5. For instance, the number of 12th graders using any illicit drug increased from 48.4 percent in 1995 to 53.9 percent in 2001. The number of 12th graders reporting they had used marijuana jumped from 41.7 percent to 49.0 percent during that same period. See Department of Health and Human Services, Monitoring the Future: National Results on Adolescent Drug Use, Overview of Key Findings (2001) (Table 1).

to the lack of evidence relating to drug use, the Court noted generally that "drug abuse is one of the most serious problems confronting our society today," and that programs to prevent and detect drug use among customs officials could not be deemed unreasonable. *Id.,* at 674; cf. *Skinner,* 489 U.S., at 607, and n. 1 (noting nationwide studies that identified on-the-job alcohol and drug use by railroad employees). Likewise, the need to prevent and deter the substantial harm of childhood drug use provides the necessary immediacy for a school testing policy. Indeed, it would make little sense to require a school district to wait for a substantial portion of its students to begin using drugs before it was allowed to institute a drug testing program designed to deter drug use.

Given the nationwide epidemic of drug use, and the evidence of increased drug use in Tecumseh schools, it was entirely reasonable for the School District to enact this particular drug testing policy. We reject the Court of Appeals' novel test that "any district seeking to impose a random suspicionless drug testing policy as a condition to participation in a school activity must demonstrate that there is some identifiable drug abuse problem among a sufficient number of those subject to the testing, such that testing that group of students will actually redress its drug problem." 242 F. 3d, at 1278. Among other problems, it would be difficult to administer such a test. As we cannot articulate a threshold level of drug use that would suffice to justify a drug testing program for schoolchildren, we refuse to fashion what would in effect be a constitutional quantum of drug use necessary to show a "drug problem."

Respondents also argue that the testing of nonathletes does not implicate any safety concerns, and that safety is a "crucial factor" in applying the special needs framework. Brief for Respondents 25–27. They contend that there must be "surpassing safety interests," *Skinner, supra,* at 634, or "extraordinary safety and national security hazards," *Von Raab, supra,* at 674, in order to override the usual protections of the Fourth Amendment. See Brief for Respondents 25–26. Respondents are correct that safety factors into the special needs analysis, but the safety interest furthered by drug testing is undoubtedly substantial for all children, athletes and nonathletes alike. We know all too well that drug use carries a variety of health risks for children, including death from overdose.

We also reject respondents' argument that drug testing must presumptively be based upon an individualized reasonable suspicion of wrongdoing because such a testing regime would be less intrusive. See *id.,* at 12–16. In this context, the Fourth Amendment does not require a finding of individualized suspicion, see *supra,* at 5, and we decline to impose such a requirement on schools attempting to prevent and detect drug use by students. Moreover, we question whether testing based on individualized suspicion in fact would be less intrusive. Such a regime would place additional burden on public school teachers who are already tasked with the difficult job of maintaining order and discipline. A program of individualized suspicion might unfairly target members of unpopular groups. The fear of lawsuits resulting from such targeted searches may chill enforcement of the program, rendering it ineffective in combating drug use. See *Vernonia,* 515 U.S., at 663–664 (offering similar reasons for why "testing based on 'suspicion' of drug use would not be better, but worse"). In any case, this Court has repeatedly stated that reasonableness under the Fourth Amendment does not require employing the least intrusive means, because "[t]he logic of such elaborate less-restrictive-alternative arguments could raise insuperable barriers to the exercise of virtually all search-and-seizure powers." *Martinez-Fuerte,* 428 U.S., at 556–557, n. 12; see also *Skinner, supra,* at 624 ("[A] showing of individualized suspicion is not a constitutional floor, below which a search must be presumed unreasonable").

Finally, we find that testing students who participate in extracurricular activities is a reasonably effective means of addressing the School District's legitimate concerns in preventing, deterring, and detecting drug use. While in *Vernonia* there might have been a closer fit between the testing of athletes and the trial court's finding that the drug problem was "fueled by the 'role model' effect of athletes' drug use," such a finding was not essential to the holding. 515 U.S., at 663; cf. *id.*, at 684–685 (*O'Connor, J.*, dissenting) (questioning the extent of the drug problem, especially as applied to athletes). *Vernonia* did not require the school to test the group of students most likely to use drugs, but rather considered the constitutionality of the program in the context of the public school's custodial responsibilities. Evaluating the Policy in this context, we conclude that the drug testing of Tecumseh students who participate in extracurricular activities effectively serves the School District's interest in protecting the safety and health of its students.

III

Within the limits of the Fourth Amendment, local school boards must assess the desirability of drug testing schoolchildren. In upholding the constitutionality of the Policy, we express no opinion as to its wisdom. Rather, we hold only that Tecumseh's Policy is a reasonable means of furthering the School District's important interest in preventing and deterring drug use among its schoolchildren. Accordingly, we reverse the judgment of the Court of Appeals.

It is so ordered.

Justice O'Connor, with whom Justice Souter joins, dissenting.

I dissented in *Vernonia School Dist. 47J v. Acton,* 515 U. S. 646 (1995), and continue to believe that case was wrongly decided. Because *Vernonia* is now this Court's precedent, and because I agree that petitioners' program fails even under the balancing approach adopted in that case, I join Justice Ginsburg's dissent.

Justice Ginsburg, with whom Justice Stevens, Justice O'Connor, and Justice Souter join, dissenting.

Seven years ago, in *Vernonia School Dist. 47J v. Acton,* 515 U.S. 646 (1995), this Court determined that a school district's policy of randomly testing the urine of its student athletes for illicit drugs did not violate the Fourth Amendment. In so ruling, the Court emphasized that drug use "increase[d] the risk of sports-related injury" and that Vernonia's athletes were the "leaders" of an aggressive local "drug culture" that had reached "'epidemic proportions.'" *Id.,* at 649. Today, the Court relies upon *Vernonia* to permit a school district with a drug problem its superintendent repeatedly described as "not . . . major," see App. 180, 186, 191, to test the urine of an academic team member solely by reason of her participation in a nonathletic, competitive extracurricular activity—participation associated with neither special dangers from, nor particular predilections for, drug use.

"[T]he legality of a search of a student," this Court has instructed, "should depend simply on the reasonableness, under all the circumstances, of the search." *New Jersey v. T. L. O.,* 469 U.S. 325, 341 (1985). Although "'special needs' inhere in the public school context," see *ante,* at 5 (quoting *Vernonia,* 515 U.S., at 653), those needs are not so expansive or malleable as to render reasonable any program of student drug testing a school district elects to install. The particular testing program upheld today is not reasonable, it is capricious, even perverse:

Petitioners' policy targets for testing a student population least likely to be at risk from illicit drugs and their damaging effects. I therefore dissent.

I

A

A search unsupported by probable cause nevertheless may be consistent with the Fourth Amendment "when special needs, beyond the normal need for law enforcement, make the warrant and probable-cause requirement impracticable." *Griffin v. Wisconsin,* 483 U.S. 868, 873 (1987) (internal quotation marks omitted). In *Vernonia,* this Court made clear that "such 'special needs' . . . exist in the public school context." 515 U.S., at 653 (quoting *Griffin,* 483 U.S., at 873). The Court observed:

> "[W]hile children assuredly do not 'shed their constitutional rights . . . at the schoolhouse gate,' *Tinker v. Des Moines Independent Community School Dist.,* 393 U. S. 503, 506 (1969), the nature of those rights is what is appropriate for children in school. . . . Fourth Amendment rights, no less than First and Fourteenth Amendment rights, are different in public schools than elsewhere; the 'reasonableness' inquiry cannot disregard the schools' custodial and tutelary responsibility for children." 515 U.S., at 655–656 (other citations omitted).

The *Vernonia* Court concluded that a public school district facing a disruptive and explosive drug abuse problem sparked by members of its athletic teams had "special needs" that justified suspicionless testing of district athletes as a condition of their athletic participation.

This case presents circumstances dispositively different from those of *Vernonia.* True, as the Court stresses, Tecumseh students participating in competitive extracurricular activities other than athletics share two relevant characteristics with the athletes of *Vernonia.* First, both groups attend public schools. "[O]ur decision in *Vernonia,*" the Court states, "depended primarily upon the school's custodial responsibility and authority." *Ante,* at 7; see also *ante,* at 3 (Breyer, J., concurring) (school districts act *in loco parentis*). Concern for student health and safety is basic to the school's caretaking, and it is undeniable that "drug use carries a variety of health risks for children, including death from overdose." *Ante,* at 13 (majority opinion).

Those risks, however, are present for *all* schoolchildren. *Vernonia* cannot be read to endorse invasive and suspicionless drug testing of all students upon any evidence of drug use, solely because drugs jeopardize the life and health of those who use them. Many children, like many adults, engage in dangerous activities on their own time; that the children are enrolled in school scarcely allows government to monitor all such activities. If a student has a reasonable subjective expectation of privacy in the personal items she brings to school, see *T. L. O.,* 469 U.S., at 338–339, surely she has a similar expectation regarding the chemical composition of her urine. Had the *Vernonia* Court agreed that public school attendance, in and of itself, permitted the State to test each student's blood or urine for drugs, the opinion in *Vernonia* could have saved many words. See, e.g., 515 U.S., at 662 ("[I]t must not be lost sight of that [the Vernonia School District] program is directed . . . to drug use by school athletes, where the risk of immediate physical harm to the drug user or those with whom he is playing his sport is particularly high.").

The second commonality to which the Court points is the voluntary character of both interscholastic athletics and other competitive extracurricular activities. "By choosing to 'go out for the team,' [school athletes] voluntarily subject themselves to a degree of regulation even higher than that imposed on students generally." *Id.*, at 657. Comparably, the Court today observes, "students who participate in competitive extracurricular activities voluntarily subject themselves to" additional rules not applicable to other students. *Ante*, at 7.

The comparison is enlightening. While extracurricular activities are "voluntary" in the sense that they are not required for graduation, they are part of the school's educational program; for that reason, the petitioner (hereinafter School District) is justified in expending public resources to make them available. Participation in such activities is a key component of school life, essential in reality for students applying to college, and, for all participants, a significant contributor to the breadth and quality of the educational experience. See Brief for Respondents 6; Brief for American Academy of Pediatrics et al. as *Amici Curiae* 8–9. Students "volunteer" for extracurricular pursuits in the same way they might volunteer for honors classes: They subject themselves to additional requirements, but they do so in order to take full advantage of the education offered them. Cf. *Lee v. Weisman*, 505 U.S. 577, 595 (1992) ("Attendance may not be required by official decree, yet it is apparent that a student is not free to absent herself from the graduation exercise in any real sense of the term 'voluntary,' for absence would require forfeiture of those intangible benefits which have motivated the student through youth and all her high school years.").

Voluntary participation in athletics has a distinctly different dimension: Schools regulate student athletes discretely because competitive school sports by their nature require communal undress and, more important, expose students to physical risks that schools have a duty to mitigate. For the very reason that schools cannot offer a program of competitive athletics without intimately affecting the privacy of students, *Vernonia* reasonably analogized school athletes to "adults who choose to participate in a closely regulated industry." 515 U.S., at 657 (internal quotation marks omitted). Industries fall within the closely regulated category when the nature of their activities requires substantial government oversight. See, e.g., *United States v. Biswell*, 406 U.S. 311, 315–316 (1972). Interscholastic athletics similarly require close safety and health regulation; a school's choir, band, and academic team do not.

In short, *Vernonia* applied, it did not repudiate, the principle that "the legality of a search of a student should depend simply on the reasonableness, *under all the circumstances*, of the search." *T. L. O.*, 469 U.S., at 341 (emphasis added). Enrollment in a public school, and election to participate in school activities beyond the bare minimum that the curriculum requires, are indeed factors relevant to reasonableness, but they do not on their own justify intrusive, suspicionless searches. *Vernonia*, accordingly, did not rest upon these factors; instead, the Court performed what today's majority aptly describes as a "fact-specific balancing," *ante*, at 6. Balancing of that order, applied to the facts now before the Court, should yield a result other than the one the Court announces today.

B

Vernonia initially considered "the nature of the privacy interest upon which the search [there] at issue intrude[d]." 515 U.S., at 654. The Court emphasized that student athletes' expectations of privacy are necessarily attenuated:

> "Legitimate privacy expectations are even less with regard to student athletes. School sports are not for the bashful. They require 'suiting up' before each practice or event, and showering and changing afterwards. Public school locker rooms, the usual sites for these activities, are not notable for

the privacy they afford. The locker rooms in *Vernonia* are typical: No individual dressing rooms are provided; shower heads are lined up along a wall, unseparated by any sort of partition or curtain; not even all the toilet stalls have doors. . . . [T]here is an element of communal undress inherent in athletic participation." *Id.,* at 657 (internal quotation marks omitted).

Competitive extracurricular activities other than athletics, however, serve students of all manner: the modest and shy along with the bold and uninhibited. Activities of the kind plaintiff-respondent Lindsay Earls pursued—choir, show choir, marching band, and academic team—afford opportunities to gain self-assurance, to "come to know faculty members in a less formal setting than the typical classroom," and to acquire "positive social supports and networks [that] play a critical role in periods of heightened stress." Brief for American Academy of Pediatrics et al. as *Amici Curiae* 13.

On "occasional out-of-town trips," students like Lindsay Earls "must sleep together in communal settings and use communal bathrooms." 242 F. 3d 1264, 1275 (CA10 2001). But those situations are hardly equivalent to the routine communal undress associated with athletics; the School District itself admits that when such trips occur, "public-like restroom facilities," which presumably include enclosed stalls, are ordinarily available for changing, and that "more modest students" find other ways to maintain their privacy. Brief for Petitioners 34.[1]

After describing school athletes' reduced expectation of privacy, the *Vernonia* Court turned to "the character of the intrusion . . . complained of." 515 U.S., at 658. Observing that students produce urine samples in a bathroom stall with a coach or teacher outside, *Vernonia* typed the privacy interests compromised by the process of obtaining samples "negligible." *Ibid.* As to the required pretest disclosure of prescription medications taken, the Court assumed that "the School District would have permitted [a student] to provide the requested information in a confidential manner—for example, in a sealed envelope delivered to the testing lab." *Id.,* at 660. On that assumption, the Court concluded that Vernonia's athletes faced no significant invasion of privacy.

In this case, however, Lindsay Earls and her parents allege that the School District handled personal information collected under the policy carelessly, with little regard for its confidentiality. Information about students' prescription drug use, they assert, was routinely viewed by Lindsay's choir teacher, who left files containing the information unlocked and unsealed, where others, including students, could see them; and test results were given out to all activity sponsors whether or not they had a clear "need to know." See Brief for Respondents 6, 24; App. 105–106, 131. But see *id.,* at 199 (policy requires that "[t]he medication list shall be submitted to the lab in a sealed and confidential envelope and shall not be viewed by district employees").

In granting summary judgment to the School District, the District Court observed that the District's "Policy expressly provides for confidentiality of test results, and the Court must assume that the confidentiality provisions will be honored." 115 F. Supp. 2d 1281, 1293 (WD Okla. 2000). The assumption is unwarranted. Unlike *Vernonia,* where the District Court held a bench trial before ruling in the School District's favor, this case was decided by the Dis-

---

1. According to Tecumseh's choir teacher, choir participants who chose not to wear their choir uniforms to school on the days of competitions could change either in "a rest room in a building" or on the bus, where "[m]any of them have figured out how to [change] without having [anyone] . . . see anything." 2 Appellants' App. in No. 00-6128 (CA10), p. 296.

trict Court on summary judgment. At that stage, doubtful matters should not have been resolved in favor of the judgment seeker. See *United States v. Diebold, Inc.,* 369 U.S. 654, 655 (1962) *(per curiam)* ("On summary judgment the inferences to be drawn from the underlying facts contained in [affidavits, attached exhibits, and depositions] must be viewed in the light most favorable to the party opposing the motion."); see also 10A C. Wright, A. Miller, & M. Kane, Federal Practice and Procedure § 2716, pp. 274–277 (3d ed. 1998).

Finally, the "nature and immediacy of the governmental concern," *Vernonia,* 515 U.S., at 660, faced by the Vernonia School District dwarfed that confronting Tecumseh administrators. Vernonia initiated its drug testing policy in response to an alarming situation: "[A] large segment of the student body, particularly those involved in interscholastic athletics, was in a state of rebellion . . . fueled by alcohol and drug abuse as well as the student[s'] misperceptions about the drug culture." *Id.,* at 649 (internal quotation marks omitted). Tecumseh, by contrast, repeatedly reported to the Federal Government during the period leading up to the adoption of the policy that "types of drugs [other than alcohol and tobacco] including controlled dangerous substances, are present [in the schools] but have not identified themselves as major problems at this time." 1998–1999 Tecumseh School's Application for Funds under the Safe and Drug-Free Schools and Communities Program, reprinted at App. 191; accord, 1996–1997 Application, reprinted at App. 186; 1995–1996 Application, reprinted at App. 180.[2] As the Tenth Circuit observed, "without a demonstrated drug abuse problem among the group being tested, the efficacy of the District's solution to its perceived problem is . . . greatly diminished." 242 F. 3d, at 1277.

The School District cites *Treasury Employees v. Von Raab,* 489 U.S. 656, 673–674 (1989), in which this Court permitted random drug testing of customs agents absent "any perceived drug problem among Customs employees," given that "drug abuse is one of the most serious problems confronting our society today." See also *Skinner v. Railway Labor Executives' Assn.,* 489 U.S. 602, 607, and n. 1 (1989) (upholding random drug and alcohol testing of railway employees based upon industry-wide, rather than railway-specific, evidence of drug and alcohol problems). The tests in *Von Raab* and *Railway Labor Executives,* however, were installed to avoid enormous risks to the lives and limbs of others, not dominantly in response to the health risks to users invariably present in any case of drug use. See *Von Raab,* 489 U.S., at 674 (drug use by customs agents involved in drug interdiction creates "extraordinary safety and national security hazards"); *Railway Labor Executives,* 489 U.S., at 628 (railway operators "discharge duties fraught with such risks of injury to others that even a momentary lapse of attention can have disastrous consequences"); see also *Chandler v. Miller,* 520 U.S. 305, 321 (1997) ("*Von Raab* must be read in its unique context").

Not only did the *Vernonia* and Tecumseh districts confront drug problems of distinctly different magnitudes, they also chose different solutions: *Vernonia* limited its policy to athletes; Tecumseh indiscriminately subjected to testing all participants in competitive extracurricular activities. Urging that "the safety interest furthered by drug testing is

---

2. The Court finds it sufficient that there be evidence of *some* drug use in Tecumseh's schools: "As we cannot articulate a threshold level of drug use that would suffice to justify a drug testing program for schoolchildren, we refuse to fashion what would in effect be a constitutional quantum of drug use necessary to show a 'drug problem.'" *Ante,* at 12. One need not establish a bright-line "constitutional quantum of drug use" to recognize the relevance of the superintendent's reports characterizing drug use among Tecumseh's students as "not . . . [a] major proble[m]," App. 180, 186, 191.

undoubtedly substantial for all children, athletes and nonathletes alike," *ante*, at 13, the Court cuts out an element essential to the *Vernonia* judgment. Citing medical literature on the effects of combining illicit drug use with physical exertion, the *Vernonia* Court emphasized that "the particular drugs screened by [*Vernonia's*] Policy have been demonstrated to pose substantial physical risks to athletes." 515 U.S., at 662; see also *id.*, at 666 (*Ginsburg, J.*, concurring) (*Vernonia* limited to "those seeking to engage with others in team sports"). We have since confirmed that these special risks were necessary to our decision in *Vernonia*. See *Chandler*, 520 U.S., at 317 (*Vernonia* "emphasized the importance of deterring drug use by schoolchildren and the risk of injury a drug-using student athlete cast on himself and those engaged with him on the playing field"); see also *Ferguson v. Charleston*, 532 U.S. 67, 87 (2001) (Kennedy, J., concurring) (Vernonia's policy had goal of "'[d]eterring drug use by our Nation's schoolchildren,' and particularly by student-athletes, because 'the risk of immediate physical harm to the drug user or those with whom he is playing his sport is particularly high'") (quoting *Vernonia*, 515 U.S., at 661–662).

At the margins, of course, no policy of *random* drug testing is perfectly tailored to the harms it seeks to address. The School District cites the dangers faced by members of the band, who must "perform extremely precise routines with heavy equipment and instruments in close proximity to other students," and by Future Farmers of America, who "are required to individually control and restrain animals as large as 1500 pounds." Brief for Petitioners 43. For its part, the United States acknowledges that "the linebacker faces a greater risk of serious injury if he takes the field under the influence of drugs than the drummer in the halftime band," but parries that "the risk of injury to a student who is under the influence of drugs while playing golf, cross country, or volleyball (sports covered by the policy in *Vernonia*) is scarcely any greater than the risk of injury to a student . . . handling a 1500-pound steer (as [Future Farmers of America] members do) or working with cutlery or other sharp instruments (as [Future Homemakers of America] members do)." Brief for United States as *Amicus Curiae* 18. One can demur to the Government's view of the risks drug use poses to golfers, cf. *PGA TOUR, Inc. v. Martin*, 532 U.S. 661, 687 (2001) ("golf is a low intensity activity"), for golfers were surely as marginal among the linebackers, sprinters, and basketball players targeted for testing in Vernonia as steer-handlers are among the choristers, musicians, and academic-team members subject to urinalysis in Tecumseh.[3] Notwithstanding nightmarish images of out-of-control flatware, livestock run amok, and colliding tubas disturbing the peace and quiet of Tecumseh, the great majority of students the School District seeks to test in truth are engaged in activities that are not safety sensitive to an unusual degree. There is a difference between imperfect tailoring and no tailoring at all.

The *Vernonia* district, in sum, had two good reasons for testing athletes: Sports team members faced special health risks and they "were the leaders of the drug culture." *Vernonia*, 515 U.S., at 649. No similar reason, and no other tenable justification, explains Tecumseh's decision to target for testing all participants in every competitive extracurricular activity. See *Chandler*, 520 U.S., at 319 (drug testing candidates for office held incompatible with

---

3. Cross-country runners and volleyball players, by contrast, engage in substantial physical exertion. See *Vernonia School Dist. 47J v. Acton*, 515 U.S. 646, 663 (1995) (describing special dangers of combining drug use with athletics generally).

Fourth Amendment because program was "not well designed to identify candidates who violate antidrug laws").

Nationwide, students who participate in extracurricular activities are significantly less likely to develop substance abuse problems than are their less-involved peers. See, e.g., N. Zill, C. Nord, & L. Loomis, *Adolescent Time Use, Risky Behavior, and Outcomes* 52 (1995) (tenth graders "who reported spending no time in school-sponsored activities were . . . 49 percent more likely to have used drugs" than those who spent 1–4 hours per week in such activities). Even if students might be deterred from drug use in order to preserve their extracurricular eligibility, it is at least as likely that other students might forgo their extracurricular involvement in order to avoid detection of their drug use. Tecumseh's policy thus falls short doubly if deterrence is its aim: It invades the privacy of students who need deterrence least, and risks steering students at greatest risk for substance abuse away from extracurricular involvement that potentially may palliate drug problems.[4]

To summarize, this case resembles *Vernonia* only in that the School Districts in both cases conditioned engagement in activities outside the obligatory curriculum on random subjection to urinalysis. The defining characteristics of the two programs, however, are entirely dissimilar. The Vernonia district sought to test a subpopulation of students distinguished by their reduced expectation of privacy, their special susceptibility to drug-related injury, and their heavy involvement with drug use. The Tecumseh district seeks to test a much larger population associated with none of these factors. It does so, moreover, without carefully safeguarding student confidentiality and without regard to the program's untoward effects. A program so sweeping is not sheltered by *Vernonia;* its unreasonable reach renders it impermissible under the Fourth Amendment.

II

In *Chandler,* this Court inspected "Georgia's requirement that candidates for state office pass a drug test"; we held that the requirement "d[id] not fit within the closely guarded category of constitutionally permissible suspicionless searches." 520 U.S., at 309. Georgia's testing prescription, the record showed, responded to no "concrete danger," *id.*, at 319, was supported by no evidence of a particular problem, and targeted a group not involved in "high-risk, safety-sensitive tasks," *id.*, at 321–322. We concluded:

> "What is left, after close review of Georgia's scheme, is the image the State seeks to project. By requiring candidates for public office to submit to drug testing, Georgia displays its commitment to the struggle against drug abuse. . . . The need revealed, in short, is symbolic, not 'special,' as that term draws meaning from our case law." *Ibid.*

Close review of Tecumseh's policy compels a similar conclusion. That policy was not shown to advance the "'special needs' [existing] in the public school context [to maintain] . . .

---

4. The Court notes that programs of individualized suspicion, unlike those using random testing, "might unfairly target members of unpopular groups." *Ante,* at 13; see also *ante,* at 4 (*Breyer, J.,* concurring). Assuming, *arguendo,* that this is so, the School District here has not exchanged individualized suspicion for random testing. It has installed random testing in addition to, rather than in lieu of, testing "at any time when there is reasonable suspicion." App. 197.

swift and informal disciplinary procedures . . . [and] order in the schools," *Vernonia,* 515 U.S., at 653 (internal quotation marks omitted). See *supra,* at 5–6, 8–11. What is left is the School District's undoubted purpose to heighten awareness of its abhorrence of, and strong stand against, drug abuse. But the desire to augment communication of this message does not trump the right of persons—even of children within the schoolhouse gate—to be "secure in their persons . . . against unreasonable searches and seizures." U.S. Const., Amdt. 4.

In *Chandler,* the Court referred to a pathmarking dissenting opinion in which "Justice Brandeis recognized the importance of teaching by example: 'Our Government is the potent, the omnipresent teacher. For good or for ill, it teaches the whole people by its example.'" 520 U.S., at 322 (quoting *Olmstead v. United States,* 277 U.S. 438, 485 (1928)). That wisdom should guide decisionmakers in the instant case: The government is nowhere more a teacher than when it runs a public school.

It is a sad irony that the petitioning School District seeks to justify its edict here by trumpeting "the schools' custodial and tutelary responsibility for children." *Vernonia,* 515 U.S., at 656. In regulating an athletic program or endeavoring to combat an exploding drug epidemic, a school's custodial obligations may permit searches that would otherwise unacceptably abridge students' rights. When custodial duties are not ascendant, however, schools' tutelary obligations to their students require them to "teach by example" by avoiding symbolic measures that diminish constitutional protections. "That [schools] are educating the young for citizenship is reason for scrupulous protection of Constitutional freedoms of the individual, if we are not to strangle the free mind at its source and teach youth to discount important principles of our government as mere platitudes." *West Virginia Bd. of Ed. v. Barnette,* 319 U.S. 624, 637 (1943).

* * * *

For the reasons stated, I would affirm the judgment of the Tenth Circuit declaring the testing policy at issue unconstitutional.

CASES INDEX

SUBJECT INDEX